RESEARCH METHODS IN FAMILY THERAPY

RESEARCH METHODS IN FAMILY THERAPY

Edited by

DOUGLAS H. SPRENKLE
SIDNEY M. MOON

THE GUILFORD PRESS
New York   London

©1996 The Guilford Press
A Division of Guilford Publications, Inc.
72 Spring Street, New York, NY 10012

Printed in the United States of America

This book is printed on acid-free paper.

Last digit is print number: 9 8 7 6 5 4 3 2 1

Library of Congress Cataloging-in-Publication Data

Research methods in family therapy / edited by Douglas H. Sprenkle,
Sidney M. Moon.
    p.   cm.
    Includes bibliographical references and index.
    ISBN 1-57230-111-2
    1. Family psychotherapy—Research—Methodology. I. Sprenkle,
Douglas H. II. Moon, Sidney M.
    RC488.5.R47 1996
    616.89'156'072—dc20

                       96-21297
                       CIP

Contributors

Douglas H. Sprenkle, PhD, is a professor of marriage and family therapy in the Department of Child Development and Family Studies at Purdue University. He was the editor of the *Journal of Marital and Family Therapy* from 1990 to 1996. He has received several major professional honors, among them the Osborne Award for excellence in teaching from the National Council on Family Relations and the Significant Contribution to Family Therapy Award from the American Association for Marriage and Family Therapy. Dr. Sprenkle has served on the Commission on Accreditation for Marriage and Family Therapy Education and is an approved supervisor and fellow of the American Association for Marriage and Family Therapy. *Research Methods in Family Therapy* is his fourth book.

Sidney M. Moon, PhD, is an associate professor of educational psychology and research in the Department of Educational Studies at Purdue University, and the director of research for the Gifted Education Resource Institute. She is also a clinical member of the American Association of Marriage and Family Therapy and has her own part-time private practice. She has taught graduate-level courses in social science research methodology in which she emphasizes a balance between qualitative, quantitative, and mixed approaches. For the past five years, she has been an active promoter and developer of multimethodological approaches to family therapy research. Her research interests include the development and evaluation of school programs for gifted and talented children, gifted children with other exceptionalities such as attention deficit disorder, and family therapy with families of the gifted.

Judith Myers Avis, PhD, is a professor of family therapy at the University of Guelph in Ontario, Canada, where she is also engaged in private practice and community consultation. She has written extensively about gender issues in family therapy practice and training and has conducted and supervised feminist research in family therapy since 1985. Most recently, she has been working on an integration of feminist and narrative ideas. She serves on the editorial boards of the *Journal of Feminist Family Therapy*, the *Journal of Marital and Family Therapy*, and *Contemporary Family Therapy*.

Richard J. Bischoff, PhD, is an assistant professor of marriage, family, and child counseling in the School of Education at the University of San Diego. He is a clinical member of the American Association for Marriage and Family Therapy with a clinical practice in San Diego, California.

Pauline Boss, PhD, is a professor of family social science at the University of Minnesota in St. Paul. She is a family therapist and supervisor of the American Association for Marriage and Family Therapy, as well as a family researcher. Her research interest is in family stress from ambiguous loss. Appreciation is expressed to the University of Minnesota Experiment Station for partial support of this project.

Dean M. Busby, PhD, is an assistant professor of marriage and family therapy at Syracuse University, where he has worked since 1990. He received undergraduate degrees from the University of Utah in both psychology and Spanish. He received his master's and doctorate degrees in marriage and family therapy from Brigham Young University. His scholarly work has been in the areas of family violence, premarital relationships, and assessment in family therapy.

Carla M. Dahl, PhD, is an associate professor of marriage and family studies at Bethel Theological Seminary in St. Paul, Minnesota. She has been a counselor and family life educator since 1982 and has conducted research in the areas of divorce, justice, and grief. Her primary research focus is an extension of her doctoral dissertation, which was based on her phenomenological exploration of how spirituality is defined and expressed within families.

Mitchell H. Dickey, PhD, is an assistant professor of marriage and family therapy at Southern Connecticut State University. He received a master's degree from Kent State University in 1982, and until 1985, was the coordinator of an outpatient counseling department, focusing on substance abuse and crisis intervention. He then received a doctorate in clinical psychology from Yale University in 1993, and taught in the Marital and Family Therapy Program at Purdue University for one year. His research interests focus on the process-outcome links in cost-effective models of family therapy and service delivery.

Denise E. Flori, PhD, is a clinical assistant professor of family medicine at the University of Oklahoma Health Sciences Center and the director of behavioral medicine for the Great Plains Family Practice Residency Program in Oklahoma City, Oklahoma. After graduate studies in geropsychology at the University of Notre Dame, she received her doctorate in marriage and family therapy from Purdue University. Her research interests include health outcomes associated with patient-centered medical care and increasing health care professionals' knowledge and interest in clinical gerontology and geriatrics. Currently, she chairs the Aging Caucus for the American Association for Marriage and Family Therapy.

Myrna L. Friedlander, PhD, is a professor of counseling psychology at the State University of New York at Albany, and an adjunct clinical assistant professor of psychiatry at Albany Medical College. Her research has appeared in the *Journal of Counseling Psychology, Psychotherapy,* the *Journal of Family Psychology,* and the *Journal of Marital and Family Therapy,* among others. Dr. Friedlander is a fellow of the American Psychological Association, the American Psychological Society, and the American Association of Applied and Preventive Psychology, as well as a member of the Society for Psychotherapy Research.

Jerry Gale, PhD, is an associate professor of child and family development at the University of Georgia and director of clinical services at the McPhaul Marriage and Family Therapy Clinic. Dr. Gale is the author of *Conversation Analysis of Therapeutic Discourse* and a coeditor of *Constructivism in Education.*

Leslie S. Greenberg, PhD, is a professor of psychology and the director of the Psychotherapy Research Centre at York University in North York, Ontario, Canada. He is a former president of the Society for Psychotherapy Research. He is also in private practice in couple and individual therapy in Toronto and trains therapists in emotionally focused approaches to treatment. He has published extensively on individual and couple therapy and is on the editorial board of a number of journals.

Laurie Heatherington, PhD, is an associate professor of psychology at Williams College. She received her doctorate in clinical psychology from the University of Connecticut in 1991 and has since combined teaching, research, and family psychotherapy. In collaboration with M. L. Friedlander and with her students at Williams, she has published numerous articles on family therapy process-outcome research, the development of measures for studying interaction and cognitive change in family therapy sessions, and studies of gender in therapy. She is on the editorial boards of the *Journal of Marital and Family Therapy*, the *Journal of Family Psychology*, *Psychotherapy*, and *Psychotherapy Research*.

Lori Kaplan, PhD, is a postdoctoral fellow in the Population Research Center of the University of Chicago. Her research focuses on family caregiving in later life, specifically caregiving to institutionalized mates and to spouses with Alzheimer's Disease. She has published nine articles and has presented her research at international, national, and regional conferences. Her dissertation was funded by the Alzheimer's Disease and Related Disorders Association.

Douglas Leber, PhD, is a research associate at the Center for Marital and Family Studies at the University of Denver. His research specialty is the prevention of violence in close relationships. He received his doctorate in personality psychology from the University of Michigan in 1991.

Kevin P. Lyness, MS, is a doctoral candidate in marriage and family therapy at Purdue University and the director of the Riverside Addictions Program at Wabash Valley Hospital in West Lafayette, Indiana. Currently, he serves on the editorial advisory board of the *Journal of Marital and Family Therapy* and belongs to the Indiana Counselors Association on Alcohol and Drug Abuse and the National Association of Alcoholism and Drug Abuse Counselors. Mr. Lyness has written or cowritten several articles and publications.

David P. Mackinnon, MBA, MA, is a doctoral candidate in marriage and family therapy at Purdue University and has a private practice in Hinsdale, Illinois. His dissertation and current research interests focus on cost effectiveness methodology as applied to the research and clinical practice of family therapy. He received the Research and Education Foundation Research Fellow Award from the American Association for Marriage and Family Therapy in 1994. Mr. Mackinnon has presented his cost effectiveness methodology at national and regional conferences and has published and presented in the area of integrating spirituality and family therapy.

Laurel F. Mangrum, MS, is a doctoral candidate in clinical psychology at Texas A&M University. She earned a master's degree from Texas A&M in 1993 and completed her clinical internship at the University of Texas Medical Center in San Antonio in 1995. Ms. Mangrum's clinical and research interests include eating disorders, multivariate research methods, and marital and family therapy.

Howard J. Markman, PhD, is a professor of psychology and director of the Center for Marital and Family Studies at the University of Denver. He is also a clinical psychologist and clinical member of the American Association for Marriage and Family Therapy, with private practices in Denver and Boulder. For the past fifteen years, Dr. Markman has specialized in research on the prediction and prevention of marital breakdown.

A. Jay McKeel, MS, is in private practice in Raleigh, North Carolina. He is a clinical member and approved supervisor with the American Association for Marriage and Family Therapy. Dr. McKeel was formerly an assistant professor of marriage and family therapy at St. Thomas University in Miami, Florida.

Thorana S. Nelson, PhD, is an associate professor and the director of the Marriage and Family Therapy Program at Utah State University in Logan, Utah. She earned her doctorate from the University of Iowa in counselor education with an emphasis on marriage and family therapy. She taught family therapy in the doctoral program at Purdue University before moving to Utah to develop and direct the master's program in marriage and family therapy.

Faye Newfield, MPH, is a project coordinator for the Behavioral Risk Factor Survey in the Hawaii State Department of Health. She was formerly a developer with the Peace Corps in their rural animation project and has also served as a consultant to a primary health care project in the Sine-Saloum region of Senegal, West Africa.

Neal Newfield, PhD, ACSW, LICSW, is an associate professor of behavioral medicine and psychiatry in the School of Medicine at West Virginia University, and director of clinical social work at William R. Sharpe, Jr. Hospital. A regional faculty member with the Family Therapy Institute of Washington, D.C., he was formerly an assistant professor of psychiatry at the Texas Tech Health Sciences Center, and a visiting assistant professor of human development and family studies and a research associate of anthropology at Texas Tech University. In previous social work positions, he worked on the Navajo and Zuni Indian reservations in New Mexico. He has five years of graduate training in anthropology.

Susan Newfield, RN, CS, is assistant professor of nursing at West Virginia University. She was formerly a clinical associate professor of nursing with the Texas Tech Health Sciences Center, School of Nursing. In a previous nursing position, she worked as a public health nurse on the Navajo and Zuni Indian reservations in New Mexico. Currently, she is completing a qualitative dissertation at Texas Tech University on ethical decision making among individual and family therapists.

Vernon P. Nickerson, MA, presently resides in Minneapolis, Minnesota. He was first exposed to focus group research while earning an undergraduate degree in industrial engineering at Northwestern University. He experienced the therapeutic value of focus groups while working in the aerospace industry as a manager and volunteering as a lay counselor in his spare time. These experiences were seminal in his decision to attend Fuller Seminary, where he subsequently earned a master's degree in theology and began graduate study in marital and family therapy.

Fred P. Piercy, PhD, is the director of the Family Therapy Doctoral Program at Purdue University. He is a clinical member, approved supervisor, and fellow of the American Association for Marriage and Family Therapy, and a fellow in the Division of Family Psychology of the American Psychological Association. His professional interests include marital therapy, family therapy of substance abuse, family therapy education, and social science AIDS research and prevention. Dr. Piercy has written over a hundred published articles and book chapters, and has received twenty funded grants. He coauthored (with Norman Lobsenz) *Stop Marital Fights Before They Start*, and (with Douglas Sprenkle and associates), *Family Therapy Sourcebook*. Dr Piercy has spent seven summers as a consultant in Jakarta, Indonesia.

Connee L. Pike-Urlacher, MS, CMFT, currently works in private practice in West Lafayette, Indiana. She earned her undergraduate degree in human development and family studies and her master's degree in marriage and family therapy, both from Colorado State University. She has published two previous articles in the area of cost effectiveness research.

Silvia Echevarria Rafuls, PhD, is an assistant professor of marriage and family therapy at the University of Florida. She earned her doctorate in marriage and family therapy at Purdue University in West Lafayette, Indiana. Her research interests include resource-based family therapy, training and supervision, culture and diversity issues in family therapy, and qualitative methodology, all of which she has written about and presented at local, state, and national conferences. She is a clinical member of the American Association for Marriage and Family Therapy, an active board member of the North Central Florida Association for Marriage and Family Therapy, and a member of the American Family Therapy Academy.

Sherry L. Rediger, PhD, is a family therapist and supervisor in private practice at the Center for Family Life Ministries in Indianapolis, Indiana. In 1988, Dr. Rediger completed her master's degree in family therapy at Hahnemann University in Philadelphia. She studied with Ivan Boszormenyi-Nagy and continues to be greatly influenced by his work. Dr. Rediger completed her doctorate in marriage and family therapy from Purdue University in 1992.

Janida L. Rice, MA, is a doctoral candidate in clinical psychology at Texas A&M University. She received both undergraduate and master's degrees from Texas Women's University. Her research interests are in the areas of women's issues and marital and family therapy.

Michelle St. Peters, PhD, is a postdoctoral trainee with the Family Research Consortium II, a multisite collaborative research program funded by NIMH to study family risk, resilience, and mental health. Dr. St. Peters earned her doctorate in developmental psychology at the University of Kansas, specializing in the influence of television on children.

Scott P. Sells, PhD, MSW, LCSW, is an assistant professor of social work at the University of Nevada and the director of the Nevada Family Therapy Institute. He is also an approved supervisor and clinical member of the American Association for Marriage and Family Therapy.

Julianne M. Serovich, PhD, is an assistant professor of marriage and family therapy at The Ohio State University. She received her doctorate in marriage and family therapy from the University of Georgia. She is a clinical member and approved supervisor of the American Association for Marriage and Family Therapy and a member of the National Council on Family Relations. Dr. Serovich has published her research in such journals as *The American Journal of Family Therapy*, *Family Relations*, *Journal of Marriage and Family Therapy*, and the *Journal of Divorce*.

Thomas Edward Smith, PhD, is an associate professor of social work and the director of the Center for Social Work Practice and Research at Florida State University. He is also a supervisory faculty member of the accredited interdivisional doctorate program in marriage and family therapy. He was formerly the director of an accredited postgraduate family therapy training program at Family Services of Milwaukee and a family therapy certificate program at the University of Wisconsin—Milwaukee.

Douglas K. Snyder, PhD, is a professor of psychology and the director of clinical training at Texas A&M University. He received his doctorate from the University of North Carolina at Chapel Hill in 1978. Dr. Snyder wrote the widely used *Marital Satisfaction Inventory* and edited the *Clinician's Research Digest*. He is a fellow of the American Psychological Association, the Society for Personality Assessment, and the American Association of Applied and Preventive Psychology. Dr. Snyder received the 1992 Outstanding Marriage and Family Therapy Research Publication Award from the American Association for Marriage and Family Therapy for his research comparing long-term effectiveness of behavioral and insight-oriented marital therapy.

Linda Stone Fish, PhD, is an associate professor of family therapy at Syracuse University. She has published three articles focusing on the Delphi method and has been involved in four Delphi studies. She has also been active in research on structural/strategic couple therapy. Her scholarly work has been in the areas of relationship development and family therapy theory.

Terry S. Trepper, PhD, is a professor of psychology and the director of the Family Studies Center at Purdue University—Calumet. He is a fellow of the American Psychological Association, a clinical member of the American Association for Marriage and Family Therapy, an AASECT certified sex therapist, and a diplomate in the American Board of Sexology. He is the editor of the *Journal of Family Psychotherapy*, and senior editor of Haworth's Series on Marriage and the Family. Dr Trepper also coauthored (with Mary Jo Barrett) *Systemic Treatment of Incest: A Therapeutic Handbook*, and *Treating Incest: A Multiple Systems Perspective*; and (with Thorana Nelson) *101 Interventions in Family Therapy*.

Jean Turner, PhD, is an assistant professor of couple and family therapy at the University of Guelph in Ontario, Canada, as well as a clinical psychologist. Her current research is on the evolution of therapeutic relationships in couple therapy, and on the transformation of gender roles in migrant families. She has recently published articles taking a social constructionist perspective on gender and power issues in family therapy and family therapy supervision.

Robert J. Volk, PhD, is the director of research in the Department of Family Medicine at the University of Texas Medical Branch in Galveston, Texas. Dr. Volk received his doctorate in family studies from Purdue University. His research interests include identifying optimal screening and treatment strategies for common problems seen in primary care settings, multivariate statistical techniques applied to primary care, and adolescent substance use.

Karen S. Wampler, PhD, is a professor of marriage and family therapy as well as the director of the Marriage and Family Therapy Program at Texas Tech University. Dr. Wampler's primary interest has been research methodology, including meta-analysis and the development of observational measures of the marriage and family process. Her current research focuses on change processes in marriage and family therapy and supervision using an attachment theory perspective.

Contents

Part III
QUANTITATIVE METHODS

Design and Measurement

Experimental Research

Relational/Predictive Research

Cost-Effectiveness Evaluations

Part IV
MIXED METHODS

Intensive Research

Survey Research

Program Evaluations

I

INTRODUCTION

1

Toward Pluralism in Family Therapy Research

DOUGLAS H. SPRENKLE
SIDNEY M. MOON

ALTHOUGH FAMILY therapy is now more than 50 years old, it is safe to say that the rapid growth of the field has depended more on its intuitive appeal than on solid research evidence for its efficacy (Nichols & Schwartz, 1995). It is still possible for a highly charismatic individual to develop a model of family therapy, get book contracts to promulgate it, and become successful on the workshop circuit without offering a scintilla of evidence beyond testimonials for the efficacy of the model. Although there are some indications that the tide may be turning (see Pinsof & Wynne, 1995), the field remains vulnerable because of its lack of attention to developing a solid foundation of research on the processes and outcomes of family therapy.

In addition, in spite of several decades of appeals to bridge the researcher–clinician gap (Olson, 1976; Breunlin & Schwartz, 1983; Liddle, 1991; Sprenkle & Bischoff, 1995), the chasm between researchers and clinicians seems as wide as ever. This is somewhat ironic given that the early family therapy pioneers considered themselves to be "family researchers" (Wynne, 1983). Family therapy had its roots in research, and such founders as Lyman Wynne, Murray Bowen, Theodore Litz, Gregory Bateson, Don Jackson, Jay Haley, and others came to family therapy through studying interactional patterns associated with problem families (Broderick & Schrader, 1981). Both Haley (1978) and Wynne (1983) have explained that in the early days there was no distinction between researchers and therapists. These "researcher–clinicians" focused on how therapeutic interventions impacted patients and their families. They would review audiotapes of their sessions, observe each other through one-way mirrors, and spend hours discussing each session and formulating hypotheses. Research had direct clinical relevance, because hypotheses were developed, tested, altered, and retested in practice settings (Wynne, 1983; Sprenkle & Bischoff, 1995). Of course, what was then considered research would not be considered rigorous by today's standards. In fact, it might be labeled rather "soft" qualitative research because it was highly impressionistic and there was not much effort to consider the role of researcher bias.

TRANSFORMATIONS IN FAMILY
THERAPY RESEARCH

The research enterprise in family therapy has undergone two major transformations since these early investigations. In the first transformation the field moved from its impressionistic beginnings to an emphasis on quantitative and experimental research. This shift forced family therapists to operationalize some of their "fuzzy" concepts. It also challenged family therapy researchers to develop reliable and valid measures, which, in conjunction with respectable research designs, helped to gain credibility for a fledgling discipline in a skeptical clinical world (Sprenkle & Bischoff, 1995).

Not surprisingly, in the early decades, there was a strong push for outcome research. Early outcome studies compared conventional treatment (often an inpatient, individually oriented treatment) with a family-oriented approach. Because some early studies found family treatments superior to conventional treatments with regard to recidivism and other important variables (e.g., Langsley, Flomenhaft, & Machotka, 1969; Langsley, Pittman, Machotka, & Flomenhaft, 1968), they gave credence to the emerging discipline (Sprenkle & Bischoff, 1995). Other early outcome studies compared one specific model of family treatment (e.g., structural family therapy) to a focused problem area (e.g., anorexia nervosa) and found the model to produce dramatic results (Minuchin et al., 1975). Even though this study had major methodological limitations (e.g., no control group), the percentage of patients improving made the rest of the clinical world take notice.

The second transformation involved a shift from a strict adherence to quantitative methods to incorporation and gradual acceptance of alternate methodologies, especially qualitative ones (Hoshmand, 1989; Moon, Dillon, & Sprenkle, 1990; Sprenkle & Bischoff, 1995). The second transformation was facilitated by powerful intellectual challenges to positivism (Anderson, 1990; Gergen, 1985; Gergen, 1991; Maturana, 1988) that have been variously called the new epistemology, constructivism, or social constructionism. Writers (e.g., Tomm, 1986) began to argue that traditional quantitative research assumed a linear causality that did not square with systemic models. Furthermore, most early quantitative research ignored the impact of the observer upon the observed and "fallaciously" assumed that one can describe an "objective" reality. Traditional quantitative research was also seen by these critics as "reductionistic." They argued that attempts to operationalize circular and systemic concepts frequently (to use Karl Tomm's colorful phrase) "kill the beast in the effort to understand it" (Tomm, 1983, p. 39).

Critics also argued that family therapy had made its quantitative leap too soon, before clearly delineating what was meant by systemic constructs (Bednar, Burlingame, & Masters, 1988). Therefore, concepts were operationalized before being truly understood and consequently seemed removed from clinical reality. They called for more attention to the context of "discovery," as opposed to the context of verification and for descriptive research which could note in intricate detail the subtleties and complexities of the therapeutic process. They also called for more attention to contextual variables (e.g., the impact of the setting in which research takes place; as well as the impact of race, ethnicity, and gender of participants). They asked that we consider the impact of the therapist and the research process itself on what was being reported. These critics pointed out that by making therapists follow treatment manuals and by utilizing other features of experimental "control," even impressive results would not necessarily relate to what happens in the real world of clinical practice (Atkinson, Heath, & Chenail, 1991).

Defenders of quantitative research were quick to point out that several of these limitations rested not with the quantitative methods themselves but rather with the field's limited understanding of how to use them. About a decade and a half ago, Alan Gurman (Gurman, 1983) argued that the correlation coefficient could be seen as a systemic statistic because it did not imply linear causality. He also argued that although the overall process of therapy is undoubtedly circular, subprocesses within therapy are linear and we should not apologize for that. After all, we expect the client to pay us rather than vice versa. Other writers have noted that such newer statistical techniques as sequential analysis and structural equation modeling can capture systemic processes with quantitative methods (Gottman, 1987; Shields, 1986; Volk & Flori, Chapter 15, this volume).

Pragmatic and ethical arguments have also been advanced for the value of quantitative methods. For example, Sprenkle and Bischoff (1995) have argued that quantitative methods are important to the field because they are widely recognized by the scientific community and funding agencies as providing valid proof of effectiveness. Convincing outcome data are essential to the survival of the field in an era of managed care, scarce resources, and calls for accountability. Finally, proponents of quantitative research have argued that we have an ethical responsibility—both to our clients and to ourselves—to demonstrate that what we do is efficacious. Because traditional quantitative research methodology is the most generally accepted way to examine issues of causality in ways that rule out alternative explanations, we have an obligation to utilize it (Gurman, 1983; Cavell & Snyder, 1991).

TOWARD PLURALISM IN FAMILY THERAPY RESEARCH

In this volume, we are arguing for a third transformation—pluralism. By pluralism we mean promulgation and acceptance of a wide variety of research methods, both qualitative and quantitative. A pluralistic society is one that values and appreciates differences. A pluralistic research community values and appreciates different inquiry paradigms, methodologies, and designs. Being pluralistic is the opposite of being provincial and an antonym for polarization. Pluralism encourages an atmosphere of understanding, openness, and tolerance. Specifically, then, a pluralistic research community asks a wide variety of research questions and answers them with a wide variety of research methodologies.

We have been identified as advocates of qualitative methods. We do believe that qualitative methods have a unique relationship with the history of our field. We also believe that qualitative designs seem congruent with systems theory, afford creative ways to investigate the actual process of therapy, and legitimize the kind of discovery-oriented research that has helped to make marital–family therapy a vibrant field. We believe that qualitative methods should be accorded respect and that their potential should be exploited. However, we do not believe that family therapy needs a *unique* research paradigm or that quantitative methods should be abandoned. What we are suggesting is that the field will benefit from additional research paradigms and that qualitative methods complement quantitative ones (Moon, Dillon, & Sprenkle, 1991).

We believe methodological pluralism is important for family therapy research because it encourages research from a wide variety of perspectives. We believe that different research questions require different methods, and different methods, in turn, give rise to different kinds of questions. Methodological pluralism will increase the tools at our disposal for understanding family therapy processes and outcomes.

GOALS AND PURPOSES OF THIS VOLUME

What do we hope to accomplish with the publication of this book? First and foremost, we hope to contribute to the development of pluralism in family therapy research and to demonstrate the advantages of being multimethodological. If one builds the structure of the family therapy research enterprise with only one or two "tools" from the methodological toolbox, one gets a cramped and confined building. We prefer an edifice that is spacious, complex, and branches out. It is just as legitimate to ask, "How does it feel to be a solo family therapist in a large private practice medical clinic?" as it is to ask, "How are heart rate, blood pressure, and galvanic skin response affected by in-session conflict?" We want to stimulate new questions as well as better answers to the old questions.

We hope that this volume will broaden the reader's understanding of what research is. Whereas most readers probably think of controlled clinical trials as "research," what about case studies? Weren't they "pooh-poohed" in my methods classes? This volume shows that the case study methodology has a long and distinguished research tradition and can be quite rigorous. Whereas white coats and "number crunching" probably fit the stereotype of research for many, what about model building from the intensive analysis of critical interventions within actual sessions with flesh-and-blood clients, as is typical of conversation analysis and event-based analysis? This volume exposes its readers to a literal smorgasbord of legitimate, rigorous research methods, all of which do not fit research preconceptions.

Second, we hope to put another plank across the researcher–clinician gap. We are well aware that clinicians are typically a pragmatic lot. Although they do ask some of the same questions that traditional researchers have asked (e.g., "Does this therapy model work?"), they are also interested in more practical concerns: "How does this family therapy approach fit with my own experience?" "How are my clients responding?" "Who should be present at the next session?" "How can I best help this substance abusing adolescent?" "Is this couple ready to terminate?" One of the aims of this book is to show that there is a method that can help answer these types of clinical questions.

Third, we hope that our readers will learn quite a bit about the methods themselves. Each chapter is designed to be a complete introduction to a particular research method. The chapters are structured similarly. Each begins with a description of the assumptions and historical development of the methodology and discusses the types of questions usually addressed. Then the authors provide a brief overview of the data collection and analysis techniques associated with the method. Each chapter concludes with a discussion of the skills needed to conduct that type of research, strengths and weaknesses of the method for family therapy research, a discussion of the ethical issues raised by the method, and thoughts about how the method can help bridge research and practice.

The "Guidelines for Chapter Authors," which were sent to the writers who contributed to this volume, are reproduced in Table 1.1. Please note that we specifically urged the authors to consider style as well as substance. We fervently hope that most of the information in this volume will be accessible to clinicians with modest training and research. We asked each author to "weave" concrete examples of the method into what otherwise might be an abstract description to make the methods more accessible and show how they apply to the field of family therapy. (After these guidelines were sent out to the authors, we suggested that authors also address the ethical issues raised by their method.)

TABLE 1.1. Guidelines for Chapter Authors

Each chapter describes a different social science methodology that is suited to the investigation of research questions in the field of family therapy. The guidelines indicate what the descriptions of the methodology in each chapter might include and provide suggestions for developing the chapters. The goal of providing chapter authors with these guidelines is to create a consistent, coherent volume on a wide variety of research methods.

I. BACKGROUND

A. Creative Introduction
Provide a creative introduction to your chapter that will "hook" the reader into wanting to know more. Make your introduction concrete and accessible to clinicians who have little formal training in research.

B. Philosophical Assumptions
What assumptions underlie the methodology? How do these assumptions shape the research? Be brief here. Just hit the highlights.

C. Historical Roots and Development
How did the methodology develop both within and without the field of family therapy?

II. METHODOLOGY

Note: In this section, we would like each author to weave at least one concrete example of the method into the abstract description. Whenever possible, this example should be from the author's own work. If currently there are no good examples of the methodology in the family therapy research literature or the author's own research efforts, the author should invent a research example to weave into the description.

A. Research Questions
What family therapy research questions are best answered by this methodology? What questions have been answered by this methodology?

B. Sampling and Selection Procedures
What is important to consider in selecting participants for family therapy studies conducted with this methodology? How is selection accomplished?

C. Data Collection Procedures
What data collection procedures are usually used? What factors are important to consider in collecting the data? How are systemic variables assessed? How are the data recorded and stored?

D. Data Analysis Procedures
What methods are used to analyze the data? Give concrete examples in nontechnical language.

E. Reporting
How are the findings reported? What does a typical research report look like? Where might it be likely to be published?

III. DISCUSSION

A. Strengths and Weaknesses of the Methodology
What are the strengths and weaknesses of the methodology when applied to family therapy research?

B. Reliability and Validity
Discuss the relevance of the concepts of reliability and validity to your tradition/method. Are reliability and validity addressed by the tradition/method? If so, how? If not, why not?

C. Skills
What special skills are needed to plan, execute, and interpret this kind of research? What are the implications for training clinicians? Researchers?

D. Bridging Research and Practice
In what ways might this methodology contribute to bridging the research and practice communities? How might clinicians best become involved in the methodology? How might the results be made more accessible to clinicians?

E. Future Directions
What future directions would you suggest for this methodology in our field?

SLICING THE RESEARCH PIE

Decisions concerning what to include in this book and how to organize it were quite vexing. We spent many hours discussing different ways of "slicing the research pie" before finalizing our list of chapters. We wanted to do justice to the diversity of research questions in the field and the pluralism we are advocating. Although we considered a variety of organizing principles, our primary focus was to develop chapters based on research "methods" being employed in the field. By methods we mean strategies or procedures that can be utilized to answer research questions. We considered a number of ways of slicing the pie before arriving at our final, somewhat eclectic, organizational scheme. In this section we first outline some of the ways we considered and then briefly describe the organizational scheme we decided to utilize.

Ways of Slicing the Research Pie

Purpose of the Research

A book on marital–family therapy research could be organized by *substantive areas*. We might have had chapters on family therapy research related to divorce, mood disorders, substance abuse, and so on. This was the approach used by William Pinsof and Lyman Wynne (1995), guest editors of the special issue of the *Journal of Marital and Family Therapy*. We chose, however, to focus on methods that could be brought to bear on the full spectrum of content areas in the field. We could have organized the book around *temporal phases of the clinical process*—such as what goes on within sessions (process research), or what happens at the end of therapy (outcome research). Although several of the methods described are ideally suited for process research (e.g. relational/predictive, event based) or outcome research (cost-effectiveness, experimental), respectively, we did not categorize these methods by their purpose except in the case of some methods especially well suited to evaluation research.

Design Features

One can divide research depending on whether an independent variable is manipulated or not (a major distinction between experimental and nonexperimental research). One can slice the pie based on studies that offer group comparisons versus those that look at the degree of relationship among variables. An example of the former would be research designed to ask the following question: *"What is the relationship between experience level of therapist and outcome?"* The latter would enable the researcher to address a question such as the following: *"Is there a relationship between therapist teaching behavior and client resistance?"* Other design features might include whether randomization is used or whether a case study employs a single versus a multiple case study format. The problem with organizing research this way is that some methods are rather easily categorized by design features, whereas others are not. For example, experimental research almost always includes group comparisons, manipulation of an independent variable, and random assignment of cases and treatments. Many of the methods described in this book, however, would be difficult to categorize by design features (e.g., most of the qualitative methods and most of the mixed methods).

Sampling and Generalization Techniques

The research pie can also be sliced depending on whether studies used probabilistic or purposive sampling. In the first case, the intent is to be able to make generalizations about a larger population from the research sample. Therefore, considerable effort must be expended to choose large, representative samples from the larger population. Purposive sampling, on the other hand, is done when probabilistic sampling is not feasible or the purpose of the research is descriptive or exploratory or the goal is analytical generalization to theory rather than probabilistic generalization to populations (Firestone, 1900). Probabilistic sampling is crucial for public opinion polls; it is not very important when one is doing exploratory research about clients' reactions to reflecting teams. Purposive sampling is used in grounded theory research and multiple-case-study research to ensure that propositions or theories that result from the analytical analysis of data will fit a wide variety of contexts.

Data Collection Techniques

The research pie can also be sliced according to whether one selects words or numbers (almost always a qualitative–quantitative distinction). Investigations can also be categorized by whether they use standardized measurement instruments, participant observation, or interviews to gather information. However, many of the research methods described in this book use such a variety of data collection techniques that it would be difficult to classify them by data collection technique alone. For example, case study researchers can collect data through observations, videotapes, standardized instruments, or interviews.

Analysis Techniques

Finally, the research pie can be sliced by looking at analysis techniques. Examples include correlational research, multivariate research, and constant comparative research. In each of these cases, a research method is being labeled by the techniques used to analyze the data.

Slicing the Pie in this Volume

After considerable discussion of the issues outlined above, we decided to group the methods in this book into three broad methodological categories: qualitative, quantitative, and mixed methods. In the qualitative section we placed methods that have traditionally been associated with the qualitative paradigm, such as naturalistic and phenomenological methods. In general, these methods are characterized by the collection of observational or verbal data that are analyzed inductively. In the quantitative section we placed methods that have traditionally been associated with the quantitative paradigm, such as experimental methods. Usually, these methods are characterized by operationalization of variables in numerical form that are analyzed statistically. However, it is important to recognize that many of the methods are actually more versatile than their place in our classification scheme might suggest. For example, although we have placed phenomenological research in the qualitative section because most phenomenological research is qualitative in nature, phenomenological research questions can be answered by mixed designs or even wholly quantitative ones (Kunkel, Chapa, Patterson, & Walling, 1995).

In this book, mixed methods are methods that tend to combine elements of qualitative and quantitative designs in a single study. Survey research is an example of a mixed method. Survey researchers can gather numerical data and analyze that data statistically. However, they might also choose to use semistructured interviews to gather qualitative data that would be analyzed inductively into categories or themes. Some of the methods in the mixed methods section have been traditionally associated more frequently with either qualitative or quantitative research. For example, case study research is typically seen as a qualitative method and survey research as a quantitative one. However, there is nothing in the methodologies themselves that requires these alignments. Case study researchers can collect quantitative data and analyze them statistically just as survey researchers can collect qualitative data and analyze them inductively.

Our organizing principles within these three major sections varied considerably. Sometimes we grouped the methods by inquiry paradigm, as in the subsections on critical theory and social constructionist research. More often, we used specific methodological features as an organizing principle. These included design features and data collection and analysis techniques. For example, overall design features were the primary grouping characteristic for the intensive and experimental methodologies. Intensive methods are those that gather and analyze data on such specific individual units of analysis as particular therapy events or certain types of cases. Typical design features in experimental research are careful operationalization and measurement of variables, manipulation of an independent variable (typically treatment), and control of alternative explanations for the results through random assignment, control groups, and/or careful pre- and post-measurement of the variables of interest. Other methodological features that influenced our groupings were the way that data are typically collected (as in the subsections on naturalistic and survey research) or the ways that data are analyzed (as in the chapter on structural equation modelling).

Occasionally we categorized a method by its purpose. For example, we categorized three methodologies (focus group research, cost-effectiveness research, and program evaluation research) first by the type of data collected and analyzed (qualitative, quantitative, or mixed) and then by the purpose of the research (evaluation research). Thus each of the major sections has a subsection on a particular type of evaluation research.

QUALITATIVE METHODS
REPORTED IN THIS VOLUME

The purpose of the qualitative part of this book is to expose the reader to existing traditions of qualitative research and to emerging approaches that are not yet well formulated. We hope that this section will spur the reader to think about ways that qualitative research can inform the field and about new qualitative methods that might be developed to answer family therapy research questions.

Naturalistic Research

This section includes two of the older, more established qualitative methods: ethnography and grounded theory research. Both methods are considered naturalistic because they emphasize collecting data in natural or field settings, as opposed to artificial settings like laboratories. In Chapter 2, Neal Newfield, Scott P. Sells, Thomas Edward Smith, Susan Newfield, and Faye Newfield provide a rich history of the development of ethnographic methods and describe several different but related traditions of ethnography that are relevant to family therapy research. They outline the essential characteristics of ethnographic research and argue that that ethnographic methods can help family therapists create a "clinical science of the humanities." Hallmarks of ethnographic research include participant observation, ethnographic or phenomenological interviewing, and various types of inductive analyses of qualitative data. Each of these hallmarks is discussed at length in this chapter so that the reader emerges with a clear understanding of key methodological concepts in ethnographic research and guidance on how to design and implement an ethnographic study. An extensive reference list provides numerous sources for further guidance for readers intrigued by Newfield et al.'s exciting introduction to the world of ethnography.

In Chapter 3, Silvia Echevarria Rafuls and Sidney M. Moon discuss grounded theory research, the methodology that gave us the constant comparative method of data analysis. They begin with Glaser and Strauss's (1967) original collaboration in the invention of grounded theory methodology and then detail the two divergent perspectives on grounded theory research that have developed as these two pioneers have emphasized different aspects of the methodology. Rafuls and Moon show how both perspectives are helpful in grounded theory research and provide step-by-step guidelines for conducting a constant comparative analysis. Their chapter is enriched by an example of an application of the initial stages of grounded theory methodology to an investigation of resource-based therapy with Latino families. The study they use to illustrate grounded theory also illustrates an eclectic approach to research design because it combines the theoretical perspective of critical theory with grounded theory and focus group methods.

Social Constructionist Research

In the social constructionist section, we have included two examples of methods that have grown out of the social constructionist inquiry paradigm: phenomenology and conversation analysis. These methods are quite different with respect to technique, but they share a focus on understanding ways that meaning is socially constructed by human beings. In Chapter 4, *The Use of Phenomenology for Family Therapy Research*, Pauline Boss, Carla Dahl, and Lori Kaplan provide a scholarly and refreshingly clear description of methodology that focuses on the essential meaning of events. They note that their purpose is "to familiarize family therapists with a method of investigation and description that is compatible with their already developed skills of observation, creativity, intuition, empathic listening, and analysis" (p. 83). Phenomenological research relies heavily on in-depth interviews for data collection and is particularly useful when researchers want to investigate insider perspectives—one or more individual's perceptions of the world and the meaning that they make of events. Boss and her colleagues outline the key features of phenomenological research and give two clinical examples of phenomenological research. Faced with the challenge of discussing where no clearly defined methodology exists, they also include such sections as "When Phenomenologists Do Not Believe in Discussing Method" and "For Those Phenomenologists Who Insist on a Method."

In Chapter 5, *Conversation Analysis: Studying the Construction of Therapeutic Realities*, Jerry Gale describes a microanalytical methodology that is particularly useful for analyzing the "talk" of therapy. Gale's chapter begins the way conversation analysis begins: with a fragment of transcript begging for analysis. He then shows the reader exactly how that transcript fragment would be analyzed by a researcher using conversation analysis to illuminate the specific therapeutic strategies that a solution focused therapist was utilizing in this portion of a marital therapy session. The remainder of the

chapter describes the relationship between conversation analysis and social constructionism and provides detailed guidance on conversation analysis methodology illustrated by concrete examples from the author's own work.

Critical Theory Research

The authors of the critical theory chapters faced a challenging task because critical theory
is an inquiry paradigm not a methodology, and there are, as yet, no particular research
strategies or methods associated with the paradigm. However, critical theory informs
the work of many family therapists, so we asked Sherry L. Rediger, Judith Myers Avis,
and Jean Turner to talk about the ways that critical theory might inform family therapy
research. In Chapter 6, Sherry L. Rediger begins by discussing the historical development of critical theory and describes essential tenets of the critical theory paradigm.
Then she describes eight aspects of critical theory methodology: identifying oppression,
authentic meeting, developing a shared commitment to know, understanding self and
other, increased consciousness, action, the responsibility to share knowledge, and self-
sustaining action. Woven into her description of these eight aspects is an extended
example showing how critical theory research might be applied to family therapy with
men who are feeling oppressed by societal values and role definitions, especially with
respect to their roles as fathers. "Critical research," claims Rediger, "is not undertaken
for the sake of knowledge but for the sake of people" (p. 136). Like family therapy, critical research uses dialogue to empower and emancipate.

In Chapter 7, Judy Avis and Jean Turner "distill ideas about feminist research from
across a variety of social science disciplines, illuminate the wide range of differing methods
of feminist inquiry now practiced and render these methods more visible and accessible
to our field" (p. 145). Their chapter is both scholarly and innovative. They describe
10 themes in feminist research and encourage feminist family therapists to be more active in the family therapy research community using a variety of inquiry paradigms and
methods. At the end of their chapter they point to possible future directions for family
therapy research in general and feminist family therapy research in particular.

Focus Group Evaluation

The final chapter in the qualitative section is on focus groups, a methodology that began as a technique for evaluating market responses to business products but is now used
in social science evaluation research and as a data collection technique in many qualitative
studies. In Chapter 8, Fred P. Piercy and Vernon Nickerson outline the historical development of focus groups, describe how focus groups might be used in family therapy
research, and give guidelines for how to conduct successful focus group research. Their
chapter provides succinct and clear guidance for researchers wishing to conduct focus
group evaluations or integrate focus group methods into other research designs.

QUANTITATIVE METHODS
REPORTED IN THIS VOLUME

The purpose of the quantitative part of the book is to expose the reader to a wide variety of purely quantitative methodologies. The quantitative methods are grouped into
four subsections, each of which is described briefly below.

Design and Measurement

This section begins with a "how to" chapter with some of the nuts-and-bolts issues of quantitative design. Mitchell H. Dickey has written a kind of "what I wish they had told me in graduate school" manual for the novice researcher which contains a lot of practical "do's and don'ts." In Chapter 9, Dickey addresses such issues as choosing a research topic and adviser, negotiating issues related to authorship, keeping your project "manageable," and some down-to-earth suggestions regarding data analysis and presentation of results. He also includes practical tips on getting your research published. To the best of our knowledge, there has never been a research chapter quite like this one, and readers are urged to digest it before tackling the more technical material that follows.

We have included a chapter on instrument and scale development because measurement is a fundamental building block of all quantitative designs. In Chapter 10, Douglas K. Snyder and Janida L. Rice take the reader step by step through the often arduous process of developing sound measurement instruments. They begin by considering assumptions that underlie structured measures. They go on to describe strategies for generating an item pool and deriving scales. They discuss how reliability and validity are established as part of the ongoing processes of scale development. The authors conclude their chapter with a discussion of the analysis and interpretation of scale scores.

Experimental Research

This section includes those methods in which there is a clear manipulation of the independent or treatment variable. Another hallmark of experimental design is the random assignment of subjects to experimental or controlled conditions (although in some designs, subjects can serve as their own control). In Chapter 11, Kevin P. Lyness and Douglas H. Sprenkle talk about the rich history of the experimental tradition and its key role in clinical research. They make the case that although built on positivist and modernist assumptions being challenged today, there is still no substitute for experimental research when it comes to making causal inferences about the efficacy of treatment approaches. Wider audiences such as the government and health care providers remain more impressed by randomized clinical trials than by any other clinical method.

Chapter 12, by Mitchell H. Dickey, "is written for family therapists who want to take an inside look at their work" (p. 264). In single-case designs, the therapist and the researcher are typically (but not necessarily) the same person. For this reason, the single-case experiment rests on the assumption of an inherent synergy between clinical work and research. Although used for decades in behaviorally oriented research, Dickey notes that there is not a single published example of a single-case experimental investigation in the family therapy literature. He believes this is unfortunate, because, when certain conditions are met, single-case experiments provide a strong basis on which to assert the benefits of therapy. Furthermore, doing this kind of research typically makes one a better therapist. Dickey demonstrates how establishing clear trends during baseline measurements is crucial to the method because inferences regarding treatment effectiveness are based on clear disparities between baseline and treatment phases. He delineates a variety of different designs strategies and allows the reader to distinguish between weak and strong designs. Although lacking the experimental criteria of control groups and random assignment, Dickey argues that method can be rigorous as well as feasible and therefore should be encouraged as a means of reducing the clinician–researcher gap.

Meta-analysis, as noted by Karen S. Wampler and Julianne M. Serovich in Chapter 13, "is a quantitative methodology for summarizing findings from different quantitative research studies on a given topic" (p. 286). It is an alternative to the typical narrative review of the literature in which conclusions are reached by summarizing statistically significant and nonsignificant findings. In meta-analysis, a common metric known as the effect size is used to analyze statistically what is known about a topic across a large number of research studies. Although not limited to experimental research, meta-analysis has been most often used to summarize the effectiveness of psychotherapy by pooling the results of a number of experimental studies. Wampler and Serovich not only detail the strengths and limitations of the methodology but offer a readable, nuts-and-bolts explanation of how to do it.

Relational/Predictive Research

This section contains two chapters that are categorized primarily by the purpose of the research and secondarily by the analytical techniques used. Relational/predictive research describes relationships between variables and/or how to predict one variable from another. Analytical techniques used range from simple correlation and regression to such complex techniques as structural equation modeling. Prediction research is research where a known variable is used to predict an unknown variable that occurs later in time. A simple example would be using Graduate Record Examination scores to predict performance in graduate school. In Chapter 14, *Approaches to Prediction: Correlation, Regression, and Discriminant Analysis*, Douglas K. Snyder and Laurel F. Mangrum describe the use of correlation and related techniques to examine factors that contribute to marital distress and couples' responses to marital therapy. The chapter is divided into two sections. The first, basic techniques, describes correlation, regression, partial and semipartial correlations, and multiple regression. The second section, advanced techniques, introduces the reader to canonical correlation analysis, multiple discriminant analysis, and the multiple cutoff approach. Although these topics may seem to be daunting, each is explained in clear English and illustrated with a clear example from the marriage and family therapy literature.

Structural equation modeling uses sophisticated mathematical techniques to analyze relationships among several variables. One of the major advantages of structural equation modeling is that it can model reciprocal causality. For this reason, it has considerable potential for family therapy research in which reciprocal or circular causal patterns are of great interest. Another advantage of structural equation modeling is that it offers one of the few alternatives to experimental research, where causality can be modeled even when random assignment to groups is not possible. Chapter 15 by Robert J. Volk and Denise E. Flori details this complex topic. Although well worth the reader's effort, this is probably the most challenging chapter in this volume. Because structural equation modeling combines elements of both factor analysis and multiple regression, readers with little knowledge of these techniques may find this chapter beyond their grasp. A careful reading of the previous chapter is highly recommended before tackling this one.

Cost-Effectiveness Evaluations

A quantitative methodology related to evaluation is cost-effectiveness research. In Chapter 16, Connee L. Pike-Urlacher, David P. MacKinnon, and Fred P. Piercy describe an exciting complement to experimental research. Just as the field needs to be concerned with the efficacy of its treatments, it also needs to focus on cost considerations.

These authors offer illustrations in which family therapy not only proved to be more effective than alternatives on treatment dependent variables but saved money in the process. The chapter makes important distinctions between cost-effectiveness and cost-benefit research, and describes the challenges of trying to measure savings when indirect costs and benefits, such as lost time from work or productivity, are at issue.

MIXED METHODS

The methods in this part of the book are inherently neither qualitative nor quantitative. In fact, the mixed methods lend themselves well to both approaches. Given our multimethodological bias, and our belief that different types of questions are best addressed with different strategies, we think that the mixed methods have great potential. The mixed methods allow researchers synergistic interplay between the quantitative and qualitative approaches to research. Of course, one can also combine more "pure" qualitative and quantitative methods within the same study, so the mixed methods are not the only way to achieve this synergy.

Intensive Research

This section brings together several related methodologies that focus on intensive examination of individual units of analysis using both qualitative and quantitative methods of data collection and data analysis. Single-subject experimental research, one of the designs in the quantitative section, is also an intensive method. We could have included single-subject research in this section but we decided that it fit better in the experimental section because it has a long tradition of association with experimental research. What differentiates the methods in this section from single-subject experimental research is a tendency to deemphasize manipulation of an independent variable and mixed methods of data collection and analysis.

In Chapter 17, *Case Study Research*, Sidney M. Moon and Terry S. Trepper discuss one of the most versatile methodologies in this volume. Moon and Trepper portray the flexibility of case study methodology in two ways. First, they divide case study methods into two types: informal and formal designs. Informal case study designs are ones that can be implemented by clinicians as a form of "action research" to improve their practice or share a clinical discovery with a wider audience through publication. Formal case study designs can be used to "develop a rich description of an individual, a system, or a therapeutic process; to discover or verify family therapy theory; or to explain how and when specific therapeutic processes work best" (p. 401). Moon and Trepper demonstrate the wide applicability of case study designs in family therapy research and dispute the notion that case study research must be purely descriptive by showing how multiple-case-study investigations can be used to verify and explain complex phenomena.

In Chapter 18, *The Events-Based Approach to Couple and Family Therapy Research*, Leslie S. Greenberg, Laurie Heatherington, and Myrna L. Friedlander describe one of the newest approaches to family therapy process research. Task analysis, the methodology described in this chapter, is one of the few methods in this volume that was originally developed by psychotherapists for psychotherapy research. We suspect that Greenberg and his colleagues will have you hooked from the first sentence of their chapter: "Imagine yourself, if you will, in the following scene . . . " (p. 411). In the pages that follow, Greenberg et al. provide step-by-step guidance for conducting task analyses of change events in family therapy. They clearly demonstrate that their methodology can illuminate the way that therapeutic events unfold over time and help build an understanding of the ways change occurs in therapy.

In Chapter 19, *Systematically Developing Therapeutic Techniques: Applications of Research and Development,* Richard J. Bischoff, A. Jay McKeel, Sidney M. Moon, and Douglas H. Sprenkle show how intensive research methods can be used to develop and refine new therapeutic techniques. Borrowing from methods used to improve products in industry and business, the authors show how systematic research and development methods allow clinicians and researchers to work together to conceptualize and refine new therapeutic techniques. The authors provide step-by-step guidance for clinician–researchers who wish to use research and development strategies to create new approaches to family therapy. They illustrate their discussion by showing how they used these methods to develop and refine a model of therapist-conducted consultations.

Survey Research

In Chapter 20, *Survey Research in Marriage and Family Therapy,* Thorana S. Nelson discusses methods "related to gathering information from samples of volunteers for the purpose of describing, explaining, and/or exploring particular aspects of the participants' experience, how these data relate to each other and other data, and how the results of the analyses of the data can be used to draw generalizations about larger populations" (p. 448). She illustrates the survey methods with reference to the Basic Family Therapy Skills Project. Her chapter describes the rich history of survey research, the various forms this methodology takes, and the strengths and limitations of survey research. This method pays a great deal of attention to sampling; the kinds of sampling techniques utilized vary considerably depending on whether the data gathered is quantitative or qualitative. Because survey research is no better than the questions asked, Nelson urges special attention to the art of asking questions. How data are reported will vary tremendously, depending on whether the focus is qualitative or quantitative.

The most clear-cut mixed method is probably the Delphi method. In every case we know of in the family therapy literature, the method has combined a qualitative analysis of a panel of experts' responses to a series of open-ended questions with a quantitative analysis of the same panels' responses to the researcher's summary of the open-ended responses. The Delphi methodology enables the researcher to formulate a consensus about an issue in the field without the expense of bringing experts together physically, with the added advantage of confidentiality and freedom from peer pressure or the undue influence of outspoken panel members. As Linda Stone Fish and Dean M. Busby put it in Chapter 21, this approach provides "a forum in which participants are able to express their opinions anonymously, gather feedback from the group about their views, obtain other views of the same ideas, and have an opportunity to revise their views" (p. 470). Delphi panelists are chosen for their expertise, rather than through a random process as in the most common form of quantitative survey research. The authors use Stone Fish and Piercy's (1987) investigation of the similarities and differences between structural and strategic family therapy to highlight the steps of this rather straightforward methodology. The authors make the case that the Delphi methodology is particularly well suited for bridging research and practice because it does not demand large samples, advanced statistical expertise, or a great amount of financial resources. This may explain why the method has become very popular for doctoral dissertations, particularly in areas in which exploratory research in underdeveloped areas is appropriate.

Program Evaluation

The last chapter in this volume, Chapter 22, *Program Evaluation Research: Applications to Marital and Family Therapy*, by Douglas Leber, Michelle St. Peters, and Howard J. Markman, sets forth a set of tools that enable practitioners and administrators to document the extent to which services are meeting the objectives for which they were designed. Some of the other methods described in this book (e.g., experimental methods or survey research) can be seen as evaluation research when their purpose is to evaluate a program or service. Therefore, the purpose of the research rather than the specifics of the design are crucial to categorizing investigations as evaluation research. Long used in educational, social service, and mental health settings, the evaluation research methodologies have great potential for family therapy. The authors weave throughout the chapter their own comprehensive evaluation of their Prevention and Relationship Enhancement Program. Although evaluation research can and does include outcome evaluation, it may focus on needs assessment, whether interventions are being implemented as planned, monitoring program delivery, and monitoring program participation. The authors outline in considerable detail the steps in the program evaluation research process. They also make it clear how qualitative and quantitative methods can be brought together to provide a comprehensive evaluation. The authors conclude by arguing that developing skills in program evaluation should become an essential part of both the practice and training of service providers. Were this to happen, researchers and practitioners would clearly communicate more effectively with one another—one of the goals to which this book is dedicated.

FINAL THOUGHTS ON APPROACHING THIS VOLUME

Although research can be a daunting enterprise, we hope that this book will help to demystify the process somewhat. For those new to quantitative research, Chapter 9, by Mitchell H. Dickey would be a good place to start, followed by, perhaps, Chapter 11, by Kevin P. Lyness and Douglas H. Sprenkle. For those new to qualitative research, good entry points might be Chapter 8 on focus groups, or Chapter 3, on grounded theory methods. These four chapters are especially clear exemplars of the quantitative and qualitative paradigms, respectively, and assume little prior knowledge. To get a feel for the mixed methods, we suggest beginning with Chapter 17, on case study research, or Chapter 22 on applications of program evaluation research to family therapy. Almost all the chapters are self-contained, so we hope that readers will be guided by their interests rather than by the "invariant" order of our table of contents.

Approached in this way, we hope that the book will make the research enterprise more exciting for clinicians. There really is almost no question a clinician might ask that is not amenable to research—provided one allows for the kind of methodological pluralism set forth here. Therefore, clinicians are advised to seek out the methods that will help them answer the clinical issues in which they have a passionate interest. Then, research will become a map to explore those issues about which you have a burning desire to learn more. Earlier we promised a literal smorgasbord of methodological options for doing family therapy research. We hope our readers will enjoy the feast!

REFERENCES

Anderson, W. T. (1990). *Reality isn't what it used to be.* New York: Harper & Row.

Atkinson, B., Heath, A., & Chenail, R. (1991). Qualitative research and the legitimization of knowledge. *Journal of Marital and Family Therapy, 17,* 161–166.

Bednar, R. L., Burlingame, G. M., & Masters, K. S. (1988). Systems of family treatment: Substance or semantics. *Annual Review of Psychology, 39*, 401–413.

Breunlin, D., & Schwartz, R. (1983). Why clinicians should bother with research. *The Family Therapy Networker, 7*(4), 22–27, 57–59.

Broderick, C. B., & Schrader, S. S. (1981). The history of professional marriage and family therapy. In A. S. Gurman & D. P. Kniskern (Eds.), *Handbook of family therapy*. New York: Brunner/Mazel.

Cavell, T. A., & Snyder, D. A. (1991). Iconoclasm versus innovation: Building a science of family therapy—comments on Moon, Dillon, and Sprenkle. *Journal of Marital and Family Therapy, 17*, 181–185.

Firestone, W. A. (1993, May). Alternative arguments for generalizing from data as applied to qualitative research. *Educational Researcher*, 16–23.

Gergen, K. (1985). The social constructionist movement in modern psychology. *The American Psychologist, 40*, 266–275.

Gergen, K. (1991). *The saturated self: Dilemmas of identity in contemporary life*. New York: Basic Books.

Glaser, B. G., & Strauss, A. L. (1967). *The discovery of grounded theory: Strategies for qualitative research*. Newbury Park, CA: Sage.

Gottman, J. M. (1987). The sequential analysis of family interaction. In T. Jacob (Ed.), *Family interaction and psychopathology*. New York: Plenum Press.

Gurman, A. S. (1983). Family therapy research and the "new epistemology." *Journal of Marital and Family Therapy, 9*, 227–234.

Haley, J. (1978). Ideas which handicap therapists. In M. M. Berger (Ed.), *Beyond the double bind: Communication and family systems, theories, and techniques with schizophrenics*. New York: Brunner/Mazel.

Hoshmand, L. L. S. T. (1989). Alternate research paradigms: A review and teaching proposal. *The Counseling Psychologist, 17*, 1–80.

Kunkel, M. A., Chapa, B., Patterson, G., & Walling, D. D. (1995). The experience of giftedness: A concept map. *Gifted Child Quarterly, 39*, 126–134.

Langsley, D., Flomenhaft, K., & Machotka, P. (1969). Follow-up evaluation of family crisis therapy. *American Journal of Orthopsychiatry, 39*, 753–759.

Langsley, D., Pittman, F., Machotka, P., & Flomenhaft, K. (1968). Family crisis therapy: Results and implications. *Family Process, 7*, 145–158.

Liddle, H. A. (1991). Empirical values and the culture of family therapy. *Journal of Marital and Family Therapy, 17*, 327–348.

Maturana, H. (1988). Reality: The search for opportunity or the quest for a compelling argument. *Irish Journal of Psychology, 9*(1), 25–82.

Minuchin, S., Baker, L., Rosman, B., Liebman, R., Milman, L., & Todd, T. (1975). A conceptual model of psychosomatic illness in children. *Archives of General Psychiatry, 32*, 1031–1038.

Moon, S. M., Dillon, D. R., & Sprenkle, D. H. (1991). Family therapy and qualitative research. *Journal of Marital and Family Therapy, 16*, 357–373.

Moon, S. M., & Sprenkle, D. H. (1992, Spring). AFTA Newsletter, 47, 29–30.

Nichols, M. P., & Schwartz, R. C. (1995). *Family therapy: Concepts and methods* (3rd ed.). Boston: Allyn & Bacon.

Olson, D. H. (1976). Bridging research, theory, and application: The triple threat in science. In D. H. Olson (Ed.), *Treating relationships*. Lake Mills, IA: Graphic Publishing Co.

Pinsof, W., & Wynne, L. (1995). The effectiveness of marriage and family therapy [Special issue]. *Journal of Marital and Family Therapy, 21*(4).

Shields, C. G. (1986). Critiquing the new epistemologies: Toward minimum requirements for a scientific theory of family therapy. *Journal of Marital and Family Therapy, 12*, 359–372.

Sprenkle, D. H., & Bischoff, R. J. (1995). Research in family therapy: Trends, issues, and recommendations. In M. P. Nichols & R. C. Schwartz, *Family therapy: Concepts and methods* (3rd ed.). Boston: Allyn & Bacon.

Stone Fish, L., & Piercy, F. P. (1987). The theory and practice of structural and strategic family therapies: A Delphi study. *Journal of Marital and Family Therapy, 13,* 113–126.

Tomm, K. (1983, July–August). The old hat doesn't fit. *The Family Therapy Networker,* 39–41.

Tomm, K. (1986). On incorporating the therapist in a scientific theory of family therapy. *Journal of Marital and Family Therapy, 12,* 373–378.

Wynne, L. C. (1983). Family research and family therapy: A reunion? *Journal of Marital and Family Therapy, 9,* 113–117.

II

QUALITATIVE METHODS

Naturalistic Research

2

Ethnographic Research Methods
CREATING A CLINICAL SCIENCE
OF THE HUMANITIES

NEAL NEWFIELD
SCOTT P. SELLS
THOMAS EDWARD SMITH
SUSAN NEWFIELD
FAYE NEWFIELD

SOME SCIENTISTS view such human activities as, for example, sharing an embrace or hugging a child as little more than a series of timed muscular contractions (Stones, 1985). Yet, an embrace may be remembered for generations, and entire literary canons are written about things of lesser import. Science can reduce an embrace to its empirical and replicable elements, but only the humanities can describe how it feels for someone to experience that same embrace. Those elements of an event that are empirically measurable can never convey the sum of human experience. Humans reflect on the meaning of events and even create meaning from them. The science of family therapy must be able to measure and apply the scientific method but also ought to examine the possibilities that a humanities dimension can add to our research and clinical work.

Science has not typically concerned itself with individuals' experience, but to be effective clinicians, we must concern ourselves with personal experience. On the other hand, the humanities cannot provide us with the tools we may need, as practicing clinicians, to predict or influence group behavior. Protagoras, one of the founders of humanism (485–410 B.C.E.), stated that "man is the measure of all things" (Plato, 1973, 160d). A clinical science of the humanities, therefore, will hold that man *is* the measure of all things and that it is legitimate and valid to measure that man. Such an approach addresses the complexity of the human experience and gains vitality from the duality/recursion between science and the humanities. As Schneirla (1972) points out, as we progress from the study of atomic particles to study at the cellular level, the molecu-

---

First authorship is shared between Neal Newfield, Scott P. Sells, Thomas Edward Smith and Susan Newfield. Together these individuals constitute the founders of the Interuniversity Qualitative Research Group.

lar level, and upward on the scale of complexity, the study of each level of organization is subsumed by that of the next higher level. Each level requires its own methods and yields its own laws and principles. This general principle of organization demands that we, as practitioners, carefully consider the methodologies we use to assist us in understanding both the science of family therapy and the families with which we work.

The science of family therapy must be linear, mechanistic, and deterministic. It should be a tool to help practitioners predict and influence behaviors. It must also be holistic/systemic, constructivist, and esthetically capable of capturing both human experience and spirit. It must simultaneously regard the individual as a part of and more than an organism. Until newer research methods are developed, the currently accepted qualitative and quantitative methods, equally respected and used, offer us the best means of developing a science of family therapy. This chapter discusses ethnography, one of the qualitative methods.

The term ethnography is derived from the Greek *ethnos*, meaning race, tribe, or people, and *graphein*, which means to write (Crane & Angrosino, 1984). An ethnography may refer to a written account that presents an overview of a culture or parts of a culture as well as the entire research process (Holly, 1984). Marcus and Fisher (1986) define ethnography as "a research process in which the anthropologist closely observes, records, and engages in the daily life of another culture—an experience labeled as fieldwork method—and then writes accounts of this culture, emphasizing descriptive detail" (p. 18). Ethnography is defined by Leininger (1985a) as a systematic means for observing, analyzing, detailing, and describing the lifeways or specific patterns of a culture or cultural subgroup within the environment in which the culture normally lives. The noted anthropologist Bronislaw Malinowski said that the ethnographer's goal is "to grasp the native's point of view, his relationship to life, to realise his vision of his world" (1922/1961, p. 25). To put it another way, each person's "stream of consciousness" is based on that person's conceptual models of the world (D' Andrade, 1976, p. 155). Ethnography is a valuable method through which practitioners may come to understand a client's conceptual models. Family therapy would be more effective and humane if family therapists and researchers could use this methodology to understand the world view and presenting problems of families in therapy.

BACKGROUND: CULTURAL INVENTORIES, MENTAL HEALTH, AND FAMILY-FOCUSED ETHNOGRAPHIES

If ethnography is first a description of people, it may be as old as writing itself. In Western tradition, Herodotus of Halicarnassus (fifth century B.C.E.) wrote systematic and distinct descriptions of cultural groups and might be identified as one of the first ethnographers. Another early ethnographer was Christopher Columbus, who wrote an account of the Carib people he encountered in the New World. His descriptions are remarkably free of the exaggerations and myths about "savages" that were commonly believed by Europeans of the period (Hodgen, 1964). The journals of missionaries and merchants, although ethnocentric and Eurocentric, are also rich sources of information about earlier cultures, some of which no longer exist.

The Committee of the Royal Anthropological Institution of Great Britain and Ireland first published *Notes and Queries on Anthropology* in 1874 (1971) in an attempt to systematize the information included in ethnographic reports. This book is still in print and is updated and revised on a continual basis. Traditionally, ethnography was concerned with describing small societies. Malinowski's (1922/1961) work is an example of that genre. Since Malinowski's day, the field of ethnography has widened considerably. Today, researchers in many disciplines use ethnographic methods to study varied types of cultural phenomena. Nursing (Leininger, 1985c; Morse, 1989, 1994; Munhall & Boyd, 1993), education (Angus, 1986; Fetterman, 1984; Ogbu, 1981), and public health (Bentley et. al., 1988; Kotarba, 1990; Nichter, 1980; Wiebel, 1988) are three professions in which the use of ethnographic research is proliferating.

A limited number of ethnographies address mental health issues. The sociologist Goffman (1961) described the culture of an asylum, and Caudill, Redlich, Gilmore, and Brody (1952) conducted a participant observation ethnography by posing as patients in order to look at the social structure of a psychiatric ward environment. Later Caudill (1958) expanded this study to include the psychiatric hospital as a small society (1958). In *Pathways to Madness*, a book rich with description, Henry (1971) describes five families, each with a schizophrenic member. *Making It Crazy* (Estroff, 1981) describes the experiences of patients with severe mental illness who attempt to negotiate the community mental health system in Madison, Wisconsin. Numerous articles exist about the experiences of drug and alcohol abusers. Spradley (1972a) has written about "beating" drunk charges and being a tramp on Skid Row. Several ethnographies concern the experience of heroin addicts (Agar, 1973; Preble & Casey, 1967; Sutter, 1966) and one was written about PCP users (Fieldman, Agar, & Beschner, 1979). Without identifying themselves, ethnographers have attended Alcoholics Anonymous meetings and described the interactions they observed at these meetings (Lofland & Lejeune, 1970). (Note: Collecting information without obtaining informed consent is a dubious practice and is discussed later in the ethics section of this chapter.)

Little has been written about family therapy from a patient/client perspective. Most accounts of therapy are written by or based on the perceptions/accounts of clinicians, theoreticians, and researchers (Kruger, 1986; Fessler, 1983). *The Family Crucible* (Napier & Whitaker, 1978) is best described as a case study or phenomenological account of what it is like to be a family therapist. More recently, Tyler and Tyler (1985) wrote an account of being a trainee at the Galveston Family Therapy Institute. This study sought to understand therapists and supervisors but failed to address the "insider" client's point of view. Ironically, the Tylers concluded that the greatest challenge trainees face is learning to understand their supervisors, not their clients. Such findings underscore the need to understand all perspectives, including those of the clients.

Wencke Seltzer, a psychologist and a student of the anthropologist Julies Henry, and Michael Seltzer, a cultural anthropologist, have attempted to develop a cultural approach to family therapy (1983, 1988). The Seltzers viewed the family as a culture and believed that through storytelling and story construction, along with other forms of fantasy work, families could be freed from stasis by "editing" any family myths with negative impact on the family or its members. Using this approach, the therapist may assist a family in building a culture of conversion to accommodate a family member with a conversion disorder. This proposed treatment approach is anthropological and transgenerational in nature (Seltzer, 1985a, 1985b, 1988). Although such work is anthropological in emphasis, it does not constitute an ethnographic description of the family's experience of the conversion disorder or of therapy. Such ethnographic research has only recently begun to develop in family therapy.

The family therapy of adolescent substance abuse has been described ethnographically (Kuehl & Newfield, 1991; Kuehl, Newfield, & Joanning, 1990; Newfield et al., 1990, 1991). More recently, ethnographic methods have been used to describe the experiences of couples and therapists who participated in reflecting team therapy (Sells,

Smith, Coe, Yoshioka, & Robbins, 1994; Smith, Sells, & Clevenger, 1994; Smith, Winston, & Yoshioka, 1992; Smith, Yoshioka, & Winston, 1993). Dissertation research conducted with the use of ethnographic methods is being seen more frequently in the field of family therapy (Brown, 1992; Gawinski, 1987; Kuehl, 1987; Love, 1992; Sells, 1993; Beer, 1993; Todahl, 1995).

ASSUMPTIONS: PHILOSOPHICAL AND OTHERWISE

McCullock asserted that a person claiming to have no epistemology had a bad one (Bateson & Bateson, 1987). Because the assumptions of ethnography are the foundation of its epistemology, it is important to review them. However, in reviewing the assumptions, Bateson's famous adage should be remembered: "The map is never the territory, the 'structure' is never 'true'" (Bateson & Bateson, 1987, p. 161). To whit, it is important to remember that the science of ethnography is bigger than its assumptions.

1. *Culture is a system of knowledge that is used by human beings to interpret experience and generate behavior* (Spradley, 1979, 1980). Ethnographers use culture as an explanatory mechanism. Every culture classifies and sorts experiences into categories. A culture also has rules and maps that are used by its inhabitants to determine which behaviors are appropriate for them and to interpret the behavior of others in the culture. The cognition that people share is their culture (Spradley, 1972b). Families share a culture, as do family therapists. Behavioral limits are at least partially determined by culture, and, because culture dictates behavioral limits, even the behavior of someone who is "crazy" is largely determined by the culture within which that person lives.

2. *People's world of experience may be discerned by the way they talk about it* (Frake, 1962, p. 74). The ethnographic methods we prefer rely heavily on language because culture is communicated among individuals. Because it is so flexible, language is both the major "signifier" and the most productive symbolic system of a culture. Although language cannot reveal the entirety of a culture, language used by informants is certainly a useful tool for constructing major portions of a culture (Goodenough, 1957; Lounsbury, 1963).

3. *People's experience should not be stripped of the context in which it occurs.* The traditional scientific method views the experiment as the ideal form of research. Under this method, all factors except the independent variable under scrutiny are held constant. To vary "context" is to threaten validity (Mishler, 1979). Ethnographic research, on the other hand, takes a holistic or systemic approach, concerning itself with the effects of the context, or naturalistic setting, on behavior. Rather than stripping an informant's responses from the context in which they occurred, ethnographic interviewers attempt, through questioning, to obtain a contextual frame of reference to assist them in comprehending the informant's point of view.

4. *Ethnography is emic rather than etic in its emphasis.* The emic view is the cultural insider's, or native, point of view. The etic view, in ethnographic terms, is the way the ethnographer views the event. The etic view deliberately excludes what the cultural native says. Ethnography emphasizes the meanings, beliefs, and world view of the natives with whom it is engaged. It seeks to comprehend their understanding of the world in which they live. Validity is not determined by measuring variance but by whether natives confirm what the ethnographer proposes as truth from the natives' point of view. However, not all qualitative research adopts an emic viewpoint. Many credible and useful qualitative methods (e.g., conversational analysis) are etic in orientation (Gale & Newfield, 1992).

5. *We must give up the doctrine of "immaculate perception"* (Sass, 1986). There has been considerable discussion of the orientation of ethnographic methodology as subjective rather than objective and constructivist rather than logical positivist (Clifford & Marcus, 1986; Leininger, 1985b; Lipson, 1989; Newfield, Kuehl, Joanning, & Quinn, 1990, 1991). We believe that "a fact is a percept viewed through a frame of reference" (Peacock, 1986, p. 67). Observers are never objective but bring their subjective points of view to the observation of any object.

An example is revealed in the experience of an anthropologist who received a copy of *Playboy* magazine while doing fieldwork in the remote Highlands of New Guinea. Because he was the first Caucasian the natives had ever seen, he was interested in how his male informants would respond to the photograph in the centerfold. When shown the picture, his informants responded enthusiastically, and a number of them even inquired about the model's marital status. The anthropologist, at first, believed that the natives' excitement was evidence of the existence of cross-cultural standards of sexual attractiveness. He later learned that it was not Miss December who generated such enthusiasm but the shiny brass pots and pans she was draped around in her modern American kitchen. The natives believed that some lucky man would get this valuable cookware as dowry if he took her as a bride.

6. *All ethnographies are low-level theories.* As Hammersley (1992) indicates, all descriptions are theoretical: "They involve concepts and are structured by theoretical assumptions" (p. 28). With regard to the "reality" of ethnographies, we do not view them as purely a story (i.e., radical constructivism), nor do we see them from the position of naive realism. Instead, we believe Hammersley's (1992, p. 52) concept of subtle reality to be useful. Subtle realism posits that the researcher can *investigate* independent knowable phenomena but that these phenomena are never *directly accessible* to the researcher. Such phenomena are mediated through cultural assumptions, purposes, and human construction.

METHODOLOGY

The ethnographic research process is inductive. It demands flexibility on the part of the researcher. In the discipline of anthropology, researchers using ethnographic methods are almost expected to change their research plans and questions after their field research is under way (Agar, 1986). After formulating working hunches, ethnographic researchers are prepared to refine the initial formulations based on what is learned under field conditions. Unlike the deductive research process, the ethnographic research process is recursive, not linear. Without a linear, externally imposed research design, the fieldworker is able to continually adapt the study to conform to shifts in local knowledge and social conditions (Spradley, 1980).

Before the 1960s, accounts of fieldwork were limited to introductory remarks in ethnographies. The pervasive belief among many professionals was that fieldwork could not be taught in the classroom but only learned through actual experience (Nader, 1970; Powdermaker, 1966). Training in ethnographic research has been considered a form of apprenticeship (Epstein, 1967). Although instructional texts are available on ethnographic research, no "cookbook" method exists that can be applied to all field conditions. Ethnographers apply specific research methods to study specific problems during fieldwork. Participant observation, interviews, life histories, conversational analysis, and case studies are some of the methods available for data collection (Holly, 1984; Clammer, 1984).

Ethnographies reflect and are shaped by theoretical presuppositions and principles that guide the process of data collection and analysis (Ellen, 1984; Herskovits, 1954). Several core paradigms are evident in ethnography. They include holistic, behavioral, and semiotic forms (Sanday, 1979). Under the "holistic" or "old" paradigm, the ethnographer focuses on a single community, its shared beliefs, practices, material culture, folklore, mythology, and behaviors (Clammer, 1984; Spradley, 1980; Holly, 1984). The theoretical premise underlying holistic ethnography is functionalist in nature. The holistic paradigm emphasizes the study of culture as an integrated whole through an examination of the relationships among institutions, populations, and events. Family therapy ethnographies, thus far, have not been holistic but rather particularistic, or what Muecke (1994) describes as focused in nature. They are concerned with the process of therapy not the relationship among institutions, populations, and events. In the mental health field, *Making It Crazy* (Estroff, 1981) comes closest to being holistic. This ethnography describes employment, general living circumstances, social life, recreation, communication, finances, family concerns, dealing with professionals in the mental health system, and much more among "psychiatric clients" in Madison, Wisconsin.

In the behavioral paradigm, the ethnographer uses operational data from preselected categories of behavior to compare the extent of variance in cultural behavior patterns. Hypotheses are developed and tested in behavioral ethnographies (Sanday, 1979). Such an approach might be useful, for instance, in studying family responses to schizophrenic behavior and what intensifies and decreases symptoms with the identified patient.

The semiotic or interpretive paradigm emphasizes symbols, meaning, and modes of thinking. The semiotic paradigm defines culture as shared cognition and the rules of behavior and belief systems associated with that shared cognition. The unit of analysis is social interaction among informants, which is why semiotic ethnography is often seen as the study of "micro" behavior and communication. Items of data collection usually include individual–group vocabulary, objects, and events (Sanday, 1979). One example of the interpretive paradigm is ethnoscience (alternate names are ethnosemantics or cognitive anthropology) (Spradley, 1979, 1980; Tyler, 1969; Werner & Schoepfle, 1987). In family therapy at least a modest amount of research is beginning to follow an ethnosemantic paradigm (Kuehl & Newfield, 1991; Kuehl et al., 1990; Newfield et al., 1990, 1991; Sells, 1993).

Ethnographic Questions

An apocryphal quote from Einstein is: "You have to itch before you can scratch." Methodology has traditionally been seen as a way to offer systematic and responsibly supportive explanations for natural phenomena. Anthropologist R. F. Ellen (1984) defines methodology as "the systematic study of principles guiding anthropological investigation and the ways in which theory informs the production of data" (p. 4). Researchers begin with a question and proceed to look for answers via the logical process of inquiry we call methodology. Students not yet completely enculturated into the proper use of methodology often begin with a method and then attempt to formulate a question. For example, knowing *t* tests, they ask questions concerning the differences between two groups. More sophisticated researchers ask questions first and then decide which methods will be most effective in their search for answers.

The methodologies with which a person is familiar will shape the type of questions that are asked. There is a recursion between the "scratch" (method) and the "itch" (question). Quantitative research is fundamentally based on an analysis of variance. How do two groups vary generically from one another, or how do the members of a single group vary on specific variables? It should not be surprising, then, that quantitative researchers ask such variance-oriented questions as: "How are couples who will divorce different from couples who will stay married after marriage counseling is completed?" and "Do patients and their families with severe mental illness have lower levels of coping and higher stress compared to patients and their families who are recovering from an addiction?"

The ethnographic approach is liberating for more traditionally trained researchers because ethnography opens up a new class of questions. The outsider's view is replaced with concern for the insider's view, and variance questions are often replaced with questions about how clients, their spouses and families, and groups/cultures experience an event. Some new questions that may arise specifically in therapy and family therapy might include the following: "In their own language and categories, what is the experience of family therapy like for family members?" "How do families make sense of a therapist's behavior?" and "Into what categories do families divide the process of therapy?" Therapists speak of the social stage, the problem stage, the interaction stage, and the ending of an interview (Haley, 1976). It is not at all certain that families will divide therapy into similar stages. Questions that might capture families' perspectives include, "How do families describe the same experience from their perspectives?" "Do families experience paradox as paradoxical?" "How do they describe paradox and similar concepts?" "Do they notice them at all?" "When therapists use enactment and raise intensity, how do the families describe these experiences?" "How do families experience directives?" and "Do they even perceive them as directives, or do they describe them as something else, such as advice giving?"

Similar questions have launched a number of family therapy ethnographies: "How do clients and families understand such therapeutic personnel and strategies as cotherapists, teaming, reflecting teams, one-way mirrors, videotaping, intakes, and assessments?" "When they talk to their friends, what do family members say about their own family therapy?" One of the authors interviewed a patient after he had been given a mental status exam by a psychiatrist. The patient believed the exam was an intelligence test and used to determine his worthiness for treatment. Clearly, patient and therapist had significantly different construals of assessment and treatment!

An ethnographic view of family therapy raises questions concerning not only the experience of therapy but also the families' experience of dysfunctional family processes and psychopathology. Most of our understanding of the family processes surrounding anorexia, schizophrenia, major affective disorders, incest, and other regular presenting problems comes from what we observe in an office setting and what our patients describe to us under the same conditions. The ethnographic approach helps us to understand the importance of context in shaping behavior. Do we honestly believe that schizophrenics and their families or families who present with incest behave and explain their behaviors in the same way when they are under our scrutiny as they do in the privacy of their own homes? A whole series of productive, participant–observer ethnographies could be developed if researchers lived with and viewed the behaviors of client families in their own environments. Henry (1971) provided a richly detailed example of this process in his study, *Pathways to Madness* when he lived with schizophrenics and their families.

Sampling and Selection Procedures

Most ethnographies rely on "purposeful" or "theoretical" sampling. Purposive, or criterion-based, sampling requires that researchers establish a set of criteria or list of attributes that the sample must possess (LeCompte & Preissle, 1993). For example, in the Sells et al. (1994) study informants were selected based on whether they were in reflecting team couples therapy; in the Newfield et al. (1990, 1991) study informants were members of families in family therapy in which the presenting problem was adolescent substance abuse and the identified patient had at least one younger sibling. Such sampling is sufficient when the primary concern of the ethnographer is to document patterns of behaviors that occur and recur in varying sets or social sets of relations (Mead, 1953). Families should also be selected based on their availability for interviews and whether they possess rich and relevant information that can be shared with researchers. The most articulate informants become key informants and are interviewed multiple times. A reader, accustomed to the random sampling used in traditional research, may question the wisdom of this approach. How can such a sample be representative?

The ethnographer's first concern is not whether the information is "representative" but whether the informant can supply relevant, complete, and sufficient information (Morse, 1989). Random sampling strategies common to quantitative research are also purposive in that they are based on specific parameters or sets of attributes. The difference is that criterion-based sampling, combined with emic-oriented qualitative interviews, is better suited for identifying unrecognized attributes and parameters that should be incorporated into research. For this reason, if population characteristics are unknown or if limited literature or research is available, criterion-based selection may identify important population characteristics and research questions for study (LeCompte & Preissle, 1993). Once research questions are formulated and the population is well described or identified, specific variables can be chosen for study, using probabilistic samples.

Purposive, or criterion-based sampling, has several variations. Basic purposive sampling requires that the researcher create a list of characteristics or attributes that are essential to answer the research questions. Typical ways to locate this sample include intensity sampling, critical case sampling, maximum variety sampling (Morse, 1994), and minimum difference sampling.

Intensity sampling emphasizes selecting informants who are authorities about a particular experience because of their extended exposure to the phenomena. Patients who have been admitted only once to a state hospital will have less breadth in their description of the experience than individuals who have had multiple admissions. The latter group may even be able to give you a history of staff attitudes and treatment strategies and how they have changed over the years.

Critical case sampling is the selection of specific examples of behaviors that are significant for the identification of incidents that may be generalized to other situations and settings. Once sampling and subsequent analysis have progressed to include other settings, data are enriched by the purposeful selection of confirming and disconfirming cases.

Maximum variety sampling requires deliberately selecting a heterogeneous sample and observing the sample for commonalities and differences. Glaser and Strauss (1967) describe this maximizing of difference sampling as a way of identifying "fundamental uniformities of greatest scope" (p. 58). After finding commonalities in a diverse sample, researchers can be confident that they are studying a phenomenon that has a strong influence or effect. Maximizing difference also ensures that categories and the properties of categories studied are well saturated and that the descriptions produced are thick. Additionally, maximizing diversity challenges the researcher to combine and integrate categories and properties as well as to clearly limit what is being studied.

If difference in sampling can be maximized, it can also be minimized. Reducing heterogeneity in sampling allows the researcher to easily identify common categories and properties of the phenomenon studied. Differences identified will probably be due to strong effects. Because the range of differences is small, the conditions under which a property exists are more clearly defined and predicted (Glaser & Strauss, 1967). Most researchers begin by studying groups with minimized difference and then, once basic categories are established, looking at diversity.

Other types of sampling include "snowball," or nominated, sampling, volunteer sampling, and enumeration, where the complete population is sampled. "Snowball" sampling (Bogdan & Biklen, 1982, p. 66; Morse, 1989, p. 119) requires that an informant refer the researcher to the next informant. With such a referral, it is easier to initiate interviews with additional informants; further, if your first informant was an insider, it is likely that your next informant will be so, as well. Volunteer sampling (Agar, 1980, pp. 156–157; Morse, 1989, p. 120) is done frequently in medical settings when perspective informants are not known to each other or the investigator. Two examples of a volunteer sample solicited through newspaper ads or some other public means include women employed out of the house who rear infants and people who want to quit smoking. Finally, enumeration is not a "sampling" method because it entails interviewing an entire group. Enumeration is only possible when the unit being studied is small.

In ethnographic research, the investigator continues to sample more people until saturation of each new category is reached (Strauss, 1987; Strauss & Corbin, 1990). As in grounded theory, the ethnographer continues interviewing informants until the stories begin to sound repetitive and no new or relevant data emerge regarding a category. Researchers must also be concerned with the breadth of their sampling. Does the sample cover the range of variation concerning a phenomenon, or is it limited in its diversity? For example, the saturation of categories necessary for a thorough description of couples' responses to marital counseling in divorce situations might be extremely limited if one's interviews were limited to upper-middle-class couples. This strategy of sampling assumes that there is not a single description of a particular phenomenon in a universal sense.

With purposive sampling as a goal, probabilistic sampling techniques are rare in ethnographic research. Instead, researchers prefer to study a few cases intensively, with a goal of generalizing to a theory, rather than generalizing to a population (Goetz & LeCompte, 1984; Yin, 1989). These ethnographic descriptions can then be tested later in quantitative designs in which probabilistic sampling is used to ensure the generalization of the findings.

Although the results of ethnographic studies can be tested later in quantitative designs, this does not mean that they must be tested. To treat such ethnographic studies as incomplete is discriminatory. This is still most obvious in many graduate programs in which students interested in doing qualitative research are permitted to do so, by ambivalent thesis and dissertation committees, as long as they do "real" quantitative research as well. Such an approach results in the student doing two research projects. Investigators using quantitative research strategies could follow up their statistical descriptions and prediction with a purposive sampling of rich descriptions of the phenomenon under measurement. The fact that they do not does not make the research inferior. Qualitative and quantitative research are complementary to each other. Research in one mode will always beg questions of the other. Sells, Smith, and Sprenkle (1995) recently described the complementary relationship between quantitative and qualitative research; they gave an example of how a qualitative study provided the foundation for a quantitative one. From this perspective, no research project is ever complete. Indeed, given the "itch," the "scratch" can continue indefinitely, using a variety of methodologies.

Data Collection

In ethnographic research, data collection means fieldwork. There are no formal rules or specific techniques for collecting valid data, working this raw data into useful information, or taking this useful information and forming predictive generalizations and explanatory principles. Fieldwork is a rite of passage for the graduate student of anthropology, and it is often accompanied by physical hardship and problems of everyday survival. It is in the field that a student of culture becomes an anthropologist (Freilich, 1970).

It is difficult to imagine that family therapists studying the behavior of clients in an office setting will have to face anything approaching the rigors of survival in the field faced by many anthropologists. Family therapists who decide to move their study of families from the office to the families homes or onto the streets where the behavior is actually occurring (e.g., when studying juvenile delinquents and their families) may find themselves facing hardships similar to those of trained anthropologists.

In doing fieldwork, the ethnographer must literally decide what to notice. There are no limits to what can be described in a culture or in a family. As Clammer (1984) points out, decisions about what to describe and what to publish are largely issues of style.

Ethnographic Styles

Encyclopedic ethnographies attempt to describe all areas of a culture: kinship, religion, material culture, political systems, performance and decorative arts, and rites of passage, including marriages and funerals, in a comprehensive manner. This type of ethnography is closely akin to phenomenological studies in that they attempt to describe the experience of another culture. Most ethnographies today are theoretical ethnographies, which attempt to answer a specific research question about a culture, such as, "How do rites of passage reduce stress during times of change and decrease the chance of regressing to a previous stage of development?" To be sure, such ethnographies can be thick with description, but they are guided by a question.

Other types of ethnographies identified by Clammer (1984) include simulations, the collection of text in a native language, and survey methods. The latter are not discussed here because they are no different from the survey methods in sociology with which most readers are familiar. Simulations are attempts to get members of a cultural group to enact a cultural event that has been abandoned as a reenactment or to perform a cultural activity out of context for the purpose of allowing the anthropologist to describe it. Minuchin's lunch with anorectics and their families (Minuchin, Rosman, & Baker, 1979) was essentially a simulation for the purpose of change rather than for observation alone.

The ethnographies mentioned above can be placed on a continuum, based on the degree of involvement with the culture required of the ethnographer. Encyclopedic ethnographies may be placed at one end of the spectrum because they require extensive involvement over long periods. Textual study and surveys require the least amount of "soaking" (Clammer, 1984), or induction into the culture, and thus may be placed at the other end of the spectrum.

Participant Observation, Ethnographic Interviewing, and Categorization

A researcher learns about a culture through observation, participation, and talking with its members in the interview process. These three methods are often collapsed into two: participant observation and ethnographic interviewing. The two methods have many commonalities. Both are inductive rather than deductive. Both are concerned with establishing the subjective world view of the native rather than that of the scientist. Both are "open" and "discovery-oriented" forms of research in which the goal is to grow hypotheses rather than to test them. Finally, both establish concepts and constructs that can be used to describe the internal workings of a culture rather than measure a set of testable variables. The details of these methodologies are far beyond the scope of this chapter. What we can provide is an overview of the processes involved in participant observation, ethnographic interviewing, data collection, and data analysis.

Participant observation is as old as travel itself. Travelers return home with a collage of impressions about the housing, social customs, ceremonies, manners, religious rites, attitudes toward family, and work practices of the cultures they have visited. The difference between world travelers and trained ethnographers is that the latter steep themselves in a culture in as systematic a manner as possible in order to draw more valid conclusions about it. In addition, ethnographers, through systematic analysis, attempt to build a theory of events to explain the behavior of members of that culture. A good ethnography provides a slice of the behavior of a culture and then interprets it within the cultural context in which it occurred (Agar, 1980).

Ethnographers learn about the culture of a people through the actions of the individual members of the culture and through discussions with them. The ethnographer learns by actively participating and observing. Thus, when ethnographers interview members of the culture, the actions in which the ethnographer took part may be more fully described and explained, and the mental processes of the people who were not directly observable may be comprehended and recorded. People are neither all that they do nor all that they say. Our verbal life may not reflect what we do, and what we do may only hint at what we think. When ethnographic interviewing concerns events that have occurred elsewhere (e.g., a fight between a husband and wife in a therapy session or another problem behavior) the informants' subsequent verbal accounts may be distorted. These distortions may occur when informants are unable or unwilling to talk about some experiences or systematically distort the experiences they do report. One may also observe a fight between a husband and wife but be unable to determine its meaning or significance. Participant observation and ethnographic interviewing thus complement each other by providing opportunities to rectify distortions caused by this interplay of cognition and behavior (Becker & Geer, 1970).

Ethnographic interviewing is a particular kind of speech event. Nominally, ethnographers explain their purpose in being there and ask more than 30 different types of ethnographic questions for the explicit purpose of aiding the informant's efforts to teach the ethnographer about designated aspects of the informant's culture (Spradley, 1979). The immediate result of ethnographic interviewing and participant observation is often an overabundance of field notes, which must be analyzed and comprehended in a systematic manner. The process of data analysis is similar for participant observation and ethnographic interviewing, although the means of collection, observation, and interviewing are quite different.

The diaries and journals of natives can be valuable sources of ethnographic texts, reflecting the world view and subjective mind of the native. *Perceval's Narrative: A Patient's Account of His Psychosis, 1830–1832*, written by John Perceval and edited by Bateson (1961), is an excellent firsthand, textual account of being psychotic. *Every Day Gets a Little Closer: A Twice-Told Tale of Therapy* (Yalom & Elkin, 1974) juxtaposes the therapeutic experiences of a patient and a therapist. Both therapist and patient kept private experiential diaries during the therapy process, which were combined into a book after the therapy was concluded.

The smart ethnographer need not wait for inspired informants who have a desire to write. Informants can be encouraged or even paid to keep journals. The texts can then be used to trigger details of events during the interview that the informant might not typically remember (Zimmerman & Wieder, 1977). With the proliferation of relatively inexpensive tape recorders, instamatic cameras, and video cameras, journaling is not limited to text. Documentary videotapes and taped interviews have been broadcast on television and radio, including such subjects as what it is like to live in a "hood" and be part of a gang, what it is like to go to public school, and what is like to be a teen mother on welfare. Modern communication technologies enable both ethnographers and informants to make valuable contributions to the field of family therapy.

Data Analysis

In quantitative research, data collection is usually demarcated as a task separate from data analysis. Ethnographic research, on the other hand, necessitates that data collection and analysis go together. The very act of writing field notes must be conducted according to a system, in order to manage the reams of notes the researcher generates. The researcher must either record entries under headings and subheadings or create a data filing system. This act of categorizing notes under headings or file names is a rudimentary form of analysis. What is said or observed is categorized, based on the native's nomenclature and ways of subdividing the world or on categories that are part of the culture of anthropology, such as those listed in *Notes and Queries* (Committee of the Royal Anthropological Institution of Great Britain and Ireland, 1874/1971). Ethnographic interviewing and participant observation are both methods for identifying cultural categories, systematically fleshing them out, establishing relationships between the categories, and identifying cultural themes between constellations of categories. In this fashion, cultural patterns and ways of responding in the culture can be understood.

The researcher works with nominal level data to determine the categories or units of study, adequate descriptions of each category, and how the categories relate to each other. As Agar (1986) points out, the ethnographer must determine what will count as a unit of analysis, and this is an interpretive issue requiring judgment and choice. The typical conditions of an experiment or survey limit the variables to be measured and the hypotheses to be tested. A typical multiple regression study will consider a few dozen variables. When it is clear which variables are to be considered, they are operationalized for purposes of the study. On the other hand, an ethnographer may generate 200 pages of field notes a week. This means that in a few weeks that researcher will be drowning in field data. How can field notes be analyzed and presented in a systematic manner? How can the ethnographer make the best use of all these field notes and ensure that the final report is not based on general impressions and memories while the "real" ethnography lies buried under a mountain of field notes? Will the ethnographer's cultural descriptions be based on representative field notes, and can the analytical process by which the ethnography was constructed be determined?

Typically, there are open-ended ethnographic interviews, semistructured interviews, and closed interviews (Leininger, 1985a, p. 54). Participant observation can be similarly characterized. Whether one is doing open-ended interview or observation or closed interviews and observation depends on whether the ethnographer is searching for cultural categories to describe a culture or a cultural scene or whether such categories have already been established and the ethnographer is seeking to elaborate on them.

Walking through a family therapy clinic, an ethnographer from another planet might observe a room with one-way mirrors, filing cabinets, a greeter, healers, teachers of healers, billing systems, and papers that those who want a healer must fill out. The ethnographer might even draw a map labeling these areas with the names that natives call them. Interviewing a client about the therapy experience, the ethnographer might ask a grand tour question, such as, "If I were your friend, and I told you that I had to go out there like you did, and I wanted to be prepared from beginning to end concerning what was going to happen in as much detail as possible, what would you tell me?" The informant might describe calling on the phone, scheduling an intake, filling out tests and questionnaires, seeing the counselor, the one-way mirror, phone calls during the meeting from people behind the mirror, meeting with the whole family, talking alone with the therapist, the ride home after the session, doing homework, and how the counselor ran the interview. Each of these would then become a category in the researcher's field notes. Future participant observation and interviewing would, at some point, become more semistructured or even closed-ended around these categories. The fieldworker might spend considerable time behind the one-way mirror noting the behaviors associated with this context and recording, as well as speculating on what those behaviors meant to participants. The researcher would want to interview clients, healers in training, and teachers of healers about one-way mirrors and the activities associated with them. By asking how the mirror is used and how informants see the mirror in relation to other activities, the native function and meaning of the mirror and the activities associated with it can be described. This search for meaning would not stop with categories.

Participant Observation and the Constant Comparative Method

Participant observation research requires a consistent, inductive method of data collection, which makes it possible to identify significant cultural categories, flesh them out, and generate the relationships between them while storing and retrieving information. This is done to help describe and explain culture or aspects of a culture. Data on the life of the natives is stored in categories. Linkages or constructs between these categories are described, and theoretical constructs are developed that instruct one on how to behave and think like a native.

Two building blocks of the constant comparative method are categories and their properties. A category is capable of standing on its own as a conceptual element of a theory. In this case, the theory is the description/explanation of how the culture functions. Properties are the conceptual aspects or elements of a category. There are four stages to the constant comparative method, as discussed by Glaser and Strauss (1967):

Stage 1. Comparing incidents applicable to each category.
Stage 2. Integrating categories and their properties.
Stage 3. Delimiting the theory.
Stage 4. Writing the theory.

In this first stage of analysis, incidents applicable to each category are compared. The researcher begins the *coding* process, with a focus on the discovery of *categories* and the generation of *memos* through the constant comparative method. The coding and memoing processes continue through subsequent stages but take a different form in each stage. The term "coding" refers to conceptualization of data into categories and relationships among categories. The term "open coding" is used to describe the initial process of unrestricted coding of data the aim of which is to produce concepts that seem to fit the data. "Open coding" is defined by Strauss and Corbin (1990) as "the process of breaking down, examining, comparing, conceptualizing, and categorizing data" (p. 61).

This may be a line-by-line and even word-by-word analysis of data collected by the participant observer. Because the goal of open coding is to open up the inquiry, it is essential to be creative and unrestricted. Errors in coding are discovered and eliminated in subsequent data analysis.

From the ethnographer's participant observation, the ethnographer describes cultural categories in detail, identifies important cultural categories, and infers or makes hypotheses about the relationships among categories and why people act in particular ways. The ethnographer will also be listening to and recording what people say about what they are doing and how their comments affect the categories under study. If it is a literate culture, the ethnographer will also study policies, memos, letters, and other texts that might contain important information about the cultural act under study. This second stage in the constant comparative method emphasizes integrating categories and their properties.

During Stage 2, units of comparison change from comparing bits of data with other bits of data to comparing data with categories generated from prior data comparisons. Although categories continue to be generated through open coding, the focus begins to narrow by investigation of proposed *core categories* through the process of *axial coding*. These investigations continue to generate memos that tend to become more relationship and theory oriented. A core category is one that accounts for most of the variation in a pattern of behavior. It functions as the center of theory inasmuch as it helps link or integrate categories together. Most other categories and their properties are related to the core category.

As the coding process proceeds and categories are discovered, researchers should intensify their analysis through axial coding. Axial coding is defined by Strauss and Corbin (1990) as "a set of procedures whereby data are put back together in new ways after open coding, by making connections between categories" (p. 96). The purpose of axial coding is to use the coding paradigm to develop a category beyond its properties and dimensions by focusing on "the conditions that give rise to it, the context in which it is embedded, the action/interaction strategies by which it is handled, managed and carried out, and the consequences of those strategies" (p. 97). It leads to the discovery of possible core categories for selective coding analysis. Axial coding may begin when the open coding process has revealed certain categories that are continually repeated for each incident.

Categories will be coded and recoded based on different characteristics, as the ethnographer's understanding of the culture shifts and changes. Often the same information may be coded into more than one category. Categories and properties of categories will emerge, take on significance, and fade as the ethnographer's understanding of the culture changes. Categories are usually studied until they reach theoretical saturation. The ethnographer knows that a category is saturated when additional observation does not produce additional information for a categorical description.

After repeated observations, the ethnographer will attempt to construct a theory (i.e., a native view of what is happening, based on what has been seen and heard). This point is called Stage 3, during which the ethnographer attempts to delimit a theory or refine the theoretical world view of the native. Stage 4, the last stage, is the actual writing of the theory or ethnography.

As the theory is reduced, the researcher reduces the categories to those contained within the boundaries of emerging theory. Coding and data analysis become more select and focused through the use of *selective coding*. During Stage 3, categories become *theoretically saturated*.

In the ethnographic research process, lower-level categories usually emerge quickly during fieldwork. Higher-level categories, overriding conceptual integration and the properties that elaborate them, usually arise later. Certain categories seem to coalesce together, and there may be natural breaks in the data, such as in sequences of incidents (Hammersley & Atkinson, 1983). Overriding conceptual integration refers to cultural themes that serve to unite cultural categories. Spradley (1979) describes such a theme as "any cognitive principle, tacit or explicit, recurrent in a number of domains and serving as a relationship among subsystems of cultural meaning" (p. 186).

Ethnographic Interviewing, Linguistics, and the Developmental Research Sequence

The consistent inductive methods of data collection used when conducting ethnographic interviews is not so different from that used in doing participant observation research. Spradley (1979, 1980) has written books on participant observation research and ethnographic interviewing in which the ethnoscience method he advocates is virtually identical in both methods of data collection. The few exceptions are the result of dealing with data generated from interviews versus that which is observed but not necessarily talked about.

If participant observation research methods and ethnographic interviewing methods can be so similar it should be no surprise that ethnographic interviewing methods also rely on the constant comparative method just recently mentioned. A comparison of the constant comparative method and ethnoscience's ethnographic interviewing data-analytical method, which Spradley (1979) calls the developmental research sequence, reveals that they are quite similar. At its core, what Spradley describes is a linguistically sophisticated version of the constant comparative method used in both participant observation and ethnographic interviewing research. First domain analysis is done, then taxonomic analysis, and then componential analysis. The method concludes with a search for cultural themes.

Domain analysis is the search for cultural categories and their properties. Taxonomic analysis uses structural questions in an attempt to linguistically create a hierarchy among the properties of a category. This may be thought of as a way to organize the information in a category according to the way a native sees it and then ensuring that the now properly organized category is well saturated. In componential analysis, linkages and the meaning of categories are established, and the categories are contrasted with each other. Through such strategies as continuous exposure to the culture, completing a componential analysis of domains and how they contrast, and a review of proverbs and sayings, the ethnographer identifies cultural themes that link categories into a meaningful relationship. This last activity is similar to what is described in the constant comparative method as hypothesizing the generation of relationships among the categories and their properties.

Domain Analysis. Descriptions of various cultural events elicited through questioning are subject to domain analysis. A domain is an informant-expressed relationship between a folk (native) category designated by a cover term and a number of other categories included under the cover term (Spradley, 1979, 1980). There is a semantic relationship based on one semantic trait between the cover term and the terms that are listed under, or "included" in, the cover term. For example, pastors, counselors, psychologists, psychiatrists, and social workers were identified in the Newfield et al. (1990, 1991) study as "*kinds of* psychos and shrinks." "Psychos and shrinks" is the folk category or cover term for types of therapists and "kinds of" is the semantic relationship.

Under a cover term is a list of symbols or included terms ("Psychos and Shrinks" include pastors, social workers, counselors, psychologists, and psychiatrists). The domain, "Psychos and Shrinks," consists of all the included terms. Although they are related to each other through one semantic relationship, they represent all kinds of psychos and shrinks. Domain analysis is an ethnographic method in which the terminology that people use and how they talk about different matters may be used to ascertain how people classify or categorize their experiences (Sturdevant, 1972). It is a basic assumption of ethnosemantics that the dimensions of meaning found in cultural experiences can be delineated through the study of these experiences as they are reflected in language (Frake, 1962).

The researcher, by asking structural questions of informants, may identify new domains or categories, verify the existence of a domain, or identify additional included terms or properties of a category to be grouped under a domain. For example:

"Are there different kinds of Psychos and Shrinks?"
"Yes" (verification).
"What are some kinds of Psychos and Shrinks?"
"Psychologists and psychiatrists are Psychos and Shrinks."

Taxonomic Analysis. With a shift to taxonomic analysis, there is a narrowing of the interviewer's investigation. Taxonomic analysis focuses on core domains and takes the analysis one step further. Taxonomic analysis examines the included terms in a domain, looking for the relationship between these terms, and establishes a hierarchy of levels, with each term at one level included under only one term at the next level. These different levels may be thought of as subsets or subdomains of the original domain. A taxonomy with only two levels is identical to a domain.

Domain and taxonomic analysis rely on unitary contrast. In the domain of Psychos and Shrinks, informants identified only two levels. Occasionally, an informant placed psychologists as a subdomain under psychiatrists. Had mental health professionals been informants, a taxonomy of Psychos and Shrinks would have included "clinical psychology," "counseling psychology," and "neuropsychology" as included terms under the subdomain of psychology and perhaps "clinical social work" and "hospital social work" as terms under social work. Expert knowledge or categories that have great significance for the native usually result in more complex taxonomies. The fourth edition of the *Diagnostic and Statistical Manual of Mental Disorders* (American Psychiatric Association, 1994) is an example of a taxonomy of interest to experts in the culture; automobiles are an example of a native category that is taxonomically complex and generates great interest among the natives in general.

Taxonomic analyses start with a domain. The semantic relationship used to define the domain is then used to search for substitute frames with the included terms. For example, psychologists *are a kind of* Psycho, social workers *are a kind of* Psycho, and counselors *are a kind of* Psycho. *Kind of* (inclusion) is the semantic relationship. The next question to informants would be, "Are there kinds of psychologists?"

In doing taxonomic analysis, it is possible to go up as well as down levels, looking for a larger domain than the one that has already been identified. In the case of a taxonomic analysis, the included terms are partitioned based on only one semantic relationship. Spradley (1979) and Werner and Schoepfle (1987) present excellent discussions of taxonomies and the questions used to develop them. The next level of analysis, componential analysis, examines how systems of symbols relate to each other on multiple contrasting dimensions.

Componential Analysis. Componential analysis is a method used to systematically identify the attributes of meaning associated with a cultural symbol. The relationship between the folk terms in a domain is examined to discover how the informants distinguish between those terms. A paradigm is then developed. A paradigm takes the attributes or dimensions of contrast associated with a domain and develops a schematic representation using the informants' world view. This helps to distinguish the included terms of a domain from each other. In the Newfield et al. (1990, 1991) study, a componential analysis of types of "psychos" was conducted. A detailed discussion of componential analysis can be found in Spradley (1979) and Werner and Schoepfle (1987).

Taxonomic analysis and componential analysis focus on core categories and are axial in their coding. The interviewer is focusing more on the relationship between domains of meaning. The idea is to examine how the core domains interrelate and comprise the native world view. This is similar to Stage 2 in the constant comparative method.

After conducting domain, taxonomic, and componential analysis, an additional step is to examine the domains for any themes that may connect them into a larger constellation or relationship (Spradley 1979, 1980). In the Newfield et al. (1990, 1991) study the ambiguity of counseling, and the informants' struggle to understand the reasons why the counselor did what he did seemed to tie the domains together. There are often multiple cultural themes that appear connected to many domains and lend continuity or uniformity to the culture. In the constant comparative model, this search for core categories and the ways they unite in patterns occurs in Stages 3 and 4.

Data Displays

Clammer (1984) has described a process of "soaking" by which ethnographers while doing fieldwork saturate themselves in the culture of another and in the process compile rich descriptions of the culture under study. Often this process of soaking feels more like drowning as the field notes pile up. A data display approach addresses this concern. Such an approach contains four, linked subprocesses (Huberman & Miles, 1994): data collection, data reduction, data display, and conclusion-drawing verification. Throughout data collection, data are reduced, displayed, and organized onto a schematic diagram in the form of structured summaries, vignettes, and matrices with text, rather than numbers in the cells. Data displays tend to become more complex as data collection proceeds. Data are condensed in one location to help the writer see patterns, revise and perceive new relationships, and possibly develop explanations that may lead to a further examination of the text or new research questions. The central notion is that valid analysis requires and is driven by displays that are focused enough to permit the viewing of a full data set in the same location and are arranged systematically to answer the research questions at hand (Miles & Huberman, 1994). This process is similar to a taxonomy in which all related domains are linked into several core categories by making a schematic diagram of relationships among the domains.

One example of this process can be found in Huberman's (1991) study of the impact of assisting teachers. Initially, Huberman (1991) brought together information from several cases into one large chart called a partially ordered metamatrix. From this chart, the consequences of assisting teachers for 12 cases (i.e., school districts) was placed on a contingency table, crossing two variables (i.e., early implementation and practice stabilization) with a third (i.e., level of assistance). With this display in hand, the researcher went back to the raw data to identify similarities and differences between the 12 cases on a high, moderate, or low level of assistance and early implementation, as perceived by informants. Such an examination then leads to another display, typically in a different form, according to information found by the researcher in the initial set of displays.

With each data display, the conclusion-drawing/verifying stage occurs as the researcher interprets and draws meaning from the displayed data. The analytical tactics range from a constant comparative method to such confirmatory tactics as triangulation with other data sources and checking findings with informants (Miles & Huberman, 1994). Data displays are an approach which can be applied when using the constant comparative method in ethnographic interviewing or participant observation research. It is equally applicable when using the developmental research sequence proposed by Spradley (1979, 1980).

Ethnographic Content Analysis

Ethnographic content analysis was first proposed by Altheide (1987) as a design that incorporated qualitative methods of ethnography with quantitative methods of content analysis. The researcher begins with a discovery-oriented ethnographic design to generate descriptive categories and theoretical concepts directly from the detailed descriptions of a group of people the researcher seeks to study within a particular setting of interest (Atkinson & Hammersley, 1989). These detailed descriptions are obtained through open-ended, exploratory interviews and observations that generate core categories (i.e., emergent themes) across all the interviews and observations collected in the study.

Once researchers have categories from the ethnographic results, a quantitative content analysis design provides a set of procedures to code the categories systematically with reliability checks to analyze, validate, and report the results (Altheide, 1987). Content analysis is similar to the observation coding procedures of process research. In most process research studies, the coder typically uses a predefined coding scheme to code specific behavioral episodes of a therapy session, either from a videotape or as they occur live in a session (Bakeman & Gottman, 1986).

In many studies, coding systems are "chosen because they are widely used or have become standard instruments, not because they provide the best test of the impact of a particular family treatment" (Anderson, 1988, p. 83). The category system used may or may not be theoretically relevant to the phenomenon under study. In ethnographic content analysis, however, the coding scheme emerges directly from the ethnographic study using a domain analysis (Spradley, 1979) or constant comparative method (Strauss & Corbin, 1990). Raters then use the coding scheme from the qualitative ethnographic study and code the sentences or paragraphs transcribed in a written format from interviews and researcher observations with quantitative content analysis procedures (Weber, 1990). Numeric frequency of categories is analyzed. Intercoder reliability is used to check, supplement, and confirm prior theoretical claims (Krippendorff, 1980). In sum, ethnographic content analysis lends itself to both qualitative and quantitative research goals and combines what are usually considered antithetical modes of analysis.

In the Smith et al. (1994) study, seven core categories were operationalized using the domain analysis procedures proposed by Spradley (1979). Interviews and field notes were coded based on these categories. Using content analysis procedures, frequency counts of categories were analyzed with a chi-square procedure. This statistical procedure was used to test the comparability of therapist and couple perceptions across all seven categories. Differences between couples and therapists within each category were calculated proportionally and compared, using a chi-square procedure to detect their significance.

A phi-coefficient contingency analysis was used to measure the correlation of the categories "spatial separateness" and "process of hearing" co-occurring together. To test whether the observed value of the phi coefficient suggested a significant association between spatial separateness and process of hearing, a chi-square procedure was computed. Texts that contained the codes "spatial separateness" and "process of hearing" were examined for the highest frequency of words. Ordered word-frequency lists were augmented with the text in which each word appeared. This database was then used to study detailed differences and similarities in semantic word use within the spatial separateness and process of hearing categories. In this way, a qualitative ethnographic analysis supported a quantitative content analysis of the data.

Computerization

The advent of computers has simplified analytic methods performed in conjunction with, or after the accomplishment of, certain mechanical tasks in the management of data (Tesch, 1991). During data analysis, the researcher must engage in such manipulative activities as locating key words or phases in the text, attaching coding categories, inserting key words or comments, and assembly of topically related segments. In the past, this was done by hand. Researchers literally took a pair of scissors, sat in the middle of a floor, cut up hundreds of pages of transcripts, and placed them in manila folders, each labeled with one code (Bogdan & Biklen, 1982).

With computers, this task can now be done quickly and with increased accuracy, as coded sections of text can be located, copied, labeled, and directed to a screen, printer, or text files (Blackman, 1992). The researcher still makes the conceptual decisions, but such software programs, as Qualpro, Ethnograph, Tap, and Alpha offer the potential for greater accuracy and thoroughness in data analysis (Fielding & Lee, 1991).

Publication

A good ethnography can be a fine piece of literature. Unfortunately, though, the same descriptions that make an ethnography a thing of literary beauty may present problems for the ethnographer seeking to publish the work. The dilemma is that space in professional journals is too limited and expensive to publish expansive ethnographic manuscripts. Another problem is that because ethnographic methods are not generally known to most readerships, valuable space must be devoted in describing the method and its rationale. These explanations are not necessary with traditional data-analytical statistical procedures. However, there appears to be an upswing in interest concerning qualitative research manuscripts. If the authors' personal experience is any indication, journal editors and reviewers are becoming sophisticated in their review of ethnographic articles and qualitative research.

Three years ago at the meeting of the American Association for Marital and Family Therapy, a group of qualitative researchers was given time to meet with editors of family therapy journals. Since that dialogue occurred, there has been a concerted effort by journal editors to increase the number of reviewers who are knowledgeable in qualitative research as well as a recognition of the problems authors face in their attempts to publish such research. Qualitative and quantitative researchers are no longer held to the same standards. This is a marked departure from past experience when ethnographies were rejected for publication with the comment that a sample size of 50 families was necessary to resubmit for reconsideration. The reviewer was apparently unaware that 50 families is an extraordinarily large sample size for most ethnographies.

Based on advice from editors and the authors' personal experiences, several guidelines for publishing qualitative research can be offered.

1. When research activities are completed, and the researchers are writing manuscripts for publication, the target audience should be carefully considered. Editors and journal reviewers consider not only whether an article has merit but also whether their readers will be interested.
2. When preparing an article for submission, collect exemplars of published ethnographic articles. Note their length, the conventions used to shorten the article, and which methods and aspects of methodologies the authors assume that a typical reader will understand without a lengthy explanation.
3. If the target journal is known, particular attention should be devoted to exemplar articles from it.
4. When in doubt, colleagues should be consulted. Good examples of resources include friends who have published ethnographic manuscripts or the author of a favored ethnographic piece. Most ethnographic researchers are pleased to recruit others interested in doing ethnography. Finally, editors frequently are helpful to beginning authors.

There are several published guides to help authors in writing ethnographies. One of the simplest and most straightforward is *Qualitative Research Proposals and Reports: A Guide* (Munhall, 1994). The manual is divided into sections with titles like doability, composability, completability, and expectability. It is clearly a "how-to" book and includes an outline for reporting a qualitative research study. Spradley's (1979) chapter on writing an ethnography is also useful, as is Volume II of *Systematic Fieldwork* (Werner & Schoepflel, 1987), which includes a more theoretical and ideological discussion of reporting ethnographies.

DISCUSSION

Reliability and Validity

Pelto (1970) asserts that research methodologies are merely trains of logic used to answer two questions: (1) How can inquiry into a particular area of the universe produce useful information, and (2) how can information disseminated by other investigators be trustworthy? To establish the trustworthiness or credibility of a research method, researchers traditionally rely on estimates of reliability and validity (Germain, 1993; Goetz & LeCompte, 1984). However, there is considerable debate about what is a valid and reliable ethnography (Goetz & LeCompte, 1984; Hammersley, 1992; McDermott, 1982; Moon, Dillon, & Sprenkle, 1990). The issues converge most deeply in the question of what criteria should be employed in assessing ethnographic studies. Hammersley (1992) lists three possible approaches for use in assessing ethnographies: (1) application of quantitative research standards, (2) application of a unique set of qualitative research standards, and (3) denial of any meaningful research standards.

In a closely argued analysis, Hammersley (1992) rejects the first and third approaches. He suggests that either extreme would do an injustice to ethnographic research traditions and methodologies. Our view is consistent with Hammersley's. Consequently, the first approach (Evans, 1983; Kirk & Miller, 1986) is not discussed and the third approach is discussed only briefly, as it pertains to family therapy qualitative research.

Supporters of the third approach argue that attempts to establish generic evaluative criteria are incompatible with the philosophical assumptions of the qualitative tradition (Atkinson & Heath, 1987; Atkinson, Heath, & Chenail, 1991; Smith, 1990; Walters, 1990). They assert that because the ethnographic approach has a philosophical underpinning in constructivist epistemology, it assumes that at any point in time there may be many equally accurate ways to describe events in the social world (Atkinson et al., 1991; Smith, 1990). Therefore, they conclude, an ethnographer "would do well to abandon the assumption that it is the researcher's job to establish legitimacy of qualitative research findings" (Atkinson et al., 1991, p. 177). These authors suggest that the legitimacy of qualitative findings come from those who read a study rather than from those who conduct it.

This position has proven difficult for qualitative researchers who try to coexist peacefully with quantitative researchers. The impact of politicized research is best described in an article by Newfield (1992). In this discussion, Newfield describes the politics of scientific inquiry with personal encounters from his experience as a qualitative researcher. He concludes that it would be best for qualitative researchers to downplay connections between qualitative research and constructivism when trying to win supporters, publish manuscripts, or achieve tenure.

Supporters of the second position advocate for a unique set of standards and present criteria they believe to be distinctive to ethnographic research and to ensure the "truthfulness" of the data (Goetz & LeCompte, 1984; Moon et al., 1990; Muecke, 1994; Werner & Schoepfle, 1987). Moon et al. (1990) present those characteristics they identify as unique to the qualitative research paradigm. These criteria include (1) clear identification of research bias and presuppositions that may have influenced data collection and analyses, (2) criterion-based sampling and selection strategies focused on generalization to theory rather than to populations, and (3) collection of data from a variety of sources to provide triangulation and thick description. Besides Moon et al.'s (1990) criteria, Muecke (1994) stresses the importance of the researcher's role in explaining or demystifying of the data rather than simply recording. Such analysis, according to this theorist, separates a good ethnography from a case study.

Researchers who adopt Hammersley's (1992) second position also reformulate traditional quantitative ideas of reliability and validity. They propose that the distinctive characteristics of ethnographies result in variations of reliability and validity, which differ from experimental research (Goetz & LeCompte, 1984; LeCompte & Goetz, 1982; Moon et al., 1990; Muecke, 1994). Instead of judging reliability by the replicability of an instrumental measurement or agreement among raters, ethnographic studies focus on replicating the studies themselves and on obtaining rich descriptions of the cultural event. The basic question to be answered is: "Can a researcher use the same methods and obtain the same results obtained in a prior study?" LeCompte and Goetz (1982) define reliability in ethnographic research as the extent to which the sets of meanings held by multiple observers are sufficiently congruent. Leininger (1985b) describes qualitative validity as concerned with confirming the truth or understanding associated with the phenomena under consideration. Therefore, validity of ethnographies is established by confirming that descriptions or categories accurately present participants' perspectives of events rather than their generalizability to other settings or whether the treatment used produced the variations in outcome.

Muecke (1994) provides support for refining these standards even more for the ethnographies in family therapy. She argues that the ethnographies currently being conducted in the health sciences do not follow the traditional ethnographic methods of prolonged and comprehensive exposure to a group of people in context and, therefore, do not always fit the criteria established for evaluating traditional ethnographic research described above (Goetz & LeCompte, 1984; Moon et al.,1990; Werner & Schoepfle, 1987). Muecke describes ethnographies in the health sciences as "focused" because they do not presuppose a long-term exposure to the society or to the goal of understanding a culture's social interaction.

Muecke's (1994) distinctions are important in the field of family therapy because current ethnographic work in the field fits this description of focused ethnographies, or what other authors have called particularistic ethnographies, miniethnographies, and microethnographies (Germain, 1993; Leininger, 1985a; Morse, 1989; Werner & Schoepfle, 1987). The goals of family therapy ethnographers have usually been to achieve a better understanding of the therapeutic process from the insiders' perspective and to improve appropriateness of professional practice. As such, they have not often included the attempt to understand the culture as a whole (Beer, 1993; Brown, 1992; Newfield et al., 1990, 1991; Kuehl et al., 1990; Sells et al., 1994; Smith et al., 1994; Smith et al., 1993; Smith et al., 1992; Todd, Joanning, Enders, Mutchler, & Thomas, 1991). Because of this narrow focus, it is difficult to apply the criteria traditionally used to evaluate ethnographic research to ethnographies done in the field of family therapy.

Muecke (1994) proposes that focused ethnographies, though brief and limited in scope, can provide valuable contributions to knowledge if they carefully address issues within their limited scope. She suggests that the greatest weakness of focused ethnographies is that they may exclude relevant information because of their narrowly defined boundaries. Muecke recommends that the research questions be carefully addressed in focused ethnographies to avoid unnecessary exclusion. A study designed to understand why a certain population group does not use family therapy resources may end up examining how families in this population resolve problems without family therapy. This broader definition helps to obtain a thick description for the area of focus and decreases the possibility that the researcher will exclude information that may unveil a powerful interpretation. The quality of the data is further enhanced when the researcher contextualizes the people studied comprehensively and accurately. In sum, the more thorough the researcher's experience in a particular context, the greater the value his or her observations will have.

Muecke's (1994) recommendations challenge family therapy ethnographers to cast their nets widely when formulating a research question and collecting data. Could a better understanding of the family's use of therapy be obtained by interviewing and observing families in their homes? Is a "one-shot interview" in the clinic or therapist's office adequate to obtain the data necessary to formulate a thick description of the cultural event in context? If the answer to these questions is no and the researcher cannot adequately address these issues, the study's needs might be better met with a phenomenological case study or a content analysis design.

Recognizing that providing a thick description is only part of the ethnographer's work, Muecke (1994) identifies a second criterion for evaluating the focused ethnography. An analysis of the information that represents more than careful observations must be provided. If this is not present, Muecke asserts that a case study and not an ethnography has been conducted. This analysis must be logically consistent and rooted in the understandings of the people studied. The goal of ethnography is development of theory about the cultural events in context, and to achieve this, analysis is unavoidable.

In a closely argued analysis, Hammersley (1992) rejects the first and third approaches and endorses the second approach. He proposes that validity and relevance ought to be the crucial criteria for the evaluation of ethnographic adequacy. Validity involves the "truthfulness" of study findings (Hammersley, 1992). This standard assumes belief in the correspondence theory of truth. Hammersley argues that what we find in studies is a selective representation of reality, although we have no ultimate, privileged access to it. The researcher is responsible for providing evidence that is plausible and credible. Having met such criteria, the researcher can conclude that claims have been established beyond a reasonable doubt. Highly theoretical or counterintuitive claims require more evidence, simply because they are more removed from informants' day-to-day experiences.

Relevance is equally important. Hammersley (1992) lists importance of topic and contribution to the literature as the major criteria for evaluation. He acknowledges that the evaluation of relevance is somewhat audience dependent. What a practitioner may deem important could vary greatly from the perspective of the researcher.

Improving Truthfulness

Because journal reviewers and editors are still more familiar with traditional concepts of validity and reliability, the following discussion of methodologies to improve the "truthfulness" of ethnographic research is presented in those terms. The information provides beginning researchers with criteria to evaluate ethnographic research and guidelines to improve the quality of their own research.

As mentioned earlier, the greatest threat to the truthfulness of a focused ethnography is the definition of boundaries that could exclude information that would provide a more informed description of the area of concern (Muecke, 1994). To provide proper boundary definition, the researcher must understand the purposes and goals of ethnography. The crucial question to be answered is: "Does the question I have asked enable the broadest description possible of the phenomena to be studied in context?" Addressing an issue from this deliberately nondirected perspective may take practice when the researcher has been trained to address these concerns from a problem-focused perspective. Rigorous ethnographic research demands that investigators be prepared to commit enough time in the field to obtain comprehensive information from a variety of sources to support a broad description from which a strong analytical report may be written (Muecke, 1994). If investigators can ensure that their project will achieve a contextualized, comprehensive, and accurate description of the phenomena being studied, they have taken the most crucial step toward ensuring the truthfulness of their work.

Two factors that can also affect the truthfulness or validity and reliability of an ethnography are socially desirable and/or acquiescent response sets (Brink, 1989). The purpose of ethnographic interviewing is to help informants describe their perspective of the phenomenon. The interviewing techniques must prevent informants from providing what they perceive researchers want as a correct answer or from offering a dichotomous, "agreement–disagreement" response.

Using a questioning process that requires informants to provide in-depth explorations of their perspective guards against the acquiescent or socially desirable response set because informants must expand on their responses to questions (Brink, 1989; Marshall & Rossman, 1989). This expansion provides researchers with the opportunity to evaluate the consistency of informants' responses. When informants are interviewed only once, identical and alternate-form questions within that interview may be used to test informants' reliability (Brink, 1989). Equivalence of response to various forms of the question provides a useful reliability check. This cross-checking process is the reliability check of choice (Brink, 1989).

Study participants' ability to enhance the validity of the collected information is also an important consideration. When the sample is theoretically representative of the role being studied, the validity of obtained information is enhanced (Brink, 1989; Leininger, 1985c). Study informants should be selected using inclusion criteria that ensure that they can provide information to fulfill the theoretical demands of the study's research questions.

A panel of experts can be used to identify key informants who will meet the study's theoretical needs or can help the investigator in deciding how to best obtain a complete description of the phenomena (Brink, 1989). Methodological issues related to interviewer characteristics and type of information needed can also be addressed by the experts. Can a male interviewer, for instance, obtain accurate information from female informants on the subject of childbirth?

Focus groups for informants can be used to validate the information obtained from individual informants. In these groups, informants may concur with each other concerning cultural perceptions, and, when there are exceptions, the ethnographer may develop rules to explain them or decide that more data are needed to provide a more thorough description. The use of multiple methods to achieve completeness of data is triangulation (Boyd, 1993; Knafl & Breitmayer, 1989).

Triangulation is another method to improve reliability and validity of ethnographies (Boyd, 1993; Knafl & Breitmayer, 1989). The concept of triangulation has two distinct meanings as it is used in the literature. Campbell (1956) first used the concept of triangulation in the social sciences and cited several methods to evaluate a single construct. Additional terms used for this process were "multiple operationism," "convergent operationism," "operational delineation," and "convergent validation" (Knafl & Breitmayer, 1989). The common thread among these approaches was the attempt to achieve confirmation of constructs using multiple measurement methods (Campbell, 1956).

Jick (1983) and Fielding and Fielding (1986) perceived triangulation as a method to gain comprehensive information about a phenomenon. They recommended that the researcher use multiple methods to enhance an overall understanding. Selection of multiple methods is not based on an ability to counterbalance one another but because they help in providing a more thorough picture. Data source triangulation entails locating independent means of verifying an assertion. However, there is no expectation that data sources will necessarily confirm one another (Knafl & Breitmayer, 1989). Because each data source may differ in perspective, a lack of confirmation may reveal the different perspectives of the data sources. Use of focus groups and experts to evaluate and respond to data is an example of data source triangulation. If researchers are committed to obtaining a thick description, this form of triangulation will be part of every ethnographic design.

In addition to the multiple method and source triangulation, two other types of triangulation have been proposed (Denzin, 1978; Knafl & Breitmayer, 1989). These methods are theoretical and investigator triangulation. Theoretical triangulation refers to the use of multiple theories to verify some artifact of information. Lincoln and Guba (1985) downplay the value of theoretical triangulation, arguing that coherence within multiple theories represents an unnecessary and unreasonable standard. They believe that because most observations by any single researcher are theory dependent, expecting theoretical triangulation is unrealistic. Investigator triangulation essentially refers to replication by different investigators. Lincoln and Guba (1985) warned that replication by entirely different researchers was unlikely unless the researchers understood the context in which data was collected. Researchers can use these methods alone or in combination to achieve triangulation.

This discussion of reliability and validity presents a broad view of the topic. Discussions related to selecting a set of standards for evaluating family therapy ethnographies provide guideposts for formulating a question and determining the appropriateness of the design. Once the correctness of the design has been decided, researchers are provided with specific methods for enhancing its reliability and validity. If family therapy researchers are sincere about obtaining useful and trustworthy information, efforts to achieve these ends will be rewarded by an increased understanding of the phenomena of "family" that can only enhance family therapy practice.

Strengths and Weaknesses

Discussions about the strengths and weaknesses of research methods can easily degenerate into polemics that only serve to polarize disputative factions. Family therapy has not been immune to these heated dialogues. Ample debate and discussion have ensued on the usefulness and value of ethnography and other qualitative methods for family therapy research (see Allman, 1982; Atkinson & Heath, 1987; Cavell & Snyder, 1991; Dell, 1982, 1985; Gurman, 1983; Joanning, Newfield, & Quinn, 1987; Kniskern, 1983; Kuehl et al., 1990; Liddle, 1991; Moon, Dillon, & Sprenkle, 1990, 1991; Newfield et al., 1990, 1991; Newfield, 1992; Shields, 1986a, 1986b; Steier, 1985; Tomm, 1983, 1986; Wynne, 1988, for key references on this debate). We believe that the best way to reduce this historical schism is in collaborative, multimethodological studies such as those described by Moon et al. (1991), Sells et al. (1995), and Smith et al. (1994). The likelihood of collaborative multimethodological research is increased when there is an understanding of the strengths and weaknesses of the methods employed. Despite the debate that has occurred, few discussions exist of the specific strengths and weaknesses of ethnographic and qualitative research methods as applied to family therapy (Liddle, 1991). Because the literature is so limited, we can only provide a beginning discussion.

In addressing strengths and weaknesses, key questions exist about using ethnographic techniques to study family therapy.

1. Given what is known about ethnography, what is the proper role and use of ethnographic research in family therapy?
2. How should family therapy researchers adapt ethnography to fit the needs and concerns of their discipline?
3. To what extent do research methods change when they are adapted to a new discipline?

First, in addressing the proper role of ethnographic research in family therapy, should ethnographic research provide basic science on family structure, dynamics, and communication patterns that clinical researchers can use to understand their clients? On the other hand, can ethnographic methods be used to study the process of therapy itself? The former role fits the traditional view of ethnographies and indeed has been conducted by sociologists and anthropologists alike. The latter role is more difficult, especially if the researcher is trained as a family therapist. The family therapist may be caught between the traditions of family therapy and the traditions of ethnography as commonly seen in anthropology and sociology.

Second, we address how family therapy researchers should adapt ethnography to fit the needs and concerns of their discipline. Given the applied nature of family therapy, researchers have had to revise traditional ethnographic methods. Ethnographies traditionally have been used by ethnographers to study culture. Today, ethnography is being adapted not to the study of culture but to the study of professions (e.g., nursing, education, public health, family therapy, and social work). When ethnographic methods are borrowed by disciplines outside anthropology and sociology, they change to fit the needs of disciplinary research and concerns. For example, the goal of family therapy ethnographies may not be, as in anthropology, to understand a culture but to serve and improve the mental health of a client population and to improve the therapy techniques of the family therapists who serve that population. Because family therapy ethnographies may involve interaction with clients who are receiving treatment, ethical considerations prevent some of the in-depth involvement for which anthropological ethnographies are noted. Because dual relationships are proscribed by the Code of Ethics of the American Association for Marriage and Family Therapy (AAMFT), family therapy researchers are understandably cautious in their level of involvement with clients who are receiving treatment. However, resolving ethical dilemmas raises methodological problems, as discussed in the next paragraph.

The third question on how ethnographies will change in their application to family therapy cannot be completely answered. The entire range of methodological problems that arise when the purpose of ethnography changes from the study of culture to the study of therapy process and outcome is unclear. For example, when the ethnographer begins with a narrowly focused question, is the ethnographer faithfully capturing the experience of the couple? If informants are telling their story of counseling should they be allowed more leeway in defining the guiding question that elicits their response? Are brief forms of therapy amenable to ethnographic research methods? Adapting ethnographic methods to the study of family therapy can evoke these difficult questions. It is likely these questions will remain unanswered until family therapy researchers gain experience in conducting ethnographies with their clienteles and develop traditions and methods based on those experiences. One solution is to develop goodness criteria for family therapy ethnographies such as those advocated by Smith, Sells, and Newfield (1995). Such goodness criteria present one construal of family therapy ethnographic traditions and standards.

Thus, discussions about the strengths and weaknesses of ethnographies are tentative because questions about methodological traditions and goodness have not been answered. Despite this lacuna, we feel confident in making several assertions about the use of ethnographic methods in family therapy.

1. *Ethnographic studies are an optimal way to begin the process of discovery and to generate theoretical concepts directly from participant descriptions.* Studies cited throughout this chapter provide evidence of how ethnographic studies can provide the foundation on which quantitative studies can build (Newfield et al., 1990, 1991; Smith et al., 1994; Sells et al., 1995). This complementarity between quantitative and qualitative studies provides a strong case for the synthesis that Moon et al. (1991) advocated. In complementary relationships between quantitative and qualitative methods, ethnographic studies either begin or contribute to the process of discovery. The recursive relationship between qualitative and quantitative methods suggests that each method can only strengthen the other method. In this vein, our ethnographic studies have also provided participant-generated theoretical assertions about family therapy practice (Newfield et al., 1990, 1991; Sells et al., 1994; Smith et al., 1992, 1993) that provide grounded research hypotheses.

2. *Ethnographic research is an excellent method for providing baseline data and identifying native explanatory models.* Ethnographic baseline data can be refined into further observation, structured interviews, and questionnaires. A large part of research in family

therapy focuses on identifying maladaptation and psychopathology, attempting to effect change, and measuring outcomes in remediation of maladaptation and psychopathology in response to these attempts at change. The naturalistic–ethnographic approach provides the family therapy researcher with a holistic description of the total phenomena. What is more important is that the use of ethnography may increasingly reveal ethnocentric biases to researchers involved in family therapy and ultimately support cultural pluralism.

3. *Ethnography can, when done optimally, reflect the world view of another person or culture.* If we are to have a humanistic side to our science, we must not only predict and influence our clients but also understand our clients' feelings about our attempts to predict and influence as they occur. There is a recursion between their experience and our attempts to help them in the process of change. As we try to change them, they are surely trying to correct and change us. It is to our advantage to understand how and why they are trying to do this. Ethnographic methods are an invaluable tool in finding these answers.

Balanced against these strengths are some weaknesses:

1. *Ethnography in the hands of non-ethnographers invites short-term research with shortened periods of participant observation and ethnographic interviewing.* From the perspective of a holistic anthropologist, such ethnographic research is quick indeed and, as such, omits the extended participant observation necessary for good ethnographic work. Family therapy ethnographies may neglect the essential element of in-depth interviewing that is characteristic of all rigorously done ethnographies. Ethnography has robust internal validity and reliability if the ethnography is based on extensive time in the field.

2. *A related weakness is the lack of generalizability (or external validity) of ethnographic studies to other groups or cultures.* If ethnographers do not choose their informants carefully, make meaningful observations, and ask thoughtful questions of their informants, the understanding that is gained through the ethnographic process may be trivial. Optimally, ethnographies provide us with insights into the broad beliefs and mores that make up the foundations of a culture. The problem with a trivial understanding is that the results do not adequately describe underlying cultural themes, beliefs, and mores and cannot be used to understand commonalities and differences that exist among members from different cultures and subcultures. Thus, in studies of therapeutic process, family therapy ethnographies may be trivial and fail to reveal important commonalities and differences among clients. The results will be shallow and unimportant.

3. *Another weakness is the difficulty in replicating either ethnographic procedures or results.* Replicating a study is a way to confirm the trustworthiness of the methodology used to collect data. Although a well-documented audit trail provides details on data collection and textual analysis and helps establish the credibility of results, family therapy ethnographies will be difficult to replicate. Because of the inherent variability in data collection and reduction, it would be nearly impossible to replicate the conditions around the participant observation or ethnographic interviewing that occurred. Without replication, there always will be some doubt as to the findings of the ethnographers.

Ethics and Adapting Ethnographic Methods to Family Therapy Questions

As discussed previously, we have wondered about the fit between family therapy research and ethnography. The business of family therapy implies an intention to help families change themselves or for therapists to change families. Ethically, it might be difficult for a family therapist to refrain from intervening if a child were in imminent danger or if family members were asking for psychoeducational interventions. Yet, family therapy ethnographers must be clear about their own intentions and boundaries when they begin their work. Ethically, the family therapy ethnographer who embraces the AAMFT Code of Ethics cannot passively allow clients to be injured. Following is a discussion of ethics that relies heavily on the traditions within anthropology to guide research behavior.

Familiarity with the principles in the Statement on Ethics developed by the Counsel of the American Anthropological Association may help anticipate and avoid serious ethical breaches and ethical dilemmas before they occur. The tradition and ethical code within anthropology helps to guide researchers' inquiry and resolve ethical conundrums. Currently the Statement on Ethics is under revision and a new version should be forthcoming (Ms. Terry Clifford, personal communication, March 1995).

Rynkiewich and Spradley (1976) present a number of case studies of ethical dilemmas in ethnographic field work. *The Ethics of Inquiry in Social Science* (Barnes, 1970) remains an excellent reference work on ethics; Werner and Schoepfle (1987) discuss the minimally acceptable ethnographic standards for generating an ethnographic report.

The ethical principles from these anthropological references are abstracted below.

1. The right to anonymity and/or recognition must be ascertained and respected.
2. Possible positive and negative consequences should be considered and communicated to potential informants. As much as possible, informants should be encouraged to give an informed consent regarding participation in an ethnography.
3. The professional identity of all ethnographic researchers should be revealed to possible informants.
4. Researchers should carefully consider how their personal values will affect their ethnographic research activities. By the same token, ethnographers should also consider how their research activities will affect their personal lives.

These ethical principles and guidelines provide some guidance to researchers but cannot resolve the ethical binds that ethnographies present. The discussion below seeks to highlight pertinent issues around these ethical binds.

Previously, non-Western, insular cultures were studied. The studies generated were, for the most part, for other anthropologists. Colonial administrations and the natives were either not aware or disinterested in ethnographers' reports. Today, the situation has changed; reports will be read by natives and those who administer to, look after, or govern them. With the boundaries of fieldwork more blurred than in previous generations, anthropologists are faced with the conflicting values of "seeking and recording facts" versus inadvertently "doing harm" (Skomal, 1994).

To learn about natives' culture, ethnographers must rely on natives' generosity and willingness. In these situations, the informants become the authority or collaborator (Osborne, 1993). The researcher must not deliberately or unwittingly harm them. As a general rule, studying individuals who are minorities, poor, powerless, institutionalized, or participating in a culturally deviant activity carries with it a greater risk of abuse. As a rule, informants who are more vulnerable because of their activities, age, class, or ethnicity require greater care in planning and implementing ethnographies.

Even innocent activities may carry with them ethical dilemmas. A friend of one of the authors was studying linguistics among Spanish-speaking heroin addicts in a small city in New Mexico. In studying phonemic variations in their speech, an apparently benign and arcane activity, she became convinced that it could be possible to distinguish addicts from nonaddicts by the way they stress certain words. The wisdom of continuing this research was reconsidered given the possibility of inadvertently causing the informants legal difficulties.

Recommendations for resolving this dilemma will be familiar to family therapists, because they reflect systems theory principles. Osborne (1993) proposes that anthropologists use "contextual ethics," evolving from an ongoing dialogue with the informants or "collaborators." Keeney (1983) refers to "a participatory ethical perspective" (p. 81) to address family therapists' concerns about the conflict between individual and group interests. An elaboration of this approach can be found in the writings of von Foerster (Segal, 1986). He addressed the solipsistic approach to contextual ethics with the principle of relativity. The perspective of each person is assumed to be valid, and the relationship between the involved parties becomes the central reference point. The principle underlying the community between people is that each benefits by optimizing choices and improving the situation of the other. For von Foerster, the guiding ethical principle was that life is not a zero-sum game and that all lose or all win. Ethics evolve from the community that occurs between the ethnographer and collaborators.

When doing fieldwork, the ethnographer may have a number of "sponsors," which adds further complexity to the ethical "community." For example, when doing an ethnography of patient violence in a state mental hospital, multiple interests will be represented. A granting agency would have particular research questions to be answered concerning the culture of violence. The administrator of the hospital would have concerns about staff–patient relationships. Ward treatment teams and medical staff would wonder about administration's perspective of the reported staff–patient interactions. Patients may hope that certain practices be deemed inappropriate or at least ineffective. Then there are the outside interest groups and their concerns. Suffice it to say that ethnographers will find themselves working within an environment of mutuality antagonistic and competitive needs.

Doing an ethnography in such an environment takes on a political dimension. The ethnographer becomes simultaneously a diplomat and a confidante whose ethics are generated by myriad dyadic relationships that constitute the key informants. It is precisely this role strain of countervailing demands that require family therapists to acknowledge a priori how their personal prejudices, values, and beliefs will affect ethnographic data collection and analysis.

For many ethnographers, the greatest challenge is suspending moral judgment and restraining interventions into natives' behavior and functioning of their culture. This prime directive in fieldwork is problematic when illegal or apparently harmful behaviors are discovered. If, in studying the hospital, the ethnographer is told about underground drug use that contributes to increased violence, the ethnographer encounters an ethical dilemma that is not easily addressed by current ethical guidelines. Does the ethnographer report the individuals smuggling drugs? The safety of staff and patients must be balanced against the right of informants to remain anonymous.

There is also the question of how far into the system one should extend this prime directive. For example, if hospital patients are the natives and we cannot interfere with them or divulge their identities, is it also wrong to interfere with the administrators of the hospital that houses the patients? Because the administrators are also native informants, the application of the rules that affect patients also should include administrators. However, what about administration at the next highest level? Should hospital administration be considered natives and administration at the state level be considered nonnatives? Is it wrong to attempt to influence the administration we are studying?

In writing the ethnographic report, who is the ethnographer obligated to protect? Although the ethical code does not provide explicit guidelines for behavior, administrators are generally less vulnerable than patients and so do not pose the same pragmatic ethical problems.

When studying foreign cultures, ethnographers had few ethical concerns. Ethnographers were visitors, had little influence on local events, and were in need of native cooperation. Furthermore, researchers were not even part of the natives' social systems. Under these circumstances, anthropologists found it easier to avoid taking action and often tried to present themselves as harmless individuals with curiosity concerning native behavior and a strong sense of cultural relativity. In studying a domestic culture, the "natives" and the ethnographer are of the same culture, and intercultural ethical neutrality becomes more difficult. Actions of informants may be illegal or subversive. The ethnographer may feel that he or she has a duty to warn, as in the use of contraband drugs among patients in the state hospital. If the ethnographer decides not to report the drugs, authorities may feel betrayed when they learn that this information was withheld.

Anthropologists have resolved this issue by either adopting a neutral stance as participant observers or taking an activist role (Skomal, 1993). The decision on which stance to adopt depends on an interpretation of the best interests of informants and who should ultimately make this determination. Making an informed choice in these ethical dilemmas requires an awareness of personal values and beliefs (Skomal, 1994).

Participant observation research and ethnographic interviewing require close association with native informants to allow the ethnographer to become saturated in their culture. Issues of neutrality and coalitions are as important in ethnographic research as they are in family therapy. If the ethnographer identifies with one group or faction, other groups may not be willing to provide information. As a consequence, the resulting ethnography will not show the cultural conflicts that are present. Compounding the need to remain neutral is that government-supported research may be viewed with suspicion. Natives may well believe, without cause, that researchers have a hidden agenda. By the same token, researchers who identify openly with informants practicing a "deviant" behavior may be held in suspicion by authorities.

Openly identifying oneself as a researcher may preclude doing the research if the activity being studied is illegal or carries a cultural stigma. This was the case with Laud Humphreys, an Episcopal priest, who did an ethnography of gay sex in public rest rooms by pretending to be a "watch queen." The watch queen gets voyeuristic pleasure from watching sex in a bathroom and keeps a close eye on doors and windows for any police or heterosexual individuals who might enter. The people he observed had no idea he was a sociologist, and only a few ever knew his purpose (Humphreys, 1970).

However, such covert research is no longer an acceptable practice, despite possible research gains. Such deception requires that a researcher knowingly enter a relationship based on fraud. Because informants have not been given an opportunity to give informed consent, their revelations may prove harmful to them. Covert research also has the potential of damaging the reputation of all ethnographers and creating barriers to subsequent investigators.

A related concern is harm that might be caused by published ethnographies. If there is little chance that informants will track down a published ethnography, publications had little danger of causing inadvertent harm to the informants. Today, researchers must determine whether informants need to be protected from the effects of a publication and, if so, do they have the means to protect them? Asking informants to read manuscripts before they are published tempers what becomes a public document. It also gives informants an opportunity to correct misunderstandings and identify information that may be personally harmful. Such reviews can be incorporated into the final report as additional information.

Preserving the anonymity of individuals or a site by giving fictitious names or changing the locations and identities are acceptable ways of protecting informants. It is important, when changing information, to guard against the reader's drawing faulty conclusions concerning the culture being studied. The researcher must advise the informant that although every effort will be made to maintain anonymity, it cannot be guaranteed (Skomal, 1994).

Consent forms were not identified in Barnes's (1970) discussion of ethical dilemmas in modern fieldwork. Informed consent in fieldwork is a dilemma (Skomal, 1994). Not surprisingly, the model for consent forms is based on a biomedical and psychological hypothesis-testing model (Wax, 1977). Using consent forms while doing ethnographic research is akin to wearing shoes that do not fit. Giving informed consent requires that researchers apprise potential participants about the possible consequences of participation in the study. Such a standard is difficult to meet because a set course of questioning and hypotheses testing can seldom be determined. Further, it is not certain who will even be part of the study when the ethnographer is conducting free-flowing interviews of people in their homes or on the street. Because ethnographic research relies on the relationship between researcher and informants, it is more difficult to list a priori what and even where information will be collected. By contrast, traditional assessment instruments and survey questionnaires administered in biomedical, psychological, and family therapy research are much more predictable in their risks and their procedures.

However, ethnographers should constantly apprise informants about who they are and their purpose for involvement and should obtain verbal consent. If possible, verbal consents should be taped; such a procedure will create less controversy for human subject review boards (Agar, 1980). When an informant consents to be taped, enough rapport exists such that formal consent undoubtedly will not be a problem. Despite the uncertainties of obtaining informed consent, it is not an academic exercise. The procedure will remind researchers about their obligations to informants. In addition, it reminds researchers about their professional responsibilities to be honest about intentions and to provide a detailed listing of what can be expected to occur during the course of the ethnography (Skomal, 1994).

Agar (1980) points out, "the only true test of ethics is if the ethnographer suffers when the informants suffer as a consequence of something he has done" (p. 185). This ethical stance is reminiscent of von Foerster's (Segal, 1986) statement that life is a non–zero-sum game. The ethical imperative in both family therapy and ethnography is to be collaborative and to work toward the benefit of all members of the community.

The Future of Ethnographic Research

Philosophically, the purpose of family therapy ethnographies may have more to do with providing a form of process research (e.g., Smith, Pereira, Sells, Todahl, & Pappagiannis, 1995) than of simply describing families when they come to therapy. Consistent with the idea that family therapy ethnography is a form of process research is the fact that both types of research focus on clients and therapists, who logically may belong to different cultures. As detailed earlier in this chapter, family therapy ethnographies are miniethnographies that do not pretend to describe the larger culture but focus instead on the therapeutic process between clients and therapists. Muecke's (1994) concept of a focused ethnography describes such family therapy ethnographies as Newfield et al. (1990, 1991), Smith et al. (1992, 1993), or Sells et al. (1994).

The purpose of family therapy ethnographies is to describe how culture affects change processes. This focus, which is much narrower than that of traditional ethnographies, has implications for how and when family therapy ethnographies will be conducted. Whether pitched as process research or as an effort to describe cultural influences on change processes, the family therapy ethnography offers an essential tool for interpreting the massive amounts of narrative and other forms of data that family therapists collect. Traditional ethnographies' level of abstraction may provide too many details and too few organizing principles to help us understand how those details fit together.

Ethnography as a Method to Bridge the Clinician–Researcher Bifurcation

As seen from the earlier discussion, family therapy ethnographers have not conducted purely descriptive studies of families. Instead, their research has focused on understanding both the intrasession process of therapy and how a family's culture affects change. In this chapter, the authors have drawn on their experiences to demonstrate their successful scholar–practitioner relationship.

Newfield et al. (1990, 1991) examined family therapy with the intent of understanding the client's perspective concerning therapy. It was found to be an ambiguous experience for clients. Moreover, although clients and therapists believed they understood each other, this was an illusion of social coherence with much room for misunderstanding. Therapists were viewed by clients as becoming resistant when they adhered to theoretical models that required them to be tenacious and not to deviate from a particular therapeutic stance despite what the clients were telling them (Kuehl et al., 1990). The concept of therapy was also examined as a strange cultural practice (Kuehl & Newfield, 1991).

Smith, Jenkins, and Sells (1995) documented how a difficult couple in therapy inspired team discussions that led to experimentation with ethnographic methods (Smith et al., 1992, 1993) and concluded with a formal miniethnography (Sells et al., 1994). In several ancillary studies, Smith et al. (1994) and Smith et al. (1995) provided further illustrations of how ongoing clinical work in reflecting teams was blended with various ethnographic interviewing and research methods. The study by Smith et al. (1995) allowed the treatment team to move beyond reiterating the tenets of a practice model and toward a systematic understanding of why it has the effect that it does. By identifying the "active ingredient," the study helped the authors to better articulate the practice theory that, in turn, allowed a differential use of interventive strategies.

Sells, Smith, and Moon (in press) described the reactions of therapists who used ethnographies to evaluate their clinical practice. The therapists' enthusiastic reactions suggest that ethnographic research methods have promise as a means to bridge the research–therapy bifurcation. The therapists focused their praise on the relevant information that ethnographic questions provided to them. In particular, the therapists' reactions spoke to the conundrum of research utilization that has troubled clinical researchers across disciplines. If therapists in other sites also warmly embrace ethnographic methods, it may help close the divide between research and clinical methods.

In addition, given the complementarity between qualitative and quantitative methods, ethnographic research methods may set a foundation from which students will seek to learn more about quantitative methods. This was demonstrated in the Sells et al. (1995) article.

In summary, the key to a successful scholar–practitioner relationship lies in applying a systematic methodology to clinical activities within a field setting. Our clinical activities helped us to develop impressions, hunches, and questions; our research activities helped us to systematically collect and analyze the field data contained in memos, individual interviews, group interviews, and personal commentaries. Our clinical activities gave us a reason to conduct research; our research helped us to refine our clinical thinking and expertise. We believe that ethnography's unique contribution to family therapy will be as a clinical science of the humanities. Within ethnographies, the arts and the sciences are joined toward a better understanding of the human condition.

REFERENCES

Agar, M. H. (1973). *Ripping and running: A formal ethnography of urban heroin addicts.* New York: Seminar.

Agar, M. H. (1980). *The professional stranger: An informal introduction to ethnography.* New York: Academic Press.

Agar, M. H. (1986). *Speaking of ethnography* (Sage University Paper Series on Qualitative Research Methods, Vol. 2). Beverly Hills, CA: Sage.

Allman, L. R. (1982). The aesthetic preference: Overcoming the pragmatic error. *Family Process, 21,* 43–56.

Altheide, D. L. (1987). Ethnographic content analysis. *Qualitative Sociology, 10*(1), 65–77.

American Psychiatric Association. (1994). *Diagnostic and statistical manual of mental disorders* (4th ed.). Washington, DC: Author.

Anderson, C. M. (1988). The selection of measures in family therapy research. In L. C. Wynne (Ed.), *The state of the art in family therapy research: Controversies and recommendations.* New York: Family Process Press.

Angus, L. (1986). Developments in ethnographic research in education: From interpretive to critical ethnography. *Journal of Research and Development in Education, 20*(1), 65–77.

Atkinson, P., & Hammersley, M. (1989). *Ethnography principles in practice.* New York: Cambridge University Press.

Atkinson, B. J., & Heath, A. W. (1987). Beyond objectivism and relativism: Implications for family therapy research. *Journal of Strategic and Systemic Therapies, 6,* 8–17.

Atkinson, B. J., Heath, A., & Chenail, R. (1991). Qualitative research and the legitimization of knowledge. *Journal of Marital and Family Therapy, 17*(2), 161–166.

Bakeman, R., & Gottman, J. M. (1986). *Observing interaction: An introduction to sequential analysis.* New York: Cambridge University Press.

Barnes, J. A. (1970). Some ethical problems in modern fieldwork. In W. J. Filstead (Ed.), *Qualitative Methodology: Firsthand Involvement with the social world.* Chicago: Rand-McNally.

Bateson, G. (1961). *Perceval's narrative: A patient's account of his psychosis, 1830–1832.* Stanford: Stanford University Press.

Bateson, G., & Bateson, C. (1987). *Angels fear.* New York: Macmillan.

Becker, H., & Geer, B. (1970). Participant observation and interviewing: A comparison. In W. J. Filstead (Ed.), *Qualitative methodology: Firsthand involvement with the social world.* Chicago: Rand-McNally.

Beer, J. A. (1993). *If you could look in a mirror through another person's eyes: An ethnography of marital therapy.* Unpublished doctoral dissertation, Purdue University, West Lafayette, IN.

Bentley, M., Pelto, G., Strauss, W., Schumann, D., Adegbola, C., De La Pena, E., Oni, G., Brown, K., & Huffman, S. (1988). Rapid ethnographic assessment: Applications in a diarrhea management program. *Social Science and Medicine, 27*(1), 107–116.

Blackman, I. (1992). *Qualpro text database and productivity tools* [Computer program]. Tallahassee, FL: Impulse Development.

Bogdan, R. C., & Biklen, S. K. (1982). *Qualitative research for education: An introduction to theory and methods.* Boston: Allyn & Bacon.

Boyd, C. (1993). Philosophical foundations of qualitative research. In P. Munhall & C. Boyd (Eds.), *Nursing Research: A Qualitative Perspective* (2nd ed.). New York: National League for Nursing Press.

Brink, P. (1989). Issues in reliability and validity. In J. Morse (Ed.), *Qualitative nursing research: A contemporary dialogue*. Rockville, MD: Aspen.

Brown, D. (1992). *A client-centered description of teamwork in family therapy*. Unpublished doctoral dissertation, Iowa State University, Ames.

Campbell, D. T. (1956). *Leadership and its effects upon the group*. Columbus: Ohio State University.

Caudill, W. (1958). *The psychiatric hospital as a small society*. Cambridge, MA: Harvard University Press.

Caudill, W., Redlich, F., Gilmore, H., & Brody, E. (1952). Social structure and interactional processes on a psychiatric ward. *American Journal of Orthopsychiatry, 22,* 314–334.

Cavell, T. A., & Snyder, D. K. (1991). Iconoclasm versus innovation: Building a science of family therapy. *Journal of Marital and Family Therapy, 17,* 167–171.

Clammer, J. (1984). Approaches to ethnographic research. In R. F. Ellen (Ed.), *Ethnographic research: A guide to general conduct*. New York: Academic Press.

Clifford, J., & Marcus, G. (1986). *Writing culture: The poetics and politics of ethnography*. Berkeley: University of California Press.

Committee of the Royal Anthropological Institution of Great Britain and Ireland. (1971). *Notes and queries on anthropology* (6th ed.) London: Routledge & Kegan Paul.

Crane, J., & Angrosino, M. (1984). *Field projects in anthropology*. Prospect Heights, IL: Waveland Press.

D' Andrade, R. G. (1976). A propositional analysis of U. S. American beliefs about illness. In K. H. Basso & H. A. Selby (Eds.), *Meaning in anthropology*. Albuquerque: University of New Mexico Press.

Dell, P. F. (1982). In search of truth: On the way to clinical epistemology. *Family Process, 21,* 407–414.

Dell, P. F. (1985). Understanding Bateson and Maturana: Toward a biological foundation for the social sciences. *Journal of Marital and Family Therapy, 17,* 167–171.

Denzin, N. (1978). *The research act: A theoretical introduction to sociological methods* (2nd ed.). New York: McGraw-Hill.

Ellen, R. F. (1984). Preparation for fieldwork. In R. F. Ellen (Ed.), *Ethnographic research: A guide to general conduct*. New York: Academic Press.

Epstein, A. L. (Ed.). (1967). *The craft of social anthropology*. London: Tavistock.

Estroff, S. E. (1981). *Making it crazy*. Berkeley: University of California Press.

Evans, J. (1983). Criteria of validity in social research: Exploring the relationship between ethnographic and quantitative approaches. In M. Hammersley (Ed.), *The ethnography of schooling*. Driffield, England: Naffferton.

Fessler, R. (1983). Phenomenology and "the talking cure." In A. Giorgi, A. Barton, & C. Maes (Eds.), *Research of psychotherapy* (Vol. IV). Pittsburgh PA: Duquesne University Press.

Fetterman, D. M. (1984). *Ethnography in educational evaluation*. Thousand Oaks, CA: Sage.

Fielding, N., & Fielding, J. (1986). *Linking data*. Beverly Hills, CA: Sage.

Fielding, N. G., & Lee, R. M. (1991). Computing for qualitative research: Options, problems, and potential. In N. Fielding & R. Lee (Eds.), *Using computers in qualitative research*. Newbury Park, CA: Sage.

Fieldman, H. W., Agar, M. H., & Beschner, G. M. (1979). *Angel dust: An ethnographic study of PCP users*. Lexington, MA: Lexington Books.

Frake, C. O. (1962). The ethnographic study of cognitive systems. In T. Gladwin & W. C. Sturtevant (Eds.), *Anthropology and human behavior*. Washington: Anthropology Society of Washington, D.C.

Freilich, M. (1970). Field work: An introduction. In M. Freilich (Ed.), *Marginal natives: Anthropologists at work*. New York: Harper & Row.

Gale, J., & Newfield, N. A. (1992). A conversational analysis of a solution focused marital therapy session. *Journal of Marital and Family Therapy, 18,* 153–165.

Gawinski, B. (1987). *Five families' descriptions of experiences with a social service agency: A mini-ethnography of father–daughter incest*. Unpublished doctoral dissertation, Texas Tech University, Lubbock.

Germain, C. (1993). Ethnography: The method. In P. Munhall & C. Boyd (Eds.), *Nursing research: A qualitative perspective* (2nd ed.). New York: National League for Nursing Press.

Glaser, B., & Strauss, A. (1967). *The discovery of grounded theory: Strategies for qualitative research.* Hawthorne, NY: Aldine.

Goetz, J. P., & LeCompte, M. D. (1984). *Ethnography and qualitative designs in ethnographic research.* New York: Academic Press.

Goffman, E. (1961). *Asylums: Essays on the social situation of mental patients and other inmates.* Garden City, NY: Anchor Books.

Goodenough, W. H. (1957). Cultural anthropology and linguistics. In P. L. Garvin (Ed.), *Report of the 7th Annual Round Table Meeting on Linguistics and Language Study* (Monograph Series on Language and Linguistics, No. 9). Washington, DC: Georgetown University Institute of Languages and Linguistics.

Gurman, A. S. (1983). Family therapy research and the "new epistemology." *Journal of Marital and Family Therapy, 9,* 227–234.

Haley, J. (1976). *Problem solving therapy.* San Francisco: Jossey-Bass.

Hammersley, M. (1992). *What's wrong with ethnography.* New York: Routledge.

Hammersley, M., & Atkinson, P. (1983). *Ethnography: Principles in practice.* London: Tavistock.

Herskovits, M. J. (1954). Some problems of method in ethnography. In R. F. Spencer (Ed.), *Method and perspective in anthropology.* Minneapolis: University of Minnesota Press.

Henry, J. (1971). *Pathways to madness.* New York: Random House.

Hodgen, M. T. (1964). *Early anthropology in the sixteenth and seventeenth centuries.* Philadelphia: University of Pennsylvania Press.

Holly, L. (1984). Theory, method, and the research process. In R. F. Ellen (Ed.), *Ethnographic research: A guide to general conduct.* New York: Academic Press.

Huberman, A. M. (1991). The professional life cycle of teachers. *Teachers College Record, 91*(1), 31–57.

Huberman, A. M., & Miles, M. B. (1994). Data management and analysis methods. In N. K. Denzin & Y. S. Lincoln (Eds.), *Handbook of qualitative research.* Newbury Park, CA: Sage.

Humphreys, L. (1970). *Tearoom trade: Impersonal sex in public places.* Chicago: Aldine.

Jick, T. (1983). Mixing qualitative and quantitative methods: Triangulation in action. In M. van Manen (Ed.), *Qualitative methodology.* Beverly Hills, CA: Sage.

Joanning, H., Newfield, N., & Quinn, W. (1987). Multiple perspectives for research using family therapy to treat adolescent drug abuse. *Journal of Strategic and Systemic Therapy, 6*(1), 18–24.

Keeney, B. P. (1983). *Aesthetics of change.* New York: Guilford Press.

Kirk, J., & Miller, M. (1986). *Reliability and validity in qualitative research.* Beverly Hills, CA: Sage.

Knafl, K., & Breitmayer, B. (1989). Triangulation in qualitative research: Issues of conceptual clarity and purpose. In J. W. Morse (Ed.), *Qualitative nursing research: A contemporary dialogue.* Rockville, MD: Aspen.

Kniskern, D. P. (1983). The new wave is all wet. *Family Therapy Networker, 1*(38), 61–62.

Kotarba, J. (1990). Ethnography and AIDS: Returning to the streets. *Journal of American Contemporary Ethnography, 19*(3), 259–270.

Krippendorff, K. (1980). *Content analysis: An introduction to its methodology.* Beverly Hills, CA: Sage.

Kruger, D. (1986). On the way to an existential–phenomenological psychotherapy. In D. Kruger (Ed.), *The changing reality of modern man.* Pittsburgh: Duquesne University Press.

Kuehl, B. P. (1987). *The family therapy of adolescent drug abuse: Family members describe their experience.* Unpublished doctoral dissertation, Texas Tech University, Lubbock.

Kuehl, B. P., & Newfield, N. A. (1991). Family listeners among the Nacerima: What the natives have to say. *Family Therapy Case Studies (Australia), 6*(1), 55–66.

Kuehl, B. P., Newfield, N. A., & Joanning, H. (1990). A client-based description of family therapy. *Journal of Family Psychology, 3*(3), 310–321.

LeCompte, M. D., & Goetz, J. P. (1982). Problems of reliability and validity in ethnographic research. *Journal of Educational Research, 52*(1), 31–60.

LeCompte, M. D., & Preissle, J. (1993). *Ethnography and qualitative design in educational research* (2nd ed.). San Diego, CA: Academic Press.

Leininger, M. M. (1985a). Ethnography and ethnonursing: Models and modes of qualitative data analysis. In M. M. Leininger (Ed.), *Qualitative research methods in nursing*. New York: Grune & Stratton.

Leininger, M. M. (1985b). Nature, rationale, and importance of qualitative research methods in nursing. In M. M. Leininger (Ed.), *Qualitative research methods in nursing*. New York: Grune & Stratton.

Leininger, M. M. (Ed.). (1985c). *Qualitative research methods in nursing*. New York: Grune & Stratton.

Liddle, H. A. (1991). Empirical values and the culture of family therapy. *Journal of Marital and Family Therapy, 17,* 327–348.

Lincoln, Y., & Guba, E. (1985). *Naturalistic inquiry*. Beverly Hills, CA: Sage.

Lipson, J. G. (1989). The use of self in ethnographic research. In J. M. Morse (Ed.), *Qualitative nursing research: A contemporary dialogue*. Rockville, MD: Aspen.

Lofland, J., & Lejeune, R. (1970). Initial interactions of newcomers in Alcoholic Anonymous: A field experiment in class symbols and socialization. In W. Filstead (Ed.), *Qualitative methodology: Firsthand involvement with the social world*. Chicago: Rand-McNally.

Lounsbury, F. G. (1963). Linguistics and psychology. In S. Koch (Ed.), *Psychology: A study of a science* (Vol. 6). New York: McGraw-Hill.

Love, J. G. (1992). *A coevolution of marriage and medicine: Systemic, constructionist and thematic voices on medical families*. Unpublished doctoral dissertation, Nova University, Ft. Lauderdale, FL.

Malinowski, B. (1961). *Argonauts of the western Pacific*. New York: E. P. Dutton. (Original work published 1922)

Marcus, G., & Fisher, M. (1986). *Anthropology as cultural critique: An experimental moment in the human sciences*. Chicago: University of Chicago Press.

Marshall, C., & Rossman, G. (1989). *Designing qualitative research*. Newbury Park, CA: Sage.

McDermott, R. P. (1982). Rigor and respect as standards in ethnographic description. *Harvard Educational Review, 52*(3), 321–328.

Mead, M. (1953). National character. In A. Krober (Ed.), *Anthropology today*. Chicago: University of Chicago Press.

Miles, M. B., & Huberman, A. M. (1994). *Qualitative data analysis: An expanded sourcebook* (2nd ed.). Newbury Park, CA: Sage.

Minuchin, S., Rosman, B., & Baker, L. (1979). *Psychosomatic families: Anorexia nervosa in context*. Cambridge, MA: Harvard University Press.

Mishler, E. (1979). Meaning in context: Is there any other kind? *Educational Review, 19*(1), 1–19.

Moon, S. M., Dillon, D. R., & Sprenkle, D. H. (1990). Family therapy and qualitative research. *Journal of Marital and Family Therapy, 16,* 357–374.

Moon, S. M., Dillon, D. R., & Sprenkle, D. H. (1991). On balance and synergy: Family therapy and qualitative research revisited. *Journal of Marital and Family Therapy, 17*(2), 173–178.

Morse, J. M. (1989). Strategies for sampling. In J. W. Morse (Ed.), *Qualitative nursing research: A contemporary dialogue*. Rockville, MD: Aspen.

Morse, J. M. (1994). *Critical issues in qualitative research methods*. Thousand Oaks, CA: Sage.

Muecke, M. (1994). On the evaluation of ethnographies. In J. W. Morse (Ed.), *Critical issuers in qualitative research methods*. Thousand Oaks, CA: Sage.

Munhall, P. L. (1994). *Qualitative research proposals and reports: A guide*. New York: National League for Nursing Press.

Munhall, P. L., & Boyd, C. O. (1993). *Nursing research: A qualitative perspective*. New York: National League for Nursing Press.

Nader, L. (1970). From anguish to exultation. In P. Golde (Ed.), *Women in the field: Anthropological experiences*. Chicago: Aldine.

Napier, A. Y., & Whitaker, C. A. (1978). *The family crucible.* New York: Bantam.

Newfield, N. (1992, Spring). Ways of knowing. *American Family Therapy Association Newsletter, 47,* pp. 51–53.

Newfield, N. A., Kuehl, B. P., Joanning, H., & Quinn, W. H. (1990). A mini-ethnography of the family therapy of adolescent drug abuse: The ambiguous experience. *Alcoholism Treatment Quarterly, 7*(2), 57–80.

Newfield, N. A., Kuehl, B. P., Joanning, H., & Quinn, W. H. (1991). We can tell you about psychos and shrinks: An ethnography of the family therapy of adolescent substance abuse. In T. C. Todd & M. D. Selekman (Eds.), *Family therapy approaches with adolescent substance abusers.* Boston: Allyn & Bacon.

Nichter, M. (1980). The lay person's perception of medicine as perspective into the utilization of multiple therapy systems in the Indian context. *Social Science and Medicine, 14,* 225–233.

Ogbu, J. (1981). School ethnography: A multilevel approach. *Anthropology and Education Quarterly, 12*(1), 3–29.

Osborne, W. (1993, December). The ethical symbiosis between anthropologists and the peoples they study. *Anthropology Newsletter, 6,* 1, 6.

Peacock, J. L. (1986). *The anthropological lens: Harsh light, soft focus.* Cambridge, MA: Cambridge University Press.

Pelto, P. J. (1970). *Anthropological research: The structure of inquiry.* New York: Harper & Row.

Plato. (1973). *Theatetus: Translated with Notes by John McDowell.* Oxford: Clarendon Press.

Powdermaker, H. (1966). *Stranger and friend.* New York: Norton.

Preble, E., & Casey, J. J. (1967). Taking care of business: The heroin user's life on the street. *International Journal of the Addictions, 4*(1), 1–2.

Rynkiewich, M., & Spradley, J. (1976). *Ethics and anthropology: Dilemmas in fieldwork.* New York: Wiley.

Sanday, P. (1979). The ethnographic paradigm(s). In J. V. Mannen (Ed.), *Qualitative methodology.* Beverly Hills, CA: Sage.

Sass, L. A. (1986, May). Anthropology's native problem: Revisionism in the field. *Harper's Magazine, 272*(163), 49–57.

Schneirla, T. C. (1972). A consideration of some conceptual trends in comparative psychology. In L. Aronson, E. Tobach, J. Rosenblatt, & D. Lehrman (Eds.), *Selected writings of T. C. Schneirla.* San Francisco: W. H. Freeman.

Segal, L. (1986). *The dream of reality: Heinz von Foerster's constructivism.* New York: Norton.

Sells, S. P. (1993). *An ethnography of couple and therapist experiences in reflecting team practice.* Unpublished doctoral dissertation, Florida State University, Tallahasse.

Sells, S. P., Smith, T. E., Coe, M. J., Yoshioka, M., & Robbins, J. (1994). An ethnography of couple and therapist experiences in reflecting team practice. *Journal of Marital and Family Therapy, 20*(3), 247–266.

Sells, S. P., Smith, T. E., & Moon, S. (in press). An ethnographic study of client and therapist perceptions of therapy effectiveness in a university-based training clinic. *Journal of Marital and Family Therapy.*

Sells, S. P., Smith, T. E., & Sprenkle, D. (1995). Integrating quantitative and qualitative research methods: A research model. *Family Process, 34,* 1–20.

Seltzer, W. J. (1985a). Conversion disorder in childhood and adolescence: A familial/cultural approach. Part I. *Family Systems Medicine, 3,* 261–280.

Seltzer, W. J. (1985b). Conversion disorder in childhood and adolescence: Therapeutic issues. Part II. *Family Systems Medicine, 3,* 397–416.

Seltzer, W. J. (1988). Myths of destruction: A cultural approach to families in therapy. *Journal of Psychotherapy and the Family, 4,* 17–34.

Seltzer, W. J., & Seltzer, M. R. (1983). Material, myth, and magic: A cultural approach to family therapy. *Family Process, 22*(1), 3–14.

Seltzer, W. J., & Seltzer, M. R. (1988). Culture, leavetaking rituals, and the psychotherapist. In O. van der Hart (Ed.), *Coping with loss.* New York: Irwington Press.

Shields, C. G. (1986a). Critiquing the new epistemologies: Toward minimum requirements for a scientific theory of family therapy. *Journal of Marital and Family Therapy, 12*(4), 358–372.

Shields, C. G. (1986b). Family therapy research and practice: Constructs, measurements, and testing. *Journal of Marital and Family Therapy, 12*(4), 379–382.

Skomal, S. (1993, October). The ethics of fieldwork. *Anthropology Newsletter, 34*(7), 1, 26.

Skomal, S. (1994, May). Lessons for the field: Ethics in fieldwork. *Anthropology Newsletter, 35*, 1, 4.

Smith, J. (1990). Alternative research paradigms and the problem of criteria. In E. Guba (Ed.), *The paradigm dialogue.* Beverly Hills, CA: Sage.

Smith, T. E., Jenkins, D. A., & Sells, S. P. (1995). Voices of diversity. *Journal of Family Psychotherapy, 6*(2), 49–70.

Smith, T. E., Sells, S. P, & Clevenger, T. (1994). Ethnographic content analysis of couple and therapist perceptions in a reflecting team. *Journal of Marital and Family Therapy, 20*(3), 267–286.

Smith, T. E., Sells, S. P., & Newfield, N. (1995). *Evaluating family therapy ethnographies using methodological goodness criteria.* Manuscript submitted for publication.

Smith, T. E., Sells, S. P., Pereira, M. G. A., Todahl, J. A., & Pappagiannis, G. (1995). Pilot process research of reflecting conversations. *Journal of Family Psychotherapy, 6*(3), 71–88.

Smith, T. E., Winston, M., & Yoshioka, M. (1992). A qualitative understanding of reflective-teams II: Therapists' perspectives. *Contemporary Family Therapy, 14*(5), 419–432.

Smith, T. E., Yoshioka, M., & Winton, M. (1993). A qualitative understanding of Reflecting teams I: Clients' perspectives. *Journal of Systemic Therapies, 12*(3), 29–45.

Spradley, J. P. (1972a). Beating the drunk charge. In J. Spradley (Ed.), *Culture and cognition: Rules, maps, and plans.* San Francisco: Chandler.

Spradley, J. (1972b). Foundations of cultural knowledge. In J. Spradley (Ed.), *Culture and cognition: Rules, maps, and plans.* San Francisco: Chandler.

Spradley, J. (1979). *The ethnographic interview.* New York: Holt, Rinehart & Winston.

Spradley, J. (1980). *Participant observation.* New York: Holt, Rinehart & Winston.

Steier, F. (1985). Toward a cybernetic methodology of family therapy research: Fifty research methods to family practice. In L. Andreozzi (Ed.), *Integrating research and clinical practice.* Rockville, MD: Aspen.

Stones, C. R. (1985). Qualitative research: A viable psychological alternative. *The Psychological Record, 35,* 63–75.

Strauss, A. (1987). *Qualitative analysis for social scientists.* New York: Cambridge University Press.

Strauss, A., & Corbin, J. (1990). *Basics of qualitative research.* Newbury Park, CA: Sage.

Sturdevant, W. C. (1972). Studies in ethnoscience. In J. P. Spradley (Ed.), *Culture and cognition: Rules, maps, and plans.* San Francisco: Chandler.

Sutter, A. (1966). The world of the righteous dope fiend. *Issues in Criminology, 2*(2), 177–222.

Tesch, R. (1991). Software for qualitative researchers: Analysis needs and program capabilities. In N. G. Fielding & R. Lee (Eds.), *Using computers in qualitative research.* Newbury Park, CA: Sage.

Todahl, J. (1995). *An ethnography of family systems medicine.* Unpublished doctoral dissertation, Florida State University, Tallahassee.

Todd, I. A., Joanning, H., Enders, L., Mutchler, L., & Thomas, F. N. (1991). Using ethnographic interviews to create a more cooperative client-therapist relationship. *Journal of Family Psychotherapy, 1*(3), 51–63.

Tomm, K. (1983). The old hat doesn't fit. *The Family Therapy Networker, 7,* 39–41.

Tomm, K. (1986). On incorporating the therapist in a scientific theory of family therapy. *Journal of Marital and Family Therapy, 12*(4), 373–378.

Tyler, M. G., & Tyler, S. A. (1985). *The sorcerer's apprentice: The discourse of training in family therapy.* Unpublished manuscript, Rice University, Houston, TX.

Tyler, S. A. (1969). *Cognitive anthropology.* New York: Holt, Rinehart & Winston, Inc.

Walters, K. (1990). Critical thinking, rationality, and the vulcanization of students. *Journal of Higher Education, 61,* 448–467.

Wax, M. (1977). On fieldworkers and those exposed to fieldwork: Federal regulations and moral issues. *Human Organization, 36,* 321–328.

Weber, R. P. (1990). *Basic content analysis* (2nd ed.). Newbury Park, CA: Sage.

Werner, O., & Schoepfle, G. M. (1987). *Systematic fieldwork* (Vol. I & II). Beverly Hills, CA: Sage.

Wiebel, W. (1988). Combining ethnographic and epidemiological methods in targeted AIDS interventions: The Chicago Model. In R. J. Battjes & R. Pickens (Eds.), *Needle sharing among intravenous drug abusers* (DDHS Pub. No. (ADM) 88-1567, Monograph 80). Washington, DC: U. S. Government Printing Office.

Wynne, L. C. (1988). An overview of the state of the art: What should be expected in current family therapy research. In L. C. Wynne (Ed.), *The state of the art in family therapy research: Controversies and recommendations.* New York: Family Process Press.

Yalom, I., & Elkin, G. (1974). *Every day gets a little closer: A twice-told therapy.* New York: Basic Books.

Yin, R. K. (1989). *Case study research: Design and methods* (2nd. ed.). Beverly Hills, CA: Sage.

Zimmerman, D., & Wieder, L. (1977). Diary-interview method. *Urban Life, 5,* 479–499.

3

Grounded Theory Methodology in Family Therapy Research

SILVIA ECHEVARRIA RAFULS
SIDNEY M. MOON

BACKGROUND

QUESTION: Are you imaginative, creative, curious, inquisitive? Do you have the courage to face the unknown, to think abstractly, to deal with ambiguity and discovery? Are you skillful in observation, in analyzing patterns and themes of interaction, in interviewing and self-examination? Are you persistent, tolerant, patient, flexible? . . . If so, not only do you have the qualities of an excellent therapist but you are also likely to be an excellent grounded theory researcher. Does that surprise you? Are we saying that the attributes and skills needed to be a good therapist are the same as those required of a good grounded theory researcher? Yes! That is the assumption on which this chapter is based and the reason why research that is guided by the principles of grounded theory is considered both fitting and useful in research with families in therapy.

The purpose of this chapter is to give an overview of the origins of grounded theory methodology and to discuss its relevance and use in family therapy research. We begin with a definition of grounded theory methodology and a description of its philosophical assumptions and its historical roots and development. We then address practical issues related to methodology by providing an example of grounded theory research from a family therapy study (Rafuls, 1994). Through this example, specifics about selection and sampling and data collection and analysis are illustrated. The study was conducted with Latin American families and their therapists in an inner-city family therapy training program in Chicago. The study's purpose was twofold. First, through qualitative interviews, the families were to identify and reflect on their own resources and strengths and determine how these might be utilized in therapy. Second, their respective therapists reflected on the information given by the families and provided suggestions about future use of the study's findings.

The discussion section addresses strengths and weakness of grounded theory methodology as it pertains to family therapy research. Strengths cover the types of research questions that grounded theory can address in family therapy and how it parallels many of the processes already known to us as therapists. Weaknesses are discussed in terms of the methodology's limitations in family therapy research. Reporting of findings is addressed in this section, as are aspects of reliability and validity of grounded theory methodology, also referred to as credibility and trustworthiness. Ways in which grounded theory bridges research and clinical practice are also considered. A section providing suggestions for future directions of grounded theory approaches in family therapy concludes this chapter.

Definition of the Methodology

Grounded theory is a methodology based on theory development from data that are collected and analyzed systematically and recursively. It is a way of thinking about or conceptualizing data as the essential element from which theory evolves. Its key feature is what is commonly known in qualitative research as the constant comparative method (Glaser & Strauss, 1967). This inductive analytical process involves a constant interplay between data collection and data analysis. Essentially, as data are collected, they are analyzed for emergent theoretical categories, which are systematically looped back into the collection of data and analyzed further for their interrelationships and meaning (Strauss & Corbin, 1990). Grounded theory emerges on reaching theoretical saturation of meanings, patterns, and categories (Glaser, 1978). Grounded theory procedure is useful to any researcher who wishes to generate inductive theory from data that is systematically collected and analyzed, whether qualitative or quantitative.

Philosophical Assumptions

In the grounded theory literature, specific theoretical tenets of the methodology are not made explicit by way of epistemological and/or ideological frameworks. In other words, grounded theory is not theoretically tied to any one specific research tradition or research paradigm but is considered theoretically consistent with several, both positivistic and nonpositivistic in nature. Thus even though grounded theory is usually associated with nonpositivistic qualitative research, theoretically, it can also be used in quantitative studies in the positivistic tradition.

Nonpositivistic research paradigms are usually, but not always, associated with "alternate" or "alternative" research paradigms (Hoshmand, 1989; Guba, 1990). For instance, in Hoshmand's (1989) treatise on alternate research paradigms (i.e., nonpositivistic, nonreductive logicodeductive research), grounded theory is discussed within the paradigm of naturalistic–ethnographic research. As such, it is associated with postpositivist philosophy, which is sometimes used to refer to naturalistic inquiry itself (Lincoln & Guba, 1985). Others like Reason and Rowan (1981), however, view grounded theory as "an excellent example of a qualitative research approach which stays firmly within the old paradigm" (i.e., positivistic), "and which stays, in terms of the Hegelian analysis, at the social 'objective' level" (p. xx). They believe grounded theory does not fall within their definition of new paradigm research because it does not reflect a "collaborative, experiential, reflexive, and action-oriented process," and is seen as divorced from the experiential knowledge of those involved in the research (p. xx). From a more constructivist viewpoint, then, the systematic and formal procedure involved in grounded theory may be interpreted as more consistent with positivism than constructivism.

We wish to express our view of grounded theory as theoretically consistent with the alternate research paradigms presented by Hoshmand (1989) (i.e., naturalistic–ethnographic, phenomenological, and cybernetic) and the alternative research paradigms as presented by Guba (1990) (i.e., postpositivism, critical theory, and constructivism). In the broader sense, alternate or alternative research paradigms differ from the positivistic research traditions in three distinct ways: (1) ontologically, by not limiting the researcher to think of social reality as "out there" known only by "truths" that are driven by natural laws and arrived at only by controlled experimentation; (2) epistemologically, by not requiring the researcher to separate the subjective and objective aspects of knowledge and the value-ladenness of facts; and (3) methodologically, by not limiting the researcher to standards of precise measurement, operationalized concepts, or deductive practices of theory testing and verification alone (Guba, 1990; Hoshmand, 1989). Alternative paradigms offer researchers new ways of approaching knowledge that may be more conducive to the types of questions they are asking. In particular, discovery-oriented approaches offer methodological options needed to address the diversity of clinical practice and families that we work with. This offers family researchers the notion that there is more than just one way of doing research, thus inviting those who perhaps might not have stepped into the research arena at all. A better understanding of how grounded theory fits within different research paradigms is presented by providing a history of its roots and development.

Historical Roots and Development

The origin of grounded theory is credited to sociologists Barney Glaser and Anselm Strauss. Together they wrote *The Discovery of Grounded Theory* in 1967. Grounded theory was created in order to "close the embarrassing gap between theory and empirical research," which Glaser and Strauss (1967) believed occurred because of the undue emphasis placed on verification of theory in sociological research at the time. Through grounded theory methodology Glaser and Strauss set out to provide researchers with a formalized framework for generating theory from empirical data. Even though grounded theory was designed with the emphasis on generating theory, it was not intended to minimize the importance of verifying theory. As Glaser and Strauss (1967) saw it, both generation and verification of theory were necessary and complementary.

Even though much of the original research using grounded theory procedures was done in sociology, the methodology is not "discipline bound" (Strauss & Corbin, 1990). Researchers in other fields such as psychology, anthropology, nursing, education, social work, and even business management have adopted grounded theory methods, and it is thought that grounded theory will continue to spread into other fields (Strauss & Corbin, 1990).

Although not noted for their use of grounded theory methods, pioneering family therapists observed families in qualitatively oriented ways. As Gilgun (1992) points out, many of the early theorists in family therapy pursued their knowledge of families through direct client–therapist interaction and postsession reflection and analysis (p. 236). Even though their qualitatively based observations formed the foothold for many of the theories they developed in family therapy, it would be a stretch to consider these pioneering efforts to be grounded theory studies without having information about their methods of data collection and data analysis. To date, despite grounded theory's congruence with the practice of family therapy, there seems to be a dearth of studies using the methodology in the field. Some of the reasons for this may be the time and labor intensiveness of grounded theory procedures and limited training in the use of grounded theory in family therapy education.

Since the inception of grounded theory in the mid-1960s, Glaser (1978, 1992) and Strauss (1987; Strauss & Corbin, 1990) have developed diverging views of grounded theory methodology. The central issue in their debate is one of emphasis on different but, in our view, equally important aspects of grounded theory methodology. Glaser emphasizes the "emergent" process of theory development, whereas Strauss emphasizes the "systematic" aspect of managing data analysis and synthesis. Glaser takes the position that grounded theory is to deal only with data that is relevant to the emerging theory, not data that is forced into a preconceived analytical framework by prescribing analysis according to certain conditions and consequences. These preconceived notions, he contends, may have nothing to do with those variables that are relevant to the emerging theory and therefore are antithetical to the very distinguishing feature of grounded theory as systematically emergent from data (Glaser, 1992).

Strauss (1987; Strauss & Corbin, 1990), on the other hand, believes that organization of the data is key to arriving at the emergent theory. As he puts it, "the excellence of the research rests in large part on the excellence of the coding" (Strauss, 1987, p. 27). Strauss's emphasis on coding grew out of experiences in teaching students how to do grounded theory research (Gilgun, 1992; Strauss & Corbin, 1990). His formalized approach in coding data is especially helpful to beginning grounded theory researchers because it helps reduce the ambiguity that generally goes along with grounded theory analysis.

We see this divergence in emphasis as a "both–and" issue and not an "either–or." We believe both Glaser and Strauss have made significant contributions. How to interpret and utilize specific procedures, as suggested by each of their differing perspectives, is best left up to the individual researcher and his or her research questions.

As a newcomer to qualitative research in general, and grounded theory specifically, the first author's (S. E. R.) experience is one of attraction to Glaser's argument on a more conceptual, epistemological level, and to Strauss and Corbin's approach on a more practical, methodological level. Procedurally, Glaser's approach is often elusive and difficult to put into "how to" terms. Ironically, the expansiveness and creativity that are a part of Glaser's view can lead to ambiguity that may limit the researcher procedurally. My first experience following Glaser's (1978, 1992; Glaser & Strauss, 1967) approach to grounded theory felt limiting because I often felt it was only possible to implement if Glaser himself, or one of his disciples, for that matter, were there to coach me all the way through. In other words, because it was less specific procedurally, it was easier to feel lost and to wonder whether I was proceeding correctly.

On the other hand, the clear-cut and specific guidelines in Strauss's approach (Strauss, 1987; Strauss & Corbin, 1990) provides newcomers to grounded theory with useful structure (especially in the throes of data analysis). Because of this, researchers who follow Strauss are more likely to be self-directed and secure with correctness of procedure. We encourage family therapy researchers to integrate both Glaser's and Strauss's approaches in a way that is congruent with their data and their own style.

In summary, we view this period of grounded theory debate and controversy as healthy because we believe it opens up more possibilities for researchers. References to the "correctness" of a method of grounded theory, or one "true grounded theory" approach, assumes ownership of a methodology that was created to get away from a one-sided perspective of research. It would seem unworthy and untrue to itself to view grounded theory in that light. Instead, we believe it is more fruitful to think of the variation in approaches to grounded theory as providing options. Which approach to use depends on the cognitive style of the researcher, the researcher's level of expertise in qualitative research, and the research questions being investigated. We might say that grounded theory is currently in its own inductive process of change and development, an emergent process within a methodology of emergent theory.

METHODOLOGY

Grounded theory methodology builds theory from data collection and analysis that emerges flexibly over time (Strauss & Corbin, 1990; Glaser, 1978; Glaser & Strauss, 1967). In grounded theory, the researcher becomes the primary instrument of data collection and analysis and it is the researcher's theoretical sensitivity that allows him or her to develop theory that is grounded in the data (Strauss & Corbin, 1990). A grounded theorist's awareness of the subtleties of meaning in data depends on personal qualities of insight, understanding, and the ability to make sense of what is pertinent.

The research study that will serve as an example of grounded theory methodology in family therapy research in this chapter is based on a study conducted by Rafuls (1994). This study employed in-depth interviews with Latino families in therapy to find out what they perceived their family resources and strengths to be and how these identified resources could be utilized as part of their therapy. Their respective therapists were also interviewed, both as individual reactants and as a reflective focus group, and asked to respond to their client-family's views and to provide suggestions about the use of resource-based interviewing in therapy. The research emphasized family resources and strengths (Karpel, 1986) within the context of ethnic-specific families, in this case Mexican American and Puerto Rican families, living in the Chicago area. Through resource-based interviewing and dialogue, the study also facilitated a reflective process between clients and therapists about the families' strengths and resources and their experiences throughout the interview process, thus providing a consultative model of inquiry and intervention. The reflective, recursive, and collaborative emphasis of this research was conceptualized from a framework of critical theory (i.e., families as experts on themselves acting as collaborative agents of change), and the methodological framework used to analyze data was based on grounded theory.

Research Questions

The research questions that are asked in a study ought to guide the research method that is used. In grounded theory, research questions are generally open-ended, flexible, and broad to begin with and then become more focused and refined as analysis occurs. Research questions in grounded theory studies generally ask about concepts that have not yet been identified or explored or whose relationships are poorly understood or conceptualized (Glaser & Strauss, 1967). Grounded theory questions also tend to be action and process oriented.

The study of Latino family strengths was guided by the following research questions:

1. What are the family resources and strengths identified by selected Latin American client-families in their own family and how would they (the families) suggest using these resources and strengths in their therapy?
2. How do the therapists who treat these families respond to the information their respective client-families share, and how do they (therapists) think this information will affect the process of therapy?

Sampling and Selection Procedures

In grounded theory research, criteria-based selective sampling is used at the beginning of a study. Selective sampling is based on a preconceived set of criteria that originates from the researcher's guiding assumptions and research questions. That is, selection is based on specific considerations which delineate appropriate unit(s) of analysis and participants depending on what the researcher is setting out to discover. Criteria based on the research question(s) generally guides the researcher to a type of selection, or selection procedure(s), which includes convenience selection, comprehensive selection, quota selection, extreme-case selection, typical case selection, unique case selection, and reputational case selection (Goetz & LeCompte, 1984).

For example, in the Rafuls (1994) study, it was important to select families with a specific ethnic identity because one of the original assumptions of the study was that ethnicity might have an influence on a family's resources and strengths. For the sake of manageability, it was thought best to start with one ethnic group (i.e., Latin Americans) and then, if necessary, increase variability with other groups.

After a grounded theory study is under way, further theoretically based sampling may occur. This theoretically based sampling is usually driven by emergent questions and themes in the data. Typically, selective sampling precedes theoretical sampling for particular reasons. First, it is highly unlikely that review boards or funding agencies would approve research that does not provide explicit criteria of the type of participant that the researcher needs to investigate. Furthermore, even researchers who approach data collection from a "not knowing" stance have some idea of questions, concepts, research strategies, and general perspectives about their area of study, generally leading them to the type of participant who would fit these considerations. In terms of a priori views, even though naturalistic inquiry would keep a researcher from preconceived notions about the phenomenon being studied, it does mandate that the researcher be explicit about those views from the beginning in the form of stated assumptions. Essentially, selective sampling allows researchers to develop their initial thoughts about a phenomenon which ultimately drives theoretical sampling as data are analyzed.

From a grounded theory perspective, the Rafuls (1994) study was limited with regard to theoretical sampling because of pragmatic considerations associated with its completion as a dissertation research project. However, if this initial study is viewed as a beginning phase of the development of a substantive grounded theory on resource-based consultation in family therapy, the limitation is minimized. That is, theoretical sampling in future research toward the development of a theory will be based on the hypotheses and categories derived from this initial study and more recursive methods of data collection and analysis will be implemented to remedy this concern.

Data Collection Procedures

Data collection and data analysis in grounded theory are exceptionally intertwined as analysis begins almost immediately after data are first collected. Data collection methods in grounded theory studies may include in-depth interviewing, participant and nonparticipant observation, and document analysis. Sources of data are numerous, including transcripts of interviews, audiotapes, videotapes, field notes, journals, theoretical and analytical memos, and documents. Generally, the "trustworthiness" of findings in a grounded theory study increases if multiple sources of data are utilized, if multiple methods of data collection and analysis are used, and if multiple investigators are involved (Lincoln & Guba, 1985). Because of the theory-guided, data-based nature of gathering information in grounded theory, data collection will not cease until theoretical saturation is reached (i.e., new data cease to yield new information). Before that point, coding and memoing, drawing on comparisons and contrasts, and arriving at analytical questions and hypotheses continue to generate additional questions for researchers which may direct them to other valuable sources of data.

Multiple data sources and methods of data collection were used in the sample study by Rafuls (1994). Data collection was divided into four phases as shown in Table 3.1. The first phase consisted of separate *interviews with the families*, followed by *individual interviews* with each of *their respective therapists*, followed by the third phase consisting of a *reflective focus group interview of the therapists*, and ending with a *reflective focus group interview of the families*. Generally, recursion in grounded theory occurs as data collection and analysis are repeatedly done until theoretical saturation is reached. In this study, recursion and emergence of data occurred in terms of process from one phase of data collection to the other as information gathered from one set of participants was shared with another set of participants.

All the interviews were audiotaped for transcription purposes. Some were videotaped as well. Phase 1 involved the videotaping and audiotaping of all four families because edited portions of family interviews were used in Phase 2 when each of the families' respective therapists were interviewed individually. Phase 3 was also videotaped and audiotaped so that edited portions of the therapists' reflective focus group could be shown to the families in Phase 4, the families' focus group.

Data Analysis Procedures

In grounded theory, data analysis begins as soon as one begins to collect data. The constant comparative method of analysis for which grounded theory is known involves a constant process of categorization, sorting and resorting, and coding and recoding of data for emergent categories of meaning (Hoshmand, 1989). Dimensions and properties of these categories are compared with other emerging categories as the researcher keeps going back to the data. Interrelationships between categories are analyzed until the researcher finds the one that is abstract enough to encompass all that has been described in the story (Glaser & Strauss, 1967). This central phenomenon is at the heart of integration process (Strauss & Corbin, 1990), the core category which is related to all the other categories and is, essentially, the basic social process that is being studied.

In the Rafuls (1994) study all the interviews were transcribed verbatim. Transcripts were reviewed for accuracy by going through the videotape or audiotape of each interview (audiotape was used only if there was no videotape of the interview). Theoretical memos (Glaser, 1978; Strauss & Corbin, 1990) were written by Rafuls (1994) after conducting and reviewing each of the interviews and throughout coding procedures. As

TABLE 3.1. The Four Phases of Data Collection in Sequential Order

Phases	Interviews		Focus groups	
	Phase 1	Phase 2	Phase 3	Phase 4
Data sources	Families (4)	Therapists (3)	Therapists	Families
Open-ended interviews[a]	Yes	Yes	Yes	Yes
Purpose	Identify resources and their use in therapy	Reactions to family data	Dialogue re: use of data	Dialogue and make recommendations
Videotaped	Yes[b]	Yes	Yes[b]	Yes
Audiotaped	Yes	Yes	Yes	Yes

[a]Flexibility and fit took precedence over standardization.
[b]Segments of this phase were used in the following phase of data collection.

data are coded, memos allow the researcher to write up theoretical ideas related to cod-ing of phenomena (i.e., incidents or indicators) and their relationships. This allows for the greater degree of integration and abstraction that is necessary in the development of categories of meaning. In the Rafuls (1994) study theoretical memos were also writ-ten by a research assistant who helped with data collection. The researcher kept a reflexive journal throughout the study as well. These different sources were cross-checked and compared for similarities and differences as categories emerged in the analysis.

Two methods of coding interview data were used in the sample study (Rafuls, 1994). The first method of interacting with the data was to display the participants' verbatim responses to the interview questions on a matrix. This data display (Miles & Huber-man, 1994) was done in column form on 12″ × 18″ sketch pad paper. An example from one of the matrix entries from the Therapist Focus Group Interview is provided in Figure 3.1.

Immediately on the left of the display is the sixth question that the therapists' group was asked. Each of the therapists' responses follow verbatim and are numbered accord-ing to the order in which they were given. Segments of these verbatim responses are underlined to highlight noticeable phenomena which are analyzed as similarities, differ-ences (or unique responses), and emerging categories, themes, or patterns on the right side of the matrix. As a form of level 1 analysis, the data display was helpful in terms of organizing phenomena and gaining perspective on emerging categories. A similar display was completed for each of the questions that were asked of respondents in each of the four phases of data collection (i.e., each question asked of families with each of their respective responses, each question asked of therapists in their individual inter-views, each question asked of the therapists' focus group as illustrated in Display 1, and each question asked of the families in their focus group interview). Again, although this provided some categorical organization and perspective with regard to "what was there," when it came time to reduce and synthesize phenomena in terms interrelated-ness, it was helpful to turn to grounded theory procedures of coding.

Before describing the method of coding used in the sample study, it is important to mention a disparity in coding procedures that exists between both the originators of formalized grounded theory. In Glaser's terms, coding is defined as substantive, theo-retical, and selective and is mostly tied to the concept of theoretical sensitivity (Glaser, 1978). Theoretical sensitivity refers to personal qualities of researchers related to their knowledge and life experience and to their ability to pick up on meaningful and perti-nent information in the area they are investigating. Strauss and Corbin (1990) refer to coding as open, axial, and selective. Open coding refers to a process of breaking down, examining, comparing, conceptualizing, and categorizing data (Strauss & Corbin, 1990). Whereas open coding is designed for the expansion of the analyst's thinking about data, axial coding is utilized in order to integrate data. Through axial coding the researcher reduces and synthesizes data by establishing the connections between subcategories and categories. Axial coding provides the foundation for selective coding. Selective coding involves the process of selecting a core category, systemically relating it to the other categories, validating those relationships, and filling in those categories that need fur-ther refinement and development (Strauss & Corbin, 1990). During this phase of cod-ing, integration of data occurs at a higher level of theoretical abstraction.

When synthesizing meaningful and pertinent information in qualitative research, analysts often reach a point when they feel like all of the massive amounts of informa-tion, floating in their head, will go nowhere. It is really an awful feeling but often a turning point in the research process. It was here, in the first author's (S. E. R.) ex-perience, when faced with connecting meaning to the relationship between categories,

Interview Questions: Therapist Focus Group	Liz	Ramona	Amy	
6. What have you come away with as a result of this experience [the study] that would be relevant to other therapists and researchers in the field?	4. "I also think that *whole area of identifying strengths is important for families to do themselves.* I think that it's easy for families and people who are in therapy to get really hooked on what they don't think is going right and to work really hard to want to change that, and *lose sight of all the good things that are already happening and strengths they can build on.*"	1. *"The opportunity to have this kind of dialogue and have someone outside to objectively interview would be helpful."* 3. *"It's a third dimension* or second dimension that's created that *allows you* to look into the level of that family and *to get a good view of* how they view *themselves."*	2. "I mean, I think, providing opportunities or seeking *opportunities to observe the family in areas other than therapy. . . .*There's something very enriching about seeing the family function. We talk about their functioning in a context that isn't therapy and where the therapist gets to be a passive kind of observer of that and allow themselves to kind of process in a way that's less direct."	**Similarities:** 1. Having family interviewed outside the context of therapy is a helpful process. 2. Interviewing of family by outsider to therapy allows for therapist to gain a different perspective of family. **Differences:** 1. Process of families identifying their own strengths is not only viewed as helpful to therapists but also helpful to families. 2. Use of "third dimension" when referring to process of resource-based interviewing conducted with families outside of therapy. 3. Use of the word "dialogue" to refer to process of talking about family interviews. **Categories/ Themes/Patterns:** 1. Impact of interviewing on (a) families and (b) therapists. 2. "Dialogue." 3. Process of dialogue akin to reflecting team experience 4. "Third dimension" denotes a metaperspective of family interview data.

FIGURE 3.1. Sample of data display (level 1 analysis).

that Strauss and Corbin's (1990) coding approach was invaluable. Although Glaser's ideas of creativity and openness resonated with the researcher ideologically, from a practical standpoint, Strauss and Corbin (1990) provided a clearer coding scheme that was modified in response to the data.

Essentially, *open coding* was done in the form of cutting up transcripts into categories of phenomena that seemed to reoccur or were unique in some way. This was accomplished by taking an analytical position and asking what each of the interview response segments was about. Subcategories describing the phenomena emerged, which then created categories as more abstract levels of analysis occurred. For example, within the responses of what became the category "Family Adaptability," there were subcategories that denoted dimensions of time (e.g., Shared Past, Shared Present, and Shared Future). Each of these dimensions emerged from phenomena related to specific aspects or examples of family life. For instance, the dimension of shared present emerged from resourceful experiences and examples of humor, togetherness, preservation of self (for the sake of family), and perception of hardship.

Categories such as Family Adaptability were filed by headings on hanging folders wherein manila folders with subcategory headings (e.g., Shared Present, Shared Past, and Shared Future) were filed with all of the pieces of transcript descriptive of each phenomenon that fell within that subcategory (e.g., humor, togetherness, preservation of self, and perception of hardship). In order to reduce and synthesize the massive amount of information compiled at that point in the analysis, a variation on Strauss and Corbin's (1990) paradigm model was used. The interrelatedness between subcategories and categories was diagrammed on 12″ × 18″ sketch pad sheets in a modified version of the *axial coding* component of Strauss and Corbin's (1990) coding model. In order to integrate data, each category was analyzed for its causal condition(s), properties, context, action/interaction strategies, intervening conditions, and consequences. These indicators were not forced on the data. Instead, they were used as a framework for analysis and adjusted according to the data set. Figure 3.2 provides an illustration of the axial coding scheme used by Rafuls (1994).

Eleven main categories of phenomena (collapsed from the original 23 file categories) were analyzed according to this paradigm model of axial coding on 12″ × 18″ sketch pad paper. Five of the 11 collapsed categories were *content related* regarding resources and strengths identified by the families (i.e., Ethnic Affiliation, Family Formation, Family Service, Family Adaptability, and Family Connectedness), and the other six were more *process oriented*, related to the impact of resource-based interviewing on the participants and on therapy itself (e.g., Interview Effects on Families, Interview Effects on Therapists [individually and in group], Consultation [therapist to researcher, researcher to therapist, etc.]).

The first step in *selective coding* was to integrate the information developed in each of the 11 categories by writing theoretical memos that fully explained all its stated *properties, dimensions, and associated paradigmatic relationships*. To create the story line that is part of this stage of theory development, each of the theoretical memos was written as sections or chapters of a book. However, not all 11 categories were developed enough to be written up at this level of abstraction (i.e., in terms of theoretical saturation). Categories having to do with family resources and strengths (i.e., the more content-oriented data) were more developed conceptually than those related to the participants' experiences of the interview process (i.e., the more process-oriented data). This difference in theoretical saturation probably occurred because theoretical saturation of content-based data requires less time than that required by process-oriented data. That is, data based on content (i.e., descriptive reporting of specific information) may be gathered

```
┌─────────────────────────────────────┐         ┌─────────────────────────────┐
│ Causal condition: Reflective focus group: │────────►│ Phenomenon: Interview effect │
│         process with therapists       │         │         on process          │
│                                       │         │        (therapist group)    │
└─────────────────────────────────────┘         └─────────────────────────────┘
```

Properties of reflective process in therapist
       focus group:

1. "Learning" about families (individual and group)
2. Expansion of context/perspective we have on family: "A different angle"
3. Multidimensional view of family; "Three dimensional mirror"
4. Synchronicity of understanding (i.e., "[therapists'] knowledge reflected in some of the things they were saying.") between therapists and families
5. Affirmation/reassurance/purpose (family to therapist; therapist to therapist)
6. Expansion of family's experience/information to therapist group level

Context of reflective process in therapist focus
       group:

1. Having families talk about themselves in different context and us talk about that (viewed as "an opportunity")
2. Able to talk about what they learned with each other—vulnerability and openness to share as a group
3. Support, question, comment on each other's work
4. Shared respect for their families' competencies

Strategies/actions of reflective focus group with
       therapists:

Dialogue
Questions and answers
Interviewing skills
    through these able to: 1. Contrast therapists' impressions with families' experiences
                     2. Share their respective family data as a group
                     3. Contrast each other's family data/ information
                     4. Therapists sharing their therapy with other therapists

Consequences

1. Therapists' comparison of families
2. Using information in therapy (with this and other families) at termination
3. Increasing use of resource-based language and interventions with families
4. More knowledge about themselves, their work, and comraderie
5. Group support, clarity, and validation re: work with families
6. Expanded view of families
7. Recommendations by Therapists:
   A. Clients are more likely to respond to outside interviewer/consultant-raised issue re: resource-based questions as therapeutic vs. non-therapeutic
   B. (Outside) interviewer would be less biased, less preconceived notions of their family strengths. (Therapists vs. interviewer to conduct interviewing)
   C. Issue raised re: timing of interviewing— during what phase of therapy—when and how to ask in relation to the family's functioning
   D. Questions asked outside context of therapy viewed as a "point of entry" to emphasize strengths in therapy
6. Increasing awareness of impact of resource-based questioning in their work

Intervening/mediating conditions

1. Time
2. Trust (in each other and in process)
3. Interest in topic
4. Commitment to research

FIGURE 3.2. Sample of axial coding.

rather straightforwardly, usually during one encounter, whereas data that is dependent on a specific process (i.e., how a phenomenon is experienced over a designated period of time during which certain events take place) would generally be gathered throughout an extended and unpredictable stretch of time. In other words, further theoretical abstraction of process related to resource-based interviewing will require an ongoing programmatic effort in order to reach theoretical saturation of this phenomenon.

The next step in selective coding was to decide on the story line, the central phenomenon around which all other categories were integrated. This required that a decision be made on a core category that was abstract enough to encompass all that was described at that point in the analysis. In the Rafuls (1994) study, the process of resource-based consultation in family therapy seemed to encompass all the categories and all that transpired in the research. It was also noted that this process consisted of two parts, the content-based information gathering of family resources and strengths, called resource-generative inquiry, and the process-oriented, reflective experiences that participants had, which came to be known as reflective dialogue. It was also noted that resource-generative inquiry was related to the first research question and reflective dialogue was related to the second research question.

To further develop a grounded theory of the resource-based consultation process, the emergent hypotheses from this initial study will need to be tested further through theoretical sampling and additional data collection and data analysis. The collection of new, theoretically based data would maximize variability and thus provide a more theoretically saturated, richer description of what has emerged thus far as the core category of resource-based consultation in family therapy (Glaser & Strauss, 1967, p. 244). It is important to note that deduction in grounded theory occurs differently than deduction in logicodeductive studies. In logicodeductive methods, deduction occurs as a process of verification of an existing theory or hypothesis. In grounded theory, deduction is based on a hypothesis or theory that emerges from data that were collected and analyzed, thus producing a relevant theoretical abstraction about what goes on in a particular area of study. Deduction in grounded theory is concerned with the verification of emergent data-based hypotheses for the sake of greater conceptual density and theoretical saturation (i.e., when analysis no longer produces any new information). Deduction in logicodeductive studies is concerned with verification or proof of previously created theory that is not grounded in data that is being studied. Because of the lack of theoretical saturation that exists with data collected so far, findings from this first stage of the project have been reported as exploratory and tentative (Rafuls, 1994).

Reporting

To report findings in grounded theory, the researcher does not need to wait for complete theoretical saturation of categories and/or testing of emergent hypotheses. In fact, because of the close connection between data collection and data analysis, reporting can begin from the time data are first collected. Initial reporting of emergent theory usually occurs during analysis in the form of informal discussions and/or presentations. We suggest, however, that reporting of initial findings go beyond personal communications and be published for reasons of exposure and critique. As Glaser (1978) asserts, grounded theory deserves publication for its rigor and value and for the stake that grounded theorists have in "effecting wider publics" (p. 128) in order to make their theories count. Strauss and Corbin (1990) concur by suggesting that publication of grounded theory studies enhances collegial communication. Usually, grounded theory is written as an integrated set of hypotheses rather than a report of findings. Although the degree of conceptualization involved in doing this requires integration of data, writing can also occur before integration occurs for the specific purpose of working one's way out of stumbling blocks of integration itself. This can be done by writing about the most relevant parts of one's theory and then analyzing them for their relationships (Glaser, 1978).

Writing grounded theory is more about the relationship between concepts than it is about the description of people or phenomena. In contrast to ethnography and phenomenology, where description is paramount and low inference descriptors substantiate credibility, description and illustration in grounded theory reporting are secondary to integrated conceptualization and are minimally utilized for support purposes. Glaser (1978) claims that the credibility of a grounded theory is achieved by its integration and relevance and not by using illustrations as proof (p. 134). Grounded theory is written so that the reader has an understanding of the conceptual work that goes into the analysis and its integration into a theoretical orientation (Glaser, 1978). This allows the reader to make reasonable judgments about the theory's "trustworthiness," which Lincoln and Guba (1985) define as the credibility and transferability of a study's findings. The trustworthiness of a study is influenced by the way that its findings are written (Lincoln & Guba, 1985). Grounded theory can be written as a paper, article, thesis, monograph, chapter, or book. Due to its origin in sociology, writing has been shaped by the style employed in sociological monographs and chapters (Glaser & Strauss, 1967; Glaser, 1978; Strauss & Corbin, 1990). This includes addressing the problem and core category that was derived from grounded theory, the methodology, and a clear analytical story about the core category.

DISCUSSION

Strengths of Methodology When Applied to Family Therapy

One of the strengths in using grounded theory methodology in family therapy research is that grounded theory is theoretically consonant to the practice of therapy. This is especially important to clinicians, who are often discouraged by how irrelevant research is to their practice. With a methodology that requires skills that parallel those required of therapists, clinicians are more likely to turn to grounded theory methodology as a way to bridge clinical practice with areas of interest that they would like to investigate further. In addition, the inductive and deductive process that occurs in grounded theory is similar to the process that therapists experience as they arrive inductively at hypotheses about clients and then deductively check out those hypotheses as therapy takes place. Therefore, the application of grounded theory methodology in family therapy research is a definite strength because of the kinship that exists between both processes.

The research questions that grounded theory can help family therapists answer is another strength because of the compatibility that exists in the way that both processes ask questions. Often clinicians ask questions that can be answered in qualitative terms. Grounded theory, in particular, is applicable to questions we ask about the process of therapy, or about our clients in therapy, because they usually refer to meanings, perceptions, and understandings of clients. Therapists' questions are also related to the sensitive topics dealt with in therapy that are usually complex, qualified, ambivalent, situational, and/or changing over time. In addition, questions may relate to alternate perspectives, diversity, and uniqueness, which fit within the paradigm of grounded theory.

Weaknesses of Methodology When Applied to Family Therapy

Application of grounded theory methodology in family therapy research presents some concerns because of the recursive nature of theoretical sampling and theory building. Theoretical sampling and theory building in grounded theory studies present concerns

regarding the programmatic efforts that they may require, how time and labor intensive these studies can be, how hard it is to delegate the analysis phase to assistants,
how hard it is to do well, and how it can potentially create role ambiguity and role
conflict if research is conducted in a clinical setting. All these concerns have implications for funding related to the denial or depletion of resources, and with regard to publication efforts, in terms of the extended length necessary to write up grounded theory
studies.

Although the compatibility of processes involved in clinical practice and grounded
theory research were previously viewed as a strength then, complementarity also presents
some concerns with regard to issues of informed consent and ethics. In other words,
there is a good chance that grounded theory research in a clinical setting can have
therapeutic influence on its participants. Usually, effects or influences of the research
are explained when informed consent is obtained. However, because therapeutic effects or influences are not predictable or known at the beginning of research, a discussion in specific terms is not possible during informed consent, thus raising ethical concerns
as a weakness of design. For that matter, any design that is inductive and exploratory
in nature, as is the case with grounded theory, would raise this concern. Besides letting
participants know that the possibility of influence on their therapy exists, there is little
else the researcher is able to do in terms of informed consent as a way of addressing
this concern.

Reliability and Validity

In the research world, the reliability and validity of a study serve as standards that determine how "good" the research really is. This presents an epistemological problem
when research paradigms digress from the positivistic traditions on which these criteria
are based. Implicit in differing modes of discovery are different standards and procedures to arrive at "good science." In qualitative terms, we might say that the reliability
and validity of a research study determine its credibility and trustworthiness (Lincoln
& Guba, 1985). Although we could discuss reliability and validity as credibility and
trustworthiness, we will stay within the language of research methodologists at large
but discuss reliability and validity as they pertain to qualitative research.

In positivistic science, reliability is concerned with the replicability of findings and
validity is concerned with the accuracy of findings. Reliability is dependent on the resolution of both external and internal design problems (Goetz & LeCompte, 1984, p.
210). Validity is also assessed in terms of internal and external aspects of accuracy related to the findings.

External reliability refers to the likelihood that an independent researcher would find
similar phenomena or generate the same constructs in the same or similar settings (Goetz
& Le Compte, 1984). The uniqueness or complexity of phenomena and individuals
that is characteristically a part of naturalistic inquiry presents some concerns with regard
to this standard of reproducibility. However, steps can be taken to safeguard against
threats of external reliability by providing readers with explicit details regarding the
researcher's theoretical perspective and the research methodology that was implemented in a study. Explication of data collection may include selection criteria of participants,
interview guide questions, descriptions of the researcher's role, and the methods of analysis
(e.g., explaining coding procedures and the development of categories and hypotheses).
Under a similar set of conditions, it is feasible for another researcher to come up with
a similar theoretical explanation about a given phenomenon.

Internal reliability refers to the degree to which another researcher would arrive at similar findings from the data that were collected in a previous study. In qualitative research, problems with internal reliability can be resolved by providing the reader with verbatim accounts or low-inference descriptors. Grounded theorists are faced with a dilemma, however, because this supportive documentation should be kept to a minimum as emphasis is placed on depth of conceptualizations rather than on description when writing grounded theory. A more reasonable approach to remedy concerns related to internal reliability in grounded theory research may be to employ members of a given "culture" that can confirm or disaffirm a researcher's findings (Goetz & LeCompte, 1984). Descriptions phrased as precisely and concretely as possible should help to remedy concerns about interrater reliability. However, qualitative research approaches do not implement standardized interview protocols because of their emphasis on discovery and open-ended interviewing. Instead, threats to internal reliability are remedied by employing multiple analysts in differing methods of peer debriefing and by providing readers with personal and professional information about the researcher which could have affected data collection, analysis, and interpretation.

For example, in the sample study, Rafuls (1994) employed the help of a research assistant throughout data collection as a peer debriefer (Lincoln & Guba, 1985) to remedy concerns about internal reliability. In addition, in grounded theory methodology, the researcher is able to develop theory that is grounded in data, thus decreasing researcher inference (Glaser, 1978). It is the researcher's theoretical sensitivity that allows him or her develop theory that is grounded in data through his or her awareness of the subtleties of meaning in the data (Strauss & Corbin, 1990). Subtleties of meaning are derived from the analytic process, from literature, and from the personal qualities and professional experiences of the researcher. In the Rafuls (1994) study, an extensive description of the researcher was provided when the role of researcher was discussed.

Internal validity refers to the authenticity of representation that exists between what researchers believe they observed and that which was actually observed (Goetz & LeCompte, 1984). Use of multiple data sources, or what is known as triangulation, is one way to address this concern (Denzin, 1978). Rafuls (1994) dealt with internal validity in her study by interviewing families and therapists in progressive phases, which built on the participants' information and interpretation from one phase to another. Multiple data sources also included videotapes and audiotapes, transcript data, the researcher's notes and journal, and theoretical memos from both the researcher and her research assistant (Rafuls, 1994). Explication of her biases and assumptions as the researcher also exemplified a "disciplined subjectivity" that Erickson (1986) refers to as a way to control for observer effects. Here too, it is important to let one's audience know about the researcher as a way of ensuring trustworthiness of findings and methods.

External validity refers to the generalizability of findings across groups. In grounded theory, the researcher is not interested in generalizations across populations but in transferability of theoretical abstractions. That is, grounded theorists are concerned with analytical generalization and transferability of findings from case to case, rather than generalizability of results from sample to population (Firestone, 1993). In grounded theory, this is achieved by maximizing comparisons across different groups of participants in differing contexts and situations through theoretical selection and saturation. The intentional sampling for theoretically relevant diversity that exists in grounded theory and its analytically based process of theory building are strengths in terms of external validity. The level of generality of a researcher's conceptualizations should be abstract enough so that it can accommodate a variety of changing situations and make them understandable but not be so abstract that they lose their sensitizing aspects (Glaser

& Strauss, 1967). According to Lincoln and Guba (1985), the burden of proof for transferability lies less with the researcher than with the reader. It is the researcher's responsibility to provide sufficiently descriptive data, or in the case of grounded theory, explanatory data, that will allow readers to make their assessment of the validity of the analysis and transferability to their own situation (Firestone, 1993).

Skills Required of the Researcher

Grounded theory researchers need to have both creative and critical thinking skills. They must also have excellent organizational and conceptual abilities, and good writing abilities. Grounded theory requires that researchers have good decision-making skills and an ability to deal with ambiguity—and lots of patience is also helpful.

Bridging Research and Practice

We began this chapter with the assumption that grounded theory and the practice of family therapy have a great deal in common in terms of the skills and qualities that each demands of its practitioner. We end here with the same assumption in discussing how this compatibility facilitates a bridge into the world of research for those clinicians who are either skeptical of, discouraged by, or disinterested in research. It is the way in which the first author (S. E. R.) was converted. No longer does research *have* to be associated with absolute truth, experimentation, quantification, and statistical significance alone. It is now also known as a creative, inductive, theory-building process that feels somewhat familiar and akin to the process of therapy.

Grounded theory questions tend to be oriented toward action and process, much like the ones that we ask as therapists (i.e. How do families respond to resource-based questions in therapy?, How does the family's response influence the therapist's view of the family?). Therefore, grounded theory facilitates a familiarity with formulation of questions for clinicians that might also prove to be useful in practice. For those therapists who are not interested in conducting research themselves, grounded theory approaches might still help bridge their practice with research by enabling them to participate in research that is conducted in groups composed of both clinicians and researchers as the sample study illustrated (Rafuls, 1994). Furthermore, even if clinicians do not participate or collaborate in studies, grounded theory is written in a way that is usually more accessible to clinicians than other more statistically oriented methods because findings are usually presented in narrative form.

The emphasis on relevance of concepts is also a shared concern among grounded theorists and therapists. In other words, just as grounded theorists are concerned about theory that develops from relevant concepts that emerge from the data, so are clinicians concerned with the question of relevant research that is meaningful and applicable to their practice.

FUTURE DIRECTIONS

Grounded theory is a methodology with widespread appeal and application to a number of fields of study in the social sciences. Family therapy is no different, as demonstrated by the Rafuls (1994) study of resource-based consultation with Latino families and their therapists. The future of grounded theory in family therapy research as a methodology lies in its congruence with evolving, cutting-edge models of family therapy (i.e., constructivist, feminist, narrative, and collaborative language systems approaches). This is especially true if these models/approaches have not developed their own research methodology. Grounded theory is also useful alongside quantitative research in studies wherein a qualitative component complements the quantitative (e.g., as part of sampling selection, brief interviews, or follow-up studies). Because of its flexibility, openness, process-oriented, and collaborative tendencies, grounded theory methodology will also be quite useful in research that addresses lived experience in cross-cultural or gender-related research.

In summary, grounded theory's compatibility with the practice and tenets of family therapy purport some interesting and fruitful research possibilities in the field. It would behoove us to take notice of this methodology in our academic programs in research methodology courses and in actual research practice with students. As for the field, it would be wise to promote this methodology through collaborative efforts between therapists and researchers and quantitative and qualitative thinkers, as well as promoting it through publication and funding efforts. Grounded theory has a definite place in family therapy.

ACKNOWLEDGMENTS

We would like to acknowledge the American Association for Marriage and Family Therapy for the 1993 AAMFT Research and Education Foundation Graduate Student Research Grant which helped fund the Rafuls (1994) study cited in this chapter.

REFERENCES

Denzin, N. K. (1978). *Sociological methods: A sourcebook* (2nd ed.). New York: McGraw-Hill.
Erickson, F. (1986). Qualitative methods in research on teaching. In M. C. Wittrock (Ed.), *Handbook of research on teaching* (3rd ed., pp. 119–161). New York: Macmillan.
Firestone, W. A. (1993). Alternative arguments for generalizing from data as applied to qualitative research. *Educational Researcher, 22*(4), 16–23.
Gilgun, J. F. (1992). Definitions, methodologies, and methods in qualitative family research. In J. F. Gilgun, K. Daly, & G. Handel (Eds.), *Qualitative methods in family research* (pp. 22–39). Beverly Hills, CA: Sage.
Glaser, B. (1992). *Basics of grounded theory analysis.* Mill Valley, CA: Sociology Press.
Glaser, B. (1978). *Theoretical sensitivity: Advances in the methodology of grounded theory.* Mill Valley, CA: Sociology Press.
Glaser, B., & Strauss, A. (1967). *The discovery of grounded theory: Strategies for qualitative research.* New York: Aldine Hawthorne.
Goetz, J. P., & LeCompte, M. D. (1984). *Ethnography and qualitative research in educational research.* San Diego: Academic Press.
Guba, E. (Ed.). (1990). *The paradigm dialogue.* Newbury Park, CA: Sage.
Hoshmand, L. L. S. T. (1989). Alternative research paradigms: A review and teaching proposal. *The Counseling Psychologist, 17*, 3–101.
Karpel, M. (1986). *Family resources: The hidden partner in family therapy.* New York: Guilford Press.
Lincoln, Y., & Guba, E. (1985). *Naturalistic inquiry.* Beverly Hills, CA: Sage.
Miles, M., & Huberman, A. (1994). *Qualitative data analysis* (2nd ed.). Thousand Oaks, CA: Sage.
Rafuls, S. E. (1994). *Qualitative resource-based consultation: Resource-generative inquiry and reflective dialogue with four Latin American families and their therapists.* Unpublished doctoral dissertation, Purdue University, West Lafayette, IN.
Reason, P., & Rowan, J. (Eds.). (1981). *Human inquiry: A sourcebook of new paradigm research.* Chichester, UK: Wiley.
Strauss, A. (1987). *Qualitative analysis for social scientists.* New York: Cambridge University Press.
Strauss, E. S., & Corbin, J. (1990). *Basics of qualitative research: Grounded theory procedures and techniques.* Newbury Park, CA: Sage.

Social Constructionist Research

4

---◆---

The Use of Phenomenology for Family Therapy Research
THE SEARCH FOR MEANING

PAULINE BOSS
CARLA DAHL
LORI KAPLAN

BACKGROUND

Are cows pink? "No," said the positivist, "they are black and white or brown—and sometimes combinations thereof." But those who have had direct experience with cows know they can be pink. We have seen them. At sunset, when the sky over a Wisconsin field is rosy and glowing, cows are pink. At that moment and in that particular context, the description of pink for cows is really true. This is phenomenology. True knowledge is relative.

We defined a phenomenon—in this case cows—by describing its essential impact on our immediate conscious experience (Becker, 1992). Artists, musicians, and poets have for ages described and recorded their interpretations of life using the phenomenological approach. In this chapter, we focus on the phenomenology of everyday life—particularly marriage and family—to familiarize family therapists with a method of investigation and description that is compatible with their already developed skills of observation, creativity, intuition, empathic listening, and analysis.

What becomes clear to us is that the phenomenon of phenomenology itself has different meanings to different people. Deutscher (1973) refers to the term broadly as a tradition within the social sciences concerned with "understanding the social actor's frame of reference" (p. 12; see also Psathas, 1973, and Bruyn, 1966). Other sociologists use the term more narrowly to refer to the European school of thought in philosophy (see, e.g., Schutz, 1960, 1967). Phenomenology has also been called the microsociology of knowledge by Peter Berger and Hansfried Kellner in their 1964 essay, "Marriage and the Construction of Reality: An Exercise in the Microsociology of Knowledge," as well as in the 1994 collection *The Production of Reality*, edited by Peter Kollock and Jodi O'Brien. Today, many might argue that the original meaning of phenomenology has been lost.

More critical, however, than one agreed-on definition of phenomenology is what we believe about the world and the people in it, so our discussion (after a brief history) focuses on *seven philosophical assumptions of phenomenology* We then discuss how research is shaped by these assumptions and what phenomenology is *not*. Finally, we focus on how to do phenomenological research, both for those who believe in using a method and for those who do not. We also discuss issues of ethics.

Because marriage, family, and close relationships are so integral a part of everyday life, phenomenologists believe they should be studied as phenomena *in that context*—in the neighborhood, at home, at mealtime, during rituals and celebrations, and so on. To be sure, empirical findings have emerged from studying families in laboratory-controlled settings or from large sample surveys, but phenomenologists believe that the phenomenon of interest, regardless of what it is, should be studied *where it naturally exists and from the actor's own perspective*. In family research, which has multiple perspectives, this means we must consider and describe diverse views—or explicitly label our work as restricted to one person's perspective of how the family or couple works. Either is acceptable—as long as it is labeled—because the phenomenologist's focus is on *whose* perspective is represented at that time and in that context.

To study the process of dyadic and familial relationships, we must first know the phenomenon we are studying. This statement is more than a truism because in family research, we have yet to agree on the definition of the family, the basic unit of study. We are increasingly unclear, for example, about what a married couple is or how a divorced family should interact. We must therefore look "in more general terms" (Berger & Kellner, 1964) at the character of the *processes* of marital and family interactions and at more diverse close relationships.

Historical Roots

Two theoretical perspectives are recommended for looking at marital and family interactions: the symbolic interactionism of George Herbert Mead (1934) and the phenomenological analysis of the social structuring of reality, especially the work of Schutz (1960, 1962, 1967) and Merleau-Ponty (1945; English translation, 1962). Although this chapter focuses on phenomenology, symbolic interactionism represents a theoretical perspective that is compatible with it.

Phenomenology originated more than a half century ago in Europe; the University of Chicago subsequently became the initial base for U.S. consideration of this European tradition. Theoretical perspectives that therapists frequently associate with phenomenology are Erving Goffman's (1959) dramaturgical model and Berger and Luckmann's (1966) sociology of knowledge. Other perspectives are found in labeling theory, existential sociology, sociology of the absurd, symbolic interactionism, and ethnomethodology. Scholars disagree as to how much these perspectives differ from each other and in what ways.

During the postmodernism of the 1990s, phenomenology is enjoying a renaissance. Family researchers of pre- and postmodern ilks are increasingly interested in how family members experience their everyday worlds and how their perceptions of what they experience lead to differing meanings.

In the 1990s, researchers as well as therapists are increasingly going into families' homes. In 1959, Hess and Handel called this the "family world" and said that interactions between individuals in a family must be viewed in the context of how the individuals define one another as relevant objects. Today, Gerald Handel is joined by Jane Gilgun, Judith Stacey, Linda Burton, and many others who reaffirm that people should be studied wherever they live their lives—in the home, in the neighborhood, in the car, at work, in school, at the mall. To a phenomenologist, then, the important reality is what individuals, couples, or families perceive it to be; their "real" world most likely is not found in the laboratory or clinic but where they naturally interact in their daily lives.

Historically, this view for studying families represents the antithesis of logical positivism and empiricism; it challenges the assumption that the scientific method is *the* one way to accumulate truth and knowledge.

Phenomenologists have criticized logical positivists in the areas of (1) verification (they say science needs common sense as well as method), (2) operationalism (phenomenologists recognize an inevitable gap between concepts and devices to measure those concepts), (3) invariance (phenomenologists see probabilistic conclusions as useful; even knowledge obtained without the scientific method is useful), (4) positive knowledge (negative findings are equally important, according to the phenomenologists), and (5) lack of reflexivity (phenomenologists see a need to regularly examine their own feelings and perceptions, an idea akin to countertransference).

When we use a phenomenological approach, our a priori assumptions about how families work—or do not work—become the core of our inquiry because no one method is prescribed in phenomenology. Our focus with this chapter therefore is on assumptions, not one particular method. Any of the methods discussed in the first half of this volume could conceivably be used with a phenomenological approach—but only *if* certain assumptions are accepted by the investigator:

Philosophical Assumptions of the Phenomenological Family Therapy Researcher

The following list comprises the basic assumptions of the phenomenological family therapy researcher.

1. *Knowledge is socially constructed and therefore inherently tentative and incomplete.* Truth remains forever relative and illusive. The use of the scientific method does not change this assumption.
2. *Researchers are not separate from the phenomena they study.* Social inquiry is influenced by the investigator's beliefs about how the world works. Subjectivity (rather than objectivity) is therefore recognized as a researcher's reality. For example, family therapists' beliefs and values (about equality, patriarchy, matriarchy, mastery over nature, acceptance of nature, communitarianism, individualism) will influence the research questions they select to study as well as their interpretation of data. The significance of subjectivity is paramount in the study of families and couples.
3. *Knowledge can be gained from art as well as science.* For example, Pablo Picasso's painting *Blue Family* shows parents and child in cold blue color, with arms entwining only themselves, and all eyes downward. There is no connection between family members. This painting, we believe, depicts the same phenomenon as David Reiss's (1981) "distance sensitive family." Reiss, however, illustrates "distance" with an empirically based technical drawing of small separated circles, while Picasso painted on canvas what he felt were symbols of distance and a lack of familial connection. Both scientist and artist depict the same phenomenon; both represent a reality of human families, but from their own experience and within their own mode of expression. Thus, both depict a form of true knowledge. We also believe that such knowledge can be gained from folk stories, folk songs, and folk art; for example, richly detailed family-of-origin stories

abound in the embroidery of Hmong refugee women in Minnesota, who, with
needle and thread, record their family's harrowing escape from their homeland
in Southeast Asia.

4. *Bias is inherent in all research regardless of method used.* Bias must be made explicit
   at the beginning. Rather than pretending to be objective, investigators should
   state, at the start of the project, what they believe and value. What we believe
   and value is less important than that we are open and straightforward about
   it. Alvin Gouldner, a sociologist of the rebellious 1960s, foreshadowed present
   postmodernism when he said that social sciences were not value-free and that
   traditional practices and assumptions of these sciences were inconsistent with
   emerging social conditions. Gouldner called for a reflexive science which would
   be self-consciously self-critical. He insisted that scholars "raise their flag" early
   in their work to let others know explicitly what their values and assumptions
   are (Gouldner, 1970). We currently see this "raising of the flag" by scholars using hermeneutics and critical theory (e.g., scholars who are feminists and/or people
   of color).

5. *Common, everyday knowledge about family worlds is epistemologically important.* The
   phenomenological approach assumes everyday knowledge is shared and held by
   researcher and subject alike. There is no hierarchy about who is the expert. All
   persons, common and celebrated, researcher and participant alike, are considered epistemologists (Gubrium & Holstein, 1993). Family therapy researchers
   may find it useful to read the essay by McLain and Weigert (1979), which was
   the first to give direction for phenomenological family inquiry per se.

6. *Language and meaning of everyday life are significant.* This is not referring to the
   science of linguistics but, rather, "the study of family discourse highlights how
   language serves to assign meaning to objects and social conditions" in everyday
   life (Gubrium & Holstein, 1993, p. 653). Language remains the primary symbol
   of human interaction and needs to be studied where it takes place *naturally*.
   Neither the laboratory nor the therapy room is a natural setting.

   Everyday life is therefore necessary for understanding how families work;
   if we only gather data at special times of crisis or stress, our knowledge will be
   skewed. Family therapists most often witness family processes at times of stress
   or crisis. It would be worthwhile when family therapists are doing research to
   visit with families at times when they are not in need of professional help. Ethical issues arise here; our solution is never to play the role of researcher and therapist simultaneously because the roles involve different goals.

   The family's language offers a source of information that is symbolically rich
   in meaning and information. The qualitative analysis of whole family conversations for themes and patterns is therefore worthwhile (see Blumer, 1969; Garwick, Detzner, & Boss, 1994; Patterson & Garwick, 1994).

7. *Objects, events or situations can mean a variety of things to a variety of people in
   the family.* Chronic illness, for example, can mean "punishment from God" or
   a "challenge from God to show one's love in a new way"—all in the same family.
   Multiple perceptions of the same event or situation are therefore important to
   hear. Although we can observe and code family acts, "it is not appearance *per
   se*, but rather what appears to be that is critical. . . . Indeterminacy derives from
   varied interpretations, which in turn is constituted by and through language"
   (Gubrium & Holstein, 1993, p. 654).

   Experiences, objects, events or situations can mean different things to different
   family members (e.g., see Frankl, 1984). Just as family therapists do, family

researchers must elicit the perceptions and views of all family members to get the total picture of a particular family. Although this makes research more complicated, it realistically reflects the diversity of gender, generation, sexual orientation, ethnicity, and culture inherent in family life. Today, in this era of frequent divorce and remarriage, it can even be difficult to get agreement in couples' reports about the number of children they have. Other more intangible experiences can also be perceived in radically differing ways.

How Research Is Shaped by Philosophical Assumptions

Phenomenological research is shaped by its philosophical assumptions in several ways: *First*, because objectivity is illusive and truth is relative, we ourselves become part of the research set; we cannot remain objectively outside. That is, our feelings, beliefs, values and responses are also data and need to be noted explicitly. The process of self-reflection is therefore a necessary part of the research process in phenomenology and often leads to midstream changes in procedure if we believe it would be more productive or ethical to do so. This may call for a new informed consent (see section on ethics for further discussion). A continuing and explicit process of self-reflexivity and self-questioning (preferably not in isolation) is required of phenomenological researchers.

Second, we consider the families we interview experts, just as we are. We listen, we observe, we note their feelings, and we note our feelings, we ask questions because it is the families, not us, who will have the answers to our research questions. For example, we could study the varying meanings of death in families by documenting their stories of loss, just as Sedney, Baker, and Gross (1994) used stories as an assessment device, as an initial intervention, and as a gauge of the progress of treatment in bereaved families.

Third, we get away from our offices to observe and interact with the families we are studying in their own natural setting (see, e.g., Liebow, 1967; Henry, 1973; and Stacey, 1990). We recommend highly the research on caring for children in high-risk neighborhoods done by Linda Burton (1991), who actually spent time in these neighborhoods.

Fourth, family therapy researchers using the phenomenological approach listen to and observe the "whole." We must not repeat the mistake of many researchers who interview mothers primarily (because they are most available) to gather data about children or families. We must attempt to hear the "family conversational voice" as a whole or to observe the "family world" as a whole. This cannot be done if we talk to only one family member. (See, e.g., Garwick et al., 1994; Pollner & McDonald-Wikler, 1985; Reiss, 1981).

Fifth, we must ask enough questions and involve enough family members to hear some differing perspectives, because in the microworld of even *one* family, there is always diversity in their gendered and generational perspectives—and often also differences in life experiences, socialization, class, beliefs and values. If, as a phenomenological researcher, you say you are studying families, whole families are what you must study. If you say you are studying couples (gay, lesbian, or heterosexual), that is precisely what you must study. If you say your are studying parents, mother and father are what you must study. But if you are studying who looks after the children, you may have to look beyond biological parents. In all cases, it is an issue of validity. We must study what we say we are studying.

Finally, our core assumptions indicate that the boundaries between when we are doing research and when we are doing therapy are more blurred in doing phenomenological inquiry than when we conduct positivist research. That is, the roles of expert researcher versus subject give way to a less hierarchical mind-set in which people simply work together to gain meaning about a particular phenomenon. However, caution must be used to protect families from our potential conflict of interest. While we are doing therapy, we cannot put the gathering of research data first; while we are doing research, we need to recognize that we are not doing therapy. The contract is different when the intent differs. This is an issue of ethics (Boss, 1991).

Some therapists, however, maintain their ethics while thinking about a new phenomenon (or an old phenomenon in a new way) and, after listening to stories and working with families for years, they induce a model of how therapists might work more productively. An example of this kind of phenomenological research is *The Invisible Web* by Marianne Walters, Elizabeth Carter, Peggy Papp, and Olga Silverstein (1988). Another example of a therapist whom we think of as a phenomenological researcher is Michael White who has, by working with many families, co-constructed a new way to be a family therapist. I (P. B.) asked Michael White if he considered himself a researcher and he said yes (M. White, personal communication, March, 1994).

We believe the women at the Ackerman Institute in New York City represent another example of phenomenological researchers. Jointly, through induction from their extensive experience, they devised a method for working to stop violence in couples who do not want to separate (Goldner, Penn, Sheinberg, & Walker, 1990). Although all these authors set out to listen to meanings, find new information, and a new way to do therapy, they may not have intended to be viewed as researchers. We believe they are. We also believe the work of Evan Imber-Black and Janine Roberts (1992) on family rituals and the work of Rosemarie Welter-Enderlin on couple passion represent phenomenological research. All these inquiries focus on meanings in some way and have added much to the effectiveness of family therapy worldwide.

Pealing Away the Onion: What Phenomenology Is Not

Is Phenomenology Different from Deconstructionism?   Although there are some similarities, especially in the rejection of the scientific method, phenomenology and deconstructionism are not the same. Both approaches recognize the indeterminacy of meaning and many from both camps believe there is regularity, order, and social organization— somewhere. For example, Gubrium and Holstein (1993) say, "The same meanings are not always attached to things, but there is regularity in the attachment process" (p. 654). Yet, other phenomenologists, as well as deconstructionists, make no assumptions about regularity and order, nor are they interested in social organization. They are, instead, interested in patterns that connect through symbols of interaction. The phenomenon of interest to them is *meaning*, not object or structure.

In the end, the difference may be that deconstructionism allows the observer greater privilege because it is based on the *researcher's* reality whereas phenomenology is a study of someone else's reality, albeit through the observer's eyes (P. C. Rosenblatt, personal communication, 1994). Also, in deconstructionism, there is no emphasis on the need for self-reflection, as in phenomenology. *Feminist* deconstructionism, however, is an exception because feminist scholarship requires self-reflection. The work of Rachel Hare-Mustin (1992, 1994) is an example.

Is Phenomenology Different from Logical Positivism?   Some say phenomenology is theorizing with a sample of one. One person's perception is the truth for that person and in that context. "The appeal to context . . . is more fundamental than the appeal to fact, for the context determines the significance of the facts" (Dreyfus, 1967, p. 43). In general, phenomenologists believe reality is within a person's private perceptions, within his or her feelings, intentions and essences. Most important, phenomenologists recognize a priori events. Fact and essence are correlative. Edie (1967) summarizes, "The 'essential' is thus what the human mind understands when it understands something in the flux of experience; what the mind adds to the world of fact is 'the necessary' or 'the essential' " (p. 9).

It becomes obvious that the quest for universal order is not as important to the phenomenologist as it is to the logical positivist. They are alike, however, in that both feel strongly about method, different though these methods are. *Instead of the scientific method of deduction, phenomenologists use the method of reduction.* The investigator begins with a generalization or a hunch and peels away (like an onion) until he or she gets closer and closer to the essence of the phenomena. The investigator keeps rejecting *what it is not* in order to get closer to *what it is.* This process of reduction—or "bracketing"—continues, as the researcher and the person being studied are in dialogue. They decide together when and how to "peel the onion."

It is apparent that reduction theorists (phenomenologists) and deduction theorists (positivists) represent two opposite points of view. There are relative strengths and weaknesses in both. Positivist researchers require theory building to be more empirically based. Parameters are clearly defined; concepts are operationalized; technical language is used. But what good is it to have a rigorous, tight methodology if the investigator is missing the point and busily, though methodically, going down a blind alley?

Consider suicide as a case in point. Sociologist Emile Durkheim (1951) observed consistent regularity in national suicide rates; based on these observations, he explained that the cause of suicide lay in societal factors. A family therapist would consider his data interesting and revealing about large aggregates of people but mostly useless regarding an individual suicide attempt of a client or a client's family member. Taking group averages tells us nothing about an individual or the meaning that specific person gives to the act of suicide. A logical positivist's primary aim to generalize may make us miss critical individual differences. Generalizations or laws may be useful in the physical sciences; they are less useful in family therapy research. The human mix is not as reliable as minerals and even more complex than chemicals.

Another case in point is schizophrenia. In the 1950s, schizophrenics were treated individually, frequently in an institution. After long therapy, the patient sometimes recovered. It was noted that when well patients returned to their families, one of two things often happened: Either they got sick again or, if they remained well, another family member developed symptoms. Traditionalists in psychiatry had researched and treated from the point of view that the system was well and the patient was ill. In the 1950s and 1960s, phenomenological investigators (or mavericks) such as Carl Whitaker, Virginia Satir, and others found in their "softer" research techniques (using feelings, hunches, intuition, and empathetic perceptions) that patients simply were acting within their context.

Using the traditionally accepted theories of the 1950s and 1960s, many of which grew out of positivism in both psychiatry and sociology, the definition of certain forms of human behavior as pathological actually served to create more pathology. R. D. Laing (1971), a radical psychiatrist of the 1960s, came to this conclusion about restrictive theorizing and research methods. Laing and others such as Carl Whitaker and Thomas Szasz were radical pioneers in their proclamations that mental illness was a socially constructed phenomenon. They were the precursors of the post modern era regarding mental health and families.

The concept of schizophrenia as *either* patient caused *or* family caused—*or* biologically caused—becomes a straitjacket that restricts therapists as well as families. By taking off the straitjacket of absolutist thinking, we see the phenomenon of family processes and chronic mental illness more clearly, albeit with more complexity.

In this example, phenomenologists served society well in bringing us closer to an accurate understanding of the everyday reality of chronic mental illness, closer to a theory that works in application and, thereby, closer to *good theory*. Through the use of their creativity, intuition, and observational skills, they brought about a paradigmatic shift in how we as therapists see the worlds of family life and mental illness.

Is Phenomenology Different from Feminist Research? Although studies about women's experiences and perspectives are still underrepresented in published family research, particularly positivist research, the method used cannot tell us whether or not a researcher is a feminist. Both positivism and phenomenology can be used for feminist inquiry; likewise, both can be used in ways that are biased against women or other disenfranchised groups. Rather than relying solely on method as the clue to a researcher's values and perspectives, we strongly recommend looking critically at the researcher's stated (or unstated) assumptions regarding the context of their inquiry, the modes of inquiry, the questions asked, the beneficiaries of the research, and so on. Simply concluding that feminists do only phenomenological study is incorrect. It is also incorrect to conclude that only feminists use this approach. We agree with Evelyn Fox Keller (1985) who wrote, "A healthy science is one that allows for the productive survival of diverse conceptions of mind and nature, and of corresponding diverse strategies" (p. 178).

Is Phenomenology Different from Content Analysis? Content analysis is a technique that allows a researcher to identify—or "code"—themes and patterns that emerge in qualitative data. Whereas phenomenological researchers *may* use content analysis, it is not necessarily their only approach to managing their data. Some, for example, may provide richly detailed accounts of their research—known as thick description—out of which only the reader draws conclusions. Some phenomenologists eschew any connection to techniques and refuse to talk of methodology. Conversely, some researchers who use content analysis techniques do so in nonphenomenological ways in order to provide some kind of frequency count, for example, or to test hypotheses.

METHODOLOGY

Within the phenomenological perspective, family therapy is perceived more as conversation than as intervention (Gubrium & Holstein, 1993). The same holds true for the family therapy researcher. That is, a phenomenological researcher extends the family's natural conversation which is already taking place as the family and individuals construct meaning and maintain that construction. Because family conversation takes place against a "taken-for-granted" backdrop within the everyday world, phenomenological inquiry—whether by researcher or therapist—involves making explicit and "reflectively bringing into nearness" (van Manen, 1990, p. 32) that which is implicit or obscured by its very taken-for-granted quality.

As with therapy, we might view the research process itself on two levels: one concerned with the principles by which the *family* has constructed its everyday world and with the contents of that everyday world and one concerned with the principles by which the therapist–researcher and the family *co-construct* meaning and interpretations within whatever is taken for granted in the therapy setting. Gubrium and Holstein (1993) note that "family is a 'project' that is realized through discourse" (p. 655); family therapy research as well as family therapy can be similarly defined, providing two levels of inquiry for the phenomenological therapist–researcher.

In both research and therapy, the phenomenological inquirer is interested in stories. Defining therapy and research as storytelling and story listening changes the emphasis from problem solving to meaning construction. In this process, both the family and the therapist are brought into a deeper understanding of the nature and meaning of the everyday world and of that one family's lived experience. Thomas Moore (1992) notes that family therapy "might take the form of simply telling stories of family life, free of any concern for cause and effect or sociological influence. . . . We might imagine family therapy more as a process of exploring the complexity of our sense of life than of making it simple and intelligible" (pp. 28–29). These stories will often include paradox and contradiction. The phenomenological therapist or researcher does not need to "smooth out" discrepancies or inconsistencies but rather looks for the meaning within them. What positivists call anomalies or statisticians call outlyers, phenomenologists call reality, even though the sample size is small or the time spent together brief. An example of such work is the work on rituals developed by Imber-Black and Roberts (1992) as well as the work of White and Epston (1990).

Research Questions

Positivists and phenomenologists take on different kinds of problems and seek different kinds of answers; thus their inquiry demands different methodologies. The positivist adopts a natural science model of research and searches for causes by using questionnaires, inventories, and scales to produce numerical data that can be statistically analyzed. In contrast, a phenomenologist seeks understanding through qualitative methods such as participant observation, in-depth interviewing, and other methods that yield descriptive data—of any kind. The phenomenologist looks for what Max Weber (1949, 1968) called *verstehen* or *understanding*. *Verstehen* refers to understanding "on a personal level the motives and beliefs behind people's actions" (Taylor & Bogdan, 1984, p. 2).

"Phenomenological questions are *meaning* questions" (van Manen, 1990, p. 23, emphasis in the original). The therapist–researcher and the family members, by understanding the meaning of complex phenomena more deeply and fully, are enabled to act with greater awareness and consciousness—to be more thoughtful, which van Manen (1990) defines in the following way: "To be full of thought means not that we have a whole lot on our mind, but rather that we recognize our lot of minding the Whole— that which renders fullness or wholeness to life" (p. 31). Within this context, then, issues such as extramarital sexual behavior, deciding to divorce, providing care for an elderly parent, or choosing to have a baby or adopt become questions to be understood and lived, not "solved" and put away. The example given by a researcher on the "Atlanta Women and AIDS Project" at the Centers for Disease Control illustrates this point: She told us that if we ever hoped to get drug-using males to begin wear condoms, the most important research question to ask them is what wearing a condom *means*.

Generally, then, phenomenological researchers avoid questions that include such predetermined categories as normal, dysfunctional, pathological, deviant, and so on. They are more likely to ask participants to define the phenomenon in question rather than defining it for them. For example, in her study, Dahl (1994) asked families to define spirituality as they understood and expressed it within their own family context.

Validity

Earlier we introduced the importance of validity in studying what we say we are studying. In phenomenological research, it is not appropriate to search for traditional kinds of measurement validity. Rather, this approach makes subjective relevance and adequacy of description of greater concern (Daly, 1992; Gubrium & Holstein, 1993). Despite the tentativeness and openness inherent in phenomenological inquiry, such research must also be evaluated by the concept of adequacy (McLain & Weigert, 1979; Schutz, 1962). Readers or listeners must see in the description of the data the validity and applicability of any concepts presented by the researcher, and participants must also agree that the analysis is an accurate reflection of their perceptions. To foster this kind of validity, participants might be asked at the time of data collection whether they would be willing to be contacted subsequently to clarify meanings, comment on findings, or participate in further data collection.

A common challenge to this kind of research from more quantitative researchers is that of representativeness and generalizability (Allen & Gilgun, 1987; Rosenblatt & Fischer, 1993). Given the complexity and diversity of the experience of a particular family, phenomenological research is more interested in accurately reflecting a given family's experience than generalizing to families in general. Such research provides data that reflect this diversity as well as enable identification of commonalities.

In order to ensure a greater degree of validity, the researcher must stay connected to those experiences of the participants and continue the back-and-forth movement between data collection and data analysis that is *so* important in phenomenological research. In addition, movement between present study, previous research, and theory development provides linkages that enhance validity (Boss, Kaplan, & Gordon, 1994; Fravel & Boss, 1992; Gilgun, 1992). Above all, the researcher must continue in dialogue with the individuals of interest. It would not be unusual for a phenomenological study to have the individual of interest participate in the formation of questions as well as in the interpretation of their answers. For example, Boss et al. (1994) asked Native American women to collaborate with them in formulating research questions and subsequently in interpretating answers and writing up results.

Required Skills

The skills most needed by phenomenologists are ones also needed by family therapists. In many ways the two endeavors are similar (see Boss, 1987). Exploring the stories of individuals, couples, and families requires the ability to listen, clarify, probe, expand, and focus. Interpreting the phenomena of everyday family life requires insight, the ability to make connections between concepts, and the ability to notice both what *is* and is *not* present. Both exploration and interpretation require respectful ways of building rapport and providing a "safe container" for the story. This safe container could be a painting, a photograph, a book, or an article in an academic journal. Finally, family therapy researchers must be aware of their own stories and the implications for everyday constructions of reality. Our own life experiences will color how we see and interpret the phenomenon of others. This idea is not foreign to family therapists today.

Clinical Examples of Phenomenological Research by Clinicians

Phenomenological research questions are questions of meaning designed to help the researcher understand the lived experience of the participant. For family therapists, these kinds of questions are familiar because they are often part of family therapy. Family therapists who wish to pursue phenomenological inquiry in a research mode might pursue any of an almost infinite range of family phenomena. Following are two examples of how a family therapist–researcher might explore common family issues.

Marital Infidelity

Robert and Carol, married 13 years and parents of an 11-year-old daughter and an 8-year-old son, agreed to participate in a research project on marital infidelity. Several months earlier, Carol had returned from a professional conference in Mexico and acknowledged to Robert that she had had an affair with a male whom she had met at the conference. The stories each partner told about the experience reflected the meanings they had constructed about marriage, sexual fidelity, and open communication.

During the process of the research interviews, these stories were frequently interrupted by other stories about hurtful incidents in the history of the marriage prior to the affair. Both partners presented different "facts" about these incidents, and arguments ensued as to which version of the story was correct. The phenomenological therapist–researcher is less interested in these facts—for instance, who said what to whom and when, what the sequence of events was, or how often similar incidents occurred. The "truth" of the stories is of greater concern: What is the meaning assigned to such events, what structures underlie the construction of that meaning, and how are those structures reinforced? The researcher consistently probed these areas with Robert and Carol rather than pursuing the "factual accuracy," which initially was so important to each partner.

The stories eventually told were ones that helped the researcher—and the couple— understand the impact of Carol's affair on them as individuals, on the balance of power within their relationship, and as part of the ongoing family themes which had begun generations earlier. The phenomenological therapist–researcher works to extract the various truths and meanings from what Moore (1992) calls "the hard details of family history and memory" (p. 32).

Infertility and Adoption

Jennifer and David, both 26 and married for 5 years, had tried unsuccessfully for 3 years to have a child and agreed to participate in a study of couples' experiences of infertility. Jennifer had had two miscarriages, and both she and David were managing the grief of those losses as well as the stressor of infertility and the accompanying medical tests and procedures. They had come to the decision to register with an adoption agency rather than to pursue further medical avenues and had decided as well to be open to adopting a child with special needs.

During the course of the research, Jennifer and David told stories of their childhood fantasies of their future family, of the children they had imagined who had been lost to miscarriage, and of the ongoing relationships they had with extended family— none of whom had struggled with similar difficulties in becoming pregnant or maintaining pregnancy and several of whom had expressed negative opinions about family friends who had adopted a child. These stories—as had Robert's and Carol's—also reflected their family-of-origin themes and myths as well as the themes that had emerged within their marital conversations over the past years. Jennifer's parents and one of David's siblings also participated in the research, enriching the understanding of both the family mythology and the phenomenon of deciding to adopt a child.

Both of the examples given reflect the two levels of phenomenological inquiry available to therapists–researchers: the dialogue *within* the family about a particular phenomenon and the dialogue *between* the family and therapist–researcher about that phenomenon. At both levels, the "facts" of the situation take on far less importance than the *meaning* of that situation. Therapists who wish to pursue phenomenological inquiry at both levels find themselves in what Max van Manen (1990) calls the "attentive practice of thoughtfulness . . . a heedful, mindful wondering about the project of life, of living, of what it means to live a life" (p. 12).

FOR PHENOMENOLOGISTS WHO DO NOT BELIEVE IN DISCUSSING METHOD

Here we look to the humanities for new knowledge because both persons and cultures construct meaning through art, music, and literature. It is the art, music, and literature that in the end describe the truth about people's experiences. The "Black Sorrow Songs," for example, describe anguish but also survival and represent the reality of competence, strength, and resilience of individuals and families against great odds (Dilworth-Anderson, Burton, & Boulin Johnson, 1993). Some phenomenologists present their results through artistic media—photography, drama, or performance art (Gilgun, 1992). In this process, the audience, whether one or many, is part of the co-construction of meaning in a very explicit way.

FOR THOSE PHENOMENOLOGISTS WHO INSIST ON A METHOD

A psychologist who turned to phenomenology to study human behavior, Amedeo Giorgi (1985), offers a method for those who do phenomenological inquiry. His method contains four essential steps in using description for psychological research, and we discuss several additional dimensions. Each is reviewed here.

1. *"Sense of the whole."* In this first step, one reads the entire description of an observation or experience many times in order to gain a general sense of the whole statement.

2. *"Discrimination of meaning units within a psychological perspective and focused on the phenomenon being researched."* Once the sense of the whole has been grasped, the researcher goes back to the beginning and reads through the text once more with the specific aim of discriminating "meaning units" from within a psychological perspective and with a focus on the phenomenon being researched. Meanings change as the interaction between narrative and the reader progresses and the context changes; meaning units reflect these shifts and progressions. Researchers acknowledge that the selection of what stands out from the text depends on their own perspectives.

3. *"Transformation of subject's everyday expressions into psychological language with emphasis on the phenomenon being investigated."* Once meaning units have been delineated, the researcher goes through all the meaning units and expresses the psychological insight contained in them more directly. This is especially true of the meaning units most revelatory of the phenomenon under consideration.

4. "*Synthesis of transformed meaning units into a consistent statement of the structure of learning.*" In this step, the researcher synthesizes all of the transformed meaning units into a consistent statement regarding the subject's experience. Giorgi, unlike other phenomenologists, states clearly, however, that one would rarely conduct this type of research with only one subject. "The more subjects there are, the greater the variation, and hence the better the ability to see what is essential" (p. 19). But he equivocates: "On the other hand, specific situated structures might still be desired, and these could be based on only one subject" (p. 19). (See Fravel & Boss, 1992, for an example of using one family only, to add new knowledge about how families cope with missing children.) This step is usually referred to as the structure of the experience and can be expressed at a number of levels (Giorgi, 1985, p. 10). We encourage therapist–researchers to go directly to Giorgi's text because he cautions us as to the misunderstanding of his phenomenological methodology (See Giorgi, 1985).

In addition to Giorgi's four steps, we present other key points regarding phenomenological method.

What Are Considered Data?

All data are words about experiences and meanings. But once we move to what the researcher observed, phenomenologists would say we are studying the *researchers' reality*. Data for the phenomenologist can therefore be family stories, family secrets, family rituals, ordinary dinner table conversations, or behaviors, letters, diaries, photographs, patterns in family behaviors or conversations, and so on. "Meaning" becomes the major source of data. Creativity and intuition lead us to the phenomenon about which we are curious. In fact, as a phenomenologist, intuition becomes a major asset rather than something to suppress (see Boss, 1987, for more on the use of intuition and creativity in family research).

Sampling and Selection Procedures

The phenomenological approach lends itself to small-*n* studies, in that it requires in-depth description of the experiences of each participant. The purpose is accurate understanding of meaning and establishing possibilities rather than generalization of findings. Randomness, therefore, is less important to a phenomenologist than to a positivist.

Because of the likelihood of small samples and the deeply personal nature of meaning questions, confidentiality becomes an especially relevant issue in phenomenological research. Using pseudonyms, altering demographic details, and allowing participants to withdraw at any stage of the process—including the presentation of results—can provide participants some protection from uncomfortable or unwanted exposure if that is desired.

Data Collection Procedures

In phenomenological inquiry, any means of collecting data might be used that allows the researcher access to the experience of another. This might include, for example, open-ended interviews, analysis of letters, diaries, oral histories, or observation of photographs or videos. The methods phenomenological researchers use must adequately and accurately represent the "expressed daily life conditions, opinions, values, attitudes, beliefs, and knowledge base of the respondents" (Cicourel, 1986, p. 249). Phenomenological methods of data collection *allow participants to define phenomena for themselves* and to describe the conditions, values, and attitudes they believe are relevant to that definition *for their own lives.* For example, Dr. Linda Coffey at the University of Chicago gives inexpensive throw-away cameras to children in the housing projects to record the relationships they believe are important to their well-being (L. Coffey, personal communication, June, 1994).

The Person of the Researcher as Instrument

If paper–pencil or other instruments are used at all for data collection, they must be carefully and thoughtfully chosen. But they are not the only instruments in a phenomenological study. The researcher is also an instrument. Although the researcher is subject to stress, fatigue, confusion, and bias, the losses due to these factors are "more than offset by the flexibility, insight, and ability to build on tacit knowledge that is the peculiar province of the human instrument" (Guba & Lincoln, 1981, p. 113). We see similarity between this idea and Whitaker and Keith's (1981) ideas of "the person of the therapist" as central in family therapy. We believe the person of the researcher also becomes the major instrument in phenomenological research.

The interpretations and theoretical links developed by phenomenological therapist–researchers are inevitably influenced by their own personal biography and family history. To increase awareness of the impact of the researcher as instrument, the therapist–researcher might keep a journal detailing experiences, emotions, insights, and questions resulting from the data collection process. This journal might contain one's affective responses to the data collection and to the analysis process, thoughts about connections and linkages among and between families, and observations from one's clinical practice that relate to the study. Patton (1990) and Reinharz (1983) note that these are also a legitimate and valuable part of the data. Clinicians call this countertransference, a phenomenon that is not absent in phenomenological research (Boss, 1987).

A prerequisite to "good" data collection is prior recognition of the content being discussed by respondents. According to Gergen and Gergen (1988), telling a story is the result of a mutually coordinated and supportive relationship between teller and listener. Further, knowledge about the culture contained in respondents' texts can only be expanded on when the researcher brings into the analysis what else is known about the participant and his or her circumstances (Mishler, 1986). This prior knowledge, however, must be evaluated against new learnings, just as new information must be integrated into prior knowledge. Otherwise, the researcher risks letting preconceptions guide and possibly obscure the meaning–discovery process of the moment.

Data Analysis Procedures

The purpose of analysis in phenomenological research is not to tie all loose ends together. Indeed, that cannot be accomplished. Rather, our purpose is to describe and understand (as in *verstehen*) the experience of the participants. Data analysis and data collection go hand in hand in phenomenological inquiry (Patton, 1990; Reinharz, 1983; Rosenblatt & Fischer, 1993). Each informs the other in a dynamic, reciprocal, nonlinear process of questioning, reflecting, and interpreting. (Here we think of Michael White's method of questioning.) Hess and Handel (1959, 1967) describe this as a back-and-forth movement from one kind of data to another, from one participant's stories to another's, and from one family's themes to another's, all the while looking for *mean-*

ings that connect and meanings that differentiate; the only rule of data analysis is to remain vitally connected to the individual and family conversations and stories.

Hess and Handel (1967) outline three assumptions regarding data gathered through phenomenological research. *First,* the researcher must attempt to connect the data with useful ideas about the data. Although phenomenological researchers attempt not to impose realities on those of the participants, they definitely impose a structure on them, one that incorporates ideas that may be useful in accurately understanding them. *Second,* these data are to be taken at more than face value; they provide information about what specific meanings families give to reality *and* information about how they do that assigning. *Third,* individual family members' stories are accurately understood only within the family context and are illuminated by other stories in that context.

Accurate understanding of participants' experiences may come through a line-by-line analysis of a story or a frame-by-frame analysis of videos or photographs. It may come through conducting a search for significant words or phrases. It may come through gathering a more global impression of thoughts and themes that occur. The significant hallmark of phenomenological analysis is that the researcher makes every effort to stay connected to the experience of the participants. This may involve checking with the participants at several points in the collection, analysis, and reporting process, letting them have input into the meaning being constructed by the researcher to see if the interpretation is on target (Dahl, 1994; Boss et al., 1994).

The process of analyzing phenomenological data, regardless of type, must include immersion in the data to observe and define what is there and to notice what is not there; it must include incubation and reflection to allow intuitive awareness and understandings to emerge; and it must include creative synthesis that enables accurate and meaningful communication of the experience of the participants (Patton, 1990; Rosenblatt & Fischer, 1993). The process must also include consideration of the researcher's intuition, because

> discovery . . . happens not with the scientific method, by magic, or by luck, but through openness to heeding one's senses and responding to one's intuition. . . . We make ourselves discovery-prone by listening, being open to feelings, and recognizing apprehensions and emotions. This state does not happen by chance; it requires the willingness to open one's mind and feelings, to make oneself prone to discovery. (Boss, 1987, p. 154)

Brown and Gilligan (1992) refer to this openness as locating both the speaker and oneself as researcher in the narrative. Rather than a goal of "objectivity" during this listening, therapist–researchers pursue the goal of connection with an internal reality different from their own. It is precisely this *connection* that provides a "way of knowing, an opening between self and other that creates a channel for discovery, an avenue to knowledge" (Brown & Gilligan, 1992, p. 28; see also Allen & Walker, 1992).

Hare-Mustin (1994), however, raises a critical question: "How does the researcher know that one's mind and feelings are open?" There is the problem of imposing one's own meanings and distorting rather than connecting. According to Hare-Mustin, this has been one of the bases for critique of Carol Gilligan's work; we cannot ignore the power of *zeitgeist* (Hare-Mustin, June, 1994, personal communication). By pointing out that family therapists and researchers are influenced by the "dominant discourse of the time," or *zeitgeist,* Hare-Mustin draws our attention to the limitations of any one person's phenomenological view. As family therapist–researchers, we hopefully are more reflexive and open to discourse than average, but we must *always* be vigilant about what we bring to the research questions we ask and to our interpretations of the words and stories we hear. Human subjectivity is an important data analysis procedural item here, but it is also a critical point relating to "the person of the researcher" as previously discussed.

Reporting Findings

The descriptions of experience form the essence of phenomenological inquiry. In them, therapists–researchers present both patterns that are present and exceptions to those patterns. Consistent with the onion-peeling nature of this approach, the research report includes both what the phenomenon under study *is* and what it *is not*.

In reporting and discussing the results of phenomenological research, therapists might follow the format suggested by Gilgun (1992). Supporting data for each pattern or exception are provided. The discussion is set in the context of previous research and theory. Such linkages enhance validity, as discussed previously. They also highlight ways in which findings "enhance previous knowledge, as correctives, as new knowledge, or both" (Gilgun, 1992, p. 26).

Reporting phenomenological research is not limited to written forms. Given the experiential nature of this inquiry, film and photography are also appropriate media for reporting. Some therapists may even find a live performance of some kind to be effective in communicating the patterns of experience they have identified. (Virginia Satir's live family sculptures come to mind.) In almost any kind of phenomenological reporting, however, the experience of the participants will be obvious—through quotations, perhaps, or translation of their stories to another medium.

Bridging Research, Theory, and Practice

The primary findings in a phenomenological study are the descriptive stories shared by the participants. The goal of phenomenological inquiry is to produce a deep, clear, and accurate understanding of the experiences of participants and of the meanings found in or assigned to those experiences. Although phenomenologists differ as to the extent to which new questions should be raised, many believe that the usefulness of phenomenological research comes out of the mutual commitment brought by researcher and reader alike to understand a phenomenon more clearly for a purpose. Such a purpose might be personal, familial, institutional, or community *change*. To facilitate this change, the presentation of phenomenological findings should be set in the context of previous research and theory. Such linkages enhance validity.

Polkinghorne (1989) summarizes the potential benefits of the clearer understanding derived from phenomenological research: increased sensitivity to the experiences of others, corrections and amplifications of empirically derived knowledge, and improved responsiveness of public policy to the realities described by participants. He encourages phenomenological researchers to maximize the effectiveness of these consequences by always including in their presentation of results the *implications* of those results for practitioners and policymakers. Here is where the therapist doing phenomenological inquiry can influence other therapists. A case in point is the innovative work of Michael White (personal communication, March, 1994; White & Epston, 1990).

Ethical Issues

Interviews affect participants.

Because qualitative methods are highly personal and interpersonal, because naturalist inquiry takes the researcher into the real world where people live and work, and because in-depth interviewing opens up what is inside people—qualitative inquiry may be more intrusive and involve greater reactivity than surveys, tests, and other quantitative approaches. (Patton, 1990, p. 356)

Several hours of reflection of one's life and values can be enlightening, inspiring, and affirming; it can also be unsettling, disturbing, and change inducing (Patton, 1990). Given that the phenomenologist explores the basic components of humanness and aspects of everyday life, it is reasonable to assume that some participants will disclose information about sensitive issues. Survivors of sexual abuse, for example, may describe the effect that experience has had on their experience of other aspects of life. The story of a participant's journey may include behaviors, past or present, which for him or her are shameful or embarrassing or which may be considered illegal or immoral by others. *Informed consent* and *confidentiality* thus become important issues for both participant and researcher. For participants, assurance must be given that responses will be kept private and will be reported in a way that will not identify them. But Patton (1990) and Doherty and Boss (1991) also caution that interviewers must be clear about when breaches of confidentiality might be legally mandated, as in cases in which abuse of children or vulnerable adults is revealed during interviews.

LaRossa, Bennett, and Gelles (1981) delineate two broad categories of ethical concerns that are relevant for phenomenological research: informed consent and establishment of a risk-benefit equation. The first category of issues can be addressed by clearly explaining the participant's rights both in the initial contact letter and consent form and at the time of the actual data collection. Because it is impossible to know in advance just where a participant's reflection may lead in any given interview (Doherty & Boss, 1991; LaRossa et al., 1981; Patton, 1990), explicit mention should be made of the right to withdraw from the project, to end the interview, or to ask that any form of taping stop at any time. Even with that option clearly established, phenomenological researchers need to be aware of the ambiguities inherent in the setting (often the participant's home) and the role (insider–outsider, therapist–researcher) (Gilgun, 1992; LaRossa et al., 1981; Olson, 1977). They should also be able to offer participants a selection of helping resources should the interviewing raise deeply unsettling issues (as recommended by Boss, 1987, and Gilgun, 1992).

Assessing potential risks and benefits is more complicated. LaRossa et al. (1981) encourage researchers to keep clearly in mind the potentially embarrassing nature of everything connected with family life, which is in our society considered "private business." Public exposure, then, can be disturbing for participants. Even if data are carefully disguised or not widely disseminated, the *feeling* of self-exposure of the individual is another consideration. Family therapists who do phenomenological research are often already skilled in the development of rapport; supportive, empathically neutral responses throughout the interview; and post-interview debriefing, all of which can help alleviate this discomfort.

These ethical considerations must be part of the researcher's awareness. Patton (1990) describes the necessity of having "the utmost respect for these persons who are willing to share with you some of their time to help you understand their world" (p. 357). At the same time, however, researchers must also remember that in-depth interviews may have a therapeutic effect on families and that the changes that may result might be desired by the family (Boss, 1987). "Our sensitivity to the costs should not obscure an equal sensitivity to the benefits that research may bring to the family as well as to us [the researchers]" (Boss, 1987, p. 152). Asking families to share their stories empowers them because it indicates we value their knowledge and their contribution to the knowledge base of a larger system.

Because of the unique characteristics of phenomenological inquiry, we add additional guidelines to protect human subjects. The phenomenologist is committed to understanding, the *verstehen* of how their world is experienced. This approach requires extra ethical guidelines which may be unique to phenomenological inquiry. No researcher, from any perspective, sets out intentionally to do harm, but for the phenomenologist, the definition of what constitutes "no harm" must include the voices and perceptions of the participants themselves. The following guidelines are suggested *in addition* to basic human subjects guidelines.

1. *Seek understanding of the participant's reality.* Overall, seek the participants' perceptions; try to get *their* story and *their* meaning of a particular phenomenon. We strive for what Max Weber in 1968 called *verstehen,* that is, "understanding on a person level the motive and beliefs behind people's actions" (Taylor & Bogdan, 1984, p. 2). For example, for the phenomenologist, outcome research is ethically more than double-blinds and control groups; it is about how family members feel and what they believe to be true about their situation. Do they feel better now than when they entered therapy? Is the quality of each family member's life better? Do they feel they can solve problems better now? Do they feel less stressed or anxious than before? Do they feel afraid or intimidated? Do they feel safe? Do they feel less violent? Whatever the research question, phenomenologists must ethically try to obtain *their* story.

We are reminded of the 90-year-old woman who dropped out of a medical study because the researcher kept insisting she answer either yes or no to every question asked. She was frustrated because they would not listen to her when she said the answer was more complex than a clear yes or a clear no. We believe it is unethical for researchers to thrust their methodology onto a participant without listening to the participant's story. After all, a 90-year-old person knows more about the everyday experience of being old than does a younger researcher. Ethically, researchers need to listen more.

2. *Revisit informed consent regularly.* Phenomenological inquiry is useful to generate new hypotheses or new constructs because its purpose is to gather understanding from patterns in the data. The research design is thus emergent. We begin, as does the artist or novelist, with only preliminary ideas. As we proceed, things become clearer and then new areas become subject to scrutiny. Here is where ethical dilemmas arise. Although the participants were informed and gave consent at the beginning of the study, this original consent may become invalid as new curiosities take researchers into new directions. How can participants give informed consent when the investigator keeps changing method and focus? How can a phenomenologist meet the criterion for informed consent when there is no allegiance to one method or goal?

When the general intent and scope of the research do not change, most human subjects committees or local institutional review boards (IRBs) do not require a new informed consent procedure for every change in method or direction. Nevertheless, we recommend that researchers err on the conservative side. We recommend that researchers inform their IRB each time they change direction or sample to make sure that a new informed consent procedure is *not* needed. The basic criterion is to "do no harm." Federal regulations for the protection of human subjects are common to all IRBs, but interpretations of these federal regulations are subject to local customs and conditions. Regional diversity will therefore influence interpretations of what is construed as harmful and what is not. What informed consent means to university professors and health professionals may not be the same as what it means to participants and their communities. We recommend therefore that phenomenologists check with their local IRBs, not only before beginning studies but every time there is a change in direction, method, or sample as their studies progress. For each change, participants must know what is happening and that they can withdraw at any time, without prejudice.

3. *Inform everyone who participates and obtain consent from all who are able to give it.* We recommend obtaining informed consent from all who participate in the study, regardless of their cognitive capacity. This may seem like a conservative position, but again, our goal is to do no harm. Dementia patients have told us that they appreciate being asked about videotaping. So have children. We go beyond the legal requirements of obtaining consent from adults and those with power of attorney and include everyone because it is more respectful. Everyone should be included in the process of informing and consenting.

This more conservative approach to informing and consenting is especially important when doing phenomenological studies because this type of inquiry is by its very nature more personal. Investigator and participant get to know each other more than with positivist research. Usually even minors and other disenfranchised people want to know what is going on and why they should participate.

4. *Avoid covert studies.* Historically, some phenomenologists have proceeded with covert research. They infiltrate a system and pretend they are one of the group they are studying. For example, in 1973, Roshenhan and 11 colleagues (three psychologists, a pediatrician, a psychiatrist, a painter, a homemaker, and a psychology graduate student) infiltrated 12 mental hospitals pretending to be patients. They wanted to answer the phenomenological question: "If sanity and insanity exist, how shall we know them?" (see Roshenhan, 1973).

Although phenomenologists could use covert research strategies in the past, their ethics would be severely questioned today. Becoming an impostor inherently negates the possibility of informed consent from participants and thus would not pass contemporary review boards which protect human subjects. Becoming a pseudo-insider also compromises the ability to hear participants as they communicate everyday lived experiences to us. That is, if we were on the inside under false pretense, we could not tell if it is our lived experience we are interpreting or if it is that of the person we are studying.

The method used by Goode (1980) avoided the ethical dilemma raised by covert observations. He wanted to understand the world of a deaf, blind, and severely retarded young girl. In addition to observing and videotaping her, he wore a blindfold and earplugs on the ward where she lived to "try on," if even for a short time, what she was experiencing. He did this openly. In addition, he let the girl organize activities for the two of them by remaining obedient and passive to her wishes. Through these techniques, he "tried to intuit, while interacting with her, what purposiveness or rationality her activities might have from her perspective" (Goode, as reported by Taylor & Bogdan, 1984, p. 11). Although informed consent could not be obtained in this case in the usual way, the girl's wishes were respected. She remained in charge of how, when, and if she and the researcher would interact, thus implying consent. Goode's method is a creative solution when chronic conditions prevent the use of traditional procedures for informing and consenting.

5. *Maintain confidentiality.* In phenomenological studies, detailed descriptions are frequently used as confidentiality becomes more difficult. Ask participants if they agree with your plan to maintain confidentiality. When one family was asked, they said they

would give consent only if their full names were used in any reports of the study (Fravel & Boss, 1992). This was a couple whose three boys had been missing for more than 30 years. Both parents wanted their names used "just in case one of the boys was still out there somewhere." Betty and Kenny Klein of Monticello, Minnesota, taught us never to take for granted what people's perceptions are regarding confidentiality.

A request for this amount of disclosure is rare, but it is not unusual to find families wanting varying degrees of confidentiality. Again, we recommend erring on the conservative side. That is, we recommend using strict confidentiality in studies of couples and families, because family members may not all agree on the need for it—or they may change their minds at a later date. There is less chance of doing harm as researches if we proceed conservatively.

FUTURE DIRECTIONS

Phenomenological research is experiencing a second summer in this period of postmodernism (read postpositivism). It opens new windows for gathering information about phenomena previously unexplored. This is especially necessary because the white middle-class families of Donna Reed, Beaver Cleaver, and Ozzie and Harriet are no longer the norm, if they ever were. In the absence of a definition of the "normal" family, family therapists can become partners in research with psychologists, sociologists, psychiatrists, family physicians, nurses, and social workers as we open ourselves to discovery about what exists, what works, what does not work, and what *can* be regarding family and individual well-being. There is much to learn using the phenomenological approach; we make ourselves more discovery prone than if we move too early to empiricism.

CONCLUSION

An old method of inquiry, phenomenology, is having a resurgence and has an intuitive appeal among family therapy researchers because it is the study of the phenomenon of everyday family processes. In 1946, Edmund Husserl said we should go back to the things themselves. The "things" were perceptions, feelings, memories, behaviors—in sum, the stuff of family life. Whether phenomenology becomes a place to start as a family therapy researcher or your research method of choice, rigor is necessary in how you proceed. That rigor depends much less on method than it does on philosophical assumptions. Assumptions therefore were the centerpiece of this chapter. They remain the main guide for doing family therapy inquiry as a phenomenologist.

In the final analysis, we need both phenomenology and logical positivism. There is a place for the creativity of dreamers and storytellers as well as for the methods of empiricists. Both have value, both can produce information about family processes, but each needs the other. We still haven't defined families, let alone how they function and how they change across the life course. Linda Burton found in her ethnographic studies that families change even in the course of one day (1991). We need to ask new questions—or ask old questions in a new way. This requires effort on our part to seek holistic, rather than microscopic pictures of family life. In doing this, we should avoid static, noncontextual, and method-bound inquiries (Cowan, Fields, Hansen, Skolnick, & Swanson, 1993). Phenomenological approaches can help.

The current renaissance of phenomenology by family therapy researchers indicates a new acceptance of diversity in research method and perspectives. This is much needed because diversity is also increasing in family structures and functions to a point where we can no longer, with validity or fairness, claim a norm. Phenomenological inquiry will help us to see new ways that families can and do work in spite of increasing complexities.

In this chapter, we have defined and described a particular approach to research—phenomenology—not new to sociologists but with new appeal to family therapists who are interested in inquiry. We focused on the assumptions underlying this nonpositivist method of inquiry rather than on methodology because a variety of methods can be used within the phenomenological approach. While a methodology is not prescribed, the core assumptions are essential in guiding how we proceed.

REFERENCES

Allen, K. R., & Gilgun, J. F. (1987, November). *Qualitative family research: Unanswered questions and proposed resolutions.* Paper presented at Theory Construction and Research Methodology Preconference of the National Council on Family Relations Annual Meeting, Atlanta, GA.

Allen, K. R., & Walker, A. J. (1992). A feminist analysis of interviews with elderly mothers and their daughters. In J. F. Gilgun, K. Daly, & G. Handel (Eds.), *Qualitative methods in family research* (pp. 198–214). Newbury Park, CA: Sage.

Becker, C. S. (1992). *Living and relating: An introduction to phenomenology.* Newbury Park, CA: Sage.

Berger, P. L., & Kellner, H. (1964). Marriage and the construction of reality: An exercise in the microsociology of knowledge. *Diogenes, 46,* 1–25.

Berger, P. L., & Luckmann, T. (1966). *The social construction of reality: A treatise in the sociology of knowledge.* New York: Doubleday.

Blumer, H. (1969). *Symbolic interactionism: Perspective and method.* Englewood Cliffs, NJ: Prentice-Hall.

Boss, P. B. (1987). The role of intuition in family research. In R. Garfield, A. Greenberg, & S. Sugarman (Eds.), Symbolic experiential journeys: A tribute to Carl Whitaker [special issue]. *Contemporary Family Therapy, 9*(1–2), 146–158.

Boss, P. (1991). Ambiguous loss. In F. Walsh & M. McGoldrick (Eds.), *Living beyond loss: Death in the family* (pp. 164–175). New York: Norton.

Boss, P. B., Kaplan, L., & Gordon, M. (1994, August). *The meaning of caregiving for Alzheimer's disease among Native American caregivers: Stories of spirituality, fatalism, and mastery.* Presentation at the Fourth Annual International Conference on Alzheimer's Disease and Related Disorders, Minneapolis, MN.

Brown, L. M., & Gilligan, C. (1992). *Meeting at the crossroads: Women's psychology and girls' development.* Cambridge, MA: Harvard University Press.

Bruyn, S. T. (1966). *The human perspective in sociology: The methodology of participant observation.* Englewood Cliffs, NJ: Prentice-Hall.

Burton, L. (1991). Caring for children in high risk neighborhoods. *American Enterprise, 2*(3), 34–37.

Cicourel, A. V. (1986). Social measurement as the creation of expert systems. In D. W. Fiske & R. A. Sheveder (Eds.), *Metatheory in social science: Pluralisms and subjectivities* (pp. 246–270). Chicago: University of Chicago Press.

Cowan, P., Field, D., Hansen, D., Skolnik, A., & Swanson, G. (1993). *Family, self and society: Toward a new agenda for family research.* Hillsdale, NJ: Erlbaum.

Dahl, C. M. (1994). *A phenomenological exploration of the definition and understanding of spirituality within families.* Unpublished doctoral dissertation, University of Minnesota.

Daly, K. (1992). Parenthood as problematic. In J. F. Gilgun, K. Daly, & G. Handel (Eds.), *Qualitative methods in family research* (pp. 103–125). Newbury Park, CA: Sage.

Deutscher, I. (1973). *What we say/What we do: Sentiments and acts.* Glenview, IL: Scott Foresman.

Dilworth-Anderson, P., Burton, L. M., & Boulin Johnson, L. (1993). Reframing theories for understanding race, ethnicity, and families. In P. G. Boss, W. J. Doherty, R. LaRossa, W. R. Schumm, & S. K. Steinmetz (Eds.), *Handbook of family theories and methods: A contextual approach* (pp. 627–646). New York: Plenum Press.

Doherty, W. J., & Boss, P. G. (1991). Values and ethics in family therapy. In A. S. Gurman & D. P. Kniskern (Eds.), *Handbook of family therapy* (Vol. 2, pp. 606–637). New York: Brunner/Mazel.

Dreyfus, H. L. (1967). Phenomenology and artificial intelligence. In J. Edie (Ed.), *Phenomenology in America* (pp. 31–47). Chicago: Quadrangle Books.

Durkheim, E. (1951). *Suicide: A study in sociology* (J. Spaulding & G. Simpson, Trans.). Glencoe, IL: Free Press.

Edie, J. (1967). *Phenomenology in America.* Chicago: Quadrangle Books.

Frankl, V. E. (1984). *Man's search for meaning.* New York: Washington Square Press.

Fravel, D. L., & Boss, P. G. (1992). An in-depth interview with the parents of missing children. In J. F. Gilgun, K. Daly, & G. Handel (Eds.), *Qualitative methods in family research* (pp. 126–145). Newbury Park, CA: Sage.

Garwick, A. W., Detzner, D., & Boss, P. (1994). Family perceptions of living with Alzheimer's disease. *Family Process, 33*(3), 327–340.

Gergen, K., & Gergen, M. (1988). Narrative and the self as relationship. *Advances in Experimental Social Psychology, 21,* 17–56.

Gilgun, J. F. (1992). Definition, methodologies, and methods in qualitative family research. In J. F. Gilgun, K. Daly, & G. Handel (Eds.), *Qualitative methods in family research* (pp. 22–39). Newbury Park, CA: Sage.

Giorgi, A. (Ed.). (1985). *Phenomenology and psychological research.* Pittsburgh: Duquesne University Press.

Goffman, E. (1959). *The presentation of self in everyday life.* New York: Doubleday.

Goffman, E. (1971). *Relations in public.* New York: Basic Books.

Goldner, V., Penn, P., Sheinberg, M., & Walker, G. (1990). Love and violence: Gender paradoxes in volatile attachments. *Family Process, 29,* 343–364.

Goode, D. A. (1980). The world of the congenitally deaf-blind: Toward the grounds for achieving human understanding. In J. Jacobs (Ed.), *Mental retardation: A phenomenological approach* (pp. 187–207). Springfield, IL: Charles C. Thomas.

Gouldner, A. W. (1970). *The coming crisis in Western sociology.* New York: Avon Books.

Guba, E. S., & Lincoln, Y. S. (1981). *Effective evaluation: Improving the usefulness of evaluation results through responsive and naturalistic approaches.* San Francisco: Jossey-Bass.

Gubrium, J. F., & Holstein, J. A. (1993). Phenomenology, ethnomethodology, and family discourse. In P. G. Boss, W. J. Doherty, R. LaRossa, W. R. Schumm, & S. K. Steinmetz (Eds.), *Sourcebook of family theories and methods: A contextual approach* (pp. 651–672). New York: Plenum Press.

Hare-Mustin, R. (1992, November). *On the need for second order change in family therapy research.* Plenary address presented at the Research/Clinical Conference of the American Family Therapy Academy, Captiva Island, FL.

Hare-Mustin, R. (1994). Discourses in the mirrored room: A postmodern analysis of therapy. *Family Process, 33,* 19–35.

Henry, J. (1973). *Pathways to madness.* New York: Vintage.

Hess, R. D., & Handel, G. (1959). *Family worlds: A psychosocial approach to family life.* Chicago: University of Chicago Press.

Hess, R. D., & Handel, G. (1967). The family as a psychosocial organization. In G. Handel (Ed.), *The psychosocial interior of the family* (pp. 10–29). Chicago: Aldine.

Husserl, E. (1946). Phenomenology. In *Encyclopaedia Britannica* (14th ed.; Vol. 17, pp. 699–702). Chicago: University of Chicago Press.

Imber-Black, E., & Roberts, J. (1992). *Rituals for our times.* New York: HarperCollins.

Keller, E. F. (1985). *Reflections on gender and science.* New Haven, CT: Yale University Press.

Kollock, P., & O'Brien, J. (1994). *The production of reality.* Thousand Oaks, CA: Pine Forge Press.

Laing, R. D. (1971). *The politics of the family*. New York: Pantheon Books.

LaRossa, R., Bennett, L., & Gelles, R. (1981). Ethical dilemmas in the detailed study of families. *Journal of Marriage and the Family, 43*, 303–313.

Liebow, E. (1967). *Haley's corner*. Boston: Little, Brown.

McLain, R., & Weigert, A. (1979). Toward a phenomenological sociology of family. In W. R. Burr, R. Hill, F. I. Nye, & I. L. Reiss (Eds.), *Contemporary theories about the family* (Vol. 2, pp. 160–205). New York: Free Press.

Mead, G. H. (1934). *Mind, self and society*. Chicago: University of Chicago Press.

Merleau-Ponty, M. (1945). *Phenomenologie de la perception*. Paris: Galimard. [Translation 1962 by C. Smith. *The phenomenology of perception*. New York: Humanities Press.]

Mishler, E. (1986). The analysis of interview–narratives. In T. Sarbin (Ed.), *Narrative psychology: The storied nature of human conduct* (pp. 233–255). New York: Prager.

Moore, T. (1992). *Care of the soul*. New York: HarperCollins.

Olson, D. (1977). "Insiders" and "outsiders" views of relationships: Research strategies. In G. Levinger & H. Rausch (Eds.), *Close relationships: Perspectives on the meaning of intimacy* (pp. 115–135). Amherst: University of Massachusetts Press.

Patterson, J., & Garwick, A. (1994). Levels of meaning in family stress theory. *Family Process, 33*, 287–303.

Patton, M. Q. (1990). *Qualitative evaluation and research methods* (2nd ed.). Newbury Park, CA: Sage.

Polkinghorne, D. E. (1989). Phenomenological research methods. In R. S. Valle & S. Halling (Eds.), *Existential–phenomenological perspectives in psychology* (pp. 41–60). New York: Plenum Press.

Pollner, M., & McDonald-Wikler, L. (1985). The social construction of unreality: A case study of a family's attribution of competence to a severely retarded child. *Family Process*, 241–254. [Reprinted 1994. In P. Kollock & J. O'Brien (Eds.), *The production of reality* (pp. 343–355). Thousand Oaks, CA: Sage.]

Psathas, G. (1973). *Phenomenological sociology: Issues and applications*. New York: Wiley.

Reinharz, S. (1983). Experiential analysis: A contribution to feminist research. In G. Bowers & R. Dueli Klein (Eds.), *Theories of women's studies* (pp. 162–191). Boston: Routledge & Kegan Paul.

Reiss, D. (1981). The social construction of reality: The passion within us all. *Family Process, 24*, 250–254. [Reprinted 1994. In P. Kollock & J. O'Brien (Eds.), *The production of reality* (pp. 356–359). Thousand Oaks, CA: Sage.]

Reiss, D. (1980). *The family's construction of reality*. Harvard University Press.

Rosenblatt, P. C., & Fischer, L. R. (1993). Qualitative family research. In P. G. Boss, W. J. Doherty, R. LaRossa, W. R. Schumm, & S. K. Steinmetz (Eds.), *Sourcebook of family theories and methods: A contextual approach* (pp. 167–177). New York: Plenum.

Roshenhan (1973). On being sane in insane places. *Science, 179*, 250–258.

Schutz, A. (1960). *Der sinnhafte aufbau der sozialen welt*, Vienna: Springer Verlag.

Schutz, A. (1962). *Collected papers: Vol. 1. The problem of social reality (1962–1966)*. The Hague: Nijhoff.

Schutz, A. (1967). *The phenomenology of the social world*. Evanston, IL: Northwestern University Press.

Sedney, M. A., Baker, J. E., & Gross, E. (1994). "The story" of a death: Therapeutic considerations with bereaved families. *Journal of Marital and Family Therapy, 20*(3), 287–296.

Stacey, J. (1990). *Brave new families: Stories of domestic upheaval in later twentieth-century America*. New York: Basic.

Taylor, S. J., & Bogdan, R. (1984). *Introduction to qualitative research methods: The search for meanings* (2nd ed.). New York: Wiley.

van Manen, M. (1990). *Researching lived experience: Human science for an action sensitive pedagogy*. Albany: State University of New York Press.

Walters, M., Carter, B., Papp, P., & Silverstein, O. (1988). *The invisible web: Gender patterns in family relationships*. New York: Guilford Press.

Weber, M. (1949). *The methodology of the social sciences.* New York: Free Press.

Weber, M. (1968). *Economy and society.* New York: Bedminster Press.

Welter-Enderlin, R. (1994). *Paare-Leidenschaft und Lange Weile [Couple passion over time].* Munich, Germany: Piper Verlag.

Whitaker, C., & Keith, D. (1981). Symbolic–experiential family therapy. In A. Gurman & D. Kniskern (Eds.), *Handbook of family therapy* (pp. 187–225). New York: Brunner/Mazel.

White, M., & Epston, D. (1990). *Narrative means to therapeutic ends.* New York: Norton.

5

Conversation Analysis
STUDYING THE CONSTRUCTION
OF THERAPEUTIC REALITIES

JERRY GALE

Exemplar 1: **The Affair is 95% Over**

((Early in a one session consultation between a solution-focused therapist, husband, and wife.))

```
221  T:  ((therapist looks at both husband and
222       wife)) Ok I mean is the but is the contact
223       with the person::: ah in the past or is
224       that still going on?
225  H:  That's ahh ((looks up and to his right))
226       (.hhh) (1.0) I would say is's ah 95 per
227       cent over (.) ((therapist nods yes)) she
228       tries to contact me at work=
229  T:  =Ok, so from your side you said ok I want to
230       put this thing back together ((wife and
231       husband nod yes)) do what I can to put it
232       back together (.hh) ((husband nods yes))
233       she still sometimes tries to ahm get some
234       contact with ((husband nods yes)) you as
235       much as possible you (.8) (.hh) you've
236       been shoving it to the side ((gestures to
237       the right)) ((husband nods yes))
```

(Gale, 1991, p. 111; see Appendix for transcript notation)

CO-CONSTRUCTING A SOLUTION NARRATIVE:
AN ANALYSIS OF THE ABOVE EXCHANGE

Using conversation analysis (CA) as the research strategy, the following analysis is provided: On lines 223–224 the therapist poses a question to the husband regarding his recent affair, "is the contact with the person::: ah in the past or is that still going on." The therapist's request, which offers several possible candidate answers (Pomerantz, 1988),

107

emphasizes past as the preferred response. This favored reply would facilitate the narrative to follow a solution focus, placing the affair as being finished and behind the couple. The husband's answer however, "I would say it's ah 95 per cent over" (lines 226–227), shifts the talk toward a problematic sequence as it suggests that the affair is not completely ended.

The therapist, who is following a solution-focused model, uses his turn to recapture a solution narrative. In his formulation (Heritage & Watson, 1979) of the husband's response, which quickly follows the husband's turn (as noted by the = sign), the therapist attributes an intention to the husband as he states, "I want to put this thing back together" (lines 229–230). This statement is noteworthy in two ways: (1) The therapist is speaking in the first person, as if he were the client making this statement, and (2) the therapist is attributing to the husband a desire to put this thing (i.e., the marriage) back together that the husband has not yet expressed.

Indeed, the therapist repeats this statement (lines 231–232), which serves to further highlight the husband's desire to put the marriage back together. The husband accepts this paraphrase and formulation of his comments as noted by his head nods of yes (lines 231, 232, 234). The therapist continues, stating to the husband, "as much as possible you (.8) (.hh) you've been shoving it to the side" ((gestures to the right)) (lines 235–236). This comment further advances the embedded premise that the husband is actively and willfully seeking to end the relationship with the other woman. The therapist's gesture to the right is also an action that is repeated throughout the session by the therapist, such that each gesture to the right is accompanied with a comment about future success.

In summary, the analysis reveals that the therapist's comments are crafted to pursue a particular agenda (i.e., solution talk). Utilizing the basic counseling skill of paraphrasing, the therapist actually reformulates the husband's comments into meaning something different than what the husband stated. The husband accepts and participates in this transformation of his original statement. In this exchange the therapist engineers, with the husband's participation, a reconstruction of the husband's statements to achieve a solution-centered narrative.

This example is presented to familiarize the reader as to how CA can be employed. This chapter covers the historical roots and philosophical assumptions of CA and demonstrates how to use CA as a research method. In addition, issues of trustworthiness, the strengths and weaknesses of this research method, and the researcher's skills are considered and the benefits of this approach for clinicians are discussed.

HISTORICAL ROOTS AND PHILOSOPHICAL ASSUMPTIONS

History

The beginning of CA is traced to the work of the sociologist Harold Garfinkel. Garfinkel (1967) was interested in understanding human action from a phenomenological perspective. He named his approach ethnomethodology, which is "the study of (ology) ordinary people's (ethno) methods" of practical reasoning (Potter & Wetherell, 1987, p. 18). Garfinkel viewed people as having a folk methodology which comprises a "range of 'seen but unnoticed' procedures and practices that make it possible for persons to analyze, make sense of, and produce recognizable social activities" (Pomerantz & Atkinson, 1984, p. 286).

Garfinkel developed his ideas in the 1950s when Talcott Parson's theory and methods were the dominant approach for studying human behavior. Garfinkel (1967), though a student of Parsons, was critical of Parsons's treatment of action which viewed individuals as "judgmental dopes" acting without self-awareness and following inaccessible normative rules. Garfinkel, influenced by the philosopher Alfred Schutz, advocated a perspective that considered people's actions a social accomplishment. In particular, Garfinkel was concerned with the issue of reflexivity, or self-awareness, in terms of how an individual's thinking impacted his or her own actions (Heritage, 1984), as well as how social selves were interactively created (Gubrium & Holstein, 1993). Garfinkel viewed language as a "reality-constituting practice" (Edwards & Potter, 1992, p. 27), not a representative code. For ethnomethodologists, understanding language means discerning actions and utterances as they are constructively interpreted within their contexts (Heritage, 1984).

This perspective is similar to the social constructionist view that knowledge of reality arises from social interaction mediated through language (Anderson & Goolishian, 1988; McNamee & Gergen, 1992). Gergen and Kaye (1992) state that "a story is not simply a story" but "is also a situated action in itself, a performance with illocutionary effects" (p. 178). Shotter (1989) states that discourse makes people socially accountable. And as R. D. Laing (1975) states, "one's self-identity is the story one tells one's self of who one is" (p. 93).

Ethnomethodology has been viewed as postmodern critical theory (Holstein & Gubrium, 1994). As the focus is on how participants use language, ethnomethodologists tend to analyze naturally occurring talk rather than conduct interviews (Adler & Adler, 1994). However, analyzing interviews as they occur in various settings (e.g., a clinical encounter) is a useful ethnomethodological activity for understanding how the participants construct a social institution (e.g., therapy).

Assumptions

Words do things and are used by speakers to achieve particular results (Austin, 1962). The study of how ordinary talk accomplishes social identities and social order became the research method of conversation analysis. CA developed from ethnomethodology in the 1960s and is linked to the work of Harvey Sacks and his colleagues Gail Jefferson and Emanual Schegloff. They developed methods for examining naturally occurring talk (Goodwin & Heritage, 1990). The basic assumptions of CA include "(1) interaction is structurally organized; (2) contributions to interaction are contextually oriented; and (3) these two properties inhere in the details of interaction so that no order of detail can be dismissed, a priori, as disorderly, accidental or irrelevant" (Heritage, 1984, p. 241).

Expanding upon the above points, first, conversations are meticulously co-orchestrated phenomena. An individual's action is not independent of the actions of others but is patterned in relationship to others' actions. Meanings are expressed and understood precisely because there are patterned structures to interactions. Second, simultaneously as speakers shape their utterances specifically for the intended recipient(s), their utterances also contribute to the continuation or closing of that context. Thus, every action both shapes the context and is constrained by the context. Third, CA examines the paralinguistic (and sometimes the nonverbal) features of talk as well as the structural sequencing of the various turn takings. Therefore, all interactional features of the context are relevant to the analyst.

CA does not assume a privileged observational perspective of behavior and avoids a priori categorization of the data. This means that the CA researcher does not try to interpret the internal or psychological state of a participant. Rather, the researcher describes how the participants' actions accomplish particular meanings. These meanings are achieved and understood through how the participants' construct and display their actions in naturally occurring speech events (Hopper, 1988).

It is relevant to note that although this chapter presents CA as a postmodern research method, conversation analysts of various disciplines do adopt other epistemological stances and different research strategies. Sociology and speech communication conversation analysts, for example, typically record and collect a large corpus of data on a particular phenomenon, such as turn-taking procedures (Sacks, Schegloff, & Jefferson, 1974), aligning actions (Stokes & Hewitt, 1976), conversation repair (Schegloff, Jefferson, & Sacks, 1977), or adjacency pairs (Schegloff & Sacks, 1973) and analyze each occurrence of that phenomenon.

Historically, CA was the study of microfeatures of talk and considered many examples of a particular speech phenomenon; discourse analysis was the study of longer narratives. In the last 15 years, the distinctions between discourse analysis and CA have become blurred (Devault, 1990). This chapter presents the employment of CA methods for examining longer narratives.

METHODOLOGY

Research Questions

Research questions for conversation analysts center around the *how* question. An open curiosity for understanding people's practical accomplishments of actions is a common thread for CA researchers (Gale & Morris, 1991). Through CA one can examine how various therapeutic realities are accomplished. CA provides a method to compare what therapists say they do in therapy with what they actually do. Questions asked by conversation analysts and ethnomethodologists have included how a solution-focused therapist achieves solution talk in therapy (Gale, 1991; Gale & Newfield, 1992); how supervisors and supervisees deal with disagreement (Ratliff, 1992); how families construct social order in the home (Buckholdt & Gubrium, 1979; Gubrium & Holstein, 1990); how family responsibility in home care of Alzheimer patients is socially constructed (Gubrium, 1988); how families decide on hospitalization of members with psychological problems (Holstein, 1988); how blame accounts are used in marital therapy (Buttney, 1990); how clients in a family therapy session construct family patterns (Stamp, 1991); and how therapy reduced a woman's social problems to personal shortcomings of the client herself (Davis, 1984).

To better describe CA research methods, features of Gale's study (1991; Gale & Newfield, 1992) are used to demonstrate the procedures of this qualitative approach. Gale's study was initiated as a dissertation. Two issues guided the study. The issues are how a solution-focused therapist achieves change via solution talk and the utility of CA as a constructionist research method.

Selecting Data

As the main focus is on how participants themselves produce and account for each other's actions, data consist of any naturally occurring interactions and are purposeful samples. One may choose a specific occurrence from a session (e.g., a positive, negative, or emotional event), or examples of similar types of occurrences (e.g., assigning tasks, beginning a session, marital conflict, and noncompliance).

CA can provide useful information even if one examines less than a 2-minute segment of a single case (Stamp, 1991). Conducting CA of an entire session is a labor-intensive activity and obviously not a useful procedure for clinicians or for many researchers. Therefore, researchers and clinicians may find it more practical to study shorter segments of therapeutic encounters. Ratliff (1992), for example, examined many brief exchanges between supervisors and supervisees. Gale (Gale, Dotson, Lindsey, Nagireddy, & Wilson, 1993) had his students do self-supervision by analyzing 10-minute segments of their own cases.

In Gale's (1991) study, a videotape of a complete therapy case was solicited. A one-session marital consultation conducted by Bill O'Hanlon was selected. This tape was chosen because the entire therapeutic dialogue was videotaped and the case was described by O'Hanlon as representative of his solution-focused therapy (O'Hanlon & Weiner-Davis, 1989). Again, it is important to stress that it is not necessary to study entire cases.

Data Collection

To collect the data, a good recording device is necessary. Although it is useful to videotape the session, it is also possible to work directly from an audiotape. The benefit of a videotape is the ability to note such nonverbal communications as facial expressions, eye contact, body movements, and gestures. It is recommended that the best possible recording device available be used to achieve a clear sound. When working with a videotape, record the audio portion onto an audiotape via a direct lead between the video cassette recorder and tape recorder to reduce extraneous noise.

The development of the transcript is part of the analytical process itself (Heritage, 1984; Sacks et al., 1974) and it is recommended that researchers–clinicians transcribe the tape themselves. Transcription is both a constructive and conventional activity. Through "soaking" of the data via repeated listening and refinement of the transcript, patterns and categories are developed. Although no transcribing method is complete, using a detailed notational system (see Appendix) can help distinguish the micropractices of the participants. Though some CA researchers have a typist write the first pass of the transcript, it is crucial that the researcher refine the transcript him- or herself. When possible, it is recommended that there be a shared listening of the tape with research colleagues. Collaborative listening and refinement of the transcript contribute to an improved transcript as well as help the analytical process.

A stenographic transcription machine, although not necessary, is very helpful. The benefits of a stenographic machine include the following: talk can be slowed down in order to better hear overlapped talk and other hard-to-hear sounds; the machine can be adjusted so that when a segment is played, the tape will automatically backtrack 1 to 5 seconds (so it is easier to pick up where you were in the transcript); and, with a foot pedal, it is easy to go forward and backward on the tape, freeing the hands to type. A foot pedal for walkman-type tape players can be purchased for under $10 from such places as Radio Shack. These devices only advance the tape forward, however.

Data Analysis

CA is a qualitative research method that is inductive, discovery-orientated, and concerned with process (the "how" question); analyzes participants' displayed understandings of interactions; and is iterative. There is continuous recursion between listening to segments of the talk, transcribing the segments, developing categories of patterns, and comparing these categories with subsequent segments of talk. This method is similar to the constant comparative method (Glaser & Strauss, 1967) and analytical induction (Taylor & Bogdan, 1984).

Pomerantz and Atkinson (1984) note that analysts should include a focus on "how participants themselves produce and interpret each other's actions" and treat each event as "worthy of serious analytic attention" (pp. 286–287). Describing how the participants themselves demonstrate their understanding of each other's actions entails that the researcher keep an open and curious perspective. It is important not to attribute hidden motives to the participants but to work from the participants' actual displays of meaning making. The analytical gaze is on how "events are **constructively described** in ways that, **for participants**, imply particular causal accounts" (Edwards & Potter, 1992, p. 10, bold in original).

Although not typically discussed in the CA literature, it is recommended that researchers keep a field journal during their research process. This journal serves several purposes. One, it is a subjectivity audit that provides a method for researchers to reflexively document and track their personal responses to experiences while involved in the research study (Peshkin, 1988). Second, it provides a method to consider how and when various themes and categories were developed, as well as which categories were not pursued (Lincoln & Guba, 1985).

Beginning conversation analysts often have difficulty deciding how to begin their analysis. There are replete distinctions possible from which to focus an analysis and it can be challenging choosing where to start. To offer several possible starting points or preliminary distinctions from which to examine clinical talk, four well-studied conversational action sequences are briefly presented. Clinical examples of these conversational sequences, as analyzed in Gale's (1991) study, are also provided. These commonly occurring micropatterns of interaction include transition relevance places (TRPs), adjacency pairs, accounts, and preliminaries. These features of talk, although presented in a piecemeal fashion, typically do not occur independent of one another but operate together.

1. Turn-taking switches or TRPs in conversations (Sacks et al., 1974) are those moments in a conversation when a transition from one speaker to another is possible. TRPs operate in all conversations and are utilized by participants as a potential end of a turn. TRPs often are accomplished when a speaker, either verbally or nonverbally, preselects the next speaker. If no choice is presented, the TRP is an opportunity for any listener to take a turn through self-selection or for the speaker to continue. A pause of a half second or more at these TRPs is meaningful. The implications of these maneuvers are significant. As conversational turn taking is interactionally managed, what one participant does affects what the others may acceptably do. For example, when the current speaker selects the next speaker, this often effectively rules out other listeners from self-selecting. Slow or hesitant speakers could be excluded from getting a turn. As Nofsinger (1991) notes:

> Many of the conversational tendencies and orientations that we commonly attribute to participants' personalities or interpersonal relationships derive (at least in part) from the turn system. For example, other participants may listen to us not because they are interested or because we are fascinating, but because they have to. (p. 89)

These interactionally managed turn transitions can influence such events as the following: (a) speaker selection, (b) number of turns to which a speaker has access to (often related to gender) (Tannen, 1989; Turner, 1993; Wilson, 1993), (c) length of turns, (d) strength of argument (as it is easier to show the relationship of one's talk to the dominant topic if that person has an adjacent turn) (Cobb & Rifken, 1991), (e) the construction of narrative accounts through the negotiation of turns; and (f) who maintains control of the turn-taking sequences (Wilson, 1993).

Exemplar 2: **TRP**

```
386  T  . . . Any moments that were
387        good, even though you knew that that was
388        happening any moments or any evenings or
389        any days that you thought were good?
390        (0.9)
391        ((Husband looks at wife))
392  W  Not really because we really didn't =
```

(Gale, 1991, p. 114)

In Exemplar 2, the therapist poses a question to the husband and wife (lines 386–389). The completion of the therapist's turn is a TRP that does not select the next speaker. There is a pause of 0.9 seconds before the wife answers (line 390). During this pause, the husband looks to the wife, as if signaling her to respond to the question. The wife completes the adjacency pair with the response on line 392. The significance of this interaction is how the husband at the TRP (line 391) maneuvers his actions to get the wife to respond. In Exemplar 1 at the beginning of the chapter, it was noted that the husband's comments regarding the affair being 95% over is a problematic response. Often during the session the husband made problematic statements prone to rebuttal and reproach (Gale, 1991). At this particular TRP, it can be seen how the husband's actions shifted the turn to his wife and provided him a way out of giving a possible problematic response.

2. Another example of a micropattern is adjacency pairs. These are sequentially paired actions that feature the production of a reciprocal response by a different speaker. They are logically organized such that a particular first-pair action must be coordinated with one of a relatively few types of second-pair parts (Schegloff & Sacks, 1973). Many clinical discursive actions are organized into adjacency pair sequences. The first action of the pair opens a slot in the conversation for the second-pair part, making the occurrence of that second action expected. As such, participants will go looking for missing second-pair parts or attempt to account for their absence.

The construction of adjacency pairs can influence such events as (a) method of question construction, (b) identification of respondents, (c) methods used to avoid questions, (d) embedded assumptions within a question or response, (e) implication of the question–response situation to the relationship between participants, (f) omission of questions, (g) presenting a candidate response in the question (Pomerantz, 1988), (h) holding the first part of an adjacency pair for an extended period of time, and (i) inserted turns before the completion of an adjacency pair.

Exemplar 3: **Adjacency Pairs**

```
01  T:  So what I need to know is (.2)
02       esse:ntially: what either::brought chew
03       for help initially: for counselling or
04       whatever it may be if (hh) you if you've
05       done I've I specifically asked (.hhh) not
```

```
06        to know anything about what > your situa-
07        tion is so I can < come with a fresh vie::w
08        and (.hhh) giveye some fresh ideas hope-
09        fully(:) and > help you move along to where
10        ever you want to go:(.hhh) < ((wife and
11        husband nod yes)) a:n: that's: what I need
12        to know, is (.hh) either what brings ya
13        toda::::y whh: and more than that maybe to
14        help me orient to where we are suppos::ed
15        to go where you hope to go (.hhh) ho:w
16        will you know ((swallowed)) if we've done
17        wonderful things here ((wife nods yes)) an
18        everything is worked out and you gotten
19        what you came for (.hh) and your relation-
20        ship for each other ah whatever it may be
21        how will you know when actually (.) things
22        are better (.hh) and ah or things are
23        where you want them to be in your rela-
24        tionship or whatever you've come for. So,
25        (.hh) I want to ask each of you > how will
26        I know < and then I may ask you some ques-
27        tions > so I make sure I understand that <
28        > in a pretty good way < (.hh) and I want to
29        know how you'll know ultimately and what
30        will be the first sign to see (.) things
31        are going in a good direction, so (.) from
32        either of you, whoever wants to start.
33        ((looks at both husband and wife))
34  H:    ((looks towards wife)) You made the call you
35        could (.8) you want to talk first?
          (Gale, 1991, p. 106)
```

In Exemplar 3 the therapist presents a series of piggy-backed questions (lines 1–33). This is a nontypical adjacency pair sequence as the therapist puts off a response from the clients for 33 lines. A careful examination of the transcript reveals that the therapist is pursuing a particular type of response. After the opening question (lines 1–3) the therapist provides clarifying statements and a focused series of questions to engineer the couple's sequenced second action (their response). The therapist presents a number of focusing questions (lines 5–7, 11–13, 13–15, 15–19, 19–22, 22–24, 25–31, 31–32). This example illustrates how the therapist pursues a solution focused response. During the therapist's turn, there are only a few accessible TRPs. Other than a 0.2 second pause in line 1, the therapist offers no discernible pauses. His inhalations and exhalations, which are possible TRPs, occur either in the middle of an utterance (lines 4, 5, 8, 12, 25, 28) or following a solution-eliciting question (lines 10, 15, 19, 22). This illustration also demonstrates a TRP (lines 34–35) and another example of how the husband shifts the responsibility to responding to the wife.

3. A third example of a micropattern is accounts. Accounts are ways that people explain actions (often unusual or unexpected types of behaviors). Accounts can be used as an excuse (when the person admits an act was wrong but he or she was influenced by some external agency) or as a justification that the actions were appropriate. In addition, accounts can be used as apologies, requests, and disclaimers. For example, apologies do not attempt to mitigate or justify an action but imply that the transgression will not recur. "Requests are accounts used before the act occurs in an attempt to license

what might be perceived as a violation" (Potter & Wetherell, 1988, p. 76). Disclaimers are preaccounts that attempt to avoid anticipated negative comments in response to statements about to be given (e.g., "I'm very committed to my husband but . . . ").

It is useful to consider how accounts are constructed to seem factual and external to the author and designed to accomplish to particular outcomes (Edwards & Potter, 1992). The externalizing nature of accounts are ways of "accomplishing versions, categorizations and explanations such that they appear as simple, uninterpreted and unmotivated descriptions" (Edwards & Potter, 1992, p. 90). Shotter, as cited by McGhee (1987), states that an account "tells us something, it informs or instructs us as to how practically to go about seeing what the 'is' is, that is, what we ought to see as the 'is' " (p. 304). Accounts can influence such events as (a) how the therapist assigns tasks that feature an explanation, (b) how participants offer explanations for their actions (past, present, and future), (c) how responsibility is accepted or rejected, (d) how history is revised, and (e) how one responds (e.g., acceptance or rejection).

Exemplar 4: **Accounts**

```
192   W:                    his:: affair went on it's been eight long
193        months that have (( )) hard on both of us and
194        (.hh) =
195                              [
196   T:                        [*right*
197   W:   = I think um (.5) there was a lot of lies a
198        lot of lot of just hateful things that
199        were done (.hhh) ((therapist nods yes))
200        and (.) he kinda pleads temporary insanity
201        which I think is a very poor excuse
202        ((therapist nods yes and no)) and I find
203        that hard to forgive him for that and =
204                              [
205   T:                        [*right*
206   W:   = (.hhh) it's I don't think it's fair that I
207        should be be asked to just forgive him and
208        pretend like that's temporary insanity
209        ((therapist nods yes)) I don't you know
210        think that's asking a lot from me (.hhh) =
211        (hhhhh)
212              [                    ]
213   T:   = And he says [look at (all) you know] this
214        is craziness I went through now its so::
215        it on tha:t (.5) idea? (.) Is it done?
216        ((therapist leans forward and looks at
217        husband as he says this, uncrosses legs
218        and sits similarly to the husband's posi-
219        tion))
```

(Gale, 1991, p. 110)

In Exemplar 4, which is the talk immediately preceding Exemplar 1, the wife's account (lines 200–203, 206–211) begins with a description of her husband's account (his excuse of temporary insanity) which he used in order to palliate his offense of the affair. The wife's account is used to explain her reluctance to forgive him (line 203). She continued with this explanation (lines 206–211), further emphasizing the unfairness of her husband's excuse and her reluctance to change. This was a key issue in the therapy process as the therapist repeatedly returns to this problem account in order to find a new solution-focused narrative for the wife.

In the following turn (lines 213–219), the therapist suggested to the husband a different account. The husband's apology was ineffective, so the therapist introduces the distinction that the affair is "done" and therefore no longer an issue. However, as seen in Exemplar 1, the husband's account of the affair does not mitigate his involvement. It is at that time that the therapist offers a new formulation of the husband's actions in order to elicit a solution-centered narrative.

4. A fourth example of a micro-pattern is preliminaries. Preliminaries, a type of presequence, are used to check out the situation before performing some action and are a strategy for communicating a no-fault response (Nofsinger, 1991). Preliminaries offer a way for the speaker to pose a question or scenario indirectly to decide whether the question should be posed directly (Levinson, 1983). "Presequences establish information relevant to how workable the projected action will be" (Nofsinger, 1991, p. 56). When multiple narratives are open, the use of preliminaries are practical microprocedures for determining which story should be pursued.

Examining preliminaries can reveal (a) methods used by the therapist to set up requests for descriptions, accounts, and tasks; (b) methods used by clients to set up issues or requests of other participants; (c) methods used to avoid issues; (d) methods used by the therapist to avoid negative responses (denial or refusal); (e) selection of particular speakers; (f) embedded assumptions used in presequenced statements that contribute to a particular narrative; and (g) use of minimal cues (verbal and nonverbal) to convey support or rejection of a presequence.

Exemplar 5: **Preliminaries**

```
246  T:   but for the most part (.) th (.hh) I
247       assume the reason you two are here
248       together is you're saying ok: if it's pos-
249       sible to put this thing back together (.)
250       to get ((wife nods yes)) (.) to some good
251       place ((husband nods yes)) that's what we
252       would like to do we would like to (.hh)
253       get the affair behind us and get back
254       ((wife nods yes)) to:: (.hh) some of
255       the things that we use to do ((husband nods yes))
          (Gale, 1991, p. 111)
```

In Exemplar 5 the therapist is proposing a particular narrative to the clients. The therapist is not just posing a direct question but is presequencing his request with a possible narrative. The therapist begins on lines 246–247 with a statement that suggests the couple's motive for therapy. However, from lines 251–255 the therapist shifts the narrative from talking *about* the couple to talking *for* the couple. This is demonstrated in his use of "we" (line 251, 252, 255) and "us" (line 253). The therapist elicits nonverbal agreement from the couple via head nods that his proposed explanatory narrative is acceptable to them. The framework of the therapist's proposed narrative is built on a solution-focused foundation. This presequence, which is the first part of a 75-line turn establishing a particular narrative, does eventually lead to a request for more information from the couple.

The four conversational action sequences presented here—TRPs, adjacency pairs, accounts, and preliminaries—provide some preliminary distinctions for beginning analysis. There are many other themes and interactional patterns that the researcher or clinician can consider. What is important to consider, as micropractices in clinical discourse are examined, is how the various discursive phenomena perform in concert with one another. The primary characteristics of conversations include an interactive reciprocity and local management by participants, so it is critical to document how the participants themselves are accomplishing and accounting for their actions.

Reporting

Reporting CA studies requires the display of actual transcripts. Because reliability is achieved through the use of exemplars (Hopper, 1988), for readers to draw their own conclusion, it is important to present instances of participants' talk. Published studies typically include a review of relevant literature, exemplars of themes being presented, and detailed analysis of these exemplars. As exemplars typically involve detailed transcript notation, it is useful to include an appendix with the transcript notation.

CA, as presented in this chapter, focuses on longer segments of interaction. Therefore, it is also useful for clinical cases to include a brief description of the case or types of instances being studied. CA is a very context-sensitive method and it is important to present relevant details of the context to the reader. These features of a CA study tend to make for long manuscripts. Also, as many readers (including journal editors) may be unfamiliar with CA, it may help to clearly but briefly articulate the analytical process and legitimacy of CA. CA papers have appeared in the *Journal of Marriage and Family Therapy* (Gale & Newfield, 1992), *Family Process* (Stamp, 1991), as well as many communication, sociology, and anthropology journals. As qualitative studies become more acceptable, it is likely that more clinical journals will accept these types of manuscripts.

DISCUSSION

Trustworthiness: Reliability and Validity Revisited

Issues of reliability and validity, to the extent in which research findings are trustworthy, are important concerns (Lincoln & Guba, 1985). Qualitative research, however, as based on a subjective paradigm of knowledge and knowing, has adopted other concepts for accessing the trustworthiness of a study (Krefting, 1991). Such terms as "credibility," "applicability," and "dependability" are concepts often associated with qualitative research.

In conversation-analytic research, credibility is achieved via prolonged engagement and persistent observation. This is accomplished through "soaking" oneself in the data via repeated listening/watching of the tape and continuously refining the transcript. Credibility is also achieved through sharing the transcript and recordings with colleagues and collaboratively refining the transcript and discussing emerging themes. Keeping an audit journal also improves credibility. Negative case examples or deviant examples help to refine category development and increase credibility. Deviant examples are those instances in the talk in which speakers depart from established patterns and show "the ways in which participants, through their actions, orient to these departures" (Heritage, 1988, p. 131).

As particular patterns and themes are classified for each substantive claim, it is necessary to show evidence not only that this instance of talk could be viewed in the way suggested but that it can be demonstrated through repeated examples. This is accomplished through constant comparisons of participant's talk with comparable examples from throughout the session. In this way, rather than speculating on speakers' real intent, the talk "speaks for itself" and credibility increases.

Providing examples of the talk in the manuscript is a method for improving dependability and applicability. Through having the extended text to read for themselves, readers are able to draw their own conclusion and can determine the trustworthiness of the data and analysis for themselves. Describing the procedures used by the researcher(s) also increases the dependability and applicability of the study. Having copies of the entire transcript available for interested readers is also beneficial.

Strengths and Weaknesses of CA

A major strength of CA of clinical talk is its focus on interaction and how participants themselves achieve and demonstrate meaning. This emphasis on the constructive nature of interactive communication (verbal and nonverbal) is consistent with epistemological assumptions of the family therapy paradigm. CA's methods are compatible with both social constructionism and second-order cybernetics. As more and more researchers and clinicians are interested in considering how language creates social identities and relationships, CA provides a method for studying these processes.

Another strength of CA, however, is also a weakness. That is, although how participants themselves accomplish and demonstrate their actions is a key goal of CA, this understanding is presented through the perspective of the researcher, who him or herself is an instrument of inquiry. As such, a researcher's biases and limitations do impact his or her study. Although researchers are encouraged to work together in refining a transcript, transcripts at best offer only a limited portrayal of interactions. No transcript can convey the richness and complexities of actual discourse. Though CA researchers do not adopt a privileged position, it is important to appreciate the limitations of a transcript and for the researchers to consider the self-reflexive nature of their work research.

As pointed out by Stamp (1991), repeated listenings to the therapeutic conversation could make the conversational features "appear to have much more relevance than they ever actually had for the participants" (p. 262). Although this chapter presents the importance of viewing discourse as accomplishing social identities, the transcripts are not identical to the phenomenological experiences of the participants.

One criticism that is sometimes leveled against CA is that it is reductionistic and therefore ignores broad issues of power and social inequities. But as Edwards and Potter (1992) note, the starting point of analysis is not of events per se but rather of a "descriptive account" of events. "It is a discursive construction, already loaded with causal formulations and attributional concerns" (p. 98). Consequently, issues of power and culture are presented and performed in the actual talk and can therefore be accounted for from that talk (see also Wetherell & Potter, 1992).

However, this response only partly addresses the concern. As Hare-Mustin (1994) points out, "Discourses do not simply describe the social world; they also categorize it. In so doing, discourses bring certain phenomena into sight and obscure other phenomena" (p. 20). Therefore, it is important for conversation analysts to be aware of cultural and social practices as well as dominant and marginalized discourses (White & Epston, 1992). Although CA can make visible the seen but unnoticed procedures of people's actions, the researcher needs to be self-reflexive, challenging, and open to alternative perspectives.

The reductionistic charge can hold for some CA research. However, although CA is microdirected, it is not necessarily only reductionistic. When segments of the conversation are considered in relationship to the broader therapeutic context, the distinction between micro and macro blur. Aspects of the micro-level can orient the analyst to new understandings of the macro-level. CA in particular can enrich such other qualitative methods as ethnography (Moerman, 1988).

One other factor to consider when undertaking a conversation-analytical study is the time component. Doing CA in a rigorous manner is a time-consuming activity. Both the transcription process and the analysis take a great deal of time and effort. One need not study an entire session, but even analyzing a 10-minute segment is labor intensive.

Skills

Useful skills include a self-reflexive stance, a willingness to challenge dominant but unseen discourse, and an openness to alternative possibilities. In addition, patience, curiosity, and the ability to synthesize are also beneficial skills for conversation analysts.

Adopting a self-reflexive stance entails a second-order cybernetic orientation, which "acknowledges that 'the same self' may be different as a result of its own self-pointing" (Steier, 1991, p. 2). Challenging the dominant discourse and being open to other marginalized discourses aids the researcher in considering unseen practices. Garfinkel (1967) noted that we often repair the indexicality of talk in that we reconstruct it to make sense to us and not necessarily the participants. Paraphrasing Hare-Mustin (1994), if the researcher is "unaware of marginalized discourses, such as those associated with members of a subordinate gender, race, and class groups, these discourses remain outside" (p.22) of their considerations and analysis.

It is important to be patient as researchers must spend much time relistening to the tape and revising the transcript. It is important to be curious in order to attend to each microdetail of the interaction and consider how that element of exchange contributes to the construction and maintenance of the context. Being open to alternative possibilities through adopting a not-knowing posture (Anderson & Goolishian, 1988) is the ability to view the text with fresh eyes and not attribute motives and meanings beyond what the participants are actually presenting. As Beer states (cited in Moerman, 1988), "Purpose is a mental construct imported by the observer" (p. 115). Finally, synthesis is the ability to examine many different themes, categories, and patterns and find threads that weave these themes into a meaningful tapestry.

Bridging Research and Practice

It is likely that on first encountering CA, clinicians will view this method as too labor intensive and microdetailed to be of benefit to their clinical practice. Upon defending my dissertation, my committee raised this very concern. This was a very important question to me. Entering a doctoral program, my preference and professional history was grounded in practice and not research (Gale, Chenail, Watson, Wright, & Bell, in press). Indeed, one goal of my dissertation was to find research methods that were user-friendly to clinicians.

CA can be advantageous to practitioners. CA can help bridge research and practice in the following five ways:

1. CA provides a method to study how clinicians achieve therapeutic success. For example, in Gale's (1991) study, the therapist's procedure of frequently overlapping his

talk with the couple to get a speaker's turn was described. Overlapped talk is a collaborative phenomenon that can significantly affect a relationship (Nofsinger, 1991). The therapist timed his communication with the couple in a precise and sophisticated manner. At no time did the couple act offended by the therapist's attempted overlaps. Yet, if another therapist were to follow this strategy without attending to his or her microactions in concert with the clients' actions, it is possible that the clients could view the therapist's actions as insensitive and thus lead to a dissolving of the therapeutic relationship.

It is these types of microprocedures that help develop (or end) interactional processes. Although many therapists are "naturally" very skilled with these microactions and are seen as highly skilled communicators, there has been little discussion in our field on these micropractices (Chenail, Zellick, & Bonneau, 1992). All too often, developing clinicians learn the theory and broad brush strokes of a therapeutic model or master but find that they do not achieve the same success with their own clients (Rambo, Heath, & Chenail, 1993).

2. CA provides a method for studying if therapists do what they say that they do. This information can improve our understanding of the strategies and skills employed by leading proponents of various schools of therapy and help articulate distinctions between different models of therapy. Although various models are organized around different assumptions, CA can examine how clinicians actually perform a particular therapeutic model.

3. CA offers a teaching method for demonstrating how utterances are practical activities that both create and maintain our social selves. For many, the concepts and utility of social constructionism and narrative therapy are difficult to describe and understand. CA demonstrates how language accomplishes social identities and social order. In addition, CA can help provide an understanding of how the accomplishment of action is an interactional phenomena. Through analysis of therapeutic discourse, it can be demonstrated how social order is a co-constructed and co-maintained phenomena.

4. CA can be used by clinicians as a type of self-supervision. In a class assignment, six doctoral students transcribed and analyzed 10-minute segments of their own therapy (Gale et al., 1993). Each reported that the analysis enhanced understanding of his or her case. As a method of self-supervision, clinicians can record and transcribe short segments of their cases. Through CA of their own clinical work, practitioners can gain a better understanding of their actions as well as the actions of the clients.

5. By using CA as a self-supervising activity, clinicians can also benefit through refining and honing their own clinical skills. Carefully attending to the microprocesses occurring in therapy can heighten clinicians' sensitivity to nonverbal and paralinguistic features of talk. This sensitivity can manifest in how clinicians attend to both clients' actions and their own actions. Further, this self-reflective practice exercises the clinician's creative discursive abilities.

In summary, this type of practitioner-generated research helps clinicians inquire about and investigate their own clinical work and allows them to get to know their data in a systematic and rigorous manner. An issue for therapy and clinicians is how to get the said and the not-yet-said to come together in a creative process (Anderson & Goolishian, 1992). Generally, therapeutic conversation pass by quickly. It is recommended that clinicians take the time to slow down this talk, via listening to and transcribing segments of sessions, in order to examine the communication weave. This procedure can facilitate a mindfulness to one's rhetorical practices and to key transitional moments that occur in therapy. While learning to do CA may seem like a daunting task, it is not unlike learning to walk or ride a bicycle. Initially it is time-consuming and awkward, but with practice, one develops a sensitivity to the many procedures involved in the micro-landscape.

FUTURE DIRECTIONS

"Psychotherapy may be thought of as a process of **semiosis**—the forging of meaning in the context of collaborative discourse" (Gergen & Kaye, 1992, p. 182, bold in original). Sluzki (1992) expressed the need for further explorations of micropractices in order to "enrich our ability to specify further theory building, clinical practice, training, and research in narrative-based systemic therapy" (p. 229). The goal of this chapter is to provide a research method for exploring micropractices. The *how* presented in this chapter entails a microlevel focus on how participants manage their talk. These micro-actions coordinate (either through binding or unraveling) the broader moves of discourse, which leads to the construction of social narratives. The narrative form "requires the detail of connections to maintain its coherence" (Edwards & Potter, 1992, p. 122).

The approach outlined in this chapter has the potential to move family therapy research into a discursive domain that is accessible, practical, and meaningful to researchers and clinicians alike. This approach also invites practitioner involvement as the data is "close to the world of the clinician" (Moon, Dillon, & Sprenkle, 1991, p. 367).

Suggestions for future directions in employing CA include the following: employing CA to study the local politics of how power differentials are constructed and utilized in a therapeutic setting; using CA to examine how gender, spiritual, and cultural factors influence the therapeutic process (Wetherell & Potter, 1992); Combining CA with interpersonal recall to elicit the participants' understanding of various events (Gale, Odell, & Nagireddy, 1995); combining CA with ethnographic interviews (Moerman, 1988); inviting the participants to collaboratively reflect on the analysis of their talk; viewing the construction of the therapeutic institution itself, that is, how participants come to create the relationship/institution known as "therapy"; and Comparing various therapy models in terms of how each approach actually constructs a therapeutic reality.

APPENDIX: TRANSCRIPTION NOTATION

(.)	A pause that is noticeable but too short to measure.
(.5)	A pause timed in tenths of a second.
=	There is no discernible pause between the end of a speaker's utterance and the start of the next utterance.
:	One or more colons indicate an extension of the preceding vowel sound.
Under	Underlining indicates words that were uttered with added emphasis.
CAPITAL	Words in capital are uttered louder than the surrounding talk.
(.hhh)	Exhale of breath.
(hhh)	Inhale of breath.
( )	Material in parentheses are inaudible or there is doubt of accuracy.
(( ))	Double parentheses indicate clarifying information, for example, ((laughter)).
?	Indicates a rising inflection.
.	Indicates a stopping fall in tone.
* *	Talk between * * is quieter than surrounding talk.
> <	Talk between > < is quicker than surrounding talk.
[	The bracket between turns indicate overlapped talk and are placed by the words overlapped.

ACKNOWLEDGMENTS

Acknowledgment and appreciation is given to students in my classes and practicum who have contributed to the development and clarity of this chapter.

REFERENCES

Adler, P. A., & Adler, P. (1994). Observational techniques. In N. K. Denzin & Y. S. Lincoln (Eds.), *Handbook of qualitative research* (pp. 377–392). Thousand Oaks, CA: Sage.

Anderson, H., & Goolishian, H. (1988). Human systems as linguistic systems: Preliminary and evolving ideas about the implication for clinical theory. *Family Process, 27*(4), 371–394.

Anderson, H., & Goolishian, H. (1992). The client is the expert: A not-knowing approach to therapy. In S. McNamee & K. J. Gergen (Eds.), *Therapy as social construction* (pp. 25–39). London: Sage.

Austin, J. L. (1962). *How to do things with words.* Oxford: Clarendon Press.

Buckholdt, D. R., & Gubrium, J. F. (1979). *Caretakers: Treating emotionally disturbed children.* Beverly Hills, CA: Sage.

Buttney, R. (1990). Blame-accounts sequences in therapy: The negotiation of relational meanings. *Semiotica, 78,* 219–247.

Chenail, R. J., Zellick, S. Z, & Bonneau, M. I. (1992, October). *How to do mediation with words: Involvement strategies.* Paper presented at the Society for Professionals in Dispute Resolution Annual Conference, Pittsburgh, PA.

Cobb, S., & Rifken, J. (1991). Practice and paradox: Deconstructing neutrality in mediation. *Law and Social Inquiry, 16*(1), 35–64.

Davis, K. (1984). The process of problem (re)formulation in psychotherapy. *Sociology of Health and Illness, 8,* 44–74.

Devault, M. L. (1990). Talking and listening from women's standpoint: Feminist strategies for interviewing and analysis. *Social Problems, 37*(1), 96–116.

Edwards, D., & Potter, J. (1992). *Discursive psychology.* London: Sage.

Gale, J. E. (1991). *Conversation analysis of therapeutic discourse: The pursuit of a therapeutic agenda.* Norwood, NJ: Ablex.

Gale, J., Chenail, R., Watson, L., & Bell, J. (in press). Research and practice: A reflexive and recursive relationship. Three narratives, five voices. *Marriage and Family Review.*

Gale, J., Dotson, D., Lindsey, E., Nagireddy, C., & Wilson, R. (1993). *Conversation analysis (CA): A method for self-supervision.* Paper presented at the 51st Annual Conference of the American Association for Marriage and Family Therapy.

Gale, J., & Morris, G. H. (1991). A window into conversation analysis. *ISSPR Bulletin, 8*(1), 9–11.

Gale, J. E., & Newfield, N. (1992). A conversation analysis of a solution-focused marital therapy session. *Journal of Marital and Family Therapy, 18,* 153–165.

Gale, J., Odell, M., & Nagireddy, C. (1995). Marital therapy and self-reflexive research: Research and/as intervention. In G. H. Morris & R. J. Chenail (Eds.), Talk of the clinic (pp. 105–130). Hillsdale, NJ: Erlbaum.

Garfinkel, H. (1967). *Studies in ethnomethodology.* Englewood Cliffs, NJ: Prentice-Hall.

Gergen, K. J., & Kaye, J. (1992). Beyond narrative in the negotiation of therapeutic meaning. In S. McNamee & K. Gergen (Eds.), *Therapy as social construction* (pp. 166–185). London: Sage.

Glaser, B. G., & Strauss, A. L. (1967). *The discovery of grounded theory: Strategies for qualitative research.* Chicago: Aldine Publishing Company.

Goodwin, C., & Heritage, J. (1990). Conversation analysis. *Annual Review of Anthropology, 19,* 283–307.

Gubrium, J. F. (1988). Family responsibility and caregiving in the qualitative analysis of the Alzheimer's disease experience. *Journal of Marriage and the Family, 50,* 197–207.

Gubrium, J. F., & Holstein, J. A. (1990). *What is family?* Mountain View, CA: Mayfield.

Gubrium, J. F., & Holstein, J. A. (1993). Phenomenology, ethnomethodology, and family discourse. In P. Boss, W. Doherty, R. LaRossa, W. Schumm, & S. K. Steinmetz (Eds.), *Sourcebook of family theories and methods* (pp. 651–672). New York: Plenum Press.

Hare-Mustin, R. T. (1994). Discourses in the mirrored room: A postmodern analysis of therapy. *Family Process, 33*(1), 19–37.

Heritage, J. (1984). *Garfinkel and ethnomethodology.* Cambridge, UK: Polity Press.

Heritage, J. (1988). Explanations as accounts: A conversation analytic perspective. In C. Antaki (Ed.), *Analysing everyday explanation: A casebook of methods* (pp. 127–144). London: Sage.

Heritage, J. C., & Watson, D. R. (1979). Formulations as conversational objects. In G. Psathas (Ed.), *Everyday language: Studies in ethnomethodology* (pp. 123–162). New York: Irvington.

Holstein, J. A. (1988). Court-ordered incompetence: Conversational organization in involuntary commitment hearings. *Social Problems, 34,* 301–315.

Holstein, J. A., & Gubrium, J. F. (1994). Phenomenology, ethnomethodology, and interpretive practice. In N. K. Denzin & Y. S. Lincoln (Eds.), *Handbook of qualitative research* (pp. 262–272). Thousand Oaks, CA: Sage.

Hopper, R. (1988). Speech, for instance. The exemplar in studies of conversation. *Journal of Language and Social Psychology, 7*(1), 47–63.

Krefting, L. (1991). Rigor in qualitative research: The assessment of trustworthiness. *American Journal of Occupational Therapy, 45*(3), 214–222.

Laing, R. D. (1975). *Self and others.* Baltimore, MD: Penguin Books.

Lincoln, Y. S., & Guba, E. G. (1985). *Naturalistic inquiry.* Beverly Hills, CA: Sage.

Levinson, S. (1983). *Pragmatics.* Cambridge, UK: Cambridge University Press.

McGhee, P. (1987). From self-reports to narrative discourse: reconstructing the voice of experience in personal relationship research. In R. Burnett, P. McGhee, & D. Cheek (Eds.), *Accounting for relationships* (pp. 289–315). London: Methuen.

McNamee, S., & Gergen, K. J. (1992). *Therapy as social construction.* London: Sage.

Moerman, M. (1988). *Talking culture: Ethnography and conversation analysis.* Philadelphia: University of Pennsylvania Press.

Moon, S. M., Dillon, D. R., & Sprenkle, D. H. (1991). Family therapy and qualitative research. *Journal of Marital and Family Therapy, 16*(4), 357–373.

Nofsinger, R. E. (1991). *Everyday conversations.* Newbury Park, CA: Sage.

O'Hanlon, W. H., & Weiner-Davis, M. (1989). *In search of solutions: A new direction in psychotherapy.* New York: Norton.

Peshkin, A. (1988, October). In search of subjectivity. *Educational Researcher,* 17–22.

Pomerantz, A. (1988). Offering a candidate answer: An information-seeking strategy. *Communication Monographs, 55,* 360–373.

Pomerantz, A., & Atkinson, J. M. (1984). Ethnomethodology, conversation analysis and the study of courtroom interaction. In D. J. Muller, D. E. Blackman, & A. J. Chapman (Eds.), *Topics in psychology and law* (pp. 283–297). Chichester, UK: Wiley.

Potter, J., & Wetherell, M. (1987). *Discourse and social psychology: Beyond attitudes and behavior.* London: Sage.

Rambo, A. H., Heath, A., & Chenail, R. J. (1993). *Practicing therapy: Exercises for growing therapists.* New York: Norton.

Ratliff, D. A. (1992). *Dangling dissensus in family therapy supervision.* Paper presented at the International Communication Association Conference, Miami, FL.

Sacks, H., Schegloff, E. A., & Jefferson, G. (1974). A simplest systematics for the organization of turn-taking for conversation. *Language, 50,* 696–735.

Schegloff, E., Jefferson, G., & Sacks, H. (1977). The preference for self-correction in the organization of repair in conversation. *Language, 53,* 361–382.

Schegloff, E., & Sacks, H. (1973). Opening up closings. *Semiotica, 7,* 289–327.

Shotter, J. (1989). Social accountability and the social construction of "you." In J. Shotter & K. J. Gergen (Eds.), *Texts of identity* (pp. 133–151). London: Sage.

Sluzki, C. E. (1992). Transformations: A blueprint for narrative changes in therapy. *Family Process, 31*(3), 217–230.

Stamp, G. H. (1991). Family conversation: Description and interpretation. *Family Process, 30*(2), 251–263.

Steier, F. (1991). Introduction: Research as self-reflexivity, self-reflexivity as social process. In F. Steier (Ed.), *Research and reflexivity* (pp. 1–11). London: Sage.

Stokes, R., & Hewitt, J. P. (1976). Aligning actions. *American Sociological Review, 41*, 838–849.

Tannen, D. (1989). *Talking voices: Repetition, dialogue, and imagery in conversational discourse.* New York: Cambridge University Press.

Taylor, S. J., & Bogdan, R. (1984). *Introduction to qualitative research methods* (2nd ed.). New York: Wiley.

Turner, J. (1993). Males supervising females: The risk of gender-power blindness. *The Supervision Bulletin, VI*(2), 4, 6.

Wetherell, M., & Potter, J. (1992). *Mapping the language of racism: Discourse and the legitimation of exploitation.* New York: Columbia University Press.

White, M., & Epston, D. (1992). *Experience, contradiction, narrative & imagination.* Adelaide, South Australia: Dulwich Centre Publications.

Wilson, R. J. (1993). *Differential treatment of men and women in marriage and family therapy.* Unpublished dissertation, University of Georgia.

Critical Theory Research

6

Critical Theory Research
THE EMANCIPATORY INTEREST
IN FAMILY THERAPY

SHERRY L. REDIGER

[Anyone] who loves his dream of a community more
than the community itself becomes a destroyer of the
latter, even though . . . personal intentions may be
ever so honest and earnest and sacrificial.
—DIETRICH BONHOEFFER, *Life Together* (1954)

RECENTLY, THERE HAS been a great deal of discussion in the family therapy field about the need to expand the boundaries of our research (Hoshmand, 1989; Griffith & Griffith, 1990; Kaye, 1990; Moon, Dillon, & Sprenkle, 1990; Atkinson, Heath, & Chenail, 1991). The effort has largely been focused on postpositivist and constructivist paradigms of scientific inquiry; with the exception of feminist research, the critical theory paradigm has been significantly absent in the family therapy literature. This chapter begins to rectify that imbalance by emphasizing the importance of critical theory for family therapy theory, research, and practice. The hope is that enthusiasm for the paradigm will spread and that others, already involved with critical theory, will be encouraged to share their visions.

BACKGROUND

Family therapy is about change. One way to conceptualize change is as a movement from constricting individual and relational life experience to an experience that is free from oppressive constraints. In this conceptualization the change family therapy seeks is emancipatory. Critical theorists partner family therapists in this way. Critical theorists are interested in raising consciousness, through self-reflection and dialogue, to the level of action in the interest of emancipation and transformation. Critical theory research, as well as the practice of therapy, cannot be value-free. Critical theory research is not pursued for the sake of knowledge—it is for human liberation. Critical theory research and the practice of family therapy are about change and change is political.

Family therapists are interested in how belief systems affect the quality of clients' lives. Intergenerational family therapists explore the emotional inheritance that occurs from generation to generation within a family (Boszormenyi-Nagy & Spark, 1973; Bowen, 1978; Pincus & Dare, 1978; Framo, 1992). Therapists such as Michael White and David Epston (1990) believe that family members' lives are limited by a dominant story or belief and can become less constrained by accessing alternative stories.

Critical theorists believe that every community, regardless of size, is powerfully and pervasively directed by its belief system or ideology. Ideology is to be "understood as an allegedly disinterested knowledge which serves to conceal an interest under the guise of a rationalisation" (Ricoeur, 1981, p. 80). Often the belief system of the community is largely unconscious; the values and agendas inherent in the beliefs are not explicit. To the degree to which these values and agendas are unnamed or unchosen, the possibility of oppression exists. The goal of critical theory research is to increase consciousness and liberate the members of a community.

Historical Roots and Development

Although the field of family therapy is just beginning to explore critical theory, critical theory itself has a history that spans nearly an entire century. The development of critical theory began in the 1920s with the members of the Frankfurt Institute of Social Research, who were interested in the work of the German philosophers Georg Wilhelm Friedrich Hegel and Karl Marx (Bredo & Feinberg, 1982). Among the members of the Frankfurt Institute were Theodor Adorno, Max Horkheimer, Herbert Marcuse, and Erich Fromm. The thoughts and writings of the Frankfurt Institute provided the foundation of critical theory. The movement has since assumed various forms, including the sociology of knowledge, liberation theology, feminism, and neo-Marxism.

Feminist research developed from the foundational perspective of critical theorists. According to Avis and Turner (Chapter 7, this volume), a feminist research perspective has been developing in the family therapy field for the past 17 years. The impact of critical theory is pervasive in the feminist family therapy research perspective (Goldner, 1985; Pilalis & Anderson, 1986; Walters, Carter, Papp, & Silverstein, 1988; Goodrich, 1991, Hare-Mustin, 1992).

Jürgen Habermas

Jürgen Habermas (1970, 1971, 1974, 1989) is one of the most prolific philosophers of the present age. Habermas came to critical theory from a background in philosophy and sociology and served, early in his academic career, as an assistant to Adorno (Held, 1980). Habermas has built a prescriptive theory which attempts to bridge the gap between knowledge and practice from his critique of the Frankfurt School's critical theorists; he has relied greatly on the works of Kant, Hegel, Marx, and Freud. His basic tenet is that human beings are unnecessarily oppressed by the hidden values of ideologies and can be freed from this oppression through self-reflection and action based on the realization of alternatives. Habermas has given great consideration to the need for the practical application of critical theory in society. He states that critical theory can find its practical realization through self-reflection and self knowledge as the means of emancipation from unnecessary constraints (Sewart, 1978).

Prior to Habermas, critical theory largely remained in the theoretical realm and was criticized for its distance from the practical problems of people and society. Influenced by Habermas, critical theorists have developed a research paradigm that has done much to close the gap between theory and practice in everyday life. One of the catalysts for Habermas's work has been his rigorous opposition to positivism. Habermas's framework for his theory is his taxonomy of scientific forms. It is Habermas's desire that the divergent approaches of the social sciences might find some greater unity within this theoretical framework.

Habermas is concerned with understanding the character of human reason and rationality by systematically analyzing the historical evolution of present-day understanding of rationality. Habermas believes that "the immediate aim of critique is insight into causalities *in the past*. It is therefore retrospective insofar as its aim is to initiate self-reflection by which we become aware of, and liberated from, the historical compulsions of the past" (Bernstein, 1976, p. 216–217). It is with the objective of consciousness and liberation that Habermas explicates and critiques a historical understanding of the evolution and impact of positivism on the social sciences.

There are various forms of positivism in the social sciences. A prevalent form of positivism arose following Comte, from the members of the Vienna Circle, a group of philosophers in the 1930s, who first conceptualized the principles of logical positivism. Although positivism is not a unified paradigm of scientific inquiry, McCarthy (1978) identifies four principles that characterize a positivistic approach to scientific inquiry: (1) the scientific method can be applied uniformly in all sciences; (2) the aim of scientific inquiry is to establish laws that explain and predict; (3) theory is separate from practice, therefore scientific inquiry is "value-free"; and (4) the testability of a scientific hypothesis is the essence of its truth.

Habermas's definition of positivism is broader than the traditional use of the word as it is associated with the thought of the members of the Vienna Circle. Habermas contends that any reduction of knowledge to a single form is a type of positivism, culminating in the belief that to "disavow reflection *is* positivism" (Habermas, 1971, p. vii). By this belief, Habermas asserts that obliterating forms of rationality for a single form is, itself, irrational.

Habermas views the impact of positivism in the social sciences as a regression to pre-Kantian thought and, inspired by the methodology of Freudian psychoanalysis, believes that the method of self-reflection is the key to the return of the theory of knowledge. In *Knowledge and Human Interests*, Habermas states that positivism has so ultimately purported objectivism that a return to a Kantian self-reflection will no longer suffice; it is only through methodology's own self-reflective process that the rational project of human beings can be furthered.

It is essential to the rational enterprise of human beings that positivism be critiqued and eliminated as a valid philosophy in the social sciences. What is at stake is any form of knowledge that does not reduce to the form that is fancied by a particular group. (Thus, Habermas accuses Marxism of being the positivism of the critical sciences and hermeneutics of being the positivism of the historical sciences.) "In Kantian terms, the synthetic achievements of the knowing subject, the constitution of the objects of possible experience and of the facts with which science deals, drop from sight" (McCarthy, 1978, p. 41). Hence, Habermas's key concern with human emancipation cannot be considered valid without his critique of positivism and analysis of the devastation that positivism has wreaked on present social science practice.

In contrast to the sciences that uphold differing forms of positivism, Habermas's theory of rationality includes several forms of knowledge. His cognitive interests of the technical, the practical, and the emancipatory reflect this consideration and he delineates three types of science that serve these interests. Most significant among these types is Habermas's science of self-reflection. Habermas asserts that "if emancipation from domination is to remain a project of humanity, it is essential to counter [positivism] and to reaffirm the necessity of self-reflection for self-understanding" (Held, 1980, p. 254). Thus, Habermas holds that the method of self-reflection is the key to the healing of the social sciences and the way to progress out of the regression that has followed positivism.

Philosophical Assumptions

A clear articulation of philosophical assumptions and values is central to critical theory; therefore, a clear articulation of the assumptions guiding critical theory is an essential aspect of this chapter. Every belief and practice is embedded in a historical context of values. False consciousness arises from adopting beliefs and practices without consideration for the underlying ideology. For example, a common occurrence in the practice of family therapy is for a therapist to read a book or attend a workshop that describes or demonstrates a new clinical technique. The therapist feels attracted to the technique or the perceived results of that technique and decides to try it out. Most often the therapist will not even be aware that the clinical technique is rooted in a particular belief system and that the belief system reflects particular values. The therapist may not have consciously articulated his or her *own* values. The therapist is often unaware that the clinical intervention he or she is trying out will perpetuate particular values—and those values that are perpetuated may be counter to the values the therapist holds. The clients' values are essential here as well. How well has the therapist articulated his or her own values? How congruent are the values that underlie his or her clinical models? What are the values of his or her clients? How clearly have family therapists articulated personal values and the values of their clinical interventions to clients so that the clients can more freely choose whether or not to work with the therapist?

A paradigm of scientific inquiry can be defined by its ontological, epistemological, and methodological beliefs (Guba, 1990). The questions of epistemology and ontology are inextricable from each other. Ontology asks the question, "What is the nature of reality and human beings?" Epistemology asks, "What is the nature of knowing?" It is not possible to state a belief about reality and being human without implying a way of knowing. It is also not possible to say something about knowing without suggesting something about reality and being human. Further, to define who we *are* as human beings and how we *know* as human beings points toward how we will *act* to gain knowledge—our methodology.

Critical theory, as a research paradigm, holds a critical realist ontology. In this ontology, reality exists apart from the observer, but no matter how great our knowledge base, that reality can never be fully known. We are limited as human beings and are not capable of capturing the totality of absolute reality. This ontological perspective differs from both the positivist ontology that science can and will eventually fully know reality, and from the constructivist ontology that reality does not exist apart from the observer.

Epistemologically, the critical theory research paradigm holds that humans interact with what they know and seek to know. The values of the inquirer are inextricable from the process of the knowing event. The critical theorist does not purport a stance of neutrality; rather, values are made explicit and are central to action. Although the epistemological position of the critical theorist is similar to constructivist epistemology, it is radically different from the positivist epistemology that the observor can stand completely apart from what is being observed.

Critical theory methodology is founded primarily on self-reflection and dialogue that will release people from oppression resulting from unnamed or unchosen values and beliefs (false consciousness). Action taken based on new knowledge is for the purpose of individual, relational, and societal transformation. These concepts and methods will be discussed further in this chapter.

According to critical theorists, we come to know what we know in dialogue with our historical and contextual experience and values (Gadamer, 1960/1975, 1976/1981). We are not able to apprehend knowledge apart from our values:

> If values *do* enter into every inquiry, then the question immediately arises as to what values and whose values shall govern. If the findings of studies can vary depending on the values chosen, then the choice of a *particular* value system tends to empower and enfranchise certain persons while disempowering and disenfranchising others. Inquiry thereby becomes a *political act*. (Guba, 1990, p. 24)

In any research, one essential question is, "Who is the research *for?*" (Reason, 1988). In 1980, a study was published by a researcher who had interviewed U.S. widows in an attempt to understand their experience (Lopata, 1980). The researcher and her research team were astonished to find that the widows who participated in the study expected to be helped in some way by the researchers. It is often the case that research is not intended for those who provide the researcher with information.

Fortunately, the researchers involved with the widows were able to hear the needs expressed and became actively involved in changing the conditions of these widows. This action is consistent with the heart of critical theory research. Critical research is for people and intends to change the conditions of the people who collaborate in the research project as well as effect change in the larger society. The action that concluded the American widows study would be the premise of a study conducted from within a critical theory research paradigm.

METHODOLOGY

Unlike traditional scientific research, critical theory inquiry has not established an exclusive, systematic methodological approach. Critical theory research is a research perspective that transcends any one methodological approach. Several creative inquiry models have been developed based on the principles of critical theory inquiry rather than formal analysis. It would be a tremendous distortion of critical inquiry for one method to be upheld as the "true" critical method. There are many ways to approach a research question critically and this chapter will only suggest one path and point toward others that might be taken.

Dialogue and Self-Reflection

Two essential dimensions of critical method are dialogue and self-reflection. "Critical theory pursues self-reflection out of an interest in self-emancipation" (McCarthy, 1978). Self-reflection is a position of understanding that knowledge is subjective and, therefore, subject to criticism. Self-reflection can lead to new awareness and an unmasking of ideology that "enables the subject of knowledge and action to project new possibilities of knowing and acting that transcend those prescribed by tradition" (Ingram, 1990, p. 110).

In 1970, Paulo Freire introduced dialogue as a method not only of inquiry but of *intervention.* It is with the intention of intervention toward liberation that dialogue becomes a method of critical research. In family therapy, the practice of dialogue as intervention is found in the contextual therapy literature (Boszormenyi-Nagy & Spark, 1973; Boszormenyi-Nagy & Krasner, 1986; Boszormenyi-Nagy, 1987) as conceived by the German philosopher Martin Buber (1958). Genuine dialogue becomes possible when individuals can maintain their own existential position ("side" or "self") while simultaneously considering the existential position ("side" or "self") of the other. Genuine dialogue exists when the other reciprocates this relational position.

In critical theory, Habermas describes the "ideal speech situation" as the normative grounding for all speech acts. It is the relational situation of two equals, being unoppressed and free, who are engaged in the mutual interest of truth. Both genuine dialogue and the ideal speech situation are anticipatory ideals that occur only in moments, but it is in naming the ideal that critique of the present is possible. "Thus the idea of truth points ultimately to a form of interaction that is free from all distorting influences. The 'good and true life' that is the goal of critical theory is inherent in the notion of truth; it is anticipated in every act of speech" (McCarthy, 1978, p. 308).

Illustration of Method

In the following paragraphs, I delineate eight aspects of critical methodology. These are not all-inclusive or definitive but do represent the principles of critical research. Furthermore, I have chosen to illustrate critical theory research methodology with a fictitious account of research with fathers. The decision to illustrate critical methodology with fathers may anger some who are rightly concerned about the experience of those who are oppressed by race, ethnicity, gender, sexual preference, economics, and so on. The intent is not to eclipse the imperative need for critical research with the overtly oppressed but to heighten awareness of the reality that *all* individuals, families, and groups experience oppression whether or not it is conscious. Critical research is relevant to all practices of family therapy.

A Critical Theory Fathering Study

I. Identifying Oppression

Kim and Joel are family therapists at a community mental health agency. Together, they have been seeing the Arden family each week for the past month. Dave and Cathy Arden sought therapy because of the increasing tension and stress in their marriage now that they are expecting their third child. In the first session Cathy was very tearful and described her joy at the prospect of another child and, at the same time, her anger and resentment toward Dave who she claimed was "no help at all" with the children. Dave became increasingly agitated as he listened to Cathy. Dave agreed that Cathy was primarily responsible for the children even though they both worked full-time outside of the home. His job required putting in more than 60 hours each week in order to advance in the company. Dave's face brightened as he talked about their children and the baby who would be born in several months. He then expressed sadness and regret that he was missing so much of being a part of his children's lives.

During the next several sessions Dave continued to explore his feelings of sadness, anger, and confusion about the bind created by his defined roles as husband, father, and employee. He felt that each role conflicted with the interests of the others and, therefore, he was unable to do well in any. Dave felt trapped—unable to meet his own needs or anyone else's. According to Dave, there was no alternative except to keep trying to hold his life and family together as he had been all along.

Identifying oppression through dialogue is an essential aspect of critical research. Dave and Cathy are unhappy and yet neither believes there are options to change their situation. In critical theory language, the perception of nonalternative arises from false consciousness—a nonawareness or distortion of the values that influence and affect daily life. Dave's despair is a direct result of his position of being alienated from his own values and unaware of the ideology underlying his lived world experience.

II. Meeting

Kim and Joel became increasingly aware that Dave and his family were experiencing oppression based on societal values and role definitions. Kim and Joel were interested in the experiences of oppression in working fathers and asked Dave if he would like to explore his situation with others. They explained that it might be helpful to understand what historical and present events contribute to the conditions fathers are experiencing; in conversation with other fathers, options for changing their situation might emerge.

Dave was cautious but intrigued. He said he knew of at least one other father in his company who seemed unhappy about having no time with his children. Together, Kim, Joel, and Dave decided to develop flyers that could be posted at several locations in the community to advertise a group for fathers who felt caught between the conflicting needs of family and work.

The evening of the first session came and nine men—as well as Kim, Joel, and Dave— were in attendance. One of the men was a coworker whom Dave had specifically invited. Everyone seemed self-conscious and a little embarrassed to be there until Kim and Joel opened the meeting with introductions and a few jokes.

Kim and Joel talked about their interest in understanding the experience of fathers and acting on alternatives that would be less constricting and more liberating for fathers. Joel shared his own experience of trying to balance his commitments to work and his family. Dave talked about the frustrations and confusion that had preceded the beginning of therapy. Other men chimed in and the group began to form through shared and diverse experience.

Kim, Joel, Dave, and the other group members are participating in creating a cooperative inquiry group (Reason & Rowan, 1981; Reason, 1988) "in which the subject is also co-researcher, being actively and openly involved on the inquiry side of the research, as well as on the action side" (Heron, 1981, p. 20). Likewise, the researcher "will also be co-subject, participating fully in the action and experience to be researched" (Heron, 1981, p. 20).

The term "meeting" is not intended here in the sense of gathering together but rather is meant as authentic meeting in which the possibility of being mutually understood and experienced exists through self-reflection and dialogue. It is through this type of internal and interpersonal relationship that new awareness and alternatives are created.

III. Commitment to Know

The group members had a lot of ideas about how to use their time together. Ten of the group participants decided to commit to each other and to understanding their experience. Two men decided not to return to the group. In the next two meetings the members talked about their common and diverse experiences of being a father. Kim and Joel initiated conversation about the importance of recording their individual and group experience and the other members agreed. Kim suggested that each member keep a journal to record individual reflections. Another member offered to videotape the meetings so that the group could refer back to the history of the group experience. These qualitative data collection methods enable the inquiry group to capture essential aspects of their experience and increase awareness.

There are many qualitative data-gathering methods such as journals, interviews, and field notes that fit critical research well. (See Lincoln & Guba, 1985; Miles & Huberman, 1994; Patton, 1990; Strauss & Corbin, 1990, for an in-depth description of qualitative research methods.) Critical research decisions about which tools to use in gathering and analyzing data must be determined mutually and collaboratively based on the needs of the researcher–participants and the participant–researchers.

Developing mutual relational commitment is important for establishing an experience in which self-reflection and dialogue are possible. Both self-reflection and dialogue require risk and vulnerability and a trustworthy relational context is essential. When researchers are also participants, as they are in critical inquiry, there is significant opportunity to participate in creating a trustworthy context by genuinely revealing personal vulnerabilities. The other research participants are not asked to risk themselves in any way that the researchers are not also risking.

Unlike traditional science, critical research is invested in the anomaly—in understanding experience that is unusual or different. The ways in which the group members' experiences are divergent will add richly to the emerging consciousness of each individual in much the same way as shared experiences will.

In the fathering study it might be helpful, for instance, to interview the two men who decided not to return to the group. Their experiences are essential to understanding the experience of oppression by fathers and, as much as possible, should not be eliminated or ignored because they did not participate in the same way that those who chose to continue in the group participated. One option would be to invite each man to a personal interview designed to understand his experience as a father as well as his decision not to continue in the group.

IV. Understanding Self and Other

Each member of the group spent time throughout the week reflecting and writing in a journal. These reflections became an important part of the meetings and provided impetus for dialogical interactions and deeper experiences of self-reflection. There often was not enough time for all the men to share in depth during a single session. After several weeks, a member suggested that each person have a partner to meet with once or twice a month to talk specifically about what each was learning through the journal writing.

As individual understanding of personal experience increased among the group members, a desire to know other perspectives developed. One of the members had a friend who was a full-time, at-home father. This father was invited to come to a group meeting to share his experiences and perspective. In another meeting, a historian from a nearby university was invited to speak to the group about the industrial revolution. A lively discussion about the impact of technology and Western values on the family followed his lecture.

Comstock (1982) specifically addresses the importance of developing educational experiences that will increase consciousness. Education involves creating opportunities to understand alternative perspectives as well as historical perspectives and influences

Freire's concept of "problematizing" is also useful. "In problematizing, the knowledge and theory of the educator is brought together through dialogue with the specific cultural experience of the educatee. The interaction gives rise to a particular way of presenting the situation. It is shown as a puzzle to be solved, a problem requiring and suggesting action" (Southgate & Randall, 1981, p. 351).

In the fathering study, Kim and Joel could utilize problematizing by sharing their perceptions of the experience of fathers in the work environment by posing or sculpting the group members. For instance, Kim and Joel could place four or five of the men in close proximity, posed at a task, and facing away from each other. While remaining in sculpt, Kim and Joel could then ask the men about their experience. Following this, the other group members could talk about their experience of observing the sculpt. From the issues that emerge from the guided sculpture, the group members have an opportunity to understand their own experience with increased consciousness. With new understanding, the opportunities for taking liberating action increase.

V. Increased Consciousness

Kim and Joel were interested in heightening awareness of the group experience. In the initial sessions, they identified their interest clearly to the other members and asked to read the journals and review the videotapes of previous meetings. The other group members agreed that it was appropriate for Kim and Joel to hold the experiences of the group together in this way.

Through a constant comparative method of qualitative analysis (Glaser & Strauss, 1967; Patton, 1990; Strauss & Corbin, 1990), Kim and Joel interpreted the experiences of the inquiry group. They invited any member who wished to be a part of the analysis and interpretation to learn the process of analysis and interpretation with them. Many times over the course of the group meetings, Kim and Joel talked with all group members about the interpretations they made from the analysis of these collections. The interpretations were modified and refined by the responses of the group members so that the interpretations were as accurate as possible.

As the group met over the course of several months, the members began to notice themselves and others differently. Common themes began to emerge from their dialogue that were reflected in the interpretations Kim and Joel were making. These themes cast light on their experience as secondary parents:

- After the birth of a child, no paternity leave was available in any of the companies in which the men worked.
- When both parents were present, the children's physicians and teachers made almost exclusive address to mothers and little eye contact or address to fathers.
- There were almost no diaper-changing tables in public rest rooms for men.
- The language used by others—and often the men themselves—disempowered fathers as parents. For example, the men began to notice how often their care of the children was referred to as "babysitting."
- Alienation of fathers from family life had resulted from the industrial revolution.
- The men felt "owned" by their employers. Most of the group members worked in environments in which it was implicitly or explicitly assumed that the employee would work 10–30 hours over the normal 40-hour workweek in order to advance in the company.
- Isolation-perpetuated oppression. The men identified the cultural pressures to present themselves as competent and independent in order to be seen as successful. This expectation alienated men from each other and from their own internal experiences.

Qualitative research concepts and methods such as triangulation, analytical induction, and constant comparative analysis can be used to analyze data gathered in critical theory research. Although it is often not possible for all members of a critical research experience to equally gather, analyze, and interpret the data, it is essential that all members have access to the process and input into the interpretation. "To understand an autonomous or conventional culture, we need to participate in it through dialogue and interaction with those who exemplify it. Any cultural explanation needs to be checked with those within the culture" (Reason & Rowan, 1981, p. 24).

Quantitative techniques are also utilized by some critical researchers. Surveys are an example of data collection methods that appear in critical theory research studies. Using quantitative techniques is controversial among critical theory researchers. Critical theorists are committed to the eradication of false consciousness and believe that the assumptions that underlie a tool or technique will inextricably influence the aim and impact of their use. Many critical theorists find the assumptions of quantitative methods antithetical to the emancipatory aim of critical theory research.

VI. Action

As each member of the group became increasingly conscious of oppression, alternatives were created and action based on these alternatives became possible. The group members consciously developed a new language by replacing phrases such as "babysitting the kids" with "taking care of the kids."

The men talked with their wives about the ways in which they abdicated parenting to their wives because of their feelings of inadequacy and fear of failure. Some of the men decided to speak directly to their children's teachers and physicians and state clearly that they are interested and involved in their children's lives.

Dave and his coworker began meeting for breakfast on the first morning of the month and invited several other men from the company to join them. Although the meetings have not yet changed company values and policies, the men are breaking out of their isolated experiences and are finding ways to live more freely in their work life.

Action is the heart of critical inquiry. The dynamic interplay of self-reflection and dialogue creates a tension that can only be satisfied through action that leads to emancipation—greater freedom from unnecessary oppression and domination. The members of this research group took action at three levels: individual, family, and community. This multileveled action will not be immediately realized in every critical inquiry, but it is important in every inquiry to build paths toward emancipation at each level.

VII. The Responsibility to Share Knowledge

The group members were energized by their new awareness and experience of liberation. Several members felt a necessity to share with others what they had experienced, learned, and acted on together. One member contacted the city newspaper and invited a journalist to meet with the group. Two other members decided to write an article together for a leading business publication. Kim and Joel talked about the professional journals in the family therapy field and the possible benefits of sharing their knowledge and experience through writing an article that would be coauthored by everyone in the group.

Critical research is not undertaken for the sake of knowledge but for the sake of people. The importance of publication in this model is not for self-advancement, as in quantitatively and hierarchically driven institutions, nor is it for the incremental accumulation of knowledge toward some greater truth. The responsibility of publishing is to share so that others might also be liberated. Therefore, publication in professional journals is important, but it is *not* enough. Professional journals are generally accessible only to the privileged. Critical research must be accessible to a greater audience. Publication in widely utilized magazines and newspapers, as well as television, video, and radio productions, is a valuable form of communicating critical experience.

VIII. Self-Sustaining Action

The members of the group began to expand their interest to other types of oppression in their day-to-day lives. Some of the group members became curious about the experiences of their wives and children. The group members challenged each other to spend individual time with each of their children and spouse to ask about their experiences in relationship to them.

John talked about an experience in which he began to tell some of his friends a derogatory joke about gay men and stopped himself halfway through the telling. John said he realized that he was creating and perpetuating oppression on an entire group of people about whom he knew little or nothing. Instead of finishing the joke, John told his friends what he had been discovering about himself and the unnecessary constraints people put on each other and themselves.

As the members of the inquiry group began to claim their own experiences of oppression, they began to see themselves, their relationships, their community—essentially, their world—differently. These men could now acknowledge and understand their own experience of oppression. Further, as a result of participating in this experience, they became much more aware of other types of oppression around them—even ways in which they were oppressive to others. Action taken toward others who are oppressed by those who have been oppressed is an essential aspect of critical research cycling. Because critical research is for people and action is taken for liberation, critical inquiry continues beyond finite research parameters.

Other Methods

It is important to the integrity of the critical research paradigm that one method not exemplify critical research. There are many other examples of critical research methodology based on the principles of critical theory. A few of these are Freire's (1970) dialogue, coding, and problematizing; Reason and Rowan's (1981) cooperative inquiry groups; and Comstock's (1982) seven steps of critical research methodology. A foundational resource, though not a methodology, is Sullivan's (1984) conceptualization of critical interpretation.

Freire's critical, liberationist method is composed of three essential aspects: (1) dialogue, (2) problematizing, and (3) coding (Randall & Southgate, 1981). Dialogue and problematizing have been described previously. Coding is the the ordering and presentation of issues that leads to increased consciousness and action among those being oppressed. An additional resource for the dialogical method is *Pedagogy of Hope: Reliving Pedagogy of the Oppressed* (Freire, 1994).

In the cooperative inquiry groups developed by Reason and Rowan (1981), the initiating researchers and participants become, together, coresearchers and coparticipants. The definitions and meanings of constraints are developed collaboratively. Researchers and participants (although the distinction becomes greatly diminished) together take action toward changing the conditions of oppression.

Comstock (1982) outlined seven steps in his critical method. In the first step, proactive groups willing to initiate emancipatory action based on research findings are identified. Next, through dialogue with participants, a conceptual framework is developed that is consistent with the understanding participants have of their current condition. Third, the history that led to the oppressive condition and the social structures that continue to oppress are studied. Fourth, the interrelatedness of conditions resulting from history, the interpretation of these conditions, and the behavior of participants based on these interpretations is described. Fifth, the contradictions inherent in action based on false consciousness are clarified. In the sixth step an educational program is implemented to raise the consciousness of participants. Finally, emancipatory action is taken to change the conditions of the participants' lives.

DISCUSSION

Limitations of Critical Methodology

Concerns have been raised about critical theory. One concern is that critical theory is, or could become, itself an oppressive ideology that purports hidden values (Bernstein, 1976; Bredo & Feinberg, 1982). Habermas believes that the ideal of the "ideal speech situation" (a genuine dialogue in which people can communicate without distortion) is the safeguard against critical theory becoming an oppressive ideology. The ideal speech situation is not an actuality, according to Habermas, but a condition that we can anticipate and strive toward in our relationships. Habermas (1980) believes that this ideal serves as a guarantee that those who attempt to approximate it will be able to uncover falseness in their factual agreements.

Another difficulty is that dialogue is a relational ideal and not a systematic method. Southgate and Randall (1981) point out that

> Sometimes dialogue is impossible because the two individuals or groups have differing interests—one desires to subjugate or control the other. Sometimes dialogue is possible, easy, creative, and fun with the exchanges flowing easily. In between these extremes lie a mass of complicated situations where dialogue is more or less difficult or complicated. . . . " (p. 61)

Critical theory research does not produce quantifications about human beings and their relationships and, therefore, may not be useful to societal institutions whose existence depends on such quantifications. Critical theory research chooses to acknowledge and embrace human limitations and freedom; therefore, critical research is not useful in "legitimizing" family therapy to third-party interests as long as such institutions base their interests on objectifications.

The overt value ladenness of critical theory research will always be offensive to some; however, values are inherent in all knowledge and all actions, though most often hidden or denied. Critical theory attempts to make these values explicit and, in doing so, less oppressive to people.

Validity

"Traditional notions of validity are all about *methods* and not much about *people*" (Reason & Rowan, 1981, p. 240); therefore, the criteria for validity in traditional research are inadequate for establishing validity in critical research. According to Reason and Rowan, "the primary strength of new paradigm research, its fundamental claim to being a valid process, lies in its emphasis on personal encounter with experience and encounter with persons" (p. 242).

Research cycling is an important feature of critical inquiry and it is a feature that speaks to the well foundedness of the inquiry process (Comstock, 1982; Heron, 1988; Reason & Rowan, 1981). The cycling process is a dynamic and continuing interplay between reflection and experience. In critical research, the interpretations and findings are subjected to the expertise of those whose experience they attempt to illuminate. Analysis is not done in isolation but in community with those whose voices are represented. This process requires the inquirers to check and recheck their impressions, to interview multiple times, and to ask those they have interviewed whether their interpretations are accurate to the interviewee's experience. (See Heron, 1988, for a complete discussion of research cycling and validity.)

Any articulation of findings or interpretations in critical research is most accurately viewed as a snapshot of a continuing, changing process. Articulations of findings are made at a point in the research cycle in which there is enough stability in the findings and when coherence exists. Coherence has been described by Heron (1988) as the ability of three constructs to mutually shape each other until their meanings are coherent with each other. These constructs are (1) "the developing research statements"; (2) "the personal, tacit, experiential meaning-making of the inquirers"; and (3) "the space and time meaning-making of the inquirers" (Heron, 1988, p. 41). The coherence criterion is completed when action is taken based on new knowledge.

Two additional aspects of the criterion of coherence are that "the research conclusions . . . be coherent with each other: they are consistent with each other, interdependent and mutually illuminating" and that "the inquirers are in agreement about these conclusions" (Heron, 1988, p. 41). It is important to bear in mind, when considering the well-foundedness of this kind of critical theory research, that the inquirers are both the initial researchers and the people whose experiences the initial researchers are interested in.

Finally, research findings are not static "truths" but are subject to continued criticism. Through cycles of critical analysis, education, and action, the aim is for research statements, through mutual accountability, to be meaningful and liberating in a personal and collaborative sense.

Skills

Many qualities are helpful for the critical inquirer in creating valid critical inquiry. Two qualities are imperative. First, the clinician–researcher must have a strong capacity for self-reflection in identifying and making explicit the personal values and beliefs that are held. Second, the clinician–researcher must be committed to nonhierarchical relationships and must develop methods of accountability to ensure that authentic meeting and dialogue are a possibility. Without these qualities, cultural invasion becomes inherent in the research process (Freire, 1976).

> Cultural invasion is the imposition of the values, belief systems, ideology, cultural norms and practices of an imperialist culture on those it has colonized and oppressed. Its basis is unequal relationship. Its object is social, economic, and political control. The opposite process, dialogue, is based on equality in relationship (which has to have a real, material base), mutual respect, and understanding. (Reason & Rowan, 1981, p. 53)

Bridging Research and Practice

The impact of critical theory on research, education, and practice has been significant in fields such as sociology and education. The impact has been less in the family therapy field, but it is growing. An important indication of the growing influence of critical theory is that marriage and family therapy doctoral programs are becoming more open to the critical theory research paradigm and several critical theory dissertations have been completed (Rediger, 1992; Rafuls, 1994).

The feminist family therapy perspective has had a significant impact on research, theory, and practice in the field of marriage and family therapy and is the most visible representative of critical theory research in the field (Avis & Turner, Chapter 7, this volume). Feminist research began to appear in family therapy journals in the mid-1980s and publications have continued to increase, though slowly, into the present decade. The *Journal of Feminist Family Therapy* was established in order to facilitate the influence of feminist researchers and practitioners on the marriage and family therapy field.

The American Association for Marriage and Family Therapy recently recognized the critical theory research paradigm by awarding its 1993 Research and Education Foundation Grant to Silvia Rafuls (1994) for her study, *Qualitative Resource Based Consultation: Resource-Generative Inquiry and Reflective Dialogue with Four Latin American Families and Their Therapists*. Rafuls's study is an excellent example of the collaborative, dialogical, and cyclical aspects of critical theory research.

In recent years, family therapy clinical practice has been affected directly by critical theory philosophy. Just Therapy is a clinical model of family therapy developed by The Family Centre in Wellington, New Zealand (Waldegrave, 1990; Tamasese & Waldegrave, 1993). This therapy model is interested in issues of justice and in creating new meaning that will bring about liberating change in individual lives. Just Therapy has developed from three founding principles: spirituality, justice, and simplicity. Its aim is overtly political.

Another clinical family therapy model that is based on the principles of critical theory is Oppression Sensitive Family Therapy (Early, Nazario, & Steier, 1994). This model is being developed at The Gainesville Family Institute in Gainesville, Florida. This model claims that therapy is never neutral and that it is always cross-cultural and political. Diversity is embraced and the aim of collaboration between the client and therapist is empowerment.

The Need for Critical Theory in Family Therapy

Why should marriage and family therapists participate in research, theory, and practice from within a critical theory paradigm? Our clients, as well as ourselves, are oppressed by unnecessary constraints and our work involves unraveling and challenging those constraints in an effort to find alternatives that clients may experience as liberating. Many of our current clinical theories and models are developed from assumptions that clients are constrained by unnecessary beliefs, structures, or conditions. The aim of therapy has been to develop alternative beliefs and relational patterns with which the clients are able to live more freely. This general description of the aim of some family therapies complements the aim of critical theory.

As Griffith and Griffith (1990) have so eloquently stated, "Ethically, we must take responsibility for the choices we make that invite the construction of different kinds of realities. When we select a particular position of observation and a particular method for observing, we are also making a choice to train ourselves in a particular style of 'readiness-to-see' " (p. 13). As researchers we are accountable for the consequences of the way we see ourselves, others, and the interest of our inquiry. A critical inquirer, theorist, and practitioner is committed to effecting change through personal self-reflection and action based on the realization of alternatives. From this paradigm, commitment is made to seeing others as history creating and able to effect liberating change in themselves and in society.

Schwartz and Breunlin (1983) challenge family therapy researchers to make research more accessible to practitioners. They contend that family therapy needs to broaden its research methods to excite the practitioner into research. Schwartz and Breunlin also ask that the researcher that exists already within the practitioner be affirmed. Critical inquiry provides a framework in which this is possible. In the critical theory research paradigm, all research is intervention and intervention is research. The act of engaging in this kind of inquiry is the act of change.

Critical theory research embraces values as inextricable from all beliefs and acts. Tomm (1983) raises the concern that science is not regulated by morals and ethics. The ideal of the critical theory research paradigm builds in a self-reflective, self-critical conscience that continually asks: "What are the assumptions and values underlying this action or belief?" "What are the consequences of these assumptions and values?" It is in the openness of this type of interaction and "truth-seeking" that we will have greater opportunity to experience ourselves and each other with greater clarity, depth, and liberation.

FUTURE DIRECTIONS

It is important to question why the field of marriage and family therapy is largely devoid of critical theory influence. Perhaps as the family therapy field strengthens in identity, the members of the profession will continue to risk venturing into new paradigms of research. The models, theories, and research practices of marriage and family therapy are in serious need of self-examination and critique. The field is in great danger of listening to feminist critiques and critical theorists with half an ear, ready to codify and categorize its message and render it inapplicable.

One of the greatest deterrents to the acceptance of critical theory in marriage and family therapy lies in the unexamined models, theories, and educational philosophies in the field. Family therapy would benefit from unpacking the hidden values and ideologies in its theories and models. To what aims and purposes do these models aspire? How can therapists utilize such models without an understanding of the values of human nature and therapy that they perpetuate? According to Held (1980), Habermas's

> ultimate objective [is] to provide a coherent framework within which a large number of apparently competing approaches to the social sciences can be integrated. . . . It is also his hope that the framework will provide a basis for bringing together the interests and findings of the ever more fragmented, individual disciplines within the social sciences. (pp. 258–259)

Family therapy lacks specific theories and often practices from models under the grand umbrella of systems theory. It is essential to note that, with few exceptions, an acceptable practice within the field has been to develop models and techniques without articulating the values and assumptions about human nature and the nature of knowledge they perpetuate. It also remains true that family therapy education lacks a rigorous format for challenging professionals to articulate personal values and assumptions and for developing congruence in research and practice based on these beliefs.

Although it is problematic that the majority of writers representing the different schools of family therapy do not clearly articulate philosophical and epistemological assumptions, the confusion is heightened by the diverse purposes that the clinical models and research paradigms appear to function under. It is premature to specify in what ways family therapy can benefit by a greater appreciation of critical theory and Habermas's cognitive interests (although such an enterprise will surely prove useful). The immediate need in the family therapy field is to unravel the theoretical groundings from which come the clinical models and interventions that we utilize. Family therapy cannot excuse itself as being a young field. It is long past time that we challenge our practice with rigorous philosophical thinking. It is long past time that we refuse to unthinkingly accept and practice from ignorance.

To that end, it is important to reemphasize the great need for the field of family therapy to take stock of its clinical models, theories, and research practices. The values and assumptions that undergird these models must be articulated in such a way that therapists can responsibly utilize or reject each. Theoretical frameworks and taxonomies, such as those proposed by Habermas, will be essential to family therapy's struggle to articulate a position in the world of human relationships. Prior to such an enterprise, it will be necessary for the educational structure in the family therapy field to be expanded to include a rigorous format for challenging students to explicate their values and assumptions about human nature and about therapy in order that our field might continue with integrity—furthering the interests of human life rather than perpetuating oppression through false consciousness.

Critical family therapy inquiry has a great deal of promise for being personally, relationally, and socially meaningful. To end, I would like to borrow from Grumet (1990), who borrows from Merleau-Ponty (1962), who quotes St. Exupéry: "Your abode is your act itself. Your act is you. . . . You give yourself in exchange. . . . Your significance shows itself, effulgent. It is your hatred, your love, your steadfastness, your ingenuity. . . . [Human beings are] but a network of relationships, and these alone matter." Such is the commitment of the critical inquirer.

ACKNOWLEDGMENTS

The author would like to thank Martha Marquez, PhD, for introductions to Oppression Sensitive Family Therapy and Ingrid Sato, NCACII, CADAC for providing literature on Just Therapy.

REFERENCES

Atkinson, B., Heath, A., & Chenail, R. J. (1991). Qualitative research and the legitimization of knowledge. *Journal of Marital and Family Therapy, 17*(2), 161–166.

Bernstein, R. (1976). *The restructuring of social and political theory.* Pennsylvania: University of Pennsylvania Press.

Bonhoeffer, D. (1954). *Life together.* New York: Harper & Row.

Boszormenyi-Nagy, I. (1987). *Foundations of contextual therapy: Collected papers of Ivan Boszormenyi-Nagy, M.D.* New York: Brunner/Mazel.

Boszormenyi-Nagy, I., & Krasner, B. (1986). *Between give and take: A clinical guide to contextual therapy.* New York: Brunner/Mazel.

Boszormenyi-Nagy, I., & Spark, G. (1973). *Invisible loyalties: Reciprocity in intergenerational family therapy.* New York: Harper & Row.

Bowen, M. (1978). *Family therapy in clinical practice.* Northvale, NJ: Aronson.

Bredo, E., & Feinberg, W. (Ed.). (1982). *Knowledge and values in social and educational research.* Philadelphia: Temple University Press.

Buber, M. (1958). *I and thou* (2nd ed., R. G. Smith, Trans.). New York: Scribner's.

Comstock, D. (1982). A method for critical research. In E. Bredo & W. Feinberg (Eds.), *Knowledge and values in social and educational research.* Philadelphia: Temple University Press.

Early, G., Nazario, A., & Steier, H. (1994, April). *Oppression sensitive family therapy: A health affirmative model.* Workshop presented at the American Orthopsychiatry Conference, Washington, DC.

Framo, J. (1992). *Family-of-origin therapy: An intergenerational approach.* New York: Brunner/Mazel.

Freire, P. (1970). *Pedagogy of the oppressed.* New York: Herder & Herder.

Freire, P. (1976). *Education: The practice of freedom.* London: Writers and Readers Publishing Cooperative.

Freire, P. (1994). *Pedagogy of hope: Reliving pedagogy of the oppressed.* New York: Continuum.

Gadamer, H. (1975). *Truth and method.* New York: Sheed & Ward. (Original work published 1960)

Gadamer, H. (1981). *Reason in the age of science* (F. G. Lawrence, Trans.). Cambridge, MA: MIT Press. (Original work published 1976)

Glaser, B., & Strauss, A. (1967). *The discovery of grounded theory: Strategies for qualitative research.* Hawthorn, NY: Aldine.

Goldner, V. (1985). Feminism and family therapy. *Family Process, 24,* 31–47.

Goodrich, T. J. (Ed.). (1991). *Women and power: Perspectives for family therapy.* New York: Norton.

Griffith, M., & Griffith, J. (1990). Can family therapy research have a human face? *Dulwich Centre Newsletter, 2,* 11–20.

Grumet, M. (1990). Show and tell: A response to the value issue in alternative paradigms for inquiry. In E. Guba (Ed.), *Paradigm dialog.* Newbury Park, CA: Sage.

Guba, E. (Ed.). (1990). *Paradigm dialog.* Newbury Park, CA: Sage.

Habermas, J. (1970). *Toward a rational society.* Boston: Beacon Press.

Habermas, J. (1971). *Knowledge and human interests.* Boston: Beacon Press.

Habermas, J. (1974). *Theory and practice.* Boston: Beacon Press.

Habermas, J. (1989). *On the logic of the social sciences.* Cambridge, MA: MIT Press.

Hare-Mustin, R. (1992, November). *On the need for second order change in family therapy research.* Plenary address presented at the Research/Clinical Conference of the American Family Therapy Academy, Captiva Island, FL.

Held, D. (1980). *Introduction to Critical Theory: Horkheimer to Habermas.* California: University of California Press.

Heron, J. (1981). Philosophical basis for a new paradigm. In P. Reason & J. Rowan (Eds.), *Human inquiry in action: A sourcebook of new paradigm research.* New York: Wiley.

Heron, J. (1988). Validity criterion in co-operative inquiry. In P. Reason (Ed.), *Human inquiry in action: Developments in new paradigm research.* Beverly Hills, CA: Sage.

Hoshmand, L. L. S. T. (1989). Alternative research paradigms: A review and teaching proposal. *The Counseling Psychologist, 17*(1), 3–79.

Ingram, D. (1990). *Critical theory and philosophy.* New York: Paragon House.

Kaye, J. (1990). Toward meaningful research in psychotherapy. *Dulwich Centre Newsletter, 2,* 27–50.

Lincoln, Y., & Guba, E. (1985). *Naturalistic inquiry.* New York: Sage.

Lopata, H. (1980). Interviewing American widows. In W. Shaffir (Ed.), *Fieldwork experience: Qualitative approaches to social science research.* New York: St. Martin's Press.

McCarthy, T. (1978). *The critical theory of Jürgen Habermas.* Cambridge, MA: MIT Press.

Merleau-Ponty, M. (1962). *Phenomenology of perception* (C. Smith, Trans.). New York: Humanities Press.

Miles, M., & Huberman, A. (1994). *Qualitative data analysis* (2nd ed.). Thousand Oaks, CA: Sage.

Moon, S., Dillon, D., & Sprenkle, D. (1990). Family therapy and qualitative research. *Journal of Marital and Family Therapy, 16*(4), 357–373.

Patton, M. Q. (1990). *Qualitative evaluation and research methods* (2nd ed.). Chicago: University of Chicago Press.

Pilalis, J., & Anderson, J. (1986). Feminism and family therapy: a possible meeting point. *Journal of Family Therapy, 8*(2), 99–114.

Pincus, L., & Dare, C. (1978). *Secrets in the family.* New York: Pantheon.

Rafuls, S. (1994). *Qualitative resource based consultation: Resource-generative inquiry and reflective dialogue with four Latin American families and their therapists.* Unpublished doctoral dissertation, Purdue University, West Lafayette, IN.

Randall, R., & Southgate, J. (1981). Doing dialogical research. In P. Reason & J. Rowan (Eds.), *Human inquiry in action: A sourcebook of new paradigm research.* New York: Wiley.

Reason, P. (Ed.). (1988). *Human inquiry in action: Developments in new paradigm research.* London: Sage.

Reason, P., & Rowan, J. (Eds.). (1981). *Human inquiry: A sourcebook of new paradigm research.* New York: Wiley.

Rediger, S. (1992). *A philosophy of education: Interdisciplinary study and innovation in marriage and family therapy.* Unpublished doctoral dissertation, Purdue University, West Lafayette, IN.

Richters, A., & Bansell, E. (1987). The relevance of Jurgen Habermas's work for counseling. *International Journal for the Advancement of Counseling, 10*(2), 85–102.

Ricoeur, P. (1981). *Hermeneutics and the human sciences* (J. Thompson, Ed. and Trans.). New York: Cambridge University Press.

Schwartz, R., & Breunlin, D. (1983). Research: Why should clinicians bother with it. *Family Therapy Networker, 4*, 23–27, & 57–59.

Sewart, J. (1978). Critical theory and the critique of conservative method. *American Sociologist, 13*(1), 15–22.

Southgate, J., & Randall, R. (1981). The troubled fish: Barriers to dialogue. In P. Reason & J. Rowan (Eds.), *Human inquiry in action: A sourcebook of new paradigm research.* New York: Wiley.

Sprenkle, D. H., & Bischof, G. P. (1994). Contemporary family therapy in the United States. *Journal of Family Therapy, 16*, 5–24.

Strauss, A. L., & Corbin, J. (1990). *Basics of qualitative research: Grounded theory procedures and techniques.* Newbury Park, CA: Sage.

Sullivan, E. V. (1984). *A critical psychology: Interpretation of the personal world.* New York: Plenum Press.

Tamasese, K., & Waldegrave, C. (1993). Cultural and gender accountability in the 'Just Therapy' approach. *Journal of Feminist Family Therapy, 5*(2), 29–45.

Tomm, K. (1983). The old hat doesn't fit. *Family Therapy Networker, 4*, 39–41.

Waldegrave, C. T. (1990). Just Therapy. *Dulwich Centre Newsletter, 1*, 5–46.

Walters, M., Carter, B., Papp, P., & Silverstein, O. (1988). *The invisible web: Gender patterns in family relationships.* New York: Guilford Press.

White, M. (1989). *Selected papers.* Adelaide, Australia: Dulwich Centre Publications.

White, M., & Epston, D. (1990). *Narrative means to therapeutic ends.* New York: Norton.

Young, R. (1990). *A critical theory of education: Habermas and our children's future.* New York: Teachers College Press.

7

Feminist Lenses in Family Therapy Research
GENDER, POLITICS, AND SCIENCE

JUDITH MYERS AVIS
JEAN TURNER

BACKGROUND

Feminist voices have been heard in the field of family therapy for more than 17 years. Although lone and sparse at first, their number and intensity have grown strong over time, reflecting back to the field the oppressive potential of many of its practices and theories. Those same voices have not been heard in family therapy research. There, the feminist presence continues to be occasional and often invisible. We have written this chapter in an effort to distill ideas about feminist research from across a variety of social science disciplines, illuminate the wide range of differing methods of feminist enquiry now practiced, and render these methods more visible and accessible to our own field. In so doing, we hope not only to draw attention to that feminist research which already exists in family therapy but also to present ideas that may encourage and support its continued development.

In exploring these ideas, we locate ourselves as both feminists and social constructionists. As feminists, we regard gender as a fundamental aspect of social relations, one that generally involves domination and asymmetric power. It can be seen as both independent from and interconnected with such other relations of domination and oppression as race and class (Flax, 1990). As social constructionists, we regard gender systems as socially constructed, both determining and determined by social organization. Further, we recognize that, in our efforts to analyze and understand gender relations, we can never be totally

This chapter represents a collaborative effort. The first author drafted the chapter with the exception of the following three sections: Program Evaluation, Strengths and Weaknesses of Feminist Approaches to Research, and Future Directions. Both authors were involved in editing, and the first author was responsible for final revisions.

free of the distorting influence of our own experiences of gender on our perceptions of the world. A social constructionist perspective leads us to be self-reflexive and critical of our own theories and presuppositions, including our feminist ones, examining them for both assumptions of "truth" and inadvertent replication of oppressive epistemologies similar to those we challenge as feminists (Flax, 1987, 1990; Gavey, 1989; McNamee & Gergen, 1992).

As feminist and social constructionist researcher–practitioners in family therapy, we are interested in studying and gaining greater understanding of all aspects of gender relations related to our field and in incorporating this understanding into our practice. We are thus interested in exploring how dominant and oppressive cultural meanings of gender may be enacted and reinforced in family therapy theory, training, supervision, practice, research, and professional publications and organizations; how gender relations in our field interact with relations of race, class, and culture; and how alternative meanings of gender may be accessed by family therapists to enable relationships based on equality, justice, and care rather than on domination and control.

We have written this chapter in a way that expresses the feminist and constructionist stances that influence our work and daily lives. We include ourselves in the discourse by writing in the first person and being transparent about our own politics and social location. Although authoring this chapter as if we have one voice creates a less cluttered text, it obscures from the reader's view areas of similarity and of uniqueness in our individual standpoints. In fact, we have many overlapping experiences and values. Both of us are white heterosexual women born in the 1940s with middle-class Canadian backgrounds. We currently work as researchers, university teachers, and couple and family therapists. Our separate histories of being deeply concerned with issues of gender equality and social justice in both our personal and our professional lives are connected by the historical–cultural context we share. Within these broad commonalities we differ significantly. The first author (J. M. A.) has stronger links with feminist theory and practice and social action (Avis, 1985, 1988, 1989, 1991, 1992); the second author (J. T.) connects herself more with social constructionist perspectives and personal reflexivity (Fine & Turner, 1991; Turner, 1991; Turner & Fine, 1995). These differences in theoretical and political positioning enrich our interactions as colleagues and add to the breadth of this chapter. At the same time, we acknowledge our biases and the partiality of our views, which limit what we have written from representing the full range of possible perspectives on this subject.

The work of writing has involved us in a collaborative process of reading, thinking, dialogue, and challenging each other's ideas over many months. The paucity of published feminist family therapy research and the dearth of discussions of feminist research in the family therapy literature made it necessary for us to turn almost entirely to other disciplines for intellectual nourishment. Our hope is that this chapter will provide a jumping off point, opening up possibilities for strong feminist voices in future family therapy research.

Philosophical Assumptions

Because the philosophical assumptions underlying feminist approaches to research are fundamental, we pay significant attention to them in this chapter. We begin with a discussion of feminist goals and critiques of traditional science, followed by an examination of three major epistemological positions developed by feminist researchers to address the problems of gender bias in traditional scientific methods.

Most feminist researchers would agree with Jane Flax (1990) regarding the primary goal of feminist enquiry:

A fundamental goal of feminist theorists is to analyze gender: how gender is constituted and experienced and how we think—or—equally important—do not think about it.
The study of gender includes but is not limited to what are often considered the dis-
tinctively feminist issues: the situation of women and the analysis of male domination
(or patriarchy). . . . Feminist theorists recover and explore the aspects of societies that
have been suppressed, unarticulated, or denied within male-dominant viewpoints. (p. 20)

Feminists in the social sciences have challenged traditional science on many levels, particularly in its claims to developing value-free, neutral, objective "knowledge."
(See Rediger, Chapter 6, this volume, for a discussion of how other critical theorists
also challenge positivism and the idea of objectivity.) Feminists point out that knowledge
is power and those who control the making and definition of knowledge control the
cultural construction of reality and meaning. Women's experiences may be seen as "subjugated knowledges" (Foucault, 1980), invisible and without credibility in a predominantly
male construction of reality which reflects and legitimates dominant ideologies, power
structures, and social interests. Feminists criticize traditional science for its insistence
on a scientific "objectivity" which involves control and distance of the observer from
the observed, decontextualization of the research, and reductionist thinking. The claim
to neutrality and the failure to acknowledge the power basis of those who produce
knowledge are seen as masking the insidious ways gender bias permeates traditional
science. These include not studying subjects of concern to women, using theories that
reflect a male standard and are biased against women (resulting in interpreting women's
behavior as negative or deficient in comparison with men's), neglecting or excluding
women's experience, ignoring sex-of-researcher effects, focusing exclusively on between-
gender rather than within-gender differences, and attributing to persons what are actually the effects of structural inequities (Flax, 1987; Harding, 1986; Hare-Mustin, 1992;
Riger, 1992).

Feminist scholars in the social sciences have attempted to address the problems
of traditional science in three different ways. These may be thought of as comprising
three distinct models of feminist epistemology: feminist empiricism, feminist standpoint
epistemologies, and feminist postmodernism (Flax, 1987; Harding, 1986, 1987; Hare-
Mustin, 1992; Riger, 1992). Each of these models embodies a particular ideology and
perspective on the construction of reality. Collectively, they indicate a diversity among
feminist scholars which is valued as promoting ongoing critique and discussion rather
than being seen as divisive. In the following discussion we summarize the major assumptions of each model as well as a critique of its limitations.

Feminist empiricists believe that there actually is an objective reality which can be
known through traditional scientific methods—the problem to be dealt with is one of
researcher bias leading to a failure in objectivity and neutrality. "This view regards science
itself as a male-oriented enterprise, but believes that existing methods can be used to
address issues of importance to women through greater sensitivity and scope" (Hare-
Mustin, 1992, p. 20). Feminist empiricists therefore advocate using existing methods
with scrupulous attention to careful design, observation, reporting and potential bias.
Feminist survey research and feminist experimental research, as well as research using
statistical formats, fall within this model. Much of this research is characterized by what
Reinharz (1992) calls a "dual vision": It simultaneously "meets the standards of the mainstream social sciences of validity, reliability, objectivity and replicability" (p. 94) while
being sensitive to feminist values and the principles of feminist research.

Critics of feminist empiricism point out the impossibility of value-free research and
the subjective bias that is necessarily embedded in all theories and research questions
(Avis, 1994). They also criticize the use of statistics which are seen as "part of patri-

archal culture's monolithic definition of 'hard facts' " (Reinharz, 1992, p. 87), and high-light the risk of sexism which frequently occurs in all aspects of statistical analysis (Oakley & Oakley, 1981).

From the perspective of *feminist standpoint epistemologies*, women's experience, knowledge, and voices have been subjugated and are therefore not visible in existing knowledge and conceptualizations. These researchers advocate using methodologies that begin with the experience of women as a subordinated group, grant women voice and the right to be heard, and develop conceptual categories appropriate to women and based on women's own experience (Smith, 1987). Stephanie Riger (1992) warns that adopting a feminist standpoint as the basis for science poses the potential risk of assum-ing a commonality of experience among all women, resulting in ignoring real differ-ences among women based on race, social class, and culture. In addition, there is a danger of creating a dominant discourse parallel to that of patriarchy by valuing women's experience and ways of being as superior to men's (Weedon, 1987).

Postmodern (or social constructionist) feminists focus on multiple meanings and social constructions of reality. (Although there are actually distinctions between the terms "postmodernism" and "social constructionism," for the purposes of this chapter we are using them interchangeably.)

> Rather than seeing a single universal standpoint that captures all women's experience, postmodern feminists see all guidelines for generating knowledge as a result of histori-cally specific interests. They accept multiplicity, uncertainty, and paradox and reject both empiricist reductionism and naive dualisms. (Hare-Mustin, 1992, p. 21)

Social constructionists assert that science does not represent reality; researchers, in fact, *create* realities. Those researchers with the most power, have more influence in defin-ing what is, and what is not, legitimate "knowledge" (Riger, 1992). Language is consid-ered particularly important because it is the vehicle through which we express our understanding of experience. Because language is not neutral, it determines what con-structions of reality are possible. For constructionists, the critical question is, "Whose interests are served by competing ways of giving meaning to the world?" Postmodern feminists' answer to this question is that "positivism's neutral and disinterested stance masks what is actually the male conception of reality; this conception reflects and main-tains male power interests" (Riger, 1992, p. 735). Feminists taking this position are most likely to advocate methodologies that allow for a deconstruction of written or spoken language (texts, written accounts, interview transcripts, case records) such as discourse analysis, content analysis, or theme analysis. Feminist postmodernists (constructionists) are committed to subverting or disrupting oppressive knowledges by analyzing both dominant and subjugated discourses. By bringing to light such subjugated discourses, contradictions within texts are revealed and alternative meanings and new choices for action are created (Weedon, 1987). Although postmodernism has powerfully increased our awareness of the relationship between knowledge and power, Riger (1992) warns of the potential danger that the focus on " 'problematizing the text' of our dis-ciplines . . . can lead to an inward emphasis that neglects the study of women in socie-ty," whereas the emphasis on language as the determiner of reality may result in "the disregard of other determinants, such as women's position in a social hierarchy" (p. 736). Questions have also been raised about whether the constructionist emphasis on mul-tiple meanings and self-reflexivity makes it impossible for these feminists to sustain their outrage about women's oppression (Gavey, 1989).

It seems clear that there is no single perfect feminist perspective. Although intended to overcome the deficiencies of traditional science, each epistemological stance has its own limitations and deviates in some way from feminist values—values which themselves lack consensus (Riger, 1992). The existence of multiple feminisms is an important and enriching source of diversity and debate, providing challenge and a range of possibilities for approaching research.

There is a growing consensus among feminist researchers that multiple and diverse methods are necessary to adequately study the complex web of factors which affect gender relations (Riger, 1992; Reinharz, 1992). What is essential is that we be aware of the values and assumptions we take on when we use a particular research method, that we systematically examine our work for its underlying values and assumptions (Riger, 1992), that we acknowledge the power relations inherent in the researcher role, and that we recognize that we are part of a larger political system including the whole network of funders, editors and reviewers surrounding the research endeavor.

Historical Roots and Development

Family therapy and the modern feminist movement began as parallel but nonoverlapping domains of thought and practice. Although both emerged at the same time in history, in the late 1950s and early to mid-1960s, they sprang from very different roots: Family therapy was initially a field dominated by (mostly male) master therapists informed by notions of expert knowledge and focused on relationships in microsystems. In contrast, feminism was initially a political movement designed to liberate women from patriarchal oppression, led by women working collectively and collaboratively without expert leaders, and focused on the relationship between the personal and the political—that is, on the relationship between micro- and macrosystems. In the ensuing years, each movement has been influenced by common social and economic forces: the rising participation of women in the labor force and the resulting concern with gender equity in both family and workplace, changing patterns of international trade and migration producing new ethnic enclaves in large cities, economic adjustment and financial squeeze resulting in greater class inequality, and emerging concern for human rights across many marginalized groups.

At the present time, family therapy and feminism have begun to develop some areas of overlap as increasing numbers of family therapists incorporate feminist perspectives into their clinical practice. Although the influence of feminist thought on family therapy practice has been significant, that of family therapy on feminism has been minimal. We will now trace the development of feminist research in these two domains in greater detail so as to place feminist research in family therapy in context.

Reinharz (1992) contextualizes the origins and development of feminist research as an outgrowth of the feminist movement. We draw on her account of the process of its development.

> During the so-called first wave of the women's movement in the United States . . . women struggled for *the right to be educated.* In the so-called second wave, women strove for additional goals related to education: *the right to criticize* the accepted body of knowledge, *the right to create* knowledge, and *the right to be educators* and educational administrators. (Reinharz, 1992, p. 11)

When the most recent feminist movement began in the early 1970s, there was no thought of feminist research as we know it today—simply discovering and critiquing the sexist bias in social science scholarship was considered revolutionary (Reinharz, 1992).

It was this discovery that set the agenda and goals of feminist scholarship, although no feminist research method had yet been identified. At first, discussions of how best to address feminist concerns occurred informally, in workshops, study and discussion groups, lectures and newspaper articles, where the framework and norms for feminist research gradually took shape. During this period, many feminists searched for ways to do research that allowed them to keep their own disciplinary methods without replicating the biases inherent in them. As feminists began to criticize dominant science, they tended to speak with one voice and to downplay their differences.

When the "second" feminist wave began in the early 1970s, research could be considered feminist simply because it focused on women—to do so was still thought to be a radical act in itself. Gradually, in the 1980s, what are now called feminist methodologies and approaches to research, the subject of this chapter, began to emerge. In the 1980s, a further development occurred, as some black feminists began to criticize white feminist scholarship for being blind to issues of racism and therefore being part of the problem (Reinharz, 1992). As a result of this criticism, during the late 1980s and the 1990s feminists have become increasingly aware of their own potential for unconsciously replicating dominant ideologies and have paid growing attention to the interrelationships between oppression related to gender and that related to other forms of oppression (e.g., race, class, culture, and sexual orientation).

In family therapy, feminism has as yet had relatively little impact on research. This situation prevails despite the development of strong feminist research in the social sciences generally, and despite the influence of feminist ideas on clinical practice in the field. Feminist research in family therapy has been slow to develop and, although present, remains almost invisible. The first feminist studies in the field, to the best of our knowledge, were two doctoral studies using the Delphi technique conducted by Dorothy Wheeler (1985) and Judith Myers Avis (1986) at Purdue University. Many of the 36 feminist family therapists who participated in these interactive studies expressed their enthusiasm at this first opportunity to identify other feminists in the field and to dialogue with them, through the Delphi process, regarding the parameters of feminist approaches to both family therapy practice and to family therapy supervision and training.

Since that time, a number of feminist studies have been conducted, many of them by graduate students, and a few of them have been published (Black & Piercy, 1991; Chaney & Piercy, 1988; Coleman, Avis, & Turin, 1990; Dienhart & Avis, 1994; Lamb, 1991). The invisibility of feminist research in the field is reflected in the *Decade Review of Marriage and Family Therapy*, where, although a paragraph is devoted to the feminist critique of family therapy, no reference is made to feminist research (Piercy & Sprenkle, 1990). When other disciplines have produced and published volumes of feminist research, we must ask why our field has been so slow to move in this direction. Perhaps, as with the feminist critique which came a decade later than it did in other fields, family therapy researchers have simply been too committed to the ideology of neutrality to be able to challenge or seriously examine assumptions about gender and power. Perhaps there is more feminist research than we know, and feminist researchers are simply having more difficulty getting their work published. Perhaps the higher concentration of women in clinical positions and men in research positions contributes. Whatever the cause, thus far the most outspoken and respected published feminist voices in the field have focused on critique and the development of feminist perspectives on clinical theory and practice rather than on research (see, among others, Bograd, 1984, 1988, 1992; Goldner, 1985, 1988, 1992; Goodrich, 1991; Hare-Mustin, 1978, 1987, 1994; Leupnitz, 1988; Walters, Carter, Papp, & Silverstein, 1988; Weingarten, 1991, 1992). Perhaps a feminist research presence is about to blossom as the feminist critique did a decade ago, indicating the greater involvement of women in the research endeavor and greater receptivity to their work in the field. We hope that the time is now past when reviewers for major family therapy journals, as the gatekeepers of the profession's literature, question the legitimacy and importance of gender as a focus for scholarly investigation. This was the experience of the first author (J. M. A.) in 1987, when a reviewer critiqued a research article on feminist supervision and training as "unbalanced in its zeal for emphasizing gender issues in family therapy training."

METHODOLOGY

Feminist Research Questions

Although there are some research questions to which a feminist lens is particularly well suited, feminists advocate that *all* research be conducted with a sensitivity to issues of gender, social context, researcher values, and the power relations between observer and observed. Questions of particular interest to feminist researchers in family therapy relate to how gender-related power imbalances and oppression are created and maintained in relationships between family members; between therapists and clients; between trainers and trainees; between researchers, research participants and consumers; between theory makers and theory users; between writers and journal editors. They are further interested in how these gender relations are differentially impacted by other relations of domination—for example, race, class, culture, and sexual orientation. Feminist researchers are concerned with issues of voicelessness, invisibility, and marginalization and with raising questions that challenge dominant constructions of gender. Feminist research most often analyzes some aspect of gender or power dynamics as they presently exist in an effort to make the invisible visible and to illuminate alternatives. Such power dynamics may operate in the control of information, knowledge, or theory, as well as in clinical practice and training.

Specifically, feminist researchers in family therapy have been asking such questions as the following: How is domestic violence perpetrated by men against women minimized in family therapy clinical accounts (Lamb, 1991)? How are training programs preparing therapists for understanding and responding to child sexual abuse (Avis, Lero, & Guldner, 1992)? To what degree do family therapy training programs integrate gender into their curricula (Coleman et al., 1990)? Do family therapists writing in major journals hold mothers more accountable than they do fathers for their children's difficulties (Haig, 1988)? To what degree does family therapy research include or ignore the category of gender (Woodard, 1991)? What distinguishes feminist from nonfeminist supervision and training (Avis, 1986)? What are the parameters of a feminist approach to family therapy (Wheeler, 1985)? What approaches do feminist-informed family therapists use for engaging men in family therapy (Dienhart & Avis, 1994)? They have also been interested in developing instruments to assess the gender sensitivity of family therapists (Black & Piercy, 1991) and the behaviors that distinguish feminist therapists from others (Chaney & Piercy, 1988).

Other questions typical of those with which feminist researchers might be concerned include the following: What kinds of experiences do abused women have when they seek the help of a family therapist? How is this experience different for white women and for women of color? For poor women and for middle-class women? What are family therapists' attitudes and beliefs about wife abuse? How do family therapists deal with couple conflicts over housework? What impact does the therapist's gender have on men's and women's experience of couple or family therapy? How is gender mediated by race, class, and culture in the family difficulties experienced by diverse families? What sexist, racist, classist, and homophobic assumptions are embedded in family therapy theories and models of practice? What special barriers do feminist, as compared with nonfeminist, writers report in getting their work accepted for publication in mainstream family therapy journals?

Feminist Approaches to Research

Themes in Feminist Research

The most comprehensive discussion we have found of research methods used by feminists, and of the themes that unite them, is Shulamit Reinharz's (1992) examination of feminist methods in social research. We highly recommend this work for its in-depth review of the variety of feminist methods across and within different social science disciplines. By analyzing a large number of investigations by self-defined feminist researchers, Reinharz (1992) specified what feminist research *includes*, rather than attempting to say definitively what it *is*. She identified 10 themes which she suggests comprise an "inductive definition of feminist methodology" (p. 240). Although not all feminist researchers act in accordance with all 10 themes, we have found them helpful in delineating the complexity and diversity of feminist research. Following is a summary of Reinharz's analysis of these 10 themes with comments on their relevance for feminist research in family therapy.

1. *Feminism is a perspective, not a research method.* Rather than being a method in itself, feminism provides a perspective on methods already present in one's own discipline. Feminist researchers work at this intersection: They learn and work within the research methods supplied by their own discipline, while criticizing or transforming them. We can see this theme clearly in family therapy, where feminist researchers have brought a feminist perspective to a range of methods commonly utilized within the field, such as qualitative interviews, survey, Delphi Technique, program evaluation, and content analysis.

2. *Feminists use a multiplicity of research methods.* "There is no single 'feminist way' to do research" (Reinharz, 1992, p. 243). Feminist researchers are adverse to defining what is methodologically correct. "Central texts" and "definitive techniques," are avoided (Reinharz, 1992, p. 246). There is greater interest in expanding methods than in narrowing definitions, and feminists increasingly emphasize multiplicity, inclusivity, and plurality of voices and methods. In keeping with this emphasis, the examples of feminist research in family therapy that we discuss in this chapter are intended as samples of the diversity that is possible rather than as exemplars of how it should be done. This emphasis on, and valuing of, multiple methods is also shared by critical theory researchers (see Rediger, Chapter 6, this volume).

3. *Feminist research involves an ongoing criticism of nonfeminist scholarship.* Feminist researchers have a continuing interest in challenging the androcentric bias of existing social science research:

> We continue to identify topics that have been male-centered and need to be rethought in terms of women's experiences. This rethinking views all social, psychological, and economic phenomena as gendered and embedded in power relations. . . . Making the invisible visible, bringing the margin to the center, rendering the trivial important,

putting the spotlight on women as competent actors, understanding women as subjects in their own right rather than objects for men—all continue to be elements of feminist research. (Reinharz, 1992, p. 248)

Thus, although feminist research is grounded in the various disciplines, at the same time it constitutes a fundamental critique of them. We see this theme in such feminist family therapy studies as Haig and Avis's (1989) content analysis of mother blaming in family therapy journals, Woodard's (1991) analysis of gender as a social variable in family therapy research, Lamb's (1991) study of how family therapy and other disciplines obscure responsibility for wife-battering behavior in their professional literature, and Avis et al.'s (1992) four national surveys examining gaps in the professional education of social workers, psychologists, and family therapists with respect to understanding and responding to child sexual abuse.

4. *Feminist research is guided by feminist theory.* Feminist research is characterized by its focus on the interaction of gender and power. Frequently "gender or femaleness is the variable and power/experience/action the relation under investigation" (Reinharz, 1992, p. 249). Feminist theory is drawn on both to develop research questions and to interpret data. From a feminist perspective, the personal is political, a vantage point that enables the feminist researcher to see and study gender politics. This perspective is particularly relevant to feminist researchers in family therapy, where unbalanced and covert power relations between men and women are constantly enacted and reproduced not only in the family system but also in the therapeutic system, the training system, and the agency system that structures the service delivery.

5. *Feminist research is often transdisciplinary.* Feminist researchers often bridge disciplinary boundaries, integrating and drawing on methods and ideas from disciplines other than their own. For family therapy researchers, this emphasis on connectedness, interdisciplinary exchange, and utilization of cross-disciplinary theories makes feminist work highly compatible with the interdisciplinary and systemic perspectives in the field.

6. *Feminist research aims to create social change.* Feminist researchers seek to contribute in ways that lead to greater gender equality as well as to the expansion of knowledge. This is the dual vision—or dual responsibility—many feminist researchers see as their mandate (Reinharz, 1992). An explicit goal of much feminist research is to promote social change leading to the transformation of gender relations, both through the consciousness raising impact of findings and through policy recommendations and practical applications of the research. They share with critical theory researchers both the view that inquiry is inherently political and the commitment to work toward social change and liberation from oppressive ideologies (see Rediger, Chapter 6, this volume). One of the goals of Haig and Avis's (1989) content analysis of mother blaming, for example, was to increase consciousness among family therapists of practices that blame mothers for their children's difficulties. Similarly, the goals of Avis et al.'s (1992) national study of professional training were to increase curriculum content related to child sexual abuse in professional training programs, to ensure greater knowledge and skills among clinical professionals, and ultimately to enhance the quality of clinical services for those affected by abuse.

7. *Feminist research strives to represent human diversity.* A recognition of women's diversity has become a cornerstone of feminist research. This recognition means acknowledging that while all women are alike in some ways, in others they are highly dissimilar. It means that feminist researchers necessarily seek to explore how relations of domination, such as those of race, class, culture, and sexual orientation, affect women's lives. As feminists struggle to increase their consciousness of their own blind spots and to

scrutinize their work for signs of hidden bias, they have attempted to diversify their samples and discuss the limitations of their research in terms of their own racist, classist, homophobic, ethnocentric, and ageist assumptions and insensitivities. Reinharz (1992) points out:

> At the same time, feminist sensitivity to issues of diversity has raised many questions. How much of the diversified world of women should be included in a particular research project? When is a group actually diverse? Do members of different subgroups speak only for themselves? Do Western feminists have a right to criticize or must they accept culturally rooted practices in other cultures that seem detrimental to women . . . ? (p. 258)

In family therapy, this sensitivity to multiple oppressions is clearly seen in the clinical and theoretical work of feminists working from a social justice perspective (Greene, 1994; Kliman, 1994; Pinderhughes, 1986; Tamasese & Waldegrave, 1993), but it has not yet become visible in feminist research. Neither debates about minorities only speaking for minorities nor questions about tolerance for gender inequality in non-Western cultures have yet appeared in mainstream family therapy literature.

8. *Feminist research frequently includes the researcher as a person.* Many feminist researchers challenge the assumption of dispassionate objectivity and detachment on which androcentric social science is based and instead emphasize their own involvement in the conceptualizing and implementing of the research. It is common for feminist researchers to present their research in their own voice (first person singular), describing the personal origins of their research questions and how their research is related to their own lives and values. They frequently describe their struggles in carrying out the study, how they have been personally affected, and what they have learned and been changed by in the process. In doing so, however, the feminist researcher must confront the positivistic biases of the journals to which she may submit her work. A feminist family therapy researcher was, for example, obliged by the editor of a major family therapy journal to remove a section of personal reflection and speculation regarding the meaning of some of the trends in gender differences in her results so that the article would conform to the more traditional (i.e., "objective" and impersonal) format.

9. *Feminist research often results in strong connections between researcher and participants.* Relationships between a feminist researcher and the people she studies are, at a minimum, highly respectful, open, and nonexploitive. In face-to-face relations, the approach often involves a high degree of researcher–participant rapport, in contrast to the distance and impersonal interactions required by traditional attempts at objectivity and control. This effort to level the power hierarchy between researcher and participants is also fundamental to critical theory research (see Rediger, Chapter 6, this volume), which by nature has more co-participatory features. In fact, feminist and critical theory perspectives have been combined in a study by Patricia Maguire (1987). Attention to relationship can be seen in feminist interview research in family therapy such as Sukie Magraw's (1992) oral history of feminism and family therapy and Kathleen Kiernan's (1994) evaluation of an intervention program for child witnesses of spousal abuse.

10. *Feminist research frequently attempts to create a special relation with the reader.* Feminist researchers often wish to establish a special relation with readers, enabling them to feel a direct connection with those studied. Quotations from interviews are often included in research reports to allow participants to speak in their own voices and to allow readers to experience participants' perspectives more directly, rather than simply through the eyes of the researcher. In family therapy we can see this theme in reports of feminist interview research such as in Kiernan (1994) and Magraw (1992).

Sampling and Selection Procedures

Most important in sampling and selection is the inclusion of women's voices as an anti-dote to the decades of research in which women's own perspectives on their experience have either not been sought directly or have been obscured by failure to recognize sex of participants as a critical variable in data analysis. Existing imbalances are addressed by giving voice to those who have been excluded or silenced in the past and by study-ing those who have not been studied previously. This approach to sampling involves a commitment to including a diversity of women's voices so as to avoid the error of believing that women of the dominant class and culture speak for all women. A con-scious choice is made of *who* is included—women, men, or both; from diverse or homogeneous races, classes, cultures—and these choices are carefully documented and explained (Collins, 1989). This practice is in sharp contrast with Woodard's (1991) finding that in many family therapy studies not even the gender of participants or researchers was specified.

Data Collection Procedures

As evident from the diverse methods described earlier, feminist researchers use a varie-ty of traditional methods of data collection. What distinguishes feminist approaches to data collection is the care that is given to establishing a highly respectful and, if possible, collaborative relationship between researcher and participants; to demystify-ing the researcher's role, values, and interest in the issue under investigation (Gergen, 1988); to ensuring that the recording of participants' experiences and perspectives faith-fully represents their meanings; and to gathering data in ways that recognize and respect the impact of social and historical context on the phenomena being studied, on the participant, and on the researcher's own perspective (Gergen, 1988). In these ways, feminist researchers express their understanding of the subjectivity of the researcher and the research and the historical and cultural contexts in which they, the participants, and the research itself are embedded (Stanley & Wise, 1979). Because feminist researchers regard participants as the authorities on their own lives (Thompson, 1992), many ask participants to review the researcher's recording of the participant's responses to ensure that they accurately capture the intended meaning. Similarly, many believe that it is important, as part of the process of collecting data, to discuss with participants how the final results will be reported and to whom they will be distributed.

There is an open acknowledgment among many feminist researchers that the research process changes both the researcher and the participants, in most cases raising their consciousness and providing complexity to their understanding of women's experiences (Fonow & Cook, 1991). In addition, the relationship between the researcher and the researched is recognized as inherently hierarchical, making it necessary to be vigilant about unintended exploitation (Stacey, 1988). Feminist researchers are mindful of tak-ing extra precautions not to betray the trust that develops, especially in qualitative studies, where women are reinterviewed a number of times (Finch, 1984).

Feminists emphasize researcher responsibility in all aspects of their work. As Ger-gen (1988) points out, the researcher is not an "innocent bystander befallen by an ex-periment" (p. 48). Each time we select a particular method, instrument, or data analysis procedure, we make particular epistemological and value assumptions (Riger, 1992). Research instruments embody specific race, class, gender, and cultural biases which will in turn be reflected in results and in their interpretation. The Marital Adjustment Scale, for example, may be critiqued for its assumption of middle-class marriage, as well as for its valuing of low conflict as a sign of high "adjustment." For this reason, feminist researchers, even those who use quantitative methods, may avoid using traditional instruments and scales as a means of gathering data.

Data Analysis Procedures

Because each feminist methodology carries with it its own procedures for data analysis, we will not attempt to discuss them in any detail here. It is important to note, however, that one of the debates among feminist scholars concerns the use of statistical approaches and quantitative methods. Some feminists who strongly criticize statistical analyses as an aspect of patriarchal control and claim to objectivity, reject quantitative methods altogether as inappropriate for feminist research purposes (Reinharz, 1992). Others advocate using both qualitative and quantitative methods so that women's subjective experience can be placed in social context within a single study (Jayartine & Stewart, 1991). Feminist postmodern researchers who rely increasingly on qualitative methods as most appropriate to their particular feminist values and goals use a variety of analysis procedures, including discourse analysis, conversation analysis, narrative analysis, interpretive biography, and thematic analysis.

Reporting

Feminist researchers take great care that the reporting of their results leads to clear understanding by the various possible audiences. A few researchers produce two versions of their research reports, one academic and one for the general public, in an effort to ensure that findings are widely accessible (e.g., Oakley, 1980a, 1980b). Other strategies used by feminist researchers to ensure that reporting reflects feminist values include involving participants in planning for distribution of findings, consulting with participants and other community members regarding interpretation of results, and reporting data in such a way as to minimize the potential for misinterpretation, distortion, and misapplication (Yllo, 1988). When there is a danger that research results could be misinterpreted by the media to the disadvantage of women, feminist researchers advocate careful interpretation of the complex meanings of their findings in context (Avis, 1994). In the case of action research, the investigator will use the results to bring forward an agenda for change by engaging with community or other governmental-level leaders.

Feminist research, by definition, involves using feminist theory to analyze gender and power relations. Occasionally, the values of a feminist researcher may clash with those of the research participants (Reinharz, 1992). Faced with this apparent dilemma, some researchers choose to make transparent these differences by sharing interpretive control and reporting diverse views (Opie, 1992). Others decide to privilege feminist interpretations and declare their textual authority as researchers (e.g., Acker, Barry, & Esseveld, 1991). Postmodern feminist researchers may acknowledge the partiality of their own interpretations by writing multiple accounts which represent their different positions on the same findings (e.g., Wolf, 1992).

Selected Examples of Feminist Research in Family Therapy

Feminist scholars outside family therapy have utilized a wide variety of disciplinary methods, as summarized by Reinharz (1992). Different research questions are addressed more effectively by different methodologies so that the choice of method depends on the issue being studied. As yet, feminist researchers in family therapy have utilized only a few of the possible methods available—interview, survey, oral history, content analysis, and multiple methods. They have also developed feminist research instruments (Black & Piercy, 1991; Chaney & Piercy, 1988). To give a flavor of both the variety of methods being used and the kinds of questions being asked, we briefly discuss three different methodologies that have been used by feminist researchers in family therapy: content analysis, survey research, and program evaluation. We present these studies as illustrations of the diversity and themes in feminist research in the field and in the hope that they will open up alternative possibilities for readers to consider.

Content Analysis

There have been at least two feminist studies in family therapy utilizing content analysis (Haig, 1988; Lamb, 1991). We discuss the first in some detail to illustrate a feminist application of the methodology in the field.

Research Goals. For her master's thesis, Cathryn Haig studied the prevalence of mother blaming in four major family therapy journals under the supervision of the first author (J. M. A.). In keeping with the feminist goal of analyzing gender and its construction, the major objective of this study was to explore the treatment of mothers and fathers in family therapy literature with respect to responsibility for child and family problems. The overriding goal was to make the covert overt—to bring into visibility family therapy authors' underlying assumptions regarding women's responsibility for the well-being of children and families and to illuminate the means by which this message may be subtly communicated in professional articles. A second goal was to effect change in the profession by raising consciousness regarding the ways in which dominant cultural beliefs about mothers might be reinforced in family therapy literature. The research was guided by feminist theory in its concern for ellucidating this aspect of gender–power relations as it is constituted by authors in the field.

Sampling and Data Analysis. Haig analyzed 93 case studies appearing in four major family therapy journals in the target years of 1978 and 1987. Content analysis was chosen as a method because it enables the researcher to deconstruct embedded messages in a piece of text. A classification system of 80 categories was developed, allowing specific characteristics of the case studies to be counted and coded. These included such categories as the number of words used to describe mothers as compared with the number used to describe fathers, the number of negative terms used to describe mothers compared with fathers, the frequency of giving psychological information about mothers compared with fathers, and the frequency with which mothers', as compared with fathers', level of over- or underinvolvement was seen as problematic.

This study is an example of empirical feminist research that integrated both quantitative and qualitative analyses. Both descriptive and inferential statistical analyses were used to analyze the categories, whereas a theme analysis of the findings related to two major categories was used to provide a clearer interpretation of the quantitative results.

Survey Research

Survey methodology has been used in several forms by feminist family therapy researchers. Here we discuss two of these forms: questionnaire and the Delphi technique.

Questionnaire Survey. Avis et al. (1992) conducted a national study in Canada involving five separate surveys of training programs, practitioners, agency directors, and treatment experts regarding the training of family therapists, social workers, and psychologists in understanding and responding to child sexual abuse. This study is an example of research in the feminist empiricist tradition, where the goal was to use existing survey methodology to study a question of serious concern to feminists—that is, the degree to which clinical professionals were being provided with adequate training in the area of child sexual abuse. Guided by a feminist perspective on sexual abuse, it examined, among other topics, curriculum content on power and gender issues and on feminist approaches to therapy. Results were fed back to all participants as well as to agencies, government ministries and professional training programs.

Delphi Technique. A second type of survey that has been utilized by feminist family therapy researchers is the Delphi technique. The Delphi is an interactive survey that allows a panel of knowledgeable participants to generate ideas and respond to each others' opinions. Its interactive nature makes it particularly well suited to feminist goals as survey items are actually generated by the participants themselves, who are then able to reflect on, endorse, or disagree with each other's ideas. This collaborative process, which sees the participants rather than the researcher as expert, was used by Dorothy Wheeler (1985) and one of the authors (Avis, 1986) in their twin doctoral studies which polled the thinking of a panel 36 of feminist family therapists. The investigations themselves were conducted in a collaborative fashion, with the two researchers developing the foundation for their studies and selecting the panel together. Wheeler (1985) explored with the participants their ideas regarding the foundations of a feminist-informed approach to family therapy while Avis (1986) explored their ideas regarding a framework for feminist-informed supervision and training. These were the first feminist studies in the field, and they represented an initial effort to bring together the thinking of feminist family therapists.

The studies were feminist in their collaborative process, in their focus on gender and power issues in practice and in training and supervision, and in their social action goal to increase the visibility and impact of feminist ideas on the field. They incorporate some elements of the feminist empiricist tradition, including careful adherence to issues of panel selection and statistical analysis. However, the Delphi itself, because of its interactive and collaborative nature, and because its results are seen as neither representative nor a reflection of "objective" reality, represents a departure from the positivist tradition.

The Delphi was also used by Dienhart and Avis (1994) to develop a beginning formulation of gender-sensitive approaches to working with men in family therapy.

Program Evaluation

Recent thesis research by Kathleen Kiernan (1994) reflects one way in which assumptions from a feminist constructionist perspective can be utilized in program evaluation. This research is described here in some detail because it embraces a number of the tenets of feminist research discussed earlier in this chapter. It can be considered a multiple-methods study because data collection involved interviews, participant observation, and analysis of records.

Focus and Entry. A community group requested that the second chapter author (J. T.) and Kiernan (a family therapy graduate student at the time) coordinate an evaluation of their rural intervention program which targeted young children who had witnessed their mother's abuse by male partners. The program providers embraced a feminist analysis of woman abuse and a family systems model for program delivery. The children, their siblings, and their mothers were participants in a combination of conjoint and concurrent intervention groups. The goals of the evaluation set by the program providers were to refine the program in a way that was accountable to all those involved and to have the client population identify their priority service needs. The evaluation outcome was expected to lead to social action, a feature of the research that is in keeping with feminist values.

From the onset of the study, Kiernan and Turner (as thesis project adviser) attended meetings of the program advisory committee, maintaining a high level of sensitivity to the experiences and diverse agendas of the research "stakeholders" who were represented on the committee. These stakeholders included program staff, members of other service delivery agencies in the community, and a woman who had participated with her children in previous program offerings.

Advisory committee members became consultants with Kiernan in a reciprocal process regarding all aspects of the research decision making, including the research questions, the sampling, data collection, analysis, and distribution of results (Guba & Lincoln, 1989). In this collaborative endeavor Kiernan was transparent with respect to her personal values and the politics of the research project, including her own feminist orientation, her power as the researcher who would interpret the results and author the final report, and her relationship with her academic advisers who supervised the work.

Sampling. The questions addressed by Kiernan's program evaluation are strongly feminist; they concern significant issues of gender and power (woman abuse) and the experience of highly marginalized individuals. To everyone's surprise Kiernan did not find in her literature search any previous studies in which children who had witnessed spouse abuse had been interviewed. Low-income rural women and children are a group whose voices have yet to be heard in the literature on woman abuse. In addition, rural families tend not only to be socially isolated but also to be disadvantaged with respect to accessible services and economic opportunities for women.

In keeping with a feminist constructionist emphasis on social context, Kiernan reviewed archival materials from the program and interviewed both key informants in the community and the service providers themselves, in addition to the women and children who had been program participants. Collection of data from multiple sources ensured that the evaluation results would be interpreted with an eye to the history of the program and the political–social context in which it was embedded. One significant outcome of the consultative process with the advisory committee was that fathers of the children were not included in the study because of safety concerns.

Data Collection and Analysis Procedures. Semistructured interviewing was chosen to enable participants to express their views in whatever sequence and style fit for them and to allow the researcher to be as sensitive as possible to their experience. Kiernan was clear with participants about her connection with the research stakeholders and the plans for distribution of the results. Kiernan shared with each adult participant her initial theme analysis of her interview with them in order to check her interpretation and ensure participant consent to having their words quoted in the final research report.

Reporting. In writing the research report Kiernan paid particular attention to confidentiality, at the same time identifying the various participant voices (mothers, children, program staff, etc.). Following a social constructionist logic, Kiernan reported the full diversity of views on the value of the program for meeting participant needs and emerging priorities, instead of reducing these to the smaller set of recommendations on which there was consensus. She added her own personal biases and program evaluation recommendations as an acknowledgment of her interpretive role in constructing the research results (Denzin, 1994). Finally, in keeping with the feminist valuing of subjectivity, Kiernan documented the experiences women shared with her about the effects of violence on their own and their children's lives, noting as well how she was emotionally affected by their accounts (Devault, 1990).

The findings of the evaluation were used by the program advisory committee to seek further funding and to raise awareness of the need for alternative programming. They were also used to facilitate an exchange of information among the participants. Reports with different formats were produced with a view to reaching a variety of audiences. Kiernan's approach to reporting results illustrates the feminist goals of promoting social action while ensuring that participants benefit from the research process.

DISCUSSION

Strengths and Weaknesses of Feminist Approaches to Research

Hare-Mustin (1992) recently concluded that "family therapy needs a new research paradigm, one that is more reflexive and more attentive to what occurs at the margins" (p. 2). Feminist approaches to research comprise such a new paradigm and demonstrate a number of strengths that could be utilized to enhance other family therapy research. Here we examine five interconnected areas of strength, and for each strength we note a corresponding weakness.

Action Orientation

Feminist researchers have a defined political agenda and commitment to social change; they believe it is important to state these social action goals clearly and show their relationship to research strategies. By making explicit their underlying values, assumptions, and goals for change, feminists draw attention to the fact that all research is inherently political. Feminist researchers ask themselves not only where they stand with regard to their values but also what their research products imply for reinforcing or critiquing oppressive ideologies. These questions encourage a new transparency in the relationships between research, practice, and ideology.

At the same time, an exclusive focus on a feminist political action agenda can lead potentially to reactionary responses, creating polarization that forestalls change, at least in the short term. Researchers who do not take into account the political context in which research participants are embedded may run into difficulties if this context is particularly conservative with respect to gender–power relations.

Attention to Power

Feminist researchers share with other critical theorists (see Rediger, Chapter 6, this volume) a fundamental concern about inequality and power. They draw particular attention to gender–power issues and in so doing highlight many potential areas of domination, control, and oppressive practices within the field of family therapy. However, an exclusive focus on power issues may result in a lack of attention to such other key elements in social relations as intimacy and connection.

Attention to History and Context

The feminist understanding of gender–power relations as processes evolving over time and influenced by political action and other social forces means that feminist researchers seek to understand the phenomena they are studying as well as their research findings in terms of historical conditions. This perspective moves research and practice away from rigid ahistorical generalizations and toward understandings and therapy practices that are congruent with current, local contexts. Few would argue that there is any drawback to a historical, contextual perspective provided that the researcher acknowledges that history is continually rewritten and that there are multiple stories about any set of historical events.

Emphasis on Inclusivity and Social Justice

As discussed earlier, North American feminism originally developed as a white middleclass movement. With the challenges presented by women of color in the 1980s came increasing awareness of feminism's lack of attention to issues of inclusivity and diversity. Since then, the growing recognition of multiple oppressions and of the interaction of gender with race, class, culture, and sexual orientation has been increasingly evident in feminist writings and research, leading Reinharz (1992) to comment that "diversity has become a new criterion for feminist research excellence" (p. 253). Sensitivity to issues of diversity has led feminist researchers to carefully examine such questions as who should be included in a particular study and why, when has a goal of diversity actually been reached, and who should speak for whom. Although maximum diversity may be more of an ideal than a practical possibility (Reinharz, 1992), it nonetheless provides a criterion against which to examine our work. Although not yet evident in feminist research in family therapy, the emphasis on diversity and social justice is a strength in other feminist research and provides a goal toward which we can strive.

A potential danger for researchers in incorporating a social justice perspective is to fail either to take into account the values of those they seek to liberate or to recognize conflict between the values of the researcher and those of participants. An example is the erroneous assumption by some white middle-class feminist researchers that impoverished black women experience gender as a greater source of oppression than race and class.

Self-Critique and Reflexivity

All research is inherently self-critical to a certain degree: Findings lead to reflection on method and theory, and evolving methods and perspectives lead to new findings. Many feminist researchers have begun to incorporate a social constructionist understanding, which leads them to be critical of their own epistemological assumptions and research practices, and to recognize that "any feminist standpoint will necessarily be partial and will to some extent merely reflect our embeddedness in preexisting gender relations" (Flax, 1990, p. 27). From this perspective, the researcher pays careful attention to any claims they may be tempted to make to absolute or neutral knowledge and to recognize that their research will always be influenced by their own gendered and social experience. They explicitly recognize the diversity of viewpoints currently influencing research and practice and include themselves and their own perspectives in the analysis of the phenomenon under scrutiny. Researchers working from both feminist and social constructionist perspectives endeavor to see the world simultaneously, or alternately, from these two viewpoints, and to welcome, tolerate, and work with the resulting "ambivalence, ambiguity, and multiplicity" (Flax, 1990, p. 183). We regard this focus on standpoint and self-awareness as a major strength of current feminist research.

There is, however, a danger that if self-reflexivity is taken to an extreme it can become a problem of infinite regress in which one's perspective on one's perspective is analyzed in terms of one's perspective, and so on. Ceaseless relativity and contextualization can lead to increasing levels of abstraction until all meaning is lost.

Reliability and Validity

Feminists working from different epistemological positions (feminist empiricism, feminist standpoint, and feminist postmodernism) work with differing notions of reliability and validity. Feminist empiricists aim to conduct research that "meets the standards of the mainstream social sciences of validity, reliability, objectivity and replicability" (Spalter-Roth & Hartmann, cited in Reinharz, 1992, p. 94), combined with a deep sensitivity to feminist values. Diana Russell (1982), for example, in discussing her study of marital rape, states that in designing her study "it was my intention to combine the most rigorous, scientifically sound methodology with a deep knowledge of, and sensitivity to, the issues of rape" (p. 28). Such feminist empirical researchers seek to use traditional approaches to reliability and validity, but with scrupulous attention to potential researcher bias (Eichler & Lapointe, 1985). They insist, for example, that the sex and statuses of both researchers and research participants be carefully documented to assess possible distortions in findings resulting from otherwise hidden influences of gender–power (Woodard, 1991). They also argue that the construct validity of measurement instruments (e.g., the Marital Satisfaction Inventory) must be validated through separate assessments of men and women.

Feminist standpoint and social constructionist researchers, on the other hand, emphasize qualitative methodologies and challenge the very idea of scientific objectivity. These feminist researchers think of reliability and validity in very different terms. As Gergen (1988) points out, "all aspects of the scientific method require acts of interpretation . . . what becomes established fact is not reflective of the world as it is, but the world as subjected to an *a priori* linguistic framework" (p. 50). Many feminists therefore challenge the positivist belief that "the only way to establish valid knowledge is through scientific procedure" (Gergen, 1988, p. 50) and focus instead on analyzing phenomena in their cultural and historical contexts, declaring personal and institutional interest in the research, and being clear about the researcher's personal values and goals in doing the research (Gergen, 1988). They suggest that "rather than abandoning objectivity, [such] systematic examination of assumptions and values in the social order that shape scientific practices can strengthen objectivity" (Riger, 1992, p. 737). These feminist researchers use concepts such as "trustworthiness" to speak of their notion of reliability and "credibility" to speak of their notion of validity (Guba & Lincoln, 1989). Olesen (1994) points out some of the difficulties facing feminists using qualitative methods in relation to reliability and validity:

> Perhaps no issue is as challenging to feminist . . . researchers as that of adequacy or credibility, the parallel to validity in quantitative work. Because they often problematize taken-for-granted situations, raise difficult and uncomfortable questions about women's contexts, and stress the importance of subjectivity, feminist[s] . . . working in the qualitative mode are particularly vulnerable to positivists' criticisms about credibility. (p. 165)

Skills

To undertake research from a feminist perspective requires the scholar to develop a variety of conceptual, perceptual, and practice skills. Most fundamental is the need for a feminist consciousness, including conceptual skills in the analysis of gender and power relations grounded in a knowledge of feminist theory and scholarship. This includes skill in analyzing gender and power relations inherent in all aspects of the research endeavor itself. Having said that, we must repeat that the complexity, multiplicity, and diversity of feminist thought means that there is no *one* or correct feminist consciousness and that feminists themselves often disagree strongly in their understanding of the dynamics of gender oppression. What is necessary, however, is an understanding of the range of feminist ideas and an ability to utilize them in conceptualizing research questions and interpreting results.

A second requirement is the possession of self-reflexive skills, which include the capacity of the researcher to know herself and her values, to locate herself in context, and to observe any phenomenon, including herself, as historically and culturally situated. This capacity includes an understanding of how her research both springs from and is affected by her own experience as a gendered person of a particular race, class, culture, and sexual orientation. It also includes an acknowledgement of these subjectivities and the partial view inherent in any research she undertakes.

We regard the ability to work collaboratively as an important skill in doing feminist research. Feminist research is often carried out by teams whose members have diverse viewpoints and different disciplinary backgrounds. In addition, the action focus of feminist research often requires collaborative skills in working closely with community groups as part of research planning, data collection, and policy implementation.

Finally, feminist scholarship requires competence in the research methodologies of one's own discipline. In family therapy, these include any or all of the various methodologies used in our field. Although those discussed earlier in this chapter may be somewhat more suited to feminist goals and questions, feminist scholars could conceivably utilize any methodology. What is important is that the researcher develop skills both in the particular method to be used and in transforming this method to be consistent with feminist values and assumptions.

From our perspective, these skills can be developed and possessed by men as well as by women. Therefore, to the question whether men can do feminist research, we would answer yes. As yet, we know of very few men in family therapy, however, who identify themselves as feminist in their research publications. We would like to think that in the future more men in our field will identify themselves as feminist, develop the skills to do research using a feminist lens, and work collaboratively with women on feminist research teams.

Bridging Research and Practice

The commitment of feminist researchers to make their research findings highly accessible has the potential for securely bridging the often disparate communities of research and practice in family therapy. Their attention to reporting results in transparent and nondistancing ways means that clinicians may more easily understand and apply the results of feminist research to their practice. This includes such reporting practices as the researcher acknowledging and discussing her personal values, assumptions, biases, and interest in the research; writing reports in the first person; contextualizing results; and presenting results in nondoctrinaire ways. Although not all these practices are followed in all feminist research, they are increasingly evident, even in empirical studies. They allow the clinician to assess the fit between the researcher's assumptions and philosophy and their own and thus to determine how much value they will place on the results. In qualitative studies, participants' voices are clearly heard, further increasing their potential to influence clinicians' thinking and practice.

The feminist commitment to creating social change means that feminist researchers are specifically interested in doing research that has social relevance for clinicians and for how therapy is done. Research questions are designed with a social change intent, and results are usually expressed in terms of their relevance for practice. In addition, the questions of greatest interest to feminist researchers concerning gender, power, abuse, and "voice" are frequently those with high relevance and interest for clinicians.

In the participatory and collaborative models of research used by many feminists, clinicians may be consulted in both research design and presenting results in ways that maximize their relevance and accessibility to clinicians. Power may be deliberately shared through making information and findings accessible to participants and participatory communities, where the results can be directly applied. Kiernan's (1994) program evaluation study, discussed earlier, is a good example of this power-sharing process through the communication of results.

We suggest, then, that by its very nature, including its commitment to making all aspects of the research process transparent and its commitment to social change, feminist research has special potential for bridging research and practice in family therapy.

FUTURE DIRECTIONS

We now move to a consideration of possible directions for feminist ideas in future family therapy research. In so doing, we examine future directions both for family therapy research in general and for feminist family therapy research in particular. We begin with the broader picture of family therapy research.

We would first hope to see an expansion and diversification in future family therapy research providing a multiplicity of methods and approaches in keeping with the feminist emphasis on methodological pluralism. The past several years have been marked by debate within family therapy regarding the relative merits of quantitative and qualitative methods. Writers other than feminists have variously recommended broadening the range of possibilities to include qualitative methods (Atkinson & Heath, 1987; Atkinson, Heath, & Chenail, 1991; Moon, Dillon, & Sprenkle, 1990), multimethods research involving both quantitative and qualitative methods (Moon & Sprenkle, 1992), a constructionist understanding of research as narrative (McNamee, 1994), and utilizing more egalitarian research processes (Beer, 1992).

We are delighted to see this discussion in the field and to see the growing recognition and legitimization of a wider range of approaches. What we would add to this discussion from our feminist perspective is a call for greater awareness of, and attention to, issues of gender and power at every step of the research process. In Carolyn Woodard's (1991) study of the treatment of gender as a social variable in research published in four major family therapy journals in 1979 and 1989, she found that 30 relevant gender-sensitive variables were not included in the majority of the 82 studies examined. Some of these variables were very basic; we list several of them here to indicate the fundamental lack of attention to gender in much family therapy research. They include failure to report the sex of participants, to report the sex of the research assistants, to discuss the possible impact of the sex of assistants on the findings, to analyze for sex differences, to note the relevance of gender to the findings, to state the researcher's own gender assumptions, to discuss gender concepts in the literature review, to state the reason for doing a single-sex study, and to discuss the gender bias of the instruments used. Woodard's investigation revealed a disturbing level of gender blindness in family therapy research which we believe must be addressed in future research in the field.

We suggest that all family therapy researchers, feminist or not, must, at a minimum, develop their awareness of their own gender values and beliefs and a sensitivity to gender as a social category if they are to avoid unconscious gender bias in their research with the consequent replication of dominant ideas about women and men. We encourage family therapy researchers to be conscious of the gender implications of the choices they make throughout the research process—in research focus, choice of participants, methods used, interpretation, and presentation of findings. We also encourage them to make explicit their own values, assumptions, and personal interest in the research question.

Future directions for feminist researchers in family therapy are somewhat more complex and involve an examination of the present state of feminist epistemology in the field. There are several feminist perspectives present and influential within family therapy, each with its own research priorities. We therefore propose several interconnected directions for the future. The initial feminist agenda in the field was concerned primarily with revealing and changing the sources of women's oppression in their experiences of family therapy. This perspective provided the foundation for the initial development of feminist thought and action; the social justice and constructionist feminisms developed concurrently and more recently. Each perspective highlights particular research concerns which we briefly discuss.

Addressing Gaps in Our Knowledge about Women and Their Experience

We are struck with how little research exists in family therapy on women, their experience and their perspectives—as therapists, as clients, in supervisory and training relationships, as employees in agencies and institutions, as authors and researchers, and as members of professional associations. The need to create space for women's voices remains important and overdue. We view it as a complement to other research priorities, such as those that follow.

Integrating Social Justice and Inclusivity into the Research Agenda

The more recently emerging social justice perspective in family therapy draws attention to the need for research that simultaneously includes multiple oppressions and increases our understanding of how gender, class, and race interact to shape family experience. As Jodie Kliman (1994) points out:

> Each of these central organizing principles of family life has been addressed (to different extents, and mostly separately from each other) in the family therapy literature. But these treatments often underestimate each variable's contribution to the social contexts in which the others are experienced and defined. Because these principles shape family life *in dynamic relation to one another*, their implications for family therapy theory and practice are best understood in their shared context. (p. 25)

Feminist research integrating a social justice perspective would have us grapple with the complex interplay of race, class and gender oppressions as they are experienced in families. Research from this perspective might focus on the impact of patriarchal ideology on men's lives as well as women's, and on the implications of multiple oppressions for family therapy processes and therapeutic relationships. It would ensure that voices from the margin are heard and that the power relations inevitably involved in therapist–client interaction and in the very nature of therapy are made transparent.

Expanding the Research Agenda to Include a Social Constructionist Feminist Standpoint

Although few investigations from a constructionist feminist perspective have emerged within family therapy, we believe that working within this frame can open new frontiers for researchers. This perspective highlights the researcher's responsibility in the construction of male and female stories and in the representation of their voices. Objectivity is always viewed from a paradoxical perspective—the observer is always part of the system being observed. Therefore, the observer must always be involved in a self-reflexive process of examining her own assumptions, beliefs, and values, which will necessarily determine what she sees and how she sees it, as well as what practices she adopts (McNamee, 1994).

This perspective provides two important directions for future feminist research in the field. It suggests that (1) research should increasingly address questions of observer standpoint and incorporate reflexive practices in developing understandings of the therapy–research process, and (2) research should give increasing attention to the ever-present gender and power relations between researcher and participant and between therapist and client. Finally, the constructionist perspective invites us to critically assess all standpoints and political positions, including the emancipatory project itself, and to use reflexivity to avoid constructing new tyrannical ideologies and practices.

CONCLUSION

We are aware of a certain irony that runs through this chapter. Although our task has been to review feminist approaches to research in family therapy, very little such research exists in spite of the presence and growing importance of feminist perspectives in the field for almost two decades. Our approach to this dilemma has been to examine family therapy and feminist research as two separate fields with an emerging area of overlap. We see this overlap as containing within it multifaceted approaches to research encompassing diverse, conflicting, and changing views on research priorities and strategies. Our objective has been to clarify the basic assumptions of the different approaches to feminist epistemology and to explore their implications for feminist research in family therapy. The discourse about feminist research in the social sciences that we have reviewed is rich with ongoing debate and critical reflection. These features, and an emphasis on self-reflexivity, ensure the transformative nature of current feminist theory. There is "a need to question all authoritative accounts, even feminist ones, otherwise they become part of the problem" (Lather, 1988, p. 577). It is our hope that this chapter will both support the efforts of family therapy researchers to examine their practices and promote strong and diverse feminist voices in the field.

REFERENCES

Acker, J., Barry, K., & Esseveld, J. (1991). Objectivity and truth. In M. M. Fonow & J. A. Cook (Eds.), *Beyond methodology: Feminist scholarship as lived research* (pp. 133–153). Bloomington: Indiana University Press.

Atkinson, B., & Heath, A. (1987). Beyond objectivism and relativism: Implications for family therapy research. *Journal of Strategic and Systemic Therapies, 6,* 8–17.

Atkinson, B., Heath, A., & Chenail, R. (1991). Qualitative research and the legitimation of knowledge. *Journal of Marital and Family Therapy, 17,* 161–166.

Avis, J. M. (1985). The politics of functional family therapy: A feminist critique. *Journal of Marital and Family Therapy, 11,* 127–136.

Avis, J. M. (1986). *Training and supervision in feminist-informed family therapy: A Delphi study.* Unpublished doctoral dissertation, Purdue University, West Lafayette, IN.

Avis, J. M. (1988). Deepening awareness: A private study guide to feminism and family therapy. *Journal of Psychotherapy and the Family, 3,* 15–46.

Avis, J. M. (1989). Integrating gender into the family therapy curriculum. *Journal of Feminist Family Therapy, 1,* 3–26.

Avis, J. M. (1991). Power politics in therapy with women. In T. J. Goodrich (Ed.), *Women and power: Perspectives for family therapy* (pp. 183–202). New York: Norton.

Avis, J. M. (1992). Violence and abuse in families: The problem and family therapy's response. *Journal of Marital and Family Therapy, 18,* 223–230.

Avis, J. M. (1994). Advocates versus researchers—A false dichotomy? A feminist, social constructionist response to Jacobson. *Family Process, 33,* 87–91.

Avis, J. M., Lero, D. S., & Guldner, C. (1992). *Meeting the challenge: Educating professionals for child sexual abuse treatment. Final Report of a national study.* Ottawa: Health and Welfare Canada.

Beer, J. (1992, Spring). Towards more useful research. *AFTA Newsletter, 47,* 57–59.

Black, L., & Piercy, F. P. (1991). A feminist family therapy scale. *Journal of Marital and Family Therapy, 17,* 111–120.

Bograd, M. (1984). Family systems approaches to wife battering: A feminist critique. *American Journal of Orthopsychiatry, 54,* 558–568.

Bograd, M. (1988). Power, gender and the family: Feminist perspectives on family systems therapy. In M. A. D. Douglas & L. E. Walker (Eds.), *Feminist psychotherapies: Integration of therapeutic and feminist systems* (pp. 118–133). Norwood, NJ: Ablex.

Bograd, M. (1992). Values in conflict: Challenges to family therapists' thinking. *Journal of Marital and Family Therapy, 18,* 245–256.

Chaney, S., & Piercy, F. (1988). A feminist family therapist behavior checklist. *American Journal of Family Therapy, 16,* 305–318.

Coleman, S. B., Avis, J. M., & Turin, M. (1990). A study of the role of gender in family therapy training. *Family Process, 29,* 365–374.

Collins, P. H. (1989). The social construction of black feminist thought. *Signs, 14,* 745–773.

Denzin, N. K. (1994). The art and politics of interpretation. In N. K. Denzin & Y. S. Lincoln (Eds.), *Handbook of qualitative research* (pp. 500–515). Thousand Oaks, CA: Sage.

Devault, M. (1990). Talking and listening from women's standpoint: Feminist strategies for interviewing and analysis. *Social Problems, 37,* 96–116.

Dienhart, A., & Avis, J. M. (1994). Working with men in family therapy: An exploratory study. *Journal of Marital and Family Therapy, 20,* 397–417.

Eichler, M., & Lapointe, J. (1985). *On the treatment of the sexes in research.* Ottawa: Social Sciences and Humanities Research Council of Canada.

Finch, J. (1984). "It's great to have someone to talk to": The ethics and politics of interviewing women. In C. Bell & H. Roberts (Eds.), *Social researching: Politics, problems, practice* (pp. 70–87). London: Routledge & Kegan Paul.

Fine, M., & Turner, J. (1991). Tyranny and freedom: Looking at ideas in the practice of family therapy. *Family Process, 30,* 307–320.

Flax, J. (1987). Postmodernism and gender relations in feminist theory. *Signs, 12,* 621–643.

Flax, J. (1990). *Thinking fragments: Psychoanalysis, feminism, and postmodernism in the contemporary west.* Berkeley: University of California Press.

Fonow, M. M., & Cook, J. A. (1991). Back to the future: A look at the second wave of feminist epistemology and methodology. In M. M. Fonow & J. A. Cook (Eds.), *Beyond methodology: Feminist scholarship as lived research* (pp. 1–15). Bloomington: Indiana University Press.

Foucault, M. (1980). *Power/knowledge: Selected interviews and other writings: 1972–1977* (C. Gordon, Ed. and Trans.). New York: Pantheon.

Gavey, N. (1989). Feminist poststructuralism and discourse analysis: Contributions to a feminist psychology. *Psychology of Women Quarterly, 13,* 459–475.

Gergen, M. M. (1988). Building a feminist methodology. *Contemporary Social Psychology, 13,* 47–53.

Goldner, V. (1985). Feminism and family therapy. *Family Process, 24,* 31–47.

Goldner, V. (1988). Generation and gender: Normative and covert hierarchies. *Family Process, 27,* 17–31.

Goldner, V. (1992). Making room for both/and. *Family Therapy Networker, 16,* 54–61.

Goodrich, T. J. (1991). *Women and power.* New York: Haworth Press.

Greene, B. (1994). Diversity and difference: The issue of race in feminist therapy. In M. P. Mirkin (Ed.), *Women in context: Toward a reconstruction of psychotherapy* (pp. 333–351). New York: Guilford Press.

Guba, E. G., & Lincoln, Y. S. (1989). *Fourth generation evaluation.* Newbury Park, CA: Sage.

Haig, C. (1988). *Mother-blaming in major family therapy journals: A content analysis.* Unpublished master's thesis, University of Guelph, Guelph, Ontario.

Haig, C., & Avis, J. M. (1989). *Mother-blaming in major family therapy journals: A content analysis.* Unpublished manuscript, University of Guelph, Ontario.

Harding, S. (1986). *The science question in feminism.* Ithaca, NY: Cornell University Press.

Harding, S. (1987). Introduction: Is there a feminist method? In S. Harding (Ed.), *Feminism and methodology* (pp. 1–14). Bloomington: Indiana University Press.

Hare-Mustin, R. T. (1978). A feminist approach to family therapy. *Family Process, 17,* 181–194.

Hare-Mustin, R. (1987). The problem of gender in family therapy theory. *Family Process, 26,* 15–33.

Hare-Mustin, R. (1992, November). *On the need for second order change in family therapy research.* Plenary address presented at the Research/Clinical Conference of the American Family Therapy Academy, Captiva Island, FL.

Hare-Mustin, R. (1994). Discourses in the mirrored room: A postmodern analysis of therapy. *Family Process, 33,* 19–35.

Jayartine, R. E., & Stewart, A. J. (1991). Women's research or feminist research? The debate surrounding feminist science and methodology. In M. M. Fonow & J. Cook (Eds.), *Beyond methodology: Feminist scholarship as lived research* (pp. 85–106). Bloomington: Indiana University Press.

Kiernan, K. M. (1994). *A diversity of voices: An evaluation of a program for child witnesses to wife abuse.* Unpublished master's thesis, University of Guelph, Guelph, Ontario.

Kliman, J. (1994). The interweaving of gender, class, and race in family therapy. In M. P. Mirkin (Ed.), *Women in context: Toward a feminist reconstruction of psychotherapy* (pp. 25–47). New York: Guilford Press.

Lamb, S. (1991). Acts without agents: An analysis of linguistic avoidance in journal articles of men who batter women. *American Journal of Orthopsychiatry, 61,* 250–257.

Lather, P. (1988). Feminist research perspectives on empowering research methodologies. *Women's Studies International Forum, 11,* 569–582.

Leupnitz, D. (1988). *The family interpreted: Feminist theory in clinical practice.* New York: Basic Books.

Magraw, S. (1992). *Feminism and family therapy: An oral history.* Unpublished doctoral dissertation, California School of Professional Psychology, Berkeley/Alameda.

Maguire, P. (1987). *Doing participatory research: A feminist approach.* Amherst, MA: Center for International Education, University of Massachusetts.

McNamee, S. (1994). Research as relationally situated activity: Ethical implications. *Journal of Feminist Family Therapy, 6,* 69–80.

McNamee, S., & Gergen, K. J. (1992). (Eds.). *Therapy as social construction.* Newbury Park, CA: Sage.

Moon, S. M., Dillon, D. R., & Sprenkle, D. H. (1990). Family therapy and qualitative research. *Journal of Marital and Family Therapy, 16,* 357–373.

Moon, S. M., & Sprenkle, D. H. (1992, Spring). Multi-methodological family therapy research. *AFTA Newsletter, 47,* 29–30.

Oakley, A. (1980a). *Becoming a mother.* New York: Schocken.

Oakley, A. (1980b). *Women confined: Towards a sociology of childbirth.* Oxford, UK: Martin Robertson.

Oakley, A., & Oakley, R. (1981). Sexism in official statistics. In J. Irvine, I. Miles, & J. Evans (Eds.), *Demystifying social statistics* (pp. 172–189). London: Pluto.

Olesen, V. (1994). Feminisms and models of qualitative research. In N. K. Denzin & Y. S. Lincoln (Eds.), *Handbook of qualitative research* (pp. 158–174). Thousand Oaks, CA: Sage.

Opie, A. (1992). Qualitative research, appropriation of the "other" and empowerment. *Feminist Review, 40,* 52–69.

Piercy, F. P., & Sprenkle, D. H. (1990). Marriage and family therapy: A decade review. *Journal of Marriage and the Family, 52,* 1116–1126.

Pinderhughes, E. (1986). Minority women: A nodal point in the functioning of the social system. In M. Ault-Riche (Ed.), *Women and family therapy* (pp. 51–63). Rockville, MD: Aspen.

Reinharz, S. (1992). *Feminist methods in social research.* New York: Oxford University Press.

Riger, S. (1992). Epistemological debates, feminist voices: Science, social values, and the study of women. *American Psychologist, 47,* 730–740.

Russell, D. E. H. (1982). *Rape in marriage.* New York: Macmillan.

Smith, D. E. (1987). *The everyday world as problematic: A feminist sociology.* Boston: Northeastern University Press.

Stacey, J. (1988). Can there be a feminist ethnography? *Women's Studies International Forum, 11,* 21–27.

Stanley, L., & Wise, S. (1979). Feminist research, feminist consciousness and experiences of sexism. *Women's Studies International Quarterly, 2,* 359–374.

Tamasese, K., & Waldegrave, C. (1993). Cultural and gender accountability in the "Just Therapy" approach. *Journal of Feminist Family Therapy, 5,* 29–45.

Thompson, L. (1992). Feminist methodology for family studies. *Journal of Marriage and the Family, 54,* 3–18.

Turner, J. (1991). Migrants and their therapists: A trans-context approach. *Family Process, 30,* 407–419.

Turner, J., & Fine, M. (1995). Postmodern evaluation in family therapy supervision. *Journal of Systemic Therapies, 14,* 57–69.

Walters, M., Carter, B., Papp, P., & Silverstein, O. (1988). *The invisible web: Gender patterns in family relationships.* New York: Guilford Press.

Weedon, C. (1987). *Feminist practice and poststructuralist theory.* Oxford, UK: Blackwell.

Weingarten, K. (1991). The discourses of intimacy: Adding a social contructionist and feminist view. *Family Process, 30,* 285–305.

Weingarten, K. (1992). A consideration of intimate and non-intimate interactions in therapy. *Family Process, 31,* 45–59.

Wheeler, D. (1985). *The theory and practice of feminist-informed family therapy: A Delphi study.* Unpublished doctoral dissertation, Purdue University, West Lafayette, IN.

Wolf, M. (1992). *A thrice-told tale: Feminism, postmodernism, and ethnographic responsibility.* Stanford, CA: Stanford University Press.

Woodard, C. I. (1991). Gender as a social variable in family therapy research: A content analysis. Unpublished master's thesis, University of Guelph, Guelph, Ontario.

Yllo, K. (1988). Political and methodological debate in wife abuse research. In K. Yllo & M. Bograd (Eds.), *Feminist perspectives on wife abuse* (pp. 28–50). Newbury Park, CA: Sage.

Focus Group Evaluations

8

Focus Groups in Family Therapy Research

FRED P. PIERCY
VERNON NICKERSON

D R. STELLA STARR received a 4.9 overall rating (on a 5-point scale) for her workshop at the American Association for Marriage and Family Therapy (AAMFT) conference. Dr. David Dweeb, on the other hand, received a 2.1. The program committee considered Dr. Starr's ratings when they invited her back the following year to do a conference institute. She eventually wrote a book, appeared on *Oprah,* and now conducts workshops across the country. Dr. Dweeb, on the other hand, now shovels manure in a stable in the small town of Tumbleweed.

Such rating systems help program committees make gross distinctions between stars and dweebs. However, what kind of research might give us a clue as to why Dr. Starr received such high ratings? And, more important, what kind of research could help us learn from her success? One approach would be for the researcher to get groups of people together who attended one of Dr. Starr's presentations and ask them to talk about what they liked. A moderator could ask them questions that might encourage them to talk about what Dr. Starr said and did that made her workshop so popular. What about the workshop captured the participants' imagination? As one participant shares a thought, another could elaborate. This, in turn, might remind another about something else Dr. Starr did. The moderator would encourage a free discussion and would ask for specific examples of the qualities the participants identified.

Immediately after these group discussions, the moderator could jot down some of the preliminary themes that emerged. Later, a secretary could transcribe the audiotapes of the discussions. The research team could review the transcript for discrete behaviors and qualities of Dr. Starr, as well as illustrative examples of each. The team would put each on a separate 3" × 5" card and again inductively categorize them in terms of themes. The researcher then would write a research article in clear, practical language that includes both themes and illustrations of workshop excellence. Dr. Dweeb, during a break at the Tumbleweed stable, could then read the article and learn to be a better presenter.

BACKGROUND

These kinds of small group discussions and data analyses are what go on in focus group evaluation. Basically, a focus group involves an interactive group discussion on a particular topic within a permissive, nonthreatening environment (Krueger, 1988). The purpose is to understand the participants' views of the topic. The open-response format and the synergistic, snowballing effect of group discussion often result in rich ideas that would be impossible through individual interviews or more quantitative methods. Focus group results are usually practical and participants typically enjoy the focus group experience.

Philosophical Assumptions

Labels carry different connotations for different people. Depending on one's politics and ideology, one develops opinions, values, and prejudices around all kinds of labels—conservative, liberal, Republican, Democrat, Baptist, Amway distributor, telemarketer. Similarly, it is natural to judge a research procedure by the philosophical label associated with it. Labels such as positivist, postpositivist, and constructivist all have their champions.

Focus group research methods, however, do not hold philosophical assumptions; focus group researchers do. For example, a positivist researcher who assumes an objective reality may use focus groups to generate ideas for quantitative items to measure that reality. A postpositivist, who believes in an objective reality and one's inability to ever know it fully, may still use focus group discussions to point toward or approximate that reality. Similarly, a constructivist may discount objective reality altogether but may still use focus groups to identify the subjective, mutually constructed community of beliefs surrounding certain topics.

In other words, there is no innate philosophical assumption implicit in the use of focus groups. It is up to the researcher to clarify his or her philosophical assumptions and how he or she uses the focus group methodology consistent with those assumptions. Then the reader can evaluate the logic of the focus group methodology within the researcher's philosophical framework and inevitably make judgments about the framework itself.

Historical Roots and Development

Social science researchers have used various types of group interviews since the 1920s (Frey & Fontana, 1993). However, the precursor to today's focus group is usually considered to have its origins in 1941, when Paul Lazarsfeld invited Robert Merton to assist him in evaluating audience response to radio programs at the Office of Radio Research at Columbia University (Stewart & Shamdasani, 1990). In their research, a studio audience listened to a radio program and pressed buttons on a polygraph-like device to indicate positive and negative responses to the program. Afterwards, the researchers asked the audience to explain their positive and negative reactions to the program, which was the beginning of the focused group interview (Merton, 1987).

In the midst of World War II, Merton used focused group interviews to analyze Army training and morale films for the Research Branch of the United States Army Information and Education Division. This resulted in a paper describing the methodology (Merton, 1946) and the book *The Focused Interview* (Merton, Fiske, & Kendall, 1956). Merton and his colleagues used focus group research findings, both during the war and later at Columbia University, in writing their classic book, *Mass Persuasion*, on persuasion and the influence of mass media (Merton, Fiske, & Curtis, 1946).

Since that time, focus group interviewing has grown to be an important research tool, particularly in marketing. For example, focus groups are the most popular method that advertisers use to evaluate television commercials. Similarly, movie studios frequently use focus groups to evaluate audience reactions to possible endings for new films. (The ending of *Fatal Attraction* was changed based on focus group feedback.)

Researchers are also increasingly using focus groups in such other applied social science areas as program evaluation, public policy, and communication. Similarly, focus groups are beginning to be used in such diverse disciplines as family studies (e.g., Pramualratana, Havanon, & Knodel, 1985) and marriage and family therapy (e.g., Polson, 1989; Polson & Piercy, 1993). Today, researchers are modifying focus group procedures to meet their own needs (Stewart & Shamdasani, 1990). For this reason, what is currently known as a focus group takes many different forms (Morgan, 1993) and does not necessarily follow all the procedures that Merton originally identified.

METHODOLOGY

Purposes and Research Questions

A research method should fit the purpose of an investigation and research questions should flow logically from that purpose. Clearly, some purposes do not fit a focus group methodology. For example, if a researcher's purpose is to test for significant differences or to generalize with statistical precision to a population, the researcher should choose more quantitative procedures. However, if the researcher wants to understand a phenomenon from the point of view of a group of people who have experienced that phenomenon, focus groups may be helpful.

The specific purposes of focus groups can vary widely. For example, they may be used to help quantitative social scientists develop questionnaires (Desvousges & Frey, 1989) or verify (i.e., triangulate) previous findings. They can also be used to generate theories and explanations (Morgan, 1993). Organizational administrators may use them to better understand what is going on in their organization, or the degree of consensus regarding a particular policy. Cross-cultural researchers may use focus groups as a respectful way to understand participants who value oral communication and/or who cannot read. Other researchers may use them to raise sensitive topics (Zeller, 1993), to understand the needs of low-income minority populations (Jarrett, 1993), and to design AIDS prevention materials (Fetro, 1990).

Perhaps the most common reason for social scientists to use focus groups is for program evaluation. Table 8.1 illustrates purposes for which family therapists might use focus groups at the beginning, middle, and end of a project (Krueger, 1988) and examples of research questions that might logically flow from these purposes.

Sampling and Selection Procedures

Focus groups are usually composed of 6 to 12 people (Stewart & Shamdasani, 1990). If a group has fewer than 6 people, it is sometimes hard to generate a diversity of ideas. If the group has more than 12 people, not everyonne gets a chance to talk and the moderator may find it difficult to keep the discussion focused on the research topic. The ideal number of participants for use is about 8. We usually invite 10, reasoning that 2 may drop out at the last minute.

TABLE 8.1. Use of Focus Group in Program Evaluation

Focus Groups before a Project Begins

Needs assessment

"What are the needs of the couples and families we want to serve? How can we meet these needs?"

Program material development

"Does this brochure get information across in the most effective manner? If not, how could it be improved?"

Marketing

"What are the best ways of reaching the group we want to serve? How can we best use media to get our message across? What kind of media?"

"What media do IV drug users and their families read/see/hear? Where could we place information about our program so that IV drug users and/or their families might see it?"

Program design

"What should be the components of our program? What components would best meet the needs of the people we want to serve? How should those components be organized?"

Strategic planning

"What are the short- and long-term goals for our program? How can we best address these goals? Which goals should we address first? Why?"

"What potential referral sources should we target? How should we contact these referral sources?"

Focus Groups during a Program

Ongoing program evaluation

"Is our program doing what it should do? What do you like about the program? What do you dislike? How should we change the program to become more responsive to client needs?"

Reducing dropouts and no-shows

"Why did you drop out of (or not show up at) our program?" How could we have done a better job of encouraging you to stay involved?"

Focus Groups after a Program

Program evaluation

"What did you like best about the program? What did you like least? What information were you most likely to use? How did you use it? What do you believe should be changed about the program for it to become more effective?"

Providing an organizational feedback loop

"What is effective about the way this organization (leader/program/department) works? What should be changed? Why? How should it be changed?"

Family Therapy-Related Focus Group Research Questions: A Few Personal Examples

Stress among family therapy graduate students and their families

"What stressors have been difficult to cope with in this graduate program? How have they affected your family? How have you coped with them? In what ways has your involvement in this program strengthened you individually and as a family? What suggestions do you have for future graduate students?" (Polson, 1989; Polson & Piercy, 1993).

Resiliency among families in Jakarta, Indonesia

"What individual and family factors have allowed certain adolescents to stay out of trouble and to excel in school even though they live in high-crime, high-poverty areas of Jakarta, Indonesia?" (Piercy, 1993).

Evaluation of a family therapy curricula for Indonesia

"Are there any aspects of these curricula and learning activities that are not sensitive to the Indonesian culture? If so, what are they? How could they be changed?" (Limansubroto, 1993).

TABLE 8.1. *cont.*

Resiliency among immigrant Hispanic families in therapy

"Do you see your shared ethnicity to be a resource for your family? What aspects of your Hispanic culture have supported you through difficult times?" (Rafuls, 1994).

[To family therapists, after they have viewed a videotape of Hispanic client families discussing strengths related to their culture] "Does this information alter your initial impressions of your client family? Will any of the information you have gained be useful to you in work with other families?" (Rafuls, 1994).

Most focus group experts emphasize homogeneity among focus group members as participants typically share more freely when they are with others from similar socioeconomic, educational, and cultural backgrounds. Even when the researcher wants to compare viewpoints of people from diverse categories, who thus may have different slants on a topic, Knodel (1993) suggests that it is better to hold separate focus groups, each homogeneous within itself but differing on what he calls "break characteristics." A break characteristic is any characteristic that differentiates one group from another. For example, it might be important to evaluate teenagers' reactions to family therapy in groups different from their parents' because the parents might inhibit the teenagers' discussion. Based on the purpose of the study, other possible break characteristics could include life stage, religion, socioeconomic status, residence (rural vs. urban), marital status, race, and gender. Also, researchers sometimes select groups based on certain break characteristics (e.g., economically disadvantaged rural women who have attended a parenting course at the local family service agency).

Subject selection is relatively easy when the purpose of the focus group study is clear. Consider, for example, our initial illustration of wanting to understand what makes Dr. Stella Starr such a good workshop leader. First, we would choose participants from people who had actually attended one of Dr. Starr's workshops. We also would want focus group participants who themselves evaluated Dr. Starr's workshop favorably. Perhaps we would also like to restrict participants to those who attended Dr. Starr's AAMFT workshop last year. It may be less compelling to form focus groups by such break characteristics as residence, religion, or even gender.

As another example, the senior author (F. P. P.) recently supervised a series of focus groups to evaluate why some children living in high-crime, high-poverty areas of Jakarta, Indonesia excelled in school and stayed out of trouble. Given this premise, focus group participants would logically be families living in these areas of Jakarta who had teens who excelled in school and stayed out of trouble. It also made sense to us to have separate focus groups for parents and teens because the parents' presence would likely inhibit some teens from talking freely. We also decided to hold separate groups of male and female teens, because a mixed group of Indonesian teens would also probably inhibit discussion. (We wanted to avoid the "peacock effect," where the boys show off for girls, which our Indonesian colleagues said was likely to happen.)

The researcher may contact subjects through the mail or by telephone. When asking subjects to take part, the researcher should explain the purpose of the study, the time requirements (usually 2 hours), and why the participant was selected. Many focus group researchers offer incentives such as money or gifts to participants and usually provide food and soft drinks at the focus group session itself. The day before the focus group session, the participants should be contacted again to be reminded of the session and their previous commitment to take part.

Researchers must be creative in recruiting and accommodating hard-to-reach participants. This often involves going where the participants are. For example, we have held focus groups related to AIDS prevention in prostitution houses. It may also be important to provide baby-sitting services, transportation, or a central location. In some cases, researchers have also used teleconferencing to bring people together from different cities (Stewart & Shamdasani, 1990).

How many focus groups should be held for a particular research purpose? Krueger (1988) suggests that researchers should hold focus groups until the issues raised by the participants become repetitive and nonproductive. This may mean scheduling four focus groups and canceling the last one if three seem sufficient. However, depending on the purpose (e.g., "What do the administrators of this agency think should be its long-term goals?"), one focus group may be enough.

Data Collection Procedures

Role of the Moderator

Most focus group researchers use moderators to lead focus group discussions. The moderator should be familiar with the research topic and skilled in group dynamics. The moderator's job is to raise questions and guide the group back to the topic when it gets off track. The moderator should be a good listener and communicator who encourages shy participants to speak and is skilled at not letting dominant participants talk on and on. He or she should establish rapport well, have a good sense of humor, and use self-disclosure in a manner that encourages self disclosure from the group. The moderator should also know when to pause and let the group process an issue and when to probe for more information (e.g., "Would you explain what you mean by that?" or "Do you have an example?"). The moderator should try not to support some opinions (through nods of approval or such comments as "That's a great idea") while ignoring others.

There is little consensus as to the training necessary to become a focus group leader. Moderators could be members of the research team, hired professionals, or even volunteers (Krueger, 1988). Krueger (1988) provides 12 hours of training for his volunteer moderators. We have found that we can use interpersonally skilled persons as moderators after we give them a thorough introduction to focus groups and opportunities to practice. We suggest that prospective moderators read *Focus Groups: A Practical Guide for Applied Research* (Krueger, 1988), observe an experienced moderator lead a focus group, and then lead a pilot focus group and receive feedback.

Krueger (1988) suggests that a focus group moderator work as a team with an assistant moderator. It is the assistant moderator's job to handle logistics (refreshments, lighting, seating), make sure that the tape recorder is working, and take comprehensive notes during the focus group. The assistant moderator may also wish to ask questions toward the end of the focus group and meet with the moderator at the end of the session for a postsession analysis of the major themes that came out during the group.

The Interview Guide

The interview guide is the set of questions the moderator asks the focus group members. These questions should flow directly from the research questions being investigated in the study. The interview guide should include from 6 to 10 written questions, with possible subpoints within each question. The moderator should be familiar with the questions and use the list only as a reminder of upcoming questions (Krueger, 1988).

The questions in the interview guide should be open-ended and should encourage group discussion. It is often helpful to begin with a welcome, a statement of the purpose of the focus group, any ground rules, and an ice-breaking question that allows each member of the focus group to talk (Krueger, 1988).

Questions should be ordered by their relative importance to the research agenda, from most important to less important, beginning with the more general, less specific technical questions. However, because a focus group discussion can take on a life of its own, it is important for the moderator to be flexible with the ordering of the questions and, when appropriate to the research topic, follow the direction of the discussion. For example, if the discussion is yielding fruitful ideas in an unexpected direction, the moderator should probe the responses and add new questions as necessary (Stewart & Shamdasani, 1990).

If more than one focus group interview is planned, the researcher may wish to consider using a "rolling interview guide" (Stewart & Shamdasani, 1990). That is, the experience of one focus group may lead the moderator to add or delete questions for the next focus group. Although this procedure has the advantage of adapting the learning from one focus group to the next one, it also has the disadvantage of lessening the researcher's ability to compare responses on the same questions across groups.

Specific Data Collection Procedures

While some focus group researchers use videotaping, one-way mirrors, and even focus meters (small boxes that let participants indicate their positive or negative feelings), most focus group researchers favor more low-tech procedures. They reason that because the main data are the themes of the group discussions, the discussion itself is best captured verbatim for subsequent analysis. This is usually done by audiotaping the focus group discussions and then transcribing them. The moderator and assistant moderator also typically keep ongoing case notes during the focus group discussions and, immediately after the focus group, discuss and write summaries of their impressions and the themes they note.

Data Analyses

When Standard Data Analyses Are Not Necessary

The primary data source of most focus group analyses is the verbatim transcripts of the focus group sessions. However, because data analyses should be consistent with the purposes of the study, there are times when a brief written or even oral summary report may be all that is needed. In such cases, the comments of the moderator and assistant moderator may suffice. For example, one of us (F. P. P.) recently held focus groups after each of a series of 5-day AIDS prevention workshops to learn about strengths and weaknesses of the workshop so our training team could improve the next workshop. For this purpose, all we really needed was a short written report and an oral summary.

There may be other times when the results of the focus group are so obvious that any additional analyses or write-up would be a waste of time and resources. For example, if the basic program evaluation question is, "Are future family intervention programs like this needed?", the answer may become quite evident as the focus group proceeds. Similarly, if administrators and decision makers are the members of the focus group itself, they may not want any additional documentation.

Standard Cut-and-Paste Analyses

Most focus group analyses involve some variation of code mapping (Knodel, 1993) or cut-and-paste techniques (Stewart & Shamdasani, 1990). Typically, the researcher reads over the transcript of the focus group once to identify those sections that are meaningful to the research questions and to get an overall "feel" for possible categories under each of the research questions. (It is also acceptable, according to Knodel [1993] to begin with hypothesized categories that can be confirmed, refuted, or added to on subsequent passes through the data.) On the second reading, initial category codes are marked in the margins. The researcher may be coding words, sentences, interchanges, or conceptual units. The researcher may need to pass through the data several times as additional units evolve. Once the coding is finished, the transcript is cut apart and sorted into meaningful categories under each of the research questions. These inductively derived categories provide the structure within which researchers will make their final interpretative analysis. Researchers typically use quotes from focus group members to illustrate the categories and assertions within the final report.

Computer software packages such as *The Ethnograph* (Seidel, Kjolseth, & Seymour, 1988) can be particularly helpful in coding and sorting categories (i.e., the "cut-and-paste" function). Also, researchers can use traditional word processing software packages as alternatives to scissors, colored pencils, tape, and 5" × 7" cards. Although computer technology can help in indexing and cross-referencing, it is still up to the researcher to make sense of the data. To minimize researcher bias, we recommend that more than one researcher be involved in the data categorization and analysis. They can categorize the data independently and then come together to discuss and resolve differences.

Also, because researchers should be as familiar with the data as possible, we believe that it is helpful for them to either moderate the focus group to at least observe the group process. This is, of course, at variance with the objectivity usually emphasized in more quantitative procedures. However, because researchers sooner or later must analyze and make sense of the data, we believe that they should try to be as acquainted with it as possible.

Content Analyses

Some focus group researchers discourage counting focus group data. Others have applied a wide range of content analyses procedures (see Krippendorf, 1980) to the transcripts of focus groups. The assumption driving the use of content analysis is that the analysis of language can provide a clue to the meanings participants ascribe to the subject of the focus group. The simplest content analysis is a finding counting sorting procedure that results in descriptive data such as counts of emotion-laden words. The problem with such an analysis is that because words are used in context, the context of the subject should also be part of the content analysis.

One computer-assisted approach, the Key-Words-in-Context technique, searches for key words and lists each along with the surrounding text (Stewart & Shamdasani, 1990). The researcher can limit the surrounding text by specifying the number of words or letters surrounding the key word and can subsequently categorize contexts as well as their relationship to key words.

Reporting the Results

Focus group research can generate a tremendous amount of data. It is not uncommon, for example, for one focus group session to generate 20 single-spaced pages of transcript. To report the results, researchers must look for statements that reflect themes, so that the trees can be seen in the midst of the forest. When the analysis focus group does not require a written report, the researcher can use a double-deck cassette player to find and record sections of the most meaningful quotes to supplement his or her oral report.

More frequently, though, data reduction and analysis occurs through some form of cut-and-paste procedure. Whether the researcher uses a word processor, or scissors, or 5" × 7" cards, the ultimate goal is to identify themes or trends, to use quotes to illustrate those trends, and to interpret these trends in the final report.

Krueger (1988) suggests three types of final reports, each using the initial research questions as the primary outline or structure. The first method of presentation, *the raw data model*, includes all participants' comments after a particular subject or research question. This involves little or no analysis by the researcher. The second method, *the descriptive model*, includes summary comments regarding themes followed by illustrative quotes by participants. The third method, *the interpretive model*, includes summary descriptions followed by illustrative quotes and the researcher's interpretations.

While Krueger's suggestions relate primarily to evaluation research, we also favor the interpretive model—use of summaries, illustrative quotes, and researcher interpretations—in writing up other focus group research studies. The appropriate journals for such reports will depend on the questions addressed and whether the focus group was used alone or in concert with other quantitative or qualitative methods. We see no reason why rigorous, good focus group research cannot be published in such top family therapy journals as *Family Process* and the *Journal of Marital and Family Therapy*.

DISCUSSION

Strengths and Weaknesses of the Methodology

One international foundation recently funded 15 research projects related to women and AIDS. All 15 of these projects employed focus groups (International Center for Research on Women, 1992). Why are such organizations interested in focus group social science research? What do focus groups have to offer family therapy researchers? What are the weaknesses of focus groups? In Table 8.2 we have summarized some of the advantages and disadvantages of focus group research.

Clearly, focus groups are not a panacea. Compared to other qualitative methods, focus groups do not allow for naturalistic observation as well as participant observation, and they do not allow for the same level of direct probing as individual interviews (Morgan & Spanish, 1984). However, they do a better job of combining these two goals than either participant observation or individual interviews alone.

Moreover, focus groups seem to have several unique advantages. They are quick and inexpensive and capitalize on the synergistic, snowballing effects of group discussion. When facilitated well, they are respectful and tolerant of diverse opinions. They encourage phenomenological, context-sensitive understanding and are usually a positive experience for the participants. Moreover, they can be catalytic in that the group may become motivated to take action regarding the topic they discussed.

The limitations of focus groups center around their inability to provide quantitative hypothesis testing or probability estimates. Potential sources of bias are also inherent in focus group research (as they are in all forms of research). In focus group research, for example, we can never know for sure whether results are generalizable or whether a strong group member, unfamiliar surroundings, or the moderator may have somehow biased the results.

TABLE 8.2. Advantages and Disadvantages of Focus Groups

ADVANTAGES	DISADVANTAGES
Format	
The setting is more naturalistic than that of a controlled experiment.	The setting is unnatural.
The format allows the moderator to probe for more information.	The procedures limit generalization.
	Participants' responses are not independent.
Synergistic group effect stimulates a wide variety of information.	The researcher has less control than in an individual interview.
Comments "snowball" or build on other comments to stimulate more creative ideas.	The moderator may knowingly or unknowingly bias the data by verbal and nonverbal clues.
Can be used with children and other samples that are not literate.	Groups can vary considerably.
	Focus groups may be difficult to assemble.
The researcher may interact directly with the participants.	Moderator must have special skills.
The method is flexible.	Anonymity of participants may not be possible within the group.
The open-response format can generate a large amount of rich data.	
Relatively low cost of time and money.	
Purpose	
Can generate theory and/or explanations.	Should not be used when statistical precision is a research goal.
Can triangulate the results of other methods.	
Can generate data on sensitive topics.	
Can support community participation and ownership when used in strategic planning.	
Can address a variety of questions.	
Provide a way for the researcher to increase the size of qualitative studies.	
Results	
Serendipitous ideas often surface during the group discussion.	The results may be affected by dominant or opinionated participants.
Participants usually enjoy the experience.	Traditional definitions of validity and reliability of data cannot be assured.
The results have high face validity.	
The results are available quickly.	
The results can serve a catalytic function in motivating participants to action.	
Interpretation	
The general results are usually easy to understand.	The wealth of data may make summarization and interpretation difficult.

Note. Data from Hess (1968), Krueger (1988), and Stewart and Shamdasani (1990).

On balance, however, if focus groups are used for appropriate purposes—such as understanding group opinion, or generating theory—family therapists should find them quite useful. Focus groups are robust, flexible, qualitative procedures that may be used on their own or in concert with other qualitative and quantitative procedures.

Reliability and Validity

Reliability

You may have guessed that traditional notions of reliability are simply not that important in focus group research. Recall our initial example. We wanted to know why Dr. Starr was such a popular workshop presenter. To find out, we speculated about using focus groups of people who attended her highly rated AAMFT workshop and inductively deriving categories of effective workshop leader qualities that might emerge during the focus group discussion. Our results would be heuristic in that they would raise possibilities of what might be effective for others, as well as future directions for more quantitative research on the subject. However, our purpose in using the focus group format would *not* be to determine whether the qualities that made Dr. Starr effective would also be the same for other presenters. All the same, Dr. Dweeb may still learn some useful presentation skills from reading our focus group results.

Reliability of procedures, on the other hand, *is* important in focus group research. Researchers should follow a standard, definable protocol for both running focus groups and analyzing focus group data. They should also summarize this protocol in published reports so that the reader can follow the logic of the analysis. This consistency serves to make focus group procedures more accountable and trustworthy.

Validity

Validity, at its most basic level, is the degree to which the data accurately reflect that which the researcher intends to measure. Because researchers use focus groups to better understand participants' view on a topic, valid data should be defined as the accurate reflection of the participants' views. Focus group results are valid, then, if they accurately reflect the views of the participants. Because the purpose of focus groups is to tap the perceived reality of participants, perceived reality *is* the reality on which the data must be considered. Do focus group data reflect perceived reality? They should, if the procedures we are advocating are followed closely.

A quantitative researcher recently asked the senior author (F. P. P.) about how marketing companies, in all good conscience, can afford to make million-dollar decisions based on focus group results that the company cannot be absolutely sure will generalize to the entire population. Good question. It is up to the researcher and sponsoring agency to decide the degree to which they wish to make program decisions based on focus group data. In many cases, the richness of these data may indeed be more compelling than statistical analyses of decontextualized, reductionistic information. In other cases, this may not be true. When external validity is a concern, we believe that marketing researchers—and family therapy researchers—would do well to use multiple research methods. This is not an indictment of focus group data, which do exactly what they are intended to do. It is simply prudent to supplement focus group data with quantitative methods when the researcher desires statistical precision.

Bridging Research and Practice

As noted earlier, researchers can use focus groups to learn about a wide range of practice issues and can then use the focus group results to improve clinical services. For example, researchers can use focus groups to assess needs, understand problems, and evaluate services in order to improve them.

Broadly speaking, though, family therapists are always engaged in focus group research when they work with families or other client groups. With this chapter in mind, we suggest that you become a more purposeful focus group researcher the next time you review a videotape of one of your therapy sessions. You can do this alone, with colleagues, or in a supervision group. What themes do you notice in the session? What categories of problems, communication patterns, emotions, and interventions emerge as you watch and listen to the tape? How can you use this information to become more effective in your own work with clients? As you can see, the perceptual and executive skills of a focus group researcher may be useful to the practicing family therapist.

FUTURE DIRECTIONS

Family therapy researchers are just beginning to discover focus groups. For this reason, the future directions of focus group research are a little like the roads out of Chicago—they go off in all directions. One "road" points toward the use of focus groups for needs assessment, another for program evaluation, and still another for more holistic and culturally sensitive interpretation of quantitative results. There are, of course, many other roads to travel for the family therapy researcher interested in focus groups.

We are excited about the generative, humanizing potential that focus group research can bring to the field of family therapy. We hope you will consider traveling down some of the roads discussed in this chapter. The ride should be fun and the destinations worthwhile.

REFERENCES

Desvousges, W. H., & Frey, J. H. (1989). Integrating focus groups and surveys: Examples from environmental risk studies. *Journal of Official Statistics, 5,* 349–363.

Fetro, J. (1990). Using focus group interviews to design materials. In A. C. Matiella (Ed.), *Getting the word out: A practical guide to AIDS materials development* (pp.37–48). Santa Cruz, CA: ETR Associates.

Frey, J., & Fontana, A. (1993). The group interview in social research. In D. Morgan (Ed.), *Successful focus groups: Advancing the state of the art* (pp. 20–34). Newbury Park, CA: Sage.

Hess, J. (1968). Group interviewing. In R. Ring (Ed.), *New science of planning.* Chicago: American Marketing Association.

International Center for Research on Women. (1992). The women and AIDS research program. *Information Bulletin,* 1–3. Washington, DC: ICRW.

Jarrett, R. (1993). Focus group interviewing with low-income minority populations. In D. Morgan (Ed.)., *Successful focus groups: Advancing the state of the art* (pp. 184–201). Newbury Park, CA: Sage.

Knodel, J. (1993). The design and analysis of focus group studies: A practical approach. In D. Morgan (Ed.), *Successful focus groups: Advances in the state of the art* (pp. 35–50). Newbury Park, CA: Sage.

Krippendorf, K. (1980). *Content analysis: An introduction to its methodology.* Beverly Hills, CA: Sage.

Krueger, R. A. (1988). *Focus groups: A practical guide for applied research.* Newbury Park, CA: Sage.

Limansubroto, D. W. (1993). *The compilation and organization of a family therapy teaching curriculum for Indonesian university students.* Unpublished master's thesis, Purdue University, West Lafayette, IN.

Merton, R. K. (1987). Focussed interviews and focus groups: Continuities and discontinuities. *Public Opinion Quarterly, 51,* 550–566.

Merton, R. K., Fiske, M., & Curtis, A. (1946). *Mass persuasion.* New York: Harper & Row.

Merton, R. K., Fiske, M., & Kendall, P. (1956). *The focused interview.* New York: Free Press.

Merton, R. K. (1946). The focussed interview. *American Journal of Sociology, 51,* 541–557.

Morgan, D. (Ed.). (1993). *Successful focus groups: Advancing the state of the art.* Newbury Park, CA: Sage.

Morgan, D., & Spanish, M. (1984). Focus groups: A new tool for qualitative research. *Qualitative Sociology, 7*(3), 253–270.

Piercy, F. (1993). *Final report of World AIDS Foundation Project, "AIDS prevention in Indonesia: Workshops for Health and Social Science Professionals."* Report to the World AIDS Foundation, Geneva, Switzerland.

Polson, M. (1989). *The exploration of program stress on trainee families in the Purdue Marriage and Family Therapy Program: A qualitatively oriented focus group study.* Unpublished master's thesis, Purdue University, West Lafayette, IN.

Polson, M., & Piercy, F. (1993). The impact of training stress on married family therapy trainees and their families: A focus group study. *Journal of Family Psychotherapy, 4*(1), 69–92.

Pramualratana, A., Havanon, N., & Knodel, J. (1985). Exploring the normative basis for age at marriage in Thailand: An example from focus group research. *Journal of Marriage and the Family, 47,* 303–310.

Rafuls, S. (1994). *The role of ethnicity in family resources: A qualitative analysis of Mexican American families in therapy.* Unpublished doctoral dissertation, Purdue University, West Lafayette, IN.

Seidel, J., Kjolseth, R., & Seymour, E. (1988). *The ethnograph: A user's guide.* Littleton, CO: Qualis Research Associates.

Stewart, D., & Shamdasani, P. (1990). *Focus groups: Theory and practice.* Newbury Park, CA: Sage.

Zeller, R. (1993). Focus group research on sensitive topics. In D. Morgan (Ed.), *Successful focus groups: Advancing the state of the art* (pp. 167–183). Newbury Park, CA: Sage.

III

QUANTITATIVE METHODS

Design and Measurement

9

Quantitative Design in Family Therapy
INSIDER HINTS ON GETTING STARTED

MITCHELL H. DICKEY

T HE VARIOUS CHAPTERS in this book provide the graduate student researcher with the most important information on each methodological tradition. This chapter does not focus on a particular research tradition per se. Rather, it offers a series of practical hints that cut across several traditions. It is a road map to help researchers avoid wrong turns and dead ends at the many intersections before a study is completed. The map begins with the decision whether to undertake the journey at all, warns of logistical dead ends and political potholes, and alerts readers to blind alleys with signposts on instrument selection and assessment strategies. It includes detailed sections on hypothesis generation and statistics and concludes with suggestions for telling the story of one's excursion in the final manuscript.

THE DECISION TO GET INVOLVED IN A PROJECT

Most graduate students begin doing research with their faculty advisers. The role of the graduate student is often to help collect data and enter it into the computer. This can be an excellent way for would-be researchers to get some exposure to the research process without much risk.

The most important decision is the first one: Should you get involved with this particular project? *The ideas behind the project simply must be innately interesting to you.* If the ideas behind the study are not innately interesting, you may decide that it is not worth the effort and quit the project.

How do you decide whether this is the project for you? If you want to focus your career on research and would be working with a nationally known researcher in an area close to your interests, I suggest you jump at the chance. If it is your first project and will require a lot of your time (e.g., to learn a faculty member's coding system), if the project could go on for several years, and if you are uncertain whether your name will ever be on a publication, you might think twice. The most important thing is not to get involved if you cannot make a commitment to the project. Ask yourself the following seven questions before you decide.

1. *What is my career path?* Am I primarily a clinician, a researcher, or (that dying breed) a scientist–practitioner?
2. *How well and in what ways does this project fit with my interests?* Is it tangential or central? Would I like to do more of this in the future? In the beginning you may not know how interested you are in a particular topic. You might try reading a few papers on this topic to see whether it piques your interest.
3. *What will I learn along the way?* Does this project further my long-term goals? Sometimes students on a research career path join a project because they will learn about a certain methodology or a certain population. Learning how to write a research report or review a paper are important skills in themselves and may justify one's time and effort. A student of mine is currently coding therapist intentions because she wants to learn about therapist thought processes. She considers it part of her clinical training.
4. *Will I get sufficient guidance?* Professors are busy and, like everybody else, they have to make good use of their time. Training you may not pay off for the faculty member if you cannot make a significant commitment. Working on faculty projects may not pay off for you if they do not have the time to guide you.
5. *What is the work structure?* How much time per week will it take, how many months (years) will the project run? What will be my role during that time?
6. *Will I be an author?* Which one? Where is the study likely to get published? This can be the most intimidating question of all. Most often it is not clear whether you will be an author or not at the start of the project. It depends on you, how much work you put in, and what role you have in the project. Universities and faculty differ greatly on this one. Fellow students are a good source of information.
7. *What about the principal investigator?* Do I enjoy working with him or her? Does he or she make the topic come alive? Is he or she well-organized and efficient? What is this professor's reputation regarding students? A professor's reputation is often a reliable guide and fellow students are often your best source of information. Ask several.

Choosing Your Own Topic

At the beginning of your career, there is no better way to begin than by working on a question you are really interested in. A question that you find personally meaningful is the only antidote (aside from the threat of not graduating) for the sheer effort it takes to undertake research. Choosing your own topic does create one problem: You will absolutely need the support of a faculty member for your project. But faculty members will choose projects that fit their interests. In this case they may not support you financially or intellectually to the degree they might otherwise. This is not mean-spirited; it is expedient. Junior faculty are under strong pressure to publish ("or perish") and must keep their efforts focused on their own work.

Faculty often test the strength of a prospective student's research ideas before they decide to take a student on. They ask themselves six questions (Zanna & Darley, 1987). You should use these same questions to test the strength of your own ideas before you ever embark on any project. Make sure you can answer them: The weak areas of your answers now are likely to be the weak areas of the paper later. If the ideas do not pass muster on these six questions, you may want to look for another topic. Test out your answers on fellow students before asking for a faculty member's time. Work through the worksheet found in the Appendix to refine your ideas before talking to potential faculty advisers. It will impress them that you are so focused and thoughtful. The questions are:

1. What is it you are interested in doing/finding out? What is the big question?
2. Why are you interested in doing this? What is so important about this topic/question?
3. How does your question relate to what is already known? What does the literature tell us?
4. How does this research differ from and/or extend previous research? What knowledge is likely to result?
5. How are you going to do this? What is the method and, possibly, the design?
6. What do you expect to find? What are the hypothesized results?

AUTHORSHIP

In recent years, a plethora of papers have been authored by three, four, or five persons and fewer papers have been authored by a single person. In a publish-or-perish world, order of authorship is important. The first author gets the most credit. In most empirical papers, the first author has originated the idea, acquired the funds, and been the primary administrator. Active collaborators are usually listed next and students who collect and score data are listed last. For the most part this is fair. At times professional hierarchy and status determine order of authorship more than one's actual contribution.

Some time ago a colleague was asked by his department chair to join him in writing a paper that the chair had been invited to write by the editor of an important journal. That meant the paper would be published. My colleague was eager to please his chair and improve his vita. He spent many hours preparing the document and when he submitted it to the chair, he was told he would be second or third author. This put my colleague in a difficult position. He could accept this order of authorship, not get his due credit, and bear his resentment or he could confront the chair, risk the chair's wrath, and still not get first authorship.

Authorship on dissertations can be a sticky issue. Faculty differ greatly regarding their expectations for authorship when you publish your dissertation. In my limited experience, senior (tenured) faculty are less insistent that they be included as an author than are junior faculty. Faculty members without tenure have extraordinary pressures to publish; time advising students on their dissertations can take away from time on their own research. Therefore, they are more likely to be interested in being included as an author. Because more widely known authors (even if listed second) tend to get the credit for the work, some students feel they do not want their advisers on the publications. *The point to be made here is that, even though it is often an awkward conversation, authorship should be discussed at the beginning of a project.* If you have questions about whether you should be included on a paper, consult the *Publication Manual* of the American Psychological Association (1994).

CLINICIAN INVOLVEMENT IN RESEARCH

At times it seems as if clinicians travel on one road and researchers take another; only rarely do they cross again. This clearly has implications for studies that depend on clinician–researcher collaboration. Collaboration works best when clinicians and researchers each take responsibility for areas within their own expertise and works worst when they do not.

For instance, when I was a graduate student, I wanted to get some experience studying the outcomes of therapy. A group of clinicians had developed what they thought was an effective, structured program of therapy for families. They wanted me to document its effectiveness so that they could use this information to advertise the program. We agreed that I would design a study, they would collect the data (as we lived in separate states), and I would score, enter, and analyze them. Initially this seemed like a mutually beneficial arrangement. Unfortunately, they collected data on only 9 of the 30 families. This is too low a percentage to consider publishing the results. I analyzed the data and gave them the results but could not agree to publish it. Our relationship soured.

Clinician Participation

In my experience clinicians will become involved in research if it does not take much time away from their practice, if they get trained in some technique, or if they can learn something from the project. In fact, I have been pleasantly surprised by the positive response from clinicians under these circumstances. In one project, treatment center staff administered various measures to inpatients during a free period in the week. They gave me the completed forms, which I coded and analyzed. Every 2 months I gave them results on their populations. This worked quite well: They got clinically relevant information on their patient population with minimal staff time; I got data.

FEASIBILITY

Topic Simplicity

The first rule for novice researchers is *to keep it simple*. Topic selection and design phases of a project are often full of optimism and excitement; ideas are fresh, obstacles have not yet been encountered, and the possibilities seem endless.

When the possibilities are endless, so are the projects. It is better to do a small project well than a large project poorly. *An overly ambitious question asked of an overly complex design is not a sign of creativity: It is a sign of inexperience.* Keep focused on one central question and, as you make design decisions, keep reminding yourself that one study can address only one question. For example, a simple question might read, "Is socioeconomic status correlated with family cohesion?" A complex question might read, "Is there a difference in the patterns of acculturation between Asian and European immigrants?" In the second question it is much more difficult to define and measure "pattern of acculturation."

Locating Participants

Can you locate enough appropriate families or therapists for your project? Where will you find them? Do not undertake a project in which you are not sure you can locate sufficient numbers of the kinds of families or therapists you want. For instance, if you want to study differences between Caucasian and Mexican American families, rural Iowa is probably not the best place to conduct it. Change topics or do the study in Chicago.

HYPOTHESIS GENERATION

One of the most important yet neglected aspects of research is the development and formulation of hypotheses. This is so often taken for granted that graduate students (and some seasoned researchers) design a study based on an idea rather than on a hypothesis. A hypothesis is a formal statement of at least two variables *and* an imputed relationship between them. It is not enough to say you want to look at family responses to systemic reframes: That is an idea. A hypothesis also includes a clearly stated relationship between two variables: Cohesive families will respond *better* to reframes than other families.

Professor William McGuire first taught me how ideas evolve and mature into researchable hypotheses. He taught me to undertake initial "thought experiments" before ever committing to a hypothesis or research design. Doing this has taught me how simplistic my original ideas often are and how to sharpen my thinking on any number of topics with this dialogical thinking. I would guess that he has probably saved me close to 500 hours of wasted work with the few hours that these "thought experiments" take.

These "thought experiments" are more fully developed in the worksheet in the Appendix to this chapter. *I strongly suggest that students go through this worksheet at least once (preferably two or three times) before designing an experiment.* As Sir Joshua Reynolds once quipped: "There is no expedient to which man will not resort to avoid the real labor of thinking." Do not begin an experiment before going through the steps described below in considerable detail. The real labor of thinking now will save you much real labor later.

DECISIONS ABOUT DESIGN

Sampling Strategies

The relevance and results of a study depend to a large extent on the samples of families included in it. You will need a referral source from which families can be solicited. Perhaps local churches or Alcoholics Anonymous groups will allow you to ask their members if they want to participate. *Be aware that the source from which families come will probably affect both your results and your ability to generalize findings.*

Survey studies depend on having a random sample of all possible people to whom the research question applies. Showing that you have a random sample is quite difficult and I suggest you not conduct such a study without adequate funds to hire staff to help you.

How do you decide which families are included in the study and which are not? At present, most family therapy studies select families for a study based on the clinical features of an individual family member, usually the identified patient (Wynne, 1988; Goldstein, 1988).

Family-Level Inclusion Criteria

Perhaps you would rather use family-level scores as a criterion to include or exclude families. How do you decide whether or not to include the family if family members disagree about how they function? Do you include a family if parents' scores meet your entrance criteria but adolescents' scores do not? You can always take a part of the family system (say, the parents) and select families for the study based on the fact that both parents rate their relationship with their adolescent as troubled.

The most convincing approach to determining family distress employs thresholds at multiple levels of the system. Gilbert, Christiansen, and Margolin (1984) defined a family as distressed if they scored above the 86th percentile on two of three levels (the individual, dyadic, or family levels). This type of definition both ensures that families in the distressed group have "real" problems and is flexible enough so that one does not have to exclude a high percentage of potential families because they do not reach the threshold.

Piloting the Procedures

Despite your diligence in going through the worksheet, it is not possible to anticipate all the possible problems with the nuts and bolts of the procedures. Many of the kinks can be worked out by testing your procedures and measures on a few families before the actual data collection begins.

For instance, suppose you really like one particular measure of family conflict because it makes crucial distinctions about the subsystem in which the conflict is located. It may be that families with less fluency in English will not be able to read such a highly refined measure. Or let us say that you are studying the effects of systemic reframes in first sessions. In piloting the procedures, you may learn that your model of reframes does not work as well the if father does not show up, and you may decide to include only cases in which all family members attend.

It is important, also, to anticipate the internal, subjective responses of whomever is responding to your questions or measures. In one of my studies, I asked therapists to choose which written interventions they preferred at given points in family interactions. They rated these interventions from most to least typical. Each category of response (e.g., "somewhat typical") had four lines under it on which therapists were to enter the intervention number. When a few therapists tried out the procedure, they said they felt constrained by having so few lines under each category and wanted to rate more than four interventions as "least typical." I changed both the instructions and the number of lines under each response category.

SELECTING INSTRUMENTS

Selecting (or developing) the best measures for your hypotheses is essential. After refining hypotheses in the worksheet, you should have a clear idea about *just what it is* you want to measure. Scales are often reviewed for their reliability and validity in journal articles and books (see especially Grotevant & Carlson, 1989).

There are also informal ways to locate instruments. When you search existing literature, note which instruments other authors have used. Shy away from measures that did not yield expected results in a fair percentage of previous studies. In addition, there is excellent informal advice available from researchers regarding which instruments are good for which purposes. Many of us have used these measures and have learned the hard way about which measures do not do what they are supposed to do. You need not learn the hard way again. I strongly urge you to talk to people (other than the scale's developer) who have used it to see if they like a scale you are thinking of using.

Instrument Fit

Having refined your variables of interest in the hypothesis-generating phase, it is now time to operationalize that variable. A "good" instrument both matches your variable as closely as possible and has good psychometric characteristics (reliability and validity): The measure should "hit the nail on the head." For instance, to measure family disengagement, we might want a measure that distinguishes between normal adolescent disengagement that comes with differentiation and emotional cutoff. *Selecting an instrument that operationalizes your construct as precisely as possible often makes the difference between statistically significant and nonsignificant findings.*

Domains of Measurement—Affects, Behaviors, Cognitions

Should you measure how family members feel about each other or their behaviors toward one another? In general, one cannot go too far wrong if one measures a person's cognitions (thoughts), affects (emotions), and behaviors. This is so common it is sometimes referred to as the ABC's of measurement: If it sounds simple, it is. Most variables can be measured in all three domains.

Self-Report versus Observation

Most variables are measured either by having participants fill out self-report questionnaires or by observing their actual behavior. These two strategies have different "side effects." Research participants must be told they are participating in an experiment. When one fills out a questionnaire, one is clearly aware of being assessed and one can easily and intentionally alter one's answers.

Measures on which responses can readily be altered or procedures which highlight the assessment process itself are called *reactive*. For instance, if you give families a questionnaire with a lot of items measuring cohesion, the family will guess the study has something to do with cohesion and may alter their answers based on their perceptions of the goals of the study. This happens quite frequently. If you use measures with the same item format (e.g., true–false), you can obscure your intent by combining a few shorter scales into one longer instrument.

In studies of therapy some researchers have asked families whether they feel their problems are better or worse than they have been. This is a bad idea. Such measures are highly reactive and may show changes over time not because the family has changed but because members want to please their therapists. Or they may show improvements simply because the participants themselves do not want to believe that they have spent all their time, energy, and money for nothing.

On the other hand, observational measures are less reactive, especially for distressed families whose members cannot "fake good" for the video camera. Most families quickly forget there is a video camera in the corner and will probably not be aware (1) that they are being measured or (2) of the dimensions on which they are being assessed.

Although observational measures often represent a more clinically valid sample of family behavior than does self-report, they are much more difficult to administer and to score. It is much easier to train coders to use coding systems that rate a family's overall performance—such as the Beavers–Timberlawn Family Evaluation Scales (see Beavers, 1982, for a description and scale scoring sheets)—than coding systems that rate each family member's statement one by one. Again, I suggest you consult your faculty adviser and some people who have used a particular coding system before ever attempting to use it yourself.

Adapting Existing Measures

Often there will be an instrument that has good reliability and validity but measures a somewhat different construct from the one you are interested in. Suppose, for example, you are interested in conflict between parents and adolescents, but the existing scale measures family conflict more generally. You are tempted to use the scale but are not sure it quite fits your construct closely enough. You may want to select a few items that fit your construct and alter a few others to make them fit better.

In general, if scales are altered only slightly (verb tense and gender), this can be a better solution than making up a new scale in which the onus is on you to show reliability and validity. The more you change the original scale or use it in a different setting (inpatient vs. outpatient) or with a different population, the less valid the instrument will likely be in your study and the greater the burden on you to show that it is similar to the original scale.

Making New Measures

At times no existing measure will do. In this case you may choose to make up your own scale. Some measures require little justification. Attendance by the whole family at first sessions is a simple behavior and you will not need to provide reliability and validity information for this measure. Similarly, you will probably not be expected to support the use of a measure such as "number of prior arrests." The validity of these variables is self-evident.

If you make up a self-report instrument with various items, you do have to justify its use by including information on the reliability and validity of the scale. It is not enough to show that the scale supported an hypothesis. Depending on your purpose, you might need to show (1) that the scale measures *one* construct (using a test for interitem homogeneity such as KR-20), (2) that the measure correlates in predicted directions with other well-known scales, but (3) does not correlate too highly ($r > .70$) or it may be redundant, (4) that the measure can be used on more than one occasion and remain stable in its performance (test-retest reliability), and, it is hoped, (5) that it shows support for the hypothesis (see also Snyder & Rice, Chapter 10, this volume, for more on instrument development).

FAMILY ASSESSMENT STRATEGIES

Assessing differences between two or more groups of individuals at one point in time is relatively easy. Assessing functioning on the family level is difficult. Assessing changes in functioning at two or three points in time for a whole family is even more difficult. Comparing differences between groups in family-level changes across time is very difficult. As you plan your design, keep in mind this simple continuum. *It is easier to measure individuals than dyads or families. It is easier to compare groups at one point in time than it is to measure change across time.*

An essential tenet of systems theory holds that behavior is mutually determined by each member of the system. Statistically, this presents a problem in analyzing family data because reports from various family members, although potentially divergent, are not independent (i.e., they correlate with each other) and should not, therefore, be analyzed as separate data points. The suggestion by some has been to analyze data for families as a whole. Bray and Maxwell (1985), for instance, discuss multiple analyses of variance (MANOVAs), which take into account the correlations among several variables and would work for family data. The higher the correlation, the more refined the measure and the more likely that one will find significant results if they are in fact there.

Number of Measures

In family research, some have advocated the use of a multimethod, multidimensional matrix assessment strategy. Using the matrix method means taking multiple measures of multiple dimensions of family functioning from multiple perspectives (e.g., family, therapist, and observer) with multiple methods (e.g., self-report and observation). I disagree for three reasons.

First, using a number of measures increases the probability that any one measure will show differences when in fact there are none (called false positives). That means that you will have to statistically adjust for this by setting higher and higher p values for each instrument you add, making it harder to find statistically significant results on any one measure. In addition, Weiss and Weisz (1990) have shown that as the number of measures in any one study increases, the average effect for each measure decreases. This would be much like having a number of tries at the high jump but every time you try again the bar gets higher and you get shorter.

Second, in studies of the outcomes of therapy, change is difficult to measure. Most measures cannot hope to tap the subtle shifts in perceptions and attitudes that are engendered by techniques such as reframes. Familywide change is, quite frankly and realistically, difficult to achieve. Many families leave therapy improved to some degree in some area of functioning, but not all families achieve clinically significant (and measurable) change in a number of areas. I would rather place my bets on changes in the presenting problem and target my therapeutic efforts clearly on that (see Weisz, Weiss, & Donnenberg, 1992, for information on targeted treatment planning): This scenario provided a better chance of finding effects due to therapy than does the matrix strategy.

Third, this multimethod, multidimensional matrix often makes interpretation of results more difficult. Typically, one measure or type of measure from one family member will yield findings that contradict other findings from other cells within the matrix. This can make the "story" of the results more difficult to tell. As a general rule, there is often more to be gained by measuring one or two constructs well than, there is in measuring several constructs with different modalities for each.

DATA COLLECTION AND SCORING

One of the most time-consuming and laborious phases in the entire research cycle is collecting, scoring, and entering data. Some methods of data collection and scoring are more efficient than others.

In one of my least efficient projects, a team of scientist–practitioners was interested in finding out about the family dynamics associated with a certain childhood disorder. My task was to get names of families from agency therapists and call these families to see whether they would participate in the study (for 2 hours and no pay). If they agreed, a colleague and I would meet them at the clinic (25 minutes away), hauling video camera, tripods, and various cords and notebooks to the agency. Often the families did not show and we would waste about 2 hours. Logistically, it would have been much easier if we had worked at the agency where the research was being conducted and if that agency had installed video equipment.

For self-report instruments, easy data scoring and entry are probably available at your university. Most universities have scanners that read sheets of dots (e.g., those for the Scholastic Aptitude Test and the Graduate Record Examination tests). All you do is coordinate items from a scale with answers on the answer sheet, then scan your answer sheets into the mainframe computer and your data are scored and entered. Be sure to run a few scoring sheets through the scanner and test to make sure you can write programs to access and analyze the data before you collect them; that is, pilot test the scanning system.

It is also important to check the accuracy of scoring and entry. Have another person check the data—probably a random check of 25% of the data will tell you whether there are errors. If there is any consistency to these errors, it will be necessary to check the entire data set. Once that is done, it is also wise to check it on the computer. In most statistical packages there is a way to look at the contents of the data set to make sure all values are appropriate for that item or scale.

Asking a statistical package to analyze data for minimum and maximum values for each variable can be extremely helpful. That way you can quickly tell whether any variable has a value that is outside the range of possible values. For instance, if socioeconomic status (SES) is rated on a 5-point scale (1–5), a maximum value of 17 means that there must be an error in the data. You can then temporarily delete all subjects with SES values below 6, list the contents again, find the subject numbers with the incorrect values, and correct them.

ANALYZING YOUR DATA: STATISTICS MADE EASY

Statistics do not have to be the reason you never want to do research again. Most colleges and universities have statistical consultation available to students and faculty for free. Sometimes the consultants are patient, speak in English (rather than "statisticalese"), and can suggest different ways of looking at your data. My best statistical advice is to find a consultant who is patient, who does not make you feel stupid, and whom you understand.

Probability Theory and Statistical Significance

The reason that you hear so much about research being based on the positivist philosophical tradition comes from probability theory. In essence, in this paradigm one can never prove that something is true but can only show that it is most likely false. So researchers set up a strawman argument. That is, we hypothesize the *null hypothesis* which means that we would say that there are *no* differences between cohesive and disengaged families on some dependent variable when we really believe these differences exist. We then try to disprove the null hypothesis by showing that the hypothesis is unlikely.

The statistics most frequently seen in social science studies are based on probability theory. Put simply, this means that you can never be 100% sure that the obtained results are valid but rather that there is a certain probability that the obtained results are an accurate representation of reality. Probability theory is a way of telling you how "confident" you can be that your results are valid or accurate.

Let us say that one group of families scores an average of 44 on a cohesion scale and another group's average score is 34 (see first graph in Figure 9.1). Are these scores different enough that you can claim your hypothesis was supported? Probability theory takes a look at the 10-point difference between the two means (or averages) and at the same time takes a look at how different the families are within each group and to see how much or how little overlap there is between the range of scores in the two groups.

If there is a lot of overlap (i.e., a small difference between the means of each group and a large variation of scores within each group), as shown in the second graph in Figure 9.1, the probability that group differences "really" exist is relatively low. If, on

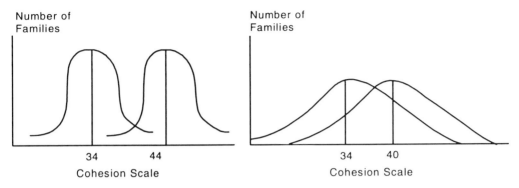

FIGURE 9.1. Graphs indicating differences between and within groups.

the other hand, there is less overlap (big differences between group averages and not much difference between families' scores within each group), as shown in the first graph in Figure 9.1, the probability that groups of families are different is high. This ratio of differences between groups to the differences among families within each group yields an F value; the larger the F value, the better p values indicate the degree of "confidence" you have that groups are different: for example, $p < .05$ indicates that if the same differences between and within groups were found 100 times, your assertion that your hypothesis is supported would be correct about 95 times out of that 100 trials for similar samples.

Rank Order and Polytomous Variables

You can measure constructs in a number of ways. First, you can rank families according to which families score higher or lower on a scale. The highest score gets the highest rank and so on. These are called ordinal scales.

You can also classify families into discrete categories such as ethnicity. Polytomous variables such as these usually have from three to eight discrete categories of response. Variables such as ethnicity are difficult to analyze because they cannot readily be ordered or ranked on a numerical scale: Who is to say whether Asian Americans or African Americans or whites should be assigned a higher or lower number than the others? The typical way to analyze such variables is to take each ethnic category in turn and to give all subjects in that category a score of 1 (one) with all other subjects receiving a score of 0 (zero). That creates a number of variables equal to the number of ethnic groups and allows you to analyze the whole set of variables together. Statistical consideration of polytomous variables such as ethnicity is beyond the scope of this chapter. Socioeconomic status, on the other hand, has five levels in the Hollingshead and Redlich (1958) classification and is by its very nature stratified. These levels can meaningfully be given numerical values indicating high to low and can, therefore, be analyzed as either categorical or continuous variables.

Analyses for Dichotomous and Continuous Variables

In most studies of family therapy or family functioning, self-report instruments will yield either dichotomous or continuous scores (see Snyder & Rice, Chapter 10, this volume, for more information on scale formation and types of measurement). "Dichotomous" means that there are only two categories of possible response (e.g., enmeshed or disengaged, male or female). Continuous means that a range of scores is possible (e.g., a family could score anywhere from 10 to 50). All hypotheses that posit a simple relationship between *two* variables can be tested with one of the three tests in Figure 9.2. Data are analyzed differently depending on whether your independent variable (IV) and dependent variable (DV) are dichotomous or continuous. This section takes you through each of the three possibilities and tells you how to analyze your data (see Figure 9.2). Here again, my thoughts derive from the work of William McGuire, who first taught me to plan analyses in advance of collecting data (see McGuire, 1983, 1989, for excellent examples of these fundamental concepts).

If both IV and DV are continuous (left-hand graph), data are analyzed with simple correlations or regressions. This is perhaps the easiest and most common way to analyze data. In this situation it is helpful if each variable has a relatively wide range of scores represented in your sample. If one or both variables has a restricted range of scores, it is more difficult for this analysis to locate associations (correlations) that "in reality" exist, and, therefore, it is less likely that your results will be statistically significant as even a little measurement error in one variable translates to a wider range of possible scores in the other axis solely because of the restricted range of scores on the first variable. For instance, if you only have moderately cohesive families in your sample, the findings might not be as strong as they would have been if you had been able to include families that are disengaged and some that are enmeshed. In essence, extreme scores are more influential in finding statistical significance than scores in the middle.

If the IV is dichotomous and the DV is dichotomous (center), you will be analyzing for differences in the average scores between two or more groups (using ANOVAs or *t* tests) and any statistical package can do this for you. This situation differs from the one above.

Let us say you are interested in showing that cohesive families are more responsive to therapy than disengaged families. To have a fighting chance of finding statistical significance, you now want them to be as different as possible on the cohesion–disengagement dimension because that is your independent variable and will influence the size of the difference between the two group averages (i.e. 44 vs. 34 in Figure 9.1).

You also want these two groups of families to be as similar as possible on a whole host of other variables (such as single- vs. two-parent households) that could affect your DV (or how they respond to therapy). Each other variable that affects the DV can increase the within-group variance and make statistical differences more difficult to obtain. (See Lyness & Sprenkle, Chapter 11, this volume, for further discussion.)

Sometimes researchers categorize families into groups by using a median split in which you take all families that score above and below the 50th percentile and separate them into two groups (i.e., high and low cohesion). *Do not use median splits* if you can avoid it because you want groups to be quite different and median splits can leave you with too much overlap. You can also use regressions with a dichotomous IV (see Cohen & Cohen, 1983).

If both the IV and DV are dichotomous (right-hand graph), you will be analyzing data for differences in the frequency with which participants naturally sort themselves into each cell. In this situation you should try to get equal numbers of families in each group (the DV will fill in as it naturally does). In the upper-right example in Figure 9.2, families can only be classified into one cell (or box). Here again, you want to make sure that families' scores are not lumped together with scores near the middle of the IV. Results will not be statistically significant if equal percentages of high- and low-cohesion families show for second sessions. Results will be statistically significant if the

VARIABLE SCALING

MAIN EFFECTS

Mode of hypothesis representation	IV Continuous DV Continuous	IV Dichotomous DV Continuous	IV Dichotomous DV2 Dichotomous
Verbal	The more cohesive the family, the greater the compliance with therapist.	Cohesive families are more compliant in therapy.	Cohesive families are more likely to comply with therapist directives.

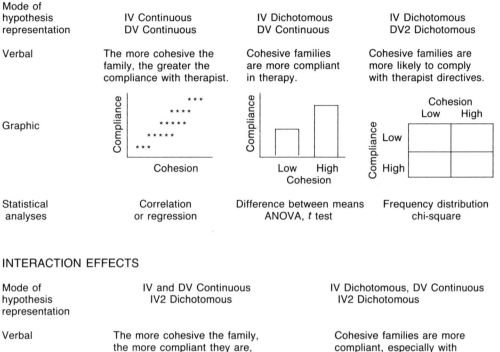

Statistical analyses	Correlation or regression	Difference between means ANOVA, *t* test	Frequency distribution chi-square

INTERACTION EFFECTS

Mode of hypothesis representation	IV and DV Continuous IV2 Dichotomous	IV Dichotomous, DV Continuous IV2 Dichotomous
Verbal	The more cohesive the family, the more compliant they are, especially with novice therapists.	Cohesive families are more compliant, especially with novice therapists.

Graphic

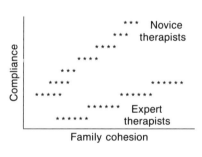 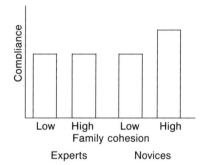

Statistical analyses	Differences between (correlations or between *b* weights)	2 × 2 ANOVA (a differential difference among means)

FIGURE 9.2. Ways of expressing hypotheses with dichotomous and continuous variables. See also Table 2.1 in Tabachnick and Fidell (1989).

percentages of rates of attendance are higher in cohesive families and lower in disengaged families.

MORE COMPLEX ANALYSES

Interaction Effects

When you have only one IV, you analyze for direct effects of the IV on the DV. When you have two or more IVs, you should analyze for the main effects of each IV on the DV and for interactions among the IVs. This is described in step 4 of the hypothesis generation worksheet. If you are not familiar with the concept of interaction effects (statistical rather than family interactions), you will need to plod through this section rather slowly and thoroughly. Skip over this section if you have only one IV.

Consider the interaction hypotheses in the bottom of Figure 9.2. When you studiously completed the various steps in the Hypothesis Generation Worksheet (see Appendix), you probably located several variables that would alter the hypothesized relationships between IV and DV. If there are additional variables you believe may influence the relationship between your two most important variables (IV and DV), you should analyze your data to detect that influence.

In this case we are adding a second independent variable, which is listed as IV2. *If the first IV and the DV are continuous but the second IV (IV2) is dichotomous* (i.e., expert vs. novice therapists), you would analyze data as a difference between correlations. In the left-hand example under interaction effects, this situation is described. In this case we are predicting that the relationship between a family's cohesion (before the family came for therapy) and its compliance with the therapist's directives is stronger for novice therapists than it is for experienced therapists.

We can determine whether therapist experience makes a difference by running separate correlations for each group (novice vs. expert therapists). We get one correlation coefficient for each group. We can then compare the size of these two correlations (see Cohen & Cohen, 1983, pp. 53–57, for an excellent description of this). In the graph, the correlation between family compliance is greater for the novice therapists than it is for the experts (which is near zero).

Similarly, *if we measure compliance as a dichotomous variable rather than a continuous one*, we change our analyses much as we did in the section on main effects above. In the right-hand example of Figure 9.1 under interaction effects, this situation is depicted. Note that, in order to get a significant interaction effect, there need not be differences between cohesive and disengaged families when therapists are experienced. Also, there need not be differences between experts and novices when the families are low in cohesion.

For an interaction to reach statistical significance, a differential difference in compliance between the two IV groups has to be found. Of course, we should have hypothesized the specific nature of that interaction before we began the experiment. We would guess that differences in the family's compliance will be greater when novice therapists treat low-cohesion families. This is a more sophisticated (and perhaps more realistic) hypothesis than the one in the section on main effects.

The statistical analysis is quite simple. Most computer programs will do this for you automatically when you list a second variable with the first IV. Interpretation of what a significant interaction term means can be more complex. In this case it is straightforward: Novice therapists have an easier time eliciting compliance from cohesive families.

Statistical References

Although the best statistical help is available in the form of some person who knows statistics, books can at times help you answer specific questions (see, e.g., Tabachnick & Fidell, 1989; Winer, Brown, & Michels, 1991; Cohen & Cohen, 1983, for the three best general references). Tabachnick and Fidell (1989) is the most user-friendly (see their Table 2.1, pp. 30–31). Winer et al. (1991) is especially good for mixed factorial designs and repeated measures, which are often used in treatment research. See Agresti (1990), for analysis of categorical variables [especially repeated measures designs with 0,1 variables]; Bray and Maxwell (1985), for MANOVA; Gibbons (1993) for nonparametrics.

ISSUES PARTICULAR TO RESEARCH ON FAMILY THERAPY

This section deals with selected conceptual and methodological issues particular to family therapy research. The issues addressed here are generic in that they apply to highly structured, funded studies, to research on your own case load, or to services research in an integrated mental health facility. If you are not doing a study on therapy, you can skip this section entirely.

Conceptual Issues in Therapy Outcome Studies

Systemic Change

As indicated earlier, most instruments measure change in specific areas of an individual's functioning. Systems theory holds that these changes do not occur in isolation but are part of a pattern of familywide changes. An important criterion for determining treatment effectiveness is the degree to which collateral changes occur. These collateral changes might occur in other family members or in other areas of the identified patient's life. For instance, remission of depression symptoms in a child may be associated with increased academic performance and improved parent–child relations.

Which Families Benefit?

Let us say you are also interested in which families are most likely to benefit from your particular brand of therapy. In that case a pre–post change score would serve as the dependent variable and several characteristics about the family would serve as the predictor (or independent variable). For example, we might find that cohesive families benefit more from therapy than do disengaged families. Enmeshment, then, would be a positive predictor of outcome. Several good examples of this exist using family therapy for children with conduct disorders (Mann, Borduin, Henggeler, & Blaske, 1990; Webster-Stratton, 1985; Webster-Stratton & Hammond, 1990).

Maintenance of Gains

The best way to determine whether families get better in therapy or not is to look at the longer-term adjustment of families several months or years after therapy. If, for instance, a large percentage of couples remain married for 4 years after marital therapy, therapy was successful (Snyder, Wills, & Grady-Fletcher, 1991). Unfortunately, for most family problems we do not have good clinical or empirical benchmarks by which we can determine whether families are likely to maintain the gains made in therapy. Survival analysis (Singer & Willett, 1991) is a method whereby you can tell what percentage of families have a remission or return of symptoms over time. One nice feature of this outcome criterion is that curves for different treatments can be compared statistically. For instance, Henggeler, Melton, Smith, Schoenwald, and Hanley (1993) were able to show that the rate of recidivism for juvenile offenders was lower when they received multisystemic therapy versus traditional family preservation services.

Cost-Effectiveness

Finally, let us say that in this cost-conscious era of mental health services, you are likely to be interested in how cost-effectively you can effect change. You might administer a shorter battery of measures much more frequently and determine how many sessions it takes families to achieve a "decent" level of functioning (i.e., a level at which medical necessity is no longer at issue). In that case you might put number of sessions on the x axis and family functioning (or child symptomatology) on the y axis. Different curves might be drawn for each type of problem. This has been done most elegantly by Howard, Kopta, Krause, and Orlinsky (1986) and can be done with equal methodological rigor for both individual families and groups of families. (See also Pike-Urlacher, MacKinnon, & Piercy, Chapter 16, this volume, on cost-effectiveness.)

Measurement of Change

Change Scores

First, let us consider the traditional change score approach. In this strategy, two or more groups complete measures at pre, post, and follow-up (i.e., before therapy begins, at the last session, and several months after termination, respectively). One then averages the scores for each group at each time period and subtracts scores at pre from those at post and than also subtracts scores at post from those at follow-up. (Subtraction is most often accomplished by forcing pretreatment scores into a regression equation first.) These are called gain scores because they tell how much the average family gained (or improved) during therapy. Then to compare brand X with brand Y, the gain scores for each treatment condition are compared with simple t tests (e.g., Kazdin, Siegel, & Bass, 1992).

Alternatively, the slopes of the lines between time periods can be compared by looking for time-by-treatment interactions. These methods test for statistical differences between two or more treatments but do not tell us about the clinical relevance of the gains or the absolute level of family functioning: It may be that families in both treatment conditions still have significant problems.

Change scores have some problems. First, the lower the test–retest reliability of the measure used to assess treatment outcomes, the greater the problem assessing change. By definition, disengaged families normally score toward the extreme on the disengagement–cohesion continuum. If an instrument is unreliable, it is a statistical likelihood that disengaged families will look less disengaged with repeated use of the instrument even though they did not "actually" change. In general, the farther a family lies from the mean at the beginning of a series of measurements over time, the larger this effect of repeated testing. This is different from a purely statistical regression to the mean even though it has the same effect. Reliabilities above .90 for interitem homogeneity, test–retest, and split-half are excellent; .80 is good, but stay away from instruments much below this.

Sensitivity to Change

Some instruments are better at describing level of functioning and others are better at measuring whether or not families change in treatment. Only a few instruments do both well. If you want to measure change, make sure you choose an instrument that is sensitive to small changes.

In my dissertation, I wanted to see whether inexperienced therapists' ratings of their own efficacy changed with level of family conflict more than they did for experienced therapists. Unfortunately, I measured efficacy with a series of adjectives that were like personality traits, not adjectives that one would expect to change with subtle shifts in subjective experience. That part of the study flopped.

PUBLICATION

The first reason to do research is to answer a question that deeply intrigues you. The second is to communicate that answer to professional colleagues. Many good studies never see the light of day (i.e., get published) either because the student has passed his or her orals and has little motivation to publish or because the final written report does not conform to the jargon or writing styles that are commonly used.

As with most of the issues covered in this chapter, writing for publication is learned by experience. The best way to learn how to write a research report is to write one with a seasoned author. When I first tried to write up a paper, I was amazed at how much better it was when my adviser edited it to fit those writing styles. Not only did he organize the ideas neatly under concise headings, but he changed individual words that I had no idea needed to be changed.

For instance, I had no idea that one should not call a study "exploratory" but rather an "initial" study. Exploratory indicates a lack of a priori hypotheses; initial indicates that this study is the first in a series of studies to be undertaken by the author. The latter sounds much more substantial.

Good Writing

My high school English teacher used to say that good writing is unmistakably clear. I believe this. When I lecture to classes and am obtuse or long-winded, I usually do not know as much as I would like about a topic. When I know the topic well, I can be both brief and clear. Try to communicate your ideas as simply and clearly as possible. The whole paper should be no longer than 20 double-spaced pages of text. Avoid jargon or define your terms clearly the first time you introduce them. There is little worse than a paper filled with obscure constructs.

Use frequent headings and small paragraphs. This way the reader can more quickly find which topics are of interest. See if you can keep no more than one idea in one paragraph.

The Abstract

The abstract sets the tone for the entire paper. Choose carefully six or seven sentences that describe the study's purpose, sample, procedures, results, and implications. Try to tell as much of the "story" as possible in the abstract.

The Introduction

The purpose of the introduction is to convince the reader (and reviewer) that your study is important; that it contributes something new to your field. To do this, you should be very careful to build a "line of argument" that takes the reader from the importance of the general topic to the importance of this study within that overall topic.

You should not try to review the entire field. That is what you do in your thesis or dissertation but not what you should do in a research report. Report only those findings and methods that bear directly on your argument for why this is an important study.

If you have more data than can comfortably fit into one paper, consider dividing it into two papers. This typically occurs in outcome studies when one paper addresses outcome and a second looks for characteristics of the clients or families that are associated with outcome.

When you review previous research, it is not helpful to describe its methodological inadequacy if you do not tell us (1) how those methods make the findings questionable, and (2) how your methods improve the likelihood of valid results. Make sure your critique of previous research is relevant to the validity of the previous findings.

The Methods Section

The sole purpose of scientific rigor is to make confident inferences under difficult circumstances. There is no other reason for all these complex and at times arcane methods.

Therefore, in the methods section you should be careful to include all information necessary for the reader to evaluate the appropriateness of the procedures, subjects, and measures to the hypothesis. In a recent review of family therapy process research (Dickey, 1994), I found that less than one-third of the studies did an adequate job of this, and the entire literature ($n = 35$ studies) suffers from this lack of information.

In most studies it is crucial to know how participants (both families and therapists) were recruited, what information they were given about the purpose of the study, when they completed assessments and in what order, and what efforts were taken to reduce reactivity. Analyses that address sample demographics should be placed in the methods section.

You do not need to include information that does not bear on the validity of the findings. For instance, if you are studying the effectiveness of therapy, you would want to include information on the test–retest reliability of each outcome measure because, as noted earlier, this is important in judging the reliability of change scores. You probably would not need to include information on split-half reliability because it probably does not bear on the findings.

The Results Section

Again, this section should be as straightforward as possible. It is often helpful to restate the hypothesis or tell us *why* you did a particular analysis before you describe the results. It is also helpful to have separate headings for main analyses, analyses of "confounds," and secondary analyses (see Kazdin et al., 1992, for a stellar example of this). Only undertake analyses that bear on specific hypotheses: The sequence of analyses should follow the logic of the hypotheses and its confounds.

Before getting to your main analyses, you may have to convince the reader that you are ready for them. You should have analyzed for differences between groups (if your IV is dichotomous) in the methods section. If you found group differences on "nuisance" variables, figure out what to do about them before you present your main analyses (again, see Kazdin et al., 1992). Do not make interpretations of the data in the results section: Save them for the discussion.

Tables are important. They are much easier to read than text and your readers will look there for the main findings. Make sure they are incredibly easy to scan and include all relevant information. I cannot stress this enough. You may want to put the most important findings in a graph or figure as is often done in oral presentations. This is easier to digest. A great book to discover how to best present your data is *Visual Display of Quantitative Information* (Tufte, 1983). Check it out.

Sending It out for Review

Before you submit a paper for publication, make sure it is ready. Most senior authors send final drafts of their papers to knowledgeable colleagues for feedback so they can anticipate reviewers concerns and address them up front before they send them to the editor of a journal. You should have at least one person read your paper before you submit it. Also, you should consider having a professional editor go over the paper for grammar, spelling, and citation style.

I recall one paper I reviewed which arrived with citations in the old *Family Process* format even though it was sent to a journal that used American Psychological Association format. Obviously the author had been rejected from *Family Process* and sent the paper to the second journal without changing the references. That is not the impression one wants to make on a reviewer.

Get the details right. Make sure you have the appropriate page margins and format for tables. Enclose a brief cover letter explaining why your article is appropriate for this particular journal. Send the requested number of copies.

After about 4 months, you should receive a letter from the editor with comments by reviewers. If the reviewers agree on the papers strengths and weaknesses, you can be relatively sure that these "concerns" are valid. If reviewers disagree, the editor should give you hints as to which problems are most important to address.

Reviewers are supposed to be critical but should also be constructive in their criticisms. Some are not. I have received some terrible reviews that seemed more like attacks than reviews and I must admit to being wary of sending manuscripts to that journal again. The most important thing is not to get too frustrated, angry, or depressed about negative reviews. When one has struggled long and hard to bring a project so far, it would be a shame to drop the ball now and neither revise it nor resubmit it somewhere else.

Realistically the editor can make three possible decisions. "Accept with minor revisions" is the most favorable review I have ever seen ("accept as is" decisions are rare). It means that if you take care of a few things, the paper will be published.

Second, "revise and resubmit" means that there is considerable merit to the paper (i.e., that it could make a contribution) but there are also some notable problems that preclude publication in its present form. Usually these require larger changes and there is a good chance of publication if you address the reviewers' concerns. There is, in this business, no guarantee of publication. Piercy, Moon, and Bischof (1994) describe one situation in which an assistant editor invited a colleague to submit a paper (which is as close as one can get to assurance of publication) but the editor rejected it over his recommendation for publication.

Third, "reject" means that the editor does not think the paper can make a contribution even with substantial improvements. If you can clearly address the reviewers' comments, however, you should not necessarily consider a "reject" decision as the final word.

Not all reviewers are created equal and it is often the case that you can persuade an editor that the reviewer is being too picky or is outright wrong. For instance, I have had reviewers tell me that I was implying causation because I used the word "predict" in a correlation analysis. Prediction in that context has nothing to do with causation but with the degree to which one can tell the score on one variable from the score on another.

However right the writer may be, harsh reviews can be a major block to reworking the paper for resubmission. You may think you should never do another research project again. If you feel in danger of being defeated by a harsh review I suggest you read Piercy et al. (1994). They surveyed family therapists about their feelings and coping strategies after hard-to-take rejections of articles they felt had a good chance of being published. Especially helpful is their advice on steps to take to keep your own internal locus of control and to keep trying. Just remember, reviewers are different, journals are different, papers after being rewritten are different. Your paper deserves to be published: You just have to find the right place.

When you revise the paper for resubmission, tell the editor exactly where and how you addressed each of the reviewers' concerns. If you chose not to change your paper in response to a reviewer concern, tell the editor exactly why you think it should not be changed. These little details are surprisingly important in getting your manuscript the attention it deserves.

FINAL THOUGHTS

In theory, researchers are judged on the quality and quantity of their work (i.e., on the significance of the substantive contribution their work makes to the field). In practice, this is not always the case. Perhaps because evaluation of someone's contribution is such a subjective process, some researchers consistently get more or less kudos than their work objectively deserves.

As in most work environments, social skills and development of professional and personal relationships come into play here. As I look at the opportunities I have had to get involved in projects and to contribute to family therapy, it has been the quality of my relationships with colleagues (which are, it must be admitted, based in part on what I know and can do) that has enabled this to happen or kept it from happening. My last hope for you is that as you meet people whose work you admire, you enjoy good personal and professional relationships with them.

APPENDIX: HYPOTHESIS GENERATION AND DEVELOPMENT WORKSHEET

Here are the steps, adapted from Professor McGuire's worksheets, to generate and refine hypotheses. (Please recall that you are often better off focusing fully on one hypothesis in one study than you would be trying to tack on a partial answer to a second question in that same study.) This worksheet is meant to work in tandem with the statistics section.

Step 1: The Initial Hypothesis

Describe an issue the strikes you as important in the functioning of families or in therapy with families. The issue should be stated in the form of a hypothesized relationship between two variables. That is, it should state an independent variable (IV), the one you can control, that is related to the dependent variable (DV), the one you cannot control.

Example. IV → DV : cohesive families are more compliant in therapy.

Step 2: Defining, Expanding, and Refining Variables

Choose one variable and "unpack" it. That is, describe it with a number of related terms, giving it alternative labels and phrases that help define it more precisely. Make distinctions between that variable and other similar constructs. Find subcategories of that variable. Identify concepts that you do not wish to include as part of that variable. Describe what the variable is not by defining its opposite.

> *Example: Cohesive families.* Emotionally connected. Members are not detached and isolated from each other. Families that spend time in each other's presence. Children enjoy weekend time with parents. High on a cohesion scale. Attend church together. No history of children being sent off to camp or living with relatives. Family members do not live parallel lives. Warmth or physical affection among members. Possible unity. Etcetera.

Step 2 Again.

Do this same process of definition, elaboration, and refinement with the second variable.

> *Example: Compliance.* Whole family shows up at first session. No member absent. Everyone living in the house (except pets) shows for up first appointment. Family members pay attention to therapist, look at therapist when he or she intervenes. Each person responds to therapist request to state a goal for treatment. Agreement regarding payment is easily reached. Family accepts therapist systemic reframe and goals are negotiated based on the reframe. Family members accept therapist interventions when small conflicts (brushfires) develop. Members express optimism about possible gains of therapy.

Step 3: Refined Hypothesis Restated

Once you have expanded each of the variables, you will probably have several subdimensions of each and implied several ways of measuring them. Select one aspect of the variable that most closely fits your interests (and is "do-able"). Write out your revised hypothesis, being as specific as you can and then represent that hypothesis in a graph.

> *Example.* Families that score high on a cohesion scale will be more likely to accept a systemic reframe than families that score low on a cohesion scale.

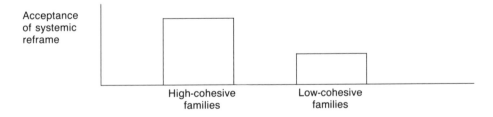

Step 4: Expanded Hypothesis—The Reasons Why

Now that you have a revised hypothesis and a concrete representation of the relationship between the two variables, it is time to think about *why*. State the IV and DV again, this time adding one reason why the hypothesis will be borne out. This reason is called a mediating variable (MV) (Baron & Kenny, 1986). (IV → MV → DV).

> *Example.* A greater percentage of high-cohesion families will have all family members accept a systemic reframe in the first session *because* they are more skilled at conflict resolution.

Step 4a.

Expand and refine this new variable, make distinctions and give it alternative labels as you did in step 2.

> *Brief example.* Conflict resolution skills. More frequent and more effective communication of problems and solutions. Consensual planning. Notes on the refrigerator.

Step 4b.

State several other mediating variables and expand and refine each of these constructs. Do not skip this step. It is very important because it helps define the conditions under which your hypotheses are most likely to be born out, and because it will help you exclude rival hypotheses later. Expand and refine each of these variables or constructs as well.

> *Brief example.* High-cohesion families will accept systemic reframes *because* family members see themselves as influencing each other in everyday life.

Step 4c.

You should now have stated your simple hypothesis several times, each with the reason why it is a solid hypothesis. In this step, state each of these mediating hypotheses (IV → MV → DV) as specifically and as clearly as you can. Represent this new mediational hypothesis with a graph.

In graph 2 the family's quality of communication (good vs. poor) and disengagement mutually influence each other. These interactions between independent variables are important to pay attention to before designing your study because it is rare that one variable affects another without the "intrusion" of several others. You will later want to argue that intruder variables are not the variables that "really" account for your results. (See Figure 9.1 for help with how to graph various combinations of continuous and dichotomous IVs, DVs, and MVs.)

> *Brief example.* Families that score high on a cohesion scale will be more likely to accept reframes during the first session than families that score low on a cohesion scale *because* high-scoring family members see themselves as influencing each other in everyday life.

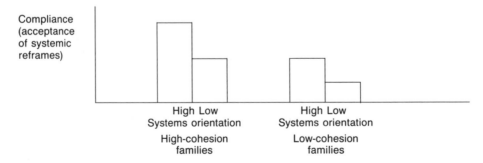

Step 5: Positing the Opposite Relationship

So far you have stated, expanded, and refined your hypotheses to account for additional variables and to specify the conditions under which your hypotheses should be tested. By now, you should already have made that simple initial thought and statement much more complex and have probably saved yourself much time. Step 5 is a way to further this. Using the same two original variables, state a new hypothesis with the opposite relationship between the variables.

Example. Cohesive families will be *less* likely to accept a systemic reframe during first sessions than low-cohesive families.

Then describe the theoretical *reason why* this new hypothesis might be true. For instance, disengaged families might be *more* likely to accept a reframe *because* they are very frustrated and desperate for help or because they might see coming to therapy as a real chance to change, or, *because* therapists who believe that the family is disengaged might make extra efforts to make the reframe fit the family. *In any event, is it important at this stage to ferret out all the possible confounding variables in the hypothesis.*

Also, in Step 5, make sure you know as specifically as possible what you mean by your new explanations (reasons why) for your reversed hypothesis. And, again, graph the new opposite hypothesis with the mediating variables.

Step 6: The Integrative Hypothesis

It is hoped that you have gotten a more complex and sophisticated set of ideas related to your original hypothesis. Take all the information you have gleaned from steps 1 through 5 and pull them together in one comprehensive hypothesis. Try to be sure that the resulting hypothesis takes into account the effects of all the "intruding" variables and specifies the conditions under which your original hypothesis should be tested. Graph this one as well.

Example. All family members of very cohesive families will respond positively after therapists introduce systemic reframes that cogently tie child symptoms to family interaction patterns. These results will obtain *if* families have (roughly) the same number of children, *if* families are headed by two parents, *if* therapist reframes are skilled, *if* families have not previously been denied treatment, and *if* parent motivation to undertake family therapy is similar between the two groups of families. In addition, this prediction will depend on (i.e., interact with) parental hierarchy such that families with ineffective parental hierarchies will be less likely to accept reframes.

Step 7: Return to Practicality

By now you have violated an essential rule of research design, the *keep-it-simple* rule. Step 6 is really an example of how complex a simple initial question can become when you think out all its implications. It is not uncommon that in doing these six steps, you will find additional hypotheses that interest you more than the original one did. This new idea often departs significantly from your original idea.

Therefore, the final step of hypothesis generation is to go back to your original idea, the one that inspired you to do the project in the first place, to see whether it has gotten lost. Check to make sure you are still really invested in your original idea. If this process has led you to another idea you like more, this is the best time to change your mind: You can easily repeat steps 1 through 6 on this new idea.

If the original inspiration has been lost or if the resulting design will violate the *keep-it-simple* rule, I suggest you not undertake the project. There are lots of interesting ideas out there—choose another. If the original idea is still exciting, consider making decisions about implementation that keep the project feasible.

If you decide that the project is worth pursuing (and believe me there is much wisdom in saying "no" at this point), you will now need to reassert the *keep-it-simple* rule and construct a practical, "do-able" hypothesis that will guide the research design. Write a final statement of the hypothesis that takes into account the most essential changes and refinements from steps 2 through 6.

At this point you do not need to take into account any issues that can be readily addressed in the design. For instance, you do not need to include all the qualifications in Step 6 above. You do not need to include all the "ifs" in the final hypothesis. You must be sure that the final hypothesis clearly states your most central and important ideas clearly and concisely. In this case the first sentence in step 6 accomplishes this. Now you are ready to begin the design phase.

Final hypothesis: All family members of very cohesive families will respond positively after therapists introduce systemic reframes that cogently tie child symptoms to family interaction patterns

REFERENCES

Agresti, A. (1990). *Categorical data analysis*. New York: Wiley.

American Psychological Association. (1994). *Publication manual of the American Psychological Association* (4th ed.). Washington, DC: Author.

Baron, R. M., & Kenny, D. A. (1986). The moderator–mediator variable distinction in social psychological research: Conceptual, strategic, and statistical considerations. *Journal of Personality and Social Psychology, 51,* 1173–1182.

Beavers, W. R. (1982). Healthy, midrange, and severely dysfunctional families. In F. Walsh (Ed.), *Normal family processes*. New York: Guilford Press.

Bray, J. H., & Maxwell, S. E. (1985). *Multivariate analysis of variance*. Beverly Hills, CA: Sage.

Cohen, J., & Cohen, P. (1983). *Applied multiple regression/correlation analysis for the behavioral sciences* (2nd ed.). Hillsdale, NJ: Erlbaum.

Dickey, M. H. (1994, February). *Methodological advances in process research with families*. Paper presented at the annual meeting of the North American Society for Psychotherapy Research, Santa Fe, NM.

Gibbons, J. D. (1993). *Nonparametric statistics*. Newbury Park, CA: Sage.

Gilbert, R., Christiansen, A., & Margolin, G. (1984). Patterns of alliances in nondistressed and multiproblem families. *Family Process, 23,* 75–87.

Goldstein, M. J. (1988). Patient status, family composition, and other structural variables in family therapy research. In L. C. Wynne (Ed.), *State of the art in family therapy research: Controversies and recommendations*. New York: Family Process Press.

Grotevant, H. D., & Carlson, C. I. (1989). *Family assessment: A guide to methods and measures*. New York: Guilford Press.

Henggeler, S. W., Melton, G. B., Smith, L. A., Schoenwald, S. K., & Hanley, J. H. (1993). Family preservation using multisystemic treatment: Long-term follow-up to a clinical trial with serious juvenile offenders. *Journal of Child and Family Studies, 2,* 283–293.

Hollingshead, A. B., & Redlich, F. C. (1958). *Social class and mental illness*. New York: Wiley.

Howard, K. I., Kopta, S. M., Krause, M. S., & Orlinsky, D. E. (1986). The dose–effect relationship in psychotherapy. *American Psychologist, 41,* 159–164.

Kazdin, A. E., Siegel, T. C., & Bass, D. (1992). Cognitive problem-solving skills training and parent management training in the treatment of antisocial behavior in children. *Journal of Consulting and Clinical Psychology, 60,* 733–747.

Mann, B. J., Borduin, C. M., Henggeler, S. W., & Blaske, D. M. (1990). An investigation of systemic conceptualizations of parent–child coalitions and symptom change. *Journal of Consulting and Clinical Psychology, 58,* 336–344.

McGuire, W. J. (1983). A contextualist theory of knowledge: Its implications for innovation and reform in psychological research. In L. Berkowitz (Ed.), *Advances in experimental social psychology* (Vol. 16). New York: Academic Press.

McGuire, W. J. (1989). A perspectivist approach to the strategic planning of programmatic scientific research. In B. Gholson, W. R. Shadish, R. A. Neimeyer, & A. C. Houts (Eds.), *Psychology of science: Contributions to metascience*. New York: Cambridge University Press.

Piercy, F. P., Moon, S. M., & Bischof, G. (1994). Difficult journal article rejections among prolific family therapists: A qualitative critical incident study. *Journal of Marital and Family Therapy, 20*, 231–245.

Singer, J. D., & Willett, J. B. (1991). Modeling the days of our lives: Using survival analysis when designing and analyzing longitudinal studies of duration and the timing of events. *Psychological Bulletin, 110*, 268–290.

Snyder, D. K., Wills, R. M., & Grady-Fletcher, A. (1991). Long-term effectiveness of behavioral versus insight-oriented marital therapy: A 4-year follow-up study. *Journal of Consulting and Clinical Psychology, 59*, 138–141.

Tabachnick, B. G., & Fidell, L. S. (1989). *Using multivariate statistics* (2nd ed.). New York: Harper and Row.

Tufte, E. R. (1983). *Visual display of quantitative information*. Cheshire, CT: Graphics Press.

Webster-Stratton, C. (1985). Predictors of treatment outcome in parent training for conduct disordered children. *Behavior Therapy, 16*, 223–243.

Webster-Stratton, C., & Hammond, M. (1990). Predictors of treatment outcome in parent training for families with conduct problem children. *Behavior Therapy, 21*, 319–337.

Weiss, B., & Weisz, J. R. (1990). The impact of methodological factors on child psychotherapy outcome research: A meta-analysis for researchers. *Journal of Abnormal Child Psychology, 18*, 639–670.

Weisz, J. R., Weiss, B., & Donenberg, G. R. (1992). The lab versus the clinic: Effects of child and adolescent psychotherapy. *American Psychologist, 47*, 1578–1585.

Winer, B. J., Brown, D. R., & Michels, K. M. (1991). *Statistical principles in experimental design* (3rd ed.). New York: McGraw Hill.

Wynne, L. C. (1988). The "presenting problem" and the theory-based family variables: Keystones for family therapy research. In L. C. Wynne (Ed.), *State of the art in family therapy research: Controversies and recommendations*. New York: Family Process Press.

Zanna, M. P., & Darley, J. M. (1987). On managing the faculty–graduate student relationship. In M. P. Zanna & J. M. Darley (Eds.), *The compleat academic: A practical guide for the beginning social scientist*. New York: Random House.

10

Methodological Issues and Strategies in Scale Development

DOUGLAS K. SNYDER
JANIDA L. RICE

SCALE CONSTRUCTION has much in common with building a new home. Although the basic principles of house construction have prevailed for years, each season brings new innovations—some cosmetic but having little impact on the basic structure, others less visible but determining both the durability and quality of the home. Most houses exhibit common features (living, sleeping, and eating areas), yet each is unique in its specific design as well as furnishings provided by the resident. Some aspects of homes (such as the foundation or roof) comprise such core elements that any compromises to these features jeopardize the integrity of the entire structure.

So it is with measurement techniques. The principles of test development have been well known for decades, although conceptual and technological innovations continue at a steady pace. The shared fundamental features of measurement techniques, particularly those of reliability and validity, comprise a foundation on which the integrity of any measurement instrument depends. And, as with the construction of a home, the ultimate value of an instrument may rest not only in the strength of its foundation or the satisfying elements of its appearance but also in its usefulness which, in turn, derives jointly from both the scale's inherent attributes and their application by the consumer.

This chapter emphasizes methodological issues and strategies in *scale development*—extending beyond initial construction to include evaluation and revision of the initial measurement device. Discussion focuses on measurement techniques in which (1) the individual is presented with structured verbal stimuli (either orally or in writing) describing either the respondent or some other person(s); (2) response alternatives are restricted to a structured, finite domain readily lending themselves to quantitative scaling; and (3) responses to individual test stimuli are combined quantitatively to provide some composite index of a clinically or theoretically relevant construct. Consequently, omitted from discussion here is consideration of nonquantitative or informal assessment approaches, nonverbal or observational measurement techniques, and behavioral or similar data gathering devices in which responses to individual stimulus items are viewed as behavioral samples and are not combined in linear fashion to yield composite indices of relevant constructs. We would assert, however, that many of the basic principles noted in our

216

discussion of scale development (e.g., issues of appropriate reference group, reliability and validity, and basis of interpretation) are relevant to these other assessment approaches as well.

The chapter begins with brief consideration of assumptions underlying structured assessment measures and their historical role in marital and family therapy research. Strategies for generating an item pool and deriving initial scales are then examined. Methodological issues related to investigations of reliability and validity are presented as ongoing processes critical to scale development. Finally, data-analytical models underlying interpretive guidelines and special issues regarding computer-based interpretive systems are discussed.

TO BUILD, BUY, OR RENT?

In choosing where to live, one must decide whether to build, buy, rent, or—for that matter—whether to live in a traditional structure of any kind. Similar alternatives accompany decisions about measurement techniques. Should we construct our own scale? Should we use an existing instrument? Should we borrow an instrument but then modify it to meet our own unique application? Indeed, should we use any formal measurement technique? Answers to these questions require consideration of attributes common to structured assessment methods and standards of scale development.

Assumptions Underlying Structured Assessment Techniques

Assumptions underlying structured, quantitative assessment techniques concern both the implied *usefulness* of this measurement approach and the *interpretation* of measurement data. The *psychometric approach* to assessment seeks to obtain reliable, valid indicators of phenomena not immediately observable or quantifiable. It derives in part from Thorndike's (1918) assertions that "if a thing exists, it exists in some amount," and "if it exists in some amount, it can be measured." The goals of this approach are to identify or derive measures facilitating objectivity, quantification, communication, economy, and scientific generalization (Nunnally & Bernstein, 1994).

However, some things such as theoretical constructs or subjective experience cannot be observed directly and can only be inferred from indirect measures. For example, how should one assess an individual's satisfaction with his or her primary sexual relationship? Diverse measurement approaches could include frequency counts of intercourse, physiological measures of sexual arousal, observational measures of verbal and nonverbal exchanges during love making, self-reports of sexual satisfaction, or reports from the individual's sexual partner. Although frequency of intercourse might be the most readily quantified index, it may also be the least related to sexual satisfaction.

This elusive quality of so many constructs of interest in the social and behavioral sciences has led to heavy reliance on *self- and other-report* techniques. Assumptions regarding the usefulness of this measurement approach in assessing couples and families have been discussed elsewhere (cf. Grotevant & Carlson, 1989; Jacob & Tennenbaum, 1988; Jacobson & Margolin, 1979; Snyder, 1982; Snyder, Cavell, Heffer, & Mangrum, 1995). Briefly, these hold that self-report strategies (1) are convenient and relatively easy to administer, obtaining a wealth of information across a broad range of issues germane to clinical assessment or research objectives; (2) lend themselves to collection of large normative samples serving as a reference or comparison group facilitating interpretation; (3) allow disclosure about events and subjective experiences respondents may be reluctant to discuss; and (4) provide important data concerning internal phenomena opaque to observational approaches including values and attitudes, expectations and attributions, and satisfaction and commitment.

However, the limitations of traditional self-report measures also bear noting. Specifically, such instruments (1) exhibit susceptibility to both deliberate and unconscious efforts to bias descriptions of oneself or others in either a favorable or unfavorable manner; (2) are vulnerable to individual differences in stimulus interpretation and errors in recollection of objective events; (3) may inadvertently influence respondents' nontest behavior in unintended ways; and (4) typically provide few fine-grained details concerning moment-to-moment interactions (Jacob & Tennenbaum, 1988).

Historical Developments in Marital and Family Assessment

Despite these limitations, the compelling advantages to self-report techniques have contributed to the development of well over 1,000 measures of marital and family functioning in the published literature (cf. Straus & Brown, 1978). The earliest efforts in this regard are reflected in the seminal work by Terman (1938) in his search for psychological and sexual correlates of marital happiness. Terman collected extensive information on marital and family functioning from 1,133 married and 109 divorced couples; he constructed self-report measures assessing individuals' sociodemographic background, descriptions of their parents and own childhood, psychological factors emphasizing emotionality and general likes and dislikes, views about the ideal marriage, and appraisals of their current marriage and sexual relationship.

Terman's own view concerning the adequacy of his approach to assessing couples is illuminating. He stressed that

> marital happiness . . . is not a single variable but rather an omnibus name that embraces an infinitude of interrelated satisfactions no one of which can be described in purely quantitative terms. . . . Its elements are in the strict sense qualitative rather than quantitative and can never be measured as linear distances are measured. But for practical purposes and for rough approximations even the most purely qualitative variables lend themselves to treatment by quantitative methods. . . . (1938, pp. v–vi)

Terman also anticipated the need to examine behavioral phenomena in marriage not investigated in his own research. Many who followed Terman modeled his approach to self-report methods of assessment. Others—beginning in the 1960s with intensive study of communication patterns of families of schizophrenics and extending to behavioral investigations in the 1970s and beyond contrasting verbal exchanges of distressed versus nondistressed couples and families—abandoned self-report techniques in favor of sophisticated schemes for coding observational data (cf. Snyder, 1982, for a review).

Still, self-reports (and to a lesser extent, structured informant reports) dominate both basic and clinical research as well as applied assessment of couples and families. New scales—as well as updated reviews of available techniques—appear regularly. Regrettably, the quality of these instruments has been decidedly mixed. Grotevant and Carlson (1989) note that "new coding schemes and measures surface frequently, often without sufficient regard for theoretical underpinnings, psychometric quality, or careful development of linkages between theory and assessment" (p. 5). Previous reviewers of the marital and family literature have noted that the vast majority of instruments (70–80%) are used only once, and only a small minority (less than 5%) are used five or more times (Schumm, 1990).

Embracing the Challenge of Scale Development

In view of these findings, one faces a real quandary in deciding whether to use an available instrument or develop one's own. With more than 1,000 marriage- and family-related measures to select from, the potential for a previously developed scale to assess constructs relevant to one's own clinical or research needs would seem quite good, yet often this simply does not hold true. In presenting a systems approach to marital and family assessment, Snyder et al. (1995) noted that formal assessment techniques are lacking almost entirely in some domains (e.g., assumptions or expectations among extended family or community regarding family behaviors); moreover, instruments developed in other domains frequently fail to meet even minimum psychometric standards.

Conversely, constructing one's own scale is replete with hazards. First, *scale development* (in contrast to initial construction) culminating in a measure with well-established psychometric properties often requires years of data collection, instrument revision, and amendment of interpretive guidelines; few clinicians or researchers have the time or interest to devote to that process. Second, separate from the issue of time, scale construction often requires resources of normative or clinical samples, independent validity criterion data, and data-analytical methods not available to the typical test consumer.

Scale development involves a sequence of essential steps, each comprising a subset of potentially lengthy procedures (Tinkelman, 1971). These include (1) articulating the scale's objectives; (2) developing specifications with regard to both content and format; (3) deriving a pool of potential stimulus items; (4) pretesting items and analyzing item characteristics (both quantitatively and qualitatively); (5) compiling preliminary scale versions and evaluating time requirements, scale distribution characteristics, and reliability; (6) administering the final version of the scale to a large representative sample for standardization purposes; (7) accrual of validity data from multiple criterion-related investigations; (8) derivation of interpretive guidelines; and (9) preparation and dissemination of descriptive findings on all scale characteristics for application and continued development by others.

Failure to recognize or embrace the entire process of scale development has contributed to the proliferation of inadequate measurement techniques precluding confidence in either clinical or research applications. Nevertheless, as discouraging as this conclusion may be, it may also impassion those committed to improving methods for understanding and enhancing marriage and family life. If the process of scale development appeals as a vehicle toward these latter objectives, read on.

COLONIAL, RANCH, OR SPLIT-LEVEL?

Item Content and Format

Initial considerations in house construction require settling on a basic structure and style. One story or two? Colonial, tudor, or French provincial? Similarly, initial considerations in scale construction involve decisions regarding both item content and format. Issues of content are driven by the objectives or applications of the measurement instrument. All content begins with some formulation—formal or informal—of the constructs or domains of interest. The assessment objective may be theoretical (e.g., the permeability of relationship boundaries) or applied (e.g., predicting couples' divorce within the next year). The domains may be singular (e.g., sexual satisfaction) or plural (e.g., satisfaction with frequency, quality, and diversity of sexual behaviors); they also may be hierarchical (e.g., specific components of life satisfaction nested under broader rubrics of work, leisure, and family) or nonhierarchical (e.g., multiple dimensions of relationship distress at comparable levels of focus and inference).

In any event, a critical component of scale development involves *mapping out assessment objectives* and content relevant to those objectives. Various information-gathering methods contribute to this process. These include reviews of both the clinical and research literature, an analysis decomposing the construct or criterion to which the measure is intended to relate, interviews with potential respondents representative of the target population, and expert opinions from potential consumers of the new scale (e.g., marital and family therapists or researchers).

In describing the process of generating stimulus items, Wesman (1971) notes that the *initial generation of "item ideas"* comprises one of the most difficult tasks of scale construction. Although no single method applies generally to all situations, several components of item writing can be identified. First, the item writer must thoroughly understand the phenomenon of interest—independent of its level of abstraction. This understanding demands familiarity with cognitive, affective, and behavioral indicators of the target construct across diverse stimulus situations. Second, appropriate items require knowledge of the population for whom the scale is intended; such knowledge implies anticipating the acceptability of item content, its impact or subjective interpretation by the respondent, and its potential to generate response variance linked to the target construct. Third, successful item generation requires mastery of language and an ability to map item ideas onto a particular item format or scale structure. For example, true–false statements discriminating respondents' behavior at one end of a construct continuum (e.g., affiliative vs. detached) require language reflecting a different level of construct intensity than statements intended to generate response variation at the other end of the construct continuum (e.g., detached vs. antagonistic).

Separate from item content, initial scale construction requires *selection of an item format*. Common formats for objective measures of marital and family functioning include true–false, Likert scale, and multiple-choice designs. The *true–false (or yes–no) format* offers several positive features, including economy of administration and scoring. Within given time and space constraints, true–false items permit broader sampling of a construct domain (and, hence, potentially higher reliability and generalizability) than a multiple-choice format (Wesman, 1971). A suitable number of true–false items varying in *response rate* (percentage of individuals answering in the scored direction) comprising a given measure typically generate sufficient variance to permit scoring of the construct along a continuous, interval-level scale. However, respondents sometimes resist responding to stimulus items they regard as "partly true, partly false" in dichotomous fashion. Moreover, dichotomous items present special difficulties in correlational procedures and, hence, should not be used if an inductive (i.e., factor-analytical) approach to scale construction is anticipated.

Likert-scale items reduce the problems of response ambivalence by permitting a range of item endorsement across a continuum (e.g., from "strongly disagree" to "strongly agree"). Although descriptors are sometimes provided for each alternative along the response continuum, anchor descriptors at the two ends of the continuum frequently suffice. Likert formats range from as few as 4-point to as many as 9-point (or more) scales. Eliminating a neutral response by using even-point scales (e.g., 4- or 6-point) has the advantage of requiring expression of at least some "tendency" along the construct continuum. A greater range of response alternatives will generally permit greater variance, all else being constant. However, greater response complexity increases the time required for a given stimulus item and, hence, potentially limits the number of items and the ability to sample as

broadly throughout the construct domain. In general, we favor a 4-point response format when using Likert items in scale construction. (See Comrey, 1988, for a contrasting opinion when using Likert items in factor-analytical procedures.)

Multiple-choice item formats occur less frequently among scales of marital or family
functioning but may be preferred when potential responses to a stimulus item are conceptualized as involving two or more alternatives along a nominal scale. Nominal scales
distinguish among response classes without implied rank (ordinal scale) or distance (interval scale). An example of such an item might be, "When my partner and I disagree
on an issue we: (1) become angry and argue without agreement; (2) avoid talking about
our differences; (3) discuss our differences calmly but usually fail to reach agreement;
(4) discuss our differences calmly and usually come to an agreement." Although one
might contend that these options comprise an ordinal scale of communication effectiveness, alternative formulations would enable response "(1)" to contribute to a scale
of verbal aggression, response "(2)" to a scale measuring withdrawal or disengagement,
and response "(4)" to a scale of conflict-resolution efficacy. By contrast, a multiple-choice
item such as, "When my partner and I disagree, we are able to resolve our differences
calmly: (1) rarely; (2) some of the time; (3) most of the time; (4) almost always," might
be better structured as a Likert item retaining the same stem and anchoring the poles
of the response continuum with "strongly agree" and "strongly disagree."

A multiple-choice item format may reduce *halo response sets* involving a tendency
to answer consistently either true or false or to respond at one end of a response continuum. Counterbalancing items within a scale for scoring direction may also reduce
this potential source of measurement error, although this approach sometimes contributes to awkwardly written items, so-called double negatives (e.g., "My partner does not
frequently fail to understand me"), or confusion in responding to a series of Likert items.

An alternative approach to reducing response sets, including individuals' tendency
to respond to items in a socially desirable direction, involves a *forced-choice format.* In
this approach, stimulus items are paired on the basis of their a priori "desirability" as
measured by their item endorsement rates in some reference group or their correlation
with an established measure of social desirability. Respondents are required to choose
between the two descriptive terms or statements that appear equally acceptable but differ
in their accuracy. Forced-choice formats are particularly useful in assessing values or
attitudes, in contrast to factual accounts of relationship experiences.

A unique feature of the forced-choice format is its potential use in developing *ipsative measures.* In ipsative measures, two or more scales comprising the measure sum to
a constant. In interpreting ipsative scores, the frame of reference is the individual rather
than some normative sample. That is, scale scores reflect the relative intensities or levels of the constructs within the respondent rather than relative intensity of a given
construct across individuals as inferred from nonipsative (normative) measures. Ipsative techniques present unique analytical and interpretive issues and, in general, have
not been adopted in measures of marital or family functioning (Hicks, 1970).

Scale Derivation from Item Pools

Once an initial pool of potential items has been developed, some method must be adopted
for grouping items into scales. The rationale for grouping items into some composite
index reflecting a target construct derives from observations that (1) most constructs
of interest are sufficiently diverse as to preclude adequate representation in one item,
and (2) both the reliability and validity of single-item measures typically suffer in comparison to multi-item indices of the same constructs. Although a variety of item-grouping

techniques have been described, in general these fall into three broad approaches: (1) deductive, (2) inductive, and (3) external (Burisch, 1984).

Deductive Approach

Deductive item-grouping techniques include methods previously labeled as rational/intuitive, theoretical, and substantive approaches. Essentially, items are grouped to form a composite index of some construct based on the apparent correspondence of manifest item content to definitions of the construct derived either from (1) the scale developer's personal or intuitive understanding of the construct (including affective, cognitive, and behavioral indicators) or (2) theoretical explications of the construct. Item grouping on rational grounds may be facilitated by having items sorted by "expert judges" and retaining those items determined to represent a given construct by a majority of judges. The deductive approach has several advantages. First, scales developed by rational or theoretical methods are more likely to possess high content validity and to facilitate interpretation based on item content. Second, some constructs are not represented well in nature by distinct index cases and, hence, may not lend themselves to contrasting groups or other external methods. However, deductive approaches are limited by the adequacy of construct definitions and items conforming to these, the scale developer's understanding of the construct, and the adequacy of the theory linking the construct to explicit indicators reflected in item content. Scales believed to be linked to some construct on the basis of item content may, in fact, not relate to that construct or any other construct of interest.

Inductive Approach

Inductive techniques to scale construction group items not on the basis of apparent item content and not on their empirical relation to some external criterion but rather on their statistical relationship to each other. Hence, inductive approaches emphasize factor-analytical or similar techniques and are frequently used when the scale developer has fairly clear ideas about what constructs to measure but remains uncertain about the manner in which these constructs may be related hierarchically. Factor analytically derived scales comprise items sharing high item loadings on one factor and, ideally, low item loadings on alternative factors. Although factors derived factor analytically are commonly rotated to orthogonal (uncorrelated) solutions, scales derived from items loading on these factors frequently are correlated. A special topic in inductive approaches involves the use of confirmatory factor analysis when a scale's internal structure is theoretically driven or guided by previous research (see Volk, Chapter 15, this volume).

Comrey (1988) provided an excellent introduction to scale development using factor-analytical methods. He suggested that for homogeneous scales developed at the lower end of a construct hierarchy, as few as 10 items may be sufficient to produce adequate reliability. Higher-order scales can be derived from factor analysis of lower-level scales, requiring at least four or five lower-level scales for each broader construct at the next conceptual level. Although items comprising factor analytically derived scales are sometimes scored in weighted fashion proportionate to their factor item loadings, research has shown that assigning unitary weights to selected items typically provides equally adequate or superior results in subsequent investigations of criterion-related validity (Wainer, 1976, 1978).

Additional considerations in using the inductive approach include minimum ratio of subjects to variables for reliable factor solutions and inclusion of an item on two or more scales. Regarding the former, recommended subject:variable ratios range from 3:1 to 10:1 and higher. Comrey (1988) proposed that a ratio of 5:1 is "reasonably good for ordinary factor-analytic work" (p. 759); a ratio of 10:1, by comparison, would permit independent analyses in two split-half samples and analysis of consistency across factor solutions. With regard to scoring an item on multiple scales the best advice is simple: do not. Doing so artifactually increases the shared variance (correlation) between two measures of different constructs developed through imperfect sampling of those constructs' respective content domains.

Advantages to the inductive approach include the derivation of scales high in internal consistency and the elucidation of scales' interrelationships and possible hierarchical organization. Factor-analytical techniques are particularly useful for reduction of large item pools of unknown structure to a smaller number of relatively homogeneous measures. However, the results of factor-analytical methods rest entirely on the adequacy of construct representation in the initial item pool (e.g., adequate sampling of a construct domain across items, and adequate sampling of the universe defined by the theory or application across construct domains). Moreover, the construct reflected by items comprising a factor analytically derived scale often remains obscure after inspection of item content (despite the ease with which factor "labels" are generated).

External Approach

Neither deductive nor inductive methods ensure that the resulting scale will relate to any nontest criterion—the ultimate measure of a scale's practical utility (Wiggins, 1973). *External approaches* to scale construction ensure that the instrument has related to *some* nontest phenomenon, although the generalizability of this observation across time, samples, and settings must be determined. Although several external approaches have been identified (cf. Dawis, 1987), the most common method involves the contrasting-groups or *criterion-keying approach.* In this approach, the scale developer attempts to identify (1) a sample of individuals (index cases) believed to exhibit or possess the target construct, and (2) a comparison sample of individuals believed not to reflect the construct. For example, a scale of marital accord could be constructed by selecting items discriminating between couples entering marital therapy and couples not in therapy sampled from the community. Appropriate comparison groups need to be carefully considered. For example, an appropriate contrasting group in developing a measure of relationship violence would be nonviolent couples in marital therapy, to control for differences between violent couples and community couples on the basis of marital distress alone.

Although inherently possessing some level of criterion-related validity, scales developed using the external approach sometimes suffer from low internal consistency, inadequate content validity, and limited generalizability to new samples or related applications. To minimize these potential hazards, Dawis (1987) suggested that in developing scales by external criterion methods (1) the contrast groups should be large, (2) mean item score differences should exhibit practical as well as statistical significance, and (3) only those items should be retained that replicate across independent cross-validation samples.[1]

Mixed Approaches to Scale Derivation

Although empirical methods of scale construction were spawned by disappointing findings from scales derived using the rational approach, well-designed comparative studies have shown no consistent superiority of any strategy in terms of validity or predictive effectiveness when scales are carefully constructed from an adequate item pool (Burisch, 1984; Hase & Goldberg, 1967). Dawis (1987) noted that in scale construction, "there can be no single 'best' method" (p. 488). In many instances, a *hybrid or mixed approach* to scale construction will yield superior results. For example, one might begin with a deductive approach to scale construction to ensure content validity but then apply criterion-keying methods to retain items relating most highly to some external indicator(s) of the target construct. Similarly, factor-analytical procedures could be used to examine the internal structure of resulting scales, to divide heterogeneous scales into a small set of more homogeneous measures, or to derive higher-order broad-band measures from lower-level, narrow-band scales.

Ultimately, regardless of the method(s) used in initial scale derivation, additional work is required to demonstrate what the scale is measuring and how reliably it measures it. It is toward these issues that we now turn our attention.

A HOUSE BUILT ON SAND . . .

Regardless of its elegance, a house built on sand will not endure. Similarly, scales possessing structural elegance or theoretical sophistication but lacking a solid foundation of reliability and validity will provide little or no practical use.

Reliability

In classical test theory, variation in scale scores is considered to reflect three components: (1) replicable score variance that relates to variation in the target construct, (2) replicable but irrelevant score variance that fails to relate to the target construct, and (3) nonreplicable score variance. *Reliability* encompasses both relevant and irrelevant replicability of scores; hence, reliability comprises an essential but nonsufficient condition for validity. The reliability or reproducibility of scores should generally be considered across three conditions: time, content, and scorers.

Temporal Stability

The consistency of scale scores across time in the absence of intervening effects is critical for evaluating changes in scores resulting from treatment or other controlled conditions. The higher the coefficients reflecting *temporal stability*, the less susceptible are scale scores to random daily changes in the respondent or assessment circumstances. Typical test–retest intervals for evaluating temporal stability hover around 4 to 6 weeks. Shorter intervals may artifactually raise reliability estimates as a result of recall of previous responses to item content, whereas longer intervals risk having uncontrolled events alter the true measure of the underlying construct. As with any correlational procedure, care should be taken to guard against truncated (restricted) range of scores at either testing.

Only measures of temporal stability are appropriate for evaluating change in scale scores across time. It seems remarkable that despite this obvious conclusion, the literature is replete with scales for which only estimates of internal consistency are available and test-retest reliability coefficients are absent. This constraint becomes evident in therapy outcome literature examining treatment gains for individual subjects. A *reliable change (RC) index* (Jacobson & Truax, 1991) for evaluating individuals' statistically reliable improvement (or deterioration) in response to treatment derives from the standard error of difference for the outcome measure which, in turn, rests on that measure's *temporal* stability:

$$RC = (X_1 - X_2) / s_{diff(x)}$$

and

$$s_{diff(x)} = s_x \sqrt{2 - 2r_{tt}}$$

where X_1 and X_2 denote pre- and posttreatment scores on the outcome measure, s_x and $s_{diff(x)}$ indicate that measure's standard deviation and standard error of difference, r_{tt} denotes the test–retest reliability coefficient, and a reliable change (RC) value of 1.96 or greater is necessary for statistical significance at $p < .05$.

Internal Consistency

Internal consistency coefficients reflect the relative homogeneity of scale content and indicate the reproducibility of scores across different item samples. Scales with a high degree of internal consistency facilitate interpretation of scores based on content. Scales developed using deductive or, especially, inductive approaches could be expected to possess higher levels of internal consistency than those derived from external methods. Moreover, narrow-band scales intended to reflect homogeneous target constructs should yield higher internal consistency coefficients than those reflecting broad-band or heterogeneous constructs.

Although generally viewed as a desirable feature of scales, it is important to note the *inverse* relationship between internal consistency and external validity. At the extreme, high internal consistency could be obtained by having an individual respond to the same item multiple times. However, many target constructs tend to be heterogeneous or multidimensional; consequently, scale construction techniques emphasizing internal consistency to the exclusion of external considerations are likely to lower rather than enhance a scale's validity and usefulness.

One approach to this dilemma is to retain individual scale items in initial scale evaluation that demonstrate high correlations with both (1) the total scale score (parceling out score variance contributed by that item) and (2) some relevant external criterion. In the absence of nontest criteria, subsequent external validity can be facilitated initially by selecting items with high item–total correlations across a broad range of item-response rates (if using dichotomous items) or mean item ratings (if using Likert items).

Before the availability of high-speed computers, estimates of internal consistency were derived from correlating scores for one-half of the scale with scores from the other half (e.g., scores for odd vs. even items). Because such correlations reflect reliability for scales only half as long as the entire scale, corrected estimates of reliability for the full scale are derived using the Spearman–Brown "prophecy" formula. However, a more adequate measure of internal consistency is provided by Cronbach's (1951) *alpha coefficient*, which reflects the mean of all split-half coefficients resulting from different splittings of a test.

The *Spearman–Brown formula* can still be useful for estimating effects of shortening or lengthening a scale with similar content. For example, in revising a scale by eliminating items with poor item–total correlations or other undesirable characteristics, one can compare the obtained internal consistency coefficient for the revised scale with what would have been predicted by shortening the original scale by randomly eliminating the same number of items where n is the ratio of the number of items in the revised

$$r_{est} = nr_{obs} / (1 + [(n - 1)r_{obs}])$$

scale to the number of items in the original scale, r_{obs} is the observed reliability coefficient for the original scale, and r_{est} is the estimated reliability coefficient for the revised scale.

Interscorer Consistency

Concerns regarding *interscorer consistency* apply primarily to scales having nonstructured response formats and to observational measures, not to scales having fixed response alternatives of the type discussed here. However, the concept of interscorer reliability can be extended to the *consistency of interpretations* across interpretive approaches or application contexts, or *consistency of decisions* based on a given score across individuals. (In a related vein, although scale scores themselves may show high test–retest stability, the consistency of interpretations may vary across time depending on the number of interpretive ranges for a scale and their respective cutting points.) When evaluating agreement for nominal data across occasions (e.g., consistency of decisions), the preferred index of reliability is Cohen's (1960) *kappa statistic*, which reflects the proportion of agreement after chance agreement is removed from consideration.

Validity

Validity denotes the extent to which scale scores measure what they are intended to measure. Not all replicable variance is valid variance. Reliability of scores is an essential but nonsufficient condition that sets the upper bounds of validity as expressed in the following:

$$r_{validity} \leq \sqrt{r_{reliability}}$$

Traditionally, validity has been conceptualized as relating to three domains: content, external criteria, and construct.

Content Validity

Content validity concerns the extent to which the content of a scale samples representatively from the domain of the target construct. As noted earlier, a critical component of scale construction involves mapping out assessment objectives and content relevant to those objectives in the initial derivation of the item pool. Thus, evaluation of content validity generally rests on a conceptual analysis of the congruence between scale and construct domains following critical review of the literature or scrutiny by expert judges.

Although content validity may be viewed as particularly relevant to scales constructed by deductive or inductive approaches, content is vital to scales constructed from an external approach as well. Contrary to Berg's (1959) deviation hypothesis suggesting that particular stimulus content is unimportant to eliciting discriminative test responses, numerous studies have confirmed that only scales constructed from an item pool sampling adequately from the domain(s) of some target construct subsequently demonstrate empirical relatedness to that construct (cf. Wiggins, 1973).

Criterion-Related Validity

Criterion-related validity refers to the ability of a scale to predict (or relate to) some external, nontest criterion or indicator of a construct. Criterion-related validity comprises the sine qua non of a scale's usefulness. As Wiggins (1973) has noted, "Regardless of the theoretical considerations which guide scale construction or the mathematical elegance of item-analytic procedures, the practical utility of a test must be assessed in terms of the number and magnitude of its correlations with nontest criterion measures" (p. 413).

Common approaches to accruing evidence of a scale's criterion-related validity include (1) documenting scores' ability to discriminate between contrasting groups; (2) convergence of scale scores with respondents' self-reports on related measures, with clinicians' or significant others' ratings of the respondent, or with observational ratings of the respondent along relevant dimensions; and (3) scores' ability to predict objective, independent events. For example, at a minimum, measures of marital satisfaction should discriminate between couples in therapy and couples from the community, measures of communication effectiveness should correspond to clinicians' evaluations or to other observational ratings of communication behavior, and a measure of treatment prognosis should relate to therapy outcome or to changes from intake to termination.

Evidence of external validity should indicate the magnitude, as well as the statistical significance, of the scale-to-criterion relationship. Presentation of group mean score differences should include discussion of effect size (Cohen, 1969). The strength of correlations should be interpreted as the square of those correlations. The correspondence of scale scores to the classification of respondents on the basis of diagnosis, treatment outcome, or some other discrete variable should include discussion of both *sensitivity and specificity* (the ability of a scale score to detect individuals having or not having some specified characteristic), as well as *positive and negative predictive power* (the proportion of correct decisions classifying individuals as having or nor having some characteristics) (Widiger, Hurt, Frances, Clarkin, & Gilmore, 1984).

Finally, not only must a scale be shown to relate to those nontest indicators it is intended to reflect (*convergent validity*), but it must also be shown not to relate to external criteria unrelated to its intent (*discriminant validity*). Of particular importance is the delineation of *moderator variables* that influence (i.e., moderate) the test–criterion relationship. Common moderators include such sociodemographic variables as age, gender, ethnicity, and marital status. It is not sufficient for demonstrating moderator effects to show that subgroups (e.g., men and women) differ in terms of mean scale scores; rather, one must demonstrate (1) group differences in the strength or direction of the test–criterion relationship, or (2) differences in optimal interpretive decision rules across groups (Cleary, Humphreys, Kendrick, & Wesman, 1975; Pritchard & Rosenblatt, 1980). Group mean differences in the absence of moderator effects may argue for the construction of separate group norms.

Construct Validity

Construct validity encompasses alternative indicators of validity and describes the extent to which a test score can be viewed as reflecting some theoretical construct or trait. Because many constructs of marital and family functioning are multidimensional or operationally difficult to articulate, evidence of a scale's relatedness to some specified construct can only be inferred from examining the complex pattern of empirical relationships linking scale scores to presumed indicators of that construct. Cronbach and Meehl (1955) have termed this network of correlations between scale scores and construct indicators the *"nomological net."* Embretson (1983) has argued that construct validity requires not only delineating empirical relationships comprising the nomological net but also identifying the mechanisms underlying these relationships.

Campbell and Fiske (1959) proposed the *multitrait–multimethod matrix* as a vehicle for examining construct variance within a nomological network. The correlational matrix comprises measures (1) believed to exhibit linkage to a common construct but differing in method of assessment (e.g., self-report, other report, and observational ratings) and (2) sharing assessment method but presumed to be theoretically distinct. Embedding the scale of interest within such a matrix permits examination of the extent to which respondents' scores on that measure reflect trait (construct) variance versus source (assessment method) variance. Volk (see Chapter 15, this volume) recommends extending the multitrait-multimethod matrix to include multiple sources (respondents) across levels of the family system—an approach consistent with the multifaceted, multilevel conceptual model for assessment proposed by Snyder et al. (1995). Confirmatory factor analysis has been used for quantitative evaluation of multitrait-multimethod matrices, although violations of assumptions underlying this approach have led to unreliable conclusions (Cole, 1987; Kenny & Kashy, 1992).

Generalizability Theory

Both reliability and validity, cornerstones of classical test theory, can be subsumed under *generalizability theory* (Cronbach, Gleser, Nanda, & Rajaratnam, 1972). Generalizability theory focuses on that universe to which a given observation (scale score) can generalize. From this perspective, test–retest reliability concerns generalizability across time, internal consistency and content validity involve generalizability across item samples from some domain of relevant construct indicators, and external validity reflects generalizability of scale scores to estimates of specific independent criteria (behaviors). The advantages to generalizability theory in evaluating scales' psychometric characteristics include (1) its amenability to factorial analyses of variance and (2) its ability to identify and estimate the magnitude of multiple sources of potential measurement error simultaneously from a given data set (Shavelson, Webb, & Rowley, 1989).

Validity versus Utility

No measure can be described as having high or low validity. Validity can only be expressed with respect to using a particular scale with a given population, for purposes of generalizing to specific nontest criteria under distinct conditions. When viewed in combination with other potential indicators or predictors of some target construct or criterion, it is a scale's *incremental validity* that matters. Incremental validity refers to that increase in criterion variance accounted for by including a predictor measure in some set of alternative predictors. For example, in multiple regression analysis, a scale's incremental validity will be limited by its covariance with other predictors in the regression model regardless of its own zero-order correlation with the criterion.

Related to the concept of incremental validity is a scale's *utility*. For example, the ability of a scale to contribute to increased accuracy of selection decisions (e.g., selecting families for a specific treatment modality based on their scores on a scale reflecting treatment prognosis) will depend on three details: (1) the validity coefficient relating scale scores to treatment outcome, (2) the prevalence (base rate) of scores falling in the favorable prognostic range among families presenting for treatment, and (3) the selection ratio or proportion of these families that can be accepted into treatment based on the adequacy of existing resources (e.g., availability of therapists trained in this treatment approach). Regardless of its validity or the integrity of information it provides, a scale possesses limited functional utility if all respondents receive uniform treatment (Hayes, Nelson, & Jarrett, 1987); conditions contributing to lack of a scale's impact on subsequent treatment may include characteristics of the respondent or significant others (partner or family), test consumer (therapist or administrator), or setting (availability of service providers or alternative interventions).

Additional criteria for evaluating scales' utility include (1) applicability to a broad range of clinical or research contexts, (2) ease and economy of administration and scoring, (3) usefulness across multiple respondents, (4) explicit interpretive guidelines across scale score ranges, and (5) ease of feedback and comprehension by nonprofessional audiences (Newman & Ciarlo, 1994).

THE HOMEOWNER'S GUIDE

To use and preserve a home effectively, the homeowner needs instructions for operating and maintaining major appliances, home heating and cooling systems, and other essential components. Similarly, to use a scale effectively in either clinical or research applications, one needs interpretive guidelines linking scale scores to relevant external criteria. Common interpretive models for expressing test–criterion relationships include regression, discriminant, and actuarial analysis.

Interpretive Models

Regression Analysis

Interpretive guidelines based on *regression analysis* posit a uniform, linear relationship between scale scores and external criteria throughout their respective ranges. Unless predicting to and from z-scores, the linear regression model requires both the means and standard deviations of the predictor and criterion measures in addition to the correlation(s) relating these measures. An advantage to interpreting scale scores from a regression model is the ability to predict a specific value along a continuous criterion measure for a given score on the predictor, thereby retaining the relative evaluation of all scale respondents. In the case of a single predictor, tables translating predictor scores to criterion scores can be readily constructed. With two or more predictors (i.e., multiple regression), such tables become impractical and criterion values must be calculated by hand or electronically.

An alternative approach to regression analysis involves converting continuous scales to dichotomous ones, using regression to identify that score on the predictor measure that discriminates individuals falling above or below some designated point on the criterion measure. This approach involving *cutoff scores* is particularly useful (1) where predictor and criterion measures are related in monotonic but nonlinear fashion, (2) when seeking a simple computational approach for combining information across multiple predictors, or (3) when seeking to limit the extent to which information from one predictor measure can override or "compensate" for contradictory information on another.

Discriminant Analysis

In cases in which the scale-to-criterion relationship is nonmonotonic, interpretive guidelines are better conceptualized from a *discriminant analysis* (or profile congruence) model. Consider, for example, an instrument comprising measures of (1) family closeness—ranging from enmeshment to disengagement and (2) family system rigidity—ranging from entropy to negentropy. Dividing each scale into three ranges and considering the nine patterns obtained by crossing scores on each, one might hypothesize on theoretical grounds that one cell (reflecting moderate scores on each scale) relates to ideal family adjustment, four cells (reflecting extreme scores on each) predict poor family adjustment, and the remaining four cells (moderate scores on one scale and extreme scores on the other) predict moderate levels of adjustment.

Discriminant analysis is a technique that forms linear combinations of predictor variables to optimally distinguish among known groups. When there are at least three groups and two predictors, one can obtain multiple discriminant functions (Nunnally & Bernstein, 1994). As with other multivariate quantitative techniques, profile analysis using this method requires complex computations not easily conducted by hand. Alternative, simpler means of developing interpretive guidelines from a profile analysis approach confine classification procedures to some restricted aspect of respondents' scores—as in the 2-point code interpretive approach common to the Minnesota Multiphasic Personality Inventory (Butcher, Dahlstrom, Graham, Tellegen, & Kaemmer, 1989).

Actuarial Analysis

Actuarial analysis refers to "procedures that derive probability estimates of criterion status from contingent-frequency tables of predictor attributes" (Wiggins, 1973, p. 80). Actuarial prediction addresses questions of the following form, "What is the likelihood that I will observe some specific characteristic about this individual, given that I already have this information about him or her?" As distinct from both regression and discriminant function analysis, actuarial models involve probability estimates of noncontinuous criteria from noncontinuous predictors. (Note, however, that in a combined approach actuarial analysis could be used to express the probability of correct classifications resulting from regression or discriminant function models.)

Procedures for developing *actuarially based interpretive guidelines* have been described as applied to the Marital Satisfaction Inventory (Snyder, 1981; Snyder & Costin, 1994; Snyder, Lachar, Freiman, & Hoover, 1991). The first step involves identifying statistically significant associations between predictors and respective criteria, typically through correlational or chi-square analyses. The second step requires the construction of *contingent-frequency tables* delineating the conditional probability of specific criterion values (e.g., presence or absence of a designated symptom) given some specific predictor value (e.g., designated range of scale scores).

Following the construction of contingent-frequency tables, the next step requires determining that predictor value for which the probability of some specified criterion departs in a significant and meaningful way from base-rate (noncontingent) probability (Meehl & Rosen, 1955). That is, at what value or scale range on the predictor measure is one significantly more or less likely to observe some criterion characteristic of the respondent than by chance alone? Once contingent-frequency tables have been constructed and *optimal cutoff scores* have been identified for each significant scale-to-criterion relationship, findings must be integrated across diverse criteria and decision rules.

Lachar and Gdowski (1979) describe this final derivation of pragmatic interpretive guidelines as "a mixture of the application of measurement theory, assessment art, and individual preference" (p. 16). Snyder et al. (1991) outline goals at this final stage as (1) identifying common cutting scores across external criteria within a given scale for distinguishing departures of criterion probabilities from base rates; (2) developing interpretive guidelines that are both accurate and complete for individual scales, while minimizing interpretive redundancy across scales; and (3) generating interpretive guidelines that satisfy both criteria of *descriptive accuracy* and *predictive utility* in improving accuracy of prediction over currently available information or base rates.

Automated Interpretation

Extensive research over several decades has demonstrated that "well-designed statistical treatment of test results and ancillary information will yield more valid assessment than will an individual professional using the same information" (American Psychological Association, 1986, p. 13). This conclusion has fostered the development of *computer-based test interpretation (CBTI) systems* across diverse assessment domains in psychology and related fields (Butcher, 1987). A recent methodological review concluded as follows:

> Computerized interpretive narratives, when developed on a broad actuarial foundation of empirical findings relating test indices to relevant external criteria, offer distinct advantages including: (a) economy of processing and more effective utilization of professional resources; (b) accuracy and consistency of scoring and implementation of interpretive decision rules; (c) virtually unlimited capacity for storage, indexing, and retrieval of relevant information from the clinical and research literature regarding test-behavior relationships; (d) ability to subject test indicators to complex, configural analyses; and (e) potential for automated collection and analysis of extensive normative data bases. (Snyder, Widiger, & Hoover, 1990, p. 470)

However, the proliferation of computer-assisted test interpretation has also generated considerable controversy (Eyde & Kowal, 1987). The widespread application of CBTI systems has far exceeded careful attention to the validity of these techniques. Methodological issues related to development and validation of CBTI systems have been reviewed elsewhere (cf. Fowler, 1987; Moreland, 1985; Snyder et al., 1990; Vale & Keller, 1987). Snyder et al. (1990) emphasized that issues and procedures relevant to test validation are all germane to the validation of computer-based test interpretation; the accuracy and practical utility of any CBTI system are constricted by the inherent validity of the measure for which it is developed.

Regardless of the interpretive model (i.e., regression, discriminant, or actuarial analysis) underlying computer-based interpretation, well-controlled validational studies of a measure's interpretive guidelines (automated or otherwise) are needed to study all components of the interpretive system. Moreover, both individual interpretive units as well as entire reports derived from an interpretive system must be examined using multiple ratings that assess (1) relevance as well as accuracy, (2) both the exclusion and inclusion of important information, and (3) usefulness in classification and treatment.

THE MODEST COTTAGE

This chapter has emphasized scale development techniques central to theory-driven measures intended for dissemination to clinical and research colleagues. Considerations involved in obtaining adequate reference or standardization samples, contrasting performance across various criterion groups, and using correlational approaches to delineate interpretive guidelines are all crucial to norm-referenced measures when an individual's scores are interpreted at least in part in reference to some comparison, standardization sample.

However, assessment objectives may vary across settings, and alternatives to norm-referenced approaches exist. Just as individuals may set out to build their own modest cottage with minimal assistance of a contractor, so too may clinicians or researchers have a need to develop a measure tailored for their own use in a specific application. Sundberg (1977) noted that non–norm-based approaches to assessment—commonly identified as *criterion-referenced measures*—fall into three categories: (1) content or performance referencing, (2) expectancy referencing, and (3) self-referencing techniques.

Content-referencing involves interpretation of a measure based on absolute (rather than relative) performance without reference to a comparison group or prediction to nontest criteria. For example, on a checklist denoting spouses' behaviors for the previous week, one might observe that the husband reported receiving 23 positive behaviors from his wife in comparison to the wife's report of only 8 positive behaviors from her husband. If an explicit goal of marital therapy has been to increase the rate of positive behaviors for each spouse from an average of less than one per day to more than two per day, results would suggest continued interventions with the husband toward meeting this criterion. Such interpretations based solely on content require assuming that (1) the respondent has understood the content of the measure in the manner intended by the developer of the measure, (2) the respondent has the capacity to provide accurate data, and (3) the respondent is motivated to provide accurate data. Considerable research indicating the tenuousness of these assumptions has been conducted in the area of personality testing, and likely generalizes to the domain of marital and family assessment as well.

Expectancy-referencing involves interpretation of scores based on predicted performance on some nontest criterion. For example, given the same checklist from the previous example and a previously identified relationship between rates of positive spousal behaviors and marital conflict, one might conclude that the wife's reports of low rates of positive behavior from her partner indicate a likelihood of her having experienced low satisfaction with the marriage during this time period. Although expectancy referencing obviates the need for a normative reference group, it still requires delineation of criterion-related validity.

Finally, in *self-referencing* an individual's performance on a measure is compared to his or her scores for a different time or situation. Continuing with the same example, one might observe that the husband's reports of receiving 23 positive behaviors from his wife during the past week reflect a threefold increase over the prior reporting period. Although still eliminating the need for a normative reference group, attributing self-referenced scores to actual change requires information on the temporal stability of the measure.

In contemplating the task of developing specialized measures for individual or local use, certain caveats should be considered. First, interpretations based on content become more tenuous as content moves from discrete behaviors sampling low-order constructs (e.g., expression of positive affection) to subjective reports intended to reflect higher-order constructs (e.g., affiliation). The importance of documenting content validity for such measures is paramount. Second, interpretations of criterion-referenced techniques extending beyond description of content to include comparisons to previous performance or expectancies regarding nontest performance require attention to the same psychometric issues of scale development as do norm-referenced measures.

To return to our metaphor, one could build a modest cottage with limited resources. But compromising on the structural integrity of the foundation will eventually bring heartbreak just as surely as a clinical or research measure tailored for individual use without adequate attention to reliability and validity.

CONSTRUCTION RESOURCES

The phrase "building a home" can imply a full spectrum of responsibilities ranging from actually pouring the foundation or nailing the roof oneself to selecting a general contractor and providing little direction beyond styles of flooring or wallpaper. Similarly, after reaching a decision to initiate scale construction, one can adopt various levels of responsibility for initial generation and evaluation of item ideas, collection of preliminary data from reference and criterion samples, scale evaluation and revision, development of interpretive guidelines or automated systems, and distribution of the measure. In most cases, consultation on both theoretical or conceptual perspectives as well as methodological or statistical ones would seem critical throughout the scale development process.

For individuals considering developing a new measure of marital or family functioning, a variety of resources specific to this domain should be consulted, including (1) conceptual models of marital or family assessment (Cromwell & Peterson, 1981; Snyder et al., 1995), (2) bibliographies of available measurement approaches in this area (Fredman & Sherman, 1987; Grotevant & Carlson, 1989; Jacob & Tennenbaum, 1988; L'Abate & Bagarozzi, 1993; Straus & Brown, 1978; Touliatos, Perlmutter, & Straus, 1990), and (3) extended discussion of selected marital and family assessment techniques (Filsinger, 1983; O'Leary, 1987; Snyder, 1982). Also essential are more general discussions of psychometric theory (Nunnally & Bernstein, 1994; Wiggins, 1973), scale construction and validation (Comrey, 1988; Dawis, 1987; DeVellis, 1991; Thorndike, 1971), and development of interpretive guidelines (American Psychological Association, 1985, 1986; Butcher, 1987; Elwood, 1993; Lachar & Gdowski, 1979; Moreland, 1985; Snyder et al., 1991).

Just as contractors need to stay abreast of new materials and construction techniques in their own field, so too clinicians and researchers alike need to remain informed of new measurement techniques and approaches to scale development. Although predicting the future presents numerous hazards, several trends are likely to characterize future research in the area of marital and family assessment. First, as theories of marital and family functioning evolve and the need for appropriate instrumentation for evaluating their tenets becomes more acute, measurement techniques in the field will become more theory driven. Reflecting this trend were the host of self-report behavioral measures developed to evaluate social learning-based approaches to marital therapy explicated in the late 1960s and early 1970s and the new generation of instruments assessing relationship aggression accompanying growing concern with domestic violence.

Second, measures of marital and family functioning are likely to become increasingly differentiated and specialized—moving from global to multidimensional measures of relationship domains. Examples in this direction include instruments assessing various components of a couple's sexual functioning and self-report measures of child–parent interactions.

Third, new measures will likely tap domains and levels of family systems previously understudied and poorly evaluated. For example, Snyder et al. (1995) observed that a broad range of formal assessment techniques have been developed at the individual and dyadic levels, in contrast to fewer techniques at the extended family or community system levels; specifically, adequate measures for evaluating the impact of community resources and cultural values or expectations on family functioning and response to family therapy have received scant attention. Similarly, increased emphasis will likely be given to developing efficient means of integrating information from multiple respondents in the extended family system.

Last, we anticipate and hope that both marital and family therapists and researchers will develop increased appreciation for the psychometric underpinnings of their measures. Above all, concerns for temporal stability and criterion-related validity should dominate decisions regarding clinical assessment and research instrumentation. Test developers will need to document specific interpretive guidelines and their empirical basis. Test consumers will need to substantiate the functional utility of their assessment techniques in increasing accuracy of decisions and enhancing treatment efficacy.

We have emphasized test development as an ongoing enterprise that begins with delineation of measurement objectives derived from theory or application, extends beyond initial construction of items and scales to include systematic appraisal of reliability and validity, and culminates with the preparation and continuous revision of interpretive guidelines based on new empirical findings.

The field of marriage and family suffers not from a lack of assessment instruments but rather from a shortage of assessment techniques having practical and theoretical utility based on their linkage to nontest criteria. The field begs for measurement approaches enriching our understanding of relationship processes and enhancing our ability to intervene effectively with distressed couples and families. Efforts toward that end require commitment to the entire process of test development.

NOTE

1. Practical significance of an item's discrimination potential can be inferred when group means on that item diverge by more than twice the item's standard error of difference.

REFERENCES

American Psychological Association. (1985). *Standards for educational and psychological testing.* Washington, DC: Author.

American Psychological Association. (1986). *Guidelines for computer-based tests and interpretations.* Washington, DC: Author.

Berg, I. A. (1959). The unimportance of test item content. In B. M. Bass & I. A. Berg (Eds.), *Objective approaches to personality assessment* (pp. 83–99). New York: Van Nostrand.

Burisch, M. (1984). Approaches to personality inventory construction: A comparison of merits. *American Psychologist, 39,* 214–227.

Butcher, J. N. (Ed.). (1987). *Computerized psychological assessment: A practitioner's guide.* New York: Basic Books.

Butcher, J. N., Dahlstrom, W. G., Graham, J. R., Tellegen, A., & Kaemmer, B. (1989). *Minnesota Multiphasic Personality Inventory-2.* Minneapolis: University of Minnesota Press.

Campbell, D. T., & Fiske, D. W. (1959). Convergent and discriminant validation by the multitrait–multimethod matrix. *Psychological Bulletin, 56,* 81–105.

Cleary, T. A., Humphreys, L. G., Kendrick, S. A., & Wesman, A. (1975). Educational uses of tests with disadvantaged students. *American Psychologist, 30,* 15–41.

Cohen, J. (1960). A coefficient of agreement for nominal scales. *Educational and Psychological Measurement, 20,* 37–46.

Cohen, J. (1969). *Statistical power analysis for the behavioral sciences.* New York: Academic Press.

Cole, D. A. (1987). Utility of confirmatory factor analysis in test validation research. *Journal of Consulting and Clinical Psychology, 55,* 584–594.

Comrey, A. L. (1988). Factor-analytic methods of scale development in personality and clinical psychology. *Journal of Consulting and Clinical Psychology, 56,* 754–761.

Cromwell, R. E., & Peterson, G. W. (1981). Multisystem–multimethod assessment: A framework. In E. E. Filsinger & R. A. Lewis (Eds.), *Assessing marriage: New behavioral approaches* (pp. 38–54). Newbury Park, CA: Sage.

Cronbach, L. J. (1951). Coefficient alpha and the internal structure of tests. *Psychometrika, 16,* 297–334.

Cronbach, L. J., Gleser, G. C., Nanda, H., & Rajaratnam, N. (1972). *The dependability of behavioral measurements: Theory of generalizability of scores and profiles.* New York: Wiley.

Cronbach, L. J., & Meehl, P. E. (1955). Construct validity in psychological tests. *Psychological Bulletin, 52,* 281–302.

Dawis, R. V. (1987). Scale construction. *Journal of Counseling Psychology, 34,* 481–489.

DeVellis, R. F. (1991). *Scale development: Theory and applications.* Newbury Park, CA: Sage.

Elwood, R. W. (1993). Psychological tests and clinical discriminations: Beginning to address the base rate problem. *Clinical Psychology Review, 13,* 409–419.

Embretson, S. (1983). Construct validity: Construct representation versus nomothetic span. *Psychological Bulletin, 93,* 179–197.

Eyde, L. D., & Kowal, D. M. (1987). Computerised test interpretation services: Ethical and professional concerns regarding U.S. producers and users. *Applied Psychology: An International Review, 36,* 401–417.

Filsinger, E. E. (Ed.). (1983). *Marriage and family assessment: A sourcebook for family therapy.* Newbury Park, CA: Sage.

Fowler, R. D. (1987). Developing a computer-based test interpretation system. In J. N. Butcher (Ed.), *Computerized psychological assessment: A practitioner's guide* (pp. 50–63). New York: Basic Books.

Fredman, N., & Sherman, R. (1987). *Handbook of measurements for marriage and family therapy.* New York: Brunner/Mazel.

Grotevant, H. D., & Carlson, C. I. (1989). *Family assessment: A guide to methods and measures.* New York: Guilford Press.

Hase, H. D., & Goldberg, L. R. (1967). Comparative validity of different strategies of constructing personality inventory scales. *Psychological Bulletin, 67,* 231–248.

Hayes, S. C., Nelson, R. O., & Jarrett, R. B. (1987). The treatment utility of assessment: A functional approach to evaluating assessment quality. *American Psychologist, 42,* 963–974.

Hicks, L. E. (1970). Some properties of ipsative, normative, and forced-choice normative measures. *Psychological Bulletin, 74,* 167–184.

Jacob, T., & Tennenbaum, D. L. (1988). *Family assessment: Rationale, methods, and future directions.* New York: Plenum Press.

Jacobson, N. S., & Margolin, G. (1979). *Marital therapy: Strategies based on social learning and behavior exchange principles.* New York: Brunner/Mazel.

Jacobson, N. S., & Truax, P. (1991). Clinical significance: A statistical approach to defining meaningful change in psychotherapy research. *Journal of Consulting and Clinical Psychology, 59,* 12–19.

Kenny, D. A., & Kashy, D. A. (1992). Analysis of the multitrait–multimethod matrix by confirmatory factor analysis. *Psychological Bulletin, 112,* 165–172.

L'Abate, L., & Bagarozzi, D. A. (1993). *Sourcebook of marriage and family evaluation.* New York: Brunner/Mazel.

Lachar, D., & Gdowski, C. L. (1979). *Actuarial assessment of child and adolescent personality*. Los Angeles: Western Psychological Services.

Meehl, P. E., & Rosen, A. (1955). Antecedent probability and the efficiency of psychometric signs, patterns, or cutting scores. *Psychological Bulletin, 52*, 194–216.

Moreland, K. L. (1985). Validation of computer-based test interpretations: Problems and prospects. *Journal of Consulting and Clinical Psychology, 53*, 816–825.

Newman, F. L., & Ciarlo, J. A. (1994). Criteria for selecting psychological instruments for treatment outcome assessment. In M. E. Maruish (Ed.), *The use of psychological testing for treatment planning and outcome assessment* (pp. 98–110). Hillsdale, NJ: Erlbaum.

Nunnally, J. C., & Bernstein, I. H. (1994). *Psychometric theory* (3rd ed.). New York: McGraw-Hill.

O'Leary, K. D. (1987). *Assessment of marital discord: An integration for research and clinical practice*. Hillsdale, NJ: Erlbaum.

Pritchard, D. A., & Rosenblatt, A. (1980). Racial bias in the MMPI: A methodological review. *Journal of Consulting and Clinical Psychology, 48*, 263–267.

Schumm, W. R. (1990). Evolution of the family field: Measurement principles and techniques. In J. Touliatos, B. F. Perlmutter, & M. A. Straus (Eds.), *Handbook of family measurement techniques* (pp. 23–36). Newbury Park, CA: Sage.

Shavelson, R. J., Webb, N. M., & Rowley, G. L. (1989). Generalizability theory. *American Psychologist, 44*, 922–932.

Snyder, D. K. (1981). *Manual for the Marital Satisfaction Inventory*. Los Angeles: Western Psychological Services.

Snyder, D. K. (1982). Advances in marital assessment: Behavioral, communications, and psychometric approaches. In C. D. Spielberger & J. N. Butcher (Eds.), *Advances in personality assessment* (Vol. 1, pp. 169–201). Hillsdale, NJ: Erlbaum.

Snyder, D. K., Cavell, T. A., Heffer, R. W., & Mangrum, L. F. (1995). Marital and family assessment: A multifacet, multilevel approach. In R. H. Mikesell, D. D. Lusterman, and S. H. McDaniel (Eds.), *Integrating family therapy: Handbook of family psychology and systems theory* (pp. 163–182). Washington, DC: American Psychological Association.

Snyder, D. K., & Costin, S. E. (1994). Marital Satisfaction Inventory. In M. E. Maruish (Ed.), *The use of psychological testing for treatment planning and outcome assessment* (pp. 322–351). Hillsdale, NJ: Erlbaum.

Snyder, D. K., Lachar, D., Freiman, K. E., & Hoover, D. W. (1991). Toward the actuarial assessment of couples' relationships. In J. P. Vincent (Ed.), *Advances in family intervention, assessment, and theory* (Vol. 5, pp. 89–122). London: Kingsley Publishers.

Snyder, D. K., Widiger, T. A., & Hoover, D. W. (1990). Methodological considerations in validating computer-based test interpretations: Controlling for response bias. *Psychological Assessment, 2*, 470–477.

Straus, M. A., & Brown, B. W. (1978). *Family measurement techniques: Abstracts of published instruments, 1935–1974* (rev. ed.). Minneapolis: University of Minnesota Press.

Sundberg, N. D. (1977). *Assessment of persons*. Englewood Cliffs, NJ: Prentice-Hall.

Terman, L. M. (1938). *Psychological factors in marital happiness*. New York: McGraw-Hill.

Thorndike, E. L. (1918). The nature, purposes and general methods of measurements of educational products. In *Seventeenth yearbook of the National Society for the Study of Education. Part II: Measurement of educational products*. Bloomington, IL: Public School Publishing.

Thorndike, R. L. (Ed.). (1971). *Educational measurement* (2nd ed.). Washington, DC: American Council on Education.

Tinkelman, S. N. (1971). Planning the objective test. In R. L. Thorndike (Ed.), *Educational measurement* (pp. 46–80). Washington, DC: American Council on Education.

Touliatos, J., Perlmutter, B. F., & Straus, M. A. (Eds.). (1990). *Handbook of family measurement techniques*. Newbury Park, CA: Sage.

Vale, C. D., & Keller, L. S. (1987). Developing expert computer systems to interpret psychological tests. In J. N. Butcher (Ed.), *Computerized psychological assessment: A practitioner's guide* (pp. 64–83). New York: Basic Books.

Wainer, H. (1976). Estimating coefficients in linear models: It don't make no nevermind. *Psychological Bulletin, 83,* 213–217.

Wainer, H. (1978). On the sensitivity of regression and regressors. *Psychological Bulletin, 85,* 267–273.

Wesman, A. G. (1971). Writing the test item. In R. L. Thorndike (Ed.), *Educational measurement* (pp. 81–129). Washington, DC: American Council on Education.

Widiger, T., Hurt, S., Frances, A., Clarkin, J., & Gilmore, M. (1984). Diagnostic efficiency and DSM-III. *Archives of General Psychiatry, 41,* 1005–1012.

Wiggins, J. S. (1973). *Personality and prediction.* Reading, MA: Addison-Wesley.

Experimental Research

11

Experimental Methods in Marital and Family Therapy Research

KEVIN P. LYNESS
DOUGLAS H. SPRENKLE

My students have spread the rumor that my idea of
the perfect study is one with 10,000 cases and no
variables. They go too far.
—Jacob Cohen (1992, p. 317)

So, you are an aspiring family therapist and researcher, maybe an assistant professor at a medium-size university, working toward tenure. You want to have an impact on the field, and you think you have some good ideas about marital and family therapy. In fact, you have created your own brand of therapy, *solution-continuum therapy* (SCT), which is based on the definition of a continuum as something that can be infinitely divided (e.g., space and time), and you believe that addressing solutions as such is beneficial for your clients. You think your therapy is different than traditional solution-focused approaches, and you think it is more effective for a broader range of subjects. But how do you go about proving this? And how can you get published and move yourself along toward tenure along the way? By using experimental design, of course. (At least, this is one way.)

BACKGROUND

Philosophical Assumptions

Essentially, experimental design is the legacy of the positivist research tradition. In experimental design, we are looking for "the truth" or some approximation of it. As Moon, Dillon, and Sprenkle (1990) point out, traditional quantitative research is at the enumerative, verificative, deductive, and objective end of the epistemological spectrum. Experimental research seeks to name and classify phenomena, verify hypotheses, and make deductions from data, and it strives to be objective. This epistemological position drives the other assumptions of experimental design—such designs are considered adequate when they can ferret out the truth unequivocally. There has been widespread debate in the field over the worth of quantitative, positivist research versus qualitative, constructivist research. We take a synthesist position that "the two methodologies are neither incompatible nor compatible; instead, they are complementary" (Moon et al., 1990, p. 358).

Given this epistemological position, the essence of experimental design is the systematic manipulation and control of variables. "In simplest terms, an experiment is performed when one variable, an independent variable, is systematically varied in order to assess its effects on another variable, the dependent variable" (Winer, Brown, & Michels, 1991, p. 3). Put another way, different treatments are given to different groups (or the same group under different condition) and performance on some response measure (or measures) is observed, recorded, and compared (Keppel, 1982).

Ideally, the groups being compared would be identical in every way save the manipulated variable, whereas the experimental conditions would be as different as possible (Kerlinger, 1986). With identical groups, we could be sure that the differences were due to the manipulation. Having the treatment conditions as different as possible maximizes the experimental variance, which is important if we are to find differences between treatment conditions. For example, comparing your SCT therapy with cognitive-behavioral therapy would maximize variance over the same comparison to traditional solution-focused therapy (SFT) because SCT and SFT are very similar.

Historical Roots and Development

Experimental design has its roots in the work of Fisher (1951), who developed experimental designs in agriculture. Much of the terminology (e.g., block designs) is still left from agriculture. Experimental design "has found widespread application in all research domains wherein control of experimental conditions is possible" (Winer et al., 1991, p. 3), including psychology and marriage and family therapy.

In fact, experimental design is the classical quantitative research design and has been used in marital therapy research from the beginning. Whisman, Jacobson, Fruzzetti, and Waltz (1989) remark that a strength "of marital therapy research methodology is its legacy of elegant sophisticated experimental designs" (p. 177). Jacobson and his colleagues have probably used and published experimental methods more than any other family therapy researchers (Jacobson, 1984; Jacobson & Addis, 1993; Jacobson & Baucom, 1977; Jacobson, Dobson, Fruzzetti, Schmaling, & Salusky, 1991; Jacobson et al., 1985; Jacobson, Follette, & Pagel, 1986; Jacobson, Schmaling, & Holtzworth-Munroe, 1987; Jacobson et al., 1989).

METHODOLOGY

Research design has two purposes: (1) to provide answers to research questions, and (2) to control variance (Kerlinger, 1986). The key assumption of experimental design is control (Keppel, 1982; Winer et al., 1991). Kerlinger (1986) refers to the "maxmincon" (p. 286) principle—"maximize the systemic variance under study; control extraneous systematic variance; and minimize error variance" (p. 286)—as the basic principle of experimental design.

Variables

Experimental designs have three types of variables—*independent variables* (IVs), *dependent variables* (DVs), *and supplementary variables* (SVs) (Winer et al., 1991). Independent variables are those variables that the researcher manipulates in order to produce change. IVs must vary either in kind or in magnitude (e.g., different treatment or different amount of treatment). Multiple IVs may be used, and when they are, this allows the study of interaction effects among the IVs. For example, it may be that age interacts with treatment type, such that treatment *A* works best for people between 25 and 30 years old, whereas treatment *C* works best for those over 55. A third level of independent variable could be added as well (e.g., gender). It is important to note, however, that with each added IV (or DV) the complexity of the design increases. Multiple IV designs are called factorial designs (Keppel, 1982; Winer et al., 1991).

Dependent variables are the outcome measures that should be affected by changes in the IV. Experimental designs with a single DV are considered univariate, even if there are multiple IVs, whereas designs with multiple DVs are multivariate designs (Winer et al., 1991). The DV chosen should be the variable that is most sensitive to the treatment condition (because you are looking for change in the DV due to changes in the IV). In addition, DVs should have small inherent variability between subjects (Winer et al., 1991). For example, when exploring SCT, your outcome measure (say, the Dyadic Adjustment Scale) should not vary much between subjects at pretest. At the beginning of the study, a group with homogeneous Dyadic Adjustment Scale scores will be more sensitive to changes brought about by SCT. Smaller between-subject variability will increase the precision of estimation for parameters and increase the power of statistical tests. DVs should also be chosen that are normally distributed because many parametric statistics are based on the assumption of a normal distribution (Winer et al., 1991).

It is important to use a measure for DVs that is sensitive to increased therapeutic efficacy. Of course, therapeutic efficacy has been defined in many different ways. Researchers may want to look at the "presenting problem" the family came in with, and the improvement in that given each added component (Wynne, 1988); they may want to look at change in family functioning from dysfunctional to functional on a measure such as the Dyadic Adjustment Scale (Jacobson & Traux, 1991), or they may want to look at objective symptom reduction (e.g., change in score on the Beck Depression Inventory) or use observational or behavioral measures of change in family functioning (Whisman et al., 1989).

Supplementary variables are often known as nuisance variables. The control of these supplementary variables is necessary because such characteristics as motivation and referral source (to name but a few), if uncontrolled, could lead to interference in interpreting group differences (Kazdin, 1994). The researcher can use direct (experimental) or indirect (statistical) methods to control SVs (Winer et al., 1991). Direct control entails the use of blocks (groups of subjects relatively equal on the SV) included in the design by using a randomized block design, which holds the SV constant over all of the treatment groups, or via randomization (random assignment) across groups. For example, in studying SCT, researchers may want to use blocks of clients based on referral source if they think that clients will differ depending on who referred them. In a randomized block design (sometimes referred to as a treatment by block design) (Keppel, 1982), the supplementary variable is used as an independent variable—in the example used, groups from referral source A and referral source B and would be randomly assigned to treatment and control groups.

Random assignment is one way to distribute nuisance variables across groups unsystematically so that they do not interfere with interpretation of the findings of interest. Indirect (statistical) control involves the use of covariates, variables that systematically covary with the dependent variable (Winer et al., 1991). Again, in studying SCT, researchers may feel that age may make a difference but they do not want to create age blocks, so they use age as a covariate. The choice of IV, DV, and SV will be determined by the research question.

Each of these strategies to control extraneous variables has strengths and weaknesses. Holding the variable constant across all groups does eliminate that variable as a source of potential problems, but it reduces our ability to generalize—we can only generalize to others with the same level of that variable. Building the variable into the design as an IV does control the variable and allows for the study of interaction effects. However, it increases complexity and needed sample size. Matching (through randomized block design) is another way of building the variable into the design. When the correlation between the matching variable and DV is high ($>$ .50 or .60), matching reduces the error term and increases the precision of the experiment (Kerlinger, 1986). Matching should not preclude randomization—that is, randomized block designs should be used if matching is going to be used. However, matching does entail potential problems. The variable on which the subjects are matched must be related substantially to the dependent variable or the matching is "a waste of time" (Kerlinger, 1986, p. 289) and can even be misleading. Trying to match on more than one or two variables at the most results in lost subjects. Matching on more than three variables is almost impossible (Kerlinger, 1986).

Randomization is the best way to control extraneous or supplementary variables (Kerlinger, 1986). It is the only method of controlling all possible extraneous variables. If at all possible, researchers should use randomization to control for SVs unless interaction effects are of interest to them. If that is the case, they should use interaction effects as IVs but still randomize.

Basic Design Considerations

The basic, classical experimental design includes two groups—an experimental group and a control group—and two evaluation periods—pretest and posttest. Figure 11.1 illustrates the classical experimental design. The two groups are compared at pretest and at posttest, and differences at posttest can be attributed to the experimental manipulation of the treatment condition (Babbie, 1986).

The classic design includes the use of a pretest, and many authors argue for the use of a pretest (Gurman & Kniskern, 1981). As an example, Jacobson (1984) uses a pretest as a covariate in the posttest analysis controlling for pretest differences in the treatment groups. Others argue that a pretest is not necessary in all conditions (Bell & Morris, 1988). The administration of a pretest is clearly indicated when you cannot control group membership (it is unethical or impossible to assign people to be, for

	Pretest	Manipulation	Posttest
Control group	X		X
Experimental group	X	X	X

FIGURE 11.1. Classic experimental design.

example, survivors of sexual abuse), when attrition from the groups is likely, or in studies with small samples. With random assignment and adequate sample sizes, pretreatment equivalence may be assumed (Bell & Morris, 1988).

Factorial designs include more than one independent variable. Figure 11.2 illustrates a factorial design including three treatment conditions (behavioral marital therapy [BMT], SCT, and a no-treatment control) and two settings (a marriage–family therapy [MFT] training center and a private practice clinic). Subjects can be randomly assigned to both treatment condition and setting. If multiple outcome measures are also used, the design becomes multivariate (and three dimensions are needed to diagram). Each box represents a subgroup or subsample. In Figure 11.2, there are six subgroups to which subjects will need to be assigned. If the researcher decides on 20 subjects per group, he or she will need 120 subjects in the total sample.

Table 11.1 lays out several questions researchers can ask themselves regarding the design. If the researcher can answer each of these questions, his or her design is probably adequate. Basically, does the design adequately measure the variables you want to measure and answer the questions you want answered, and is it valid? These questions should be addressed before a researcher undertakes an investigation and reports findings.

Inadequate Designs

There are a variety of designs that look experimental—they may have a pretest and a posttest, they have a control group, and so forth—but are inadequate and uninterpretable within a positivistic paradigm (Cook & Campbell, 1979; Kerlinger, 1986). There are four common inadequate designs.

The first is the "one-shot case study" (Kerlinger, 1986, p. 295), which Cook and Campbell (1979) call the "one-group posttest-only design" (p. 96), of which there are two forms. In the first, the IV is manipulated between pretest and posttest, but there is no control group. For example, suppose you have developed a new family therapy intervention in your solution-continuum approach, the *solution-continuum diagram* (SCG). You have a group of clients with whom you have used the SCG, and you give them the Dyadic Adjustment Scale. They all score in the functional range, and you assume that they have improved because of your intervention. This looks experimental (sort of) because you manipulated a variable—the SCG intervention. However, because there was no control group, your IV is not really variable—it has only one value. An even poorer one-shot case study includes the measurement of your DV after an event over which you have no control. For example, you wish to understand the steps leading up to divorce so you study a group of people who are divorced. Without any comparisons—either pretest or control group—this design is scientifically worthless (Kerlinger, 1986). It is important to note that such a design is scientifically worthless when examined from the epistemological position underlying experimental designs (i.e., positivism). The

	BMT	SCT	Control
Training clinic			
Private practice		(Outcome measures)	

FIGURE 11.2. Factorial experimental design. This is a two-by-three factorial design, with two settings and three treatment conditions. There could be multiple outcome measures as well.

TABLE 11.1. Criteria of Research Design

Questions to ask of your research design

Does the design answer the research questions? or Does the design adequately test the hypotheses?

Does the design adequately control independent variables so that extraneous and unwanted sources of systemic variance have minimal opportunity to operate?

Can we generalize the results of a study to other subjects, other groups, and other conditions? That is, are our results generalizable beyond the groups in the study?

Did the experimental manipulation really make a significant difference? That is, is the study *internally valid?*

Are the variables of this research representative? That is, is the variable the same for the two groups under study or does it have different meanings?

Note. Data from Kerlinger (1986, pp. 298–301).

in-depth (i.e., qualitative) study of a single group may be very useful given a different position. Indeed, a synthesist position holds that these separate methodologies are complementary.

The second inadequate design is the "one-group, pretest–posttest" (Kerlinger, 1986, p. 295) design, which also has two forms (again, one with an IV that the researcher manipulates; another with an IV he or she assumes, but cannot manipulate). As an example of the first, suppose you have a group of clients whom you wish to test with the SCG. You remember that your last try (the one-shot case study) was inadequate. So you give them the Dyadic Adjustment Scale before the intervention, perform the SCG, then give them the DAS again as a posttest. All the couples got better, and you conclude that it was your intervention. Unfortunately, there are a large number of other factors that may have produced your results: measurement, history, maturation, the regression effect, and so forth (Cook & Campbell, 1979, expanded on later in this chapter, and in Table 11.4), and there is no way to tell whether they or your intervention produced the results.

The third inadequate design is the "simulated before–after" (Kerlinger, 1986, p. 297). In this design, there are two groups which are assumed to be similar. The pretest is given to one group with the intervention and posttest is given to another. The pretest and posttest are then compared, and differences are attributed to the intervention or to manipulation. Although this design does have a control group of sorts, there is no way to ensure that the two groups were equivalent, and therefore the controls are weak.

Finally, there is the "two groups, no control" (Kerlinger, 1986, p. 297) design. In this design, there are two groups, and one is administered the treatment while the other group is not. At posttest, the groups are compared, and differences are attributed to the treatment. The groups are not randomly assigned, and there is no pretest measure. Once again, the groups are assumed to be equal, but there is no assurance—even if the groups are matched on a number of variables. Without randomization, control cannot be assumed (Kerlinger, 1986).

Ethical Considerations

General Considerations

Babbie (1986) discusses some of the most general ethical considerations in social research. These are directly applicable to experimental designs in MFT outcome research.

The first ethical principle is voluntary participation—people have the right to refuse to participate in research projects and should not feel compelled to participate. In therapy research, this is important because clients may feel that as their therapist is asking them to do this research, they should comply. Informed consent is important in ensuring that this principle is upheld in that it ensures that potential subjects understand the risks and benefits of participating or not participating in the research.

The second principle is that the research should do no harm to the participants. For this reason, it is unethical (as common sense would also dictate) to assign people to groups that include negative life events (e.g., survivors of sexual abuse). As such, control in research with these types of problems is compromised and other control methods have to be used. In addition, this principle brings into question the use of no-treatment control groups, as receiving no treatment may result in harm. This issue is discussed in more depth in the next section.

The identity of the participants in research needs to be protected, through either anonymity or confidentiality (the difference being that in an anonymous project the researcher him- or herself does not know the identity of the participants). Therapy outcome research needs to take pains to ensure the confidentiality of the participants. Professional organizations such as the American Psychological Association and the American Association for Marriage and Family Therapy have codes of ethics for research.

Control Group Selection and Withholding Treatment

There are several ways to decide what type of control group to have. First, it is important to consider that denying or postponing treatment may be problematic; yet, a no-treatment or waiting list control is often used. Alternatives to this include *treatment on demand* (TOD) (Gurman & Kniskern, 1981). In TOD, clients in the comparison group are also assigned a therapist and told they can have access to therapy on demand, whenever they want a session. If a client requests more than a preset cutoff number of sessions, he or she would be dropped from the TOD condition. This design results in four groups: (1) clients (families or couples) receiving treatment; (2) TOD remainers who have not requested any sessions; (3) TOD remainers who have received fewer than the cutoff number of sessions; and (4) TOD dropouts who received more than the cutoff number of sessions. Todd and Stanton (1983) criticize this design because of difficulties with self-selection—clients themselves determine into which of groups (2), (3), or (4) they fall. Although it is possible to make comparisons between group (1) and a combination of (2), (3), and (4), this comparison is less than desirable. The advantage is that treatment is available for those who need it.

Another possible solution to withholding treatment is to compare parallel treatment groups (Todd & Stanton, 1983). In this design the untreated control group is eliminated. This design can take two forms: (1) comparison between two or more equally valued treatments and; (2) an add-on, or constructive, design in which a new component is added on to a previous treatment. In the first, the problem is determining whether the two treatments are truly equally valued. In the second, there may be an interaction between the new method and the existing treatment, where they might add to one another or even cancel each other out, and it would not be possible to tell which was the case. In addition, it is difficult to make parallel groups truly parallel (Todd & Stanton, 1983). Finally, in both cases, if no differences between parallel groups are found, does this mean they are equally effective or equally ineffective (Todd & Stanton, 1983)? This design may be acceptable if previous research has shown that the researched treatment is better than a no-treatment control.

Research Questions Addressed by Experimental Design

A wide variety of research questions can be answered through experimental methods, and the question dictates the design (Kazdin, 1994; Kerlinger, 1986). Table 11.2 (reproduced from Kazdin, 1994) shows different treatment strategies, the research questions asked, and the basic requirements of the design.

Basically, using experimental methods, we can answer questions regarding a therapy's overall effectiveness or comparative effectiveness, we can examine what components of that therapy are most (and least) effective, and we can examine the therapist, client, and process variables that affect treatment—questions basic to family therapy research.

Each of the strategies listed in Table 11.2 suggests different independent and dependent variables. For example, in a *constructive strategy*, the purpose is to find out what components can be added to a treatment package to improve therapeutic efficacy. The independent variable will be the added components. That is, the component will be varied by group and compared across groups on the outcome measure. The number of components added will determine the number of groups required. To continue with SCT example, you may feel that the idea of the continuum is an added component to traditional SFT, so you would compare a group receiving SFT with a group getting SFT plus the idea of continuum. If you further thought that you could add a narrative component to make your therapy even more successful, you could add another group.

The literature may also tell you something about *supplementary variables* for which you wish to control in addition to your constructive strategy (although if you use randomization, this is less likely to be of interest). There are a wide range of client (Garfield, 1994) and therapist (Beutler, Machado, & Neufeldt, 1994) variables that have been associated with psychotherapy outcome. For researchers interested in therapist experience as it interacts with their treatment model in producing outcome, a randomized block design with therapists of different experience would allow this analysis. Indeed, Gurman, Kniskern, and Pinsof (1986) have called for multidimensional research that examines interactions among variables, and particularly for research examining the interaction between client and therapist variables. Several researchers have also suggested that mediational research, which looks at the interaction of therapist and client variables with treatment and outcome, is more important than pure comparative outcome research which merely compares two treatments (Beutler, 1991; Greenberg & Pinsof, 1986; Jacobson, 1985; Parloff, 1986).

Experimental designs in family therapy research have been used for comparative research, to compare a specific treatment model to a nonspecific control in which clients receive treatment that only includes the common factors of therapy but not the specific interventions of a model (Jacobson, 1978), to compare a treatment package to a minimal treatment (Singer, Irvin, Irvine, Hawkins, & Cooley, 1989; Strayhorn & Weidman, 1989), or to compare a treatment package to a control group that receives no treatment (Hahlweg & Markman, 1988)—all to determine the effectiveness of the treatment. Experimental design has also been used to examine a specific goal of family therapy, such as engagement in the process (Szapocznik et al., 1988), to examine the added benefit of social intervention to psychopharmacological intervention with schizophrenics (Leff, Kuipers, Berkowitz, & Sturgeon, 1985), to compare treatments for the same presenting problem (Jacobson et al., 1991), to examine what types of couples respond to couple therapy (Snyder, Mangrum, & Wills, 1993), and to examine the process of change in couple therapy (Johnson & Greenberg, 1988).

Wynne (1988) suggests:

TABLE. 11.2. Alternative Treatment Evaluation Strategies to Develop and Identify Effective Interventions

Treatment strategy	Question asked	Basic requirements
Treatment package	Does treatment produce therapeutic change?	Treatment vs. no-treatment waiting-list control
Dismantling strategy	What components are necessary, sufficient, and facilitative of therapeutic change?	Two or more treatment groups that vary in the components of treatment that are provided
Constructive strategy	What components or other treatments can be added to enhance therapeutic change?	Two or more treatment groups that vary in components that are provided
Parametric strategy	What changes can be made in the specific treatment to increase its effectiveness?	Two or more treatment groups that differ in one or more facets of the treatment
Comparative outcome strategy	Which treatment is the more or most effective for a particular population?	Two or more different treatments for a given population
Client and therapist variation strategy	Upon what patient, family, or therapist characteristic does treatment depend for it to be effective?	Treatment as applied separately to different types of cases, therapists, and so on
Process strategy	What processes occur in treatment that affect within-session performance and may contribute to treatment outcome?	Treatment groups in which patient and therapist interactions are evaluated within the sessions

Note. From Kazdin (1994, p. 21). Copyright 1994 by John Wiley. Reprinted by permission.

Elaborate clinical trials with global outcome comparisons between models are not only expensive and difficult to organize, but they are apt to be less informative than is hoped unless component variables relevant to competing hypotheses first have been identified and included in the study. (p. 257)

Wynne suggests that at this point in the development of family therapy, we should focus our attention on within-model experimental research—comparing components and dismantling treatment packages—in order to find out what parts of our models work, before comparing overall models.

Introduction to an Illustrative Example

Jacobson and colleagues (Jacobson, 1984; Jacobson et al., 1985, 1987) provide an excellent illustrative example of experimental design in family therapy clinical research. Jacobson (1984) began a component analysis, comparing BMT with two of its major components, behavior exchange (BE) and communication/problem-solving training (CPT), as well as to a waiting-list control group. Thirty-six married couples were randomly assigned to one of the three treatment groups or to the control group. Six-month, 1-year, and 2-year follow-up measurements were also reported (Jacobson, 1984; Jacobson et al., 1985, 1987, respectively).

Previously, Jacobson had found that BMT was more effective than a nonspecific control group. In this study, then, Jacobson (1984) attempted to dismantle the BMT treatment package via examination of its two major components to find which components are most effective. The independent variable is treatment component (none, CPT,

BE, or complete package). The dependent variables included global marital satisfaction, presenting problem checklists, and spouse reports of behavior at home. We will revisit this example throughout the chapter.

Sampling and Selection Procedures

Experimental designs are by their nature comparisons of groups. As such, assignment of subjects to the various research groups is important. The researcher is trying to discover differences between groups due to a treatment (or comparison of treatments), and these differences should be to the treatment, not to extraneous factors. The groups should be equivalent before the treatment is given. Groups should also be of similar or equal size in order to meet the assumptions of many of the statistics used in analysis.

Randomization (specifically random assignment) is the mechanism used to distribute characteristics of the sample across groups. However, random assignment does not ensure equivalent groups in the short run, as noted earlier. With small samples in particular, equivalence across groups may not be assumed (Kazdin, 1994). Use of larger samples (more than 40 subjects per group) or precise and rigorous preassignment blocking (see below) can increase confidence in group equivalence. Given small samples, pretests to compare groups are particularly necessary. "Preassignment blocking involves grouping subjects: . . . into sets or blocks that are similar in the characteristic(s) of interest. . . . Subjects within each set or block of subjects are randomly assigned [to] conditions" (Kazdin, 1994, p. 35). Randomized block designs are infrequently used in psychology research (Keppel, 1982) but are an important possible design.

To generalize findings beyond the experiment, researchers should use random selection of subjects from a population. Random selection ensures that each person in the population has an equal chance of being selected for the study. With random selection, the researcher can justify statistically any generalizations made to the larger population (Keppel, 1982). However, most of our samples in therapy research are convenience samples—we cannot just pick people at random to receive family therapy. If previous research has shown similar results using subjects from different populations, it becomes easier to assume that those population differences are unimportant and that valid generalizations can be made (Keppel, 1982). However, caution should always be used in making generalization beyond the treatment sample.

Data Collection Procedures

There is no one "experimental design data collection procedure." However, there is consensus that outcome assessment needs to be multifaceted, involving differing perspectives, characteristics of the participants, areas of functioning, and method of assessment (Gurman et al., 1986; Kazdin, 1994; Whisman et al., 1989).

Issues in data collection include relating your measures to the goals of treatment (e.g., using the Dyadic Adjustment Scale to measure changes in couple functioning), choosing what to assess, assessing multiple viewpoints, choosing appropriate assessment methods, reducing of error variance, and making choices regarding follow-up assessments, cost-effectiveness, and data screening (all discussed below).

Kazdin (1994) suggests that outcome measures should relate to the goals of the treatment, should measure symptom reduction, and should also examine increases in "prosocial behavior" (p. 41). Wynne (1988) and Jacobson (1985) argue that the presenting problem should be the primary outcome measure in family therapy research. Kniskern (1985), on the other hand, believes that too much reliance is placed on change in presenting problem, and that outcome should also focus on change in family interaction patterns. There are other variables that may be of interest in psychotherapy research as well, including measures that examine the link between in-session process and outcome (see also Greenberg & Pinsof, 1986), client reactions to treatment, and measures concerning the administration of treatment—including the cost of treatment, requirements for training therapists, ease of application, and so forth.

In addition, outcome can be assessed from multiple viewpoints: the client's, the therapist's, and observers' viewpoints (Gurman et al., 1986). Shields (1986) notes that there are two sources of variables, the family and the therapist; three dimensions for variation, behavioral, cognitive, and emotional; and two methods of measurement, observational and self-report. These can be combined in myriad ways to measure family therapy outcome. Gurman and Kniskern (1981) provide yet another way of conceptualizing this complexity of assessment within the family. They identify seven "familial unit(s) of assessment" (p. 766) and place them in a typology with treatment context, resulting in a 7-by-5 table of possible assessments. Although the overall typology would be much too complex to research, specific rows or columns may help conceptualize the units of assessment. For example, one row is "cross-generation of identified patient: individual as a unit of assessment." If the treatment context is family therapy with a parent as the identified patient (one column), the children would be the target of assessment in this case (see Table 11.3).

Whisman et al. (1989) suggest that family therapy outcome studies should focus on measurement of marital satisfaction as well as on measures of the skills being taught or the behavioral changes that are the focus of therapy (to measure the effectiveness of the intervention). They explore the debate between those advocating the use of observational/behavioral methods versus the use of self-report methods. Whisman et al. (1989) note that proponents of observational measures claim that they are less open to bias than are self-report measures. Observational measures may be susceptible to perceptual biases, depending on who is doing the observing. Many observational coding systems require spouses to report on each other, yet attributions may affect that assessment. Indeed, spouse's ratings and the subject's ratings are often unrelated (Whisman et al., 1989). Spouse ratings and observer ratings may also differ. Thus, the benefits and drawbacks of observational and self-report measures need to be considered.

There are two ways to reduce error variance in experimental design: reduce errors of measurement through controlled conditions, and increase the reliability of measurement (Kerlinger, 1986). If variables are sufficiently unreliable, the findings may reflect nothing but measurement error (Tabachnick & Fidell, 1989).

In marital and family therapy research, control over conditions usually occurs through manualized treatments (Kazdin, 1994), and such manuals have been recommended strongly for family therapy research (Gurman & Kniskern, 1981). In marital therapy research, Jacobson has been noted as having strong treatment manuals (Whisman et al., 1989). Having a treatment manual and measuring the therapist's adherence to the manual is one way of ensuring equal conditions for all subjects—important for reducing error variance. Unfortunately, most real-world therapy is not manualized. As therapists, we tailor our therapy to fit our clients, and it may be that each client receives a different therapy from the same therapist.

Jacobson et al. (1989) looked into this. They compared "research-structured versus clinically flexible" (p. 173) treatments, and found at posttest that there were no differences in efficacy between the two. However, at 6-month follow-up, the couples who received research-structured therapy were more likely to have deteriorated. On the other hand, Shadish, Ragsdale, Glaser, and Montgomery (1995) found in a large-scale meta-

TABLE 11.3. A Priority Sequence for Assessing Therapeutic Change in Couples and Families

Familial unit assessment	Treatment context and family constellation				
	Family therapy I: Child as IP		Family therapy II: Parents as IP	Marital therapy: Spouse/parent as IP	
	Family with more than one child	One-child family		Marriage with child(ren)	Childless marriage
I. Identified patient (IP)	IP child	IP child	IP parent	IP spouse	IP spouse
II. Marriage	Marriage	Marriage	Marriage	Marriage	Marriage
III. Total system	Family	Family	Family	Family	(Marriage)
IV. Same generation of IP: individual	IP's siblings	–	Non-IP spouse	Non-IP spouse	Non-IP spouse
V. Cross-generation of IP: individual	Each parent	Each parent	Each child	Each child	–
VI. Same generation of IP: relationship	IP child and non-IP child(ren)	–	(Marriage)	(Marriage)	(Marriage)
VII. Cross-generation of IP: relationship	Parents and IP child: Child 1 = IP	Parents and IP child	Child(ren) and IP parent	(Parents and child[ren], i.e., family)	–
	Parents and non-IP child(ren)	(Parents and IP child)	Children and non-IP parent	(As above)	–

Note. Parentheses indicate that this familial unit has already been accounted for at an earlier level of assessment priority. Blank spaces indicate that assessment of this familial unit is logically impossible. IP, identified patient. Adapted from Gurman and Kniskern (1981, p. 766). Copyright by Brunner/Mazel. Reprinted by permission.

analysis that manualized "laboratory" research has consistently higher effect sizes than does clinic-based research. So, whereas manualized treatment provides better control and higher effect sizes, clinic-based treatment may have more real-world efficacy. As researchers, we need to weigh the benefits of a structured therapy in reducing error variance (and increasing the sensitivity of our research) against the weakness of a potentially weaker treatment (which may mask real benefits of a flexible treatment). Although the structured, manualized treatment reduces error variance, it may also reduce experimental variance and may result in weaker research into the efficacy of the treatment as it is practiced. The debate on this topic is ongoing (Jacobson et al., 1989; Shadish et al., 1995). Jacobson (1991; Jacobson & Addis, 1993) states that studies that match treatments to client characteristics will be an important future direction for marital therapy research.

It is important in experimental designs to have multiple posttreatment assessments (Kazdin, 1994). Most important is the immediately posttreatment assessment. This is the primary characteristic of experimental designs and this is where the bulk of important outcome information comes from.

In our ongoing example, Jacobson et al. (1985) report a 1-year follow-up and Jacobson et al. (1987) report a 2-year follow-up in which important information was gathered.

At the 6-month follow-up, statistically significant differences between the BE, CPT, and complete package groups were found on outcome measures (including marital satisfaction and behavioral reports). These disappeared at 1- and 2-year follow-ups. However, at both the 1-year and 2-year follow-up, couples treated with the complete package were most likely to be happily married and least likely to be separated or divorced. This type of follow-up information is important in evaluating the overall efficacy of any treatment model—we need to know how long the benefits of our treatment last.

In addition, recent changes in the health care market have led to increased interest in cost-effectiveness research. Cost-effectiveness research may become an integral part of all outcome research (see Pike-Urlacher, Piercy, & Mackinnon, Chapter 16, this volume, for an in-depth discussion of cost-effectiveness research).

Finally, it is important, particularly in multivariate analyses, to screen the data prior to engaging in analysis. Tabachnick and Fidell (1989) make several recommendations for data screening. Researchers should inspect descriptive statistics for accuracy of input, checking for out-of-range values and plausible means and standard deviations. The amount and distribution of missing data should be examined and dealt with if possible. They should identify nonnormally distributed variables, and these can be transformed, if desirable (see Tabachnick & Fidell, 1989, pp. 83–87 for recommendations on data transformations). Outliers should be examined as well. Researchers should first check to see whether they were entered correctly, If so, they must check to see whether one variable is causing most of the outliers. It may a poor variable and the analysis might be better served if the researcher eliminates that variable. The researcher may also need to decide whether the outlier falls within the population he or she intended to sample. If not, the case can be deleted without loss of generalizability to the intended population. Finally, researchers may need to transform the data or change the scoring to minimize the impact of the outliers on their analysis (Tabachnick & Fidell, 1989).

Generally, data collection methods should derive from the research question and should address the goals of the treatment (Kazdin, 1994). The Jacobson (1984; Jacobson et al., 1985, 1987) study provides an example of this. Jacobson and colleagues were testing BMT—designed to promote marital satisfaction by changing behaviors to enhance quality of life at home and to teach communication skills to help couples handle conflict more effectively. The BE component was geared only toward changing behaviors, whereas the CPT component was geared toward improving communication. The complete package includes both components.

Jacobson (1984) used three measures of outcome: the Dyadic Adjustment Scale, the Presenting Problem Checklist, and the Spouse Observation Checklist. The Dyadic Adjustment Scale was used to examine changes in global relationship satisfaction, the Presenting Problem Checklist was used to rate change in the presenting problem over time, and the Spouse Observation Checklist was used to examine changes in spousal behavior over time. Together, these measures adequately tap the constructs of interest— that is, change in marital satisfaction, change in presenting problem, and change in behavior.

Data Analysis Procedures

There are several data analysis procedures to be addressed. The basic analysis to experimental design is analysis of variance (ANOVA). Considerations in ANOVA include the basic design as well as planned comparisons (i.e., between-group comparisons planned ahead of time in ANOVA). There are broader considerations as well. The researcher needs to decide on the unit of analysis and criteria for assessment. Power is another vital issue in family therapy research. Finally, the clinical significance of the finding is important.

ANOVA (and multivariate analysis of variance [MANOVA]) is the analysis used with experimental designs. ANOVA is the analysis of the difference between two groups: "the extent to which to the groups do differ is compared with the standard of random distribution: could we expect to obtain such differences if we had assigned cases to the various groups through random selection?" (Babbie, 1986). Put another way, "analysis of variance is used when two or more means are compared to see if there are any reliable differences among them" (Tabachnick & Fidell, 1989, p. 37).

In analysis of variance, in order to find significance, the between-group variance needs to be larger than the within-group variance. Consider Figure 11.3 as a concrete visual example. In Figure 11.3, there are four groups of data (A, B, A', and B'). Groups A and A' and B and B' have the same mean value (groups A and A' mean = 10.375, groups B and B' mean = 21.125). However, the within-group variation, or standard deviation, is very different (A = 2.33, A' = 7.05, B = 1.73, B' = 13.57). When looking at the scatter plot, it is much easier to tell that group A and group B are different than it is to tell that A' and B' are different because of the differences in the variation. Groups A' and B' overlap considerably, and this obscures differences between them.

As noted earlier, we can use multiple IVs and DVs in designing our research. If we have a single DV, regardless of number of IVs, our analysis is considered univariate, and ANOVA is the appropriate analysis. If we have more than one IV, our analysis of variance would be a factorial ANOVA, otherwise it would be a one-way ANOVA. If we have more than one DV, our analysis is considered multivariate, and we use MANOVA. Factorial MANOVAs are also possible. In addition, analysis of covariance (ANCOVA and MANCOVA) can be used. In analysis of covariance, linear regression is used to adjust the results of an experiment for differences existing between subjects before the start of the experiment (Keppel, 1982). This reduces error variance and increases the sensitivity of the experiment. Very complex designs can be examined using multivariate analysis of variance and covariance.

Let us go back to the Jacobson example (Jacobson, 1984; Jacobson et al., 1985,

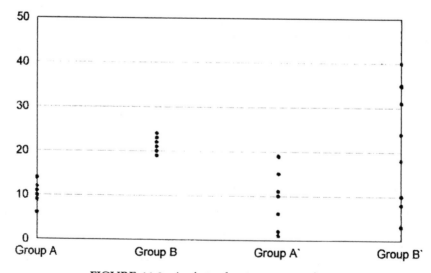

FIGURE 11.3. Analysis of variance scatterplot.

1987). Treatment effects were evaluated using seven criteria: the Dyadic Adjustment Scale, three measures of the presenting problem (total residual change [TC], percentage of problem elimination [%E], and percentage of problem reduction [%R], and three measures of positive and negative behaviors exchanged between spouses (daily frequency of positive behaviors [+/day], daily frequency of negative behaviors [−/day], and the ratio of positive and negative behaviors [+/−]. Overall treatment effects were evaluated with one-way MANCOVAs using five of the measures (Dyadic Adjustment Scale, TC, +/day, +/−, −/day) with pretest scores on each serving as covariates to control for pretest level. These were one-way MANCOVAs because there was only one IV—treatment group—and multiple DVs. (To extend the example, if you used Therapist as a randomized factor, you would use a two-way analysis of variance). These tests were followed by univariate F tests for three planned comparisons reflecting the major hypotheses of the study: (1) results immediately after treatment were expected to favor BE and complete package conditions, especially on the behavioral measures; (2) at follow-up, CPT couples were expected to have "caught up" to and even surpassed BE couples; and (3) a greater proportion of complete package couples would use their problem-solving skills subsequent to termination compared with CPT couples, and would therefore show the most substantial long-term effects. For %R and %E, t tests of correlated means were calculated because, as percentage change, they were already adjusted for pretest and did not lend themselves to MANCOVA analysis. The couple was the unit of analysis, with husbands and wives scores added together.

The planned comparisons involved comparing the three treatment groups to the waiting list, the complete package with the component groups, and one component versus the other using all outcome measures. The overall MANCOVA was used to establish that there was an overall treatment effect, whereas the planned comparisons were used to pinpoint the nature of the treatment effect. The global satisfaction (Dyadic Adjustment Scale) measure provides a good example of how this was done. Given that the overall MANCOVA was significant, Jacobson then examined change in the Dyadic Adjustment Scale scores for all four groups. Only the three treatment groups showed change in Dyadic Adjustment Scale between pretest and posttest (tested using t tests). One-way analyses of variance were used to test the planned comparisons. The three treatment groups were significantly more effective than no treatment, but there were no differences between the complete package and the two components, nor were the two components significantly different from each other in terms of Dyadic Adjustment Scale change. Jacobson (1984) concludes that "it appears that all three versions of BMT generate significant but equivalent increases in global marital satisfaction immediately after treatment" (p. 299).

It is necessary with multiple dependent variables to use a MANOVA instead of a series of univariate ANOVAs particularly when the dependent variables are correlated. In family therapy research, most DVs will be correlated to at least some extent. MANOVA takes into account and controls for such correlations. (See Tabachnick & Fidell, 1989, for an excellent resource, on data analysis.)

Whisman et al. (1989) make several suggestions for improving methodology and reporting in family therapy research. They suggest that attention be paid to the unit of analysis in analyzing couple data. If the couple is the unit of analysis, how should the researcher deal with individual's scores on such measures as the Dyadic Adjustment Scale? Commonly, such scores are averaged, but that average may mask major discrepancies between the two spouses' scores. There are a number of alternatives, such as calculating the absolute difference between spouses' scores, using both spouses' scores as multiple dependent measures for the couple, and conducting analyses based on the scores of the spouse who exhibits the greater marital distress at the end of therapy (Baucom, 1983). Another question to be answered is, "Should couples be defined as distressed if the average of their scores places them in the distressed range or only if both spouses' scores fall in the distressed range" (Whisman et al., 1989)? Researchers should be aware of these questions as they prepare data for analysis.

There are two additional areas of analysis that also need to be addressed in this chapter: power and clinical significance. According to Kazdin (1994), "a critical research issue is the extent to which an investigation can detect differences between groups when differences exist in the population" (p. 45). Power is the probability of rejecting the null hypothesis when in fact it is false. Power is a function of the criteria set for statistical significance (alpha), sample size, and effect size or the difference between the groups (Cohen, 1992). A large number of outcome studies provide weak tests, particularly in studies with small to moderate effect sizes, because they lack sufficient power (Kazdin, 1994). Different types of studies are likely to yield different effect sizes. For example, comparisons of treatment groups and no-treatment control groups are likely to produce large effect sizes, whereas dismantling or comparative outcome studies are likely to produce smaller effect sizes. The smaller the effect size, the larger the sample needed to gain adequate power to find differences.

One consideration in research design is sample size: "How large a sample will I need to have adequate power?" Given an alpha level, power level, and estimated effect size, we can calculate the needed sample size (in fact, given any three, we can calculate the fourth). Tradition puts alpha = .05, and power = .80. Effect size can be estimated mathematically from previous studies (see Jacobson & Traux, 1991). Estimates of effect sizes can be obtained from published research or from knowledge about the type of study being conducted. If a comparative outcome study is being conducted, a medium effect size of about .40 would be estimated (Kazdin, 1994). Given these three (alpha = .05, power = .80, effect size = .40) we can use tables (e.g., Cohen, 1988) to look up the appropriate sample size or a computer program designed to provide power analyses to get our sample size. Given the above figures, a sample of 40 subjects per group would be needed (Kazdin, 1994). Loosening the requirements on alpha or power or increasing the effect size estimate would lower the necessary number of subjects per group. Power analyses will become increasingly important as we seek to establish the effectiveness of family therapy. Cohen (1992) states that "failure to subject your research plans to power analysis is simply irrational" (p. 329).

Finally, there is the consideration of clinically significant change. Jacobson and Traux (1991) lay out a statistical approach to defining meaningful change in psychotherapy research. They make the point that even large effect sizes may not yield clinically significant results. Subjects may have moved from really dysfunctional to just dysfunctional. If they are still dysfunctional, treatment may not have been successful. They propose that for clinically significant change, "the level of functioning subsequent to therapy places that client closer to the mean of the functional population than it does to the mean of the dysfunctional population" (Jacobson & Traux, 1991, p. 13). Jacobson and Truax (1991) also provide a Reliable Change Index (p. 14), which is a measure of how much change has occurred as a result of therapy; a measure particularly useful when the distributions of normal and dysfunctional populations overlap. (See Jacobson & Truax, 1991, for methods on calculating the Reliable Change Index.)

Reporting

The findings in experimental design are reported in traditional research report format. The methods section should include information about sample characteristics, the design of the study, treatment conditions, therapists, measures and assessment, administration and scoring procedures, and hypotheses and the plan for data evaluation (Kazdin, 1994). The results section should include information on the data analysis: data screening, preliminary analyses, treatment effects, planned comparisons, and follow-up data. A discussion section should follow that describes the significance of the findings.

Gurman et al. (1986) summarize recommendations for family therapy research reports. They recommend using the clinically significant change statistics developed by Jacobson (and refined by Jacobson & Traux, 1991). They also suggest going beyond reporting only group data, which hides information relevant to clinicians. They suggest reporting the proportion of cases showing clinically significant improvement, clinically insignificant improvement, and clinically significant worsening for each outcome criterion measure and also reporting the breadth of treatment effects, shown as the number and percentage of change criteria on which each case improves, shows no change, or shows deterioration, presented as a series of frequency distributions.

Whisman et al. (1989) note that few studies in family therapy publish exclusion criteria for subjects or the number of subjects who were excluded. Because such exclusion limits the generalizability of the study, such criteria should be carefully specified and examined.

Cohen (1992) makes some suggestions for research reporting and design. First, Cohen recommends the principle that "less is more, except of course for sample size" (p. 316). He suggests studying few independent variables and even fewer dependent variables. Because a great many of our variables in family therapy research are correlated, the more variables used, the more likely a type I error—rejecting the null hypothesis when in fact it is true. Large numbers of variables also tend to become redundant. Cohen (1992) notes too that the less-is-more principle applies to reporting of results. Four or five decimal places for statistics are not necessary in family therapy research—so much detail is actually detrimental in that it creates clutter and distraction.

Cohen (1992) also recommends the principle "simple is better" (1992, p. 318)—in representation, analysis, and reporting of data. A picture is worth a thousand words, and graphic representations often make our findings easier to understand. In fact, the act of diagramming findings may help in understanding of the data. Cohen holds that we should use the simplest statistic that will get the job done, as well, but not at the expense of information (e.g., simplifying a factorial ANOVA by reducing all cell sizes to the size of the smallest by dropping cases).

Finally, Cohen recommends being descriptive. Rich description will engage an audience and will make one's research more accessible and more understandable.

So, where will such research reports appear when they are published? Family therapy research reports based on experimental designs are likely to be published in the leading family therapy and psychotherapy journals, provided they are rigorous and well done. Journals that have published such designs in the past include *American Journal of Family Therapy, Behavior Therapy, Behavior Research and Therapy, Journal of Consulting and Clinical Psychology, Journal of Marital and Family Therapy,* and *Family Process,* to name but a few. (See Jacobson, 1984; Jacobson et al., 1985, 1987, for an illustrative example of multiple reports on a long-term research project.)

DISCUSSION

Strengths and Weaknesses of the Methodology

The chief advantage of experimental designs lies "in the isolation of the experimental variable and its impact over time" (Babbie, 1986, p. 199). Because of the control involved in experiments, we can have a good deal of confidence in our interpretation of the results that the groups were different due to the independent variable. True experiments with perfect control would meet the three requirements to determine causality: First, the cause must precede the effect in time; second, the two variables must be empirically correlated with one another; and third, the observed empirical correlation between the two must not be able to be explained away as being due to the influence of some third variable that causes both.

In family therapy, this degree of certainty is greatly needed. Family therapy needs to prove its effectiveness, particularly in this day of managed health care. Not only do we need to know whether family therapy works (although we have a pretty good idea that it is effective in many situations), but we need to know how it works and for whom it works best. Experimental research in family therapy has "led to a considerable increment in knowledge obtained over the past 20 years" (Whisman et al., 1989, p. 177).

The main weakness of experimental research is that it may not reflect real-world therapy and may not be as relevant for clinicians. Treatments used in experimental designs are typically manualized (Kazdin, 1994), and this rigidity is different than typical clinical practice (Jacobson et al., 1989). However, it may that as experimental research becomes more sophisticated, clinically flexible therapies may be used. In addition, if we follow Jacobson's (1991) call for matching studies, we may find which treatments are best for which clients and which problems—clinically relevant research.

Experimental designs are also seen as complicated and as needing a great deal of resources. The example in Figure 11.2 might require as many as 240 subjects (with 40 per group—not an unrealistic number depending on alpha, power, and effect size), and this is beyond the scope of many research projects. Multivariate analyses are also somewhat complex, although computer programs such as SPSS continue to make this less of an issue. Single-case experimental designs (Crane, 1985; Dickey, Chapter 12, this volume; Kazdin, 1994) may be useful in clinical settings, although the conclusions drawn from them are not as strong as those drawn from full experimental designs (Crane, 1985).

The biggest concern may be that experimental designs are firmly rooted in positivism and do not fit well with the new epistemology of family therapy. Traditional family therapy research has been attacked as "nonsystemic" (Morris, 1987, p. 2) and too linear. In fact, the cause–effect model is a linear model, but there may be questions that such family therapy research can answer. Morris (1987) argues that knowing that two groups differ significantly is not informative about the process of family therapy, and that the meaning of such differences are indiscriminate. Atkinson and Heath (1987) note that traditional science attempts to measure an objective reality, whereas constructivists believe that such a reality does not exist, or that we cannot know an objective reality even if it does exist, because observations are always influenced by the perspective of the observer. However, Atkinson and Heath (1987) recognize that the categorization of data for understanding is inevitable, and they suggest that by laying out the process of constructing such categories in our research reports, we can better meet the requirements of a constructivist view. Can researchers adequately address the subtleties and complexities of therapy? Dell (cited in Hunsley, 1993), a noted constructivist, stated while although our explanations of phenomena should be systemic, our descriptions of the same phenomena must be linear. What this means is that description itself is reductionistic, which is unavoidable. By adding the level of explanation to description, systemic issues are addressed. Hunsley (1993) goes on to say that this difference between explanation and description applies equally to research. Experimental design is but one of the research options open to family therapists and seems to have its place.

Reliability and Validity

Reliability, per se, is not addressed in experimental designs except as a means of reducing error variance. The more reliable the measures used, the less error variance introduced into the design, and the more sensitive the analysis will be.

Validity, however, is another story. Both internal and external validity are important considerations in experimental design. In internally valid studies, findings are due to what we think they are (i.e., our IV) and not to some other source. However, there are a number of threats to internal validity. Several common threats to internal validity are laid out in Table 11.4. History, maturation, testing, and selection can be controlled via random assignment to groups. Instrumentation can be controlled easily through maintaining either the same instrumentation or by maintaining rigorous standards for coding if using observation. Statistical regression and mortality will have to be examined during analysis. Mortality should be reported and assessed as a potential threat.

External validity is a tougher criterion to satisfy (Kerlinger, 1986). By external validity, we mean the representativeness or generalizability of our findings. Can we apply these findings to all distressed married couples? To all behavioral marital therapists? We recommend caution in making sweeping claims as to the representativeness of findings, unless there is a similar demonstrated effect on multiple samples or the researcher has randomly sampled from the population to which he or she is generalizing.

Skills Needed to Execute Experimental Design

What special skills are necessary to be successful at experimental design? First, researchers need to be able to think using the logic of experimental design. Researchers need to be able to be critical of their design. Experimental designs are carefully planned to answer specific research questions. Researchers should be familiar with statistics, or at least be friends with someone else who is familiar with statistics. They should be able to do a power analysis, MANOVA, follow-up comparisons, and so forth. They should be able to write well, so that they can disseminate the results. If a researcher can write

TABLE 11.4. **Threats to Internal Validity**

Threat	Definition
History	An event takes place between the pretest and posttest which is not the treatment of interest but which affects the posttest scores.
Maturation	An effect might be due to the respondent's growing older, wiser, stronger, etc.
Testing	An effect might be due to the number of times participants responses are measured.
Instrumentation	An effect might be due to a change in the measuring instrument between pretest and posttest.
Statistical regression	An effect might be due to respondents' being classified into experimental groups at, say, the pretest on the basis of pretest scores, but if the measures are unreliable, high pretest scorers will score lower at posttest and low pretest scorers will score higher, resulting in regression to the mean and washing out effects.
Selection	An effect may be due to differences between the groups when groups are not controlled.
Mortality	An effect may be due to different kinds of persons dropping out of a particular treatment group.

Note. Data from Cook and Campbell (1979, pp. 51–52).

clearly and simply, his or her audience will have an easier time understanding the findings. A researcher probably will need to have many resources as well. However, even
in a private practice setting, researchers may have a waiting list to use as a no-treatment
control, although they are not likely to randomly assign clients to a waiting list. As
long as subjects are randomly assigned to control and treatment groups, a relatively
small number of subjects can yield a powerful study given a small number of variables.

The skill needed most of all is probably confidence that you can do this type of
research and do it well. It may look intimidating and overwhelming, but it is not as
bad as it looks. Collaborate with someone and divide the work. Find a mentor and (to
borrow a popular line from the advertising media) Just Do It!

Bridging Research and Practice

Although this research model is based in the positivist tradition, it has given us a great
deal of information about therapy. With the addition of clinically significant change
criteria, experimental designs are telling us more about how much therapy actually helps
people. As we become more sophisticated, we will begin to address the specificity question: what therapy works for which clients and for which therapists for what problems
under what conditions? Matching studies and clinically flexible treatments are moving
us in this direction.

One way of bridging this gap is to use mixed methods (Moon et al., 1990). By adding rich descriptions to our "dry" experimental research, and by getting at multiple viewpoints, our research can be of interest to a broader audience. Practicing ecologically
sound (Gurman et al., 1986) research—that is, research that is multidimensional and
examines multiple perspectives—will also broaden the audience we wish to reach.
However, it is important to note that experimental design is not the only form of family therapy research, as this volume so aptly demonstrates. Experimental design has its
place, but other forms of research do as well.

Results should be reported simply, richly, and descriptively. It is hard to relate to
numbers, but if the researcher can link those numbers to people, his or her audience
may be more interested. Researchers should talk about the implications of their findings for clinicians. The *Journal of Marital and Family Therapy* strongly encourages authors
to include clinical implications in all research studies submitted to the journal. A large
portion of the readership of the *Journal of Marital and Family Therapy* are clinicians,
and these additions help make research more accessible.

If clinicians were to get involved in research, perhaps this research would then be
more relevant. It may be up to the researchers to reach out to clinicians and get them
involved. Offer your expertise as a researcher and collaborate with a clinician. Together,
your research will be more relevant.

FUTURE DIRECTIONS

Gurman and Kniskern began promoting multiperspective multimethod "ecologically
sound" research in 1981. Unfortunately, this is still a future direction for the field. Few
studies have been sophisticated enough to go beyond the question, "Is this research
effective?" Jacobson and his colleagues have done component research that begins to
ask the question, "What parts of this therapy are effective?" Some research has examined
which clients respond to treatment, and there is some research on the process of therapy. However, all these areas need further development.

There is also a need to research therapist variables (Piercy & Sprenkle, 1990; Sprenkle & Bischoff, 1995). Sprenkle and his associates state that future comparative research should use different therapists, matched on variables such as therapeutic allegiance, experience, and skill (Sprenkle & Bischoff, 1995), or at the least researchers should discuss therapist bias (Piercy & Sprenkle, 1990).

Jacobson and Addis (1993) summarize future directions for couple therapy research, and these can be expanded to family therapy research in general. They suggest that intramodel comparisons are needed—that is, constructive, dismantling, and component analyses. They say:

> We would like to see further combinations of experimental and correlational designs, where specific treatment components are under experimental control, and the processes presumably affected by those components are measured separately from outcome. Not only do such designs test important theoretical hypotheses regarding change mechanisms, but they also often shed light on basic processes underlying couple conflict and distress. In terms of payoff and cost effectiveness, these types of designs seem to offer clear advantages relative to between-model comparisons. (p. 89)

They go on to suggest several other priorities for family therapy research: increased attention to prevention, research on gender issues, research on domestic violence, and assessment of therapist competence. Jacobson (1991) further suggests matching studies and the intensive analysis of therapy process.

Mixed methods may be another area of growth in family therapy. In addition, fitting family therapy research to a systemic model is an exciting growth area for the field.

Alexander, Holtzworth-Munroe, and Jameson (1994) note three additional directions for family therapy research. First, most family therapy research is biased toward white males. Multicultural perspectives and gender perspectives are poorly represented. Second, there is a lack of attention to developmental issues. Finally, family therapy outcome research has ignored issues of comorbidity.

Family therapy is underresearched. Find an area of great interest to you and begin researching it. You will be able to fill a gap because there are more gaps than filled in places.

REFERENCES

Alexander, J. F., Holtzworth-Munroe, A., & Jameson, P. (1994). The process and outcome of marital and family therapy: Research review and evaluation. In A. E. Bergin & S. L. Garfield (Eds.), *Handbook of psychotherapy and behavior change* (4th ed., pp. 595–630). New York: Wiley.

Atkinson, B. J., & Heath, A. W. (1987). Beyond objectivism and relativism: Implications for family therapy research. *Journal of Strategic and Systemic Therapies, 6*(1), 8–17.

Babbie, E. (1986). *The practice of social science research* (4th ed.). Belmont, CA: Wadsworth.

Baucom, D. H. (1983). Conceptual and psychometric issues in evaluating the effectiveness of behavioral marital therapy. *Advances in Family Intervention, Assessment and Theory, 3*, 91–117.

Bell, N. J., & Morris, J. P. (1988). The pretest in experimental family therapy research: Practical and statistical considerations. *Journal of Family Psychology, 2*, 105–110.

Beutler, L. E. (1991). Have all won and must all have prizes? Revisiting Luborsky et al.'s verdict. *Journal of Consulting and Clinical Psychology, 59*, 226–232.

Beutler, L. E., Machado, P. P. P., & Neufeldt, S. A. (1994). Therapist variables. In A. E. Bergin & S. L. Garfield (Eds.), *Handbook of psychotherapy and behavior change* (4th ed., pp. 229–269). New York: Wiley.

Cohen, J. (1988). *Statistical power analysis for the behavioral sciences* (2nd ed.). Hillsdale, NJ: Erlbaum.

Cohen, J. (1992). Things I have learned (so far). In A. E. Kazdin (Ed.), *Methodological issues and strategies in clinical research* (pp. 315–333). Washington, DC: American Psychological Association.

Cook, T. D., & Campbell, D. T. (Eds.). (1979). *Quasi-experimentation: Design and analysis issues for field settings.* Chicago: Rand McNally.

Crane, D. R. (1985). Single-case experimental designs in family therapy research: Limitations and considerations. *Family Process, 24,* 69–77.

Fisher, R. (1951). *The design of experiments.* New York: Hafner.

Garfield, S. L. (1994). Research on client variables in psychotherapy. In A. E. Bergin & S. L. Garfield (Eds.), *Handbook of psychotherapy and behavior change* (4th ed., pp. 190–228). New York: Wiley.

Greenberg, L. S., & Pinsof, W. M. (1986). Process research: Current trends and future perspectives. In L. S. Greenberg and W. M. Pinsof (Eds.), *The psychotherapeutic process: A research handbook* (pp. 3–20). New York: Guilford Press.

Gurman, A. S., & Kniskern, D. P. (1981). Family therapy process research: Knowns and unknowns. In A. S. Gurman & D. P. Kniskern (Eds.), *Handbook of family therapy* (pp. 742–775). New York: Brunner/Mazel.

Gurman, A. S., Kniskern, D. P., & Pinsof, W. M. (1986). Research on the process and outcome of marital and family therapy. In S. L. Garfield & A. E. Bergin (Eds.), *Handbook of psychotherapy and behavior change* (3rd ed., pp. 565–624). New York: Wiley.

Hahlweg, K., & Markman, H. J. (1988). The effectiveness of behavioral marital therapy: Empirical statues of behavioral techniques in preventing and alleviating marital distress. *Journal of Consulting and Clinical Psychology, 56,* 440–447.

Hunsley, J. (1993). Research and family therapy: Exploring some hidden assumptions. *Journal of Systemic Therapies, 12*(1), 63–70.

Jacobson, N. S. (1978). Specific and nonspecific factors in the effectiveness of a behavioral approach to the treatment of marital discord. *Journal of Consulting and Clinical Psychology, 45,* 92–100.

Jacobson, N. S. (1984). A component analysis of behavioral marital therapy: The relative effectiveness of behavior exchange and communication/problem-solving training. *Journal of Consulting and Clinical Psychology, 52,* 295–305.

Jacobson, N. S. (1985). Family therapy outcome research: Potential pitfalls and prospects. *Journal of Marital and Family Therapy, 11,* 149–158.

Jacobson, N. S. (1991). Toward enhancing the efficacy of marital therapy and marital therapy research. *Journal of Family Psychology, 4,* 373–393.

Jacobson, N. S., & Addis, M. E. (1993). Research on couples and couple therapy: What do we know? Where are we going? *Journal of Consulting and Clinical Psychology, 61,* 85–93.

Jacobson, N. S., & Baucom, D. H. (1977). Design and assessment of nonspecific control groups in behavior modification research. *Behavior Therapy, 8,* 709–719.

Jacobson, N. S., Dobson, K., Fruzzetti, A. E., Schmaling, K. B., & Salusky, S. (1991). Marital therapy as a treatment for depression. *Journal of Consulting and Clinical Psychology, 59,* 547–557.

Jacobson, N. S., Follette, V. M., Follette, W. C., Holtzworth-Munroe, A., Katt, J. S., & Schmaling, K. B. (1985). A component analysis of behavioral marital therapy: One-year follow-up. *Behavioral Research and Therapy, 23,* 549–555.

Jacobson, N. S., Follette, W. C., & Pagel, M. (1986). Predicting who will benefit from behavioral marital therapy. *Journal of Consulting and Clinical Psychology, 54,* 518–522.

Jacobson, N. S., Schmaling, K. B., & Holtzworth-Munroe, A. (1987). Component analysis of behavioral marital therapy: 2-year follow-up and prediction of relapse. *Journal of Marital and Family Therapy, 13,* 187–195.

Jacobson, N. S., Schmaling, K. B., Holtzworth-Munroe, A., Katt, J. L., Wood, L. F., & Follette, V. M. (1989). Research-structured vs. clinically flexible versions of social learning-based marital therapy. *Behavioral Research and Therapy, 27,* 173–180.

Jacobson, N. S., & Traux, P. (1991). Clinical significance: A statistical approach to defining meaningful change in psychotherapy research. *Journal of Consulting and Clinical Psychology, 49,* 12–19.

Johnson, S. M., & Greenberg, L. S. (1988). Relating process to outcome in marital therapy. *Journal of Marital and Family Therapy, 14,* 175–183.

Kazdin, A. E. (1994). Methodology, design, and evaluation in psychotherapy research. In A. E. Bergin & S. L. Garfield (Eds.), *Handbook of psychotherapy and behavior change* (4th ed., pp. 19–71). New York: Wiley.

Keppel, G. (1982). *Design and analysis: A researcher's handbook* (2nd ed.). Englewood Cliffs, NJ: Prentice-Hall.

Kerlinger, F. N. (1986). *Foundations of behavioral research* (3rd ed.). New York: Holt, Rinehart, & Winston.

Kniskern, D. P. (1985). Climbing out of the pit: Further guidelines for family therapy research. *Journal of Marital and Family Therapy, 11,* 159–162.

Leff, J., Kuipers, L., Berkowitz, R., & Sturgeon, D. (1985). A controlled trial of social intervention in the families of schizophrenic patients: Two year follow-up. *British Journal of Psychiatry, 146,* 594–600.

Moon, S. M., Dillon, D. R., & Sprenkle, D. H. (1990). Family therapy and qualitative research. *Journal of Marital and Family Therapy, 16,* 357–374.

Morris, J. P. (1987). Non-systemic assumptions about family therapy research. *Journal of Strategic and Systemic Therapies, 6*(1), 2–7.

Parloff, M. B. (1986). Frank's "common elements" in psychotherapy: Nonspecific factors and placebos. *American Journal of Orthopsychiatry, 56,* 521–530.

Piercy, F. P., & Sprenkle, D. H. (1990). Marriage and family therapy: A decade review. *Journal of Marriage and the Family, 52,* 1116–1126.

Shadish, W. R., Ragsdale, K., Glaser, R. R., & Montgomery, L. M. (1995). The efficacy and effectiveness of marital and family therapy: A perspective from meta-analysis. *Journal of Marital and Family Therapy, 21,* 345–360.

Shields, C. G. (1986). Critiquing the new epistemologies: Toward minimum requirements for a scientific theory of family therapy. *Journal of Marital and Family Therapy, 12,* 359–372.

Singer, G. H. S., Irvin, L. K., Irvine, B., Hawkins, N., & Cooley, E. (1989). Evaluation of community-based support services for families of persons with developmental disabilities. *Journal of the Association for Persons with Severe Handicaps, 14,* 312–323.

Snyder, D. K., Mangrum, L. F., & Wills, R. M. (1993). Predicting couples' response to marital therapy: A comparison of short- and long-term predictors. *Journal of Consulting and Clinical Psychology, 61,* 61–69.

Sprenkle, D. H., & Bischoff, R. J. (1995). Research in family therapy: Trends, issues, and recommendations. In M. P. Nichols & R. C. Schwartz (Eds.), *Family therapy: Concepts and methods* (3rd ed., pp. 540–580). Boston: Allyn & Bacon.

Strayhorn, J. M., & Weidman, C. S. (1989). Reduction of attention deficit and internalizing symptoms in preschoolers through parent–child interaction training. *Journal of the American Academy of Child and Adolescent Psychiatry, 28,* 888–896.

Szapocznik, J., Perez-Vidal, A., Brickman, A. L., Foote, F. H., Santisteban, D., Hervis, O., & Kurtines, W. M. (1988). Engaging adolescent drug abusers and their families in treatment: A strategic structural systems approach. *Journal of Consulting and Clinical Psychology, 56,* 552–557.

Tabachnick, B. G., & Fidell, L. S. (1989). *Using multivariate statistics* (2nd ed.). New York: Harper & Row.

Todd, T. C., & Stanton, M. D. (1983). Research on marital and family therapy: Answers, issues, and recommendations for the future. In B. B. Wolman & G. Strickler (Eds.), *Handbook of family and marital therapy* (pp. 91–115). New York: Plenum.

Whisman, M. A., Jacobson, N. S., Fruzzetti, A. E., & Waltz, J. A. (1989). Methodological issues in marital therapy. *Advances in Behavioral Research and Therapy, 11,* 175–189.

Winer, B. J., Brown, D. R., & Michels, K. M. (1991). *Statistical principles in experimental design* (3rd ed.). New York: McGraw Hill.

Wynne, L. C. (1988). The "presenting problem" and theory-based family variables: Keystones for family therapy research. In L. C. Wynne (Ed.), *The state of the art in family therapy research: Controversies and recommendations,* (pp. 89–108). New York: Family Process Press.

12

Methods for Single-Case Experiments in Family Therapy

MITCHELL H. DICKEY

BACKGROUND

Gauging the effectiveness of our work as family therapists is difficult. What are our implicit criteria for good therapy? What benchmarks do we use to judge whether we are good therapists? Our case loads are full. Clients keep appointments and do not terminate after two sessions. Families discuss difficult issues. Our colleagues seem interested when we talk about our work. Mostly, things are going well. For many therapists, the absence of problems provides a measure of reassurance. For others, it represents success.

In the restaurant business, if steaks do not come back with complaints, the cook is doing well. What looks like medium rare on the outside to the cook is medium rare on the inside to the customer. For some cooks, the absence of problems is not enough. They want to make a thin slice in the underside of the steak so that they can take an inside look at their work.

This chapter is written for family therapists who want to take an inside look at their work. It offers a series of general guidelines from which interested cooks can become more creative in developing their own recipes. It provides a set of flexible tools from which interested family therapists can become more creative in refining and expanding their own skills and become more certain about their effectiveness.

Doing good work with families is a central, defining feature of our professional lives, yet the signposts to tell us how we are doing are indistinct. Rarely do we know how things have gone for families after termination; rarely do we know whether they make continuing use of what they learned in our offices. We might like to know how they would describe their work with us to the next therapist they see. At least researchers have statistics to evaluate their results.

Gauging effectiveness can also be difficult because in the "real" world, outcome for a particular therapy is rarely as clear or as "good" as it is in edited videotapes at conferences or as it appears to be in sanitized research reports. In fact, for the individual family, there are few reliable criteria or benchmarks for successful therapy.

Our cases simply do not look like the public or published accounts of successful therapy. This chapter outlines one important, objective way that therapists can gauge (or demon-

strate) their effectiveness. Personal curiosity or questing is not the only reason single-case research is important for family therapists. Proving the clinical effectiveness of systems-oriented therapies to the general psychotherapy community and to businesses and insurance companies undertaking health care reform will be increasingly important. In the larger agenda of health care reform, insurance companies have a clear mandate to cut costs and are looking for feasible ways to do so. Although the debate about the role of research in influencing social policy will continue for years to come, there is no doubt that treatment models that have proven effective with major mental disorders will be more difficult to exclude from coverage.

It is unlikely that the current political struggles in Washington will persuade family therapists to research the single case. In fact, the view that research per se is inimical to systems theories is widespread in family therapy (Liddle, 1991). In this view, the ultimate validity of any approach rests with its stakeholders and empirical evidence does not matter (Colapinto, 1979).

These views are not without historical precedence. Not long ago psychoanalysts held such an opinion of their future and eschewed the importance of traditional research in demonstrating efficacy. Today psychoanalysis has been dropped from the list of reimbursable treatments by many insurance companies and it is increasingly difficult to get patients for analysis or trainees for analytic training. Establishing effectiveness matters.

Philosophical Assumptions

Experimental designs with a single family rest on the same philosophical assumptions as other social sciences. Traditional social science methodology holds that claims of support for a particular hypothesis are stronger if alternative explanations are less plausible than the hypothesis of interest. *In other words, if one's results could just as easily have been caused by something other than the variable of interest to the researcher, that is not a strong finding. This is of particular interest when we would like to show that improvements in families are the result of therapy.*

In single-case designs, the therapist and the researcher are often, but not necessarily, the same person. Thus, single-case experiments rely on objective measures to reduce the possibility of therapist bias regarding therapeutic gains. As far back as 1931, the call for measuring the effects of therapy were heard: "I appeal to you. . . . Measure, evaluate, estimate, appraise your results, in some form, in any terms that rest on something beyond faith. . . . Out of such evaluations will come, I believe, better service to the client" (Cabot, 1931, as cited in Bloom & Fischer, 1982, p. ix).

Finally, single-case experiments are based on the assumption of inherent synergy between clinical work and research. As noted later, the skills required are of service to both the researcher and the client or family. They can be employed in the offices of individual clinicians without compromising clinical care and are designed to be flexible regarding treatment approach, duration, and needed shifts in focus.

Historical Roots and Development

Single-case experiments are rare in family therapy research. To my knowledge, not one single-case experiment has ever been published in the marital or family therapy literature. Case studies, on the other hand, are quite common in family therapy and have been a staple way to advance clinical theories for three generations of family therapists. Most of these case studies have relied heavily, if not exclusively, on the clinician's perception of both process and outcome for their validity. Case reports have traditionally been written by the therapist without reference to what the family thought was important. Recently, this practice has been questioned (Tomm, 1990).

Within the larger field of psychotherapy, the history of using single cases to develop clinical theory and technique predates Freud. Then, in the early 1950s, behaviorally oriented psychologists began to use more rigorous methods for testing the efficacy of therapy, including the single-case experiment.

METHODOLOGY

Research Questions

One of the most important issues for any model of psychotherapy or family therapy is alleviating distress. Do symptoms remit and does family functioning improve? The clear advantage of experimental designs for the single case is that it is less likely that the clinician–investigator will unwittingly make false claims for the effectiveness of therapy. *When certain conditions are met, single-case experiments provide a strong basis on which to assert the benefits of therapy.*

The range of possible questions to be answered and approaches to be undertaken through experimentation with the single case can quickly overwhelm. An illustrative case example is offered to distinguish among and expand on the various avenues of inquiry available to clinical researchers with this methodology. This fictitious example has been invented for heuristic purposes and will continue throughout the chapter.

> The identified patient, we will call him Mark Young, is a 9-year-old boy from a single-parent, middle-class, Caucasian family. He has one younger sister. Recently he has been suspended from school for fighting and disruptive behavior in the classroom and has also been difficult to manage at home. Mrs. Young, Mark's mother, works locally as an office manager. She scheduled an appointment after having been referred by his teacher at school. At the Family Clinic, he was evaluated and given a provisional diagnosis of conduct disorder, solitary aggressive type.

Sampling and Selection

A cogent method for determining clinical efficacy begins with initial assessment of the family. Because there is only one case to be selected, inclusion criteria can and ought to be stringent and carefully considered. Selection of essential elements of family and individual functioning relevant to the presenting problem is crucial. Here, as with treatment planning, a knowledge of basic research on the psychological functioning and contextual factors associated with conduct disorders can guide selection of the relevant domains to be assessed.

The purpose of the study is the primary consideration in selection. If the investigator is interested in asserting that findings from this particular case generalize to other families with similar problems, the investigator would select a family in which several essential features of family functioning are typical of that problem. If, on the other hand, the investigator is interested in generalizing from previous studies to different kinds of problems, it would make sense to choose a client or family that is quite different from the types of families previously studied with this approach. If the investigator is interested in showing that symptomatic improvement in an individual family member is related to familywide changes, he or she should choose a family in which there is a relatively clear "function of the symptom" for the family (Haley, 1987; Madanes, 1981).

Whatever the investigator's intent, it is still not feasible to select a family for study on the basis of the family's functioning per se because there is currently no consensus among family therapists or researchers regarding a typology of family functioning (Wynne, 1988). *The presenting problem (or symptomatology of the identified patient) remains the most widely used and reliable criterion available.* Nonetheless, it is possible and desirable to assess functioning at the family level and to incorporate that information into selection and treatment planning.

Sample Description

A reasonably thorough and valid assessment of child and family functioning includes self-report and observational measures of both individual and family functioning. The validity of the assessment can be augmented by information from sources outside the family. For instance, many studies have asked teachers to complete the Child Behavior Checklist—Teacher Form (CBCL-TRF) (Achenbach & Edelbrock, 1986) to corroborate parent reports. Often referred to as multimatrix, multimethod assessment, this standard is rarely met in family therapy outcome studies.

In the case illustration, the Young family completed several self-report measures that assessed both child and family functioning. Mark completed the Self-Report Delinquency Checklist (Elliott, Dunford, & Huizinga, 1987), which measures a variety of delinquent behaviors in the home, at school, and in the community. Mrs. Young completed two self-report instruments: the Parenting Stress Index (PSI) (Lloyd & Abidin, 1985) and the cohesion and control subscales of the Family Environment Scales (Moos & Moos, 1981). Mrs. Young was also interviewed about her son's behavior with the Interview for Antisocial Behavior (Kazdin & Esveldt-Dawson, 1986). These measures described Mark as evincing a moderate degree of delinquent behaviors primarily at home and school. Mrs. Young described herself as highly stressed in her dual role as wage earner and parent and as lacking control and cohesion on the FES. She was also introduced to the Parent Daily Report (PDR) (Chamberlain & Reid, 1987), a brief telephone interview used to assess presence of conduct problems during the most recent 24 hours.

In addition, after having completed the questionnaires and interviews, Mark and Mrs. Young were observed for three 10-minute interaction periods. They completed three tasks: plan a meal together, resolve a recent conflict, and free play. These interactions were coded for task completion, parental facilitation of decision making, leadership, and discipline. In general, the interactions were led by Mark and tasks were not completed.

Data Collection

In addition to a thorough assessment of individual and systemic functioning before treatment begins, information about change is collected continuously over the course of therapy. Typically, client and family reports of specified behaviors, moods, or cognitions are obtained throughout treatment, sometimes on a daily basis. This information serves as the primary marker for therapeutic effectiveness.

Subsequent to initial assessment and selection, information is collected as to the frequency and stability of problems. Called a baseline, this information typically accrues for several weeks preceding the onset of treatment and is fundamental to inferences that treatment (or therapy) is effecting change. To develop a stable baseline, observations regarding Mark's behavior were obtained daily from Mrs. Young on the

PDR for 3 weeks between assessment and onset of treatment. The PDR was also used during treatment as the main method of assessing change.

Figure 12.1 portrays five possible baselines. Each of these hypothetical baselines illustrates a different type of problem stability. Higher scores represent greater problems. Baseline 1 indicates deterioration, baseline 2 indicates improvement, baseline 3 indicates a stable level of problem behaviors (and a return to baseline levels when treatment is withdrawn), baseline 4 indicates large fluctuations in problem behaviors, and baseline 5 hints at possible episodic fluctuation in problems. If reports indicate improvement (baseline 2), treatment may be unnecessary. If reports indicate deterioration, the baseline period may be shorter and treatment begun immediately. Solid lines represent actual performance and dotted lines represent expected performance based on continuation of baseline trend.

Projections of future levels of problem are anticipated from the baseline trend. For instance, deterioration would be expected to continue in baseline 1. When no slope or trend occurs (as in baseline 3), neither exacerbation nor diminution of symptoms would be anticipated.

Once treatment has begun, data are collected continuously throughout the course of therapy at regular intervals, usually daily or weekly. Unlike typical outcome studies, decisions regarding duration of treatment are made by the investigator and clinician during treatment. Once begun, measures and frequency of data collection do not change. Because of this, it may be wise to collect baseline measures on at least one domain of family functioning relevant to presenting problems. As systemic therapists, we would be keenly aware of the influence of context on behavior and might be interested in showing how changing parent–child interactions affects symptomatology in the identified patient.

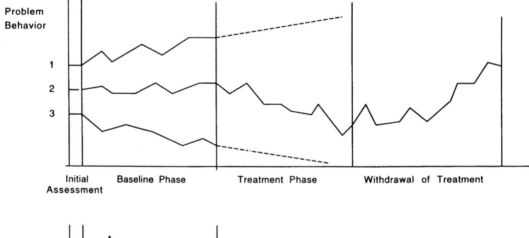

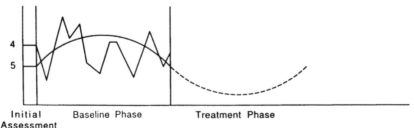

FIGURE 12.1. Examples of possible results.

In our case illustration, specific items from the PSI which were endorsed during the initial assessment were extracted from the much longer PSI and used as target items during the baseline and treatment phases. To show associations between parenting and child behavior, it would be necessary to collect information on Mrs. Young's parent management skills during baseline and to collect information on changes in these skills over the course of therapy. Figure 12.2 indicates baseline levels of Mark's behavior problems and Mrs. Young's parent management practices. Each baseline has its own scale. The target items from the PSI were completed by Mrs. Young on a weekly basis. After each session the therapist rated Mrs. Young's parent management skills on these same PSI items. Other than the initial assessment, there was no baseline for the therapist's rating of Mrs. Young's parenting: Rather, these data were used to corroborate Mrs. Young's self-report.

Data Analyses

Effects of treatment are shown by observing differences in severity or frequency of problems between baseline and treatment phases. *Establishing clear trends during baseline is crucial because inferences regarding treatment effectiveness are based on clear departures in slope between baseline and treatment phases* (see Figure 12.1, treatment lines 1 and 3). In general, these inferences are stronger or more valid when large and immediate changes in slopes occur. When smaller or less immediate changes are observed, claims of treatment efficacy are open to alternative explanations. That is, observed changes in trend or slope may stem from intervening life events or a regression to the mean based solely on the scale's reliability. This method of observing changes in slope or trend between baseline and treatment phases is called the visual inspection method and traditionally has not relied on statistical analyses. (Colloquially, when large and immediate changes occur,

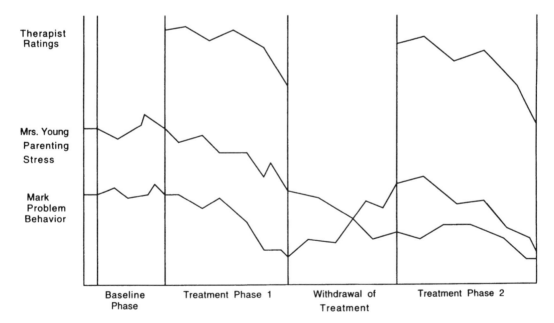

FIGURE 12.2. Fictitious data for the Young family. Therapist ratings occurred only during treatment phases. Mrs. Young's and Mark's lines cross. Each baseline has its own scale or level and the therapists' ratings do not indicate higher stress because they are located above Mrs. Young's ratings on the graph. Each scale is relative only to its own baseline.

the data are often said to pass the "intraocular trauma test"; that is, the data "hit you between the eyes.")

If the identified patient's behavior were deteriorating, as represented by baseline 1 in Figure 12.1, a change to stabilization of the problem (treatment line 1) would be considered beneficial. This inference is strengthened if previous research on this disorder or problem has shown that deterioration is expected without treatment. For example, if a treatment were able to arrest the development of Alzheimer's disease, that would be of considerable benefit to patient and family.

Similarly, the clinical significance of the gains of therapy can be gauged if previous research has determined clinical levels for which recurrence is unlikely. For example, levels of antibodies below a certain level for 2 years is considered a "cure" for some lymphomas. For Mark, cutoff scores on the CBCL—Total Problem Scale could be used to determine clinical significance of changes because this scale has been widely used in treatment studies of child conduct disorders.

Stability and direction of baseline performance are crucial in making valid inferences about effects of treatment. Trends or slopes in baseline levels of symptoms may pose difficulties in interpreting results. In baseline 2, a decrease in symptoms may be anticipated from the projection of baseline performance and it would be difficult to attribute decreases during the treatment phase as having resulted from the intervention. Similarly, in baseline 4, large fluctuations over several weeks are observed. In this case the confidence with which inferences about effectiveness can be made are attenuated because changes during treatment could have resulted from natural fluctuations rather than improvement.

Treatment Plan

The case illustration focuses on family treatment of a 9-year-old boy with conduct problems and his highly stressed, single mother. A relative abundance of information exists on the psychological functioning of children with conduct disorders and their families. First, such children exhibit poor interpersonal problem-solving skills as seen in premature attribution of hostile intent in others, in relative inability to generate nonaggressive solutions to social-conflict situations, in the inability to take the perspective of the other, and in their trouble deferring to authority (Dodge, 1985; Hinshaw, 1992; Kendall & Brasswell, 1985; Spivack & Shure, 1982). Second, parents of these children are less likely to monitor child behavior closely, and parenting is often inconsistent, harsh, and punitive (Kazdin, 1987; Patterson, 1982, 1986; Rutter & Giller, 1983). Third, families that do not respond well to treatment tend to be economically disadvantaged, stressed, socially isolated, single parents from minority groups with psychological problems of their own (Dumas & Wahler, 1983; Hinshaw, 1992; Kazdin, 1990, 1993; Webster-Stratton, 1985; Webster-Stratton & Hammond, 1990).

In the case illustration described in Figure 12.2, Mark and Mrs. Young achieved a stable baseline by about 3 weeks. Given the current status of knowledge regarding family functioning of children with conduct disorders and given initial information from the Young family, treatment was aimed at two primary targets. First, Mark received 15 sessions of problem-solving skills training. This training focused primarily on generating a greater variety of solutions for interpersonal conflicts, inhibiting aggressive impulses, and monitoring attributions of aggressive intent in others (Dumas, 1989; Kazdin, Esveldt-Dawson, French, & Unis, 1987; Kazdin, Siegel, & Bass, 1992). These skills were taught with Mrs. Young, Mark, and the therapist present. As treatment progressed, Mrs. Young was encouraged to help Mark acquire and practice these skills.

In separate sessions, Mrs. Young received 15 weeks of parent management training. This focused on learning to monitor Mark's behavior more closely, giving consistent and timely punishments, and paying explicit attention to good behavior (Patterson, Chamberlain, & Reid, 1982). The point to be made here is not whether this treatment adheres to a particular school of family therapy but that knowledge from basic and applied research can fruitfully be brought to bear in planning treatment to maximize likelihood of success.

Treatment Outcome

In Figure 12.2, clinical improvements were observed, but the reason for improvement was ambiguous. From both the therapist's and Mrs. Young's perspective, Mrs. Young's child management skills began to improve quickly, but Mark's aversive behaviors did not decrease until 6 to 8 weeks later. From a methodological perspective, this raises questions about overall treatment efficacy in that other variables (e.g., positive life events) could plausibly have influenced the overall decrease in aggressive behavior evinced by Mark. To address the likelihood of this, a post hoc interview about family life events was conducted. No such event was found and no larger historical event occurred during this time. From a family systems perspective, changes in one part of the system (i.e., Mrs. Young) could be seen to affect other parts (i.e., Mark). The claim that treatment was responsible for the improvement, then, appears more plausible.

Reporting

Reporting results of single-case experiments is straightforward. Typically, clinician–investigators provide a graph of problem levels during baseline, intervention, and nonintervention phases as in Figure 12.2. With single-case experiments, the data often "speak for themselves"; that is, they pass the intraocular trauma test. As earlier, it is helpful to include possible alternative explanations for the findings and relevant information about the likelihood of influence from these other variables.

Because single-case experiments are often the source of innovative clinical techniques, more importance can be placed on description of the actual intervention and the context in which it was delivered. Strong statements regarding efficacy which arise from single-case experiments can generate controversy and, subsequently, encourage investigations of similar cases by additional clinicians and researchers (see deShazer, 1988). In this regard, a thorough description of the clinical techniques and context is warranted. Two journals publish case studies exclusively: *Family Therapy Case Studies* and the *Journal of Family Psychotherapy*. Currently, single-case experiments are most likely to be published in behavioral journals such as *Behavior Therapy*.

Alternative Designs

The design in the case illustration describes a simple multiple baseline design with two related constructs being assessed—mother's parenting and child's aggressive behaviors. These simple designs can be expanded to include additional features which strengthen judgments about efficacy.

So far, the example of the Young family does not meet the traditional definition of an experiment because participants are not randomly assigned to one of several conditions that are set up (or manipulated) by the investigator. Because random assignment is not possible with only one case, designs are most typically quasi-experimental.

That is, manipulation of the independent variable (usually some aspect of treatment) is accomplished not through comparisons between two alternative treatments but through comparisons between one treatment and another version of itself. Treatments can be applied, removed, and reapplied; they can be applied in different settings, by different persons, or at different times of day; one technique can be combined with other techniques given in different orders; different treatments can be targeted at different problems within the same family. Each of these design decisions represents a different way of manipulating the independent variable.

Reversal (A-B-A-B) Designs

In single-case designs, the most plausible threat to conclusions that an intervention effected change is the possibility that improvement might have occurred despite the intervention because of history, maturation, repeated testing, intervening life events, and normal remission of symptoms (see Bloom & Fischer, 1982; Cook & Campbell, 1979). To diminish the plausibility of these alternative explanations, investigators have undertaken designs in which treatment is discontinued for a period of time after the changes have stabilized. Manipulation of the independent variable is accomplished by the application or removal of treatment. The clinician–investigator decides at what point and for how long treatment is withheld. The parameters of treatment are typically not determined at the outset of the study, but decisions regarding type, intensity, and duration of treatment are made in response to the needs of client or family as intervention progresses.

At some point, however, treatment is discontinued. During this phase, the trend of symptoms may reverse and the client or family may return to the level of symptoms previously in evidence during baseline. If this occurs, the treatment begins again until symptoms have reached acceptable levels. If the problem waxes and wanes as treatment is withdrawn and reinstituted, this more strongly suggests that treatment has effected gain. Ethical and clinical considerations in using reversal designs are discussed below.

In our case illustration, Mrs. Young and the clinician jointly decided when to take a "vacation" from therapy. In Figure 12.2 that decision is indicated by a withdrawal-from-treatment phase. Daily phone calls assessing Mark's behavior and weekly reports of Mrs. Young's parenting continued during this time. Four weeks after treatment was discontinued, Mrs. Young reported that her child management skills remained intact but that Mark's behavior was getting worse. After 2 additional weeks, the decision was made to return to treatment. This is represented by the second treatment phase in Figure 12.2. During this time, a lack of correspondence was noted between the therapist's in-session rating of Mrs. Young's parenting skills and Mrs. Young's rating of her own skills at home during the week. After 4 weeks of this, the clinician and investigator decided to refocus treatment to help Mrs. Young regain her parent management skills. Six weeks later, agreement was reached between therapist's and mother's ratings of parenting skills and treatment was discontinued a second time.

Multiple-Baseline Designs

The case illustration exemplifies one type of multiple-baseline design. In this case, one dimension of functioning is assessed for each of two individuals. Typically, several dimensions of functioning are assessed for one client and one dimension is targeted for intervention at a time. Manipulation of the independent variable occurs when treatment techniques are changed. These designs are undertaken when the investigator is interested in showing that specific techniques are effective for specific target symptoms. Presumably the intervention is specific enough to influence only one of the specified symptoms and is inert with respect to the other symptoms.

When, however, two or more dimensions of family functioning are naturally associated with each other, baselines are not independent. With correlated dimensions of family functioning, several related dimensions may be affected by intervention. This is especially likely to occur when baselines represent several behaviors within one person. For instance, both anxiety and depression may respond to intervention aimed at increasing self-esteem.

Family systems theory would view the multiple-baseline design as "ecology chopping." Systems theory asserts not only that the whole is greater than the sum of the parts but that smaller elements of a system can affect larger ones. Family systems theory would predict that a shift in one baseline would affect baselines for other family members in a relatively short time (i.e., that independence of baselines among family members would be unlikely). In these designs, the dual goals of showing systemic change and specificity of intervention are at odds.

Taken in this pure form and given the realities of developing stable baselines for each family member, it would be nearly impossible to show with confidence both reciprocal influence among subsystems and the effects of specific interventions on specific targets. On the one hand, if intervention aimed at one person or subsystem did not affect performance of another person or subsystem and if later intervention did affect that person or subsystem, inferences suggesting that treatment is responsible for improvement are strengthened but the tenets of family systems theory are not.

On the other hand, if a pattern is observed between the performance of one family member or subsystem and another member or subsystem during baseline (i.e., if baselines among members were not independent), or if intervention aimed at one person or subsystem also affected other persons or subsystems in a clinically meaningful way (Mann, Borduin, Henggeler, & Blaske, 1990), support for systems theory would accrue but arguments for the efficacy of the intervention would be weakened. In essence, the observation of second-order change—fundamental change in the implicit rules by which families govern themselves—would weaken the argument that therapy was effective on methodological grounds.

Simultaneous-Treatment Design

Baselines on one symptom can also be collected across settings (e.g., at home, in the classroom, and during after-school sports). To test for differences in effectiveness, different treatments can then be implemented within the separate settings. These designs work better when the behavior in question can change from one minute or hour to the next without affecting the probability of that same behavior occurring later. More generalized problems such as conduct disorders are unlikely to show treatment differences.

Different persons in each of these settings can administer interventions at different times of a day. The resulting set of three intervention lines, depicted in Figure 12.3, show different responses to intervention and thereby show differential efficacy of treatment. The strongest intervention can then be administered by these three persons across all three settings and further decreases in problem behaviors assessed during a final intervention phase (see Ollendick, Shapiro, & Barrett, 1981).

There are four main practical and methodological difficulties with these designs. First, as different persons administer the intervention, it may be that one person is more

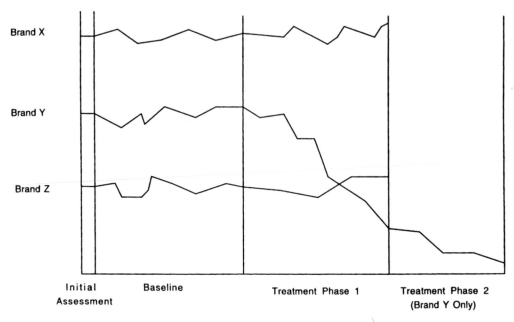

FIGURE 12.3. Comparative treatment example.

suited to this role or begins with a better relationship with the client. If so, differential improvement may not be due to a particular kind of technique but rather to the person or his or her general skill. Second, interventions administered in the morning may carry over to the afternoon, thereby making the afternoon treatment appear more effective than it actually was. These two problems can be addressed by having more than one subject in the study and by counterbalancing the therapists and settings across subjects. For instance, with additional cases, therapists can switch from morning to afternoon and vice versa.

Third, some behaviors are triggered by certain settings or social stimuli. In this case the three baselines developed for each of the three settings may be qualitatively and quantitatively different enough to make comparisons among treatments less tenable. Fourth, as with all group comparisons between alternative treatments, the possibility that treatments are similar in some important way is considerable. Often termed "nonspecific factors," these generic ingredients of therapy include alliance with client or family, empathy, warmth, and general interpersonal skills. Generic ingredients have generally obscured differences in effectiveness between treatments.

Changing-Criterion Design

Unlike multiple-treatment designs, these designs are appropriate for problems that (1) typically change slowly and (2) can show relatively large changes. Based on baseline levels, specific criteria are established for performance during an initial treatment phase. When these expectations are met, criteria are altered to reflect further improvement during a second treatment phase. When met, these criteria are altered again and again until symptoms or problems are vastly reduced (see Figure 12.4). Without discontinuities of treatment, these designs are unable to eliminate several rival hypotheses to the reason for change. Only when performance matches criterion closely are inferences about efficacy strong. Thus, these designs would be likely to work better with behaviors that are under the control of the individual (e.g., compulsive hand washing) than with interpersonally triggered behaviors such as aggression.

DISCUSSION

Strengths

These methods evidence several strengths. First, and clearest, they allow the clinician–researcher to be relatively sure that obtained results are due to therapy and not to misperception by the investigator. This provides a significant advantage over case studies which could, but often do not, employ checks for validity.

In fact, the history of case studies is one of premature, grand claims for effectiveness. For instance, an entire approach to therapy to help adult children leave home is reputed to have been based on clinician's impression of one case (Haley, 1980) and has not been tested empirically. Freudian theories of infantile sexuality and penis envy, which dominated a half century of therapeutic services, were based on subjective data from case studies. Without reasonable empirical testing, the likelihood that fallacious clinical theories and iatrogenic techniques will be developed from subjectively assessed case studies that then get incorporated into everyday clinical practice by therapists eager to be up-to-date on the latest innovation but unfamiliar with ways to judge the validity of such claims is historically high. (See Moon & Trepper, Chapter 17, this volume, for qualitative methods of empirical testing of case study findings.)

An important asset of single-case experiments is that they are relatively easy to undertake and do not require large amounts of funding to implement. Strong designs can be carried out in the offices of individual clinicians without compromising standards of clinical care. Few other methods of psychotherapy research can make such claims.

Third, single-case experiments often provide important innovations in clinical prac-

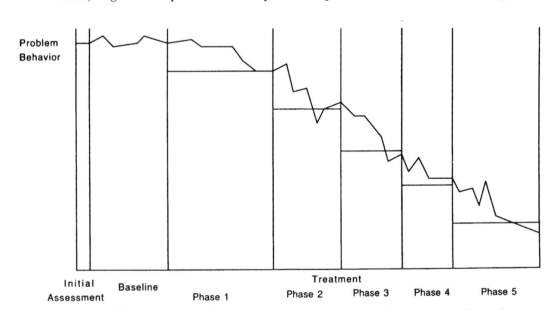

FIGURE 12.4. Changing criteria example. Horizontal lines represent shifting criteria regarding each new target for behavior performance.

tice. New techniques can be developed and tested for a wide variety of clinical problems within a relatively brief time. Ineffective treatment can be identified quickly because information about progress is available on a continuous basis. This can prevent iatrogenic effects.

Fourth, objective feedback on improved performance can itself have a beneficial impact on clients. This visual information about changes in functioning can promote increased self-efficacy of clients and families and encourage them to take note of and responsibility for change. When the signposts of improvement are indistinct—clients often say things are "better" but have greater difficulty saying in what ways or to what degrees they are better—this information can help clients and families be more sensitive to change and thereby foster optimism about and motivation for treatment.

Fifth, a common complaint clinicians have about research on therapy in general is that treatments are poorly specified in written reports and cannot easily be translated to the individual case in practice (Morrow-Bradley & Elliott, 1986). In single-case experiments, treatments are usually well specified and can be employed by other clinicians.

Sixth, theories regarding reciprocal influence and second order change can be tested with designs that incorporate baselines for each family member. Symmetrical and complementary interactions that occur over several days can be reliably charted and points for intervention can be identified with daily assessments. For example, spouses could rate their own pursuing and distancing behaviors and compare them to their spouse's ratings to locate points at which they can interrupt frustrating sequences.

Seventh, as payers of health insurance demand increasing information about treatment efficacy from individual clinicians about individual cases, accountable professionals may find these methods to be the strongest and most flexible way currently available to document success. These methods are much stronger than the satisfaction surveys beginning to be used by payers: They are stronger because of the response bias likely in anonymous questionnaires and the lack of a clear connection between satisfaction and symptom reduction across diagnoses.

Limitations and Considerations

As in all studies of psychotherapy outcome, the claim of efficacy in single-case experiments can be challenged by the presence of other factors which may, in fact, have been responsible for the change. Methodology influences the validity with which inferences can be drawn regarding treatment effectiveness.

It is possible to speak generally about ways to improve methods. Table 12.1 portrays aspects of methodology that affect the likelihood of drawing valid inferences regarding the influence of treatment. Weaker methods are generally open to criticism, primarily based on threats to internal validity (noted in the right-hand column) and stronger methods address them. In general, designs that use objective measures continuously, and that show immediate and large effects for chronic problems in more than one case, are less susceptible to concluding that treatment is effective when it is not. Immediate and large effects for chronic problems are a lot to ask of any treatment. In addition, if the investigator is interested in demonstrating that a particular technique or approach is effective for a number of different problems, results must be obtained across heterogeneous types of cases.

Some problems are less amenable to single-case experimentation. Some behavioral disorders are episodic in nature, such as binge eating or drinking. Thus, a stable baseline may take many months to develop and withholding treatment for this amount of time is generally ill advised. In addition, periods without excessive eating or drinking

TABLE 12.1. Methodological Choices in Single-Case Experiments

Design feature	Weaker methods	Stronger methods	Validity concerns addressed
Size of effect	Small	Large	Regression to mean, maturation
Timing of effect	Delayed	Immediate	History, maturation
Nature of problem	Episodic or improving	Chronic, stable	Natural remission, regression to mean
Measurement	Anecdotal	Objective and/or observational	Reactivity, response bias
Timing of assessment	Pre–post	Continuous with baseline	Testing, regression to mean, history
Number of cases	One	Several	History, idiosyncratic outcome

may appear as rapid and large changes when, in fact, they are intermittent periods in between binges.

As noted earlier, reliable assessment of specific problems is crucial to determining outcomes. Theoretically, nothing prohibits these methods from being used with all sorts of problems, even with such client–therapist variables as transference. Practically, however, behaviors are probably more reliably rated than moods or cognitions because they are more amenable to observation by others. This point becomes especially salient when the identified patient is a child and problems are rated by parents. In our case illustration, Mrs. Young rated Mark's aversive behavior, which leaves open the possibility that Mrs. Young's ratings may have been influenced by her own moods and attributions. For instance, if Mrs. Young experienced a period of higher stress at work, her ratings of Mark may have been affected, independent of how that period influenced her own parenting skills.

Crane (1985) has commented that the sole use of self-report is inappropriate for family therapy research. When moods, affects, or cognitions are targeted for intervention, observational coding, however reliable, cannot account for the client's internalized response or the meaning of it. Here the person experiencing the affect or making the attribution is the best rater. Measures of subjective experience may be reactive to the subject's understanding of the purpose of assessment. For instance, a person diagnosed with a dependent personality disorder might not want to displease the therapist and might rate his or her mood as better than it actually is. In the hopes of avoiding treatment, an adolescent mandated to therapy may rate progress worse than it is. Similarly, such important aspects of interpersonal and insight-oriented therapies as development of a working alliance, which is thought to develop in stages over the course of longer treatment, are unlikely to meet the criteria of large and immediate change. It may not be surprising in this regard that many extant single-case experiments involve behavior therapy with children. The complexity of measuring internalized, subjective experiences and analyzing data at the family level has not been resolved.

Ethical Considerations

In general, the benefits of undertaking single-case experiments outweigh the potential costs primarily because treatment failures are identified quickly and different treatment could be readily substituted.

Recall that in the A-B-A-B designs, treatment was withdrawn to determine stability of treatment gains. Withdrawal of treatment contains ethical dilemmas. If reduction of symptoms is stable (i.e., if treatment is beneficial), problems may not return to baseline levels. In fact, some clients and families may use what they have learned in therapy and continue to improve on their own. Theories of brief therapy are predicated on this. For clinicians and families this is a desired outcome; it reflects successful treatment. For the researcher it is more difficult to argue for a causal role for treatment because rival explanations cannot be eliminated. If problems return to baseline levels, the clinician and researcher may have discontinued treatment prematurely and, thereby, reinforced distress. The psychological consequences of instituting, removing, and reinstituting treatment are unknown, but it stands to reason that client or family motivation for treatment might be diminished by this process.

On the other hand, it is often noted that clinicians can keep clients or families in therapy longer than is necessary. (Recent cost-containment strategies by insurance companies are based on this view.) Testing family readiness to terminate treatment through trial periods when no sessions occur is a common technique in brief strategic and systemic therapies (Fisch, Weakland, & Segal, 1982; Palazzoli, Boscolo, Cecchin, & Prata, 1978). Such natural breaks in treatment as therapist or family vacations offer the opportunity to monitor stability of change for return of problems.

In addition, current policy in health maintenance organizations is aimed not at achieving long-term maintenance of treatment gains but at subclinical levels at which dose–effect ratios (Howard, Kopta, Krause, & Orlinsky, 1986) indicate cost-effectiveness. In other words, discontinuation of treatment before the clinician or investigator believes it to be optimal may become a reality and obviate the ethical concerns described earlier.

Finally, participants in any research project are entitled to be informed clearly about the nature of the project and what will be expected of them. They must be informed of the potential risks of interventions (especially innovative ones) and of the intentions and techniques of treatment. This might ruin some strategic interventions that depend for their efficacy on the family not knowing the therapist's intention. (Human subject committees increasingly frown on statements in consent forms that indicate that deception might be used in the study.) Participants are also entitled to know beforehand who will have access to the data and how their anonymity will be protected if the study is published.

Investigator Skills: Bridging Research and Practice

In the oft-lamented gap between research and practice, single-case experiments hold large promise to build bridges. As noted earlier, it is often the case that one person acts as both clinician and researcher: That is, the therapist investigates the efficacy of his or her own work. It should not be surprising, therefore, that the skills required of clinician and researcher are as similar as they are.

First, the clinician–investigator should be armed with a broad knowledge of both research and clinical theory on how families function. It is especially important that the clinician–investigator be familiar with basic research on family functioning in the area pertinent to the specific case. In the case illustration, it was helpful in planning treatment that so much information is currently available on families of children with conduct disorders.

Second, the clinician–investigator should be able to define a single, specific, solvable problem from among the many vague "issues" offered by the family (see Haley, 1987;

Fisch et al., 1981, among others). Defining central family problems is also important so that appropriate means can be found to operationalize these problems with reliable measures. In this regard, the clinician–researcher must also be skilled in assessing which aspects of family interaction bear most directly on presenting problems. (Beginning clinicians often generate interesting hypotheses about family dynamics but do not tie them clearly to the onset or maintenance of symptoms in the identified patient [Papp, 1980].)

Third, once defined, the clinician must be able to articulate goals for treatment and build consensus with the family about these goals and the means to achieve them. In structural theory this is termed "constructing a workable reality" (Minuchin & Fishman, 1981). To ensure that ratings are completed regularly and in good faith, the clinician–researcher must develop collaborative relationships with family members.

Fourth, once the treatment plan has been established, the clinician–researcher must be able to execute it proficiently. He or she must become accomplished in the skills required and remain faithful to the stated goals of treatment rather than allowing the family to change the focus of treatment every week (Haley, 1987; Madanes, 1981). At the same time, the clinician–researcher must also be open to the weekly or daily information from the family about progress and decide when and how to refocus a treatment that is not achieving the desired results.

Finally, the clinician–researcher must possess enough restraint to wait for initial successes to be maintained throughout a follow-up period or further verified by success with additional cases. This reduces the potential for false claims.

Each of these research skills also fosters clinical skills. This suggests that these activities may be of considerable utility in training family therapists. To my knowledge, no study currently exists of the efficacy of training family therapists by having them undertake single-case experiments in their training clinics. Such a study could test the hypothesis that therapists can be efficiently trained in family therapy skills.

Using traditional research methods, one might randomly assign therapists to a training-as-usual group and a single-case training group, assess in clinical skills before and after training, and look for differences in the gains achieved by therapists in these two training groups. Using single-case designs to test this same hypothesis would not be as straightforward. One would not expect clinical skill to return to baseline after training is withdrawn. Therefore, one could alter the design such that one therapist received training as usual for a specified time and then received training with single-case experiments for a specified time. A second therapist could receive training with single-case experiments first and then training as usual second. Figure 12.5 describes two possible findings. In the top graph, both therapists learned the most during the initial training phase and less during the second phase no matter which form of training was received. In the bottom graph, both therapists gained more skill in the experimental training condition.

FUTURE DIRECTIONS

In that there are currently so few single-case experiments extant in family therapy, the possible avenues of exploration are many. Not all will prove fruitful. Where feasible, information as to which avenues are likely to prove fruitful can be gleaned from the past 40 years of individual psychotherapy research. The following suggestions for future research are sequential in that they represent possible steps in an overall program of research.

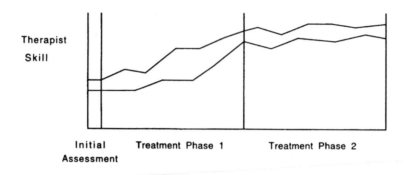

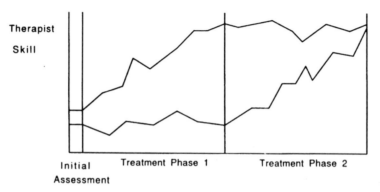

FIGURE 12.5. Focus on therapist instead of family.

Single-Case Designs for Context-Dependent Behavior

Several possible avenues for small-sample and single-case research depend on under-standing family influence on individual behavior. Throughout, emphasis has been placed on the connections between family interactions and individual symptoms in develop-ing effective family-based treatments. For many problems the nature of the relationship between family and individual functioning is not clear (Olson, Russell, & Sprenkle, 1989).

Nonetheless, within an individual family, it is possible to describe the clinical mean-ing of family interactive contexts which elicit specific behaviors. For example, Crits-Christoph et al. (1991), studied the family interactional antecedents to crying and non-crying episodes in a 17-year-old, superlabile diabetic girl. They demonstrated that cry-ing episodes were more likely when discussions (1) focused on the patient, (2) involved other family members, (3) had been hostile and rejecting, or (4) had concerned the avail-ability of supplies. Information of this sort can be invaluable in developing focused treat-ment plans. These designs do not require that treatment occur.

Session Outcome and Single-Case Process Research

In the evolution of successful treatments, investigating smaller, incremental shifts within sessions can provide valuable clues as to the constituent processes of an overall ther-apeutic success. Instead of looking at one case as the unit of analysis, this related ap-proach posits one type of session outcome as the unit of analysis and looks for therapist techniques that foster a particular session outcome over several similar cases

(Elliott, 1985; Elliott, James, Reimschuessel, Coslo, & Sack, 1985). Good outcomes for individual sessions can be articulated within a conceptually clear overall approach to a particular problem, again based on a knowledge of the problem and of psychosocial processes associated with it. For instance, in the Young family, sessions in which Mark was able to generate a greater number of alternative solutions for conflicts with peers or a greater ability to regulate his own affect would be rated as good sessions. In these variants of single-case experiments, the percentage of good sessions becomes the dependent variable. Techniques prevalent within good sessions can be refined to further "goodness of session" (Mahrer, 1988; Mahrer, Lawson, Stalikas, & Schachter, 1990).

Delineating Phases of Treatment

With relatively isolated and circumscribed problems, one may proceed in a straightforward fashion with such circumscribed treatments as extinction schedules. With embedded problems (which often occur when family interactions maintain symptoms), treatment may have to be multidimensional and shift focus from time to time while keeping the overall blueprint intact. Models of treatment, therefore, must be informed by time course of therapy and the tasks essential to each phase (Alexander, 1988). Within the first few sessions, one would hope to see client or family satisfaction and optimism at high levels but would not expect to see changes in symptomatology.

After that, one would next hope to see initial shifts in family interaction sequences implicated in symptom maintenance (Fisch et al., 1982). Later in treatment, one might expect to see stabilization of improvement and collateral changes in other family subsystems. Multiple-baseline designs, as illustrated in Figure 12.6, are especially appropriate for these kinds of questions because changes in specific target areas are expected in different time frames. Note that a second treatment for depression was implemented after no improvement during the first trial.

Symptomatic and Systemic Change

Central tenets of family systems theory hold that influence among family members is reciprocal, that symptoms in one person are maintained by familywide interaction sequences, and that changes in these interactions provide for more enduring remission of symptoms. The unit of analysis for research, then, becomes the entire set of interpersonal behaviors associated with the problem behavior, rather than the problem behavior per se (Watson, Henggeler, & Borduin, 1985). When sequences of interaction among family members are the problem, it begs the question of who is objective enough yet physically present enough to reliably rate their occurrence. Each family member could rate an aspect of the problematic sequence. Criteria could be set as to which family members must rate changes in which behaviors to what degree for systemwide change to have occurred.

In the case illustration, Mark's sister might rate Mark's aversive behavior directed toward her, his teacher might rate classroom behavior, and Mrs. Young and the therapist might rate successful parent management events during the week and in session, respectively. When both Mark's and Mrs. Young's behavior have met criteria for several weeks, systemic change would be said to have occurred. A strong case could be made for the importance of systemic change when a sufficient number of cases in which systemic change occurred show greater improvement at follow-up than cases with similar changes in identified patient problems without concomitant systemic change. That is,

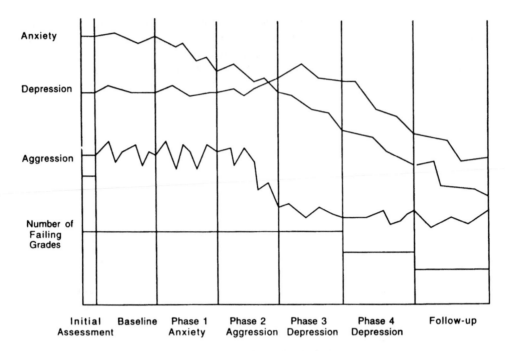

FIGURE 12.6. Multiple baseline design.

if changes in the identified patient last longer when accompanied by changes in family interaction, that implies the importance of these systemic shifts.

Mechanisms of Change: N of 4 Designs

Most of our discussion has focused on demonstrating that clinically significant change has occurred and on how to show that treatment was responsible for change. That is fundamental per se. Once a treatment has been established as effective for a specific problem, the domain of inquiry can be expanded to focus on understanding the therapeutic mechanisms implicated in that change and whether these mechanisms would also be helpful in alleviating other types of problems. This question is especially important for family theorists and clinicians because champions of a particular model have tended to maintain that their approach is beneficial across a broad spectrum of problems.

N of 4 designs begin with two dissimilar types of problems. Then two different kinds of treatment are developed, each of which should be particularly well suited to one of the two types of problems. For example, structural family therapy with its emphasis on parental hierarchy would be a natural fit for child conduct disorders. Similarly, a Satir-like therapy might be expected to work well for a family with a depressed child because it focuses on clear, positive communication and self-esteem. In N of 4 designs, the two treatments are administered to both of the conditions.

That means that one family with conduct problems receives structural therapy and another receives Satir-like therapy and that one family with a depressed child receives structural therapy and another family receives Satir-like experiential therapy. The hypothesis that structural therapy would work better with conduct disorders and that Satir-like experiential therapy would work better with childhood depression is represented in Figure 12.7. In the two cases in which therapy was not going well, treatment would

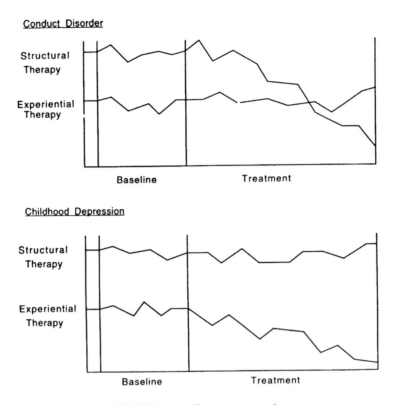

FIGURE 12.7. Treatment specificity.

be switched to a presumably more effective treatment after a short period for ethical reasons.

If the results approximated those in Figure 12.7, it would be strong support for matching treatment to family. Although matching treatment to the family may sound clinically simplistic, to the best of my knowledge no family therapy study has ever shown that one form of family therapy is superior to another with different family problems. Far from being simple, this type of differential treatment effectiveness for different problems is one of the thorniest issues in all psychotherapy research and most clinicians would be surprised to discover how much easier it is to say than to do.

CONCLUSION

This chapter has sketched fundamental design issues involved in showing therapy outcomes with single families. Interested clinicians will find the learning that comes from a careful empirical consideration of their work to be both refreshing and challenging. Family therapists who have become deeply involved with research on effectiveness of therapy say, almost to a person, that it changed the way they do therapy. I hope that some of you will take up the invitation to confront your own work in a way that enriches it by conducting single-case experiments.

REFERENCES

Achenbach, T. M., & Edelbrock, C. S. (1986). *Manual for the Child Behavior Checklist and Revised Child Behavior Profile.* Burlington, VT: University of Vermont.

Alexander, J. F. (1988). Phases of family therapy process: A framework for clinicians and researchers. In L. C. Wynne (Ed.), *State of the art in family therapy research: Controversies and recommendations.* New York: Family Process Press.

Bloom, M., & Fischer, J. (1982). *Evaluating practice: Guidelines for the accountable professional.* Englewood Cliffs, NJ: Prentice-Hall.

Chamberlain, P., & Reid, P. (1987). Parent observation and report of child symptoms. *Behavioral Assessment, 9,* 97–109.

Colapinto, J. (1979). The relative value of empirical evidence. *Family Process, 18,* 427–441.

Cook, T. D., & Campbell, D. T. (1979). *Quasi-experimentation: Design and analysis issues for field settings.* Boston: Houghton-Mifflin.

Crane, D. R. (1985). Single-case experimental designs in family therapy research: Limitations and considerations. *Family Process, 24,* 69–77.

Crits-Christoph, P., Luborsky, L., Gay, E., Todd, T., Berber, J., & Luborsky, E. (1991). What makes Susie cry? A symptom-context study of family therapy. *Family Process, 30,* 337–345.

de Shazer, S. (1988). *Clues: Investigating solutions in brief therapy.* New York: Norton.

Dodge, K. A. (1985). Attributional bias in aggressive children. In P. C. Kendall (Ed.), *Advances in cognitive-behavioral research and therapy* (Vol. 4, pp. 73–110). Orlando, FL: Academic Press.

Dumas, J. E. (1989). Treating antisocial behavior in children: Child and family approaches. *Clinical Psychology Review, 9,* 197–222.

Dumas, J. E., & Wahler, R. G. (1983). Predictors of treatment outcome in parent training: Mother insularity and socioeconomic disadvantage. *Behavioral Assessment, 5,* 301–313.

Elliott, D. S., Dunford, F. W., & Huizinga, D. (1987). The identification and prediction of career offenders utilizing self-reported and official data. In J. D. Burchard & S. N. Burchard (Eds.), *Preventing delinquent behavior* (pp. 90–121). Newbury Park, CA: Sage.

Elliott, R. (1985). Helpful and nonhelpful events in brief counseling interviews: An empirical taxonomy. *Journal of Counseling Psychology, 32,* 307–322.

Elliott, R., James, E., Reimschuessel, C., Coslo, D., & Sack, N. (1985). Significant events and the analysis of immediate therapeutic impacts. *Psychotherapy, 22,* 620–630.

Fisch, R., Weakland, J. H., & Segal, L. (1982). *Tactics of change: Doing therapy briefly.* San Francisco: Jossey-Bass.

Haley, J. (1980). *Leaving home.* New York: McGraw-Hill.

Haley, J. (1987). *Problem-solving therapy.* San Francisco: Jossey-Bass.

Hinshaw, S. P. (1992). Externalizing behavior problems and academic underachievement in childhood and adolescence: Causal relationships and underlying mechanisms. *Psychological Bulletin, 111,* 127–155.

Howard, K. I., Kopta, S. M., Krause, M. S., & Orlinsky, D. E. (1986). The dose–effect relationship in psychotherapy. *American Psychologist, 41,* 159–164.

Kazdin, A. E. (1987). Treatment of antisocial behavior in children: Current status and future directions. *Psychological Bulletin, 102,* 187–203.

Kazdin, A. E. (1990). Premature termination from treatment among children referred for antisocial behavior. *Journal of Child Psychology and Psychiatry and Allied Disciplines, 31,* 415–425.

Kazdin, A. E. (1993). Risk for attrition in treatment of antisocial children and families. *Journal of Clinical Child Psychology, 22,* 2–16.

Kazdin, A. E., & Esveldt-Dawson, K. (1986). The Interview for Antisocial Behavior: Psychometric characteristics and concurrent validity with child psychiatric inpatients. *Journal of Psychopathology and Behavioral Assessment, 8,* 289–303.

Kazdin, A. E., Esveldt-Dawson, K., French, N. H., & Unis, A. S. (1987). Problem-solving skills training and relationship therapy in the treatment of antisocial child behavior. *Journal of Consulting and Clinical Psychology, 55,* 76–85.

Kazdin, A. E., Siegel, T. C., & Bass, D. (1992). Cognitive problem-solving skills training and parent management training in the treatment of antisocial behavior in children. *Journal of Consulting and Clinical Psychology, 60,* 733–747.

Kendall, P. C., & Braswell, L. (1985). *Cognitive-behavioral therapy for impulsive children.* New York: Guilford Press.

Liddle, H. A. (1991). Empirical values and the culture of family therapy. *Journal of Marital and Family Therapy, 17,* 327–348.

Lloyd, B. H., & Abidin, R. R. (1985). Revision of the Parenting Stress Index. *Journal of Pediatric Psychology, 10,* 169–177.

Madanes, C. (1981). *Strategic family therapy.* San Francisco: Jossey-Bass.

Mahrer, A. R. (1988). Discovery-oriented psychotherapy research: Rationale, aims, and methods. *American Psychologist, 43,* 694–702.

Mahrer, A. R., Lawson, K. C., Stalikas, A., & Schachter, H. M. (1990). Relationships between strength of feeling, type of therapy, and occurrence of in-session good moments. *Psychotherapy, 27,* 531–536.

Mann, B. J., Borduin, C. M., Henggeler, S. W., Blaske, D. M. (1990). An investigation of systemic conceptualizations of parent-child coalitions and symptom change. *Journal of Consulting and Clinical Psychology, 58,* 336–344.

Minuchin, S., & Fishman, H. C. (1981). *Family therapy techniques.* Cambridge, MA: Harvard University Press.

Moos, R. H., & Moos, B. S. (1981). *Family Environment Scales Manual.* Palo Alto, CA: Consulting Psychologists Press.

Morrow-Bradley, C., & Elliott, R. (1986). Utilization of psychotherapy research by practicing psychotherapists. *American Psychologist, 41,* 188–197.

Ollendick, T. H., Shapiro, E. S., & Barrett, R. P. (1981). Reducing stereotypic behaviors: An analysis of treatment procedures using an alternating treatments design. *Behavior Therapy, 12,* 570–577.

Olson, D. H., Russell, C. S., & Sprenkle, D. H. (1989). *Circumplex model: Systemic assessment and treatment of families.* New York: Haworth.

Palazzoli, M. S., Boscolo, L., Cecchin, G., & Prata, G. (1978). *Paradox and counterparadox.* Northvale, NJ: Jason Aronson.

Papp, P. (1980). The Greek chorus and other techniques of paradoxical therapy. *Family Process, 19,* 45–57.

Patterson, G. R. (1982). *Coercive family process.* Eugene, OR: Castalia.

Patterson, G. R. (1986). Performance models for antisocial boys. *American Psychologist, 41,* 432–444.

Patterson, G. R., Chamberlain, P., & Reid, J. B. (1982). A comparative evaluation of a parent-training program. *Behavior Therapy, 13,* 638–650.

Rutter, M., & Giller, H. (1983). *Juvenile delinquency: Trends and perspectives.* New York: Penguin.

Tomm, K. (1990, June). *Ethical postures that orient one's clinical decision-making.* Paper presented at the annual meeting of the American Family Therapy Association, Philadelphia.

Watson, S. M., Henggeler, S. W., & Borduin, C. M. (1985). Interrelations among multidimensional family therapy outcome measures. *Family Therapy, 12,* 185–196.

Webster-Stratton, C. (1985). Predictors of treatment outcome in parent training for conduct disordered children. *Behavior Therapy, 16,* 223–243.

Webster-Stratton, C., & Hammond, M. (1990). Predictors of treatment outcome in parent training for families with conduct problem children. *Behavior Therapy, 21,* 319–337.

Wynne, L. C. (1988). An overview of the state of the art: What should be expected in current family therapy research. In L. C. Wynne (Ed.), *State of the art in family therapy research: Controversies and recommendations.* New York: Family Process Press.

13

Meta-Analysis in Family Therapy Research

KAREN S. WAMPLER
JULIANNE M. SEROVICH

INTRODUCTION

Definition and Importance

Meta-analysis is a quantitative methodology for summarizing findings from different quantitative research studies on a given topic. It stands in marked contrast to the typical narrative review of literature in which conclusions are reached based on a general summary of statistically significant and nonsignificant findings. In meta-analysis, a common metric, known as effect size, such as the product–moment correlation or the standardized difference between two groups—for example, $(M_e - M_c)/SD_{pooled}$—is used to represent a study finding. The study finding, as represented by this number, becomes a data point and can be used in any number of creative ways to statistically analyze what is known from many different research studies on a topic.

Meta-analysis is a precise and powerful way of providing information important to the field of family therapy for any question on which multiple relevant quantitative studies have been conducted. Its purposes are to (1) summarize what is known; (2) assess relations between study findings, variables, and methodology; (3) suggest recommendations for future research, including identifying areas in which little further research is needed; (4) develop and test models and theoretical propositions across samples; and/or (5) generate policy and practice implications (Carson, Schriesheim, & Kinicki, 1990; Durlak & Lipsey, 1991).

One important function of meta-analysis has been to summarize the effectiveness of psychotherapy. Rather than reading numerous separate studies, the clinician and the policymaker can read a summary of the research that is in terms of easily understood numbers. Two examples of interest to marriage and family therapists are the article by Lipsey and Wilson (1993) summarizing over 302 different meta-analyses of treatments in psychotherapy, prevention, and education and the comprehensive meta-analysis by Shadish, Montgomery, Wilson, Wilson, Bright, and Okwumabua (1993) of marriage and family therapy outcome studies. The information generated by a meta-analysis is often put in terms easily understood by clinicians. For example, Shadish et al. (1993) report an average effect size of .51 based on 71 studies comparing outcomes for those in marital and family therapy with controls. An effect size of .51 means that, on average, a client in marriage and family therapy was better off than 70% of those in the control condition (Shadish et al., 1993). Clinicians might be interested in specific questions as well, such as, "On average, how effective is strategic therapy as compared with parent training for conduct disorders in children?" Such questions can also be addressed by meta-analysis (cf. Shadish & Sweeney, 1991).

Another reason meta-analysis is so useful to the field of family therapy is the difficulty in conducting primary research on issues meaningful to clinicians and policymakers. Of necessity, most important family therapy research is intensive and expensive, involving observational methodologies, extensive self-reports and interviews, and relatively small treatment and control samples. Small sample sizes mean that most family therapy research studies have low statistical power, making it harder to detect true differences when they do exist. In contrast, meta-analysis may be less important in a field such as demography, which can access a large volume of meaningful data through national telephone surveys or existing data archives. Given the complexity of the phenomena of interest in family therapy, the field of necessity depends on an *accumulation* of knowledge from studies involving relatively small samples and a wide range of methodological rigor. Evaluation of the relation of different types of methodological problems to study findings is included as part of a good meta-analysis and greatly helps the reader evaluate results.

Assumptions

As a quantitative methodology, meta-analysis rests on the same assumptions as quantitative research in general: that knowledge can be gained from scientific study of phenomena and that quantifying or representing phenomena in terms of numbers is meaningful. It is assumed that knowledge integrated across a number of studies is superior to that from separate studies and that the common metric used is meaningful. In essence, meta-analysis produces information that is far more general than that in an individual study. For example, scores for several different measures of marital satisfaction would likely be reported in terms of standard deviation units instead of reporting something specific such as "the mean score on the Dyadic Adjustment Scale for this sample was 105."

Meta-analysis is a general methodology and is not associated with any one theory. Whether a particular meta-analysis is consistent with a particular theory, such as systems theory, would depend on the conceptualization the researcher used to guide the meta-analysis. The most important and the most controversial assumption of meta-analysis is that the individual studies on which the meta-analysis is based have yielded meaningful and valid results. Critics have argued that meta-analysis produces a "garbage in–garbage out" problem and can make meaningless and invalid results look important by aggregating across several studies (Michelson, 1985; Wanous, Sullivan, & Malinak, 1989). Meta-analysts agree that the ultimate value of the meta-analysis rests on the validity of the individual studies included and has developed quantifiable ways to assess the impact of methodological inadequacies on study findings.

Historical Development

Although quantitative methods for combining results across studies have existed since the 1930s, the term "meta-analysis" was coined by Glass (1976). The meta-analysis by

Smith and Glass (1977) on the effectiveness of psychotherapy (later expanded into a book, Smith, Glass, & Miller, 1980) was the first widely cited study labeled "meta-analysis," even though other quantitative literature reviews had been published before the famous Smith and Glass meta-analysis. Meta-analysis is really a "family" of approaches to quantitative integration of research studies (Bangert-Drowns, 1986). Influential books (Cooper & Hedges, 1994; Glass, McGaw, & Smith, 1981; Hedges & Olkin, 1985; Hunter & Schmidt, 1990; Rosenthal, 1991; Wachter & Straf, 1990; Wolf, 1968) discuss important variations of meta-analysis.

Meta-analysis grew out of the increasing recognition that advancement of knowledge was relying much too heavily on the statistical significance test, which boils down findings to a "yes" or "no," resulting in the loss of much relevant information (Cohen, 1969; Rosnow & Rosenthal, 1989). Research information summarized and integrated in terms of the significance statistic, as in the traditional narrative review, obscures information on the magnitude of effects, information of critical interest to clinicians and other family practitioners. Overreliance on the statistical significance test results from exaggerated concern with type I error (the probability of finding a significant difference when there is none) and the neglect of issues of statistical power and type II error (the probability of finding no difference when there is one). This imbalance is the reason most narrative reviews, based as they are on significance tests (yielding yes–no conclusions concerning whether any difference exists), reach much more conservative and less accurate conclusions about the impact of treatment than meta-analytic reviews that use effect size estimates. (See Beaman, 1991; Lipsey & Wilson, 1993; Rosenthal, 1991; and Schmidt, 1992, for a more extended discussion.)

The rapid development and acceptance of meta-analysis as a methodology can be seen in the number of articles referenced in *PsychLit* between 1976 and 1993 with meta-analysis as a keyword (see Figure 13.1). Meta-analysis is well accepted by researchers and editors in many fields, but particularly in medicine, where meta-analysis is used to integrate results from clinical trials (Cook et al., 1993; Thompson & Pocock, 1991), in psychology, and in education. Meta-analysis has not been used extensively in family studies or in marriage and family therapy although some meta-analytical studies exist (cf. Giblin, Sprenkle, & Sheehan, 1985; Shadish et al., 1993; Wampler, 1982).

Articles specifically on the methodology of meta-analysis are also proliferating as meta-analytical techniques continue to become more complex and sophisticated. Indeed, Schmidt (1992) believes that some researchers will begin to specialize in meta-analysis rather than in primary research (individual research studies where data are collected directly data from research participants). Although meta-analysis continues to have its critics, it has become more and more accepted as a crucial and valid methodology for the advancement of knowledge. Unfortunately, many researchers receive no training in meta-analytical techniques. Knowledge of the meta-analytical approach will be increasingly expected of both researchers and consumers of research.

METHODOLOGY

We have identified eight steps in performing a meta-analysis (see Table 13.1). These steps are similar to those of a primary research study but with a focus here on obtaining data from already completed research studies rather than directly from research participants. In the following sections, each step and the decisions associated with that step are discussed in turn.

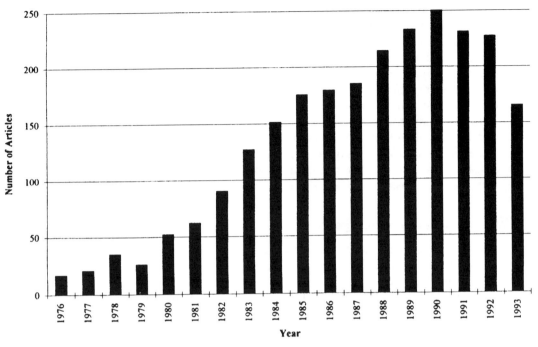

FIGURE 13.1. Number of meta-analysis articles in *PsychLit,* 1976–1993.

Research Questions

The first step is to select an appropriate research question to test based on a thorough knowledge of the research literature on a topic. The purpose of the research question may be description or hypothesis testing (Durlak & Lipsey, 1991). The following sections address three common types of research questions tested by meta-analysts.

To illustrate the steps used in meta-analysis, two examples are used throughout this section. One based on differences between group means and one involving correlations. The first example, experimental in nature, is outcome research on the Couple Communication (CC) Program, a four-session communication program for couples (Miller, Miller, Wackman, & Nunnally, 1991). Wampler completed a meta-analysis of research on CC in 1982, again as an illustration of the use of meta-analysis as a methodology. Examples from the original meta-analysis involving 20 studies are used as well as an

TABLE 13.1. Steps to Performing a Meta-Analysis

Step 1: Selection of an appropriate research question to test.

Step 2: Identification of relevant studies.

Step 3: Establishing criteria for inclusion and exclusion of studies.

Step 4: Data collection and coding.

Step 5: Data entry.

Step 6: Determining and calculating the common metric.

Step 7: Data analysis.

Step 8: Report writing.

update of that meta-analysis with an additional 15 studies. CC research involves one common independent variable (the CC program itself) and a set of pre–post designs that are easy to conceptualize in terms of effect size. Examples of research questions for the CC meta-analysis were as follows: (1) How effective is the CC program? (2) Does CC have an impact more on women's or men's views of the couple relationship?

A contrasting correlational example is research on knowledge of HIV and AIDS developed to test a model involving several different independent and dependent variables. In this study, the researchers were interested in the relationship between the independent variables of knowledge of HIV/AIDS and attitude toward HIV/AIDS with the dependent variables of risky behavior and perceptions of vulnerability. Instead of investigating pre–post designs, this model seeks to condense extensive literature investigating the relationship between these variables.

Effectiveness-of-Treatment Questions

Meta-analysis is a general methodology for integrating information across research studies and, as such, is not limited to any particular type of question. A limitation on meta-analysis arises from the availability of basic research on a topic. For example, many family therapists would be interested in the question of the relative effectiveness of solution-focused as compared to problem-focused approaches to a problem, but a meta-analysis on such a question would not be appropriate because insufficient primary research has been done on this topic.

Meta-analysis has been used most often to address the question of the effectiveness of some treatment. Information about differences between experimental and control groups in terms of effect size is obtained and summarized across studies. Here effect size is simply the standardized difference between two groups, for example, $(M_e - M_c)/SD_{pooled}$. Meta-analysts can focus on specific questions, such as, "What is the impact of a team calling into the therapy room?" to very general questions, such as, "What is the effectiveness of marriage and family therapy?"

All the meta-analyses completed in the area of marriage and family therapy have been summaries of treatment effectiveness focused at the level of general questions. Meta-analyses have been completed on the general effectiveness of marital and family therapy (Hazelrigg, Cooper, & Borduin, 1987; Shadish, et al., 1993), on behavioral marital and/or family therapy (Hahlweg & Markman, 1988; Shadish, 1992), and on marital or parenting enrichment programs (Cedar & Levant, 1990; Giblin et al., 1985; Wampler, 1982). Examples of closely related meta-analyses include those of psychotherapy effectiveness in general (cf. Lipsey & Wilson, 1993; Smith & Glass, 1977; Smith et al., 1980) and comparisons of marital satisfaction and parental well-being by family status (Amato, 1991; Amato & Keith, 1991; Vemer, Coleman, Ganong, & Cooper, 1989). All these meta-analyses are of experiments; that is, they examine the impact of some condition (e.g., treatment or family structure) on a set of outcomes.

Methodological Questions

Study quality is addressed in meta-analyses on substantive issues. Meta-analysis can also be used, however, primarily to address a methodological issue. Meta-analysis can be used to help establish reliability and validity for a measure by summarizing information about a particular scale across studies. For example, in a meta-analysis of primary research on a personality measure, a procedure was used to integrate results of factor analyses of the measure across several studies (Bushman, Cooper, & Lemke, 1991). In another, outcome measures used in agoraphobia studies were identified, effect sizes for different types of measures were calculated, and the most promising instruments were identified. As part of a summary of meta-analyses on psychological and educational treatments, Lipsey and Wilson (1993) included a meta-analysis of methodological biases that might lead to inflation of effect sizes. Although most methodological biases were found not to substantially inflate effect sizes, study designs using only one group (the experimental or treatment group) pre and post were found to have inflated effect sizes compared with studies including both an experimental and a control group. In a more fine-grained analysis, Ambady and Rosenthal (1992) examined the accuracy of predictions based on length of behavioral observation and found that accuracy did not increase with longer length of time observed, suggesting that brief observations can provide as much useful information as longer ones.

The usefulness of meta-analysis for examining methodological issues has barely begun to be exploited. Such recurrent methodological issues in family therapy research as the similarity of constructs measured by different family measures, gender differences in perceptions of the marriage and family, and the appropriateness of different family measures across cultures could be effectively addressed with meta-analysis. Such studies are important to the field of marriage and family therapy and can offer valuable information to future researchers.

Theoretical Questions

Perhaps the most exciting use of meta-analysis, one that is being increasingly developed, is testing theoretical models (Cooper & Lemke, 1991). Meta-analysis can be used to test main effects (e.g., all couples will benefit from CC) as well as interactions (e.g., middle-class couples will benefit more from CC than working-class couples). Generally, in this type of meta-analysis, the researcher develops a model and then tests the model by summarizing the evidence for each of the hypothesized relations using meta-analytical techniques. The correlation is usually the common metric used to summarize across studies (Rosenthal & Rubin, 1982). Providing a good example of meta-analysis used to test theory, Shadish and Sweeney (1991) present evidence for a model investigating moderators and mediators affecting marital and family therapy outcome.

Sampling and Selection Procedures

As in any methodology, there are few definitively correct answers but, rather, a series of choices that must be made, justified, and tested. A great deal of the controversy about meta-analysis has centered on the choice of studies to be included (high quality vs. all; published vs. all) and the unit of analysis to use (study finding, study, subject).

Identification of Relevant Studies

Step 2, and a crucial part of meta-analysis, is identification of the population of relevant studies. The goal is to identify and sample studies in a way that those studies included in the meta-analysis are an unbiased sample of the primary research studies available on a topic. In essence, the studies included in a meta-analysis must have something in common related to the research question. The "something in common" may be an independent variable (e.g., participation in a CC group), a dependent variable (e.g., knowledge of HIV/AIDS), a measure (e.g., use of Family Adaptability and Cohesion Evaluation Scales, or FACES), or a set of variables (e.g., all studies on strategic family therapy and conduct disorder).

As with any research process, the research question and the methodology constantly influence each other. For example, the researcher may not be able to locate enough studies on a particular topic, making the meta-analysis inappropriate for that research question. As relevant articles are identified and reviewed, the research question may need to be modified. For example, one possible research question on the CC research is a comparison of the effectiveness of CC for middle-class and working-class couples. Unfortunately, not enough studies are available with data separated by social class for such a comparison to be made. Similarly, one of the problems in the knowledge of HIV/AIDS meta-analysis has been the lack of a common measure of knowledge. Comparing results of studies that used different measures is commonly referred to as the "apples and oranges" problem of meta-analysis.

In meta-analysis, the researcher strives to identify *all relevant research studies*. Sources are painstakingly searched manually and by computer and include reference lists of relevant articles and book chapters, standard social science abstracts (*Psychological Abstracts, Sociological Abstracts*), compilations of unpublished material (*Educational Resources Information Center, Dissertation Abstracts International*), and other databases (*Social Science Citation Index*). Although computers have helped immensely in identifying studies, there is no substitute for a thoughtful and dogged approach to the search, including, inevitably, manual searches. The search may include contacting key researchers for references and, sometimes, even for unpublished data. The care and time needed for this step are crucial to the quality of the meta-analysis. Sources vary widely in terms of identifying key studies. For example, Shadish, Doherty, and Montgomery (1989) in their search of the marriage and family therapy outcome literature identified 165 randomized controlled studies, many more than were included in other reviews and meta-analyses of the marriage and family therapy outcome literature. Shadish et al. (1989) document the nonoverlap of studies identified through different methods and caution especially against relying solely on key word searches of bibliographic data bases for identifying relevant studies.

> *CC Example.* CC research was fairly easy to locate. Manual and computer searches were made using combinations of keywords (COUPLE, COMMUNICATION, ENRICHMENT, MARITAL/MARRIAGE, PREVENTION). The major sources for research studies were *Psychological Abstracts* and *Dissertation Abstracts International*. The main developer of the program (Sherod Miller) was contacted and asked to identify research studies. *Social Science Citation Index* was searched using a few, early key articles on CC that most authors would cite. Some researchers were contacted directly because it was understood that they were engaged in CC research. This located some articles in press. Articles were obtained through inter-library loan or the University library. Most CC research is in dissertations, and these were purchased from the University Microfilms International, at a relatively expensive per item charge.

> *HIV/AIDS Example.* To identify relevant HIV/AIDS studies, *PsychLit, Sociofile,* and ERIC were searched using combinations of the key words AIDS, HIV, KNOWLEDGE, ATTITUDES, PERCEPTIONS, and BEHAVIOR. In addition, *Dissertation Abstracts International* was searched for unpublished data along with a thorough check of the reference sections of each of the articles found for presented papers and those in review.

Inclusion and Exclusion Criteria

Step 3 is determining which inclusion and exclusion criteria to use to select exactly which of the identified studies should be included in the meta-analysis. The key is to be *explicit* and to give a *rationale* for the choices made.

Basic criteria include (1) relevance to the research question; (2) sufficient similarity of variables, design, sample, and/or measures (apples-and-oranges problem); (3) availability of the research report; (4) inclusion of appropriate and sufficient data and statistical findings in the research report; and (5) elimination of nonindependent data sets (e.g., two studies drawn from the same database). The researcher might add other specific criteria as well, for example, including only studies on distressed (clinical) populations or only studies with data on more than one family member. Some may want to specify a relevant time period (e.g., only research done since 1985). Again, the researcher needs to defend each decision just as the primary researcher would defend sampling decisions made in other types of research.

The validity of the conclusions reached in a meta-analysis depends on the quality of the primary research studies included. The predominant view in meta-analysis is to include studies with a range of methodological rigor and then systematically assess the relation of various methodological problems to meta-analysis results. It is particularly important to include unpublished research studies, especially dissertations, and even studies completed but never published (sometimes called "file drawer data") (Cook et al., 1993; Rosenthal, 1991). Meta-analysts have provided clear evidence that effect sizes for published data are larger than effect sizes for unpublished data because of a publication bias toward significant findings (Cook et al., 1993). Thus, if unpublished data are eliminated, effect size estimates are likely to be inflated.

Once other criteria are met, there is no set criteria in terms of number of studies to be included in a meta-analysis. In fact, the number of studies in each separate meta-analysis included by Lipsey and Wilson (1993) ranged from 5 to 475.

Data Collection and Coding Procedures

Once research studies are identified and evaluated in terms of inclusion and exclusion criteria, step 4 is to obtain the data needed from each study. The most important data are the relevant effect sizes (discussed in the next section). Additional data are coded having to do with the characteristics of the study. These variables will be used in describing the studies included in the meta-analysis as well as in analyzing variables related to effect size. Particular variables differ according to the nature and purpose of the meta-analysis, but most include data related to (1) sample characteristics, (2) methodological quality, (3) independent variables, (4) dependent variables, and (5) moderator or mediator variables. Detailed information about measures must be included along with appropriate numerical results.

To collect the data needed from each study, it is important to develop a detailed codebook specifying what and how data are to be collected. Many published meta-analyses state that the codebook is available from the author. Texts on meta-analysis include examples as well. The codebook developed for the CC study is included as the Appendix. It is divided into sections corresponding to study characteristics, ratings of methodological quality, and results in terms of effect sizes for each measure at pretest, posttest, and follow-up. The quality rating scale for the correlational meta-analysis to test a model of HIV/AIDS knowledge is included as Table 13.2.

As with any data collection and coding task, training of coders and reliability checks are essential. It is important, therefore, for a second coder to retrieve data from at least a subset of studies in order to document accuracy and interrater agreement. This is also important for ratings of methodological rigor. Information on interrater agreement would be reported as part of the methods section of the meta-analysis. Yeaton and Worthman

TABLE 13.2. Quality Rating for Study: Correlational Studies

Criteria	Points
Used established measures	5
Used multiple measures of dependent variable(s)	1
Multiple vantage points	1
Appropriate statistical analysis	5
Reported past reliability of measures	1
Reported current reliability of measures	2
Reported information on validity	2
Sufficiently describes measures	1
Sufficiently describes sampling	1
Sufficiently describes results	1
Accounted for response set bias	1
Replicability of procedures	1
Sufficient power/sample size	3
Tested for confounds; accounted for covariates	5

Range: 0–30

Score: _____

(1993) have written about different ways to think about and calculate interrater agreement for a meta-analysis.

Step 5 is actual data entry. At this point, the meta-analyst usually enters the information into a computerized database. Meta-analysts have two options for data entry. One option is to enter the data into computer programs written specifically for meta-analysis (cf. Johnson, 1993; Mullen, 1989). These programs have limitations, but potential users may obtain a demonstration program from the publisher for a nominal fee to examine the utility of the program. A second option would be to enter the data into commonly used database programs or files created through statistical software.

Data Analysis Procedures

Determining and Calculating the Common Metric

After the data from each study are collected, coded, entered, and checked for accuracy and reliability, step 6 is to determine and calculate the common metric to be used in combining data across studies. Again, there is no one correct common metric to use. The choice of the common metric depends on the type of meta-analysis and on the type of data produced at the level of the individual study finding.

Although there are numerous variations, the common metric used in most meta-analyses is either a standardized difference between group means—$(M_e - M_c)/SD_{pooled}$—or the product–moment correlation coefficient. The major sources on meta-analysis (cf. Cohen, 1969; Glass et al., 1981; Hedges & Olkin, 1985; Rosenthal, 1991) provide formulas for computing the different measures of effect size, as well as formulas for converting different statistics (e.g., t, F, and chi-square) into either of the two basic types of common metric. Difference-between-means statistics can easily be converted to the product moment correlation and vice versa (Rosenthal, 1991). The computer programs available for meta-analysis (cf. Johnson, 1993; Mullen, 1989) are designed to convert different statistics into effect sizes, although the researcher can also write the necessary computer programs using statistical packages such as SPSS and SAS or do the calculations by hand.

The major sources on meta-analysis also contain ways of estimating the common metric when some information is missing (e.g., report means, but not standard deviations). This occurs somewhat often, unfortunately, but there are ways to take available information and convert it to an effect size. In other situations—for example, when results are only labeled "not significant"—the meta-analyst may choose to set the effect size to 0. Again, the key is to be explicit about your decision rule and to provide a rationale.

Interpreting Effect Sizes

How an effect size is interpreted depends on the common metric utilized for that particular study. Effect sizes are generally categorized as small, medium, or large. Studies using the r statistic produce effect sizes varying in magnitude from between $+1.00$ and -1.00 reflecting the range of a correlation. According to Cohen (1969), an effect size using the r statistic is large if above .50, medium at .30 and small at .10. Using the standardized difference between two groups (d statistic), however, effect sizes vary in magnitude from $+3.00$ to -3.00 reflecting the normal curve. These would be interpreted as being the difference between groups expressed as the percentage of a standard deviation and considered large if above .80, medium at .50, and small at .20 (Cohen, 1969). A positive effect size indicates that the treatment group improved over the control group; a negative effect size indicates the opposite with improvement on the part of the control versus treatment group. The interested reader might consult Cohen (1969, 1992) for additional information on statistical power interpretations.

Unit of Analysis and Weighting

Before further analysis, data may be combined or weighted. It is rare that the unit of analysis is each separate effect size because studies that use many measures would be weighted most heavily in the results of the overall meta-analysis and the effect sizes are not independent. For example, number of possible effect sizes generated for each CC study ranged from 1 to 14 for each type of contrast. To avoid this problem, some meta-analysts use the study itself as the unit of analysis by combining into one all effect sizes within a study prior to proceeding with analyses across studies. Unfortunately, this means much precision can be lost. A compromise alternative is to combine related effect sizes according to a few key constructs, thus limiting the number of effect sizes but still leaving more than one effect size per study. This alternative allows for meaningful flexibility and precise model testing while still being responsive to the issues of independence and overall weighting of studies within the meta-analysis. In the CC meta-analysis, for example, it would make sense to compute an effect size for self-report measures and a separate one for observational measures rather than combining effect sizes across all measures in a study. Before proceeding further, some meta-analysts weight the individual data points according to certain study criteria, whereas others do not. For example, one common weighting is by sample size using the inverse of the variance (Hedges & Olkin, 1985, p. 81, equation 10). Weighting for sample size is especially important for samples under 30. On the other hand, some meta-analysts will use unweighted effect sizes or correlations and then compare results by sample size. Others do not weight but, instead, turn this issue into an empirical question, for example, comparing effect sizes for studies with random assignment to those without random assignment. (See Hedges & Olkin, 1985; Durlak & Lipsey, 1991; Hunter & Schmidt, 1990; National Research Council, 1992; Rosenthal, 1991, for discussions of the issue of weighting.)

Statistical Analyses of Research Questions

At this point the meta-analyst is ready move to step 7 to analyze the data in terms of the research questions guiding the meta-analysis. Techniques specifically designed for meta-analysis have become increasingly sophisticated (Hedges & Olkin, 1985; Hunter & Schmidt, 1990). Careful consideration is given to meeting statistical assumptions, particularly those of homogeneity of variance.

As in a primary research study, statistical analysis moves from description (central tendency, variation, range, distribution) to analysis of the research questions in terms of independent and dependent variables using analysis of variance and/or regression techniques, depending on how the research questions are stated. A unique aspect of meta-analysis is that it affords the opportunity to perform statistical analyses related to methodological questions (e.g., comparing effect sizes for controlled vs. noncontrolled studies) as well as substantive questions (e.g., comparing effect sizes at posttest with those at follow-up).

Format for Reporting the Meta-Analysis

Step 8 is writing up the results of the meta-analysis. Meta-analyses have appeared in a wide variety of journals, including those of the highest quality. Although still not common in family studies and in marriage and family therapy, a large number of meta-analyses and articles on technical aspects of meta-analysis have appeared in *Psychological Bulletin*, one of the most prestigious social science journals.

The format of an article reporting a meta-analysis is more similar to that for a quantitative study than for a narrative review article. The introduction of the research question(s) and the relevant review of literature is followed by the methods section, the results section, and the discussion of results. The reference section often, but not always, includes two parts, one for those mentioned in the article and a second for those research studies included in the meta-analysis itself.

Although the form and intent of each section of the report are the same as for a primary research study, the content differs. In the methods section, instead of describing a sample, the meta-analyst describes the identification and retrieval of studies, inclusion and exclusion criteria, and characteristics of the studies. The latter often includes a section on research participants as well (e.g., gender, age, social class, and race/ethnicity), but across all the studies involved, not study by study. Instead of measures, a description of how independent and dependent variables were grouped is included along with a description of the means of calculating effect sizes. Measures of methodological adequacy are described along with procedures to ensure accuracy and reliability of coding. The results section contains the statistical analyses across studies. The discussion section, as with any research report, contains an evaluation of results, connections back to the literature, and implications for research and practice (if in a clinical area).

EVALUATION

Strengths and Weaknesses

Meta-analysis has clear advantages over the narrative review of the literature including precision, objectivity, and replicability. The major summary of meta-analyses of treatment completed by Lipsey and Wilson (1993) is an example of the kind of power meta-analysis provides as a methodology. In one article, the results of 302 meta-analyses, themselves representing many research studies, are summarized in terms of effect size (the standardized difference between an intervention and a control group), in a straightforward manner that is easily translated into terms understood by the clinician. An extensive evaluation of these results allows the reader to review the validity of the findings. Meta-analysis lessens the probability of type II error by taking more information into account than simply whether results reach a certain level of statistical significance, avoiding the problems with narrative reviews and analyses that overemphasize avoidance of type I error.

Meta-analysis is not as useful in less developed areas of research. Unfortunately, this includes several areas of interest to marriage and family therapists. Until the primary research is done, many of the important questions will not be amenable to meta-analysis. Thus, it is not a problem with the method but, rather, a problem with the availability of basic research in the field. Of course, meta-analysis cannot be used to aggregate across qualitative studies. Of necessity, meta-analysis focuses on general questions, of broad interest and lacks the detail that the reader might desire. For example, a detailed examination and description of individual measures and treatments would not usually be included in a meta-analysis, nor would case examples or excerpts from transcripts illustrating the study findings.

Most problematic, a meta-analysis, even one done poorly, can be impressive and influential because the results are said to represent a large number of research studies and a large number of research respondents. Boiling down research in an area to a single number, say, 70% rate of success, presents an obvious danger of being taken out of context and separated from the important cautions that would accompany such a statement. Because of its potent influence, perhaps even more than with primary research, it is important for the consumer of meta-analyses to be able to look beyond the results and critically consider the meta-analytical methodology that generated them. Only such a careful and knowledgeable approach to meta-analytical research can help ensure clinical and policy interpretations and conclusions that neither misinterpret nor overstate the weight of meta-analytical findings. This, of course, speaks to the importance of educating researchers, clinicians, and policymakers in the basics of meta-analytical research, just as we do now with primary research, so that they *can* be critical consumers.

Reliability and Validity

An important way to assess the quality of a meta-analysis, as with a primary research study, is the extent to which the authors make their methodology clear and explicit, so that the meta-analysis could be replicated. The reader should be able to evaluate the meta-analysis based on the information given in the research report. Important documentation criteria include reporting (1) procedures for retrieval of all relevant studies, (2) clear standards for study inclusion, (3) procedures for assessing accuracy and reliability of information retrieval from the individual studies, and (4) assessment of the relation of individual study methodological quality to the results of the meta-analysis.

It is important to remember that the validity of the meta-analysis ultimately rests on the quality of the individual research studies that are included. That is again why it is crucial that the meta-analyst present data on how methodological characteristics of individual studies relate to the results of the meta-analysis.

Skills Needed

Conceptual and analytical skills are most important in meta-analysis. The researcher must be able to derive important questions from existing literature and then determine how to organize the results of many studies in a way that is meaningful and clear. While paying attention to the details of individual studies, the meta-analyst cannot be caught up in detail. A meta-analysis also requires the attitude of a detective. It takes a persistent, dogged, and creative effort to identify, locate, and obtain the studies that become the basis of a meta-analysis. The meta-analyst needs to maintain an objective attitude and be committed to reporting the results and evaluating them regardless of outcome.

Basic training in both primary research and meta-analytical methods is important to the researcher undertaking meta-analysis. The meta-analyst must thoroughly review and critically evaluate each primary research study. The extensive literature on meta-analysis as an approach, and the number of examples of meta-analysis, makes it possible for someone trained in primary research to undertake a meta-analysis, although specific training in meta-analysis is necessary.

Bridging Research and Practice

As with any research, the results of a meta-analysis provide information to help the clinician in decision making but do not provide answers as to how to treat a particular couple or family. As Thompson and Pocock (1991) state in reference to the usefulness to physicians of meta-analyses of clinical trials, meta-analysis does not provide simple answers to "complex clinical problems" (p. 338).

Meta-analysts provide important information on broad issues to clinicians and policymakers. Probably the most important functions of meta-analysis are to integrate, summarize, and evaluate the results of a large number of individual studies in a way that is accessible to practitioners. By "boiling down" results into a few findings expressed in the metric of effect size or correlation, the meta-analysis provides an accessible and effective overview. Effect size can be translated into terms easily understood and evaluated by the clinician. For example, knowing that attending four sessions of the CC program, on average, produces an effect size of .52 means that, on average, couples completing CC were half a standard deviation more improved in terms of relationship satisfaction than were control couples not attending CC.

Other methods are being developed to translate effect sizes into terms meaningful to clinicians. Rosenthal and Rubin (1982) developed the binomial effect size display, which puts effect sizes in terms of the proportion of control and treatment subjects above a specified level. It is also possible to put results in terms of cost-benefit (Durlak & Lipsey, 1991).

FUTURE DIRECTIONS FOR META-ANALYSIS IN FAMILY THERAPY RESEARCH

To date, meta-analysis has been used in marriage and family therapy only to evaluate overall treatment effectiveness. As more research is done, that function of meta-analysis will remain important. More evidence is needed as to the basic effectiveness of marriage and family therapy as opposed to other approaches. Unfortunately, in many areas, the use of meta-analysis will have to await further basic research. In others, however, enough research is already available to make meta-analysis appropriate. For example, family psychoeducational approaches to severe mental illness, spouse-aided therapy, and family approaches to drug and alcohol treatment are already good candidates for meta-analysis.

Meta-analysis is also useful for looking at components of therapy, conditions under which therapy is more or less successful, fit between problem type and therapy, and characteristics of the therapist and training related to outcome. The analysis by Shadish and Sweeney (1991) is an excellent example. Finally, meta-analysis can be effectively used now to evaluate methodological issues in family therapy research, particularly the validity of different observational and self-report measures of marital and family functioning.

APPENDIX: CODEBOOK FOR COUPLE COMMUNICATION STUDIES

Identification

STUDY IDENTIFICATION NUMBER _____
YEAR OF PUBLICATION _____
FORM OF PUBLICATION ____
  1. Dissertation
  2. Journal article
  3. Book or book chapter

  4. Unpublished manuscript
  5. Other

Sample

MARITAL STATUS ____
  1. Married
  2. Engaged
  3. Other

SOCIAL CLASS ____
  1. Middle class
  2. Working class
  3. Mixed

SETTING ____
  1. Urban
  2. Suburban
  3. Rural
  4. University
  5. Unspecified/general
  6. Mixed

RACE/ETHNICITY ____
  1. Nonminority
  2. Minority
  3. Mixed
  4. Unspecified

DISTRESS LEVEL ____
  1. General population
  2. Distressed
  3. Not distressed

  4. Mixed
  5. Unspecified

Methodology

STUDY DESIGN ____
  1. CC only, Pre–post
  2. CC plus control, Pre–post
  3. CC plus comparison, Pre–post
  4. CC plus control plus comparison, Pre–post
  5. CC only, Pre–post–follow

6. CC plus control, Pre–post–follow
7. CC plus comparison, Pre–post–follow
8. CC plus control plus comparison, Pre–post–follow

TYPE OF COMPARISON GROUP ____
1. Growth/enrichment group
2. Behavior training
3. Communication skills/other

4. Concurrent CC
5. Sex therapy
6. Relationship enhancement (RE)

LENGTH OF FOLLOW-UP IN MONTHS _____

TYPE OF CC ____
1. Standard, described
2. Standard, not described

3. Modified

Note: Leave blank if missing or not applicable

NATURE OF ASSIGNMENT TO CONDITION ____
1. Random
2. Matched then random/stratified random
3. Not random
4. Not specified

Quality Ratings

(Adapted from Gurman & Kniskern, 1978, pp. 820–821)
1. Controlled assignment to conditions (5 points) __.__
2. Pre–post measurement (5 points) __.__
3. IV not contaminated, experience level, therapist per treatment group, competence (5 points) __.__
4. Appropriate statistical analysis (1) __.__
5. Follow-up: None (0), 1–3 mos. (.5) 3 mos + (1) __.__
6. Treatments equally valued (1) __.__
7. Treatment carried out as planned: Presumptive evidence (.5), clear evidence (1) __.__
8. Multiple change indices used (1) __.__
9. Multiple vantage points in assessing outcome (1) __.__
10. Outcome not limited to only IP (1) __.__
11. Data on concurrent treatment: none or equivalent across groups (1), mention, but no documentation (.5) __.__
12. Equal treatment length across conditions (1) __.__
13. Outcome allows for both positive and negative change (1) __.__
14. Therapist–investigator nonequivalence (1) __.__
15. Sufficient power/sample size (1) __.__
16. Dropouts/attrition followed (1), followed and analyzed (2) __.__
17. Check on equivalence of groups (1) __.__

TOTAL QUALITY SCORE _____.__

Effect Sizes

FOR EACH EFFECT SIZE:
ID _____
EFFECT SIZE NUMBER _____
TYPE _____
01. CC only, Pre–post
02. CC only, Pre–follow
03. CC plus control, Pre–post
04. CC plus control, Pre–follow
05. CC plus control, Post only

06. CC plus control, Follow only
07. CC plus comparison, Pre–post
08. CC plus comparison, Pre–follow
09. CC plus comparison, Post only
10. CC plus comparison, Follow only

DOMAIN OF MEASURE _____
01. Observation of marital interaction (B)
02. Self-report of relationship satisfaction (R)
03. Self-report of communication (C)
04. Self-report of other relationship quality (OR)
05. Self-report of individual quality (OI)
06. Other (O)

EFFECT SIZE _____._____
SAMPLE SIZE ON WHICH EFFECT SIZE IS BASED
CC _____ CONTROL _____ COMPARISON ____

ACKNOWLEDGMENT

The authors appreciate the assistance of Mark H. Butler and Judy A. Kimberly.

REFERENCES

Amato, P. R. (1991). Parental divorce and adult well-being: A meta-analysis. *Journal of Marriage and the Family, 53,* 43–58.

Amato, P. R., & Keith, B. (1991). Parental divorce and the well-being of children: A meta-analysis. *Psychological Bulletin, 110,* 26–46.

Ambady, N., & Rosenthal, R. (1992). Thin slices of expressive behavior as predictors of interpersonal consequences: A meta-analysis. *Psychological Bulletin, 111,* 256–274.

Bangert-Drowns, R. L. (1986). Review of developments in meta-analytic method. *Psychological Bulletin, 99,* 388–399.

Beaman, A. L. (1991). An empirical comparison of meta-analytic and traditional reviews. *Personality and Social Psychology Bulletin, 17,* 252–257.

Bushman, B. J., Cooper, H. M., & Lemke, K. M. (1991). Meta-analysis of factor analyses: An illustration using the Buss–Durkee hostility inventory. *Personality and Social Psychology Bulletin, 17,* 344–349.

Carson, K. P., Schriesheim, C. A., & Kinicki, A. J. (1990). The usefulness of the "fail-safe" statistic in meta-analysis. *Educational and Psychological Measurement, 50,* 233–243.

Cedar, B., & Levant, R. F. (1990). A meta-analysis of the effects of parent effectiveness training. *American Journal of Family Therapy, 18,* 373–384.

Cohen, J. (1969). *Statistical power analysis for the behavior sciences.* New York: Academic Press.

Cohen, J. (1992). A power primer. *Psychological Bulletin, 112,* 155–159.

Cook, D. J., Guyatt, G. H., Ryan, G., Clifton, J., Buckingham, L., Willan, A., McIllroy, W., & Oxman, A. D. (1993). Should unpublished data be included in meta-analyses? *Journal of the American Medical Association, 269,* 2749–2753.

Cooper, H. M., & Hedges, L. (Eds.). (1994). *Handbook of research synthesis.* New York: Russell Sage Foundation.

Cooper, H. M., & Lemke, K. M. (1991). On the role of meta-analysis in personality and social psychology. *Personality and Social Psychology Bulletin, 17,* 245–251.

Durlak, J. A., & Lipsey, M. W. (1991). A practitioner's guide to meta-analysis. *American Journal of Community Psychology, 19,* 291–332.

Giblin, P., Sprenkle, D., & Sheehan, R. (1985). Enrichment outcome research: A meta-analysis of premarital, marital and family interventions. *Journal of Marital and Family Therapy, 11,* 257–271.

Glass, G. (1976). Primary, secondary and meta-analysis of research. *Education Researcher, 5*, 3–8.

Glass, G., McGaw, B., & Smith, M. (1981). *Meta-analysis in social research.* Beverly Hills, CA: Sage.

Gurman, A. S., & Kniskern, D. P. (1978). Research on marital and family therapy: Program, perspective, and prospect. In S. Garfield & A. Bergin (Eds.), *Handbook of psychotherapy and behavior change: An empirical analysis* (pp. 820–821). New York: Wiley.

Hahlweg, K., & Markman, H. J. (1988). Effectiveness of behavioral marital therapy: Empirical status of behavioral techniques in preventing and alleviating marital distress. *Journal of Consulting and Clinical Psychology, 56*, 440–447.

Hazelrigg, M. D., Cooper, H. M., & Borduin, C. M. (1987). Evaluating the effectiveness of family therapies: An integrative review and analysis. *Psychological Bulletin, 101*, 428–442.

Hedges, L. V., & Olkin, I. (1985). *Statistical methods for meta-analysis.* Orlando, FL: Academic Press.

Hunter, J. E., & Schmidt, F. L. (1990). *Methods of meta-analysis: Correcting error and bias in research findings.* Newbury Park, CA: Sage.

Johnson, B. T. (1993). *DSTAT software for the meta-analytic review of research literature.* Hillsdale, NJ: Erlbaum.

Lipsey, M. W., & Wilson, D. B. (1993). The efficacy of psychological, educational, and behavioral treatment. *American Psychologist, 48*, 1181–1209.

Michelson, L. (1985). Editorial: Introduction and commentary. *Clinical Psychological Review, 5*, 1–2.

Miller, S., Miller, P., Wackman, D., & Nunnally, E. W. (1991). *Couple communication.* Littleton, CO: Interpersonal Communication Programs.

Mullen, B. (1989). *Advanced BASIC meta-analysis.* Hillsdale, NJ: Erlbaum.

National Research Council. (1992). *Combining information: Statistical issues and opportunities for research.* Washington, DC: National Academy Press.

Rosenthal, R. (1991). *Meta-analytic procedures for social research.* Beverly Hills, CA: Sage.

Rosenthal, R., & Rubin, D. B. (1982). Comparing effect sizes of independent studies. *Psychological Bulletin, 92*, 1165–1168.

Rosnow, R. L., & Rosenthal, R. (1989). Statistical procedures and the justification of knowledge in psychological science. *American Psychologist, 44*, 1276–1284.

Schmidt, F. L. (1992). What do data really mean? Research findings, meta-analysis, and cumulative knowledge in psychology. *American Psychologist, 47*, 1173–1181.

Shadish, W. R. (1992). Do family and marital psychotherapies change what people do? A meta-analysis of behavioral outcomes. In T. D. Cook, H. Cooper, D. S. Cordray, H. Hartman, L. V. Hedges, R. J. Light, T. A. Louis, & F. Mosteller (Eds.), *Meta-analysis for exploration: A casebook* (pp. 129–208). New York: Russell Sage Foundation.

Shadish, W. R., Doherty, M., & Montgomery, L. M. (1989). How many studies are in the file drawer? An estimate from the family/marital psychotherapy literature. *Clinical Psychology Review, 9*, 589–603.

Shadish, W. R., Montgomery, L. M., Wilson, P., Wilson, M. R., Bright, I., & Okwumabua, T. (1993). Effects of family and marital psychotherapies: A meta-analysis. *Journal of Consulting and Clinical Psychology, 61*, 992–1002.

Shadish, W. R., & Sweeney, R. B. (1991). Mediators and moderators in meta-analysis: There's a reason we don't let dodo birds tell us which psychotherapies should have prizes. *Journal of Consulting and Clinical Psychology, 59*, 883–893.

Smith, M. L., & Glass, G. V. (1977). Meta-analysis of psychotherapy outcome studies. *American Psychologist, 32*, 752–760.

Smith, M. L., Glass, G. V., & Miller, T. I. (1980). *The benefits of psychotherapy.* Baltimore, MD: Johns Hopkins Press.

Thompson, S. G., & Pocock, S. J. (1991). Can meta-analyses be trusted? *Lancet, 338*, 1127–1130.

Vemer, E., Coleman, M., Ganong, L. H., & Cooper, H. (1989). Marital satisfaction in remarriage: A meta-analysis. *Journal of Marriage and the Family, 51*, 713–725.

Wachter, K. W., & Straf, M. L. (Eds.). (1990). *The future of meta-analysis.* New York: Russell Sage Foundation.

Wampler, K. (1982). Bringing the review of literature into the age of quantification: Meta-analysis as a strategy for integrating research findings in family studies. *Journal of Marriage and the Family, 44,* 1009–1023.

Wanous, J. P., Sullivan, S. E., & Malinak, J. (1989). The role of judgment calls in meta-analysis. *Journal of Applied Psychology, 74,* 259–264.

Wolf, F. M. (1986). *Meta-analysis: Quantitative methods for research synthesis.* Newbury Park, CA: Sage.

Yeaton, W. H., & Worthman, P. M. (1993). On the reliability of meta-analytic reviews: The role of intercoder agreement. *Evaluation Review, 17,* 292–309.

Relational/Predictive Research

14

Approaches to Prediction
CORRELATION, REGRESSION, AND DISCRIMINANT ANALYSIS

DOUGLAS K. SNYDER
LAUREL F. MANGRUM

PHILOSOPHICAL AND HISTORICAL UNDERPINNINGS

In many ways, scientific understanding of couples and families progresses in a manner similar to children's knowledge of their surrounding world. Like a child's first impression of the parent, science begins with an awareness of some phenomenon not yet understood but sensed to be important for further exploration. Exploration leads to efforts to refine the ability to recognize and define instances of occurrence and nonoccurrence, and this ability promotes efforts to quantify. Like the child's insight that parents provide nurturance, science progresses with the recognition that certain phenomena go hand in hand; the occurrence of one denotes the likelihood of the other, the absence of one the improbability of the other. It is this recognition of covariation between events that precedes the last stage of understanding reflected in the ability to influence or control one phenomenon by manipulating another. Thus, awareness leads to exploration, exploration to measurement, measurement to observation of covariation, and covariation to manipulation and influence.

We do not imply by this proposed progression that marital and family dynamics are either singular or unidirectional. Most phenomena are influenced by multiple other phenomena, and directions of influence are often recursive: A affects B, and B affects A. Nor does this progression acclaim quantitative approaches to the exclusion of qualitative ones; we have argued elsewhere that both play critical roles in the generation and verification of knowledge (Cavell & Snyder, 1991). Indeed, efforts to delineate covariation using quantitative techniques often proceed best when the phenomena selected for study have been identified through intensive qualitative methods. Rather, we propose that prediction strategies based on correlation and related procedures provide a useful bridge between observation of existing phenomena—whether qualitatively or quantitatively based—and attempts to modify the same.

Science based on covariation is as timeless as civilization. The recognition that seasons covary with celestial patterns prompted early astronomy as a basis for predicting optimal occasions for planting. Quantitative techniques emphasizing covariation took hold in the behavioral sciences in the late 1800s with the efforts of Sir Francis Galton, an English biologist, to establish an anthropometric laboratory in order to accumulate a systematic body of data on individual differences. Galton (1888), whose interest lay in the heritability of physical and simple psychological functions, suggested principles of the correlation coefficient as a method of expressing the extent to which two variables covary; Karl Pearson (1896), Galton's student, operationalized the product–moment correlation coefficient now known as the "Pearson r." The investigation of individual differences and covariation of abilities in both Europe (Binet & Simon, 1905; Spearman, 1910) and the United States (Cattell, 1890; Terman, 1916; Thurstone, 1947) anticipated advanced correlational techniques of multiple regression and factor analysis already well established by 1950. It was Terman's initial interest in individuals with distinguished intellectual abilities that subsequently led to his use of correlation in a study of psychological factors predicting marital happiness (Terman, 1938).

METHODOLOGY

In this chapter, we emphasize the use of correlation and related techniques to examine factors contributing to marital distress and couples' response to marital therapy. Throughout our discussion, we draw heavily on examples linking depression and relationship difficulties. Our emphasis on depression and marital unhappiness derives partly from convenience (specifically, our previous research efforts in this area) and partly from the literature. Numerous studies have identified marital distress as a vulnerability factor, precipitant, concomitant, consequence, and potentiator of depression (cf. Jacobson, Holtzworth-Munroe, & Schmaling, 1989). Moreover, the co-occurrence of depressed affect and marital distress has been examined from a broad range of theoretical perspectives and correlational techniques.

This section is divided into two parts. The first section, reviewing basic techniques, begins with a brief discussion of the kinds of data lending themselves to correlational analysis. Assumptions underlying correlation, techniques of computation, and associated interpretive issues are examined at length because these also apply to more advanced techniques derived from correlation. The relationship of correlation to prediction is examined using simple linear regression. "Third variables" affecting correlation coefficients are discussed in terms of moderator and suppressor variables and from the perspective of partial correlations. These concepts are extended to the technique of multiple regression analysis. The second part of this section introduces more advanced techniques used in prediction. Canonical correlation analysis offers an approach for relating multiple predictors to multiple criteria. Multiple cutoff and multiple discriminant function analysis are then presented as alternatives to the regression approach. Throughout our discussion, the emphasis is on conceptual rather than statistical understanding of these research methodologies.

Measurement Levels and Distributions

What measurement characteristics are important to consider in correlation? Variables can typically be considered as being measured at one of four levels, each progressively more demanding in terms of data requirements and more generous in terms of potential analytic procedures (Stevens, 1946). At the simplest level are nominal scales, by which events are grouped into discrete classes for which no assumptions regarding order or distance are made; examples include classifying individuals by ethnicity or marital status. At the next level are ordinal scales, by which individuals are grouped into discrete classes presumed to reflect rank order; examples include classifying individuals by social class (low, middle, high) or by family life stage (childless, oldest child less than 5 years old, and so on). Lacking in ordinal scales is information about the "distance" or degree of difference between categories.

Interval-level scales imply not only that classes are ordered by rank but also that the distances between categories are defined in terms of fixed and equal units. Examples include typical measures of relationship satisfaction (e.g., the Dyadic Adjustment Scale [Spanier, 1976] or Marital Satisfaction Inventory [Snyder, 1981]). Interval scales may be discrete (e.g., indicating level of marital happiness by circling 1 of 7 points on a scale anchored by "extremely unhappy" on one end and "extremely happy" on the other) or continuous (e.g., indicating level of marital happiness along the same scale by marking an " × " anywhere along the line). Finally, ratio-level scales have all the properties of an interval scale plus a meaningful "zero point" inherently defined by the measurement scheme and construct. Examples of ratio scales include length of marriage or number of agreements expressed during a 5-minute discussion. Ratio scales permit proportional comparisons (e.g., a husband may express twice as many agreements as his wife) whereas interval scales do not (e.g., one would not describe a wife as being "twice as maritally happy" as her husband).

Levels of measurement have important implications for the kinds of analytic procedures that can be applied to the data. For example, assessing covariation between variables measured along nominal or ordinal scales requires nonparametric approaches (e.g., chi-square or rank-order correlations), whereas variables measured using interval- or ratio-level scales lend themselves to more powerful parametric approaches including product–moment correlation (Pearson r) and regression. Variables measured as dichotomies present special consideration in correlation and related techniques, depending on whether the underlying construct is viewed as dichotomous (e.g., using "husband" and "wife" to reflect gender) or continuous (e.g., using "divorced" vs. "still married" to reflect effectiveness of marital therapy). For most correlational procedures, dichotomies can be treated as interval-level measures.

In addition to level of measurement, different approaches to assessing covariation make different assumptions about the manner in which observations on some variable are "dispersed" or distributed around the center of those observations. For example, the Pearson correlation coefficient assumes that each of the two variables being related are continuous and that measurement error for each is normally distributed; normal distributions are those reflecting the familiar bell-shaped curve. Variables whose distributions deviate significantly from normality may require less powerful, nonparametric approaches to examining covariation.

Basic Techniques

Correlation

Conceptual Basis. At its simplest level, correlation denotes the extent to which two variables "co-relate" or covary. For example, do high levels of depressed affect go hand in hand with high levels of marital distress? It is important to emphasize that correlation reflects only association, not causality. For example, depression may contribute to marital distress, or marital distress may contribute to depression, or each may contribute to the other, or each may be influenced by some third variable or set of variables, or all of the above may be true. The propensity to attribute causality to correlational findings constitutes probably the most frequent and conceptually most problematic interpretive error in the use of correlation and related techniques.

Correlations can be depicted graphically as in Figure 14.1. In this example, individuals are measured on two variables: depression (DEP) and global marital distress (GDS). For each variable, the distribution of subjects' scores can be summarized using two statistics: (1) a measure of central tendency (typically the arithmetic mean) and (2) a measure of dispersion (typically the variance or standard deviation). In Figure 14.1, each circle or sphere denotes the variability of subjects on the corresponding variable. The covariability of observations or covariance (i.e., the extent to which high scores on one variable systematically denote either high or low scores on the other) is indicated by the area of the two circles' overlap.

Pearson's product–moment correlation is simply a "standardized" index of covariation that ranges from −1.0 to +1.0. If two variables have a correlation of 1.0, then high scores on one variable covary perfectly with high scores on the other; a correlation of −1.0 would denote that high scores on one variable covary perfectly with low scores on the other. In either case, the two circles in Figure 14.1 would overlap completely. By contrast, a correlation of .00 would indicate a complete absence of covariation between the two variables, and their corresponding circles in Figure 14.1 would not overlap at all. The amount of overlap depicted between DEP and GDS in Figure 14.1 denotes a modest correlation (approximately .60).

The strength of association between two variables is best inferred not by the correlation coefficient itself but, rather, by the *squared* correlation coefficient. Specifically, the squared correlation between two variables reflects the percentage of variance (variability of observations about the mean) in one variable that can be explained or predicted by knowledge of individuals' variance (or variability in scores) in the other variable. Referring to Figure 14.1, if the correlation between DEP and GDS is .60, then 36% of the variability in individuals' scores on the depression measure can be explained by their scores on the measure of global marital distress. (Similarly, 36% of the variability in marital distress can be predicted by individuals' scores on depression.)

The squared correlation coefficient constitutes the most prevalent but fairly rigorous interpretation regarding the *meaningfulness* (rather than statistical significance) of one's findings. (For contrasting views, see Abelson, 1985, and Ozer, 1985.) Correlations approaching .70 in absolute magnitude—typically regarded as relatively large—explain only half the variance (49%) in one variable from another; more common correlations in the research literature ranging from .30 to .40 permit explanation or prediction of only 10% to 15% of the variability in one variable from the other.

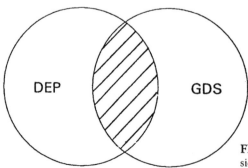

FIGURE 14.1. Simple correlation between depression (DEP) and global marital distress (GDS).

Assumptions. What requirements should the data satisfy before using correlational techniques? Nunnally and Bernstein (1994) list three assumptions underlying use of the Pearson product–moment correlation. First, the relationship between the two variables should be monotonic (consistently positive or consistently negative) and, preferably, linear (see Figure 14.2). Although prediction models can be derived for nonlinear relationships, the Pearson r is not appropriate to these situations. For example, Figure 14.3 depicts a hypothetical curvilinear relationship between level of family functioning and level of cohesion or intrafamily attachments (ranging from disengaged, at one extreme, to enmeshed at the other), where optimal family functioning occurs at a middle range of attachment. In this example, level of family functioning can be predicted perfectly from level of attachment, yet the two variables would still obtain a Pearson r of .00. Alternative methods exist for assessing curvilinear relationships.

A second assumption underlying the Pearson r is that errors of estimate in predicting one variable from the other should be approximately the same across all levels of both variables. (This condition is known as homoscedasticity, and its absence as heteroscedasticity.) Prediction error is depicted by the distance between actual sample observations (depicted by individual data points) and the regression line for predicting scores on the dependent variable from scores on the independent variable. For example, in Figure 14.2, the average error in predicting levels of DEP from variance in GDS remains fairly constant throughout the entire range of GDS (with some increase in average error at higher levels of GDS). By contrast, in Figure 14.4, the scatterplot linking probability of seeking marital therapy to level of global marital distress shows considerable variability across the range of GDS. Low levels of marital distress are reliably linked to low likelihood of seeking marital therapy, whereas high levels of GDS relate less predictably to couples' behavior; some highly distressed couples may enter marital therapy while others may pursue divorce. A common regression line derived for the entire sample underestimates the degree of predictability from low scores on GDS and overestimates the degree of predictability from high scores on GDS.

Finally, use of the Pearson r assumes that measurement error affecting each of the

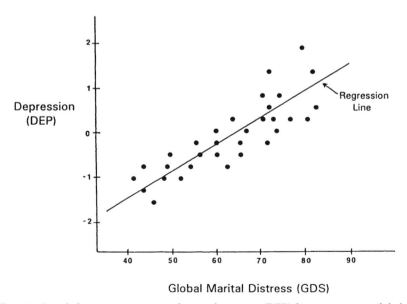

FIGURE 14.2. Simple linear regression, predicting depression (DEP) from variance in global marital distress (GDS).

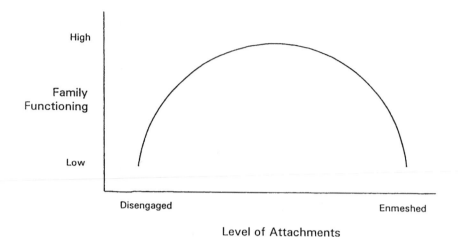

FIGURE 14.3. Hypothetical curvilinear relationship between level of family functioning and level of intrafamily attachments.

variables must be normally distributed; that is, differences between measured levels of a construct and the true, underlying levels of the construct for individuals in the sample must have a normal distribution. This also implies that the construct underlying each measure is presumed to be continuous. When all three assumptions of linearity, homoscedasticity, and normality are met, the two variables being related are said to reflect a bivariate normal distribution.

Fortunately, inferences drawn from the Pearson r are fairly robust to violations of these assumptions. That is, moderate degrees of skewness, nonlinearity, or heteroscedasticity may not greatly affect the magnitude of r or its interpretation. However, when clear

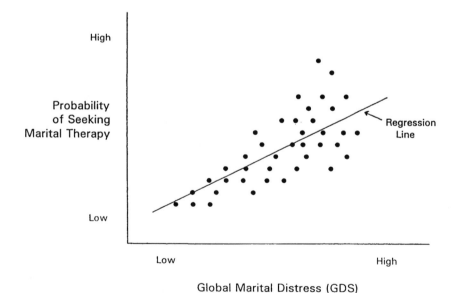

FIGURE 14.4. Scatterplot reflecting heteroscedasticity. The average error in predicting probability of seeking marital therapy is greater at higher levels of global marital distress (GDS).

violations of these assumptions exist, or when data reflect ordinal- rather than interval-level measurement, alternative approaches to examining covariation should be used. These are summarized in Table 14.1. For example, the phi coefficient (ϕ) is used when both variables are dichotomous (e.g., gender and employment). Although ϕ and r are computationally equivalent, ϕ can be expected to underestimate the value of r that would have been obtained from continuous data that have been dichotomized. The point–biserial correlation (r_{pb}) is used when one variable is dichotomous and the other is continuous. Like ϕ, r_{pb} is computationally equivalent to r. However, whereas both ϕ and r can reach values of 1.0, the maximum size of r_{pb} between a dichotomous variable and a normally distributed variable is about .80 (Nunnally & Bernstein, 1994).

Alternative correlation coefficients have been proposed as estimates of the Pearson r where the two underlying (latent) variables are presumed to be continuous but one or both of the measures of these variables has been dichotomized (e.g., coding expressed emotions as positive or negative). In the case of one continuous and one dichotomized measure, the biserial correlation (r_{bis}) can be computed; in the case of two dichotomized measures (reflecting two continuous constructs), the tetrachoric correlation (r_{tet}) can be used. Generalizations of these two coefficients (polyserial and polychoric correlations) have been developed for use where continuous constructs have been measured using three or more categories. In general, polyserial and polychoric correlations (including r_{bis} and r_{tet}) will always be somewhat higher than values of r derived from the same data. These estimates may or may not be accurate and should be used only with caution and with clear justification.

Finally, two alternative correlation coefficients should be considered where the data reflect ordinal-rather than interval-level data. The Spearman rho (ρ) and Kendall tau (τ) coefficients are used where observations on two variables reflect rank order without implied equal distance between adjacent ranks. Both coefficients assume a relatively

TABLE 14.1. Measurement Characteristics and Assumptions Underlying Selection among Alternative Statistics Reflecting Degree of Association

Statistic	First variable		Second variable		Comments[a]
	Measure	Construct	Measure	Construct	
Pearson r	Interval or ratio	Continuous	Interval or ratio	Continuous	Assumes bivariate normal distribution
Spearman rho (ρ)	Ordinal	Continuous	Ordinal	Continuous	Approximates r when number of tied ranks is small
Kendall tau (τ)	Ordinal	Continuous	Ordinal	Continuous	Preferred when number of tied ranks is large
Phi (ϕ)	Dichotomy	Dichotomy	Dichotomy	Dichotomy	Underestimates r when data are dichotomized
Point–biserial (r_{pb})	Dichotomy	Dichotomy	Interval or ratio	Continuous	Maximum value = .80
Biserial (r_{bis})	Dichotomy	Continuous	Interval or ratio	Continuous	May overestimate r
Tetrachoric (r_{tet})	Dichotomy	Continuous	Dichotomy	Continuous	May overestimate r
Chi-square (χ^2)	Nominal	Nominal	Nominal	Nominal	Also appropriate for ordinal-level measures

[a]See text for clarification of comments.

large number of categories and relatively few tied observations (ranks) on each varia-ble. Spearman's ρ provides a closer approximation to the Pearson r than Kendall's τ when the number of categories is large and the number of tied ranks is small (i.e., the data are more or less continuous). Kendall's τ is more appropriate when a fairly large number of cases have been classified into a relatively small number of categories. (When a small number of categories have been measured for each variable at a nominal rather than ordinal level of measurement, the chi-square (χ^2) statistic should be used.) Although both ρ and τ can range from -1.0 to $+1.0$, the absolute value of Kendall's τ tends to be smaller than that of Pearson's r.

Interpretive Issues. Several properties of data can render interpretation of correla-tion coefficients difficult or inappropriate. For example, we have already noted that the absolute magnitude of r is likely to be compromised to the extent that the two vari-ables (1) are noncontinuous in measurement, (2) have nonsimilar distributions, or (3) are related in nonlinear fashion. An additional factor potentially contributing to spuri-ously low correlations involves restricted range of observations. In general, such restricted range may result from methodological limitations in either measurement or sampling. Measurement sources of restricted range occur when the measuring technique is insuffi-cient to adequately reflect construct variation actually present in the sample. For ex-ample, if one wished to examine the relationship of spousal differences in personality style to global marital accord in a nonclinic sample, the Minnesota Multiphasic Person-ality Inventory–2 (MMPI-2) (Butcher, Dahlstrom, Graham, Tellegen, & Kaemmer, 1989) would be a poor instrument to use because its construction is oriented toward individu-al differences in psychopathology rather than variation in personality style within the nonpathological spectrum; most scores for a nonclinic sample could be expected to cluster at the low end of MMPI-2 scales.

Sampling sources of restricted range emerge when respondents are selected in such a way as to minimize potential covariation between the two variables of interest. For example, if one wished to examine the relationship of individual psychopathology to couples' response to marital therapy, then initially excluding couples where one or both partners exhibit a thought disorder, severe personality disorder, or substance abuse could be expected to limit variability on measures of psychopathology and, consequently, the covariability (correlation) between these measures and any measure of treatment outcome.

We have noted that the squared correlation coefficient provides the best index for evaluating the strength of the relationship between two variables and, hence, the corre-lation's meaningfulness. Meaningfulness differs from statistical significance; with a suffi-ciently large sample ($n > 100$), a correlation of only .20 (and explaining less than 5% of the variance in one variable from the other) may be statistically significant (i.e., not due to chance) at a probability level of $p < .05$. Similarly, one should avoid discussing the "difference" between correlations based on (1) their absolute magnitude, or (2) one reaching statistical significance and the other not. In citing the difference between two correlations, one should first determine their statistically significant difference using Fisher's (1921) r-to-Z transformation described in most intermediate-level statistics texts.

Finally, the ease with which correlations can be computed and the tendency of researchers to examine large numbers of variables requires consideration of errors in statistical inference. Specifically, a type I error involves falsely concluding that a corre-lation is significant; the probability of such an error is set by the "alpha" or probability level (denoted by p) adopted for hypothesis testing. Thus, citing a correlation as signifi-cant at $p < .05$ implies that there is a 5-in-100 chance that the correlation has reached statistical significance due to chance alone (i.e., sampling error) rather than resulting from true covariation between the two variables in the population of interest. If one were to correlate the scores for husbands on 15 variables with the scores for wives on these same variables, a correlation matrix with 105 unique correlations would result. Suppose 10 of these reach statistical significance at $p < .05$. Given that we could expect approximately 5 of the 105 correlations to reach significance by chance alone, which 5 of the 10 significant correlations should we attribute to covariation generalizable to the population of interest and which 5 to chance? Unfortunately, there is no way to determine the answer to this question.

One method of controlling overall type I errors when computing numerous correlations is to split one's sample in half, compute the same correlation matrices for both halves, and then consider only those correlations that replicate across split-half samples. If one were to use a probability level of $p < .05$ in each sample, the likelihood of a correlation between the same two variables being significant *by chance* in both samples is roughly .0025 (less than 3 out of 1,000 and considerably less than 1 out of 100). The benefits of replicating results across independent samples cannot be overstated.

Regression

Conceptual Basis. How does correlation relate to prediction? Whereas a correlation expresses the direction and strength of relationship between two variables, it does not by itself permit predicting an *individual*'s score on one measure from that person's score on the other. The method one uses to accomplish this is simple linear regression.

In discussing correlation, we described a hypothetical relationship between individuals' level of depression (DEP) and global marital distress (GDS), where the two variables have a correlation of $r = .60$. Given this relationship, how could one predict spouses' level of depressed affect from level of marital distress? Using regression analysis would require the following information: (1) the means and standard deviations of the distributions of scores for each variable, (2) the correlation between the two variables, and (3) the individual's score on the marital distress measure from which to predict that person's score on the depression measure. If marital distress and depression are represented by X and Y, respectively, then predicting an individual's level of depression (Y′) from his or her level of marital distress (X) can be fairly easily computed from the following:

$$Y' = r_{XY}(s_Y/s_X)(X - \overline{X}) + \overline{Y}$$

where Y′ is the predicted level of depression, r_{XY} in the correlation between depression (Y) and marital distress (X), s_Y and s_X are the standard deviations of Y and X, and $\overline{Y}$ and $\overline{X}$ are the means of Y and X, respectively. This formula is much simplified if one uses standardized z-scores for each of the two variables. The advantage of z-scores is that they constitute a simple linear transformation of raw scores, have a mean of 0 and standard deviation of 1, and can be interpreted relative to the unit-normal distribution. If z_X is the individual's standardized score on X and z_Y' is the predicted standardized score on Y, then:

$$z_Y' = r_{XY}z_X$$

Interpretive Issues. Figure 14.2 shows a scatterplot of scores from a small sample of couples on a standardized measure of depression (DEP) and global marital distress (GDS). The bivariate distribution of these scores reflects a modest correlation between these two variables (approximately .60). The line passing through this distribution reflects the best-fitting line for predicting levels of depression from marital distress, where "best fit" minimizes the sum of squared distances from each point to the line (commonly called the least-squares solution). This line is defined by the regression formula cited earlier. From Figure 14.2, one can observe that a score of 50 on GDS predicts a standardized score of approximately −1 on DEP, equivalent to the 15th percentile of individuals' scores on the depression measure; similarly, a score of 80 on GDS predicts a standardized score of approximately +1 on DEP, equivalent to roughly the 85th percentile of individuals' scores on the depression measure.

Several features of prediction from regression analysis bear noting. First, when the correlation between two measures is ± 1.0, the relative distance of the predicted criterion score from the mean of the criterion measure will be precisely equal to the relative distance of the predictor score from the mean of the predictor measure. For example, with a correlation of $r = 1.0$, if a wife's marital distress score were at the 85th percentile for that measure, her predicted depression score would also be at the 85th percentile. Second, the lower the absolute magnitude of the correlation between two measures, the closer the predicted criterion score will be to the mean of the criterion measure compared to the distance of the individual's score on the predictor measure relative to the mean of the predictor variable. The tendency of predicted scores, Y', to converge on the mean of the criterion measure was termed "reversion" by Galton and was the basis of Pearson's identifying the product–moment correlation as the "r" coefficient. Thus, with a correlation of $r = .60$ if a wife's marital distress score were at the 85th percentile, her predicted depression score would only be at the 73rd percentile. Third, if the correlation between two variables is 0, the best prediction of an individual's score on the criterion measure is the *mean* of the criterion measure, regardless of that individual's score on the predictor measure.

Finally, given a correlation between two variables with absolute magnitude less than 1.0 and the inevitability of some error in predicting Y' from X, one can specify a level of confidence that an individual's actual criterion score is within some interval bounding the predicted criterion score. The statistic used to establish this "confidence interval" is the standard error of estimate, defined as follows:

$$s_{est(Y)} = s_Y \sqrt{1 - r^2_{XY}}$$

One could state with approximately 68% confidence of accuracy that the actual criterion score should fall within ± 1 $s_{est(Y)}$ of the predicted criterion score, and with approximately 95% confidence that the actual criterion score should fall within ± 2 $s_{est(Y)}$ of the predicted criterion score.

Third Variables

Moderator Variables. How can correlations between two variables be influenced by individuals' scores on some other variable? When the correlation between a predictor (X) and criterion (Y) measure varies systematically as a function of some third variable (M), that third variable is termed a "moderator" variable. The effect of a moderator variable is depicted in Figure 14.5. Again, as in Figure 14.1, the overall covariability between depression (DEP) and global marital distress (GDS) is reflected by the overlap between the two circles reflecting variability in individuals' scores on each respective measure. In Figure 14.5, we have indicated husbands' and wives' scores on each measure by the letters "H" and "W," respectively. Although an equal number of H's and W's appear in each circle, the area of these two measures' overlap (representing covariability) is

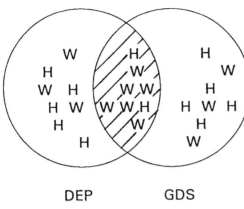

FIGURE 14.5. Gender as a moderator variable. The relationship between depression (DEP) and global marital distress (GDS) is stronger for wives (W) than for husbands (H).

DEP   GDS

determined primarily by wives' (W) scores. In this example, the overall correlation between DEP and GDS for the combined sample of husbands and wives would underestimate the correlation between these two measures for wives alone and overestimate the correlation between these two measures derived separately for husbands.

Moderator effects are quite common. In fact, this example reflects a common finding that women's overall level of affect is more strongly influenced by relationship concerns than is men's affect (Formanek & Gurian, 1987). Although common moderators include such sociodemographic indices as gender, age, ethnicity, marital status, and economic class, *any* variable including discrete behavioral observations or indirectly measured psychological constructs can function as a moderator variable. Moderator variables are identified most readily by testing for the statistical significance of difference between correlations of predictor to criterion measures for two or more subgroups (e.g., husbands vs. wives, or Caucasian Americans vs. African Americans).

If one were to graphically depict the scatterplot of individuals' scores on criterion and predictor measures for subgroups defined by some moderator variable (e.g., distinguishing scores for husbands and wives by "H" and "W" as in Figure 14.6), moderator effects would be noted from regression lines having unequal slope. Finally, in multiple regression analysis, moderator effects are reflected by significant prediction from "interaction terms" between two or more predictors. Typically, one investigates potential moderator effects for variables hypothesized on the basis of theory, clinical experience, or previous research to possibly influence the covariability between predictor and criterion variables for different subgroups.

Suppressor Variables. How can we reduce error in predicting from correlations? When two variables are imperfectly correlated, there is some variability in individuals' scores on the predictor variable X that does not systematically covary with individuals' scores on the criterion variable Y. Therefore, if we were to use simple linear regression to predict scores on Y from scores on X, there would be some error in our prediction due to variance in X uncorrelated with variance in Y. In Figure 14.1, that portion of the circle denoting variance in GDS that does not overlap with the circle denoting variance in DEP constitutes error in predicting DEP from GDS.

One method of improving our prediction of depression from variance in global marital distress is to find some third variable (S) that correlates with that portion of GDS that constitutes error (i.e., that portion of GDS that does not overlap [correlate] with DEP). Such a variable is termed a "suppressor" variable because its effect is to covary out or

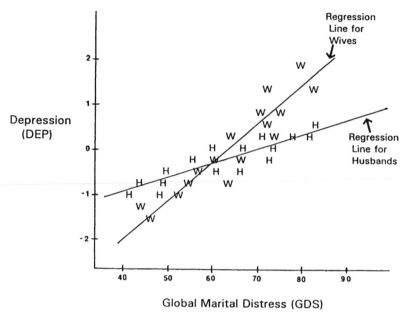

FIGURE 14.6. Separate regression lines showing a stronger relationship in predicting depression (DEP) from variance in global marital distress (GDS) for wives (W) than for husbands (H).

suppress that portion of variability in a predictor measure that is irrelevant to prediction of the criterion. Figure 14.7 provides an example of such a suppressor variable. In this example, the suppressor variable is marital commitment (COM), reflecting the extent to which an individual has an emotional stake in maintaining the marriage. As depicted in Figure 14.7, commitment (COM) is significantly (and negatively) correlated with GDS but uncorrelated with DEP. If depression covaries with some portion of marital distress *not* related to level of marital commitment, we can improve our prediction of depression by first subtracting (covarying out) from GDS that portion of global distress that covaries with commitment. Improvement in prediction occurs because of the remaining (residual) variance in GDS, proportionately more covaries with DEP than does the total variability in GDS; that is, we have subtracted out (suppressed) nonpredictive variance in GDS. The prediction equation will have the following general form:

$$DEP = b_1 GDS - b_2 COM + c$$

where b_1 and b_2 denote some weighting (regression coefficients) of the two predictor variables GDS and COM, respectively, and c denotes some value of a constant.

Suppressor variables are identified in multiple regression analysis when significant standardized weights are given to some variable correlating minimally with the criterion variable and significantly with one or more predictor variables. It bears noting that it is the absolute magnitude of these correlations and standardized weights (regression coefficients) that are important rather than their direction (valence), because the direction of the correlations is an artifact of the manner in which the measurement instrument is scored.

Partial and Semipartial (Part) Correlations. Up to this point, we have emphasized primarily zero-order correlations—that is, the unadjusted or simple correlation between

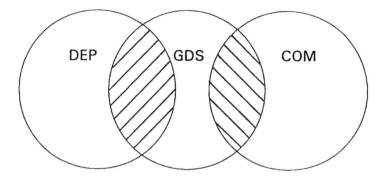

FIGURE 14.7. Commitment as a suppressor variable. A portion of the error in global marital distress (GDS) in predicting depression (DEP) is suppressed by controlling for committment (COM).

two variables ignoring (i.e., not controlling for) the effects of any third variable. By contrast, partial correlations provide an index of the association between two variables, X and Y, while adjusting for the effects of one or more additional variables on *both* X and Y. Semipartial correlations provide an index of the association between two variables, X and Y, while adjusting for the effects of one or more additional variables on *either* X or Y, but not both variables.

For example, Figure 14.1—discussed earlier—depicts the "zero-order" (or simple) correlation between depression (DEP) and global marital distress (GDS), which we described as being approximately .60. By comparison, Figure 14.8A depicts the intercorrelations or overlap among three variables: depression, global marital distress, and attribution of marital difficulties to one's own behavior (AOB). Each of the three variables is shown to be correlated (to varying degrees) with each of the remaining two. Consider the situation in which the zero-order correlation between GDS and AOB and between AOB and DEP is approximately .30. To what extent does attributing marital difficulties to one's own behavior (AOB) correlate with depression (DEP) *after* controlling for covariance of both variables with global distress (GDS)? The partial correlation of AOB with DEP, controlling for GDS, can be derived using formulas provided by Pedhazur (1982, p. 116). If one literally covers up that area in both DEP and AOB overlapping with the circle denoting variance in GDS, one observes that the remaining portion of DEP overlapping with AOB is relatively small (see Figure 14.8B); in this case, the partial correlation equals .16. The semipartial correlation of AOB with DEP, controlling only for the covariance of GDS with AOB but not with DEP, is only slightly smaller (.13) (see Figure 14.8C).

Partial and semipartial correlations facilitate an understanding of suppressor variables. For example, if in Figure 14.7 the correlation of DEP with GDS is .60 and the correlation of GDS with COM is .50, the semipartial correlation of global marital distress with depression, controlling for effects of commitment to retaining one's marriage, increases to .69. Similarly, as we will see shortly, partial and semipartial correlations provide the key to understanding multiple regression analysis.

Multiple Regression

Conceptual Issues. What techniques permit us to combine information from several variables to predict some criterion? For example, can prediction of spouses' depressed affect from their level of marital distress be improved by considering other potential

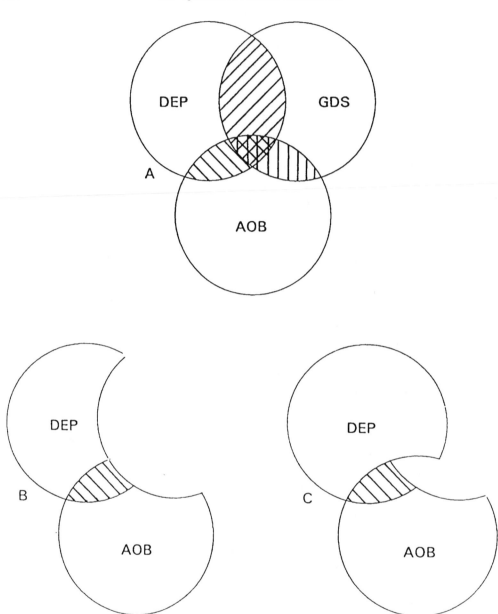

FIGURE 14.8. A. Relationships among depression (DEP), global marital distress (GDS), and attribution of marital difficulties to one's own behavior (AOB). B. DEP correlates with GDS at r = .60; DEP and GDS both correlate with AOB at r = .30. The partial correlation of DEP with AOB is lower (r = .16) after controlling for the correlation of both variables with GDS. C. The semipartial correlation of DEP with AOB is also lower (r = .13) after controlling only for the correlation of AOB with GDS.

contributing factors? Multiple regression is a general statistical procedure for investigating the relationship of a single criterion variable to two or more predictor variables. Multiple regression can be used to derive the best linear prediction equation from some set of predictor variables and to evaluate the overall accuracy of that equation. It can also be used to control for possible confounding effects of one or more variables to evaluate the predictive contribution from some other specific variable or set of variables. Finally, multiple regression can be used to discover structural relations among complex multivariate data sets.

Essentially, the objective of multiple linear regression (or multivariate prediction) is to identify multiple predictors associated with different or unique components of criterion variance. This objective will be met to the extent that predictors are significantly correlated with the criterion and minimally correlated with each other. The correlation between a criterion variable and the linear composite of predictor variables derived from multiple regression analysis is called the multiple correlation (R); the square of the multiple correlation, R^2, denotes the total proportion of criterion variance explained by the linear combination of predictor variables.

Figure 14.8, discussed earlier from the perspective of partial correlation, also provides an example for considering multiple regression. In attempting to predict individuals' scores on the criterion measure of depression (DEP), multiple regression will ordinarily select as the *first* predictor that variable that has the highest zero-order (simple) correlation with the criterion—in this case, global marital distress (GDS) with a correlation of .60 with DEP. If two or more additional predictors remain, multiple regression will then ordinarily select as the *next additional* predictor that variable with the highest partial correlation with the criterion, controlling for the effects of the first predictor (GDS) on both the criterion and remaining possible predictors. As noted earlier, the partial correlation between depression and attributing marital difficulties to one's own behavior (AOB), controlling for GDS, is only .16—which may or may not add significantly to predictive accuracy beyond prediction from marital distress alone.

Multiple regression becomes decidedly more complex when three or more predictor variables are considered, as depicted in Figure 14.9. In this example, two additional variables are available as potential predictors of depression—namely, life event stressors (LES) and attribution of marital difficulties to the partner's behavior (APB). Consider the situation in which LES are correlated with depression at .15, and APB is uncorrelated with DEP but is correlated with AOB at .60. GDS would ordinarily be selected as the first predictor of DEP because of its highest zero-order correlation with the criterion. Although AOB has the next highest zero-order correlation with DEP (.30), LES would likely be selected as the second predictor because its partial correlation with DEP controlling for GDS (.19) is higher than AOB's partial correlation with DEP controlling for GDS (.16).

If these three predictors were the only ones being considered, their order of entry into the multiple regression equation would likely be GDS first, then LES, and then AOB (presuming all added significantly to the prediction of depression). However, as depicted in Figure 14.9, APB acts as a suppressor variable in that it subtracts out that portion of variance in AOB not related to the criterion—perhaps a general tendency to attribute marital problems to both partners' behavior. In this example, the partial correlation of AOB with DEP, controlling for effects of both GDS *and* APB, would be .20. Thus, in a regression equation selecting the best combination of three predictors, the variables entered might be GDS, AOB, and APB (weighted negatively)—with LES subsequently being entered as the fourth predictor.

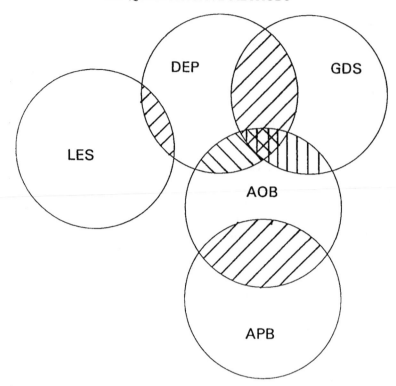

FIGURE 14.9. Multiple linear regression reflects covariation between the criterion (depression [DEP]) and multiple predictors (global marital distress [GDS], life event stressors [LES], and attribution of marital difficulties to one's own behavior [AOB]), including suppressor variables (attribution of marital difficulties to partner's behavior [APB]).

Procedural Issues. The results of multiple regression depend not only on the correlations of predictors with the criterion and with other predictors but also on decisions regarding the specific procedures used in the regression analysis. For example, the Statistical Package for the Social Sciences (SPSS, Inc., 1990) requires a series of decisions regarding various options for conducting multiple regression. The first decision involves the method of entering predictors into the prediction equation. Three basic options exist: (1) forcing entry of all possible predictors to examine their cumulative predictive accuracy, (2) controlled entry of subsets of predictors in hierarchical fashion to test specific hypotheses, and (3) stepwise entry or deletion of predictors based solely on covariance structure among predictors and criterion.

Forced entry of all predictor variables is used when the investigator has no specific hypotheses regarding subsets of predictors and wishes to examine the overall utility of predictor variables considered in their entirety. For example, one might be interested in the overall relationship between the five personality dimensions measured by the NEO Personality Inventory—Revised (NEO-PI-R) (Costa & McCrae, 1992) and the global distress scale of the Marital Satisfaction Inventory (Snyder, 1981) as an index of the relationship between personality and marital functioning. The squared multiple correlation between GDS and the regression equation incorporating ideal weightings of the five NEO-PI-R scales would provide the best measure of this relationship.

Hierarchical entry is used when one wants to test specific hypotheses regarding some subset of possible predictors. For example, if an important hypothesis concerns the effects of marital distress (GDS) on depression (DEP) *after* the effects of life events (LES) have already been accounted for, one would compare (1) the squared multiple correlation (R^2) for the regression equation predicting DEP entering LES first and GDS second, with (2) the R^2 for the equation entering LES alone.

Stepwise entry of predictors is used when the investigator wishes to derive an optimal prediction equation using the smallest possible set of the strongest combination of predictors. Several stepwise procedures are possible: (1) forward inclusion in which predictors are added if they satisfy certain statistical criteria determined by the investigator, (2) backward exclusion in which predictors are eliminated one by one (again, on the basis of specified statistical criteria) from a regression equation that initially includes all predictors, and (3) forward inclusion combined with deletion of variables no longer meeting predetermined statistical criteria at each successive step. The most common of these stepwise procedures is the first (forward inclusion).

If selecting stepwise procedures for the regression analysis, the investigator must specify criteria for entering or deleting predictors from the regression equation. The first criterion specifies the maximum number of predictor variables to be selected (e.g., the best 3 of 10). The second criterion specifies the minimum F ratio computed in a test for significance of a regression coefficient for that variable to be included in the next step. The third criterion specifies the proportion of variance in a potential predictor *not* explained by predictors already selected for the regression equation that is required for consideration of that predictor for possible inclusion. Most statistical packages have default values for these statistical criteria so that stepwise regression can be executed without these criteria being specified by the user; however, default values tend to be very liberal toward inclusion of predictor variables with minimal incremental predictive utility, leading to a number of interpretive difficulties concerning results.

Interpretive Issues. Multiple regression analysis constitutes an important statistical tool for developing prediction models, testing specific prediction hypotheses, and enhancing overall predictive accuracy. However, use of multiple regression requires familiarity with assumptions and limitations of the technique bearing on interpretation of results (cf. Nunnally & Bernstein, 1994, pp. 185–193).

First, because of their complexity, reporting of multivariate results requires attention to both their applicability and verification by the informed consumer. When presenting results of multiple regression analysis, both standardized and unstandardized weights should be presented; standardized weights permit interpretation of the relative contribution of predictor variables to some linear function, whereas unstandardized weights provide the means for actually computing linear composites without transforming predictor variables to standardized scores.

Second, multiple linear regression makes all the same assumptions as correlation and simple regression, namely, that the bivariate distributions between predictors— and between predictors and the criterion—satisfy conditions of linearity, homoscedasticity, and normality. In addition, multiple regression is optimized when predictor variables are relatively independent (i.e., uncorrelated). When two or more of the predictor variables are highly intercorrelated (e.g., $> .80$)—a condition termed "multicollinearity"— derivation of the regression equation may not be possible; if calculation of the equation does proceed, results may be highly unreliable from one sample to another.

Third, in addition to multicollinearity, the likelihood of unreliable results increases when (1) the ratio of subjects to predictor variables is relatively small (e.g., $<5:1$), (2) predictors are selected without careful consideration of theory or previous empirical findings, or (3) nonlinear solutions (e.g., exponential or log transformations of predictor variables) are used that capitalize on chance covariation between predictors and the criterion. An important means of guarding against spurious (chance) findings involves cross-validating results of a multiple regression equation derived from one sample by applying the same equation to an independent sample and assessing the amount of shrinkage in the squared multiple correlation (R^2). Another means of minimizing chance findings involves using stringent criteria for entering and retaining predictor variables in a stepwise procedure.

Finally, it is critical that the standardized weights (regression coefficients or "beta" weights) applied to predictor variables not be interpreted as reflecting the "importance" of predictor variables *outside the context of multivariate prediction*. When predictor variables are highly correlated relative to their correlation with the criterion, regression coefficients may be poorer indicators of predictors' importance than zero-order (simple) correlations. A more useful concept than importance in evaluating a multiple regression equation concerns predictor variables' "uniqueness." The uniqueness of a specified predictor variable is the difference in R^2 when (1) all predictors are included in the regression equation, versus (2) the predictor in question is excluded from the equation.

Advanced Techniques

Canonical Correlation Analysis

Conceptual Issues. Suppose one wants to relate multiple predictors to multiple criteria simultaneously. For example, one might wish to examine the relationship of marital distress to children's adjustment, using scales from the Marital Satisfaction Inventory (Snyder, 1981) as predictors and scales from the Personality Inventory for Children—Revised (Wirt, Lachar, Klinedinst, & Seat, 1984) as criteria. Canonical correlation permits such prediction by combining elements of both regression analysis and factor analysis. We have noted that multiple regression analysis permits consideration of multiple predictor variables and their intercorrelations in predicting some single criterion variable. Canonical correlation differs from multiple regression in that rather than relating two or more predictor variables to one criterion variable, canonical analysis examines the relationship(s) of two or more predictor variables to two or more criterion variables. Factor analysis is a statistical procedure for reducing some set of variables to a smaller number of dimensions by examining the correlations or shared variance among those variables. Canonical correlation analysis differs from factor analysis in that whereas the latter generates linear combinations of variables to account for as much variance as possible *within one* set of variables, canonical analysis generates linear combinations of variables to explain the maximum amount of covariance *between two* sets of variables.

Objectives of canonical correlation analysis can be depicted graphically as in Figure 14.10. In this example, five predictor scales from the Marital Satisfaction Inventory (conflict over childrearing [CCR], dissatisfaction with children [DSC], affective communication [AFC], problem-solving communication [PSC], and disagreement about finances [FIN]) have been related to three criterion scales from the Personality Inventory for Children–Revised (social skills [SSK], academic achievement [ACH], and delinquency [DLQ]). Canonical analysis first forms two linear combinations, one of the predictor variables and one of the criterion variables, by differentially weighting them so that the maximum possible correlation between them is obtained. This correlation is referred to as the first canonical correlation or canonical variate. As depicted in Figure 14.10, the first canonical variate reflects a strong relationship between a predictor composite made up of marital communication difficulties (AFC and PSC) and conflict over

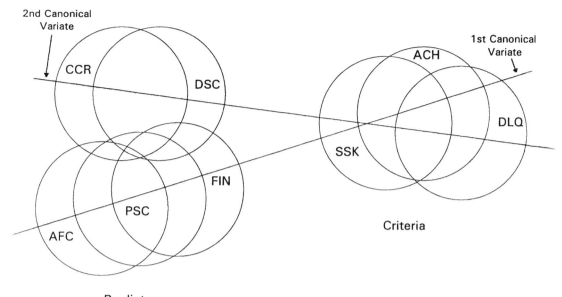

2nd Canonical Variate

1st Canonical Variate

Criteria

Predictors

FIGURE 14.10. Canonical correlation analysis. Two canonical variates account for covariation between five predictor measures reflecting dimensions of marital satisfaction (conflict over childbearing [CCR], dissatisfaction with children [DSC], affective communication [AFC], problem-solving communication [PSC], and disagreement about finances [FIN]) and three criterion measures reflecting dimensions of child adjustment (social skills [SSK], academic achievement [ACH], and delinquency [DLQ]).

finances (FIN) and a criterion composite made up primarily of deficits in social skills (SSK) and academic achievement (ACH).

Canonical analysis then partials out variance in each variable accounted for by the first pair of linear combinations and forms a second pair of linear combinations that provides the maximum possible correlation between remaining (residual) variance in each variable; this second correlation constitutes the second canonical correlation. In this example (see Figure 14.10), the second canonical variate reflects a strong relationship between a predictor composite made up of spousal conflict over childrearing (CCR) and dissatisfaction with children (DSC) and a criterion composite determined primarily by deficits in social skills (SSK), delinquent behavior (DLQ), and—to a lesser extent—academic difficulties (ACH). The number of canonical correlations that can be derived in canonical analysis is one fewer than the smaller of: (a) the number of predictors, or (b) the number of criteria. In the present example, the maximum number of canonical correlations that could be derived is two (one fewer than three).

Interpretive Issues. A major advantage to canonical correlation analysis is its ability to examine intricate relationships among multiple sets of variables typical of theories concerning family systems. However, interpretation of canonical correlations is more complex than interpretation of multiple correlations from regression analysis. First, the meaning of squared canonical correlations differs from the meaning of squared multiple correlations in regression. Because canonical correlations reflect covariation of linear combinations of predictor and criterion variables, one could obtain a large canonical correlation if one predictor variable were highly correlated with only one criterion variable, even if the total variability among predictors was only marginally related to the total variability among criteria. Fortunately, "redundancy analysis" (Stewart & Love, 1968) provides a means for determining the proportion of the total variance in a set of criterion variables accounted for by the total variance in a set of predictor variables for each successive canonical correlation. The overall proportion of variance in a criterion set accounted for by a predictor set is then reflected by the sum of redundancy indices across all possible canonical variates.

Second, interpretation of the underlying constructs reflected by canonical variates is rendered difficult by the complexity of linear combinations on *both* sides of the prediction equation. Further, although the overall variability in a criterion set accounted for by variability in a predictor set may be fairly stable across samples, the canonical weighting of specific variables comprising each canonical correlation may be highly unstable. Therefore, cross-validation is even more critical to interpretation in canonical analysis than in multiple regression analysis, due to sample-specific covariation.

Multiple Discriminant Analysis

Conceptual Issues. Regression analysis techniques are restricted to situations in which the prediction criterion involves a continuous, interval-level variable (e.g., extent of depressed affect or relationship dissatisfaction). What can we do if this requirement is not satisfied? When the criterion variable involves nominal-level measurement (e.g., distinguishing among individuals from different ethnic groups or among intact, separated, and divorced couples), regression procedures can no longer be used. Multiple discriminant analysis is a statistical procedure for distinguishing among individuals comprising two or more groups. Whereas regression techniques lead to prediction of individuals' scores along some continuous interval-level measure, discriminant analysis techniques emphasize classification of individuals into a relatively small number of discrete groups. Discriminant analysis can also be used when scores on an interval-level criterion are related in nonlinear fashion to the predictors (e.g., when optimal family functioning occurs at intermediate levels of attachment between family members, and scores at either end of the attachment continuum—very high or very low—reflect impaired functioning).

Consider, for example, a situation in which we would like to identify predictors of couples' response to marital therapy. Potential predictors of treatment outcome in a hypothetical data set might include the following measures obtained at the beginning of treatment: (1) global marital distress (GDS), (2) commitment to the marriage (COM), (3) additional life event stressors (LES), (4) attribution of marital difficulties to the partner's behavior (partner-blame) (APB), and (5) attribution of marital difficulties to one's own behavior (self-blame) (AOB). In this example, multiple discriminant analysis can be used either for prediction (classification) or for delineating complex multivariate relationships reflected in group differences (theory exploration). As an example of the former, multiple discriminant analysis might be used to identify predictors of treatment response in order to predict outcome (or alter treatment strategy) among a new sample of couples entering therapy. Alternatively, results of the discriminant analysis might be used to examine hypotheses regarding the role of relationship attributions in contributing to or maintaining marital distress.

In multiple discriminant analysis, the investigator identifies a set of predictor variables hypothesized to provide a basis for distinguishing among groups or classes of individuals. Discriminant analysis derives one or more weighted linear combinations of predictor variables (multiple discriminant functions, or MDFs) that optimally discriminate among groups. The maximum number of discriminant functions that can be derived is either (1) one less than the number of groups, or (2) equal to the number of predictor variables if there are more groups than variables. After the first discriminant function has been determined, each successive discriminant function attempts to explain (predict) group differences not already accounted for by previous discriminant functions.

Consider again the example in which discriminant function analysis is used to predict treatment outcome from measures of marital distress, commitment, life event stressors, partner-blame, and self-blame. Figure 14.11 depicts hypothetical results of this analysis where treatment outcome is reflected in spouses' classification into one of three groups: (1) divorced (D), (2) unhappily married (U), and (3) happily married (H). In this example, two discriminant functions have been derived to distinguish among these three criterion groups. The first multiple discriminant function (MDF-1) is determined primarily by weights given to three predictor variables: global distress (GDS), life event stressors (LES), and partner-blame (APB). Individuals' composite scores on this first function discriminate primarily between happily married couples and those who either have divorced or are unhappily married. Scores on this function above 0 identify all the divorced and most of the unhappily married individuals, and scores below 0 identify all the happily married spouses. However, scores on the first discriminant function do not distinguish well between distressed spouses who remain married and those who divorce; for example, with a score of 1 on this function subjects are about as equally likely to end their marriage as to remain unhappily married.

In Figure 14.11, a second discriminant function (MDF-2) has been derived by giving weight primarily to two predictor variables: commitment (COM) and self-blame (AOB). Like the first MDF, this second function distinguishes between divorced and happily married individuals. However, unlike the first MDF, this second discriminant function also distinguishes fairly well between divorced and distressed married spouses. Among the maritally distressed, individuals low on commitment and self-blame (below a score of 0 on this second function) are likely to divorce, whereas those high on

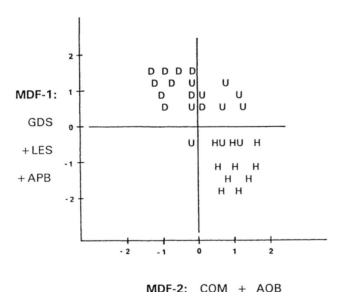

FIGURE 14.11. Classification of happily married (H), unhappily married (U), and divorced (D) couples using multiple discriminant function (MDF) analysis. Predictor variables include global marital distress (GDS), life event stressors (LES), attribution of marital difficulties to partner's behavior (APB), commitment (COM, and attribution of marital difficulties to one's own behavior (AOB).

commitment and self-blame (above a score of 0 on MDF-2) are more likely to retain their marriage.

Procedural Issues. In conducting multiple discriminant analysis, the investigator must first decide how to measure or categorize the criterion variable. For instance, in the example considered earlier, we could have combined divorced with unhappily married couples and retained happily married couples as a separate category to form two groups distinguished primarily by level of relationship distress; alternatively, we could have combined unhappily and happily married couples, retaining divorced couples as a separate category to form two groups distinguished by marital status. In addition, depending on our sample, we might instead identify a fourth group of separated but nondivorced couples. Results of the multiple discriminant analysis will depend on which two-, three-, or four-group classification scheme for the criterion variable we select. Given a sufficient number of valid predictors, the larger the number of criterion groups, the larger the number of discriminant functions that may be derived and the more complicated the interpretation of results will be.

As in multiple regression analysis, the objective of selecting predictor variables in multiple discriminant analysis is to choose the smallest number of predictors that maximally distinguish among groups and minimally correlate with each other. The larger the number of correlated predictors, the more unstable (unreliable) will be the weights given to predictor variables defining the multiple discriminant functions and the interpretations given to these functions. Potential predictor variables should be selected on the basis of theory, previous research, or their relative statistical independence (low intercorrelations).

Also as in regression analysis, results of multiple discriminant analysis depend in part on specific procedures and criteria used for entering and retaining predictor variables in each successive discriminant function. For example, all potential predictors could be entered simultaneously if the objective of the analysis is to delineate structural relationships among predictors as they relate to the criterion for theoretical purposes. Alternatively, a variety of stepwise procedures for entering predictor variables are available that differ primarily in (1) methods used to compute the distances among groups, and (2) criteria for determining the statistical significance of predictor variables' incremental predictive utility. As with multiple regression procedures, the default values for selection criteria set by many statistical packages are quite liberal, often leading to inclusion of marginally useful and unreliable predictors in the discriminant function. Users of these statistical routines should consider options for defining more conservative inclusion criteria.

In addition to deriving multiple discriminant functions, most statistical packages provide the option of applying results to the original sample (or an independent cross-validation sample) to determine the percentage of cases correctly classified by these discriminant functions. Plotting of cases along the discriminant functions, as done in Figure 14.11, can facilitate interpretation of results—particularly when only two or three functions have been derived.

Interpretive Issues. Unlike multiple regression analysis in which a single linear composite predictor equation is derived, discriminant function analysis may produce multiple predictive equations (functions). An initial interpretive task involves deciding how many discriminant functions should be considered; both statistical significance and interpretive meaningfulness enter into this decision. Procedures exist for determining the proportion of criterion variance explained by any given discriminant function relative to the complete set of discriminant functions, as well as for determining the proportion of discriminant function variation explained by group membership.

Interpretive meaningfulness may also be evaluated by considering the theoretical implications of predictor variables weighted highly on a particular discriminant function. Standardized discriminant function weights assigned to predictor variables (called standardized coefficients) denote the relative contribution of each variable to that function. They also possess the nice feature of producing discriminant function scores having a mean of 0 and standard deviation of 1, so that any individual's score on the discriminant function can be easily translated into percentile rank (using a table of *z*-scores for the unit-normal distribution).

As with regression and canonical analysis, individual discriminant function coefficients must be interpreted *within the context of multivariate prediction;* they do not necessarily denote the relative strength of predictors that would be observed in univariate prediction. In addition, as with canonical correlation analysis, discriminant function analysis becomes increasingly complex as the number of functions increases. Moreover, the likelihood that weights assigned to individual predictors will reflect chance covariation increases as (1) the number of predictor variables, criterion groups, and discriminant functions increase; and (2) the number of subjects in the sample of derivation decreases. As with other multivariate procedures, cross-validation of results in an independent sample is highly desirable.

Multiple Cutoff Approach

Conceptual Issues. We have considered prediction situations in which the criterion variable is measured (1) at a nominal level (discriminant analysis), or (2) at an interval level and is related to predictors in linear fashion (regression and canonical analysis). A multiple cutoff approach to prediction is useful when neither of these two situations exists. Specifically, the multiple cutoff technique may be preferable when: (1) the relationship of criterion to predictor(s) is monotonic but nonlinear, (2) the relationships among predictors are nonadditive (noncompensatory), or (3) the application of results mitigates against complex weighting schemes derived from alternative multivariate techniques.

Monotonic but nonlinear relationships occur when higher values of one variable consistently denote either higher or lower values of a second variable, but *not to the same degree* across ranges of the two variables. For example, commitment to one's marriage may remain at a fairly high level across both low and moderate ranges of marital distress but then drop sharply as marital distress reaches a high level (see Figure 14.12). Nonadditive relationships among predictors occur when scores on one predictor variable do not offset (i.e., do not compensate for) the effects of scores on another predictor variable on some criterion. For example, marital distress and commitment may both be related to decisions for divorce; however, in cases in which commitment is very low, even low marital distress may not offset a spouse's propensity to end the marriage.

Specific applications or settings may also argue for using a multiple cutoff approach to combining information from predictors, rather than multiple regression or discriminant analysis, when the consumer of results lacks the means for applying complicated weighting schemes in calculating criterion scores. In such instances, it may be preferable to identify cutoff scores dichotomizing each predictor variable (e.g., more likely versus less likely to divorce) and then determine the number of predictor scores exceeding cutoff required to reach some interpretive decision.

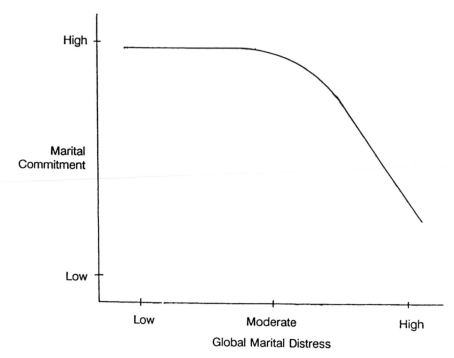

FIGURE 14.12. Monotonic, nonlinear relationship between marital commitment and global marital distress.

Interpretive Issues. An example of the multiple cutoff approach to predicting treatment outcome is provided in a study by Snyder, Mangrum, and Wills (1993) investigating couples' response to marital therapy at termination and 4 years following treatment. Snyder et al. (1993) examined several classes of predictor variables, including (1) demographic measures, (2) self-report measures of relationship functioning, (3) self-report personality measures, (4) observational measures of communication behaviors, and (5) treatment characteristics. Generalized predictors of treatment response were determined by identifying replicated correlations between predictor and outcome across both husbands and wives.

For each generalized predictor of treatment response, a cutoff score was identified that optimally distinguished happily married from distressed married or divorced couples. Subsequent to identifying cutoff scores, additional analyses were conducted to determine the conditional probability of marital distress or divorce as a function of the number of predictors exceeding cutoff (designated as "hits"). An example of these analyses is shown in Table 14.2. Predictor variables in this analysis included (1) MMPI K (Correction) scale, (2) MMPI Depression scale, (3) Feminity scale (Baucom, 1976), and (4) Dyadic Adjustment Scale (Spanier, 1976).

Overall, the base-rate (unconditional) probability of divorce or marital distress in this sample 4 years after completing marital therapy was .35 (11 couples divorced, 8 couples maritally distressed, and 36 happily married couples). However, as shown in Table 14.2, the probability of divorce or marital distress at 4-year follow-up was relatively low for individuals or for couples exceeding only 0–1 cutoff scores on predictor measures (conditional probabilities ranging from .07 to .22); by contrast, poor long-term treatment outcome was considerably more likely for individuals and couples exceeding

TABLE 14.2. Conditional Probability (CP) of Divorce
or Marital Distress 4 Years after Therapy as a Function
of Number of Predictors Exceeding Cutoff at Intake

Predictors	n	CP
Husbands		
0–1	29	.14
2–4	26	.58
Wives		
0–1	32	.22
2–4	23	.52
Couples		
0–1	15	.07
2–4	29	.34
5–7	11	.73

cutoff scores on a majority of predictor measures (conditional probabilities ranging from
.52 to .73). Applying this approach to clinical settings provides an efficient method
for therapists to identify critical areas of vulnerability for tailoring treatment strategy
to the specific needs of a couple.

DISCUSSION

Correlation itself is a simple concept. Some things go hand in hand; they covary. The
techniques reviewed here, ranging from simple correlation to more complex multivariate procedures, all stem from this basic interest in describing how fluctuation in one
phenomenon relates to fluctuation in another.

Correlational techniques can become more complex because of issues concerning
how we measure the things we're interested in, how many things we're predicting to
and from, how predictors overlap and influence each other, how many observations
we're able to obtain, how well these observations reflect other situations of interest,
and our ability to make use of what we discover.

Issues of Sampling

Throughout our discussion we have noted three issues regarding the sample of individuals
for whom data are collected: size, range, and representativeness. Because of the potential for multivariate techniques to capitalize on chance covariation among predictor
and criterion variables, it is critical that the sample be large relative to the total number of variables being considered. Subject-to-variable ratios of 10:1 are encouraged, with
5:1 being a minimum standard. At the same time that large samples contribute to the
stability of findings, they also enable relatively small correlations to reach statistical
significance. Consequently, one should consider the meaningfulness of correlations
(reflected in r^2 or R^2) as well as their statistical significance.

The ability of two variables to covary depends in part on the degree of variability
in each independently. When the range of observations on one or both variables is
restricted, the observed correlation between them may underestimate their true correlation in the larger population. Restricted range may result from either inadequate measurement techniques or inadequate sampling.

However, it is also critical that the sample be representative of the population to which findings will be applied. If the sample of application has a restricted range, generalizing a correlation derived from a sample with unrestricted range to the sample with restricted range will lead to faulty conclusions. For example, although depression and marital distress may covary in the general population, they may not correlate among couples entering marital therapy, when levels of marital distress tend to be restricted to moderate or high levels.

Issues of Reliability and Validity

Considerations of sample size relate directly to issues of reliability. Using multivariate correlational procedures in studies with low subject-to-variable ratios will inevitably lead to unstable results. Even when the overall magnitude of relationship between criterion and predictor(s) remains stable, the weights assigned to individual predictors may vary considerably across samples. The problems of unstable weights are magnified when multiple linear composites are derived as in canonical correlation or discriminant function analysis, or when predictor variables are highly intercorrelated (the problem of multicollinearity).

The reliability of findings also suffers from "fishing" expeditions—when the investigator searches for significant correlations in a relatively large matrix without specifying prior to the analysis which correlations are predicted to reach significance and in which direction. For example, even a relatively small matrix of intercorrelations among 10 variables produces 45 unique correlations, two or more of which may be expected to reach statistical significance at $p < .05$ by chance alone. Cross-validation of findings across split-half samples greatly reduces the likelihood of attributing meaningfulness to chance findings.

Even reliable (replicable) findings may not be valid; that is, they may not really mean what we believe they mean (or may not represent what we propose them to represent) and thus may not generalize to some intended application. There are numerous sources of compromised validity. First, the investigator must identify variables likely to correlate with other variables of interest based on theory, prior research, or subjective experience; inadequate selection of constructs may compromise either prediction strategies or efforts to delineate structural relationships of theoretical relevance. Second, once relevant constructs are identified, we need to select appropriate measures of those constructs—a task that can only be accomplished by examining what those measures have previously been shown to relate to on an empirical basis.

Third, the validity of findings depends on the appropriateness of the statistical procedures applied to the data. For example, variables with bivariate distributions departing significantly from requirements of normality, linearity, and homoscedasticity may require alternative statistical procedures from those reviewed here. In addition, specific criteria and procedures adopted in multivariate correlational techniques may be inappropriate to either the measures, the sample, or intended application of results.

Finally, the meaningfulness of multivariate correlational techniques often depends on the extent to which linear composites of variables (as in multiple regression, canonical correlation, or discriminant function analysis) lend themselves to unambiguous interpretation. Unfortunately, it is not uncommon for investigators to seize upon the weights of one or two variables meeting their theoretical bias for "labeling" a canonical variate or discriminant function while ignoring significantly weighted variables not meeting their bias. The proportion of variance in linear composite scores accounted for by all predictor variables contributing to that composite should be carefully considered.

Issues of Application

Misinterpretation of correlations as reflecting causal relationships constitutes the most common abuse of correlational techniques. Covariation demands further explanation. The functional relationship between two related phenomena—that is, the extent to which one variable influences another—must always be established by observing effects of controlled manipulation.

The second most common error in using multivariate techniques is to interpret weights assigned to predictor variables as reflecting their relative importance separate from the multivariate prediction context. We have noted in our discussion that a predictor variable correlating highly with the criterion may receive no weight in a multivariate analysis because of its overlap with other predictors, whereas another predictor correlating not at all with the criterion may receive a strong weighting because of its role as a suppressor variable. An implication of this principle is that univariate (simple or zero-order) correlations should always be presented along with multivariate results. Also, as we noted earlier, when presenting results of regression or discriminant function analysis, both standardized and unstandardized weights should be presented.

Despite these limitations, multivariate correlational techniques provide powerful tools for exploring and discovering important relationships among variables of interest. Even simple correlation allows us to confirm or disconfirm the relatedness of two phenomena that *appear* informally to co-relate and to establish the magnitude of this relationship. More sophisticated multivariate procedures permit hypothesis testing of the relative importance of specific factors in the context of related factors through hierarchical approaches to data analysis.

In addition to articulating criteria for including and retaining predictor variables in any given analysis, the meaningfulness of predictors should be communicated by presenting information about the change in R and R^2 resulting from inclusion of any specific predictor. In canonical correlation and discriminant function analysis, the percentage of criterion variance explained by each linear composite should be specified.

Graphic presentation of results can dramatically facilitate their interpretation. Plots of simple regression lines, with confidence bands for prediction indicated by including lines reflecting $\pm 1 \, s_{est(Y)}$, effectively depict both the nature of the bivariate distribution and prediction accuracy. In multiple discriminant function analysis, plots of cases on respective functions indicate the accuracy of classification and enhance interpretation of discriminant functions' utility in distinguishing among specific criterion groups.

Finally, when correlational techniques are intended to facilitate clinical intervention as well as theoretical understanding, methods should be used to maximize efficient application of results. Multiple cutoffs and contingent probability analysis reflect one approach toward this end (cf. Snyder, Lachar, Freiman, & Hoover, 1991). Alternatively, investigators could make available simple spreadsheets on floppy disk in which clinicians or other consumers could enter subjects' raw scores on measures and the spreadsheet would compute predicted criterion scores, confidence intervals for estimated scores, and interpretive guidelines for score ranges.

FUTURE DIRECTIONS

We began this chapter by suggesting that correlational techniques provide an important bridge between observation of two or more phenomena and efforts to modify the same. We noted that considerable research has established the linkage of depressed affect and marital conflict, although the precise nature of this complex relationship remains unclear (Snyder & Heim, 1992). As with other areas of correlational research involving marital and family dynamics, findings relating depression to marital discord have led to new treatment approaches aimed at the co-occurrence of these two clinical concerns and experimental investigations of these treatments' efficacy (Beach, Sandeen, & O'Leary, 1990; Clarkin, Haas, & Glick, 1988; Jacobson, Dobson, Fruzzetti, Schmaling, & Salusky, 1991). We anticipate that other correlational studies of couples and families regarding other clinical phenomena will similarly facilitate development and validation of more effective intervention approaches.

A variety of texts provides good introductions to multivariate correlational techniques (e.g., Bernstein, 1988; Harris, 1985; Tabachnick & Fidell, 1983); others offer more detailed presentations of these same procedures (e.g., Cohen & Cohen, 1983; Pedhazur, 1982). Similarly, several statistical packages provide excellent discussions of multivariate procedures for the unsophisticated user, including SAS (SAS Institute, 1992) and the Statistical Package for the Social Sciences (SPSS, Inc., 1990); both provide software for personal computer as well as mainframe applications.

More sophisticated multivariate prediction techniques are being developed on a regular basis. Others already developed in the agricultural, economic, and physical sciences are finding their way into the behavioral sciences. Although we expect new techniques to become available, we anticipate that the greatest development over the next decade will be the increasing use of such current techniques as multiple regression and discriminant function analysis by marital and family researchers.

Finally, we anticipate that future investigators will retain a keen appreciation for the application of their findings in the typical clinical setting. Conscientious efforts must be made to bridge research and practice. These include development of theory with explicit implications for overt operations of assessment and intervention, use of measures accessible to the modal clinician, and translation of complex multivariate findings into specific applications.

REFERENCES

Abelson, R. P. (1985). A variance explanation paradox: When a little is a lot. *Psychological Bulletin, 97*, 129–133.

Baucom, D. H. (1976). Independent masculinity and femininity scales on the California Psychological Inventory. *Journal of Consulting and Clinical Psychology, 44*, 876.

Beach, S. R. H., Sandeen, E. E., & O'Leary, K. D. (1990). *Depression in marriage: A model for etiology and treatment.* New York: Guilford Press.

Bernstein, I. H. (1988). *Applied multivariate analysis.* New York: Springer-Verlag.

Binet, A., & Simon, T. (1905). Methodes nouvelles pour le diagnostic du niveau intellectuel des anormaux. *Annee Psychologique, 11*, 191–244.

Butcher, J. N., Dahlstrom, W. G., Graham, J. R., Tellegen, A., Kaemmer, B. (1989). *Manual for the Minnesota Multiphasic Personality Inventory–2.* Minneapolis, MN: University of Minnesota Press.

Cattell, J. M. (1890). Mental tests and measurements. *Mind, 15*, 373–380.

Cavell, T. A., & Snyder, D. K. (1991). Iconoclasm versus innovation: Building a science of family therapy—Comment on Moon, Dillon, and Sprenkle. *Journal of Marital and Family Therapy, 17*, 167–171.

Clarkin, J. F., Haas, G. L., & Glick, I. D. (Eds.). (1988). *Affective disorders and the family: Assessment and treatment.* New York: Guilford Press.

Cohen, J., & Cohen, P. (1983). *Applied multivariate analysis/linear regression* (2nd ed.). Hillsdale, NJ: Erlbaum.

Costa, P. T., & McCrae, R. R. (1992). Normal personality assessment in clinical practice: The NEO personality inventory. *Psychological Assessment, 4,* 5–13.

Fisher, R. A. (1921). On the "probable error" of a coefficient of correlation deduced from a small sample. *Metron, 1*(P. 4), 3–32.

Formanek, R., & Gurian, A. (Eds.). (1987). *Women and depression: A lifetime perspective.* New York: Springer.

Galton, F. (1888). Co-relations and their measurement. *Proceedings of the Royal Society, 45,* 135–145.

Harris, R. J. (1985). *A primer of multivariate analysis.* Orlando, FL: Academic Press.

Jacobson, N. S., Dobson, K., Fruzzetti, A. E., Schmaling, K. B., & Salusky, S. (1991). Marital therapy as a treatment for depression. *Journal of Consulting and Clinical Psychology, 59,* 547–557.

Jacobson, N. S., Holtzworth-Munroe, A., & Schmaling, K. B. (1989). Marital therapy and spouse involvement in the treatment of depression, agoraphobia, and alcoholism. *Journal of Consulting and Clinical Psychology, 57,* 5–10.

Nunnally, J. C., & Bernstein, I. H. (1994). *Psychometric theory* (3rd ed.). New York: McGraw-Hill.

Ozer, D. J. (1985). Correlation and the coefficient of determination. *Psychological Bulletin, 97,* 307–315.

Pearson, K. (1896). Mathematical contributions to the theory of evolution: Regression, heredity, and panmixia. *Philosophical Transactions, 187a,* 253–318.

Pedhazur, E. J. (1982). *Multiple regression in behavioral research: Explanation and prediction* (2nd ed.). New York: Holt, Rinehart & Winston.

SAS Institute. (1992). *SAS/LAB software: User's guide.* Cary, NC: Author.

Snyder, D. K. (1981). *Manual for the Marital Satisfaction Inventory.* Los Angeles, CA: Western Psychological Services.

Snyder, D. K., & Heim, S. C. (1992). Marriage, depression, and cognition: Unraveling the Gordian knot—Reply to Ettinger et al. *Journal of Marital and Family Therapy, 18,* 303–307.

Snyder, D. K., Lachar, D., Freiman, K. E., & Hoover, D. W. (1991). Toward the actuarial assessment of couples' relationships. In J. P. Vincent (Ed.), *Advances in family intervention, assessment, and theory* (Vol. 5, pp. 89–122). London: Kingsley Publishers.

Snyder, D. K., Mangrum, L. F., & Wills, R. M. (1993). Predicting couples' response to marital therapy: A comparison of short- and long-term predictors. *Journal of Consulting and Clinical Psychology, 61,* 61–69.

Spanier, G. B. (1976). Measuring dyadic adjustment: New scales for assessing the quality of marriage and similar dyads. *Journal of Marriage and the Family, 38,* 15–28.

Spearman, C. (1910). Correlation calculated from faulty data. *British Journal of Psychology, 3,* 271–295.

SPSS, Inc. (1990). *SPSS reference guide.* Chicago, IL: Author.

Stevens, S. S. (1946). On the theory of scales of measurement. *Science, 103,* 677–680.

Stewart, D., & Love, W. (1968). A general canonical correlation index. *Psychological Bulletin, 70,* 160–163.

Tabachnick, B. G., & Fidell, L. S. (1983). *Using multivariate statistics.* New York: Harper & Row.

Terman, L. M. (1916). *The measurement of intelligence.* Boston, MA: Houghton Mifflin.

Terman, L. M. (1938). *Psychological factors in marital happiness.* New York: McGraw-Hill.

Thurstone, L. L. (1947). *Multiple factor analysis.* Chicago, IL: University of Chicago Press.

Wirt, R. D., Lachar, D., Klinedinst, J. K., & Seat, P. D. (1984). *Multidimensional description of child personality: A manual for the Personality Inventory for Children* (1984 revision by D. Lachar). Los Angeles, CA: Western Psychological Services.

15

Structural Equation Modeling

ROBERT J. VOLK
DENISE E. FLORI

BACKGROUND

The tradition of structural equation modeling (SEM) in family therapy research is a brief one, as the technique is only beginning to show up in the empirical literature. SEM applications are more common in the family studies and family psychology literatures, where studies have focused on testing models of family or individual functioning (Braver et al., 1993; Deal, Wampler, & Halverson, 1992; Dumka & Roosa, 1993; Floyd & Wasner, 1994; Fowers, Applegate, Olson, & Pomerantz, 1994; Gottman, 1993; Lussier, Sabourin, & Wright, 1993) or validating existing measurement instruments and methods for assessing family functioning (Bray & Harvey, 1992; Cole & McPherson, 1993; Kurdek, 1992). Some of the more powerful applications of SEM in family therapy process and outcome research have not yet been realized.

SEM is a general class of data analytic strategies that combines multiple regression and factor analysis. Multiple regression is described in detail by Snyder and Mangrum (Chapter 14, of this volume). In brief, it is a technique whereby an investigator attempts to predict a percentage of the variance in a dependent variable from a group of independent variables. Factor analysis is described in the chapter on scale development (Snyder & Rice, Chapter 10, this volume). Factor analysis is a statistical technique that enables researchers to determine which items of an instrument are sufficiently positively correlated with each other, and sufficiently negatively correlated with the other items of the instrument, to be considered a cohesive "factor" or subscale of the instrument.

Historically, SEM developed from work in two different fields. Economists have used SEM and multiple regression to estimate the effects of independent variables on dependent variables as mediated by intervening variables. At the same time, psychometricians have used factor analysis to examine properties of measurement tools and theoretical constructs.

These two traditions came together in several areas, including studies of adolescent drug use where large, longitudinal datasets where available. The historical development of SEM has run parallel to the development of statistical software packages for analyzing increasingly complex models. A widely available package is EQS (Bentler, 1985). This package relies on specifying models as a series of equations including the parameters to be estimated. It is a highly flexible package with numerous estimators for nonnormal data. (A Windows version is now available.) LISREL is a second, popular package (Jöreskog & Sörbom, 1989). Unlike EQS, LISREL requires respecifying a model using LISREL Model notation, including Greek symbols for various parameter estimates and pattern matrices following the structural equations. (The most recent version of LISREL allows for editing path diagrams interactively, avoiding cumbersome matrix specifications.)

The purpose of this chapter is to provide clinicians with a nontechnical introduction to SEM and to highlight potential applications of SEM for the family therapy researcher. Emphasis is placed on the composition of a structural model (e.g., variables, relationships among variables), and conceptual issues in model development and hypothesis testing, while reference is made to more technical overviews for interested readers. Our presentation is balanced to reflect applications of greatest utility to family therapy researchers. SEM requires large datasets (200 subjects or *more* is a general rule, although smaller samples can be used as well). When the variables are not normally distributed, which is often the case in research on families, much larger datasets are needed. Thus, we pay greater attention to applications involving the evaluation of measurement instruments and constructs, where large datasets are more readily available, while we provide a briefer overview of applications in prediction and outcome research. The construct of *expressed emotion* and its relationship to health and functional status is used as a backdrop for reviewing applications of SEM. An example of confirmatory factor analysis is given through validation of the Family Emotional Involvement and Criticism Scale (FEICS) (Shields, Franks, Harp, McDaniel, & Campbell, 1992), using data from a study of National Guard personnel collected shortly after their return from the Persian Gulf War. The chapter concludes with a brief discussion of the strengths and weaknesses of SEM in family therapy research.

Some initial comments are in order before we begin our overview of SEM. Investigators interested in applications of SEM should consider the following issues. A background in factor analysis and regression is essential before considering any type of modeling in which latent variables (i.e., factors) are incorporated and relationships among latent variables are estimated. In the context of graduate training, SEM might be considered an advanced statistics course, taken after regression/analysis of variance and psychometrics/factor analysis training is completed. Second, as mentioned earlier, SEM requires large datasets. If the variables included in a model are not normally distributed, even larger datasets are needed. Third, evaluating the fit of a model, although always driven by substantive concerns, can be difficult as there are many different indicators of goodness of fit. Decisions about modifying a model must be made, weighing the improvement in fit of a model on both theoretical/substantive grounds and statistical grounds. Neither alone is sufficient to demonstrate that one model is better than another. Finally, the statistical software, although greatly improved, still requires a great deal of knowledge about structural equations. Clearly, the statistician and theoretician must work closely throughout the entire process of model testing and modification.

An Overview of SEM

Structural Equation Modeling by Another Name

SEM is a general class of analytic strategies for testing causal theories using nonexperimental data (Martin, 1987). Recently, applications have been extended to experimental data as well (Aiken, Stein, & Bentler, 1994). SEM encompasses a number of techniques: covariance structure modeling, latent variable modeling, confirmatory factor analysis, path analysis and linear structural relations. Each technique shares a common strategy of simultaneous estimation of correlational data.

The term "covariance structure modeling" refers to testing theoretical models of the causal relationships among variables, where such relationships are expressed as variances and covariances among observed variables (i.e., there is some "structure" to the variances and covariances). A theoretical model can be represented by the variability of each variable (i.e., variances) and the relationship among each pair of variables (i.e., covariances). When expressed as a matrix of variances and covariances, a theory is said to impose a "structure" on the matrix, and if the theory is a good one, the difference between observed variances/covariances (the data we collect) and those produced within the constraints of a theory should be small. This term is synonymous with structural equation modeling. *Latent variable models* include constructs that are measured indirectly through such observed variables as items on an assessment questionnaire or observations from a rating scale. The observed variables (the data we collect) are considered indicators of underlying, indirectly observed constructs. In these models, latent constructs can be predicted by, and serve as predictors of, other observed and latent variables. *Causal modeling* implies some causal nature to the model, often through the use of time-ordered (longitudinal) data. Causal modeling is often used, inappropriately, to describe the more general structural equation modeling. *Confirmatory factor analysis* (CFA) is a general analytic strategy for evaluating the factor structure of measurement instruments or theoretical constructs. It also serves as the measurement model in latent variable models. *Path analysis* refers to traditional techniques of regression-based analysis, with the addition of simultaneous estimation, affording additional indicators of goodness of fit. In traditional path analysis, a separate regression equation is solved for each dependent variable. In path analysis using SEM, the relationships among the variables are estimated simultaneously in a single equation. Path analysis uses only observed variables (as opposed to latent variables) and emphasizes estimating direct and indirect effects. Finally, *linear structural relations*, or LISREL (*LI*near Structural *REL*ations), is a modeling strategy that relies on Greek notation and matrix algebra in specifying and testing structural equation models. LISREL is also a common SEM software package (Jöreskog & Sörbom, 1989).

Path Diagramming Conventions

Diagramming conventions for structural equation models follow those used in path diagrams. These conventions are depicted in Figure 15.1. Squares (or rectangles) represent *observed* variables. The observed variables might be scores from a self-report assessment tool, individual items from a questionnaire, ratings from observations, laboratory test values, or any other observed measure. Circles represent *latent* variables, which are measured indirectly through the observed variables. Straight arrows represent cause and effect or predictive relationships. In the figure, the first latent variable predicts the second latent variable. In this case, the first latent variable is considered an *exogenous* variable (i.e., it predicts, but is not predicted by, other variables in the model). The second latent variable is considered an *endogenous* variable (i.e., it is predicted by other variables. Endogenous variables can also predict other endogenous variables). In addition, there are six observed variables, three each *loading* on the two latent variables. Finally, curved arrows represent correlations or covariances, and assume no directional or causal relationships.

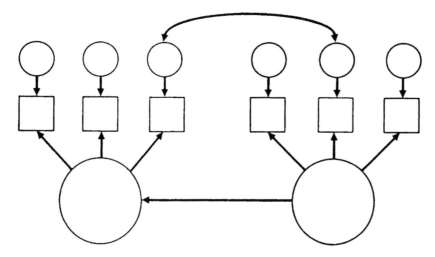

FIGURE 15.1. Path diagramming conventions used in SEM.

The Logic of SEM

In a sense, SEM might be seen as a combination of factor analysis and regression. First, consider the regression-based aspects of SEM. The multiple regression approach follows the general linear model. In multiple regression, a single, normally distributed dependent variable is regressed on one or more independent variables. The regression coefficients represent the unique association of each predictor variable with the dependent variable, controlling for other variables in the model. Goodness of fit is evaluated based on the proportion of variance in the dependent variable explained by the predictor variables, expressed as R^2 (the squared multiple correlation). The greater the proportion of variance explained, the better the model. When certain variables are hypothesized to have an effect on other variables both directly and through influence on intervening variables, the modeling strategy is referred to as path analysis. Again, though, there is a single dependent variable for each equation estimated.

In the regression model, it is assumed that all variables are measured perfectly reliably, and hence there is no measurement error. Yet, this is rarely the case. The problem can be demonstrated using classical test theory. Following classical test theory, the variance of any variable can be expressed as reliable variance (true score variance) and unreliable variance (error variance). Figure 15.2 depicts this relationship for a single variable, X, denoted by a square. The larger circle represents the proportion of reliable variance of X, whereas the smaller circle represents the proportion of unreliable variance (or error). In the case of multiple regression, the loading from the larger circle to the observed variable is assumed to be equal to 1.0—that is, all the variance of X is assumed to be perfectly reliable, and there is no measurement error. Figure 15.3 extends this assumption to the regression model, where three observed variables, mea-

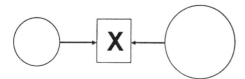

FIGURE 15.2. Reliable (larger circle) and error (small circle) variance of observed variable X.

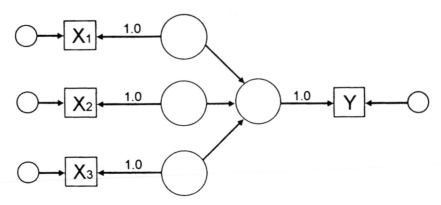

FIGURE 15.3. Regression model, with implicit structure and no measurement error.

sured without error, predict a dependent variable, also measured without error. This figure is the regression model, including the assumed perfect reliability of the measures. However, the assumption of perfect reliability is rarely met. The result is biased regression coefficients and less variance explained in the dependent variables.

As measurement error is almost always a concern, accounting for unreliability must be considered when estimating the relationships among variables. Again following classical test theory, error variances are assumed to be randomly distributed and should not covary between variables. Thus, any covariance among variables (i.e., the degree to which variables are correlated) is assumed to be error-free. By using multiple indicators of a variable, the common variance (the factor) can be retained and then used to both predict and be predicted by other variables. Thus, rather than using standard multiple regression with observed variables, SEM uses *factors* in regression analyses. Although there are many variations to this theme in SEM, this combination of factor analysis and regression is generally the common strategy.

To explain the factor-analytic aspects of SEM, it is helpful to consider an example. Marital quality is a construct in that it cannot be measured directly and objectively (there is no blood test for determining a quality marriage). Thus researchers have created questionnaires or assessment tools that serve as "indicators" of the construct. By asking a series of questions in a questionnaire (e.g., "How satisfied are you with your marriage?" "How much time do you spend with your spouse?"), the researcher is taking a number of "shots" at the construct, as though trying to triangulate on the true underlying state. In this sense, the construct is being measured indirectly through the questions (i.e., the construct is latent), and the questions are simply indicators of the construct. What they have in common (called factors) must be the construct.

The Measurement and Structural Models

This section describes the anatomy of a structural model. The measurement model is important because it depicts the relationships between the observed variables and the constructs, whereas the structural model depicts the relationships among the constructs. The concepts presented here will become clearer as we use them throughout the various applications that follow.

Measurement Model. Measurement models depict the relationships *between* observed variables and latent variables. The measurement model includes the data we collect.

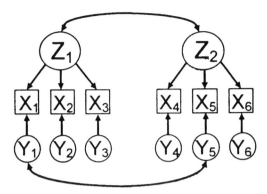

FIGURE 15.4. Measurement model.

Figure 15.4 gives a hypothetical measurement model. There are six observed variables (X_1 to X_6), also called indicators. To return to our previous example, these observed variables might be questions from a questionnaire or observations from a coding scheme for assessing marital quality. These variables are considered observed because these are the data we collect. Three of the observed variables load on one latent variable (Z_1), and the remaining three load on another latent variable (Z_2). The latent variables are the constructs we are trying to measure, in this example marital quality of husbands (Z_1) and wives (Z_2). They are latent because we observe them indirectly by asking lots of questions or rating them using a coding system. The curved arrow between the two latent variables indicates they are correlated, although no directional influence is specified. Residual variances (the error variances, also called unique factors) are noted as Y_1 to Y_6, and represent the proportion of the variance of each observed variable is not shared with other observed variables loading on the same latent variable.

The relationships among the observed and latent variables may not be entirely obvious to readers less familiar with factor analysis. The direction of the arrows is from the latent variable to the observed variables. The observed variables serve as imperfect measures of the underlying construct. This specification assumes there is some underlying construct, measured indirectly and representing common aspects of the indicators. The construct is assumed to "drive" scores of the observed variables. The measurement model also includes residual variances or unique factors (Y_1 to Y_6), again with the direction of effects from the unique factor to the observed variable. A unique factor represents the proportion of a variable that is not shared with the other observed variables loading on the same common factor. This unique factor contains error variance (assumed to be random) and may also contain reliable variance that is not shared with the other variables loading on the same common factor. At the same time, unique factors can be correlated, Y_1 with Y_5 for example, if such a relationship is substantively meaningful.

Structural Model. Figure 15.5 gives a hypothetical structural model. The structural model specifies the relationships among the latent variables and does not include the observed variables from the measurement model. In other words, the structural model specifies relationships among factors. Note there are several *exogenous* variables (Z_1 and Z_2), in this case specified as latent variables, predicting three latent *endogenous* variables (Z_3, Z_4, and Z_5). The structural model might also be specified using *only* observed variables (squares), in which case the model would represent a path model and path analysis with SEM might be chosen as the appropriate analytic strategy. (When there is no measurement model, the analysis is a path analysis.) As with multiple regression, the exogenous variables are correlated. Unlike a regression-based model, the endogenous

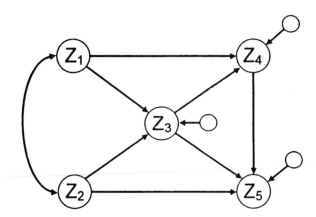

FIGURE 15.5. Structural model.

variables can also serve as predictors of other endogenous variables. Directional relationships among what are traditionally considered dependent variables are allowed in the structural model. The smaller circles associated with each endogenous variable represent the proportion of variance not explained by the exogenous predictors.

General Structural Model. The general structural model combines both the measurement and structural models in specifying the entire relational structure. It is within the general structural model that the mix of factor analysis and regression can be seen. Figure 15.6 gives a general structural model, combining the measurement and structural models from Figures 15.4 and 15.5. This is a desirable specification for several reasons. First, as all structural variables (the Z variables) are latent, they are theoretically assumed to be free of measurement error. In effect, by specifying a measurement model, the proportion of reliable common variance in the observed variables is partitioned from unreliable (error) and unique variance, resulting in error-free latent constructs. For example, rather than using responses to a single question as a measure of a construct, the model might include several questions as indicators of a construct. All paths predicting relationships among latent variables will be adjusted for measurement error, typically increasing the magnitude of the path coefficients. At the same time, only error-free variance is retained in endogenous variables, also tending to result in a greater proportion of explained variance (higher R^2). This latter point is a crucial one, as regression and analysis of variance fail to account for unreliability in independent and dependent variables, imposing a "ceiling" on the proportion of variance that is available to be explained and on the magnitude of the regression coefficients. In addition, the paths will be differentially adjusted for measurement error, as the observed variables that serve as indicators of latent constructs will be unreliable to different degrees.

A second advantage of the general structural model is simultaneous estimation of the parameter values (path coefficients, factor loadings, etc.). That is, a single analysis is run, as opposed to running many analyses to estimate the relationships among the predictors. Through estimating the model simultaneously, we can evaluate the fit of the entire model. The measurement model can also be tested using simultaneous estimation procedures, which is often done prior to estimating the entire general structure model. By estimating model parameters simultaneously, a host of goodness-of-fit indices can be computed, in contrast to multiple regression where the proportion of variance explained in the dependent variable is the typical measure of goodness of fit. This array

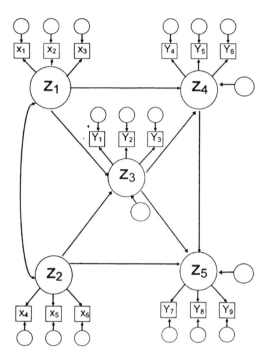

FIGURE 15.6. General structural model (measurement and structural model).

of fit indices can be used in testing hypotheses about competing alternative models or the equivalence of models across samples.

METHODOLOGY

Steps in the Process of SEM

This section provides an overview of the steps taken in the process of SEM. Table 15.1 outlines each step for the reader. We then take the reader through an example of confirmatory factor analyses using the FEICS.

Step 1: Model Specification—"The Way Things Appear to Be"

As SEM is a general analytic strategy for testing theoretical models, the researcher always starts with a theory. Concepts central to understanding a phenomenon must be identified and organized such that their relationships are clearly delineated. It makes no sense to test poorly developed theories. There must be a model representing how the investigator perceives things to be. *Step 1A* in the process is to express the theoretical model using the path diagramming conventions described earlier. Observed variables should be indicated, it should be clear which constructs load on which observed variables, and the relationships among the variables should be depicted. The result should be a path diagram with rectangles, circles, curved and straight lines, specifying all relationships in the model.

TABLE 15.1. Steps in the Process of Structural Equation Modeling

---

Step 1: Model Specification—"The Way Things Appear to Be"
  Step 1A: Begin with a theoretical model. Express model using path diagramming conventions.
  Step 1B: Prepares the model for analysis. (Re-express path diagram as structural equations or using ma-
            trices, depending on software package used.)
  Step 1C: Assess the identification status of the model. Can a unique, best solution be achieved, or are
            there too many relationships to be estimated?

Step 2: Model Estimation—"Testing Our Model against the Real World"
  Step 2A: Design a study, collect some data.
  Step 2B: Examine distributions of the variables included in the model. Select an appropriate estima-
            tion strategy for the level of measurement and distribution of the data. (A larger sample is
            needed if data are not normal; correlations should be used when variables are measured on
            an ordinal level.)
  Step 2C: Write the program and test the model against the data.
  Step 2D: Examine the fit of the model. Consider global indicators of fit and indicators for specific vari-
            ables in the model.

Step 3: Compare to Viable Alternative Models—"Is There a Better Model Out There?"
  Find the most parsimonious model, which provides an acceptable fit to the data.

Step 4: Model Modification and Reestimation—"Making Things a Little Better"
  Consider meaningful modifications which improve the fit of the model, both substantively and statistically. Reestimate the modified model, compared to previous models.

Step 5: Validation—"Can We Do It Again?"
  When a modified model is accepted, the study should be repeated again, in an attempt to "confirm"
  the new model.

Step 1B prepares the model for analysis. Depending on the software package selected, the model must be reexpressed as structural equations or, in the case of LISREL,
in LISREL Model form with Greek symbols. From this point on in the process, it is
important to involve a statistician or someone knowledgeable in SEM. *Step 1C* is to
determine whether or not the model is "identified." Simply, the model must not include so many paths that a unique best solution cannot be found. If there are too many
paths, the model may not be identified. Parsimony is always the goal in specifying and
testing a model. Again, a statistician should be involved at this point.

Step 2: Model Estimation— "Testing our Model against the Real World"

Implied in this discussion is that somewhere in the process the researcher needs to acquire some data (*step 2A*). This is not a chapter on research design and data collection,
but we assume that the researcher has selected a good design given the research question and has drawn a sample representative of the population of interest. In *step 2B*,
the researcher should consider the distributions of the variables included in the model.
Ideally, all variables are measured on an interval level and are normally distributed.
In practice, this is rarely the case. Much like linear regression, models can be tested
with less concern about level of measurement of the independent variables if the dependent variables are continuous and normally distributed. When they are not, different estimators need to be selected (nonnormal theory estimators) and much larger sample
sizes are required (in excess of 200 cases) (Jöreskog & Sörbom, 1988). It is also preferred
that the dependent variables be measured at an interval level (e.g., infant birth weight

in grams), so that covariances rather than correlations can be used. When interval-level measures are used, the units are meaningful and the relationships among variables are easier to describe. Correlations should be used when ordinal measures are used (e.g., marital quality). When correlations are used, the magnitude of effects can be compared within the model but not to effects in other models.

The program is then written and the model tested against the data (*step 2C*). In *step 2D*, the fit of the model is examined. The researcher needs to make some assessment of how well the theoretical model fit the observed data. Many indicators of fit use differences between the observed variances and covariances and those reproduced in the analysis based on restrictions imposed by the theoretical model. These differences are referred to as residuals. For example, if in the model two variables are hypothesized to be uncorrelated, any observed correlation is unexpected. If these residuals are big, the model is said to provide a poor fit. There are numerous indicators of fit available to the investigator, some evaluating the model as a whole and others considering individual coefficients (e.g., Bentler & Bonett, 1980; Jöreskog & Sörbom, 1989; Tucker & Lewis, 1973).

Step 3: Compare to Viable Alternative Models— "Is There a Better Model Out There?"

In model testing, it is crucial to consider alternative models. The logic of model testing is to accept a model until a better one comes along. The goal is always parsimony, and simpler specifications should also be considered. There may be competing theories about how variables are related. These competing models should be tested with the same data, and the fit of each model compared.

Step 4: Model Modification and Reestimation— "Making Things a Little Better"

It is often the case that an initial model specification, while good, could be improved upon by adding or deleting paths, loadings, correlations, and so forth. MacCallum, Roznowski, and Necovitz (1992) have referred to this process as the *specification search*. The task is to considered meaningful modifications that improve the fit of the model without capitalizing on chance. At this point, SEM becomes more of an art than a science. The entire process needs to be driven by theory, while the model testing simply provides additional information on how likely the result is due to chance.

Step 5: Validation—"Can We Do It Again?"

This step is missing from most model testing. Any time modification is considered, the testing moves from confirmation to exploration, and an exploratory model needs to be reconfirmed on a new sample. The concern is that the modified model is simply a chance finding that would not be replicated if the study were conducted again using a new sample.

Validation of the FEICS Using Confirmatory Factor Analysis

The Expressed Emotion Construct and the FEICS

To demonstrate various applications of SEM for family therapy research, we use the *expressed emotion* construct and its relationship to health and functional status. The construct of *expressed emotion* was first identified in Great Britain as an important predictor of relapse among schizophrenics (Booker, 1990). High *expressed emotion,* and in particular frequent critical comments, was found to be related to relapse in schizophrenic patients following hospital discharge. Recently, the construct has been applied to other clinical problems, including relapse by patients with unipolar depressive disorders (Hooley & Teasdale, 1989), heightened depressive symptoms (Florin, Nostadt, Reck, Franzen, & Jenkins, 1992), and diabetic control in children (Koenigsberg, Klausner, Pelino, Rosnick, & Campbell, 1993). Shields and colleagues have used the concept to study mental health and healthy cardiovascular behaviors in primary care patients (Franks, Campbell, & Shields, 1992).

The FEICS was developed by Shields et al. (1992) to operationalize two constructs from *expressed emotion* theory: *perceived criticism* and *emotional involvement.* Although *expressed emotion* has typically been measured using behavioral rating schemes with skilled observers, the FEICS provides a self-report measure of *expressed emotion* from the subject's perspective. Even-numbered items from the 14-item scale are indicators of *perceived criticism* whereas odd-numbered items are indicators of *emotional involvement.* Items are scored on a 5-point scale, ranging from "almost never" to "almost always." Initial psychometric analyses supported the internal consistency, factor consistency, and criterion-related validity of the scale. Here the FEICS is used to demonstrate construct validation using confirmatory factor analysis.

Data for this application come from a study of the health-related quality of life of Oklahoma National Guard shortly after return from the Persian Gulf War. Approximately 700 Guard members completed self-report questionnaires about their current health and functional status, their employment experiences before and after the war, and their deployment experiences. A major focus of the survey was the impact of family functioning (*expressed emotion* and perceived coping during deployment) on the mental and physical health of the Guard members upon return from the war. The FEICS served as the measure of *expressed emotion* in this study. It was hypothesized that family functioning would predict both poorer mental health (i.e., depression, anxiety disorders, and somatization) and physical health (i.e., perceptions of poorer health and greater limitations in physical functioning) among Guard personnel, controlling for age and injury status.

Step 1: Model Specification

Dual-Factor Model. The FEICS operationalizes two constructs of expressed emotion: *emotional involvement* and *perceived criticism.* Figure 15.7 is a confirmatory factor model of the FEICS, representing the hypothesized factor structure of the scale as developed by Shields et al. (1992). In this specification, all odd-numbered items load on the factor *emotional involvement,* whereas all even-numbered items load on the factor *perceived criticism.* The two factors (common factors) are correlated; the unique factors are uncorrelated. The unique factors represent the proportion of variance in the item that is not shared with the other items and includes measurement error. This specification represents how the FEICS should perform.

Alternative Specification: Single-Factor Model. An argument based on parsimony could be made for the FEICS actually measuring a single construct, *expressed emotion,* with the dual-factor model representing an unnecessarily complex specification of the factor structure. In fact, in most validation studies it is important to compare the fit of a more complex model to a simpler specification. The single-factor model includes 14 indica-

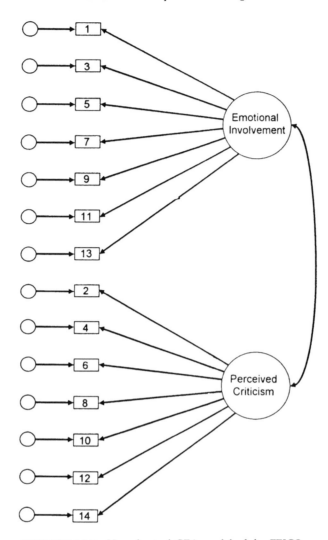

FIGURE 15.7. Hypothesized CFA model of the FEICS.

tors of a single, common factor (*expressed emotion*) with uncorrelated unique factors. For the dual-factor specification to be accepted, it should provide a superior fit to the data compared to the more parsimonious single-factor model (i.e., it is hypothesized that the dual-factor model will provide a superior fit to the data than the single-factor model).

Steps 2 and 3: Model Estimation and Comparison with Viable Alternative Models

The FEICS items are measured on 5-point Likert scales, producing ordinal indicators. For these analyses, we used PRELIS (PRE-processor for LISREL), a companion software package for LISREL, to compute correlations for the FEICS items (Jöreskog & Sörbom, 1988). The first model tested was the single-factor model, the most parsimonious specification of the FEICS (our alternative model). The χ^2 for the single-factor model was 1770.85, with 77 degrees of freedom ($p = .000$), indicating a poor fit. Unlike conventional hypothesis testing, evidence of acceptable fit comes from a nonsignificant χ^2 (i.e., the p-value exceeds the conventional $p < .05$ level). A nonsignificant χ^2 suggests that the model should not be rejected as providing an acceptable fit. (There are many other indicators of fit which should be considered by the investigator. See Hayduk, 1987, and Bollen, 1989, as a start.)

The dual-factor model was then considered. χ^2 for this model was 1207.17, with 76 degrees of freedom ($p = .000$). Along with the other indicators of fit, this model was a poor specification of the FEICS factor structure, although it was superior to the single-factor model.

Step 4: Model Modification and Reestimation

Whenever model modifications are proposed, both statistical and substantive issues must be considered. For example, allowing a variable to load on an additional factor must be consistent with the empirical literature and the theory serving to organize the researcher's thinking. Our preliminary, exploratory factor analyses suggested that the FEICS measured three correlated factors rather than two. (Note this model could have been considered a second, alternative specification.) Specifically, items 1 and 11 ("I am upset if anyone else in my family is upset." and "If I am upset, people in my family get upset too.") load together on a factor, given the label *upset*. The remaining odd items load on *emotional involvement* and even items load on *perceived criticism*, as in the dual-factor specification. The common factors are correlated whereas the unique factors are independent. This model is a more complex specification of the FEICS structure than represented by either the dual-factor or single-factor models, and to accept this model it must provide a superior fit to either of the previous models. If indeed the three-common factor model provides the superior fit, it would suggest that the FEICS *emotional involvement* construct is actually multidimensional, with odd scale items serving as indicators of two (or more) correlated but distinct constructs.

It is important to recognize that the three-common-factors specification is derived from an exploratory factor analysis, suggesting a factor structure somewhat different from what has been proposed by the developers. In addition, the analytic plan here takes the same data used in the exploratory analyses and attempts to validate the hypothesized structure with a CFA. This approach is not ideal, as whenever the same data is used to develop and validate an instrument, a better fit would be expected than when the validation is done on an independent sample. Thus, we must be cautious in evaluating the fit of the three-common factors model given these concerns and not be too quick in accepting the model when other, simpler specifications also seem reasonable.

The final, confirmatory factor model of the FEICS is shown in Figure 15.8. Note that the final specification differs from the hypothesized specification in a number of ways. First, there are three common factors rather than two. *Upset* and *emotional involvement* are moderately correlated. A smaller correlation was observed between *upset* and *perceived criticism*, whereas the correlation between *emotional involvement* and *perceived criticism* was very small though statistically significant. Items 1 and 11 are indicators of the common factor *upset*. The two *approval* items ("My family approves of most everything that I do." and "My family approves of my friends.") load on *perceived criticism* and *emotional involvement*, but in opposite directions. In this model, less frequent approval by one's family is related to greater *perceived criticism*, as suggested by previous studies using the scale (recall these items are reversed scored). At the same time, less frequent approval is associated with less *emotional involvement*. This latter finding might

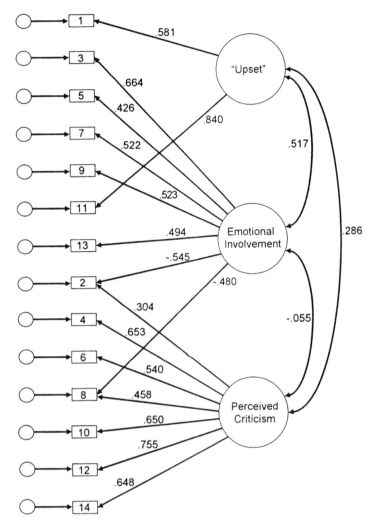

FIGURE 15.8. Final CFA model of the FEICS.

be interpreted as greater emotional distancing by other family members who are less approving of a member's behavior and friends.

Step 5: Validation

After completing this extensive construct validation of the FEICS, what happens next? The appropriate next step would be to conduct a validation study, collecting more data on the FEICS and testing the new three-factor model against the original two-factor specification. From there, attention could turn toward using the instrument in a causal model. For example, a latent variable model of expressed emotion as mediating the effect of injury and socioeconomic status on mental health and functional status might be tested.

Applications of SEM for Family Therapy Research

There are many general applications of SEM. Rather than providing a broad overview of these strategies, this section highlights applications of apparent greatest utility for family therapy research. When appropriate, reference is made to examples of applications from the clinical literature.

Evaluating Measurement Instruments and Theoretical Constructs

This first set of applications uses CFA to evaluate the validity and reliability of measurement instruments and as a method for validating theoretical constructs. The distinction between evaluating measurement instruments and theoretical constructs is an important one. Certain hypotheses can be tested about measurement instruments (e.g., testing the fit of the expected factor structure, invariance of the structure across groups or time, validity of the instrument, and hypotheses about measurement error). Testing the validity of theoretical constructs, although using the same analytic techniques, deals more with identifying the dimensions of theoretical constructs and with the consistency of these dimensions across groups or time (Byrne, 1989).

Historically, CFA is the precursor of the more common and familiar exploratory factory analysis. Only recently have statistical packages been available for estimating confirmatory factor-analytic models. In the case of CFA, the researcher has some a priori expectation for how a measurement instrument should perform or which observed variables are indicators of which underlying theoretical constructs. That is, the researcher expects certain observed variables to load on specific common factors and knows how many factors should be specified, whether or not common factors are correlated, the relationships among the unique factors, and perhaps the magnitude of the relationships. The researcher then tests the CFA model by restricting the solution (hence the term "restricted" factor analysis) to reflect the hypothesized structure. In contrast, the traditional approach of exploratory or "unrestricted" factor analysis ignores all information about how an instrument should perform or which observed variables are indicators of a theoretical construct. Exploratory factor analysis is akin to "starting over" and basing the analysis on little more than ignorance. Unfortunately, it is not uncommon to see a series of studies examining the measurement properties of an instrument, each conducting a separate exploratory factor analysis and erroneously concluding that the scale does not perform as expected. Such differences may be based entirely on sampling variation.

Instrument Validity. The validity of a measurement instrument deals with expectations for how an instrument should perform. Hoyle and Smith (1994) identify two types of instrument validity. *Structural validity* concerns expectations for the factor structure of an instrument. From our example, an instrument might be developed to operationalize central constructs of *expressed emotion*, identified as the degree of conflictual interactions and the degree of emotional reactivity and overinvolvement in a family. In fact, this is what was done by Shields et al. (1992) in developing the FEICS. A researcher attempting to validate the factor structure of the FEICS (as we did in the previous section) would specify a confirmatory-factor analytic model (a measurement model), including two common factors, with the questionnaire items serving as indicators of the latent constructs. Still further restriction might be placed on the model, such as equating all the loadings (which is actually what is being done when a scale is summed without item weighting) or fixing the correlation between the latent constructs to a certain value (in fact, by not estimating the correlation, it is fixed to zero).

A second approach to instrument validation is testing for *construct validity*. After the structural validity of the instrument has been demonstrated, it is important to consider the relationships of the construct to other measures or theoretical variables. Whereas structural validity involves the measurement model, construct validity involves both measurement and structural models. The general strategy involves first estimating the measurement model for a given instrument and then correlating the latent constructs (common factors) with other criterion latent constructs. For example, Figure 15.9 shows a general structural model, testing the construct validity of the FEICS. In this case, two latent constructs (*emotional involvement* and *perceived criticism*) representing *expressed emotion* are correlated with several criterion constructs measured by another self-report measure (family *cohesion* and *adaptability*). Moderate to high correlations between the *expressed emotion* constructs and *cohesion* and *adaptability* would provide evidence for the instrument's construct validity, demonstrating an association between the constructs.

Another approach to construct validity which may prove to be of particular interest to family therapy researchers involves an extension of multitrait–multimethod (MTMM) analysis, a method for testing convergent and discriminant validity. In conventional MTMM analysis, several traits are measured using different methods, such as measuring *emotional involvement* and *perceived criticism* using self-report questionnaires and observational rating schemes (Campbell & Fiske, 1959). Evidence of instrument validity comes from observing large correlations across methods within traits (convergent validity) and smaller correlations across different traits within methods (discriminant validity). Such an approach should be attractive to family therapy researchers as there are observational and self-report measures of many family systems constructs already available.

A limitation of conventional MTMM analyses is the reliance on visual inspection of the correlation coefficients when evaluating convergent and discriminant validity. Confirmatory factor analysis allows for more direct hypothesis testing of the MTMM matrix. A six-factor CFA model is given in Figure 15.10. There are three trait factors (*emotional involvement, perceived criticism,* and *adaptability*) and three method factors (the FEICS questionnaire, a second questionnaire, and a rating scale). Note that in this specification, trait variance is being partitioned from method variance for each observed variable. First the overall fit of the model would be evaluated. Evidence of discriminant validity would come from nonsignificant correlations among the trait factors. Evidence

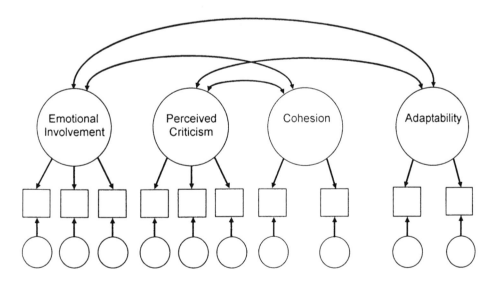

FIGURE 15.9. CFA model testing the construct validity of expressed emotion constructs.

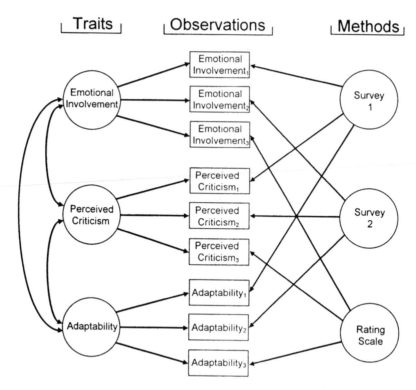

FIGURE 15.10. Multitrait–multimethod CFA model.

of convergent validity would come from significant loadings of the observed variables on the trait factors across methods. An extension of this approach would be to then use the trait factors in a structural model. The *expressed emotion* constructs would be free of method variance, which in this case might be considered insider as opposed to outsider perspectives.

There are several derivations of the MTMM approach afforded by SEM (Cole, 1987, provides an overview of these techniques). First is the *monotrait–multimethod* design, which tests convergent validity by examining the loadings of each method on the factor. The *multitrait–monomethod* design, most common in family therapy assessment, can be used to test for discriminant validity, where it is hypothesized that the traits are not correlated. The *monotrait–monomethod* design represents a "poor-person's test of convergent validity" (Cole, 1987, p. 584). This type of design can provide some information about convergent validity if the indicators are different items from a scale or different measures. A further application of the MTMM approach involves collecting data for multiple systems within a family. As an example, Martin and Cole (1993) tested the construct validity of adaptability and cohesion in dyadic relationships using a sample of families with developmentally disabled children. They specified two CFA models: one for adaptability and the other for cohesion. In each model there were three "system" factors (mother–father, mother–child, father–child), each measured from three perspectives or "methods" (child, mother, and factor). This application can be considered *multisystem–multimethod* and also suggests such other approaches as *multisystem–multitrait* (*emotional involvement* and *perceived criticism* might be assessed for various dyads) and *multisystem–multitrait–multimethod* (*emotional involvement* and *perceived criticism* assessed for various dyads using self-report and observational methods). Clearly, such applications would require complex research designs and extensive data collection efforts. These types of applications have yet to be explored in family therapy research.

Stability and Reliability. Structural equation models can be used to estimate the stability of a measurement instrument across time using a test–retest design. The typical approach to assessing test–retest reliability involves collecting data at one point in time and then readministering the instrument at a second point in time, assuming that the variable of interest will not have changed over the time lag. The problem with such approaches is that they confuse stability (or change) with reliability. When test–retest designs are used with observed variables, it is not possible to disentangle reliability from real change (or lack of change).

Figure 15.11 shows a model of the stability of a construct measured at two points in time. The construct, *expressed emotion,* is measured at one point in time (time *a*) and then again at a later point in time (time *a* + 1). The correlation between *expressed emotion* at time *a* and time *a* + 1 is interpreted as the stability of the construct across the specified period of time. (The stability coefficient is a measure of rank stability, although the group means may change.) As this is a latent variable model (in this case, two measurement models with correlated common factors), the latent variables are assumed to be free of measurement error. Also, note that the unique factors (smaller circles) are correlated across time, or autocorrelated. These correlations assume that there may be some portion of each observed variable that is expected to be correlated across time. The stability coefficient is only due to the correlation of the common factors and not to any additional correlations among the residuals. The stability coefficient serves as an indicator of rank stability (larger coefficients indicate that "subjects scoring high initially score high later, and subjects scoring low initially score low later," whereas a smaller coefficient would suggest a great deal of variability in change across time).

Measurement Invariance. Applications where instrument validity and reliability come together involve tests of measurement invariance. Perhaps one of the most crucial aspects of measurement in clinical research, measurement invariance is rarely considered (Hoyle & Smith, 1994). Conceptually, the problem is one of consistency in the composition of constructs or measurement instruments when used repeatedly with the same group, or when used to compare different groups.

Measurement invariance across time is crucial in clinical research as it sets the stage for comparing means across time (such as in pretest–posttest outcome studies) and by

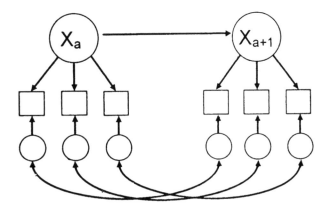

FIGURE 15.11. CFA model testing the stability of a construct across time.

itself demonstrates how a construct might change or remain stable across time. In outcome studies in which the same measures are used in repeated measures designs, it is important to demonstrate measurement invariance before testing for treatment effects. For example, in a study of adolescent drug use treatment, a latent outcome variable "problem drug use" might be operationalized using measures of marijuana use, other illicit drug use, heavy alcohol use, and cigarette smoking. Thus, a CFA model would be specified, and change in problem drug use would be assessed from pre- to postintervention. Yet, the intervention may target only illicit drug use, and no change in cigarette use would be expected. Prior to intervention, it would be expected that cigarette use and other drug use would be highly correlated. After intervention, the association might be quite low, as illicit drug use would decrease for most adolescents as a result of treatment, yet many adolescents would continue to smoke. The latent variable model of problem drug use would not be invariant across time (i.e., the factor loadings were not invariant across time), and comparisons of means might not be appropriate. At the same time, the change in factor structure could be of substantive interest to the researcher. Other applications might include testing for change in the factor structure of such constructs as marital quality across the course of therapy.

Measurement invariance across groups is also crucial in clinical research, but for different reasons. Anytime cross-cultural differences are considered, measurement invariance must first be established. For example, it would be erroneous to infer any differences in degree of *expressed emotion* among African American and Mexican American families by testing for mean differences in scores on the FEICS. Any observed difference may be explained entirely by differences in the structure of *expressed emotion* between the two groups, or by differences in measurement error. The application would involve multiple group comparisons, where the same CFA model is specified for each group and then the groups are compared simultaneously, with increasing constraints placed on the comparisons. The first step might be to test for the same number of factors and patterns in the loadings across groups. Further constraints could then be considered, such as equating the correlations among the factors for each group, providing a test of whether or not the factors have the same degree of association in each group (Byrne, 1989). As with testing for measurement invariance across time, the observed differences in models may be of substantive interest to the researcher.

Validating a Theoretical Construct. The logic of model testing when the goal is to validate a theoretical construct follows that used in validating measurement instruments. The difference is that rather than evaluating the measurement properties of an instrument, the composition of a construct is of interest. Take the construct of *expressed emotion*. It might be hypothesized that expressed emotion is multidimensional, with *perceived criticism* and *emotional involvement* serving as first-order constructs and *expressed emotion* serving as a higher-order construct. An alternative model might suggest that *expressed emotion* is unidimensional, and any measure of *expressed emotion* is a measure of a single construct. The issue might be further complicated by hypothesizing differences among various ethnic groups, where emotional closeness and criticism are highly associated in one group yet distinct in another. Again, the analytic strategies are the same as those used when evaluating a measurement instrument, but the focus is on the construct rather than the scale.

Testing Causal or Predictive Relationships

SEM has been used most extensively to test causal or predictive relationships among variables. In the family studies and family psychology literatures, SEM has been used in testing models of marital dissolution and stability (Gottman, 1993), predicting non-custodial parents' contact with their children (Braver et al., 1993), identifying predictors of commitment in dating relationships (Floyd & Wasner, 1994), the role of blame attributions in marital adjustment (Lussier, Sabourin, & Wright, 1993), mediators of problem drinking affecting mothers' personal adjustment (Dumka & Roosa, 1993), and testing the construct of similarity in marital relationships (Deal, Wampler, & Halverson, 1992). Three applications of SEM for family therapy research are highlighted here.

As mentioned above, the use of the term "causal modeling" is unfortunate. Fancy modeling does not equate with establishing causality. The argument for causality must be developed by the researcher, who must meet a host of criteria (e.g., temporality of the cause and effect, a logical relationship, a dose–response effect, and an absence of spuriousness). SEM provides an analytic strategy for testing models which the researcher presumes are causal. Consider the products of model testing: (1) estimates of the magnitude of relationships among variables, (2) the statistical significance of the relationships, and (3) indicators of the fit of the model relative to alternative models. SEM contributes by estimating the strength of the relationships among variables and the relative fit of competing models, but little more. It remains a task of the researcher to assert and defend causality.

In the first application, more complex models of the relationships between *expressed emotion* and health-related quality of life might be considered after testing hypotheses about measurement validity and reliability. Figure 15.12 gives a model from the National Guard study in which postwar functional status is predicted by injury during deployment, using cross-sectional data. In this example, *expressed emotion* is modeled as a mediating variable, with injury and socioeconomic status (SES) having an indirect effect on mental health through *expressed emotion* as well as direct effects (dashed lines). Injury and SES also have an indirect effect on functional status through *expressed emotion* and mental health. (See Baron & Kenny, 1986, for a discussion of the distinction between moderator and mediator variables.) Thus, the total effect of injury and SES on functional status is mediated by *expressed emotion* and mental health. This type of model is a latent variable model rather than a path model. There is a measurement model for each construct (the observed variables are implicit in the figure), and the relationships among the constructs constitute the structural model. An alternative hypothesis might be tested in which the total effect of injury and SES on mental health is entirely indirect through *expressed emotion* (paths indicated by dashed lines would be fixed to zero).

Although this example uses cross-sectional data, a superior design would involve collecting data across at least three periods. This specification might be considered the

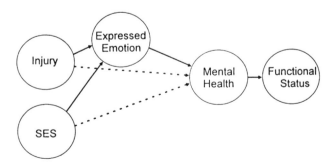

FIGURE 15.12. Latent variable model predicting mental health and functional status.

classic design for testing causal models using nonexperimental data. At baseline assessment, some event occurs, such as being deployed for the Gulf War, following our example (see Figure 15.13). Associated with this event is a change in income for the deployed person (possibly a decline). Such sociodemographic factors as marital status, number of young children, and gender might also be considered at baseline. Then, mediating variables would be assessed during the period of deployment or shortly after return. In this example, these mediating variables would be family *emotional involvement* and *perceived criticism*. Finally, outcomes would be assessed after the member had returned from deployment. These outcomes might include measures of mental health (anxiety and depressive symptoms) and perceived functional status. Hypotheses would be tested in which the effect of change in income as a result of deployment on mental health and functional status is mediated by family functioning. An alternative specification (step 3) might be that the effect of change in income on mental health and functional status is entirely direct, and family functioning has no impact. The advantages of this type of specification are obvious—the predictor variables temporally precede the outcomes of interest while mediating factors are assessed at some intermediate point in time. In this way, there is a clear temporal ordering of the events, mediators, and outcomes.

A third application involves an adaptation of longitudinal modeling. The following example is used to demonstrate this type of application. The researcher is interested in identifying "therapist factors" (i.e., gender, race/ethnicity, years of training, and practice) that predict initial change in family functioning after the first few sessions of a brief family therapy program, in this case for adolescent drug abuse. It might be hypothesized that a greater change in family functioning would be observed for more experienced therapists. Therapist gender and race/ethnicity would be included to explore these relationships. Again, the dependent variable is *change* in family functioning. A longitudinal, latent variable model would be specified in which family functioning conceptualized as conflictual exchanges (coded using a behavioral assessment scheme for measuring *expressed emotion*) is measured at an initial evaluation and then during the fourth session of treatment (see Figure 15.14). When specified in this way, the therapist factors are predictors of *change* in family functioning, as the effect of initial family

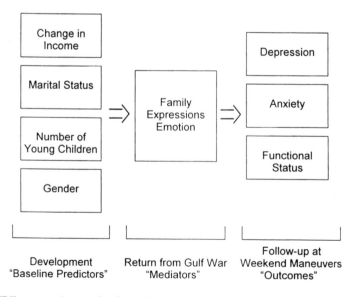

FIGURE 15.13. Longitudinal model predicting mental health and functional status.

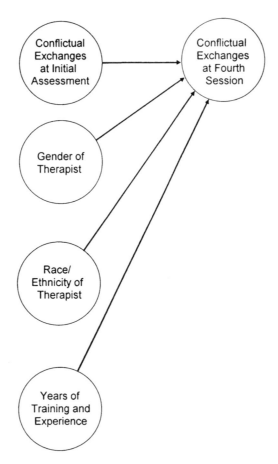

FIGURE 15.14. Latent variable model predicting change in conflictual exchanges during early stages of treatment.

functioning on functioning at the fourth session accounts for *stability*, leaving only change and measurement error to be explained. As this is a latent variable model, the measurement model accounts for measurement error, leaving only reliable variance to be predicted by the therapist factors. Obviously, there are many other applications of longitudinal models in family therapy process research, such as predicting change in functioning across the entire course of treatment and modeling changes in mental health for husbands and wives in marital therapy, to name a few.

Estimating Treatment Effects in Outcome Studies

In outcome studies, researchers typically test the effect of one or more treatments (e.g., pharmacotherapy plus brief family therapy) compared to alternative treatments or controls (e.g., pharmacotherapy alone or placebo). The design standard is a randomized, controlled trial (RCT) in which eligible subjects are randomly assigned to treatment arms, baseline assessments are taken, and subjects receive an intervention and then are reassessed at specified follow-up periods. Group differences at follow-up or differences in change from preintervention to follow-up are examined to determine the effect of treatment on outcomes. Such approaches provide limited information about how change in family functioning affect treatment outcomes. For example, an outcome study of adolescent drug abuse treatment might be undertaken in which a brief family therapy intervention is compared to a no-treatment control group. The treatment outcomes might include drug use at 6 months postintervention. Again, the traditional approach would be to look at differences in drug use at follow-up for the two intervention groups or to consider change in drug use from preintervention to follow-up. A more powerful approach would be to directly model the hypothesized therapeutic process. Two methods are described here.

Dummy Variable Coding. Figure 15.15 extends the pretest–posttest design to include dummy variables and other variables hypothesized to be influenced by the intervention. Dummy variables are variables coded "1" if something is present or "0" if something is absent, and they are particularly helpful with categorical variables. Each category of the variable becomes a separate dummy variable, which has a value of "1" or "0." In the case of two treatment groups (e.g., brief family therapy and control), only one dummy variable is needed (for each additional treatment group, another dummy variable could be added to the model) (Hawkins, Abbott, Catalano, & Gillmore, 1991). The dummy variable is coded "1" for families receiving the intervention and "0" for the controls (the "Treatment Group" variable in Figure 15.15). The simplest model would be a two-group, posttest design in which the effect of the dummy variable on postintervention functioning would be equal to the mean difference between the treatment and control groups. The result would be the same if multiple linear regression was used, where postintervention functioning was the dependent variable, preintervention functioning was a covariate, and treatment group was an independent variable.

The dummy variable approach, when used with latent variables in the pretest–posttest design, has the advantage of testing for change in functioning accounting for measurement error (Aiken, Stein, & Bentler, 1994). At the same time, the model does not directly reflect the process of how change occurs. For example, it might be hypothesized that the brief intervention would directly affect the degree of emotional involvement among family members (decreasing overinvolvement) and the degree of perceived critical exchanges. The model might be respecified so that the intervention variable directly predicts *emotional involvement* and *perceived criticism* at termination of treatment (or any period during treatment) and has an indirect effect on drug use outcomes through change in *expressed emotion*. The effect of the intervention on postintervention functioning is mediated by family *emotional involvement* and *perceived criticism*. Although a simplified representation of the therapeutic process, this application of SEM more directly represents the process of change and influence, providing estimates of treatment effects including those family functioning variables targeted by the intervention.

Multiple Group Comparisons. A more complex approach to testing for treatment effects is to test for the equality of relationships among the variables for different groups. There are several approaches available to the researcher. In the posttest design with latent outcome variables, measurement models are specified separately for each treatment group. After setting equality constraints on the loadings (i.e., they are the same for each group), an additional constraint is added in which the means are equal across groups. A significant difference in the fit of the models would indicate that the means are not equivalent. This type of approach is referred to as a structured means analysis (Hoyle & Smith, 1994). In the pretest–posttest design with latent outcome variables, models are again specified for each group, this time representing change in the outcome variable across treatment. After appropriate constraints are placed on the mea-

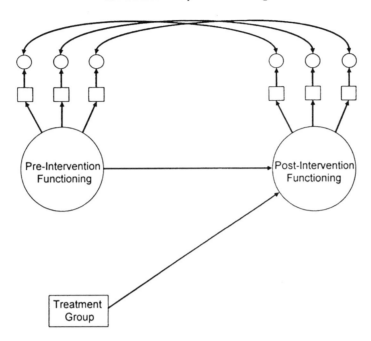

FIGURE 15.15. Latent variable model estimating treatment effects in a pretest–posttest outcome study.

surement models, an additional constraint is added in which the pretest and posttest means are equated across groups. The advantage of SEM over analysis of variance or regression in estimating treatment effects and testing hypotheses is that latent outcome variables can be specified, thus controlling for measurement error.

After testing for mean differences both across time within treatment groups and then between treatment groups, the researcher might want to look more closely at the patterns of relationships among predictor and outcome variables across groups. For example, it might be hypothesized that the relationship between drug use and school performance would differ for the brief family therapy and control groups, where the two outcome variables remain highly correlated at 6-month follow-up for the control group (i.e., problem behaviors tending to be associated), but in the treatment group the association would be lower (i.e., decreased drug use with subsequent though not immediate change in academic performance). Multiple group analysis would be used to test this hypothesis, where the correlation between school performance and drug use would be specified invariant and the fit of this model would be compared to a model in which the correlations are free to differ. The magnitude of the correlation coefficients might also be of substantive interest.

SUMMARY

SEM has many strengths and applications, several of which have been presented in this chapter. Although methodologically complex, SEM is always theory driven. SEM requires the researcher to specify a priori a theoretical model and to be explicit about the hypothesized relationships among variables. Such theoretical models often have their origins in observations made by clinicians about how families function. The technique may very well provide family therapy researchers with a host of new analytic tools for testing hypotheses about family functioning and change.

Although SEM has many strengths, it is certainly not without its weaknesses. The results of any model testing should always be considered temporary and only acceptable until a better model comes along. Validation is crucial in SEM, yet in practice it is rarely done. Whenever a new specification is considered, a validation study should be undertaken to test the new model against other competing models. At the same time, the goal of any structural modeling is parsimony, and a simpler model that fits the data equally as well as a more complex model should be selected as the superior model.

Generally, large samples are required, which may be difficult to obtain in family therapy research. Convention suggests that sample sizes of 200 are optimal, yet most outcome studies have great difficulty enrolling and retaining such a large number of clients. Smaller samples can be used, but simpler models are required (fewer variables and parameters to be estimated) and the precision of the estimates can be lost (Tanaka, 1987).

Perhaps a greater concern involves the assumptions of many estimators used in SEM (i.e., the methods used to estimate the model parameters). The estimators based on normal theory require random samples and variables measured at interval or ratio level, and that distributions of the variables be multivariate normal. Random sampling is often not feasible in clinical research. The requirement of interval level measures poses more difficulty, as many variables in family therapy research are ordinal or categorical. The FEICS, for example, yields ordinal measures of *expressed emotion*. Measures in family therapy outcome research are often categorical, such as relapse in substance use trials. The typical approach to such problems is to use nonnormal theory estimators with correlations rather than variances and covariances. It is important to keep in mind that wherever correlations are used, the estimates are standardized and cannot be compared across models or samples. Thus, direct multiple group comparisons are not possible.

There are also many concerns regarding how researchers go about using SEM. Although SEM is often referred to as causal modeling, inferences of causality cannot be made solely on the basis on the analytic techniques used (Baumrind, 1983). The onus is still on the researcher to develop an argument for causal relationships, ideally through the use of longitudinal designs and tests of alternative explanations for relationships among variables. Furthermore, the technique is subject to "fishing expeditions," where the investigator quickly moves from model testing to exploration without considering substantive issues in proposing new models.

A major drawback in developing applications of SEM for family therapy research is that the technique is methodologically complex. The analytic software relies on Greek notation, in the case of LISREL, or specifying equations, in the case of EQS (two of the more popular SEM packages). SEM has been described as a methodologic black box by its critics, greatly limiting its applications in areas of health services research (Bergner, 1990). Few clinicians have the training needed to conduct these types of analyses. Few graduate training programs offer courses in these advanced techniques. At the same time, it is not necessary to have these analytic skills to use SEM. Rather, the researcher need only specify a model to be tested, along with competing alternative models, and then work closely with a methodologist/statistician in designing the study and analyzing the data. The theorist's role is crucial in SEM, as the technique is one of hypothesis testing. All modifications must be both substantively and statistically driven.

Our goal in this chapter has been to provide an overview of the many potential applications of SEM in family therapy research and to give a general overview of the steps involved in the process of structural modeling. Future directions for the application of SEM in family therapy research will undoubtedly be limited by the feasibility of collecting enough data to meet sample size requirements. Although estimating treatment effects in outcome studies using structural modeling allows for a more direct test of the intervention, few investigators will be in the position to conduct such large-scale studies. It may be that most applications of SEM in the near future will involve testing measurement tools for consistency across cultures, developing latent variable models of salient constructs in family theory, and developing causal models of family functioning. Such analyses are crucial in illuminating family processes and developing theory-driven interventions. Although SEM is a "newcomer" to family therapy research, it has the potential to play an important role contributing to the empirical foundation of the discipline.

ACKNOWLEDGMENTS

Preparation of this chapter was supported in part by a grant from the National Institute on Drug Abuse (DA06514). Data used in the chapter come from the study "Health Consequences of Rapid Deployment for the Persian Gulf War: Impact of Mobilization of Oklahoma National Guard and Reserve Personnel," funded by University of Colorado Hazards Research Center and the Society for the Psychological Study of Social Issues. Appreciation is expressed to Jon C. McFather and Kristy E. Smith for assistance in preparation of the manuscript.

REFERENCES

Aiken, L. S., Stein, J. A., & Bentler, P. M. (1994). Structural equation analysis of clinical subpopulation differences and comparative treatment outcomes: Characterizing the daily lives of drug addicts. *Journal of Consulting and Clinical Psychology, 62,* 488–499.

Baron, R. M., & Kenny, D. A. (1986). The moderator–mediator variable distinction in social psychological research: Conceptual, strategic, and statistical considerations. *Journal of Personality and Social Psychology, 51,* 1171–1182.

Baumrind, D. (1983). Specious causal attributions in the social sciences: The reformulated stepping-stone theory of heroin use as an exemplar. *Journal of Personality and Social Psychology, 45,* 1289–1298.

Bentler, P. M., & Bonett, D. G. (1980). Significance tests and goodness-of-fit in the analysis of covariance structures. *Psychological Bulletin, 88,* 588–600.

Bentler, P. M. (1985). *Theory and implementation of EQS: A structural equations program.* Los Angeles: BMDP Statistical Software.

Bergner, M. (1990). Latent variable structural equation modeling in health services research. In L. Sechrest, E. Perrin, & J. Bunker (Eds.), *Research methodology: Strengthening causal interpretations of nonexperimental data* (DHHS Publication No. (PHS) 90-3454). Rockville, MD: Agency for Health Care Policy and Research.

Bollen, K. A. (1989). *Structural equations with latent variables.* New York: Wiley.

Booker, C. (1990). Expressed emotion and psychosocial intervention: A review. *International Journal of Nursing Studies, 27,* 267–276.

Braver, S. L., Wolchik S. A., Sandler, I. N., Sheets, V. L., Fogas, B., & Bay, R. C. (1993). A longitudinal study of noncustodial parents: Parents without children. *Journal of Family Psychology, 7,* 9–23.

Bray, J. H., & Harvey, D. M. (1992). Intimacy and individuation in young adults: Development of the young adult version of the personal authority in the family system questionnaire. *Journal of Family Psychology, 6,* 152–163.

Byrne, B. M. (1989). *A primer of LISREL: Basic applications and programming for confirmatory factor analytic models.* New York: Springer-Verlag.

Campbell, D. T., & Fiske, D. W. (1959). Convergent and discriminant validation by the multitrait–multimethod matrix. *Psychological Bulletin, 56,* 81–105.

Cole, D. A. (1987). Utility of confirmatory factor analysis in test validation research. *Journal of Consulting and Clinical Psychology, 55,* 584–594.

Cole, D. A., & McPherson, A. E. (1993). Relations of family subsystems to adolescent depression: Implementing a new family assessment strategy. *Journal of Family Psychology, 7,* 119–133.

Deal, J. E., Wampler, K. S., & Halverson, C. F. (1992). The importance of similarity in the marital relationship. *Family Process, 31,* 369–382.

Dumka, L. E., & Roosa, M. W. (1993). Factors mediating problem drinking and mothers' personal adjustment. *Journal of Family Psychology, 7,* 333–343.

Florin, I., Nostadt, A., Reck, C., Franzen, U., & Jenkins, M. (1992). Expressed emotion in depressed patients and their partners. *Family Process, 31,* 163–172.

Floyd, F. J., & Wasner, G. H. (1994). Social exchange, equity, and commitment: Structural equation modeling of dating relationships. *Journal of Family Psychology, 8,* 55–73.

Fowers, B. J., Applegate, B., Olson, D. H., & Pomerantz, B. (1994). Marital conventionalization as a measure of marital satisfaction: A confirmatory factor analysis. *Journal of Family Psychology, 8,* 98–103.

Franks, P., Campbell, T. L., & Shields, C. G. (1992). Social relationships and health: The relative roles of family functioning and social support. *Social Science in Medicine, 34,* 779–788.

Gottman, J. M. (1993). A theory of marital dissolution and stability. *Journal of Family Psychology, 7,* 57–75.

Hawkins, J. D., Abbott, R., Catalano, R. F., & Gilmore, M. R. (1991). Assessing effectiveness of drug abuse prevention: Implementation issues relevant to long-term effects and replication. In C. G. Leukefeld & W. J. Bukoski (Eds.), *Drug abuse prevention intervention research: Methodological issues* (NIDA Research Monograph 107). Bethesda, MD: National Institute on Drug Abuse.

Hayduk, L. A. (1987). *Structural equation modeling with LISREL: Essentials and advances.* Baltimore: Johns Hopkins University Press.

Hooley, J. M., & Teasdale, J. D. (1989). Predictors of relapse in unipolar depressives: Expressed emotion, marital distress, and perceived criticism. *Journal of Abnormal Psychology, 98,* 229–235.

Hoyle, R. H., & Smith, G. T. (1994). Formulating clinical research hypotheses as structural equation models: A conceptual overview. *Journal of Consulting and Clinical Psychology, 62,* 429–440.

Jöreskog, K. G., & Sörbom D. (1988). *PRELIS: A preprocessor for LISREL.* Chicago: Scientific Software, Inc.

Jöreskog, K. G., & Sörbom D. (1989). *LISREL VII: Analysis of linear structural relationships by maximum likelihood, instrumental variables, and least squares methods.* Chicago: Scientific Software.

Koenigsberg, H. W., Klausner, E., Pelino, D., Rosnick, P., & Campbell, R. (1993). Expressed emotion and glucose control in insulin-dependent diabetes mellitus. *American Journal of Psychiatry, 150,* 1114–1115.

Kurdek, L. A. (1992). Dimensionality of the dyadic adjustment scale: Evidence from heterosexual and homosexual couples. *Journal of Family Psychology, 6,* 22–35.

Lussier, Y., Sabourin, S., & Wright, J. (1993). On causality, responsibility, and blame in marriage: Validity of the entailment model. *Journal of Family Psychology, 7,* 322–332.

MacCallum, R. C., Roznowski, M., & Necovitz, L. B. (1992). Model modifications in covariance structure analysis: The problem of capitalization on chance. *Psychological Bulletin, 111,* 490–504.

Martin, J. A. (1987). Structural equation modeling: A guide for the perplexed. *Child Development, 58,* 33–37.

Martin, J. A., & Cole, D. A. (1993). Adaptability and cohesion of dyadic relationships in families with developmentally disabled children. *Journal of Family Psychology, 7,* 186–196.

Shields, C. G., Franks, P., Harp, J. J., McDaniel, S. H., & Campbell, T. L. (1992). Development of the Family Emotional Involvement and Criticism Scale (FEICS): A self-report scale to measure expressed emotion. *Journal of Marital and Family Therapy, 18,* 395–407.

Tanaka, J. S. (1987). "How big is big enough?": Sample size and goodness of fit in structural equation models with latent variables. *Child Development, 58,* 134–146.

Tucker, L. R., & Lewis, C. (1973). A reliability coefficient for maximum likelihood factor analysis. *Psychometrika, 38,* 1–10.

Cost-Effectiveness Evaluations

16

Cost-Effectiveness Research
in Family Therapy

CONNEE L. PIKE-URLACHER
DAVID P. MACKINNON
FRED P. PIERCY

After months of letters and phone calls, Jill finally secured an appointment with the director of the largest employee assistance program (EAP) in her county. Jill's family therapy practice has been slow to build because so many of the mental health care referrals in her area come from the EAPs in the region, and Jill is not yet approved for referrals at any of the large EAPs. As excited as she is about the appointment, Jill knows that to receive referrals from the EAP, she must make a presentation on both what she does and the effectiveness with which she does it. But, this alone will probably not be enough because many other mental health practitioners in her area already enjoy coverage by this and other EAPs. To be competitive, Jill must also demonstrate that family therapy is *cost*-effective.

We live in a time of expanding health care costs and shrinking dollars. Policymakers, insurance companies, EAPs, and individuals are all demanding that health services be not only effective but also cost-effective. The field of mental health care is no different. Consumers are asking whether mental health services are justified considering the cost. Managed care providers are seeking mental health care services that can prove their effectiveness (Aderman, Bowers, Russell, & Wegmann, 1993). Third-party reimbursers are concerned with cost-effectiveness, as they annually pay substantial money to maintain the health, including mental health, of insurees. Family therapists, like other practitioners, must demonstrate that the benefits of family therapy are worth the costs. Furthermore, as a field, we must find concrete, monetary methods to communicate with insurance companies and other agencies—to speak their language. It is up to us to demonstrate both the efficacy and cost efficacy of family therapy if we are to secure our future within the changing health care reimbursement and funding establishment.

However, we do not know much about the cost-effectiveness of family therapy. It is essential that family therapists be able to demonstrate which family interventions with which populations, in which contexts are not only effective but also cost-effective. This chapter attempts to demystify cost-effectiveness methodology and suggests ways to use cost-effectiveness procedures as routine components in family therapy outcome research.

We demonstrate how to use cost-effectiveness research, when to use it, and which methods to use. Finally, we show how to be good consumers of cost-effectiveness research; our hope is that the reader will not only understand this research but also be able to speak the language of cost when talking about programs, arguing for policy changes, or advocating for the field and practice of family therapy.

BACKGROUND

Two key terms to which we frequently refer throughout this chapter are "cost-benefit analysis" (CBA) and "cost effectiveness analysis" (CEA) (Parloff, 1980; Levin, 1975). Each is a specific analysis method in cost-effectiveness research. The researcher examines the treatment modality in terms of whether it achieved the desired purpose (cost-effectiveness) and at what cost (cost-benefit). The primary distinction between these analyses is the questions asked. CEA evaluates whether the benefits of a particular program are worth the costs. CBA evaluates whether the benefits of a particular course of action exceed its cost. Among the differences of approach are the way benefits are valued. In CBA, all potential benefits are defined in monetary terms, most frequently in dollar values. CEA, on the other hand, measures the benefits gained in units other than monetary ones.

In CBA, researchers compare costs, expressed in monetary terms (e.g., salaries of providers), with monetary benefits (e.g., cost of fewer days missed from work). The monetary costs are then compared to the monetary benefits of each program to determine whether the benefits of a particular course of action exceed its costs. The net benefits can be expressed in two ways: (1) as a *net monetary benefit* (total benefits less total costs), or (2) as a *net benefit ratio* (total benefits divided by total costs). If the net monetary benefit is positive (e.g., 1.3), benefits exceed costs; if the net monetary benefit is negative (e.g., .07), costs exceed benefits and there is a net monetary loss. In a net benefit ratio, the benefit exceeds the costs with a positive ratio (e.g., 3:1); whereas when it is negative (e.g., 1:2) there is a loss. The researcher can then assess the inherent worth of a program in simple monetary terms: Do the financial benefits exceed the financial costs? Second, because the costs and benefits are measured in the same (monetary) unit, comparisons can be made across programs (e.g., inpatient hospitalization vs. intensive outpatient family therapy).

CEA does not require monetary values as the unit of comparison. Instead, costs are tied to certain outcomes (e.g., for family therapy services costing $10,000 per year, three adolescents can be kept out of jail). In CEA, the total cost of the project is expressed in monetary terms and compared to the measured effects or results of that program. This permits comparison of cost per unit of effectiveness between treatments designed to accomplish the same purpose or goal. However, a clear value judgment is necessary to evaluate the worth of a program in terms of nonmonetary benefits (e.g., Is it worth $10,000 to keep three adolescents out of jail?).

Later in the chapter, we discuss CBAs and CEAs in further detail, outlining how and when to use them.

History of Cost-Effectiveness Research

Cost-effectiveness research has a long history, in the military, business, and policymaking fields (Levin, 1975). According to Levin (1975), CBA was the original analysis used to examine costs and benefits, and it was from this history that CEA evolved.

The military may have been the first to use CBA for public decision making in its 1936 evaluation of water resource projects (Levin, 1975). The Flood Control Act of 1936 required that the Corps of Army Engineers certify whether projects were feasible based on the ratio of benefits to costs. As a result, numerous techniques were developed for measuring costs and benefits of public investment in flood control. Because monetary values for costs and benefits could be applied to evaluate water resource projects, regardless of their purpose or geographical location, projects could be evaluated and ranked according to their net estimated contributions to social welfare (benefits minus costs). This information was then used to allocate the water-resource investment budget so that only those projects were funded that maximized the net value of expected benefits (Levin, 1975).

CEA was developed because many social policies and decision making projects involve benefits that could not be translated into monetary terms. Levin (1975), also credits the military with developing CEA procedures. Military analysts needed a method to evaluate weapon systems, choices about war, and national defense decisions. The cost analysis framework was aimed at achieving particular "objectives" at minimal cost. Objectives included the destruction of enemy targets whereas costs included not only money and machinery but loss of human life. Readers can appreciate the difficulty in assigning a monetary value to human life or national freedom and security.

Panzetta (1973) credits the field of industrial economics for developing some of the first CBA procedures. Within a competitive economy such as ours, goods and services compete for the dollar. Because of our competitive marketplace, market analyses of costs of goods, and what these goods offer, has a rich history in the field of economics, which in turn has filtered into every facet of business.

Analysis procedures that examine costs for services (CEA), rather than things (CBA), have not developed as quickly, or in the same detail. Two areas receiving high attention are health studies and education and manpower training (Levin, 1975). Several types of health-related CEAs have been completed. The first type compares different methods to treat the same problem. For example, Maidlow and Berman (1972) compared different treatment for heroin addicts. They first examined differential effectiveness and then examined the cost of providing these services. A second type of CEA involved estimates of the costs of particular diseases. For example, Fein (1958) estimated the costs related to mental illness and Klarman (1965) examined the various costs related to syphilis. Another type of health-related CEA examined the economics of disease prevention. Forst (1973), for example, examined the cost-effectiveness of periodic health exams on future well-being and utilization of health services.

In education and manpower training, researchers used similar cost-effectiveness analysis. For example, researchers compared the costs and benefits of a variety of educational programs to ascertain the relative effectiveness and cost of each. For example, Perl (1973) compared the effectiveness and cost-effectiveness of differentially educated teachers and different class sizes on student test scores. Another type of study, similar to those in health services, examined the cost of inadequate education. One series of studies, for example, focused on the costs of students not completing high school (Weisbrod, 1965). Finally, the field of education has also examined the cost-effectiveness of prevention programs. For example, studies have examined the costs and benefits of programs designed to prevent dropouts versus the cost of not having such a program (Becker, 1964).

Although the present state of psychotherapy evaluation has reached a high degree of sophistication, it has paid surprisingly little attention to measuring social effects and benefits, especially in terms of cost-effectiveness (Krupnick & Pincus, 1992).

Generally in the field of mental health, there have been relatively few studies comparing types of treatment for specific disorders. Paul's (1967) specificity question of what therapy is effective for what presenting problem under what circumstances is also quite relevant when researching cost-effectiveness. Pike and Piercy (1990) and Krupnick and Pincus (1992) call for the inclusion of cost questions in outcome research, which examines the effects of specific treatments on specific problems. This has been done in a few cases. For example, behavioral therapy was found to be both effective and cost-effective with phobias and obsessive–compulsive disorders (Ginsberg & Marks, 1977). It is much easier to evaluate programs that are clearly described and specifically administered. There is also less risk of inaccurate conclusions when one knows which services or combination of services is most effective and cost-effective with which populations in which contexts (Krupnick & Pincus, 1992).

A great deal of time has been spent examining the costs of various disorders in the mental health field. For example, Regier et al. (1988) report that in 1988, psychiatric illness affected nearly one-third of the U.S. adult population. Rice, Kelman, Miller, and Dunmeyer (1990) estimate the cost of psychiatric illness in one-third of adult Americans to be approximately $273 billion in 1988 dollars. Researchers have also examined the costs of specific psychiatric illness. For example, Stoudemire, Frank, Hedemark, Kamlet, and Blazer (1986) found that depression cost society about $16.3 billion in 1986 dollar values.

Researchers have also estimated the cost of psychiatric illness in other areas of functioning. For example, psychiatric disorders are the major cause of nonpsychiatric illness, disability, and death in the United States. They also lead to the use of costly medical resources, productivity loss, motor vehicle accidents, and incarceration (Krupnick & Pincus, 1992). For example, epidemiological studies show that patients with psychiatric disturbances often seek treatment at primary care sites for medically unexplained symptoms, make at least twice as many health care visits as comparison subjects (Katon, 1991), and experience longer hospitalizations—incurring greater costs than patients without psychiatric problems (Verbosky, Zrull, & Franco, 1991).

Cost-Effectiveness Research and Family Therapy

As in other mental health fields, family therapy researchers have done little to examine the cost-effectiveness of family therapy treatment. They have also done little to develop the technology needed to evaluate the cost-effectiveness of specific family therapy treatments with specific populations (e.g., distressed marital couples and families with delinquent teens). A few studies have been conducted that specifically examine the cost-effectiveness of family therapy treatment. The most common type of study compares types of treatment. For example Cardin, McGill, and Falloon (1985) compared home based-family therapy with individual management in the treatment of schizophrenic clients. They found no difference in the outcome or benefits between the two types of treatment modalities. However, they found that the total costs for the family treatment group was 19% less than that of the individual treatment group—a savings of approximately $2,000 per patient (Cardin et al., 1985).

A second type of family therapy cost-effectiveness study examines the costs and benefits of a specific prevention program. Lipsey (1984) evaluated the cost-effectiveness of an adolescent offender prevention program. He compared the costs, benefits, and outcomes of family counseling to similar data from research studies on other prevention programs with the same population. Lipsey's work represents a creative way to evaluate cost-effectiveness by comparing his results with other published treatment methodologies.

Only four cost-effectiveness studies in the field of family therapy had been published at the time of this writing (Langsley, Kaplan, et al., 1968; Langsley, Pittman, et al., 1968; Langsley, Flomenhaft, & Machotka, 1969; Lipsey, 1984; Cardin et al., 1985; Tarrier, Lowson, & Barrowclough, 1991). Each of these family therapy cost-effectiveness studies, along with their strengths and weaknesses, is summarized later in this chapter. In addition, virtually no studies have examined the long-term costs of chronic marital and family problems (Krupnick & Pincus, 1992). The popular media commonly cites a litany of societal problems related to the family: high divorce rates, problems with single-parent families, increasing rates of child abuse, rampant adolescent drug abuse, and gang-related violence. Unfortunately, the family therapy field has made few efforts to document either the costs of such problems or the cost savings of family therapy in addressing them.

All family therapists have an intuitive sense of the effectiveness of their work. We too believe that family therapy can play an important role in addressing the many concerns our society faces. We also believe that marital and family health is not a luxury but relates directly to a wide range of other physical and mental health issues that can be addressed through family therapy. Family therapy researchers must begin to document in dollar and cents the cost-effectiveness of family treatments. To paraphrase an old legal maxim, if it is not documented, it does not exist. Thus, unfortunately we must say, then, that until family therapy cost-effectiveness is examined thoroughly and specifically across treatments, presenting problems, and contexts *and documented*, it does not exist in the eyes of the external world.

Assumptions of Cost-Effectiveness Research

As suggested earlier, we generally assume that family therapy can benefit family members. This issue is not *if* but for whom and under what conditions. We further assume that outcome research will help us answer these questions. In addition, we assume that ideal outcome research will address differential cost-effectiveness questions as well as questions related to differential outcome. Cost-effectiveness research, of course, assumes comparison of treatments, costs, and benefits. We must assume, therefore, that we can find ways to quantify outcome. Furthermore, we assume we can quantify those costs and benefits in such a way as to make meaningful cost comparisons regarding outcome (Panzetta, 1973). CBA assumes that we can use all monetary symbols to do so, whereas CEA offers more leeway to find nonmonetary methods to document benefits.

One important assumption of cost-effectiveness research is that costs and benefits have some common value (Levin, 1975). The dollar does not carry the same weight on a day-to-day basis. Because of the time value of money (a concept discussed in detail later in this chapter), a dollar of cost or benefit paid or realized today is worth more than a dollar of cost or benefit paid or realized at a later date. In order to compare costs and benefits that are realized at different times, costs and benefits must be converted to a common base. (This process is also discussed later in the chapter.) The assumption is that this conversion can be accomplished. Another assumption relates primarily to benefits and is most critical in CEA. That is, we assume that all benefits being compared are equivalent, or can at least be made comparable (Panzetta, 1973). For example, if the benefit is the same (e.g., number of delinquents kept from being placed in training school), whichever service costs less is the most efficient. But because the benefits are typically not exactly the same (e.g., differential rates of placement in different types of facilities and different scores on different standardized tests), it is critical that they are made comparable or comparison between services have no meaning. We assume that the researcher will address this issue early in the design of the research project, particularly if more than one outcome is to be examined.

Finally, we assume that cost-effectiveness research has as its goal identifying treatments with the highest efficiency and not merely lowering costs (Glass & Goldberg, 1977). Everything in life has a cost. Cost-effectiveness research examines which treatment maximizes benefits because it is not enough to lower costs. Many programs have suffered budget cuts and resource losses that negatively affect outcome. It is our assumption that, with thorough evaluation, the researcher can discover the best and most efficient combination and use of resources to answer such questions.

METHODOLOGY

Research Questions

What questions are best answered by cost-effectiveness research? Historically, as described earlier, four types of questions have been evaluated by the health and mental health fields. The first examines the comparison of alternative methods of treatment for the same presenting problem. The second type of question examines the costs of particular diseases (such as depression) if left untreated. The third type of question examines the cost of illness on such other areas of functioning as work and wage loss and medical health if such illnesses are left untreated. The fourth type of question relates to the prevention of disease and the estimated costs and benefits of such prevention. These four types of questions create the foundation for cost-effectiveness research. Most questions addressed by family therapy cost-effectiveness research will fall under the umbrella of one of these broad questions.

There are several specific research questions that cost-effectiveness research can be used to answer in the field of family therapy. These questions are built on two primary questions: What are the relative costs to the benefits obtained and does any method used to achieve a particular outcome, do so more cost-effectively than other possible treatments. The following is a sample of questions that could be asked:

1. Is a particular treatment that has been found to be effective through outcome research also cost-effective?
2. Are the benefits of a particular treatment worth the costs of achieving those benefits?
3. Do the benefits of a particular treatment exceed the costs of that treatment enough to warrant continuing the treatment program?
4. Do the benefits of a particular treatment exceed the costs for that treatment when compared with other possible treatments?
5. What is the efficiency of a treatment program (i.e., benefits divided by costs) when compared to other programs?

Many researchers and practitioners are also calling for cost-effectiveness research that compares the effect of providing or not providing family therapy (Letich, 1993). This type of research forms a bridge across all four of the questions historically examined through cost-effectiveness research. It investigates how family therapy can be effective, as well as the costs of not providing family therapy on health, mental health, work, and myriad other issues directly affecting society. Of course, many of these costs and effects can be measured monetarily, which provides data for decisions regarding policy and third-party reimbursement, to name a few. Finally, such research can also address estimated savings in terms of preventing future problems. Such prevention may affect related fields such as medicine (e.g., future hospital stays for stress-related illness) and education (additional years of education or the societal expense of dropping out of school).

Within broad questions such as these, many variables may be examined in terms of cost-effectiveness. In planning cost-effectiveness research, it is important to use the same skills and attention to detail as in planning any good outcome research (Krupnick & Pincus, 1992). (See Leber, St. Peters, & Markman, Chapter 22, this volume, for detailed information regarding outcome research.)

Several variables are particularly important to consider. They include variables related to clinical, personal, economic, and societal changes. The researcher must first ask, "What are the clinical perspectives and techniques used to provoke change? Who, in fact, is the one that changes? Is it the family? Is it the drug-abusing adolescent? What changes are most important?" In other words, who receives the direct personal benefit of treatment and how is that benefit defined? Who pays the cost and who receives the benefit? (Krupnick & Pincus, 1992).

Keeping these ideas in mind, cost-effectiveness studies are best used when questions of efficacy or outcome are already being asked. Cost-effectiveness questions, then, can be added to the questions already asked.

It is important to remember that the questions best addressed by cost-effectiveness research relate to choice or comparison (e.g., what are the differential cost and benefits of family therapy vs. individual treatment for drug-abusing adolescents and their families?) Similarly, cost-effectiveness research is a good tool for evaluating the efficiency of various programs (Glass & Goldberg, 1977). By asking questions of comparison it is possible to look at both the efficacy and cost efficacy of the components of any given treatment program and evaluate which combination of components not only demonstrates the best outcome for the client but how these components can do so with the highest benefit and lowest costs. For example, a researcher might ask whether family therapy for drug-abusing adolescents works best in combination with self-help groups, tutoring, and/or parent education? How much does each of the services cost? What is the effect of not providing one or more of these services? Is there an increase in benefits or cost to provide family therapy or tutoring in the adolescent's home rather than office? Is it worth the increased cost considering the cost of missed appointments when the entire family must travel to the therapist's office?

Finally, it is important to mention again that the goal of cost-effectiveness research is not merely to lower costs but to find the maximum benefit from any given program, whether it be family therapy alone or in combination with other treatments. The overall goal is to discover what treatment(s) maximize benefits in the most efficient way possible. This does not mean that the best program is always the cheapest. We must, however, recognize the limitations of resources and make evaluations that encourage the best management of those resources to obtain the best results. This goal is at the heart of cost-effectiveness research.

Steps in Conducting Cost-Effectiveness Research

Generally, cost-effectiveness studies should be crafted in the same careful manner as well-designed outcome studies (Krupnick & Pincus, 1992). However, we acknowledge that cost-effectiveness research also has its differences. We recommend that researchers use the following 10 general steps in planning cost-effectiveness research (Parloff, 1980; Pike & Piercy, 1990).

Define Problem

Ideally, it is best to begin with a broadly defined problem which is later defined in specifics. This is the stage of question formation and subsequent hypotheses. For example, the researcher might begin by asking which of three outpatient methods for treating schizophrenics is most cost-effective. A possible hypothesis could be that a combination of medication and home-based family treatment will be more cost-effective than medication and office-based individual treatment.

State Objectives

Research objectives need to be stated explicitly and to flow logically from the problem definition. In cost analysis the objectives are typically stated in terms of examining the degree to which a desired outcome (benefit) is achieved with the highest efficiency (i.e., most benefit per dollar cost). For example, a legitimate objective related to the problem defined above would be to determine which treatment has fewer monetary costs and higher benefits.

Objectives must be determined through quantifiable data, no matter which cost analysis (CBA/CEA) is used. The way data are operationalized will determine the technical design of the study as well as the interpretation of the results. Therefore, the researcher must determine precisely what the desired changes or effects are (e.g., decrease hospitalizations for schizophrenic patients or decrease in family stress for families of schizophrenic patients). The researcher can then determine the appropriate costs and benefits that will need to be measured in the study.

Identify Alternatives

In all cost analyses, some type of comparison is made, whether that is within a program, between two programs, or with no treatment. Therefore, it is important to determine the many alternative methods available. The ultimate question to be answered is whether a given treatment is "cost-effective compared to . . . [what]." This "what" is important. If viable alternatives are ignored, the results become less compelling.

Analyze Benefits/Effectiveness

At this point, the researcher must choose CBA, CEA, or some combination of both. This choice should be based on the objectives of the study and the cost analysis methods' "fit" with the chosen outcome measures. Fortunately, the methodologies themselves determine the contexts in which either a CBA or CEA can be used. As defined earlier, CBA examines all costs and benefits strictly in monetary terms. Therefore, whatever benefits are being examined in a CBA they must be able to be measured monetarily (e.g., the amount of money saved by avoiding inpatient hospitalization).

If benefits cannot be measured monetarily, the researcher must choose a CEA. This is because CEA does not require monetary values for benefits as the unit of comparison. Instead, costs are tied specifically to nonmonetary units of outcome. For example, the researcher may wish to examine outcomes related to increased marital satisfaction and its subsequent impact on the school performance of the couple's children. CEA allows the researcher to compare the cost of a program to one or more units of outcome. If it is possible, we recommend using both CEA and CBA together to measure both monetary and nonmonetary outcomes. This allows the results to be used more widely because different interest groups (e.g.: funders of national health care, couples in therapy, and school boards) will be more interested in certain outcomes than others.

In planning a cost-effectiveness study, special attention must be paid to the benefits being measured. When creating the research design, the researcher should identify all possible benefits and state them clearly. We suggest that the researcher explore benefits within the following categories (Pike & Piercy, 1990):

1. *Personal benefits* pertain to the individual client or family and can include increased physical and mental health, decreased medical costs, and decreased symptomatology.
2. *Family benefits* pertain to benefits the family gains as a result of the program or treatment. Benefits can include increased closeness, lowered stress levels, and increased marital satisfaction.
3. *Health resource benefits* usually refer to such health care expenditures as insurance claims and hospitalization costs.
4. *Social benefits* are common to and generally agreed upon by community or society. Examples include fewer crimes, decreased need for police intervention, reduced incarceration costs, lowered welfare costs, lowered insurance rates, and lowered community expenditures.
5. *Other economic benefits* represent secondary and less obvious benefits. Examples include increased capacity for work, increased productivity increased contributions to society, and increased ability to contribute to the pool of taxes.

Once all possible benefits are identified, the researcher determines the applicability of each benefit to the research project and then considers two issues: measurement and valuation.

Measurement

Benefits should be measured in units appropriate to the problem and objectives defined. In CBA, the unit will be dollars. In CEA, an appropriate outcome measure will be chosen. The effectiveness value derived from that measure will then be compared across treatments to the different costs required to achieve it. For example, the effects of two treatments for schizophrenic patients may be compared by examining the number of days of emergency hospitalization required during the year after treatment.

Valuation

Valuation is the process of determining the worth of each chosen benefit. In CBA, monetary values are used to make the comparison. For CEA, the issue is more complicated and vulnerable to differing evaluation methods and perspectives because such easily measurable terms as money are not used (Office of Technology Assessment [OTA], 1980). Instead, benefits may be marital satisfaction or lowered conflict. These values could be evaluated differently depending on who is doing or using the research. For example, a family researcher may put more value on change in marital satisfaction and the subsequent benefits than do national health care planners.

Three areas of potential distortion should be addressed to allow both the researcher and the consumer to understand clearly the costs and benefits using the same assumptions and measures. This reduces the possibility that the researcher, or those who are using the data, will overstate the results. Valuation allows the researcher to adequately define the terms being used and to be clear about the subsequent values placed on each outcome.

The first potential distortion for which valuation is needed is that of the *time value of money*. Because many costs and benefits of psychotherapy occur over time, they must be placed in some type of long-term perspective. For example, rather than comparing 1990 costs and 1994 benefits, the researcher must choose and make explicit a common value (e.g., costs and benefits at 1994 values). (More specific information about this concept is given within the section on discounting.)

The second type of potential distortion the researcher must address is the *valuation of multiple outcomes*. Because many legitimate outcomes of family therapy treatment are possible, it is important to find a common ground that will allow the researcher to sum and/or compare different outcome measures. However, just as researchers cannot compare apples and oranges, neither can they compare increases in marital satisfaction with decreases in depression. Using a score standardization system can help address this issue. For example, an overall measure of effectiveness can be derived from transforming selected outcome measures into standard scores and calculating a "summary degree of change score." Costs can then be compared to summary scores within and across treatments to determine which program has the highest ratio of benefits to costs (OTA, 1980; Parloff, 1980).

Smith and Glass's (1977) classic meta-analysis is a good example for employing standard scores to multiple outcome measures to allow for comparisons across different treatments. In their work, Smith and Glass (1977) examined nearly 500 studies of psychotherapy. By transforming outcomes into standard scores called effect sizes, they were able to compare the relative effects of various psychotherapy treatments even though different studies used different outcome measures.

Finally, *intermediate outcomes* could be given values if planned during the design of the study. Intermediate outcomes are smaller measures of the change ultimately desired. For example, compliance with curfews is an intermediate outcome that could both reflect and support the ultimate goal of reduced delinquent activity.

Analyze Costs

There are two types of costs to be measured: direct and indirect. Direct costs relate to the actual resources used, such as the amount paid for therapy sessions. Indirect costs are other costs not directly measured, such as the therapist's loss of income due to missed appointments or the cost of child care. Direct and indirect costs can be summed and used as a total score, or a subscore of indirect costs can be created.

Initially, the researcher lists all possible costs so all possible cost components of a given program can be assessed. These components can include such costs as personnel, facilities, materials and equipment, baby-sitting, and the value of client's time. The researcher then chooses the costs appropriate to the questions being evaluated. Because doing cost analysis is new to the field of family therapy, presently no standardization exists regarding which cost variables should be chosen and how they should be evaluated. Therefore, it is important when cost variables are chosen that the same ethical guidelines involved with choosing benefit variables be used, because it is easy to take cost data and make the figures change depending on how they are presented and which ones are included. Therefore, we suggest that researchers examine studies using a cost-effectiveness component as an initial starting point for developing cost variables. We also suggest consulting with peers familiar with cost-effectiveness research both in family therapy and cost accounting prior to finalizing research plans as a check for methodology. (Peer resources could include the authors of this chapter, the Research and Education Foundation of the American Association for Marriage and Family Therapy, local businessmen, and accountants familiar with the principles of cost analysis.) Levin (1975) strongly recommends that cost information be gathered as an integral part of the original outcome research design, rather than post hoc, because this allows measurement and monitoring of costs to be both timely and precise.

There will be several perspectives regarding both costs and benefits. These perspectives should be stated explicitly in the definitions, valuations, and analyses. For example, who incurs the cost and who receives the benefits? If a client is paying $60 per therapy session and feels less depressed, the decrease in depression will be examined in terms of client cost of $60 per session. However if the client's insurance company pays 80% of that cost, how should client cost and benefit be valued? If the client no longer misses work due to depression-related problems, the company gains increased productivity for the 80% cost paid. Or, the client may decrease his or her utilization of other primary health care and thus decrease overall medical claims per year, saving the company money in other costs. Valuation choices abound. It is therefore important to delineate who pays what cost and who receives what benefit so that the analysis is clear.

Decide on the Perspective of the Analysis

The researcher must determine from whose perspective a cost analysis will be done. It is natural, for example, for clients and insurance companies to have different ideas about how to use and evaluate cost-effectiveness data. Other possible perspectives to consider include those of the therapist, administrators, funding agencies, advocacy organizations, taxpayers, government agencies, private businesses, and researchers (Yates, 1980). Ideally, the issue of perspective should be decided at the time the study is planned and should be clearly stated in the methods section of research reports.

Discounting

Costs and benefits usually do not occur simultaneously, yet these data must be given values so comparisons can be made. Thus, as stated earlier, it is helpful to discount all future costs and benefits to a chosen present value so accurate comparisons can be made (Pike & Piercy, 1990).

As previously discussed, the time-value-of-money principle suggests that benefits received today are assumed to be worth more than benefits received at a later date, and costs paid today are assumed to be more "costly" than costs paid in the future. The dilemma that must be addressed is how to compare a dollar of today's cost or benefit with a dollar of cost or benefit at a later date because these dollars are apparently of a different value. The business and economic communities found a way to solve this problem through the use of *discounting*.

Discounting is the procedure by which future payments are given present valuations so that they can be compared to the present payments. For example, $100 offered today is worth more than $100 offered a year from now because the money can be placed in a savings account and draw interest, making it worth more one year from now. If the present value of the $100 offered in the future can be adjusted, comparisons at the present value of the future payment to the payment offered right now can be made. Discounting provides a method to do so.

Discounting takes the $100 offered in the future and reduces it by a factor that represents the amount of interest that will not be earned. In other words, the $100 offered in the future is composed of some amount given now which is invested for a year. At the end of the year, the total sum is the initial amount given plus earned interest which equals $100. Discounting finds out what the initial amount is that results in a total sum of $100 available at the end of the first year.

This process allows the researcher to evaluate in the present total program costs and benefits even though many of these costs and benefits will be realized in the future. For research purposes, we recommend using a standard formula to create a common value from which to make comparisons. Pike and Piercy (1990), Yates (1980), and Levin (1975) offer the following mathematical formula for discounting:

$$PVC = \sum_{t=1}^{n} \frac{X_t}{(1 + i)^t}$$

where *PVC* represents the present value of the future payment, X^t denotes the future payment in year t, i represents the appropriate interest rate that is used to discount the future payment, and n reflects the number of periods or years between now and the year in which the future payment will be received. The equation is set up to provide the present value or the sum of multiple future payments of varying amounts received (or paid) at various times.

A critical discounting factor is the choice of interest rate used to discount future costs and benefits to the present. The business and economic communities recommend that the interest rate reflect the time period over which the cost of benefit is to be discounted. For example, if a cost is projected to occur 6 months from now, a currently prevailing 6-month interest rate should be used to discount that cost. Other costs and benefits will be discounted with interest rates appropriate to their discounting periods.

Due to periods of interest rate fluctuations, we recommend sensitivity analysis. Sensitivity analysis, as a general rule, is the comparison of costs and benefits under different hypotheses and/or assumptions. In other words, cost analysis is done using several different figures for costs and benefits. Each of these figures is then compared to provide a thorough and ethical examination. The sensitivity analysis used is one in which various interest rates are used for discounting to evaluate the range of potential present values for the costs and benefits. This analysis provides not only additional information on the relative sensitivity of the overall costs and benefits to fluctuations in specific costs and benefits but also sensitivity to movements in interest rates.

Analyzing Uncertainties

Another type of sensitivity analysis that we recommend involves examining "uncertain events" (benefits) under different assumptions (e.g., discounting figures) (Yates, 1980). Because methodology and technology can affect the outcome of cost-effective research, it is important to test the outcome under different circumstances to see whether the outcome varies with methodology. Such a sensitivity analysis demonstrates the dependence of the results on certain assumptions (e.g., discount rates) and, we hope, that an assumption does not significantly affect the results (OTA, 1980). For example, reduced delinquency can be measured in several ways such as family report or number of arrests. In a sensitivity analysis both measures would be used in the cost analysis and then compared to see whether the type of measure used affects the outcome of the cost analysis. If differences do occur, the researcher must examine the cost analysis using both outcomes and offer hypotheses concerning the difference.

Addressing Ethical Issues

Researchers conducting experimental studies often face ethical issues around the definitions and methodologies they choose. Because cost-effectiveness research depends on the same assumptions as outcome research, the same ethical issues must be considered when creating the basic research design, even before the components are considered. For example, the researchers must weigh the ethical ramifications of using no-treatment controls in experimental studies.

In cost-effectiveness research, another area of ethical concern relates to how to interpret and present results. This concern arises because the decisions of the researcher related to valuation and discounting can easily skew the results in one direction or another. Regarding valuation, disclosure is the key. The researcher must be clear and specific about how costs and benefits are assigned, the weighting of those values chosen, the rationale employed, and the perspective that guides interpretation. Such clarity will make it less likely that the researcher will mislead the consumer. Furthermore, the researcher must carefully examine the way he or she obtains and presents results.

Similarly, the discounting figure the researcher uses can greatly affect the results. Therefore, readers must be able to understand how and why the particular discounting figure was derived. Sensitivity analysis is an important way to ensure that the researcher does not choose a favorable discounting figure that supports a selective interpretation of the data. With sensitivity analyses, readers can see how different results are quite dependent on the figures used.

Once appropriate precautions are taken, it follows that the researcher will present the results in a clear and readable manner and point out any problems the reader should anticipate in using the results. It is important that the researcher take the time to explain everything, including the various sensitivity analyses performed, and not oversimplify results that may sound catchy and convincing but actually be quite misleading.

Reporting Findings

The researcher can report the results of CEAs and CBAs in a variety of ways, depending on the analysis conducted. The most straightforward way to present results is through the use of tables or matrices that compare the differential costs and benefits, line by line, of different treatments. For example, in Table 16.1, we use fictitious data to present a comparison of the costs and benefits of two treatments (Pike & Piercy, 1990). As the reader can see, Treatment 1 prevented 80 days of hospitalization for a savings of $40,000, whereas treatment 2 prevented 50 days of hospitalization for a savings of $25,000. When the initial costs of personnel and facilities are factored in, the total savings relative to the costs for treatment 1 is $22,000, whereas the total costs and savings for treatment 2 are equal.

In Table 16.2, we use fictitious data to demonstrate a method of presentation developed by Newman (cited in Parloff, 1980) for use in psychotherapy research (Pike & Piercy, 1990). This method presents the range of clients' functioning on a normed instrument (e.g., the Dyadic Adjustment Scale [Spanier, 1976]) for different treatment groups at the beginning and the end of treatment. In this case, we used Jacobson, Follette, and Revenstorf's (1984) concept of clinical significance to classify clients as functional

TABLE 16.1. Comparison of the Costs and Benefits of Two Treatments

	Treatment 1 (n = 50)	Treatment 2 (n = 50)
Costs		
Personnel	$12,000	$15,000
Facility	$ 6,000	$10,000
One day of hospitalization	$ 500	$ 500
Benefits		
Total number of hospital days prevented by each treatment	80	50
Total savings (cost of 1 day × days saved)	$40,000	$25,000
Total		
Ratio: Cost to benefit	$18,000 to 80 days prevented	$25,000 to 50 days prevented
Total savings relative to costs (total savings − summed costs)	$22,00	$ 00.00

(within one standard deviation of the mean of the normative sample) and dysfunctional (outside one standard deviation of where the normative sample scored). Table 16.2 allows the reader to see whether more subjects in treatment 1 moved from a dysfunctional range to a functional range than those in treatment 2. Also, we summarize the cost of the treatments for each client and divide this number by the number of clients who in fact moved from a dysfunctional to a functional level of functioning. We then present the cost of each treatment to bring one client from the dysfunctional to the functional category on the Dyadic Adjustment Scale. Obviously, such a presentation could be used with a variety of dependent variables. It is then up to the reader to determine whether a particular outcome is worth the money to bring it about.

TABLE 16.2. Cost Comparison of Client Functioning

	Treatment 1	Treatment 2
Pretest (Dyadic Adjustment Scale) group means	85	87
Posttest group means	125	101
Clinical significance[a]	50	60
Average treatment costs (average number of sessions × $60 per session)	$ 600 (average 10 sessions)	$ 3,000 (average 50 sessions)
Total cost (n = 100 each treatment group)	$60,000	$300,000
Cost per patient ratio (total cost of treating patients/number of patients achieving clinical significance)	$ 1,200	$ 5,000

[a]"Number of subjects moving from dysfunctional range to functional range during the course of therapy" (Jacobson, 1984, p. 340). For more information about clinical significance see Jacobson, 1985).

Linear methods may also be used to present the mixture of factors that contribute to outcome, along with their costs (Parloff, 1980). These processes allow administrators to make a judgment regarding the degree to which certain factors are crucial to outcome and to weigh their importance in light of their costs.

Finally, the typical way to present CBA results is in terms of monetary values. Usually, the researcher creates a ratio by dividing the total benefits (in dollars) by the total costs for each treatment (Parloff, 1980). If the ratio is larger than 1, the benefits exceed the costs. If the ratio is less than 1, the costs exceed the benefits. The net benefits (benefits in dollars minus the costs in dollars) may also be presented for each treatment for comparison.

Space limits us from presenting all the ways that cost analyses results can be presented. We suggest that the reader examine a number of cost analyses studies to determine which of a range of presentation methods best fits his or her particular study.

Where should family therapy researchers submit cost-effectiveness studies for publication? Because cost-effectiveness analyses should be an integral part of all family therapy outcome research, we believe that cost-effectiveness information should also be an integral part of any published research study. Thus, any journal now publishing family therapy outcome research would be an appropriate outlet for family therapy cost-effectiveness research. Beyond that, cost-effectiveness results can and should find their way into agency newsletters, yearly reports, and policy fact sheets for legislators.

SUMMARY OF COST-EFFECTIVENESS STUDIES IN FAMILY THERAPY

Only a handful of cost-effectiveness studies exist to date in the family therapy field. To help readers see how cost-effectiveness has been used to date, each published study from the literature is summarized to offer concrete examples of potential studies. A brief summary of the strengths and weaknesses of each study has also been included, again to provide guidance for future studies.

The Langsley Group

Langsley and his colleagues (Langsley, Kaplan, et al., 1968; Langsley, Pittman, et al., 1968; Langsley, Flomenhoft, & Machotka, 1969) were perhaps the first to examine the cost-effectiveness of family therapy. Their initial interest was in comparing outcome results between standard inpatient treatment and short-term, family-centered crisis therapy (CT).

Langsley, Kaplan, et al. (1968) developed a family crisis model to treat families in which one member would ordinarily be admitted into a psychiatric hospital. To test the effectiveness of this treatment approach, Langsley, Kaplan, et al. (1968) conducted an experimental study with 150 families randomly assigned to each of two experimental conditions: family CT and hospitalization. In each group, one member of the family presented with symptoms serious enough to warrant hospitalization. Patients and their families assigned to the CT received the family crisis treatment and the patient was *not* hospitalized. In the control group, the patient was hospitalized and given treatment as usual. Langsley and associates (Langsley, Kaplan, et al., 1968; Langsley et al., 1969) then completed a cost analysis based on the premise that family CT kept clients from being hospitalized in spite of their initial presentation with psychiatric disturbances.

To test this premise, Langsley, Kaplan, et al. (1968) examined the relative cost-effectiveness of the family therapy crisis treatment (experimental group) to the hospitalized group (control group) by examining the costs and benefits of avoiding hospitalization. (They acknowledge that their study was not a complete comparison of the results of treatment but instead focused on differential costs.) They employed a simple cost accounting method. They assessed the average cost per day for hospital treatment and multiplied this by the average number of days patients spent in the hospital to determine the average cost per patient. In the late 1960s, the actual cost per control group patient per day at Colorado Psychiatric Hospital was $50. The average stay for the controls was 26 days for a total of about $1,300 per hospitalization.

The cost of family CT was estimated by examining the costs of personnel, overhead, supplies, and travel costs. This figure was then divided by the number of cases the team *could potentially treat* in one year (not the actual cases treated in one year). They found that the annual budget for personnel costs was $65,000 and the overhead, supplies, and local travel were estimated to add $5,000 to those costs. Langsley, Kaplan, et al. (1968) estimated that the team of therapists could treat seven new cases per week or approximately 350 cases per year. Therefore, if the $70,000 is divided by the number of cases potentially seen per year (350) the total cost per client approximates $200.

Their conclusion, then, was that it costs $1,300 to provide hospital treatment and only $200 to provide family CT. In a ratio form, they concluded that it cost six times less to provide family CT to obtain similar outcome results than to provide hospital treatment.

The strength of this study lies more in when and how the study was conducted than in the methodology itself. This study introduced the concept that family therapy, if compared to other forms of treatment, may obtain better or at least the same outcome at significantly less cost than more traditional treatment modalities.

However, several mistakes were made in examining the cost-effectiveness of both programs. First, the costs for each program were not approached from the same perspective. The control group was measured using direct costs (hospitalization) whereas the experimental group was measured using indirect costs (annual budgets). Furthermore, it is unclear who actually incurred the cost—the patient or the hospital. It appears that the patient incurred the hospital costs while the hospital incurred the budget costs for the family therapy. In measuring the costs for the control group, only average scores were used so that the cost estimations were based on the average number of hospital days not the mean of the costs actually incurred by each patient. Also, rather than measuring the ratio between the costs and benefits of the *actual* number of CT patients treated, the researchers examined the maximum number of patients that *could* be treated. Therefore, the real cost–benefit differential between the control and experimental groups was left unreported. The cost ratio for actual numbers may have been less impressive.

Second, many important details were ignored when measuring the costs that may have offered a more complete picture (e.g., How much financial loss did the patient and family incur due to loss of job when the patient was hospitalized? How much did it cost the patient and his or her family to attend family therapy?). Similarly, because the costs were not measured in parallel fashion for the two treatments, it is inappropriate to compare them.

Cardin et al.

Cardin et al. (1985) conducted a cost analysis as part of a larger study on the efficacy of family management in the community care of schizophrenics. They compared the relative costs and benefits of family and individual management. They began with three hypotheses and collected data accordingly. Costs and benefits were acquired for each patient over a 2-year period. This was done, in part, by each patient's therapist, who kept track of treatment-related costs (emergency visits, phone calls, day treatment visits) and societal costs (law enforcement, welfare, health insurance). The therapist kept a record of the patients' earnings, as well. A retrospective review of hospital admission records, emergency room attendance, rehabilitation counseling, medication, and psychotherapy records was also conducted. No attempt was made to assess the societal costs. Their unit of analysis was the individual schizophrenic patient.

The researchers employed both CEA and CBA methodologies. They began by examining the direct and indirect treatment costs, community costs, and the benefits accrued for each patient during the first year in the study. Monetary values were given to each. Figures used were obtained from the cost allocation system employed by the Health and Mental Health Services of Los Angeles County from 1980 to 1981. The researchers obtained indirect costs for residential rehabilitation and day treatment programs directly from the appropriate facilities. An extra cost, equal to 60% of the basic cost, was added to family therapy treatment because it was a home-based program and included extra staff and travel costs. Community maintenance costs were obtained directly from patient and family reports. Law enforcement costs were obtained from local government statistics.

Benefits were calculated by tabulating the earnings from competitive employment, government-sponsored job programs, and shelter workshops. The researchers also included the savings associated with reductions in hospital utilization. They calculated savings by measuring the number of days of hospitalization before and after treatment. The number of days after treatment was subtracted from the number of days prior to treatment. The researchers then multiplied this figure by the daily cost of hospital care.

However, they did not use discounting. The researchers then tabulated this information in a matrix and made comparisons. Cardin et al. (1985) found no difference in direct treatment costs between family management and traditional individual management. However, indirect treatment costs were significantly lower for family management. Therefore, when they examined total costs they found that the cost of family management was 19% less—a savings of about $2,000 per patient. The $2,000 figure was obtained by dividing the total costs by the sample size to find the dollar difference per patient for the two treatment modalities. The researchers found no significant difference in benefits between the two modalities. However, family management produced greater savings in light of the costs, so benefits favored family management. Furthermore, the costs were higher for individual treatment at the end of the first year, and at the second year follow-up the costs for individual treatment remained high while those for family treatment had lowered.

Cardin et al. (1985) also conducted a CEA. They derived an index of effectiveness from the combined changes in three outcome areas: (1) psychopathology, (2) social functioning, and (3) family functioning. For each area of outcome, they derived a standardized scale and then created a standard score for each scale, with change measured from 0 to 3. Next they combined the scores from each scale to form an index of effectiveness and divided the total cost of each approach by the total units of therapeutic effectiveness to ascertain the cost efficacy of the two treatment modalities. For the family management condition, Cardin et al. (1985) found an average of 4 units of therapeutic effectiveness per patient during the first year at a cost of $2,220 per unit; the individual treatment condition accumulated only a total of 38 units of effectiveness at a cost of $5,167 for each patient. They concluded that of the patients and families in family therapy, more than two-thirds showed moderate gains. In contrast, two-thirds of patients and families in individual treatment showed only slight gains. Therefore, family management was more than twice as cost-efficient as the traditional individual-based treatment condition.

Cardin et al. (1985) used straightforward methods which could be replicated in other studies designed to examine the efficacy of family therapy. This research team utilized local sources and therapist recordkeeping to attain costs and benefits. They did a specificity analysis by using both CBA and CEA analyses to examine the cost-effectiveness of the treatments. The primary weakness in this study was the lack of discounting. The differences may have been larger or smaller had discounting been employed. Nevertheless, this study had several strong design features. It began with specific objectives which were then tested. The design was consistent with those objectives. Finally, the study was performed and presented in a way that allowed comparisons and informed conclusions.

Lipsey

Lipsey (1984) examined the cost-effectiveness of a family-based Los Angeles delinquency prevention program to learn what, if any, the savings were for local and state government as a result of this program. Lipsey (1984) began with a model containing four propositions about delinquency prevention. From these propositions and cost savings, he created an equation to examine the data in his study. The three components in his equation were delinquency risk (R), success rate (S), and cost differential (C). His equation was as follows: cost benefit = R × S × C.

Lipsey employed several methodologies to obtain data for each of the variables in the equation. For the delinquency risk factor (R), he identified four groups from which delinquent clients were drawn. These groups were based on studies done in Sacramento, Philadelphia, and Los Angeles County. Success rate (S) was defined as the proportion of clients with delinquency potential and one or more arrests who have been prevented for further crime by the treatment intervention. The cost differential was estimated by comparing the juveniles' delinquency to the average cost of the prevention treatment for those juveniles.

Lipsey took several steps to measure the cost differential. He devised direct costs by calculating the total budget from all sources and dividing by the total number of clients. Estimating the costs saved (benefits) was more difficult. He did this in several ways. First, he calculated direct costs for an arrest (average gross costs were obtained). Next, Lipsey estimated the amount of money saved in the prevention of subsequent arrests. Lipsey also calculated savings from the perspective of potential victims, with the assumption that these savings indirectly benefit the government. He also calculated savings to victims from undetected offenses. Finally, using these figures, Lipsey performed a sensitivity analysis to determine the savings that result from the prevention of a juvenile arrest using each of the possible measures of benefits.

Once Lipsey gathered the information for each of the equation variables, he calculated the range of possible cost–benefit ratios. He then summarized the range of savings by the Los Angeles County delinquency program. Lipsey's conclusion was that the savings by the program was $0.82 to $1.40 for every dollar spent. Thus, at the program's worst it approximately breaks even in terms of costs and benefits. At its best, prevention returns 40% of direct costs on every dollar invested in law enforcement and juvenile justice. Lipsey concluded that the cost–benefit ratio of delinquency prevention can be favorable even with realistic assumptions about delinquency prevention. However, Lipsey found the cost–benefit ratio to be highly dependent on the interaction among the three variables, with the selection of clients being critical. That is, the cost–benefit ratio improves with youth who are more at risk for delinquency. The range of savings can change depending on how each variable is defined and its interaction with the other equation variables.

Perhaps the greatest strength of this study is its thoroughness of plan and use of sensitivity analyses. Lipsey was able to make several conclusions because of his multifaceted, well-planned analyses (e.g., he included a range of savings using different figures and he examined the interaction of the equation variables in determining the cost–benefit ratio). His design is also consistent with his model and equation. Finally, he described his methodologies clearly and presented the results clearly so the reader can draw clear conclusions.

The primary weakness is the lack of attention paid to the variable of time. He did not specify over what period the study occurred, and he did not use discounting techniques.

Tarrier et al.

Tarrier et al. (1991) evaluated the costs of adding family intervention to the treatment of schizophrenia. They chose to examine the financial implications of this family intervention associated with a previously reported successful family treatment of schizophrenia.

They began with a primary hypothesis that the extra costs of the family intervention would be offset by the savings in the reduced use of other facilities of the mental health services by the intervention patients compared to a control group. The study therefore, focused only on direct costs.

They used the Korner cost accounts (a publically available standard cost system) for acute psychiatric care (Salford Health Authority, 1988) and only 1987–1988 prices for comparisons. They included only direct costs (e.g., medical nursing, drugs, dressings, paramedical, and diagnostic input). Hospital admission was costed according to the total number of days per patient multiplied by the cost per inpatient day, taken from the Korner cost accounts for acute psychiatric care. Similarly, the cost of outpatient treatment was calculated on the cost per outpatient visit from the Korner cost accounts multiplied by the number of outpatient visits for each patient. They made a similar calculation for day-care attendance. They also calculated the salaries for nurses, social workers, and psychologists using a midpoint salary from their standard salary scale for each title.

They then compared the treatment groups for each expenditure category of the established services. They confirmed their hypothesis, finding that patients with family therapy treatment added to standard treatment reduced the cost per patient by 27% compared to patients with no family treatment. Thus, the total costs due to the added family intervention component of treatment was outweighed by the decrease in use of other mental health care services.

The strength of this study is that the researchers completed the cost analysis in a succinct manner based on a clear hypothesis. Standard figures were used and the variable of time was considered with all costs derived from the same annual year. However, many more variables could have been examined and the benefits, both direct and indirect, could have been costed. If this was done, the results would likely have been even more impressive.

DISCUSSION

Strengths and Weaknesses of the Methodology

Cost-effectiveness research involves a practical, treatment-oriented methodology, and one might wonder why it has not been used more in the field of family therapy. One reason may be that our field is dominated by practitioners with little interest in such research. And even those practitioners who are interested in using cost-effective methodologies to evaluate their treatment programs may not know how to do so. Few family therapy researchers have a background in accounting or business. For this reason, the ideas and concepts of cost-effectiveness can sound like a foreign language.

The technology itself also has weaknesses. It will be a challenge to adapt and update cost-effectiveness methodology to better fit the field of family therapy. Perhaps the thorniest issues of methodology lie in the area of measurement. For example, it is difficult to quantify qualitative variables. How do you quantify the outcome of marital satisfaction? And should you? Some would maintain that marital satisfaction is not a valid outcome to evaluate in terms of costs and benefits. After all, marital satisfaction could be thought of as a luxury, not a costly illness. Is marital satisfaction worth putting money into? This is a good cost analysis question. The answer, of course, will depend on who is asked and how much money brings about how much marital satisfaction and the savings accrued as a result of marital satisfaction. We need to address such questions, but we will also need better ways to quantify such mental health outcomes in economic terms, which may require changing cost-effectiveness methodology.

Another weakness of cost-effectiveness research is the room for error that comes with valuation, measurement, and interpretation. It is easy to manipulate results; they can appear different under different circumstances. For example, choosing one discounting figure over another can make a program appear cost-effective. So can the way costs and benefits are standardized. Anyone who has dabbled in the house market knows what a difference an interest rate can make on the subsequent mortgage rate paid for the same priced loan. The same kind of differences can appear in cost-effectiveness research, depending on which rate is chosen for discounting. Choosing which values to use and how to use them can be tricky, especially for the business novice. Yet, how they are used will greatly affect the results.

The way results are presented can also skew their meaning. It would be helpful if the way results are presented could be standardized. However, it is likely that standardization will never occur in family therapy, as it does in accounting, because of the numerous viewpoints, questions, and treatment programs that can be evaluated from a cost-effective perspective. At this point, we must rely on the ethics of researchers to examine their questions from several perspectives and to present each of these perspectives so that others can examine the data and draw their own conclusions.

Perhaps, it is this last weakness that lends itself to the greatest strength of cost-effectiveness research—the adaptability of the methodology across fields and contexts regardless of the questions. As long as questions are well grounded in the context and rules of outcome research methods and used as a method of comparison, the possibilities are limitless. And as long as each researcher is clear in the presentation of cost-effectiveness data, many comparisons, decisions, and policies can be created from the use of these studies.

Cost Analysis Skills

There are several skills needed to conduct cost-effectiveness research. The first, mentioned throughout the chapter, is a familiarity and comfort with the rules and methodologies of outcome research. This is the frame on which cost-effectiveness research relies; knowledge must begin here.

The second set of skills involves direct knowledge about costs and benefits. To begin to create cost-effectiveness research, researchers must look for obvious and subtle costs and benefits within their own projects. We suggest that researchers begin by examining the rich history of cost-effectiveness research and develop an understanding of how costs and benefits have been examined by others. Searching the psychology and business literature with the following key words can assist in this literature review: cost-effectiveness, costs, cost-analysis, and cost of medical care. Also, obtaining publications about cost-effectiveness printed by the OTA (1980) can also help the researcher develop an eye for costs and benefits in a multitude of contexts.

Another important skill lies in the field of cost accounting. As mentioned earlier, valuation and discounting are essential aspects of cost-effectiveness research. Yet, they are often confusing concepts to the accounting novice. An important skill, then, would be to understand and develop comfort with valuation techniques. Historically, cost and benefit valuation has been the domain of cost accountants. We recommend that the family therapy researcher explore this field—perhaps through basic accounting courses and texts—to better understand the concepts of valuation and discounting. A thorough reading of previous cost-effectiveness studies will also help.

Bridging Research and Practice

Cost-effectiveness research is practical in that it tackles real programmatic concerns. Yet it also requires knowledge and skills in outcome research methods and accounting principles. It is through this sophisticated knowledge that practical cost-effectiveness decisions can be made. Thus, cost-effectiveness research serves as a natural bridge between the researcher and the practitioner.

For years, Douglas Sprenkle (1976), one of the editors of this book, has been discussing this need to bridge research and practice. The 1990s are providing additional impetus in this direction, as people are becoming more interested in what about family therapy is effective and cost-effective. At the same time, the lives and practices of clinicians are being profoundly affected by the need for accountability.

We believe that this is as it should be. For too long, family therapy has emphasized rhetoric over results. The charismatic master has held more sway than the conscientious researcher, and accountability has had more to do with enthusiasm than data. Things are already changing. The field of family therapy is facing some tough questions: Does family therapy work? For whom does it work? How much does it cost? Is it worth it? As we sort out answers to these questions, practice issues will be affected as never before. Consequently, the question is not whether practice and research should be bridged but how we should best address this inevitability. Cost-effectiveness research provides one important answer.

We believe that cost-effectiveness data will generally support and add credence to our field's collective belief that family intervention provides a key to resolving many presenting problems. Legislators, policymakers, and insurance carriers will be important audiences for this information, and their decisions will further affect how family therapy is practiced. At the same time, what clinicians know intuitively, and what they are doing, will continue to inform future cost-effectiveness research. And so the circle goes.

FUTURE DIRECTIONS
FOR COST EFFECTIVENESS RESEARCH

Our vision for cost-effectiveness research has many dimensions. In the immediate future, family therapy researchers must educate themselves about the intricacies of this research. To this end, we need workshops that teach cost-effectiveness research methods at state and national conferences. University programs must begin teaching cost-effectiveness methodology as part of their research methods courses. We also need written material that demystifies the process and lays out procedures that are easily transferable to other settings. We need good models of cost-effectiveness in our journals.

Our vision also includes the evolution of a family therapy research culture that routinely asks cost-effectiveness questions. For example, we see a day when every family therapy outcome study will have a cost-effectiveness component. We believe that with education about the methodology, this day is coming and in this time of shrinking resources, there is no other choice.

The practice of family therapy requires that we do a better job of getting the results of cost-effectiveness research into the hands of the people that can use them. Clinicians must have access to cost-effectiveness research to improve their services. They also need to find ways to persuade others accurately and convincingly that their services are not only needed but imperative. Policymakers, insurance carriers, and government and private funding agencies all need accurate information to make informed decisions on how to spend their money efficiently.

REFERENCES

Aderman, J., Bowers, M., Russell, T., & Wegman, N. (1993, October). *Making the cut: Family therapists and managed care.* Panel discussion, AAMFT Annual Conference, Anaheim, CA.

Becker, G. S. (1964). *Human capital.* Princeton, NJ: Princeton University Press.

Cardin, B., McGill, C. W., & Falloon, I. R. H. (1985). An economic analysis: Costs, benefits, and effectiveness. In I. R. H. Falloon (Ed.), *Family management of schizophrenia — A study of clinical, social, family, and economic benefits.* Baltimore: Johns Hopkins University Press.

Fein, R. (1958). *Economics of mental health.* New York: Basic Books.

Forst, B. E. (1973). An analysis of alternative periodic health examination strategies. In W. A. Niskanene, A. C. Harberger, R. H. Haveman, R. Turvey, & R. Seckhauser (Eds.), *Benefit-cost and policy analysis 1972.* Chicago: Aldine.

Ginsburg, G., & Marks, I. (1977). Costs and benefits of behavioral psychotherapy: A pilot study of neurotics treated by nurse–therapists. *Psychological Medicine, 7,* 685–700.

Glass, N. F., & Goldberg, D. (1977). Cost-benefits analysis and the evaluation of psychiatric services. *Psychological Medicine, 7,* 701–707.

Jacobson, N. S., Follette, W. C., Revenstorf, D. (1984). Psychotherapy outcome research: Methods for reporting variability and evaluating clinical significance. *Behavior Therapy, 125,* 336–352.

Klarman, H. E. (1965). Syphilis control program. In R. Dorfman (Ed.), *Measuring benefits of government investments.* Washington, DC: Brookings Institution.

Krupnick, J. L., & Pincus, J. A. (1992). The cost-effectiveness of psychotherapy: A plan for research. *American Journal of Psychiatry, 149,* 1295–1305.

Langsley, D., Kaplan, D., Pittman, F., Machotka, P., Flomenhaft, K., & DeYong (1968). *The treatment of families in crisis.* New York: Grune Stratton.

Langsley, D., Pittman, F., Machotka, P., & Flomenhaft, K. (1968). Family crisis therapy—results and implications. *Family Process, 7*(2), 145–158.

Langsley, D., Flomenhaft, K., & Machotka, P. (1969). Follow up evaluation of family crisis therapy. *American Journal of Orthopsychiatry, 39*(5), 753–759.

Letich, L. (1993, May/June). Judgment day for health care. *Family Therapy Networker*, pp. 65–68.

Levin, H. M. (1975). Cost-effectiveness analysis in evaluation research. In M. Guttentag & E. L. Struening (Eds.), *Handbook of evaluation research.* Beverly Hills, CA: Sage.

Lipsey, M. W. (1984). Is delinquency prevention a cost effective strategy? A California perspective. *Journal of Research in Crime and Delinquency, 21*(4), 279–302.

Maidlow, S. T., & Berman, H. (1972). The economics of heroion treatment. *American Journal of Public Health,* 1397–1406.

Office of Technology Assessment. (1980). *The implications of cost-effectiveness analysis of medical technology. Background paper 1: Methodological issues and literature review.* Washington, DC: U.S. Government Printing Office.

Panzetta, A. F. (1973). Cost-benefit studies in psychiatry. *Comprehensive Psychiatry, 14*(5), 451–455.

Parloff, M. (1980). *The efficacy and cost effectiveness of psychotherapy.* (U.S. Government Printing Office Document 052-003-00783-5). Washington, DC: Office of Technical Assessment.

Paul, G. L. (1967). Strategy of outcome research in psychotherapy. *Journal of Consulting Psychology, 31,* 109–118.

Perl, L. J. (1973). Family background, secondary school expenditure, and student ability. *Journal of Human Resources, 6,* 156–180.

Pike, C. L., & Piercy, F. P. (1990). Cost effectiveness research in family therapy. *Journal of Marital and Family Therapy, 16,* 375–388.

Regier, D. A., Boyd, J. H., Burke, J. D., Rae, D. S., Meyers, J. K., Kramer, M., Robins, L. N., George, L. K., Karno, M., & Locke, B. Z. (1988). One month prevalence of mental disorders in the United States. *Archives of General Psychiatry, 45,* 977–986.

Rice, D. P., Kelman, S., Miller, L. S., & Dunmeyer, S. (1990). *The economic costs of alcohol and drug abuse and mental illness: 1985.* San Francisco: University of California, Institute for Health and Aging.

Salford Health Authority. (1988). *Annual Accounts—Korner Costs Accounts.* Salford, United Kingdom: Authors.

Smith, M., & Glass, G. (1977). Meta-analysis of psychotherapy outcome studies. *American Psychologist, 32,* 752–760.

Spanier, G. B. (1976). Measuring dyadic adjustment: New scales for assessing the quality of marriage and similar dyads. *Journal of Marriage and the Family, 38,* 15–28.

Sprenkle, D. H. (1976). The need for integration among theory, research, and practice in the family field. *Family Coordinator, 24,* 261–263.

Stoudemire, A., Frank, R., Hedemark, N., Kamlet, M., & Blazer, D. (1986). The economic burden of depression. *General Hospital Psychiatry, 8,* 387–394.

Tarrier, N., Lowson, K., & Barrowclough, C. (1991). Some aspects of family interventions in schizophrenia II: Financial considerations. *British Journal of Psychiatry, 159,* 481–484.

Verbosky, L. A., Zrull, J. P., & Franco, K. (1991). Cost-effectiveness of psychiatric consultation [abstract]. *Journal of the American Medical Association, 265,* 664.

Weisbrod, B. A. (1965). Preventing high school dropouts. In R. Dorfman (Ed.), *Measuring benefits of government investments.* Washington, DC: Brookings Institution.

Yates, B. T. (1980). The theory and practice of cost utility, cost effectiveness, and cost benefit analysis in behavioral medicine: Toward delivering more health care for less money. In J. M. Ferguson & C. Taylor (Eds.), *The comprehensive handbook of behavioral medicine.* New York: SP Medical & Scientific Books.

IV

MIXED METHODS

Intensive Research

17

Case Study Research

SIDNEY M. MOON
TERRY S. TREPPER

BACKGROUND

The purpose of this chapter is to describe two basic types of case study research that we think hold promise for research in the field of family therapy. First, we discuss "informal" case studies: clinical action research that is undertaken by clinicians who wish to think more systematically about their cases and disseminate their clinical innovations to a wider audience through publication. Second, we discuss "formal" case studies. By formal case studies we mean case studies designed by a researcher for the purpose of advancing knowledge in the field.

History and Assumptions

As a research method, the case study has a checkered history. Early in the 20th-century case study research was common and well respected (Platt, 1992; Mitchell, 1983; Runyan, 1982). However, as quantitative methods gained ascendancy in the social sciences, the case study fell into disrepute. For a long time experimental researchers incorrectly equated the case study with one of the weakest types of quasi-experimental designs: the "one-shot case study," a posttest only, one-group design (Cook & Campbell, 1979; Yin, 1989). Case studies were shunned by social scientists in the 1960s and 1970s (Platt, 1992; Trepper, 1990; Yin, 1989). Recently, however, there has been a revival of interest in case study research in several fields, including education (Merriam, 1988; Moon, 1991; Stake, 1994; Lancy, 1993), sociology (Hamel, 1992, 1993; Platt, 1992), psychology (Ericsson & Simon, 1984; Kazdin, 1992; Yin, 1989), and family therapy (Trepper, 1990).

This reawakening of interest in case study research has come about for several reasons. First, historically, case studies have had tremendous impact on the social sciences (Kazdin, 1992; Platt, 1992). Second, methodologists have advanced powerful arguments for the value of case study designs (Bradshaw & Wallace, 1991; Kazdin, 1982; Miles & Huberman, 1994; Yin, 1989, 1992). Third, the growing interest in qualitative methods in the social sciences has led to increased interest in qualitative case study methods (Merriam, 1988; Moon, 1991). Fourth, critiques of the extensive paradigm have led to renewed interest in such intensive methods as the case study (Safran, Greenberg, & Rice, 1988). Fifth, case studies have been promoted for their potential to bridge the gap that has developed between research and practice in applied social science fields (Kazdin, 1992; Moon, Dillon, & Sprenkle, 1990; Trepper, 1990).

Although case study research is gaining in popularity, there is little agreement about either the definition of case study research or the underlying philosophical assumptions that guide such research. Some methodologists feel case study research is a qualitative method (Merriam, 1988) whereas others see it as a mixed method (Miles & Huberman, 1994; Moon, 1991; Runyan, 1982; Yin, 1989). Some define case studies as studies of contemporary phenomena (Yin, 1989); whereas others use the term to refer to retrospective life history research (Wallace, 1989). Some would reserve the term "case study" for studies of clearly bounded systems (Stake, 1988, 1994); others believe that less well-defined units of analysis such as events or time periods can be "cases" (Miles & Huberman, 1994; Yin, 1989). Some approach case study research from constructivist or phenomenological assumptions (Lincoln & Guba, 1985; Merriam, 1988); others approach it with realist, positivist, or postpositivist assumptions (Lancy, 1993; Miles & Huberman, 1994; Yin, 1989).

In spite of these many areas of disagreement, there are also areas of agreement. Most writers believe that the two essential characteristics of case study methodology are (1) in-depth study of (2) a small number of purposively selected cases (Anderson, 1990; Hamel, 1992; Miles & Huberman, 1994; Moon, 1991; Safran et al., 1988; Stake, 1994; Yin, 1989). Similarly, most writers agree that case study research departs from the traditional experimental research paradigm in eschewing statistical generalization in favor of analytical generalization (Firestone, 1993; Lincoln & Guba, 1990; Yin, 1989).

In this chapter, we define case study research broadly in terms of these areas of agreement, embracing in the process all the areas of disagreement. For example, we believe that case study research can be conducted from a variety of philosophical positions, that the "cases" studied can be either clearly bounded systems or less well-bounded systems such as events, that both retrospective and prospective studies can be called case studies; and that case studies can be conducted using qualitative, quantitative, or mixed methods of data collection and analysis.

We have divided the methodological section of this chapter into two parts. The first, "informal" case studies, describes case study methodology appropriate for clinical action research conducted by therapists on their own therapy. Most informal case studies are descriptive and discovery oriented. Causal inferences must be made cautiously, if at all, with this type of research. The second part of this section covers "formal" case studies. Formal case studies are designed by researchers to investigate specific phenomena and advance scientific understanding of the human condition. Three types of formal case studies are discussed: descriptive, discovery oriented, and explanatory.

INFORMAL DESIGNS

Consider the extent of clinical innovations which occur daily in therapeutic practice, through either design or serendipity. These might be novel interventions, applications of an older technique to a new clinical problem, or changes in the structure of the therapy process. Now consider that almost all these discoveries go unnoticed, except by clinicians and their clients. Many innovative "solutions" to the problems associated with the human condition reside in the experiences of a single therapist. However, therapists, particularly nonacademic ones, simply do not consider the work they do part of the process of clinical research. As a result, their innovations go untested, undisseminated, and ultimately unused by anyone other than themselves.

Those who may have the most to offer in terms of clinical innovation—practicing clinicians—are often not comfortable with doing research. They usually think of research as being statistically based, requiring access to large university libraries, being exceptionally time-consuming, and requiring large samples. Although these are the characteristics of many important research methods, informal case study research does not require any of these and, therefore, can be an attractive alternative for the clinician interested in doing research.

Informal case study research offers an approach for clinicians who wish to systematically examine their own clinical innovations and present these to other clinicians. Unlike formal case study research, which uses a rigorous methodology, informal case study research is more flexible, and is more concerned with hypothesis generation than hypothesis testing. Like other qualitative methods, informal case study research allows for greater interaction between the case being studied and the investigator, increasing the possibilities for new and important information being discovered. Informal case study research usually is descriptive and discovery-oriented.

Methods

Preliminary Steps

One of the best ways to begin is for clinicians to reflect back over the cases they have seen over the past year and try to identify either (1) a case in which something interesting or unique happened that might be worth further scrutiny or (2) a theme that has been noted in several cases. Examples include (1) serendipitous interventions, (2) a change in the sequence of a standardized clinical program, (3) obtaining assessment information from an unplanned source with an unexpectedly useful outcome, and (4) discovering that all the cases with a particular presenting problem have benefited from the same intervention. The possibilities are endless. An excellent source for initial ideas is *101 Interventions in Family Therapy* (Nelson & Trepper, 1993), which offers brief clinical interventions with case examples by practicing clinicians.

From the initial reflection, the next step is to understand the essence of the observation. What is the meaning of the observation? Was the discovery real (i.e., might it occur again under similar circumstances) or was it a fluke? Has it been done, in another form, many times before, or is it something truly unique? Why did it happen? That is, is there some basic explanation possible, or was it purely idiosyncratic?

Finally, a decision is made whether to pursue this as an informal case study. If the observation seems exciting, unique, and of important consequence to the field but more preliminary study is needed, an informal case study is in order.

Questions

Once the general *idea*—that is, what the clinician wishes to examine—is clear, the next step is to turn the idea into a research question. When doing informal case study research, questions should (1) get at the core of the research idea, (2) be broad enough to allow for flexibility during data collection, and (3) allow for new questions to be generated. Although there are myriad possible questions, most will fall in the following four categories:

1. *What's going on here?* These questions focus on testing the reality that the clinician believes exists. Is there indeed a change based on this novel intervention?

Is what I see across cases really a theme, or am I overgeneralizing? Is the family really getting better, or am I engaging in wishful clinical thinking?

2. *What if . . . ?* These questions seek to clarify relationships and understand how changing those relationships may make a difference. What if I sent letters to therapy dropouts? What if I shortened treatment to 6 weeks? What if I do couple counseling with only one spouse?

3. *How . . . ?* How questions focus on the *process* of change. How exactly do communication exercises improve communication within a family? How does the gender of the therapist affect the comfort level of opposite-sex clients in sex therapy? How are "joining" interventions during a first session actually perceived by clients?

4. *Why . . . ?* Why questions seek to offer explanations for observed situations. Why do some women drug abusers seek treatment while others do not? Why are many incestuously abused daughters more angry at their mothers than their abusing fathers? Why do couples respond better to an intervention when it is offered conjointly than when it is offered individually?

Although a number of questions can steer an informal case study, it is best if the clinician asks just one or two major guiding questions. Case studies, like other qualitative methods, are best when they allow for the greatest flexibility. One broadly based guiding question usually allows for more investigative nimbleness than many more specific questions, which may have a tendency to narrow the focus of the research too much and too soon.

Selection

For many informal case studies, the choice of which case to examine is easy because it was one unique case that stimulated the research and would be the focus of the study. A one-session strategic intervention that was used to ameliorate an HIV hypochondriac obsession is a good example (Wetchler, 1994).

Multiple case studies may be used to present a theme across a number of different cases to demonstrate the consistency and/or differences in the theme. An excellent example of this is an article that describes how recovery from sexual abuse trauma can alter not only the foundation of individual identity but also that of the marital relationship (McCollum, 1993). Four marital therapy cases were selected for this informal case study project. The cases were alike in that the sexual abuse recovery process of one partner was affecting the marital relationships of all four the couples but different in the way that they responded to the therapist's intervention. The therapist used the metaphor of renegotiating the marital contract to try to help these four couples understand the impact of sexual abuse recovery on their relationship. In two cases, the contract was easily renegotiated; in the other two, renegotiation was much more difficult and/or not possible. By describing one case from each of these two subgroups in depth, McCollum (1993) was able to illustrate some of the variations in couple response to both sexual abuse recovery and intervention based on renegotiation of the marital contract.

The decision to study one case or a number of cases depends on the research questions being asked and the ultimate purpose of the research. For example, a therapist may have access to a unique case, one for which little has been written. An informal intensive case study would be an excellent approach to learning more about that case, generating hypotheses about the case, and serving as a first step for future research on the topic. As another example, a therapist may "realize" that he or she uses an innovative technique in certain clinical situations and wish to study this further. An informal multiple case study would be appropriate here, where the therapist examines the technique across many cases. However the cases are selected, it is important to pay attention to ethical concerns such as informed consent and confidentiality. These issues are discussed in greater depth toward the end of the chapter.

Data Collection

Whereas with a formal case study the data collection phase should be rigorous, informal case studies have a lot more latitude. This does not mean that the data collection methods should be sloppy. On the contrary, the methods used should be sound, reliable, and accurate. However, informal case studies are usually characterized by *pragmatics* in data collection. They can be simple and not necessarily time-consuming.

It should be noted that data can be collected *prospectively* or *retrospectively*. In the former, a research question is developed, a decision on which future case or cases to examine is made, and then data are collected as the case progresses. In the latter, the research question is developed, a decision on which previous case or cases to examine is made, then data already collected on that previous case or cases are examined.

Case Notes. Written case notes are most commonly used as the basis for data collection in the informal single-case study. If the clinician plans a prospective study, he or she can take even more detailed case notes than usual. In a retrospective study, the clinicians will have to use the notes that are available. How complete and accurate the notes are may determine whether the study can realistically be done with a particular case. For a prospective study, the clinician can plan to take more detailed progress notes than usual and then write periodic summaries of the case.

Project Journals. An alternative to formal case notes are project journals. Whereas case notes have a primary purpose of supporting the clinical work, project journals include materials not appropriate for the client's chart. These might include detailed information related to the research question, personal reflections of the clinician, or collateral information provided by another source.

Audio and Video Chronicles. Increasingly, therapists are audiotaping or videotaping many of their sessions. For those interested in doing informal case study research either now or at a later date, chronicling cases via audio- or video-taping is an excellent way to ensure an accurate record of the sessions, particularly if the tapes can be transcribed for detailed analysis. Videotape has the added advantage of preserving both verbal and nonverbal exchanges.

Interviews with Extended Family or Friends. Sometimes a clinician doing informal case studies can obtain important information from sources close to the clients. These extended family, friends, work acquaintances, and so on can provide important information related to the research question that may not be obtained from direct observation of the clients themselves.

Memories of the Sessions. One undervalued but often used method of data collection in informal case studies is simply the memories of the clinician. Written information offers contemporaneous support for the information about the case, but memories of sessions are also valid. Sometimes, in fact, retrospective review of case material can be even more insightful by offering a clearer picture of the whole case. There is nothing wrong in taking advantage of the 20–20 vision of hindsight.

Data Analysis

As with data collection, the analysis of informal case study data can be simple, not necessarily requiring an inordinate amount of sophistication. The purpose of data analysis is to answer the guiding research questions and to generate new hypotheses for further research.

Intensive Case Review. Complete case reviews are often used as a form of data analysis. With this method, the clinician intensely reviews the progress notes or the videotapes, looking for patterns consistent throughout, changes as a result of interventions, and important clinical themes. A written case summary is then made to help consolidate the findings for the clinician. Usually it is helpful for a colleague to read the first draft of the case summary to help validate the clinical impressions.

Peer Debriefing and Supervision. One of the difficulties with the informal case study method is that the clinician usually works alone. This isolation may result in less than accurate or useful results. A partial solution is for the clinician to present the case to colleagues, including videotapes of sessions if available, along with the research questions and initial hypotheses and impressions. The colleagues can validate and help refine the findings as the case moves along and also help clarify the results of the project.

Asking the Clients. Although not appropriate for all informal case study projects, sometimes the best interpreter of the results are the clients themselves. Certainly if the research question involves therapy outcome, asking the clients if certain interpretations are accurate is reasonable. Also, the various clinical hypotheses that might be generated could well be discussed with the clients, who may be able to clarify, expand, or even reject certain speculations. Some authors of informal case studies routinely ask their clients for feedback on articles that were based on those case studies.

Dissemination

The ultimate purpose of all research, including informal case studies, is to disseminate the findings to those for whom the results would be useful. In marital and family therapy, there are a variety of forums in which informal case studies can be shared with colleagues.

Conferences. There are many local, national, and international conferences for marriage and family therapy. A quick scanning of the conference brochures will convince a fledgling informal case study researcher of the interest in this method. The majority of presentations made at these conferences are based on informal case studies—certainly more than those based on experimental or even formal case study research. This is because these conferences are primarily for practicing therapists who find presentations on innovative methods based on informal case material the most helpful to their work.

Most conference presentations based on informal case studies follow a similar format. First the presenter, who usually developed the practice method being presented, offers an historical overview to the problem, including other clinical methods commonly used. Next, the presenter gives the theoretical underpinnings of the method and details the method itself (be it an intervention, assessment device, a complete treatment program, etc.). Then he or she presents a case that exemplifies the use of the method, usually through video vignettes but sometimes through a formal written case presentation. Finally, the presenter offers a summary of the case, its relevance to the new method, and some limitations.

Journals. Many family therapy journals will accept articles based on informal case studies. The best outlet for informal case studies are journals that publish case studies *exclusively*, such as the *Journal of Family Psychotherapy* and *Case Studies in Family Therapy*. Most of the omnibus journals, such as the *Journal of Marital and Family Therapy* and *Family Process*, publish case studies occasionally, usually as brief reports. Finally, some content-specialized journals, such as the *Journal of Feminist Family Therapy and the Journal of Systemic and Strategic Therapies*, also publish articles based on informal case studies that relate to their particular specialty focus.

Format. Just because a case study was informally conducted does not mean it should be informally presented. On the contrary, a fairly standardized format for written presentation of the informal case study has evolved.

The article should begin with *a review of any relevant literature.* This section should only include previous research that relates to the theoretical underpinning or supports the argument for the novel approach or method described in the case study. The literature review should be relatively brief and include only citations that relate directly to the argument. It should not be encyclopedic or attempt to be all-inclusive. As a rule of thumb, the introduction and literature review should not be more than four manuscript pages.

A description of the problem being addressed by the case study should logically flow from the literature review. This description corresponds to the "purpose of the study" paragraph found in most empirical articles and sets the stage for the case presentation itself. It alerts the reader to the goals of the study, where the study fits in the larger research arena, and the orientation and biases of the author. If a new intervention is being proposed, this is the section in which its the overall purpose and description of are offered.

The second section is usually the case study itself. It begins with *any clinically relevant information concerning the family.* Authors always question how much detail to include in a case study. The answer relates to how informal case studies are to be ultimately evaluated by professional peers. There clearly needs to be enough detailed information about the case for readers to evaluate the reliability and validity of the findings and interpretations of the author. This is even more crucial in an informal case study than in an empirical presentation because the data are not objective. However, if too much information is presented (i.e., the case presentation itself is just too long) the author runs the risk of overloading the reader and making reasonable assessment of the material impossible. Generally, in informal case studies, the actual case presentation is usually no more than five or six manuscript pages.

After the overall case presentation, if an intervention as proposed, *a description of the intervention in enough detail as to be replicable* is given. The description should include *an illustrative dialogue* to help readers understand not just the purpose and theory of the intervention but how it should be implemented. Either dialogues can include verbatim transcripts from actual sessions or they may be made up by the author to exemplify how the interchange between client and therapist might go. Made-up dialogues should maintain the precise flavor of the therapist–client interaction without using the exact words.

The last section of the article is the Discussion section. In this, the author offers his or her interpretation of the findings made in the case study. It is always wise to be humble in the presentation. For example, a paragraph that begins, "This case study has shown the XYZ intervention to be highly effective in the treatment of depressed women," is inaccurate and naive. Instead, an author might begin the paragraph with, "In this case study it was shown that the XYZ intervention was helpful for a depressed woman client, and may be promising as an intervention for others," and then go on to summarize the strengths of the intervention. However, the paper should end with a section on *limitations and suggestions for future research*, where the reader is reminded that this is a case study, with a sample of one, with uncontrolled factors, and interpreted and presented by one or two people. Future research should then be suggested that would further examine the efficacy of the intervention.

Discussion

Informal case studies offer clinicians an opportunity to become researchers by using that with which they are most familiar—their own cases—as data. The informal case study method is an excellent choice for those who (1) have limited formal research training and experience, (2) have a primary interest in clinical service delivery but also wish to contribute to the larger field as a whole, (3) have access to a specific or unusual population, (4) have truly made some exciting clinical discoveries; and/or (5) wish to move from clinical work to research in an orderly, step-by-step fashion.

The major strength of informal case study research lies in its flexibility. Whereas formal research is limited by its method, structure, and rules, informal case study research encourages the novel, serendipitous, and creative. Because this method is not limited to testing certain hypotheses, new hypotheses can be generated. And whereas formal research methods discourage that which is uncontrolled, informal methods encourage the seeking of seemingly unrelated phenomena, looking at novel explanations, and being more subject centered during the research itself.

Of course, all of this "openness" comes at a price, and that price is the major limitation of informal case study research: *control*. Without *control*, generalizability is limited to case-to-case transfer (Firestone, 1993). Without *control*, replicability is difficult. And without control, ultimately the validity of the findings comes into question. Why is this important? Family therapy, like all forms of medical–psychological–social interventions, is susceptible to charlatans, quacks, and even good-spirited but misinformed practitioners. These people may intentionally, or unintentionally, mislead the public through "testimonial" research—that is, the presentation of "case studies" that imply efficacy. Family therapy in recent years has come under attack by some who argue the claims made are based more on "testimonials" than research, thus marginalizing the field (Shields, Wynne, McDaniel, & Gawinski, 1994). It is imperative that informal case study researchers do not contribute to this situation. They must be realistic as to the purpose and uses of the method. They must be humble in their presentations, both at conferences and in journals, and they must at all times communicate the limitations of any approach developed through informal case studies. Finally, they must remain cognizant that the informal case study method is just one research type, which has its strengths and limits. At all times, informal case study researchers should encourage further testing and investigation of their ideas.

FORMAL DESIGNS

Formal case study research is designed to investigate a specific phenomenon for the purpose of advancing knowledge about that phenomenon. In family therapy, formal case study research can be used to develop a rich description of an individual, a system, or a therapeutic process. It can also be used discover or verify family therapy theory and to explain how and when specific therapeutic processes work best. It is a rigorous methodology characterized by in-depth study of a few purposively selected cases using multiple sources and methods of data collection.

Methods

Designs

Many designs are possible in formal case study research. The first step in designing a formal case study is to decide on the unit of analysis. The unit of analysis can be an individual, a system, or an event. Some case studies have one unit of analysis, such a single therapist. Others have multiple embedded units of analysis such as a family, the subsystems of the family, and individual family members. The unit of analysis is the focus of study and is always purposively selected. In other words, the particular case or cases studied are selected for clearly defined reasons according to specified criteria. For example, in a case study conducted by the first author of a child with co-occurring learning disability, giftedness, and physical impairments (Moon & Dillon, 1995), the unit of analysis was the child and the child was selected for study because he was unique— he had a unique combination of exceptionalities and had been home schooled.

The second step is to make a preliminary decision about how many cases will be needed. In the example above, only one case was needed because the purpose was to develop a rich description of the developmental history and learning characteristics of one child. In Bischof's (1993) study of the development of a model of self-consultation, on the other hand, several cases were needed in order to investigate how the model being developed worked under a variety of conditions for a variety of therapists. The third step is to decide how to collect information about the case or cases. Case study research usually employs multiple methods of data collection. Often qualitative and quantitative data are combined in a single study. Finally, a decision must be made about how many stages the research will have. Many case study designs have multiple stages and/or recursive waves of data collection and analysis. These aspects of case study research are discussed in more detail in the data collection and analysis sections below.

Questions

A wide variety of questions can be answered with case study research. These questions can be divided into three categories: descriptive, discovery oriented, and explanation oriented. *Descriptive questions* are questions that ask for a rich description of some naturally occurring event. They are often answered by an in-depth examination of a single, interesting case. Examples of descriptive questions include the following:

1. What does the therapy of an expert in structural–strategic therapy look like?
2. What issues are being raised in therapy by a divorcing woman and how do her perceptions of these issues compare to those of her therapist?
3. What are the unique characteristics of XYZ clinic?

Discovery-oriented questions are similar to descriptive questions but go one step further—they attempt to discover generalizable principles or models. Discovery-oriented questions usually require a comparison of several cases. Examples of discovery-oriented questions include the following:

1. What do trainees and supervisors believe are the characteristics of effective supervisory relationships?
2. What therapeutic approaches seem to be most helpful to couples in the decision making stage of divorce?
3. How might we develop a model for the systemic treatment of incest?

Explanation-oriented questions focus on developing an explanation for how or why something occurs. Explanation-oriented questions require fairly elaborate, recursive research designs with multiple methods of data collection/analysis. Examples of explanation-oriented questions suitable for case study research include the following:

1. Why does solution-focused therapy help some clients and not others?
2. Why do Hispanic families at XYZ clinic drop out of therapy more often than black families?
3. Why do medical doctors resist the assistance of family therapists when working with terminally ill patients?

Data Collection

One of the hallmarks of case study research is multiple methods of data collection. By collecting data from many perspectives, case study researchers use the principle of triangulation (Denzin, 1978) to increase confidence in their findings. Common methods of data collection include observation, interviews, and assessment instruments of all kinds.

A variety of kinds of *observation* are possible. Structured quantitative protocols can be used or the observations can be more qualitative and open ended. The observer can be a participant observer or a nonparticipant observer. Therapist–researchers conducting case study research on their own cases would be participant observers. Therapist–researchers conducting research on the cases of others might observe by watching sessions through one-way mirrors, sitting unobtrusively in a corner of the therapy room during sessions, or watching videotapes of sessions.

Interviews are often used to explore differing perceptions among clients, therapists, and supervisors. Interviews can be structured or unstructured, formal or informal. They are usually audio- or videotaped and then transcribed prior to analysis. Interviews can be used to explore the history of a concern, to elicit perceptions of therapy processes, or to explore the thoughts and feelings of participants at specific points in therapy. They can also be used to develop "expert systems" (i.e., to explore the specific decision-making processes of expert therapists).

The full spectrum of *assessment instruments* can be used in case study research. Case study researchers can use such archival information as case notes and intake files as part of the data for their studies. They can collect new assessment information as a part of the research; administer such psychological and family assessment devices as the Dyadic Adjustment Scale, FACES, or the Beck Depression Inventory; and also create quantitative questionnaires, goal attainment scales, or other assessment instruments as part of their data collection strategy.

The first author (S. M. M.) conducted a multiple-case study of the social, emotional, and learning characteristics of children with co-occurring giftedness and attention-deficit/hyperactivity disorder using muliple metehods and sources of data collection. Both quantitative and qualitative data were collected in this study. Sources of information included children, parents, and teachers. Quantitative instruments administered to the participants included the Family Environment Scale, the Classroom Environment Scale, the Child Organization Scale (student, parent, and teacher versions), the Conners Behavioral Rating Scale, the Home and School Situations Questionnaires, and the Group Inventory for Finding Creative Talent. Most of these instruments were filled out in parallel forms by children, parents, and teachers in order to provide information about the differences in perspectives among these three subsystems. In addition, such archival quantitative data as achievement and IQ test scores were examined. Qualitative data were collected in this study through semistructured interviews with the children, their parents, and their teachers. For pragmatic reasons, observation was not used. However, the study would have been richer and more powerful if observation of the children in both the home and school setting had been included in the design.

Data Analysis

In formal case study research, data analysis is a complex and time-consuming task. Usually, voluminous amounts of data are collected and it can be hard to make sense of it all. The analytic task is complicated by the fact that there are no well-accepted conventions for how case study data analysis should proceed (Yin, 1989). In this section, we outline general guidelines for case study analysis and suggest resources for further study.

The first step in analyzing case study data is to decide whether the analysis will be conducted simultaneously with data collection or only after all the data has been collected. The primary advantage of the simultaneous method is that it enables the researcher to alter data collection techniques as needed to address issues that arise from the initial analyses. The simultaneous method is particularly useful for case studies that are designed to discover theory or develop explanations for complex phenomena. Advantages of the end-of-study method of analysis are that (1) the researcher can make choices about which data sources/methods should be examined first, (2) all the data from a given study can be analyzed in a short time and data from all sources and methods can be compared at that time, and (3) this method is often more efficient.

Once the timing of the analysis has been determined, the analyst must decide what types of analyses to conduct. The analytic task is simpler in single-case studies than in multiple-case studies. In a single-case study, only two broad types of analysis are possible: (1) a within-case analysis and (2) a comparison of the case with the literature. In a multiple-case study, three types of analysis are possible: (1) within-case analyses, (2) one or more cross-case analyses, and (3) comparisons of the cases with the literature.

Within these broad types of analyses, specific strategies are utilized. Usually, the quantitative data collected in case studies are analyzed with descriptive statistics. The information generated by these descriptive analyses is then incorporated into the qualitative within and cross-case analyses of the cases.

Data analysis strategies developed for qualitative research are also used in case study research. These strategies include analytic induction; constant comparison; and open, axial, and selective coding (Glaser & Strauss, 1967; Goetz & LeCompte, 1984; Strauss & Corbin, 1990). In addition, Yin (1989) suggests using pattern matching, explanation building, or time-series analyses as core analytic strategies for case study research that is designed for theory building or explanatory purposes. These strategies are discussed in depth by Dickey (Chapter 12, this volume, on single-case behavioral research). In the second edition of their text on qualitative data analysis, Miles and Huberman (1994) describe numerous analytic strategies that are appropriate for case study research with a particular emphasis on the use of "data displays." Data displays are matrices or diagrams that summarize data in a compact and understandable fashion.

A retrospective, multiple-case study of high school seniors who had participated in an enrichment program for gifted and talented children in elementary school that was conducted by Moon, Feldhusen, and Dillon (1994), illustrates the way these different techniques can be combined in a single study. This study was conducted when the participants were seniors in high school and involved two stages of data analysis. During the first stage, results of a questionnaire containing both a Likert scale and open-ended items were analyzed. The questionnaire had been completed by former participants ($n = 23$) and at least one of their parents ($n = 23$). Archival documents including test scores and progress reports from the elementary school years were also incorporated into this analysis.

The first step in the data analysis was to analyze the Likert scale using descriptive statistics. Then, all data sources for each case (archival student data, Likert scale composite and raw data for students and their parents, and responses to the open-ended questions on the questionnaire from students and their parents) were analyzed in 23 separate case analyses. After each case analysis was completed, a theoretical memo (Strauss & Corbin, 1990) was written summarizing the findings and comparing the findings to all previously analyzed cases. Each case analysis took approximately 4 hours to complete.

When all the case analyses had been completed, a cross-case analysis of the responses to each of the open-ended questions was conducted using the techniques of open coding followed by axial coding and a quantitative content analysis. The cross-case analysis of each question also took approximately 4 hours to complete.

After the first-stage analyses were completed, 10 families were selected using purposive sampling for intensive family interviews. Discrepant and negative cases were deliberately included in the interview sample. The data analysis for the second stage of the research concentrated on the interview transcripts and was conducted after all interviews had been completed. Again, case analyses were conducted first and were followed by cross-case analyses. Because the families who had participated in this stage of the research were purposively selected to help develop theory about the effectiveness of the enrichment program in developing talent in participating students, strategies used for this analysis included comparison of positive and negative cases; careful analysis of discrepant cases; open, axial, and selective coding; and comparison of the findings with the literature on talent development.

This example shows how case study research incorporates multiple methods of data collection (records, written questionnaires, and interviews) from multiple sources (former teachers, participants, and their families) which are then analyzed by a variety of different techniques (descriptive statistics, content analyses, inductive analyses, and constant comparison) in order to produce rich descriptions, generalizable theories, and/or comprehensive explanations of social science phenomena.

Reporting

Writing up case study research is both exhilarating and exhausting. The researcher must ask: "What is the best way to communicate my findings?" "What audiences do I hope to reach with my findings?" The answers to these questions will shape the report. As usual, there are decisions to be made. For example, the researcher must decide whether to present the findings in book or article/chapter form. Often, case studies yield so much data that it is difficult to condense them to the length of a conventional journal article. Many case study researchers choose to bypass journals and develop their findings into a book.

After the "genre" decision is made, the next step is to decide how to present the findings. There are numerous alternatives; thus we discuss three of our favorites here. One of the most common approaches is to develop a *narrative description* about the central phenomenon of the study (Strauss & Corbin, 1990). This approach works particularly well for exploratory and descriptive case study research where the goal is to tell the "story" of the findings. Selecting a story line allows the researcher to integrate all the findings around a central theme and to produce a coherent, highly readable, and interesting research report.

A second approach is to organize the findings by *assertions plus supporting evidence* (Erickson, 1986). An assertion is a one-sentence statement of a finding that is supported by evidence. For example, in the retrospecive case study of the long-term effects of an enrichment program for gifted and talented children described earlier (Moon et al., 1994), one of the assertions developed in the final research report was that *the program had been an appropriate "early years" talent development experience.* This assertion was supported by evidence from the questionnaires, the intensive family interviews, and a comparison of the overall findings of the study with the findings of a study reported by Bloom and his colleagues (1985) on talent development processes in world-class experts in six fields. The assertion emerged in the final stage of data analysis and represented a way of looking at enrichment programs that differed from prevailing theories at the time.

A final approach to presenting the findings from case study research is the *explanatory display.* This approach is particularly appropriate when case study research has been conducted in order to develop a causal explanation. Miles and Huberman (1994), describe a variety of possible explanatory displays. One of the simplest is a case dynamics matrix. "A case dynamics matrix displays a set of forces for change and traces consequential processes and outcomes" (Miles & Huberman, 1994, p. 148). A more powerful type of explanatory display is a causal network, "a display of the most important independent and dependent variables in a . . . study . . . and of the relationships between them" (p. 153). A causal network is a qualitative path diagram that looks similar to the path models developed as a result of quantitative causal modeling. Qualitative causal modeling is similar to quantitative causal modeling in that both methods facilitate the investigation of causal relationships among variables that are not easily manipulated (e.g., thoughts and feelings) and permit consideration of the interrelationships among variables systemically so complex, reciprocal relationships can be identified. However, the processes involved in developing a qualitative causal network display are different from those involved in quantitative causal modeling in that they are grounded in an understanding of events over time in a concrete, local context rather than in probabilistic statistical analyses (Miles & Huberman, 1994).

Discussion

Strengths and Weaknesses

It is difficult to discuss the strengths and weaknesses of formal case study research in general terms because case studies can be conducted from a number of different inquiry paradigms (Guba, 1990) or orientations (Krathwohl, 1993). Often what is perceived as a weakness in one inquiry paradigm–orientation is seen as a strength in another. For example, a constructivist–particularist might perceive that a strength of descriptive case study research is the development of rich, contextual descriptions of unique social science phenomena. A positivist–analyzer, on the other hand, might view the same type of study as weak because it would not generalize beyond the specific situation described. We believe that case study research can be conducted from a variety of perspectives and inquiry paradigms and that it is important for case study researchers to be explicit about the paradigm that is informing their research and to be evaluated by criteria that fit that paradigm.

Inquiry paradigms aside, what are some general strengths of case study research when applied to the field of family therapy? Case study research is similar in many ways to clinical work. It allows for holistic, systemic approaches to research questions and for the incorporation of multiple sources of data and multiple perspectives. All these characteristics are a good fit for family therapists and similar in many ways to the clinical practice of family therapy. Case study research is also useful for observing change over time—a major goal of much family therapy research. Finally, case study research can yield findings that are readily accessible to practitioners and relate directly to clinical practice.

Case study research has a number of pragmatic weaknesses. The biggest is that it is extremely time-consuming. The data collection, data analysis, and reporting stages of formal case studies all take a great deal of time. In addition, it is difficult to delegate case study data collection and analysis to assistants or computers. Publication can also be a problem because of the difficulty of compressing narrative findings into a journal-length manuscript. A weakness of the exploratory types of case study research is that, as with all explorations, it is possible to spend a great deal of time and effort and fail to find anything of value. This weakness is not applicable to theory-driven explanatory case study research.

There are also some research purposes for which case studies are not well-suited. Survey research is more appropriate than case studies for finding out the perceptions or beliefs of a large number of people about a particular issue. Case studies are also of limited value in the later stages of instrument development, when specific, quantifiable, normative information about the psychometric qualities of the instrument is needed. When treatment variables can be easily manipulated, large samples are available and a few, easily quantified and operationalized variables are being investigated, experimental research is more appropriate than case study research, especially if randomization to treatment and control groups is ethical and feasible.

Reliability and Validity

Perceptions of issues of reliability and validity differ in different social science inquiry paradigms (Guba, 1990; Lincoln & Guba, 1985) and orientations (Krathwhol, 1993). Our view here is that reliability and validity are important in case study research but are often addressed in different ways than they are in probabilistic research. Tactics for enhancing the *reliability* of case study research include using multiple observers, persistent observation (e.g., watching a videotape repeatedly), systematic maintenance of a research database, establishment of a chain of evidence, and the use of interview protocols (Asher & Moon, 1993; Miles & Huberman, 1994; Yin, 1989).

Tactics for enhancing the *validity* of case study research include observing naturalistic settings, triangulating data methods and sources, prolonged engagement in the setting, using low-inference descriptors when reporting findings (e.g., quotes), member checks (checking perceptions and conclusions with participants and/or letting participants read the final report), disciplined subjectivity (actively monitoring potential researcher biases), using of systematic data analysis techniques (e.g., open, axial, and selective coding; constant comparison; data displays; pattern matching; and time-series analysis), and peer debriefing (discussing emerging conceptions of the case/theory with colleagues) (Asher & Moon, 1993; Miles & Huberman, 1994; Yin, 1989).

Issues of generalizability in case study research need to be addressed in terms of case-to-case transfer or analytical generalization rather than through probabilistic generalization from a sample to a population (Firestone, 1993). Usually, case-to-case transfer is the most appropriate method of generalization for descriptive case studies, especially single-case studies, whereas analytical generalization is most appropriate for discovery-oriented and explanatory case studies. In most circumstances, multiple-case studies have greater generalizability than single-case studies (Yin, 1989).

Skills

Different types of case study research require different types of skills. For example, the skills most needed for descriptive case study research are curiosity, motivation, good powers of observation, good inductive thinking skills, and strong writing abilities. For discovery-oriented case study research, the researcher needs to have strong analytic, creative, and conceptual powers. The researcher needs to be good at analyzing, synthesizing, and evaluating large amounts of data. In addition, he or she needs to be good at divergent and imaginative thinking to generate many ways of looking at the data and to develop strong conceptualizations that fit the data. For explanatory case study research, a good theoretical grounding in the literature, disciplined subjectivity, and strong analytic skills are particularly useful.

Skills needed during the data collection phase of all all three kinds of case study research include observation, interviewing, and self-monitoring skills. Family therapists are usually highly trained in all these areas and are thus well-equipped for case study data collection. For the data analysis stage, researchers would benefit from formal training in such specific techniques as analytic induction, constant comparison, data displays, pattern matching, and descriptive statistics.

When it comes to report writing, case study researchers need excellent writing and organizational skills. They must be able to condense the vast amounts of data collected without losing the richness of that data. For descriptive case study research, narrative writing skills of the sort that a novelist might employ are helpful. In discovery-oriented and explanatory case study research more formal writing is usually appropriate. These types of case study research call for strong organizational and conceptual writing similar to that used in preparing legal briefs.

ETHICAL ISSUES

There are two major ethical issues which must be addressed in all forms of case study research. The first is *informed consent*. It would be unethical to alter treatment, add a new procedure or device, or in any way conduct therapy in any experimental way without the complete informed consent of the client. In a retrospective study in which the clinician–researcher is analyzing existing data on a previously treated case where no alteration of the treatment program was made and anonymity of the client family is preserved in the research report, informed consent of the client family beyond that typically required for the therapy process itself is usually unnecessary. However, in prospective studies in which the research is planned in advance and may affect treatment, clients should be informed about the research in advance and given the opportunity to decide whether they wish to participate. In prospective case studies all the usual ethical guidelines for informed consent when working with human subjects apply (need for signed consent of all participants, parental consent for minors, and right to withdraw at any time for any reason). When dealing with issues related to informed consent, the researcher should err on the side of conservatism. When in doubt, inform.

The second issue is confidentiality. When presenting a case study, either at a conference or in print, the identities of the family, family members, and extrafamilial participants in the case must be fully disguised. This means not only that the names must be changed but that any other possibly identifying information, such as occupations, ages of family members, and even the sex of the children, should be altered. As a guide, researchers should ask, "Would a family friend reading the article be able to identify the family?" If there is any doubt, the identity should be disguised further. If you are going to use verbatim transcripts, it is a wise idea to obtain the family's written permission. Although at this writing is unclear legally as to who owns the words said in a therapy session, ethically we believe the clients do, and that they should be allowed to determine whether they want their words used or not. In single-case studies, when it can be difficult to disguise the identity of the client family without affecting the accuracy of the research report, an alternative strategy is to ask client/participants to read initial drafts, provide feedback on their accuracy, and then sign a written consent for publication. In addition to addressing ethical issues of informed consent and confidentiality, such "member checks" (Lincoln & Guba, 1985) can enhance the reliability and validity of the research.

An ethical dilemma has emerged in the last few years which crosses both the *informed consent* and *confidentiality* issues. Most people who present videotape case study material at conferences are well aware that they must obtain the written consent of all participants prior to showing the tape. A more confusing area relates to children used in a videotape. Even though parents or guardians sign a consent form for the children, it is probably wiser to block out the faces of the children. Ask yourself the question: If a case study videotape were made of you as a child, would you want it shown at conferences now? From an ethical standpoint, we believe small children cannot give informed consent for themselves and should therefore have their identities hidden even more carefully than adults who can give more reliable consent.

FUTURE DIRECTIONS

Both informal and formal case study research holds tremendous promise for elucidating therapeutic processes. Informal case studies are especially useful for developing retrospective reports of serendipitous clinical discoveries. Both informal and formal case studies can be used for exploratory work in such new areas of the field as underresearched special populations and for discovery-oriented investigations of innovative treatment methods. Formal case study research can also be helpful in addressing the specificity question (i.e., what treatments are most effective for what clients under what conditions). Single-case explanatory research allows for in-depth examination of the inner workings of specific therapeutic processes in specific circumstances. Multiple-case explanatory research is even more powerful because it allows for simultaneous analysis of the idiosyncrasies of particular cases and the common themes that recur across cases.

In addition, case study research has the potential to help bridge the infamous gap between theory and practice because of its innate similarities to clinical practice. The methodology of case study research requires similar skills to those of clinical practice and has a familiar feel for most clinicians. Observations, interviews, inductive analysis, constant comparison—these are foundational techniques in both case study research and the clinical practice of family therapy. As a result, family therapy clinicians usually make excellent case study researchers. The research reports generated from case study investigations are generally written in an accessible narrative style that is clinically relevant and easy for clinicians to understand. This is especially true for single-case studies and exploratory/discovery-oriented work. Multiple-case explanatory studies, on the other hand, can be extremely technical, highly abstract, and difficult to understand.

There is a need for more published examples of formal case studies in the family therapy literature. There are some good examples of informal case study research, especially in journals that specialize in publishing case study research (e.g., *Journal of Family Psychotherapy* and *Case Studies in Family Therapy*). However, there are few good examples of formal case study research in the family therapy literature. The field needs good exemplars of a variety of case study designs: exploratory, discovery-oriented, and explanatory. Because case study methodology is a rapidly growing area of social science research design, case study researchers will need to work to stay abreast of the newest methodological developments and to take an inventive approach to research design so that they can contribute to the ongoing development of case study methods. We hope that this chapter will spur (1) greater interest in case study methodology among family therapists, (2) a wide variety of case study investigations of family therapy, and (3) improved training in case study methodology in family therapy doctoral programs.

REFERENCES

Anderson, G. (1990). *Fundamentals of educational research*. London: Falmer Press.

Asher, J. W., & Moon, S. M. (1993). Quantitative and qualitative guidelines for research in gifted education. *Quest, 4*(1), 7–10.

Bischof, R. (1993). *The development of a model of self-consultations*. Unpublished doctoral dissertation, Purdue University, West Lafayette, IN.

Bloom, B. S. (Ed.). (1985). *Developing talent in young people*. New York: Ballantine.

Bradshaw, Y., & Wallace, M. (1991). Informing generality and explaining uniqueness: The place of case studies in comparative research. *International Journal of Comparative Sociology, 32,* 154–171.

Cook, T. D., & Campbell, D. T. (1979). *Quasi-experimentation: Design and analysis issues for field settings*. Chicago: Rand McNally.

Denzin, N. K. (1978). *Sociological methods*. New York: McGraw-Hill.

Erickson, F. (1986). Qualitative methods in research on teaching. In M. Wittrock (Ed.), *Handbook of research on teaching* (Vol. 3, pp. 119–161). New York: Macmillan.

Ericsson, K. A., & Simon, H. A. (1984). *Protocol analysis: Verbal reports as data*. Cambridge, MA: MIT Press.

Firestone, W. A. (1993). Alternative arguments for generalizing from data as applied to qualitative research. *Educational Researcher, 22*(4), 16–23.

Glaser, B. G., & Strauss, A. L. (1967). *The discovery of grounded theory: Strategies for qualitative research*. New York: Aldine.

Goetz, J. P., & LeCompte, M. D. (1984). *Ethnography and qualitative design in educational research*. San Diego: Academic Press.

Guba, E. G. (1990). The alternative paradigm dialog. In E. G. Guba (Ed.), *The paradigm dialog* (pp. 17–27). Newbury Park, CA: Sage.

Hamel, J. (1992). Introduction: New theoretical and methodological issues. *Current Sociology, 40,* 1–15.

Hamel, J. (1993). *Case study methods*. Newbury Park, CA: Sage.

Kazdin, A. E. (1982). *Single-case research designs*. New York: Oxford University Press.

Kazdin, A. E. (1992). Drawing valid inferences from case studies. In A. E. Kazdin (Ed.), *Methodological issues and strategies in clinical research* (pp. 475–490). Washington, DC: American Psychological Association.

Krathwohl, D. R. (1993). *Methods of educational and social science research: An integrated approach.* New York: Longman.

Lancy, D. F. (1993). *Qualitative research: An introduction to the major traditions.* New York: Longman.

Lincoln, Y. S., & Guba, E. G. (1985). *Naturalistic inquiry.* Beverly Hills, CA: Sage.

Lincoln, Y. S., & Guba, E. G. (1990). Judging the quality of case study reports. *Qualitative Studies in Education, 3,* 53–59.

McCollum, E. E. (1993). The effects of recovery from childhood sexual abuse on marital relationships: A multiple case report. *Journal of Family Psychotherapy, 42*(2), 35–46.

Merriam, S. B. (1988). *Case study research in education: A qualitative approach.* San Francisco: Jossey-Bass.

Miles, M. B., & Huberman, A. M. (1994). *Qualitative data analysis: An expanded sourcebook* (2nd ed.). Thousand Oaks, CA: Sage.

Mitchell, J. C. (1983). Case and situation analysis. *Sociological Review, 31,* 187–211.

Moon, S. M. (1991). Case study research in gifted education. In N. K. Buchanan & J. F. Feldhusen (Eds.), *Conducting research and evaluation in gifted education* (pp. 157–200). New York: Teachers College Press.

Moon, S. M., & Dillon, D. R. (1995). Multiple exceptionalities: A case study. *Journal for the Education of the Gifted, 8,* 111–130.

Moon, S. M., Dillon, D. R., & Sprenkle, D. H. (1990). Family therapy and qualitative research. *Journal of Marital and Family Therapy, 16,* 357–373.

Moon, S. M., Feldhusen, J. F., & Dillon, D. R. (1994). Long-term effects of an enrichment program based on the Purdue Three-Stage Model. *Gifted Child Quarterly, 38,* 38–48.

Nelson, T. S., & Trepper, T. S. (1993). *101 interventions in family therapy.* New York: Haworth Press.

Platt, J. (1992). "Case study" in American methodological thought. *Current Sociology, 40,* 17–48.

Runyan, W. M. (1982). In defense of the case study method. *American Journal of Orthopsychiatry, 52,* 440–446.

Safran, J. D., Greenberg, L. S., & Rice, L. N. (1988). Integrating psychotherapy research and practice: Modeling the change process. *Psychotherapy, 25,* 1–17.

Shields, C. G., Wynne, L. C., McDaniel, S. H., & Gawinski, B. A. (1994). The marginalization of family therapy: A historical and continual problem. *Journal of Marital and Family Therapy, 20,* 117–138.

Stake, R. E. (1988). Case study methods in educational research: Seeking sweet water. In R. M. Jaeger (Ed.), *Complementary methods for research in education* (pp. 253–269). Washington, DC: American Educational Research Association.

Stake, R. E. (1994). Case studies. In N. K. Denzin & Y. S. Lincoln (Eds.), *Handbook of qualitative research* (pp. 236–247). Thousand Oaks, CA: Sage.

Strauss, A., & Corbin, J. (1990). *Basics of qualitative research: Grounded theory procedures and techniques.* Newbury Park, CA: Sage.

Strauss, A., & Corbin, J. (1994). Grounded theory methodology: An overview. In N. K. Denzin & Y. S. Lincoln (Eds.), *Handbook of qualitative research* (pp. 273–285). Thousand Oaks, CA: Sage.

Thorensen, C. (1978). Making better science intensively. *Personnel and Guidance Journal,* 279–282.

Tomm, K. (1983, July/August). The old hat doesn't fit. *Family Therapy Networker,* 39–41.

Trepper, T. S. (1990). In celebration of the case study. *Journal of Family Psychotherapy, 1*(1), 5–13.

Wallace, D. B. (1989). Studying the individual: The case study method and other genres. In D. B. Wallace & H. E. Gruber (Eds.), *Creative people at work* (pp. 25–43). New York: Oxford University Press.

Wetchler, J. L. (1994). Brief strategic treatment of a male with HIV hypochondriasis. *Journal of Family Psychotherapy, 5*(4), 1–12.

Yin, R. K. (1989). *Case study research* (2nd ed.). Newbury Park, CA: Sage.

Yin, R. K. (1992). The case study method as a tool for doing evaluation. *Current Sociology, 40,* 121–137.

18

The Events-Based Approach to Couple and Family Therapy Research

LESLIE S. GREENBERG
LAURIE HEATHERINGTON
MYRNA L. FRIEDLANDER

I MAGINE YOURSELF, if you will, in the following scene. It is your 10:00 A.M. session with Mother and Father "Harrison," who have sought help for their 14-year-old son because of his increasingly angry, noncompliant, and disruptive behavior at home. Two sessions have already taken place in which you explored the problem and potential solutions along with the relevant family history. All family members responded cooperatively to your questions, discussing their perceptions and opinions in a reasonable, measured way, but this reasonableness was in stark contrast to the chaos they described taking place at home.

Today's session is markedly different. From the outset, indeed the moment the family enters the room, you are aware that emotions are running high—everyone is feeling at once outraged and helpless. Mother and Father trip over one another in their pointed criticism of their son's escalating hostility. Apparently every time he has an argument with his girlfriend on the phone, he explodes in anger at his parents. This pattern dominates every evening they spend together. Mother is particularly vehement about the change in her son's behavior since the girlfriend came on the scene. The boy sits sullenly and silently throughout his parents' harangue. Their challenges to him, as well as your own carefully delivered questions, are met with shoulder shrugs or a barely audible, "I don't know." At this point—roughly 15 minutes into the session—your thoughts are running something like this. First, you realize that a frustrated pursue–distance cycle is being played out in front of you, and it is going nowhere. Second, you sense that the real drama is between Mother and Son. Father's interruptions seem only to diffuse the intensity between her and the boy. Third, you have the feeling that, under her anger, Mother is very hurt by her son's all-consuming interest in his girlfriend. Your task—at this point—is to move the session forward toward a resolution of the stalemate. The therapeutic alliance seems good but insecure, as the treatment is in an early stage. The parents are likely to be embarrassed about showing their emotional turmoil like this after

411

the two controlled sessions in weeks past. The son probably distrusts you, another authoritative adult, feeling that you would never take his side in a disagreement with his parents. Your own emotions are running high as you realize that failure to provide a new understanding or a behavioral shift in this session could seriously derail the treatment. A lot is riding on this session. What to do? Just then, Mother explodes, "He's just so different from how he used to be!" This remark prompts you to a decision—you will try to help these family members sort it out together, right here and now.

Based on your assessment of what might be underlying their feud, you direct Mother and Son to discuss their relationship. Son mutters, "Just stay out of my life," and Mother turns to you to complain further about him. Hearing this, Father interrupts, bringing in some irrelevant point. Now you are more certain about the task of this session. It is not about formulating rules for talking to the girlfriend on the telephone. Rather, it is about promoting a meaningful discussion between Mother and Son concerning the changes in their relationship now that he has moved into adolescence. This is a red-hot issue, and the family is at an impassè. Mother and Son cannot have a meaningful conversation about their changing relationship until they are able to stay engaged long enough on the topic without Father's interference. You turn to the son and gently say, "Can you talk to your mom about that . . . that you want her to sort of stay out of your life—is that the way you put it? Can you talk to her about how you feel about it?"

Let's leave that session for now and take a look at your next session, at 11:00, a couple treatment with "Alec and Elaine Kaufman." You've been seeing them for a couple of months and, while they both seem to like and trust you, there has been minimal change in their relationship. You feel much more kindly disposed toward Elaine than Alec, and this imbalance worries you. Their arguments in the sessions have steadily become more heated. When the last session ended, the tension was very high. Today Alec, uncharacteristically, begins the session by forthrightly asserting the idea that maybe they should be pleased with the small improvement they've made thus far and not risk tackling the "real, underlying problems." For him, that means Elaine's mismanagement of money and her sexual unresponsiveness. Maybe, he says, he should just accept the status quo, not rock the boat, and realize that his marriage is not great but better than that of many of his friends. His manner, verbal and nonverbal, disqualifies Elaine. She responds by disqualifying him in return, "You know you don't really feel that way! You know you could never just let it be. You've said a million times that unless things change, you'll leave." Now they begin to argue in earnest about what he "really" meant to say, and the process of contemptuous blame and disqualification overwhelms them even before they tackle one of the "real" problems. You have seen this pattern of mutual blame many times before. You realize that an emotional shift needs to take place here, regardless of the topic of discussion. The issue is how to move Alec, who is verbally quick and cutting, from attacking Elaine, the more nonverbal, uncertain one of the pair. The problem is complicated by your dislike for Alec's tactics, and you sense that you have lost virtually all empathy for him at this point. But you know that if the balance of emotions does not shift in this session, this couple may go beyond the point of no return. What to do?

In each of these two sessions you, the therapist, need to accomplish a specific clinical task. With the Harrisons, you need to break the pursue–distance cycle that is keeping Mother and Son from productively discussing the changes in their relationship. With the Kaufmans, you need to break the cycle of mutual blame, defensiveness, and disqualification that keeps them from having an intimate encounter.

These clinical dilemmas are common ones. We selected these vignettes to illustrate the value of the events-based approach to studying couple and family therapy.

As we proceed through this chapter, we will be referring back to the two sessions to illustrate the research paradigm. The events-based approach to process research provides a way to describe and explain the accomplishment of clinical goals such as these. In contrast to traditional therapy research, the outcome of interest is not global client improvement. After all, when conducting a session like the one with the Kaufmans, you are unlikely to be thinking about reducing their symptoms. Rather, you are pondering what needs to be done—at the moment—to give these people a new experience of one another. You assume that a new emotional experience, right now in the room with you, will be a catalyst to facilitate all kinds of novel experiences for them, as individuals and as a couple. If Alec can show himself to be vulnerable and hurting, you think, maybe Elaine will not want to withdraw. If Elaine can stop disqualifying Alec, maybe he can speak more lovingly to her.

After your 11:00 A.M. session, you are unlikely to wonder whether the Kaufmans' marriage is satisfactory (the general treatment goal), but you are likely to wonder whether they experienced one another differently today. In thinking about your session with the Harrisons, you wonder whether Mother and Son really feel engaged with one another. These kinds of clinical goals have to do with proximal outcomes (Greenberg, 1986). They are not distal, global treatment outcomes. Rather, proximal goals tend to be suggested by something specific that occurs in the session—a statement or a particular kind of interaction—that prompts you, the therapist, into action. The period of time in the session devoted to accomplishing a specific clinical goal like this is an "event" or an "episode."

As clinicians, because we recognize that the repeated, successful completion of therapeutic events is what makes for a successful treatment, we try to improve our skills to achieve important in-session goals. That is, not only does our interest lie in selecting the immediate goal for a particular family at a particular moment in treatment, it lies also in figuring out how to achieve that goal. The events-based approach to process research is a way to identify important events that promote change and to study the steps in the process that lead up to that change.

In this chapter, we first describe the philosophical assumptions of the events-based approach to family therapy research and the history of its development. Next, we describe in more detail one type of change process research, task analysis (Greenberg, 1984, 1986; Rice & Greenberg, 1984). The overview of task analysis is followed by a description of practical methodological aspects of this research strategy and an actual research example. The chapter concludes with a summary of the strengths of the events-based research paradigm, including issues of reliability and validity.

PHILOSOPHY AND BACKGROUND

Essentially, events-based research involves the isolation and description of meaningful episodes in order to investigate how change occurs in therapy. Using the events paradigm, researchers isolate "key episodes" in therapy in order to gain a better understanding of change processes in the context of clinically meaningful units. This approach draws on a tradition of critical incident research (Flanagan, 1954) in which key events are selected for study as a means of understanding phenomena of interest. It also draws on a tradition of protocol analysis or process research in which specific verbal behaviors or interactions are investigated in order to understand the nature of change or problem-solving performances. (Greenberg & Pinsof, 1986).

Events-based studies began appearing in the individual psychotherapy literature when investigators came to recognize that traditional research methods were inadequate to illuminate and explicate the complex events that occur during a single therapy hour, let alone over a course of psychotherapy (Greenberg, 1975; Rice & Greenberg, 1984). Many authors pointed out that psychotherapy research was not able to capture the complexity of the phenomena under study, (e.g., Greenberg, 1984, 1986a; Stiles, Shapiro, & Elliott, 1986). Earlier studies that sought to determine whether psychotherapy was effective perpetuated "uniformity myths" whereby the major variables—the therapist, client, and outcome—were incorrectly regarded as homogeneous (Kiesler, 1973). Even the most carefully controlled outcome studies did not specify "what treatment, by whom, is most effective for this individual with what specific problem, under which set of circumstances and how does that change come about?" (Paul, 1969/1989, p. 44).

Early process research also operated under a uniformity myth. The assumption that the process is uniform throughout treatment was reflected in the common procedure of random sampling, within and across therapy hours, of verbal behaviors. We know, however, that process is not randomly distributed. Other uniformity assumptions were reflected in the prolific use of aggregation, whereby ratings of process variables were averaged across sessions and treatments without regard for the contexts in which they occurred.

One fundamental assumption underlying change event research is that therapist and client behaviors, rather than being randomly distributed occurrences, are complex, meaningful, and multidimensional performances. It is the patterning of the multidimensional features of a given performance that needs to be specified to capture the complexity and provide a more adequate understanding of the therapeutic process (Greenberg, 1975; Rice & Greenberg, 1984; Stiles et al., 1986). The patterned multidimensionality may also differ at different stages of the therapeutic process and for different therapist–client systems. Notwithstanding a trend in the last two decades toward specificity in psychotherapy research—in terms of client problems, therapeutic interventions, and targeted outcomes—many researchers still tend to look at variables in isolation. Variables tend not to be seen as embedded in a complex therapeutic process but are isolated and taken out of context (Greenberg, 1986b; Heatherington, 1989). The result of this static approach to psychotherapy research is that the dynamic interaction between therapist, client, technique, and environment is ignored. Neither the experimental approach of manipulating conditions nor the correlational approach of studying individual differences apart from the differential demands of the situation has proved particularly productive. A strategy is required that is sensitive to the transactional nature of the person and situation, enabling client and therapist performances to be studied over time (Greenberg, 1991).

In 1984, Rice and Greenberg proposed an alternative research paradigm that advocated the study of meaningful "events" in therapy (Greenberg, 1975) and further suggested that the methods of task analysis be applied to study those events. Task analysis originated in the 1940s as a procedure for analyzing the important components of industrial tasks and more recently has been used by cognitive psychologists to study the nature of specific information-processing activities (Newell & Simon, 1972; Pascual-Leone, 1976a, 1976b). By the early 1990s, several task-analytical studies of individual (e.g., Clarke, 1990; Greenberg, 1983, 1991; Greenberg & Safran, 1987; Rice & Saperia, 1984; Safran, Crocker, McMain, & Murray, 1990) and family (Friedlander, Heatherington, Johnson, & Skowron, in press; Greenberg, Ford, Alden, & Johnson, 1993; Heatherington & Friedlander, 1990) therapy had appeared in the literature.

Task analysis is one events-based strategy that illuminates the component steps or stages involved in the solution of a clinical task. After a small sample of events has been isolated, the episodes are subjected to analysis to identify the components of suc-cessful performances that lead to in-session resolutions of particular client problems. The analysis is facilitated by comparing the clients' performances in successful and un-successful change events (e.g., Friedlander et al., in press; Greenberg, 1984, 1986b). This method for selecting and studying change episodes has been a useful way to resolve the central difficulty in process research, that of information overload, in which one has a vast amount of process, all of which is potentially meaningful.

The task in the Harrisons' session was to engage Mother and Son in a meaningful discussion of changes in their relationship. The task for the Kaufmans, on the other hand, was to shift from blaming and defensiveness to nurturance and affiliation. The assumption is that these clinical tasks are meaningful not only for the Harrisons and the Kaufmans but for many other families who are similarly "stuck." In other words, we assume some regularity to the change process within identifiable events across clients.

In this approach, we also assume that the therapeutic process is more meaningfully understood when specific change events are suggested by a particular theory of treat-ment. One of the major points, then, is that the events chosen as "key" should reflect the theoretical orientation of the treatment approach under study. An analytical ther-apist, for example, might view the Kaufman event as one of gaining insight into the projective identification that motivates each spouse's set of feelings toward the other. A cognitively oriented therapist, on the other hand, might see this same episode as one in which one partner's schema for, or perception of, the other is changed. An in-teractional therapist might focus on the steps by which the more hostile spouse shifts to a nurturant and affiliative position, thereby initiating a new interaction.

In applying task analysis to psychotherapy research, Rice and Greenberg (1984) and Greenberg (1986a, 1986b) made several assumptions, the most important of which is that the complex flow of interaction between the client and therapist can be segment-ed into discriminable, recurring problem-resolution events that are crucial to bringing about therapeutic change. A second assumption is that different processes have differ-ent meanings in different contexts. A frequency count of particular behaviors—like blam-ing or withdrawal—does not take into account at what point in an interaction the behavior occurs or whether its occurrence varies over time. Thus, in order for a process description to be meaningful to the clinician, it is necessary to specify clearly the con-text in which it occurs. It would be insufficient, for example, to stipulate that more self-disclosure by partners in marital therapy is related to marital satisfaction. If we are to understand how change can take place for a specific couple, like the Kaufmans, we must at least specify when and in what context their self-disclosure takes place and what that disclosure should be about. Based on this assumption, Greenberg (1986a, 1986b) specified a number of different contexts that should be taken into account in studying therapeutic change (e.g., the speech act, the episode, and the relationship). He further suggested that the midlevel context, an episode or event, is highly important. Begin-ning with a "marker" (Greenberg, 1984) and ending with a "resolution," the event or episode is an "island" of clinical work in a particular therapeutic context. Particular moment-by-moment processes at the level of the speech act (e.g., blame, criticize, agree, or paraphrase) can then be studied in their episodic context. The context for the Harri-son family was a pursue–distance struggle. For the Kaufmans, it was mutual blame. Par-ticular therapeutic intervention strategies (e.g., focusing on underlying feelings or interpretation of psychogenetic material) can also be stipulated to define the episodic context. Within different episodes, a given behavior (e.g., a warm compliment) is like-ly to have different meanings. Episodes in turn should also be placed in a particular relationship context. An episode of conflict resolution between a highly cohesive couple is different from an episode of conflict in a highly disengaged couple. Similarly, an episode of conflict resolution in which both parties have a good working alliance is different from a conflict episode in which there is a poor alliance with the therapist or a coalition between one partner and the therapist. The Harrisons were in the early stage of family therapy with a tenuous but positive relationship with the therapist. The Kaufmans, on the other hand, were at a midpoint in their treatment, and their therapist was more closely aligned with one spouse.

Another assumption concerns the need to covary relationships of several process variables at a particular point in time, and over time, in order to identify clinical phenomena that are important in particular contexts. For example, the softening of a harsh critical stance in Alec Kaufman, the blamer, could be identified by a change in the pattern of his voice, in his depth of experiencing, in his verbal responses to Elaine, and so forth. These indicators are important in episodes of conflict resolution. In other words, it is crucial that the basic unit of measurement be a sequence of interactions between family members rather than isolated responses. A minimal measurement unit would be a two-step (AB) interaction between members of a couple. A three-step interaction (ABA) is, however, preferable, with expanded sequences being most desirable. A dance metaphor illustrates this point. Consider studying a dancing pair by counting how many times Partner A moved her left foot forward and how many times Partner B moved her right foot backward, and trying to correlate that with how well each person liked the dance. Perhaps they were moving their feet in coordination with each other and having a great dance. Or, perhaps they were one move off in their coordination and stepping on one another's toes. The researcher would not know whether they were having a smooth dance or were tripping on each other unless A's behavior was studied in relation to B's preceding behavior and vice versa.

The final assumption is that therapeutic processes are investigated in order to explain how change occurs in psychotherapy. The events-based approach emphasizes description and explanation over prediction. It involves isolating phenomena of interest and selecting key episodes that are change events and that recur across people and time. The main design strategy involves comparing successful and unsuccessful events in order to discriminate the components of a successful event. The next section describes in more detail the methods and procedures involved in task-analytical research.

METHODOLOGY

To reiterate, task analysis of therapeutic change relies on the identification and examination of recurring change events to provide a better understanding of clinical processes in the context of clinically meaningful units. From this perspective, the therapeutic encounter is viewed as a set of significant events, or episodes, that capture aspects of treatment that are potent and effective in producing change.

A change event was defined initially (Greenberg, 1975; Rice & Greenberg, 1984) as an interactional sequence between client and therapist consisting of a client problem marker, followed by a series of therapist interventions and the ongoing client performance which, if successful, culminates in the client's achieving an effective resolution to the problem. The marker—the first component in the event—is the family "dance" (Minuchin, 1974), which allows the therapist to recognize the immediate task that needs to be accomplished. Many tasks and subtasks occur in the course of a single session (indeed, in the treatment as a whole), but specific markers suggest that a particular kind of event is about to take place. In the case of the Kaufmans, the marker is the cycle of mutual blame and recrimination. In the case of the Harrisons, the marker is the disengagement impassè between Mother and Son, followed by three unsuccessful attempts on the part of the therapist to direct them to discuss their relationship (Friedlander et al., in press).

Once a marker is selected and defined, the best therapist operation for this type of problem has to be stipulated as clearly as possible in the form of a set of linked interventions to achieve a particular goal. Although this level of theorizing has been slow to develop, theorists interested in marital therapy are now in the process of stipulating such interventions and operations (Greenberg & Johnson, 1988; Jacobson & Gurman, 1986; Snyder & Wilson, 1989).

After the marker and the therapist intervention have been specified, the third component of the event, the ensuing client performance, can be studied. In marital therapy, the client performance consists of each individual's cognitive/affective information-processing about self and other, and the interactional sequences that take place between them. It is in these aspects of client performance that the change process resides and can be observed. Research should focus on measuring this performance to identify what processes lead to the fourth event component, the in-session outcome or resolution of the problem. In the Kaufman session, the resolution of the mutual blame cycle was an intimate encounter in which each spouse described, with feeling, a fear of losing the other. In the Harrison session, the resolution involved both Mother and Son disclosing feelings of loss around the boy's increased need for autonomy (Friedlander et al., in press).

There are two major phases within a task-analytical research program. These are, first, the completion of a rational–empirical analysis of the event and its components, and, second, the verification of the rational model of change. These two phases are described next and exemplified by our study of the resolution of conflict—mutual blame such as that experienced by the Kaufmans—in emotionally focused couple therapy. (Greenberg & Johnson, 1988; Johnson & Greenberg, 1988).

Rational–Empirical Phase

In this first phase of the research, the moment-to-moment performance of the therapy participants as they resolve a specific clinical task is examined to identify the components of a successful performance (Greenberg, 1984; Pascual-Leone, 1976a, 1976b). In this phase, the clinician–researcher attempts to describe the actual flow of the performance and organize it into temporal sequences of actions. This process involves working backward from the end performance (the resolution) to the starting situation (the marker), by identifying smaller and smaller performances until the event description that is generated is coherent and clinically meaningful. This procedure has as its goal the development of a conceptual model of the interactions that produce successful performances.

The actual steps of this rational–empirical phase of a task analysis are:

1. The explication of the clinician's cognitive map.
2. The description of the task.
3. The specification of the task environment.
4. The evaluation of the potency of the task environment.
5. The rational task analysis.
6. The empirical task analysis.
7. Construction of a rational-empirical model.

The aim of the whole procedure is the construction of the conceptual model in step 7.

Initially, the clinician needs to spell out as clearly as possible the nature of the event and the problem or task and how he or she thinks change occurs. This is called the "cognitive map" (step 1). Next, the task must be selected and described as clearly as possible (step 2). This involves delineating the precise behavioral components of the client marker and developing a system for identifying its presence or absence. For example, the specific behaviors in the Kaufmans' negative interactional cycle would need to be specified. In our research with the Harrison family (Friedlander et al., in press), we identified a set of specific behaviors that we believed signaled disengagement, both direct (e.g., refusing to speak and leaving the room) and indirect (e.g., frequently changing the topic and making small talk). Once the starting point for the problem that is to be resolved has been operationally defined in this way, the task environment can be specified (step 3). This is accomplished by compiling a manual of suitable therapist interventions for facilitating the resolution of the clinical task. Once this manual has been developed, adherence can be checked so that the event can be studied in a quasi-controlled fashion. That is, if the therapists in the sample behave in a similar fashion when confronted with that marker, the family performances can be observed relatively free from therapist "noise." This simplification strategy (Bordin, 1974) allows the researcher to (at least for the time being) ignore the therapist's contribution because it is assumed to be roughly similar across events.

The fourth optional step involves testing to see whether a change of some type does, in fact, occur when the task one has identified is "worked on" in the environment specified by the therapist manual. Comparative or controlled study can be undertaken to confirm that something potent is occurring (i.e., that client problems are resolved or that progress is made).

The next three procedures are at the heart of the task analysis. The fifth step requires the investigator to construct a rational model of task resolution by conjecturing about how this task could, ideally, be solved and by specifying ways in which family performances, of the types imagined to be associated with task resolution, could be measured. This step distinguishes this research approach from purely empirical task analyses in that the investigator develops an idealized performance model of possible resolution strategies. This model makes explicit the investigators and expert therapists' implicit knowledge and this guides the investigator in subsequent observations of how actual families successfully resolve their problems. It provides an initial understanding of how systems perform, which is then checked against actual performances. It is often helpful to diagram the hypothesized performance.

The sixth step involves observing actual performance. This is the empirical task analysis. At this point, the investigator observes an actual performance of a family involved in task resolution in order to identify and diagram the sequence of steps family members take as they move through the event, from the marker to the resolution. In step 7 the empirically generated model is then compared with the rational model to correct any mistakes in the latter. Qualitative descriptive methods can be used and observational measures can be applied (i.e., those that were identified in step 5) to capture any differences between the two models. This procedure is followed by repeated observations of successful performances. This allows the investigator to successively reformulate the initial empirical model and refine the measurement procedures. At the conclusion of this phase of the task analysis, a revised rational–empirical model of the clients' performance is generated that acts as the current best version of the model. This ends the model-building and discovery-oriented phase.

At this point, it is necessary to attempt to verify the model on a new data set. The following section describes some of the specific issues, practices, and procedures in this second verification phase of a family therapy task analysis project.

Verification Phase

In this phase, more traditional research methods (i.e., those that are based on the logic of refutation and hypothesis testing) are used. Although the major investigative strategy in task analysis is the inductive discovery-oriented cycling between hypothesized, possible performances, the verification of the models constructed by this method is essential.

In general, a group of resolution and nonresolution performances of a particular event are compared to determine whether the specified components of the model discriminate between successful and unsuccessful performances at a statistically significant level. Then, client processes are related to outcome (e.g., a pattern of in-session softening in the blamer and disclosure in the withdrawer to increased marital satisfaction at termination of treatment). The advantage of relating process to outcome at this stage of the research program is that one now has a complex model of how change occurs, and this model allows increased control and explanation of the variability in family performances. The design investigates answers whether clients who engage in the hypothesized in-therapy processes have better outcomes than those who do not. We turn now to the specifics of data collection.

Data Collection

Task analysis and other event-based research methods require actual videotapes (in some cases, audiotapes) of psychotherapy sessions. These can be procured in several ways depending on the nature of the research questions and the opportunities available. The researchers themselves may collect the data, either in-house or as the guests of a cooperating clinic. The latter requires obtaining informed consent and being responsible for the taping. Alternatively, the researchers might arrange for therapy sessions to be taped by the clinic staff. Another possibility is to obtain tapes from an archive of previously collected data, from a commercial tape library (e.g., the American Association for Marriage and Family Therapy), or directly from "expert" therapists themselves.

Each of these alternatives has its own advantages and challenges which should be carefully considered in the planning stages of the study. Issues to consider include the availability of research assistants, the time frame of the study, the amount of control over the data collection that is needed, the practicalities of obtaining informed consent either before the taping or at a later date, and the extent to which videotaping and/or research is being done routinely at the clinic. Particularly when studying couples or families, obtaining informed consent can be complicated. Sometimes the family's dynamics or problems interfere with their decision making about whether or not to participate in research.

Sampling of Events

One of the challenges of this type of research is to have at one's disposal a pool of sessions in which the event of interest might have occurred. Ideally, the researcher is able to videotape, or have access to videotapes, of all therapy sessions conducted during the data collection period. Then, rather than sampling randomly, the researcher can screen all available tapes for the presence of the clinical event of interest. This is a form of theoretically guided sampling. It is important, when working with a cooperating agency, that the staff provide not only their "best" sessions, or their most "successful" cases, but all the sessions that were taped. Once the tapes are procured, sampling of events proceeds. In the discovery oriented rational–empirical phase, there are two major approaches to selecting key events: theoretically-guided sampling and discovery-oriented sampling. The latter involves inquiries into participants' experience of what they found helpful or change producing in a particular session. Theoretically guided sampling, on the other hand, refers to the selection of an event for intensive study that is regarded as significant from clinical or theoretical perspectives. Whereas theoretically guided sampling allows for the building of explanatory models of key events, discovery-oriented sampling is oriented toward description of the types of events clients find meaningful. That is, discovery-oriented research requires "purposive sampling." This refers to selecting observations that are "believed to facilitate the expansion of the developing theory" (Bogdan & Biklen, 1992, pp. 71–72). This is an analytical induction method, which begins only with a "rough definition of the phenomenon to be explained" (Taylor & Bogdan, 1984, p. 127). As the observers watch many sessions, a model of the event of interest (including more concrete definitions of the marker and resolution) evolves.

In the verification phase, however, the event (including the marker and resolution) will have already been defined and data collection proceeds as in any comparative study. The sampling, then, requires at least two independent observers who work with that operational definition of the marker or of the resolution and select a sample in which the event has occurred and been resolved and a sample in which resolution has not occurred in order for the performance in the two groups to be compared. For example, in our study of disengagement in family therapy, the observers looked for the marker of clear directives to family members to discuss a specific topic, followed either by engagement in the task or by direct or indirect refusals to engage. In an analysis of marital conflict, a marker of a three-step escalatory interaction established a conflict event, whereas resolution was measured by affiliative interaction between partners.

Data Analysis

Data-analytical procedures for task analysis and other types of events-based research are varied and depend on the research questions and the nature of the observational coding. In the later stages of the empirical analysis and in the verification phase, successful observational coding requires a reliable and valid coding system that is sensitive to the kinds of variables in which one is interested. The most sophisticated coding system is useless if it is not relevant to the affects, cognitions, or behaviors that are hypothesized to change during the event. Thus the Structural Analysis of Social Behavior (SASB) (Benjamin, 1974) was chosen by Greenberg et al. (1993) in the study of conflict events in emotionally focused therapy with couples because it measured affiliation and interdependence and these were viewed as highly relevant. The Family Relational Communication Control Coding System (Friedlander & Heatherington, 1989; Heatherington & Friedlander, 1987), on the other hand, was selected to study family members' movements from disengagement to engagement interactional behaviors in structural family therapy (Heatherington & Friedlander, 1990) because this best measured issues of control in communication, which was seen as highly relevant to resolving family problems.

Successful observational coding of this type requires well-trained and motivated judges who are closely supervised. Some instruments, such as the SASB, require more clinical sophistication than others; this should be considered in selection of coders. In general, the requirements for good observational coding in this research paradigm are the same as in more traditional research. There are a number of publications that provide excellent advice on the practical details involved in observational coding (e.g., Hill, 1991).

Researchers, however, need to be especially open in the initial, inductive phase of the research in steps 2, 3, and 6 to discovering patterns of behaviors that might hold the key to change or to successful resolution of tasks. Perhaps the success of a family member's response to the therapist's attempts to facilitate engagement depends on another family member's indirect support of the engagement. Like a juggler, the family therapy process researcher must keep an eye on several moving targets (the family members) and their behavior with each other as well as with the therapist. Moreover, the researcher sometimes must attend to several variables at once (e.g., keeping an eye on engagement vs. disengagement behaviors while monitoring the affect of each family member). In many ways, the researcher's task is similar to the task of the family therapist.

Representing and recording these types of data are both challenging and exciting. It is often useful in the discovery-oriented or inductive stages of the research to make visual representations of the data. Long sheets of computer paper can be used to map out a session, or a portion of the session, that is of interest, from the first speaking turn to the last. Then the individual therapist and client behaviors of interest can be recorded wherever they occur in that stream. Such visual inspection facilitates finding interesting patterns of behavior within events because it gives the "human synthesizer" a chance to work. It may be noted, for example, that therapists' challenges to family members' blaming constructions tend to be followed by clients' self-questioning of their constructions. Is this pattern reliable? That is, does self-questioning occur more during a certain time frame following therapist challenges (a conditional probability) than in general over the course of the entire session (an unconditional probability)?

Sequential analysis techniques can sometimes be useful in this research in attempting to identify or verify patterns, but they also have a serious limitation. It is the study of actual sequences in concrete interactions that is crucial in the identification of patterns in the inductive discovery-oriented phase, not the study of the statistical attributes of a group of sequences. That is, to discern the pattern of variables associated with particular change processes, we need to capture the configuration of the process itself and not lose it by averaging across episodes. Interactional rules are not based on probabilities. There are unlikely to be laws of interaction that depend on time lags in sequences. Thus, to determine whether a particular event occurs at a particular "lag" in time assumes that the lag is a significant variable in the interaction. This is not the case. In the Kaufmans' quarrel, what is of significance is not at which lag Elaine and Alec deescalate, but the fact that they deescalate at all and the effect this has on their subsequent interaction. The events of interest are the more subtle patterns. We may find, for example, that when Alec deescalates and Elaine deescalates, this sequence is followed by a reescalation by Alec, followed by another deescalation by Elaine. This pattern, unless it was hypothesized beforehand or is incredibly robust, would be lost by averaging techniques based on interactional lags.

Reporting Results

On the completion of the study, the researcher is faced with a final decision—where to send it for publication, for dissemination to the clinical/research community at large? The challenge is wrought by the fact that (depending on the stage of the research program) the final product of discovery-oriented task analysis may look like a different beast from the traditional, familiar journal articles. Operational definitions may have not been set until somewhere in the middle of the study. The "results" may be linguistic or pictorial models rather than numeric. The "discussion" may be a model rather than an interpretation of statistical test results. The published articles using this approach described in this chapter serve as examples of the variety of ways in which task analyses and other events-based research studies can be reported.

Although a completed program of research on a specific event may well lend itself to book or chapter, the early studies are more likely to be published in journals. A number of psychotherapy or general clinical journals (e.g., *Psychotherapy, Psychotherapy Research, Journal of Counseling Psychology, Journal of Consulting and Clinical Psychology*, and *Psychotherapy Integration*) and family journals (e.g., *Journal of Marital and Family Therapy* and *Journal of Family Psychology*) have published some of the change events research referred to in this article. Perusal of the editorial policy statements and of the articles already published in these and other journals is recommended.

Finally, as family therapy process researchers, we sometimes feel like neither "fish nor fowl" (or perhaps sometimes we feel like both) because of the paucity of family research in the psychotherapy journals and the paucity of process research studies in the family therapy journals. The decision about where to publish often comes down to a political or ideological consideration about where one thinks the work would have the most impact. Also, presenting one's work at conferences—either research or clinically oriented conferences—can help to communicate the work to the widest possible audiences. We turn now to an illustration of the methodology presented thus far, followed by some concluding remarks.

DISCUSSION: HELPING COUPLES LIKE THE KAUFMANS

In this example, we describe a number of interrelated events-based studies of emotionally focused therapy (EFT), which has proven to be especially successful in helping couple like the Kaufmans.

In an intensive task analysis of the process of marital conflict resolution (Plysiuk, 1985) in EFT (Johnson & Greenberg, 1988), five episodes of conflict resolution in specific sessions were intensively analyzed using task-analytical methods (Greenberg, 1984) in an attempt to build a model of the process of conflict resolution. This study is an example of the discovery-oriented descriptive approach, which attempts to describe the observed phenomena of change to reveal underlying regularities (Greenberg, 1986a, 1986b). In this case, four successful resolution performances were compared with one unsuccessful performance to identify components that were common to successful performance. The task analysis procedure used involves the generation of a rational model of the hypothesized components of resolution and the comparison of this rational model with a number of actual resolution performances in which the interactions are scored on process measures. This comparison of actual performances with hypothesized performances leads to the development of an empirically grounded, refined model of conflict resolution performance.

In the rational analysis, it was hypothesized that a typical negative interactional sequence, which begins with a pursuer blaming a withdrawing partner, would shift in the following fashion: (1a) the pursuer (e.g., Alec) would begin to express underlying vulnerability; (2) the withdrawer (e.g., Elaine), seeing the partner's vulnerability, would make contact; (3) the pursuer, seeing the other as accessible, would ask for reassurance or state personal need; and (4) the withdrawer would respond with acceptance. At this point, both partners would be operating from a new view of self and other, and there would be an increase in security and responsiveness.

Having generated this hypothesized model, we transcribed a videotape of each resolution event. Then, each statement in the interaction was coded by two raters on the Experiencing Scale (Klein, Mathieu-Coughlin, & Kiesler, 1986) and on the SASB (Benjamin, 1974). Information was also gathered from some couples on their view of what had occurred during the event using interpersonal process recall (IPR) (Elliott, 1986). Using the IPR, the couple reviews a tape of the event and is asked to recall what each was thinking and feeling at different moments in the interaction. In this way, the investigator gains a picture of each spouse's internal processes and perceptions.

Using the coded data and IPR information, performance diagrams of the moment-by-moment interactions were graphed. These diagrams were inspected and compared with each other to reveal identifiable interaction patterns that occurred consistently across all resolution events. Consistent patterns were found. These were interpreted within the framework provided by the rational model to reveal four discriminable stages or components of the task resolution of conflict events.

The pattern of resolution that emerged from the data was described as follows. First, the pursuer blames and the withdrawer either avoids, protests, or appeases. Second, one of the partners openly discloses his or her feelings or needs and the other responds with understanding or comforting. Here an unexpected pattern emerged. The pursuer (e.g., Alec) temporarily reverted to blaming, but the withdrawer did not revert to protesting or defending. Rather, the withdrawer continued to affirm the partner. In each resolution event, pursuers appeared to "test" their partners in this way. If the withdrawer remained positive and did not respond to the pursuer's escalating by counterescalating, the couple then proceeded to the next stage. Finally, both partners trustingly disclosed feelings or needs at a deep level while the other responded with empathy and affirmation. These four patterns were labeled "escalations," "deescalation," "testing," and "mutual openness."

Next, a comparison of the rational analysis with the actual performance events resulted in the construction of a four-step interactional model of the resolution of a problematic blame–withdraw sequence in marital conflict. The four steps were measured by specific process indicators, and each stage was characterized by a unique configuration of indicators over time (i.e., a pattern). The final stage, mutual openness, for example, differed from the deescalation stage in that both partners were observed to have reached higher levels of experiencing and to have maintained these levels over a number of interactional sequences.

In a subsequent study of the process of change (Greenberg et al., 1993), episodes of conflict interaction in the second and seventh session of therapy (treatment consisted of eight sessions) were compared to test the hypothesis that EFT, when successful, leads to change in negative interactional cycles. Conflict episodes from 22 successful couples were transcribed and coded on the SASB. Findings showed that EFT brought about a significant reduction in the frequency of disaffiliative behaviors and sequences and an increase in affiliative behaviors and sequences, whereas negative reciprocal and complementary sequences decreased. This study focused on the verification of hypotheses of what changes in therapy rather than on the discovery of change processes themselves. However, it illustrates the overlapping nature of outcome and process research (Greenberg, 1986a, 1986b) in that certain processes, like shifts in interactions, are proximal outcomes.

A study of clients' perception of change processes was also completed using a critical incident approach (Greenberg, James, & Conry, 1988). Twenty-one couples who had received EFT were interviewed 4 months after therapy and asked to describe critical incidents that stood out for them as most helpful and to describe how change had taken place in these incidents. The incidents were sorted into categories by 37 coders and analyzed using latent partition analyses (Wiley, 1967), which revealed five underlying or latent categories. The main finding of interest in this study was that the couples reported that the expression of underlying feeling was related to changes in spouses' perceptions of each other and seemed to evoke new and more supportive interactions. Other change factors reported by couples were that they felt more entitled to their feelings and needs, developed more understanding, focused more on self, and felt validated by the therapist.

A study relating in-session performances to client outcome compared the process of therapy in key events in the best session of successful and unsuccessful couples, as measured by change in Dyadic Adjustment Scale (Spanier, 1976) scores at the end of the therapy (Johnson & Greenberg, 1988). It was hypothesized that in successful couples, blamers in peak sessions would exhibit high levels of experiencing and more quadrant one (disclosing self, affirming other) scores on the SASB. This hypothesis arose from the clinical theory of EFT in that an identified change event occurs when the blaming spouse reprocesses intense affective experience and discloses such experience, which then evokes a new response in the partner. The occurrence of this event, labeled "softening" and identified by a precise pattern of process variables, was also delineated.

Peak sessions of the three most improved and the three least improved couples (as identified by therapist and client postsession report) were compared. The peak sessions of the improved couples showed generally deeper experiencing and more affiliative responses. In addition, five softening events were identified in the improved couples; none were observed in the unimproved group. This event, resulting in a shift in a negative interaction cycle, represents the first two stages described in the first descriptive study (Plysiuk, 1985). This kind of study represents a beginning in identifying key ingredients in the change process in one approach to marital therapy.

In a third study (Greenberg et al., 1993), events in peak and poor sessions of 22 couples were compared. Peak and poor sessions were identified by a combination of postsession therapist and client reports of change and progress in the session. An event that began with the couple engaged in an escalatory sequence and was followed by the therapist operation of focusing on underlying feelings was identified in each session. Twenty minutes of process which followed was then rated on the SASB and the Experiencing Scale. Reported peak sessions showed significantly greater depth of experiencing, more affiliative interaction, and more "focus on self" as opposed to "focus on other" statements. These studies provide evidence to support the idea that depth of experiencing and more affiliative interaction are involved in the change process in EFT.

This research design essentially answers the questions about whether clients who engage in the hypothesized in-therapy processes have better outcomes than those who do not. Moreover, it specifies the steps between client behaviors and outcomes, providing information about individual differences in patient performance. It should be able, for example, to explain just where the process went awry with one couple but was successful for another.

Research Skills

How can the reliability and validity of events-based research studies be evaluated? From the previous discussion, it should be clear that some traditional methods for evaluating research are appropriate here, particularly at the verification stage of the research. For example, the reliability of observers' ratings should be ensured by careful training and evaluated using interjudge reliability assessments that take into account chance agreement (e.g., kappa [Cohen, 1960]).

In addition, other demonstrations that one's claims are believable are required in task analysis research. At the rational–empirical stage particularly, the researcher is "immersed" in the data of the sessions. The researcher abstracts ideas and observations from the data, but the data will (typically) not be fully presented in its entirety for others to check. Steier (1988) noted that because the researcher is actually the instrument used to analyze the data, the researcher's theoretical orientation and other biases should be presented along with the data. Reliability is demonstrated by showing that the patterns of changes which are proposed by the model repeat themselves consistently throughout the data set and, ideally, in studies conducted by other research groups.

Validity is further demonstrated by contrasting successful versus unsuccessful events and showing that the patterns of change in the former are different from those in the latter, again in a manner that conforms to the model. In task analysis, the conceptual model of change is repeatedly subjected to "reality checks." If certain elements of the model are found not "to discriminate between successful and unsuccessful events, the model is modified and re-tested. In this way, validity is enhanced by grounding the model in actual clinical material throughout the research process. This gives the conceptual model clinical relevance and coherence" (Stiles, 1993). Other means of enhancing validity include (1) using independent researchers to identify the events, (2) involving the clinic staff or other practicing therapists in evaluating the accuracy and clinical meaningfulness of the event selection criteria, and (3) checking the findings against relevant clinical literature (Stiles, 1993). Thus, for example, if the model specifies that a certain intervention by the therapist at a critical juncture will lead to greater depth of experiencing by a blamer such as Alec Kaufman, is this consistent with what is already known about softening events in EFT?

Every method of research has a "range of convenience" (Kelly, 1955), that is, a set of questions or situations for which it is well suited and others for which it is not useful as a tool for understanding. Other methodologies are better suited to pure outcome questions, such as whether Treatment A "works" better than Treatment B or whether it works faster. Although events-based research does not require "expert" therapists, it does require (especially at the verification stage) therapists who are carefully trained and monitored for adherence to the model. Events research is close, intensive work, and most research programs unfold slowly, over a number of years.

On the other hand, change event investigations are well suited for studying basic and advanced questions about what exactly it is, in the therapy hour, that leads to proximal and then to distal outcomes. For this reason, events-based methods are excellent for theory testing and for specifying clinical strategies. Researchers using task analysis methods have now reported a number of models of the change process in individual therapy, including the resolution of problematic reactions (Rice & Saperia, 1984), conflict splits (Greenberg, 1984), unfinished business (Greenberg, 1991), allowing of painful experiences (Greenberg & Safran, 1987), creation of meaning (Clarke, 1990), alliance ruptures (Safran et al., 1990) and misunderstanding events (Rhodes, Geller, Greenberg, & Elliot, 1992). The work in couple and family therapy is just beginning (cf. Greenberg & Johnson, 1988; Heatherington & Friedlander, 1990; Friedlander et al., in press), but it is already clear that events-based methods have the potential to facilitate many new kinds of studies of those treatments. For example, event-based intervention studies allow the comparison of interventions for such commonly occurring challenges as diffusing blame, dampening escalating interactional cycles, moving from an intrapsychic to a relational focus, creating new bonds, restructuring alliances, facilitating forgiveness, promoting intimacy, and resolving disengagement issues. Both the type of client performance in these events that leads to change and the nature of postsession change could be clarified.

Bridging Research and Practice

Until recently, family theorists have been better at describing dysfunctional couples and family interactions than they have at specifying just how the therapist should intervene to change them. Beginning family therapists, too, are often better at detecting and conceptualizing a couple's or family's problems than they are at knowing how to intervene. This state of affairs is not surprising. In the past decade much has been written about how the practice of marital and family therapy has run ahead of theory, and about how the burgeoning quantity of strategies and techniques are becoming more and more sophisticated yet less and less connected to theories of change. Many voices are calling for an empirically based research literature that is also relevant in the clinic (i.e., one that links therapist's and clients' behaviors directly to each other, and one that links process to client outcome). The kind of rational–empirical, discovery-oriented, model-building studies that we have described here provide a means by which clinically relevant theoretical propositions can be refined, developed, and tested. Without specific mini-theories and the empirical evidence to support them, marital and family therapy risks becoming an ever-growing castle in the air. Task analysis and other events-based research approaches can help to provide a solid foundation, a grounding, for that "castle."

FUTURE DIRECTIONS

The study of therapeutic events or episodes although, in and of itself, illuminating will be strengthened by studying the unfolding of the events over time. Events can be viewed as aspects of an unfolding narrative and as relating to core themes. A study of events in the context of specified narratives, where key events may produce critical shifts in the narrative would be most useful. Specifying the narrative themes that emerge during treatment and their key constitutive episodes and studying how change in episodes over time leads to change in the narrative appear to be a most promising direction for future research.

REFERENCES

Bogdan, R. C., & Biklen, S. K. (1992). *Qualitative research for education* (2nd ed.) Needham Heights, MA: Allyn & Bacon.

Benjamin, L. S. (1974). Structural analysis of social behavior. *Psychological Review, 81,* 392–425.

Bordin, E. S. (1974). *Research strategies in psychotherapy.* New York: Wiley.

Clarke, K. M. (1990). Creation of meaning: An emotional processing task in psychotherapy. *Psychotherapy: Theory, Research, and Practice, 26,* 139–148.

Cohen, J. (1960). A coefficient of agreement for nominal scales. *Educational and Psychological Measurement, 20,* 37–46.

Elliott, R. (1986). Interpersonal process recall (IPR) as a psychotherapy process research method. In L. S. Greenberg & W. M. Pinsof (Eds.), *The psychotherapeutic process: A research handbook.* New York: Guilford Press.

Flanagan, J. C. (1954). The critical incident technique. *Psychological Bulletin, 51,* 327–358.

Friedlander, M. L., & Heatherington, L. (1989). Analyzing relational control in family therapy interviews. *Journal of Counseling Psychology, 36,* 139–148.

Friedlander, M. L., Heatherington, L., Johnson, B., & Skowron, E. (1994). Sustaining engagement: A change event in family therapy. *Journal of Counseling Psychology, 41,* 438–448.

Greenberg, L. S. (1975). *Task analysis of psychotherapeutic events.* Unpublished doctoral dissertation, York University, Toronto, Ontario.

Greenberg, L. S. (1983). Toward a task analysis of conflict resolution in Gestalt therapy. *Psychotherapy: Theory, research, and practice, 20,* 190–201.

Greenberg, L. S. (1984). Task analysis: The general approach. In L. N. Rice & L. S. Greenberg (Eds.), *Patterns of change: Intensive analysis of psychotherapy process.* New York: Guilford Press.

Greenberg, L. S. (1986a). Research strategies. In L. S. Greenberg & W. M. Pinsof (Eds.), *The psychotherapeutic process: A research handbook.* New York: Guilford Press.

Greenberg, L. S. (1986b). Change process research. *Journal of Consulting and Clinical Psychology, 54,* 4–9.

Greenberg, L. S. (1991). Research on the process of change. *Psychotherapy Research, 1,* 14–24.

Greenberg, L., Ford, C., Alden, L., & Johnson, S. (1993). In-session change processes in emotionally focused therapy for couples. *Journal of Consulting and Clinical Psychology, 61,* 68–84.

Greenberg, L., James, P., & Conry, R. (1988). Perceived change processes in emotionally focused couples therapy. *Journal of Family Psychology, 2,* 1–12.

Greenberg, L. S., & Johnson, S. M. (1988). *Emotionally focused therapy for couples.* New York: Guilford Press.

Greenberg, L. S., & Safran, J. (1987). *Emotion in psychotherapy.* New York: Guilford Press.

Greenberg, L. S., & Pinsof, W. M. (1986). *The psychotherapeutic process: A research handbook.* New York: Guilford Press.

Heatherington, L. (1989). Toward more meaningful clinical research: Taking context into account in coding psychotherapy interaction. *Psychotherapy, 26,* 437–447.

Heatherington, L., & Friedlander, M. L. (1987). *The Family Relational Communication Control Coding System Manual.* Unpublished manuscript.

Heatherington, L., & Friedlander, M. L. (1990). Applying task analysis to structural family therapy. *Journal of Family Psychology, 4,* 36–38.

Heatherington, L., Friedlander, M. L., & Johnson, W. (1989). Informed consent in family therapy research: Ethical dilemmas and practical problems. *Journal of Family Psychology, 2,* 373–385.

Hill, C. E. (1991). Almost everything you ever wanted to know about how to do process research on counseling and psychotherapy but didn't know who to ask. In C. E. Watkins, Jr. & L. J. Schneider (Eds.), *Research in counseling.* Hillsdale, NJ: Erlbaum.

Jacobson, N. S., & Gurman, A. S. (Eds.). (1986). *Clinical handbook of marital therapy.* New York: Guilford Press.

Johnson, S. M., & Greenberg, L. S. (1988). Relating process to outcome in marital therapy. *Journal of Marital and Family Therapy, 14,* 175–183.

Kelly, G. (1955). *The psychology of personal constructs.* New York: Norton.

Kiesler, D. (1973). *The process of psychotherapy: Empirical foundations and systems of analysis.* Hawthorne, NY: Aldine.

Klein, M. H., Mathieu-Coughlin, P., & Kiesler, D. J. (1986). The experiencing scales. In L. S. Greenberg & W. M. Pinsof (Eds.), *The psychotherapeutic process: A research handbook.* New York: Guilford Press.

Newell, A., & Simon, H. (1972). *Human problem solving.* New York: Prentice-Hall.

Pascual-Leone, J. (1976a). Metasubjective problems of constructive cognition: Forms of knowing and their psychological mechanisms. *Canadian Psychological Review, 17,* 110–122.

Pascual-Leone, J. (1976b). A view of cognition from a formalist's perspective. In R. Riegel & J. Meachan (Eds.), *The developing individual in a changing world* (Vol. 1). The Hague: Mouton.

Paul, G. (1989). Behavior modification research: Design and tactics. In C. M. Franks (Ed.), *Behavior therapy: Appraisal and status.* New York: McGraw-Hill. (Original work published 1969)

Plysiuk, M. (1985). *A process study of marital conflict resolution.* Unpublished masters thesis, University of British Columbia, Vancouver, BC.

Rhodes, R., Geller, J., Greenberg, L., & Elliot, W. (1992). *Preliminary task analytic model of resolution of misunderstanding events.* Panel presented at the meeting of the Society for Psychotherapy Research, Berkeley, CA.

Rice, L. N., & Greenberg, L. S. (Eds.). (1984). *Patterns of change: Intensive analysis of psychotherapy process.* New York: Guilford Press.

Rice, L. N., & Saperia, E. P. (1984). Task analysis of the resolution of problematic reactions. In L. N. Rice & L. S. Greenberg (Eds.), *Patterns of change: Intensive analysis of psychotherapy process.* New York: Guilford Press.

Safran, J., Crocker, P., McMain, S., & Murray, B. (1990). Therapeutic alliance rupture as a therapy event for empirical study. *Psychotherapy, 27,* 154–165.

Snyder, D., & Wills, R. (1989). Behavioral versus insight-oriented martial therapy: Effects on individual and interpersonal functioning. *Journal of Consulting and Clinical Psychology, 57,* 39–46.

Spanier, J. (1976). Measuring dyadic adjustment: New scales for assessing the quality of marriage and similar dyads. *Journal of Marriage and the Family, 38,* 15–28.

Stiles, W. B. (1993). Quality control in qualitative research. *Clinical Psychology Review, 13,* 593–618.

Stiles, W., Shapiro, D., & Elliott, R. (1968). Are all psychotherapies equivalent? *American Psychologist, 41,* 165–180.

Steier, F. (1988). Toward a coherent methodology for the study of family therapy. In L. C. Wynne (Ed.), *The state of the art in family therapy research: Controversies and recommendations.* New York: Family Process Press.

Taylor, S. J., & Bogdan, R. (1984). *Introduction to qualitative research methods* (2nd ed.). New York: Wiley.

Wiley, D. E. (1967). Latent partition analysis. *Psychometrica, 32,* 183–193.

19

Systematically Developing Therapeutic Techniques
APPLICATIONS OF RESEARCH AND DEVELOPMENT

RICHARD J. BISCHOFF
A. JAY McKEEL
SIDNEY M. MOON
DOUGLAS H. SPRENKLE

MARRIAGE AND FAMILY therapy research has typically been limited to studying existing therapeutic procedures. This chapter describes a strategy for using research to develop and improve therapeutic interventions and models.

The research strategy described here is based on the research and development (R&D) tradition (Borg, 1987; Borg & Gall, 1989; Williams, 1991), and blends several qualitative and quantitative research approaches. This research strategy formally replicates what a clinician might do informally to design or improve a therapeutic technique. A therapist first develops ideas about a new intervention or ways to improve an existing intervention. Then, the therapist uses the intervention with several clients, modifies the intervention based on the clients' response and feedback, tries the modified technique, and continues this process until the therapist is satisfied the intervention is effective or decides to discard the idea. Because this research strategy is flexible and recursive and uses multiple perspectives, family therapists may be especially comfortable with this approach to developing clinical interventions.

With an almost infinite number of treatment possibilities from which to choose, clinicians, clients, and third-party payers are increasingly asking for evidence of clinical effectiveness to guide the selection of treatment strategies. Process and outcome studies provide one strategy for demonstrating clinical utility. However, using a systematic system to develop, improve, and evaluate clinical techniques provides an earlier opportunity to formally evaluate the effectiveness of therapeutic ideas and speeds the development of promising techniques.

Using a systematic strategy to develop therapeutic interventions has several benefits. First, new ideas can be more quickly developed and modifications can be discovered

429

that will improve the initial idea. Second, ineffective interventions can be discarded rather than introduced into the pool of interventions available to the clinician. Third, the applicability of the intervention and its limitations can be identified.

BACKGROUND

Traditionally, new treatment interventions and models evolve from a therapist's clinical experience, informal observations, creativity, and theoretical perspectives. Therapists introduce interventions to the clinical community, with perhaps only anecdotal evidence of effectiveness, through journal articles, books, workshops, or word of mouth. In general, this informal process has been accepted by the therapeutic community. Critics, however, observe that although scientific research is sometimes used to study the effects of treatments, treatment development has been very unscientific (e.g., Anderson, 1986; Bednar, Burlingame, & Masters, 1988).

To overcome the shortcomings of the traditional way of developing and communicating therapeutic strategy, we have combined several research traditions. The result is a systematic and rigorous method of model and technique development.

Research and Development

Those in the industrial sector have recognized that often products are developed but are not used by consumers because they do not address consumer needs. Also, many products that are poorly developed are often gobbled up by consumers because they are packaged so that they appear to meet consumer needs. When the latter occurs, the product typically loses its appeal because it was poorly developed or the limitations to its use were not accurately or clearly articulated. In psychotherapy, packaging rather than scientific development of therapeutic interventions typically determines initial appeal (Anderson, 1986; Mahrer, 1989). This is unfortunate because it is an intervention's ability to meet therapeutic needs that determine durability. R&D attempts to bridge the gap between product development and product use by accurately assessing the needs of the consumer and attempting to meet those needs (Adams, 1983). The process of R&D is one in which investigators determine a need, produce a product, test it, refine it, and test it again. Investigators repeat this cycle of testing and refining until they develop a product that adequately meets the needs of the consumers of the product.

Although R&D has been used primarily in the industrial sector (Williams, 1991), it has also been used in the field of education to develop educational programs and teaching strategies for use in classrooms with real life situations (Borg & Gall, 1989). Williams (1991) has shown the advantage of applying R&D technology to make basic and applied research more meaningful to clinicians. Through our research, we have used R&D to develop therapeutic strategies.

R&D is a process in which the investigator determines a need, plans a strategy for filling the need, develops a preliminary model of the strategy, field tests this model, refines the model based on the results of the field test, and field tests the model again. R&D researchers recursively move from model development to field testing and back to model development until a product of proven effectiveness emerges (Borg & Gall, 1989). Although various proponents do not agree about the number of steps involved in the R&D process (e.g., Borg & Gall, 1989, identified 10 steps whereas Williams, 1991, identified five), we conceptualize R&D in terms of four stages. We believe that these stages, although fewer than those identified by other authors, embody the essence of the R&D process. These four stages are (1) identifying the consumer and determining needs; (2) generating ideas for meeting the perceived needs; (3) developing, field testing, and revising the preliminary model; and (4) finalizing the model and disseminating the product.

To apply this process to therapeutic model and technique development, we found it useful to combine aspects of various research traditions. We borrowed heavily from task-analytical methodology (Greenberg, 1984; Greenberg, Heatherington, & Friedlander, Chapter 18, this volume), grounded theory research (Glaser & Strauss, 1967; Rafuls & Moon, Chapter 3, this volume; Strauss & Corbin, 1990), focus group interviewing (Anderson, 1990; Morgan, 1989; Piercy & Nickerson, Chapter 8, this volume), survey research (Nelson, Chapter 20, this volume), and clinical outcome research. To familiarize the reader with these research traditions, a brief description of each is found below.

Task Analysis

Task analysis was originally developed in the area of industrial and work psychology (Greenberg, 1984) but has been successfully applied to the study of change processes in therapy (Greenberg et al., Chapter 18, this volume; Greenberg & Johnson, 1988; Heatherington & Friedlander, 1990; Rice & Greenberg, 1984) and to the development of therapeutic strategy (Bischoff, 1993; Bischoff & McKeel, 1993; Bischoff, McKeel, Moon, & Sprenkle, 1996). Task analysis involves the intensive, inductive analysis of in-session therapeutic events (Greenberg et al., Chapter 18, this volume; Greenberg, 1984). The research procedure involves repeatedly going back and forth between two different types of analysis (Bischoff et al., 1996; Greenberg et al., Chapter 18, this volume; Greenberg, 1984). In the first type of analysis, the rational analysis (RA), the investigator constructs an idealized model of the event without the aid of direct observations. The idealized model is created from the investigators' ideas about what underlies similar therapeutic situations. This idealized model is used to inform later intensive observations of the event. The second type of analysis, the data-based analysis (DBA), is an intensive observation and analysis of the therapeutic event. Investigators intensively examine a sample of task situations and isolate the essential patterns that form the structure of the task. This is an emergent, evolving process with several iterations. In each DBA, investigators immerse themselves in the data to develop an increasingly refined model of the task situation. Each series of RAs and DBAs is considered a cycle of research with a typical investigation involving more than one iteration.

The cyclical nature of task-analytical methodology closely parallels the process of conducting an R&D investigation. The repetitive movement from the DBA to the RA resembles the process of developing, field testing, and revising models within the third step of the R&D process. It is probably for this reason that task-analytical methodology has long been used as an adjunct to R&D in the industrial sector (Borg & Gall, 1989).

Grounded Theory Research

Grounded theory research was developed in the early 1960s (Glaser & Strauss, 1967) as an alternative to deductive theorizing that was not grounded in data (Strauss, 1987). The approach has as its premise the inductive development of theory through immersion in the data (Rafuls & Moon, Chapter 3, this volume; Strauss, 1987). The investigator inductively derives linkages, themes, and concepts from the data to reconstruct the richness of the phenomena under study (Rafuls & Moon, Chapter 3, this volume; Strauss & Corbin, 1990). These reconstructions are then verified in the data.

Through this approach, theory is generated through constant comparison analysis (Glaser & Strauss, 1967). Using this technique, investigators inductively derive themes and categories that make sense of their observations of the data, continuously comparing and contrasting these with the themes, categories, and observations that preceded them. In this way, the theory is constantly being enhanced, refined, and verified.

Particularly during the early phases of the R&D process, theoretical sensitivity to the data (Strauss & Corbin, 1990) is crucial. Grounded theory research encourages the use of multiple perspectives and multiple methods which aid the researchers in the careful exploration of the evolving therapeutic technique. Therefore, grounded theory research complements R&D by allowing the flexibility in research method necessary to deal with the evolving nature of the developing therapeutic strategy.

Focus Group Interviewing

Although focus group interviewing began in the social sciences, it has been used extensively as an investigative procedure in marketing research (Morgan, 1989). Focus groups consist of persons who have some common characteristic or experience, brought together to focus discussion on some relevant topic area (Anderson, 1990; Piercy & Nickerson, Chapter 8, this volume). The primary advantage of focus group interviewing is to access data and depth of understanding that can only result from the interactional processes within a group (Anderson, 1990; Morgan, 1989). Focus groups are often used as a way to provide formative evaluations (Anderson, 1990). Focus group interviewing becomes an important compliment to the R&D process because it provides a vehicle for accessing consumer needs and for product evaluation. Focus groups also allow researchers to check out their reconstructions of the data (Lincoln & Guba, 1985) with therapists and clients who have contributed data for the investigation. Appropriate use of focus groups can help ensure that the clinical richness of the procedure can be captured in the product that is being developed.

Survey Research

Survey research strategies (Nelson, Chapter 20, this volume) can be used throughout the R&D process to guide the evaluation and modification of therapeutic techniques. Surveys can include both qualitative (e.g., open-ended) and quantitative (e.g., Likert-type) questions. Brief surveys, specifically designed to examine the intervention under study, can serve as a quick assessment of the clinician's and/or clients' views. For instance, a short questionnaire can be given after the session in which the intervention is used or at the beginning of the following session. Surveys may also include standardized therapeutic assessment instruments such as the Dyadic Adjustment Scale (Spanier, 1976). When used appropriately, these instruments can help the investigator make determinations throughout the R&D process about the effectiveness of the developing strategy and the client and therapist perceptions of it on a case-by-case basis.

Clinical Outcome Research

Research is often used in the fields of psychotherapy to evaluate the effectiveness of treatment programs and approaches to therapy. In conducting outcome studies, investigators typically evaluate the effectiveness of a therapeutic event or treatment by comparing the effects of the treatment against some standard (e.g., an alternative treatment or the pretreatment condition) (Kerlinger, 1973). Using these methods, data are traditionally quantified and subjected to statistical analysis. Outcome measures are particularly appropriate during the latter phases of the R&D process. R&D researchers can use these methods to determine the effectiveness of the model of therapeutic intervention that evolves from the R&D investigation.

METHODOLOGY

As described previously, R&D involves moving through several stages. These stages progress from (1) evaluating consumer needs; (2) generating ideas about how consumer needs can be met; (3) developing a preliminary model of the idea, testing, evaluating and refining the product until a usable model emerges; to (4) finalizing the model and disseminating it in a user-friendly way. This section addresses each stage of the R&D process and what is involved in each. To illustrate the R&D process as it applies to the development of models of therapeutic strategies, we provide an example of a study we conducted that resulted in a model of an in-session therapeutic procedure called a therapist-conducted consultation (TCC) (Bischoff et al., 1996). A brief rationale for the TCC study is presented below.

The TCC

During the past 10 years or so, a trend has developed to conceptualize therapy as a narrative event in which therapist and client collaborate in developing new descriptions of the client's problem situation (Anderson & Goolishian, 1988, 1992; de Shazer, 1994; White, 1986; White & Epston, 1990). Although these approaches to family therapy are gaining in popularity, previous to our investigation little had been done to operationalize strategies for developing and enhancing collaborative relationships. The TCC attempts to engender therapeutic collaboration by setting up a dialogue between the client and therapist about their experience of therapy. As clients see their experience of treatment, whether positive or negative, being validated by a caring therapist, they become more willing to overtly participate in treatment decision making. Treatment can then be altered to more accurately represent client agendas.

The TCC is a brief (20-to-30-minute) discussion initiated by the therapist about the clients' and therapist's experience of the process of therapy. During the TCC, the discussion focuses both on what the therapist and client identify as helpful in therapy and what they want to change. The therapist shares his or her perceptions of therapy with the clients and asks the clients to do the same. Clients are asked to identify what they have liked and disliked about treatment and how their experience of treatment could be improved in the future. The purpose of the consultation is to identify the direction therapy can take to best meet client goals. This procedure enhances therapeutic collaboration by inviting clients to participate more fully in making the decisions effecting the course of their treatment.

Stage One: Identifying the Consumer and Determining Needs

The outcome of good R&D research is dependent on an accurate assessment of consumer needs. It is not surprising that different consumer groups have different and sometimes contradictory needs. This is especially true with consumers of therapeutic interventions. For example, potential consumers of a method of therapeutic intervention might include clinicians, clients, research funding organizations, insurance companies, governmental agencies, training facilities, other mental health professions and related disciplines, lobbying groups, and state and national government bodies. Clearly, each of these "consumers" of the final product may have very different needs. Consequently, it becomes imperative for the R&D researcher to specifically identify the target audience of his/her research and the needs of this audience (Adams, 1983).

Once the target consumer has been identified, investigators attempt to assess the needs of the consumer so that the therapeutic strategy can be designed to meet those needs. Although many strategies can be used to assess consumer needs, there is probably no substitute for directly asking members of the consumer group what their needs are and how these needs can be met (Williams, 1991). Focus groups, interviews, and questionnaires are often good media for directly eliciting consumer needs.

Complementing but not replacing a direct assessment of consumer needs is a thorough review of the pertinent literature. Determining what has already been written about the subject, who has been doing the writing, and where the material is being published will help the investigator get a good idea about who has been targeted before, how the product has been marketed, and why the current literature is not filling the consumer needs.

For example, we became interested in developing a strategy for enhancing therapeutic collaboration after noticing that therapists we were supervising, although interested in developing collaborative relationships, were unsure about what they could do to engender collaboration. Consequently, we interviewed clinicians with whom we were working and found that they needed suggestions and strategies for how to enhance collaboration. We also turned to the literature that emphasizes collaborative relationships and talked with clinicians and theoreticians associated with these models. Two key findings resulted from these inquiries.

First, relatively few published works detailed strategies designed to enhance collaborative relationships. One of the few attempts was made by Wynne, McDaniel, and Weber (1986) in conceptualizing therapy as consultation. A primary motivation for using the term "consultation" was that this term seemed to have a more collaborative feel to it than "therapy" or "counseling." The term "consultation" clearly identifies the client as in control of the changes made and yet still acknowledges the therapist–consultant as the expert. Although Wynne et al. (1986) attempted to identify what takes place in these types of consultations, the descriptions are primarily anecdotal and from the perspectives of the authors reflecting on their own work. Considering the lack of published strategies for developing collaborative relationships, it was no wonder that our supervisees and other clinicians were struggling with this issue. Consequently, we determined that a need existed for specific and easily applied descriptions of strategies designed to enhance therapeutic collaboration. Through our needs assessment, we also found that our target consumers would be therapists attempting to learn collaborative styles of therapy.

Second, in discussing this issue with Kate Kowalski (personal communication, 1990), the second author (A. J. M.) learned that Brian Cade sometimes invites a colleague into a session to lead a discussion with the therapist and client about the process of therapy. This idea, coupled with the type of consultation proposed by Wynne et al. (1986), peaked our curiosity and provided a foundation for our investigation.

To ensure that the final product met the needs identified, we continued this type of assessment throughout the project. At the conclusion of each cycle of research we conducted a focus group of participating and nonparticipating therapists to find out whether our product was meeting their needs and to receive feedback on our reconstructions of the data. If the model was not meeting their needs, we asked them to give us suggestions for what needed to be done differently to meet those needs.

Stage Two: Generating Ideas for Meeting the Perceived Need

After determining need, the R&D researcher engages in a process of generating potential solutions for meeting the perceived need. Three strategies for generating ideas at this stage include the use of brainstorming, focus groups, and the existing literature.

Through brainstorming (Adams, 1986; Isacksen & Treffinger, 1985; von Oech, 1983, 1986) the investigator identifies as many potential ideas for meeting the perceived need as possible. Using this strategy, the investigator should entertain any idea, no matter how ridiculous, unusual, or impractical. Although most ideas generated with this strategy will not be usable, it does allow the investigator to entertain potentially fruitful ideas that would not have been considered otherwise because of restraints imposed by individual preconceptions, the existing literature, or social sanctions.

In using focus groups at this stage, the investigators invite a small group (or several small groups) of potential consumers of the product to discuss potential solutions to the need. Brainstorming strategies are often appropriate to stimulate idea generation within focus groups. Discussions during focus groups may also include strategies that the individual clinicians are currently using to meet the need.

Finally, the existing literature can help generate ideas for meeting the perceived need. The literature may suggest a solution to the need but not adequately address the need. For example, we found that although there is a burgeoning literature that emphasizes the importance of developing collaborative therapist–client relationships, there was very little in this literature that provided concrete strategies for developing collaborative relationships.

We generated ideas for the TCC by discussing needs and solutions with other clinicians in both focus groups and individual interviews. We also scanned the pertinent literature for ideas. After talking with clinicians and turning to the literature, we decided that applying ideas associated with consultations would be fruitful in enhancing therapeutic collaboration. Although we found the ideas shared by Kowalski (personal communication, 1990) particularly appealing (see Bischoff & McKeel, 1993), we also felt that it might be impractical in most therapeutic settings to expect that a professional colleague would be readily available to come into a session to conduct an interview with the therapist and client about the process of therapy. Consequently, we attempted to develop a therapeutic strategy where the therapist could conduct a process oriented interview of the clients' experience of therapy without the aid of a colleague.

Stage Three: Developing, Field Testing, and Revising the Preliminary Model

This phase of the R&D methodology consists of two processes: (1) developing a preliminary model and (2) field testing and revising the model. We have combined these two processes into the same stage because in practice the distinction between them becomes blurred. When using R&D to develop models of intervention, investigators move recursively from the model to the testing stages. In fact, typical investigations would entail multiple iterations of tentative model, implementation, testing, and revision. The essence of these stages is to take crude undeveloped ideas and develop and refine them into an effective, coherent, and easily communicated model of intervention.

Task-analytical methodology is often used within R&D in both industry and education (Borg & Gall, 1989). This may be because task analysis closely parallels the R&D process at this point in an investigation. The RA is similar to the development of the preliminary model stage and the DBA is similar to the field-testing stage. Because of these parallels, we use task-analytical terminology to describe the structure of the research process at this phase of an R&D project. The task-analytical terminology conveys what is taking place at any given point during this phase of the R&D process. Within this structure we have integrated aspects of grounded theory research, focus group interviewing, and other research traditions.

This phase of R&D consists of four overlapping steps: (1) the development of a tentative model of therapeutic intervention, (2) implementation of the model for purposes of data collection, (3) data collection and analysis, and (4) organization of results into a revised model of the therapeutic intervention. Steps 1 and 4 are best thought of in terms of the RA, whereas steps 2 and 3 are best thought of in terms of the DBA. These steps are repeated until theoretical saturation (Lincoln & Guba, 1985) has been reached and a final model of the therapeutic intervention emerges. In developing the TCC, four iterations, moving from RA to DBA, were undertaken with each cycle of research resulting in an increasingly refined idealized model of the TCC.

Developing the Tentative Model

First, the R&D process at this phase of the investigation begins with the investigator organizing his or her ideas for meeting the perceived needs identified during stage one. These ideas are formalized as a tentative, initial model of therapeutic intervention. This model is an idealized representation of what the therapeutic strategy is expected to look like based on a familiarization with the need assessment, pertinent literature and personal experiences. The development of this model constitutes the RA. This tentative, idealized model serves (1) as a guide or treatment manual for the therapists providing data for the investigation and (2) to inform intensive observations that take place during the DBA of that cycle of research.

In the development of the TCC, the initial rational model was modified from a model for collegial consultations that was previously published in Bischoff and McKeel (1993). Collegial consultations are designed to accomplish the same goals as the TCC, but do so by inviting a colleague of the therapist into the session to conduct the discussion about the therapist's and clients' experience of therapy.

Implementing the Preliminary Model

The second step of this phase of the R&D process consists of implementing the preliminary model for purposes of data collection. During the first iteration of this research process the model is typically carried out under conditions that are quite artificial and limited in scope (Borg & Gall, 1989; Williams, 1991). This makes sense; it would not be wise to invest time, money, and resources into a therapeutic strategy without evidence that it will meet the identified needs (Williams, 1991). During subsequent cycles of research, however, the model is applied in a wider variety of conditions and to conditions that more accurately represent lived clinical experience.

Implementation during the first cycle of the TCC project was tightly controlled and not representative of the real world of therapeutic intervention. This was done to test the viability of the technique and the project before substantial resources and energy were expended. During the first cycle, only three therapists were asked to conduct the TCC with their clients. These therapists were specifically selected because they were expected to produce the most useful data. Selection of these therapists was determined by previous therapeutic experience and interest in therapeutic models that emphasize collaboration. The initial rational model (Bischoff & McKeel, 1993) was shared with these therapists so they had an idea of what was to be accomplished by the procedure. The therapists were instructed to conduct the TCC in the way they believed would most benefit their clients and the therapy system and that would best contribute to the enhancement of therapeutic collaboration. After finding that the procedure held promise, the scope of implementation was expanded during subsequent cycles of research to different therapists working from various theoretical orientations and to different client presenting problems and situations.

Data Collection and Analysis

This is the heart of the analytical procedure. This step consists of relevant data collection and immersion in the data for purposes of systematic data analysis. Although any number of research techniques can be used, we recommend that the investigator use a combination of qualitative and quantitative research methods and focus group interviewing in this step of the research process.

In data collection, data should be elicited from a number of different sources and through a variety of methods. This technique, known in qualitative research as triangulation (Denzin, 1978), enhances theoretical sensitivity to the data (Strauss & Corbin, 1990) and is a primary method of ensuring the credibility of a qualitative study (Denzin, 1978; Hoshmand, 1989; Lincoln & Guba, 1985; Yin, 1989). In our study of the TCC, we obtained data from five different sources using six data collection methods (Figure 19.1).

For data analysis, we recommend that primarily qualitative methods be used during the preliminary cycles of research when emphasis is primarily on exploration. During the early cycles of research, investigators need to be open to previously unforeseen possibilities within the data. Grounded theory strategies provide the attention to inductive analysis needed during these early cycles of research. In the TCC study, four cycles of research were conducted that consisted of case and cross-case analyses (Yin, 1989) of videotaped consultations. The constant comparative method of data analysis (Glaser & Strauss, 1967) was used to code and analyze the data.

As a complement to this grounded theory approach, surveys can be used to assess clinicians' and clients' views of the intervention. Investigators may construct a short questionnaire designed to specifically address issues identified in the needs assessment

	Videotaped session	Therapists	Clients	Model commentator	Peer debriefer
Observation	X				
Questionnaire		X	X		
Interview		X	X		
Focus group		X			
Reflection session				X	X

FIGURE 19.1. Matrix of data sources by data collection methods for the TCC study.

phase of the R&D process. Responses to these questionnaires can be evaluated on a case-by-case basis to provide direction in analysis. In the TCC study, clients and therapists answered 10 Likert-type questions to help determine their views of the intervention. This information was useful in two ways. First, when questionnaires were matched with the case being analyzed, they provided additional information about the intervention and gave specific direction to the analysis. Second, when responses across clients and therapists were combined through summary statistics, they provided the investigators with an idea about the success of the intervention at each stage of the research. Overall, this data revealed that more than 80% of the clients and therapists found the TCC useful.

After initial observations of the TCCs in each cycle were completed, a subsample of these cases was chosen using theoretical and practical criteria (Glaser & Strauss, 1967; Lincoln & Guba, 1985; Strauss & Corbin, 1990) for intensive observation, coding, and comparison against the rational model that informed the cycle of research. During this step of each cycle, the investigator(s) observed the videotaped consultation sessions chosen for intensive analysis and analyzed them according to the constant comparison procedure (Glaser & Strauss, 1967). The rational model that began the research cycle informed these observations and analyses.

During later cycles of research, after theoretical saturation has been met and the model begins to adopt its final form, we recommend that R&D researchers incorporate quantitative methods. These methods are most appropriate for evaluation of the finalized model. Through probability sampling strategies and quantification of data and analysis, the effectiveness of the model of intervention can be more reliably determined.

For example, it would be helpful to compare pre-TCC with post-TCC scores on a measure of therapist–client collaboration to determine whether a noticeable change in collaboration resulted from the use of the TCC. Comparing treatment outcomes or satisfaction with therapy ratings from clients who received the TCC and those who did not would also prove valuable. Information gained from these type of evaluations would speak to the clinical utility and general effectiveness of the procedure.

Revision and Development of an Idealized Model

To conclude each cycle of this step of an R&D project, the investigator organizes the data and the results of the data analysis and compares this against the rational model that informed the cycle of research. This leads to a new RA and results in a rational model to end the cycle of research. This resulting model informs the next iteration.

The cyclical process described above continues until theoretical saturation (Lincoln & Guba, 1985) is reached. In other words, the investigator continues to recursively move from the RA to DBA until new data adds little or nothing new to the model.

Stage Four: Finalizing the Model and Disseminating the Product

The result of this phase of the R&D process is an idealized yet realistic version of the model of therapeutic intervention. This model should be in a form that is easily accessible and that can be readily disseminated to the potential consumers of the final product.

In the case of the TCC, the idealized model consisted of three stages (Bischoff, 1993; Bischoff et al., 1994). Descriptions of these stages were written in such a way that specific aspects of the procedure were communicated with enough detail that a beginning therapist could read the description and be able to carry out the therapeutic intervention.

In addition to writing an easily communicable description of the therapeutic strategy, it is equally important that the model be disseminated to the potential consumers of the investigation. This is different from what typically occurs in the development of treatment manuals for research purposes. These manuals are typically developed explicitly to serve the research purposes and consequently often have limited applicability beyond the study for which they were developed (Borg & Gall, 1989). The treatment manual that results from the R&D study, however, is designed to have broader applicability and to be accessible to the potential consumer of the research. It is important then that the investigators seek out a medium for dissemination that will make the model accessible to the consumers.

Potential media for dissemination of an R&D project include clinical journals and texts that have a readership that includes the consumers of the product. Too often, good products are developed but not disseminated (marketed) properly and so are not accessible to those who could most use the product.

In the case of the TCC and the related procedure, the collegial consultation, we disseminated the product first to the therapists with whom we were working. After all, this was the group that expressed the need and desired the product. Second, we sought publication of the final product in clinical journals that have a readership that includes beginning therapists and trainers interested in therapies that emphasize therapeutic collaboration.

DISCUSSION

The methods described in this chapter provide the investigator with access to rich clinical experience that can inform the development of treatment strategies. Using R&D strategies to develop models of therapeutic intervention can improve the transferability of technique descriptions and consequently make them more useful for training, practice, and research purposes.

Advantages of the R&D Methodology

There are several advantages to using R&D as a systematic method of developing models of therapeutic intervention. The first advantage is that it provides the investigator with clear direction for developing therapeutic strategies. Successful R&D research explicitly determines consumer needs and then allows these needs to drive the study. In applying R&D to the development of therapeutic intervention, we have emphasized the importance of continuing to assess consumer needs throughout the research process. As the evolving model of intervention is repeatedly presented to samples of the consumer group and these participants are invited to comment on how well the model meets their needs, consumer needs become increasingly clarified and the ability of the evolving model to meet those needs is improved. Using this methodology allows investigators to decide early in the research process the merit of an idea and allows them to modify viable ideas throughout the research process. So, although the R&D process may appear time-consuming, it results in a more useful product and may reduce the time it takes to move a product from idea to market. By attending to consumer needs and allowing these to influence the final product, the systematic development of therapeutic intervention becomes a more efficient process.

A second advantage to this research protocol is that both the investigators and the consumers can have greater confidence in the results; the final product is based in a systematic and rigorous study of the phenomena using both qualitative and quantitative methods, not on anecdotal evidence. For example, eliciting and analyzing data repeatedly through the various cycles of research allow for the saturation (Lincoln & Guba, 1985) necessary to piece together a coherent and useful model of therapeutic intervention. Combining this analysis and interpretation of data with member checking and continued assessment of how the evolving model is meeting consumer needs allows for a trustworthy (Lincoln & Guba, 1985) description of the therapeutic event to emerge. Evaluations of the effectiveness of the model through outcome measures can also help ensure the utility of the model. The result is a therapeutic strategy with greater credibility and robustness than one developed by informal methods and sold with evangelical hype. This process addresses concerns by critics of family therapy by developing therapeutic intervention through a systematic and rigorous research protocol.

Third, R&D facilitates the identification of the intervention's essential ingredients. Relying on informal observation and individual experience, developers of therapeutic models may emphasize elements of strategies that are not necessary for the successful implementation of the intervention. Or, they may overlook elements that are essential but that are more difficult to identify. The R&D process overcomes this weakness in traditional methods of technique development by emphasizing the microanalysis of the key elements to the therapeutic strategy as well as the macroanalysis of the intervention in relation to consumer needs and participant perceptions of the evolving model. The recursive nature of this process allows both the investigator and study participants to identify those elements that are most important to successful implementation of the intervention. This process of identifying key elements makes it easy for investigators to completely and accurately describe the steps necessary to implement and carry out the intervention. Consequently, R&D methodology improves transferability (Lincoln & Guba, 1985). Communicating the therapeutic procedure accurately and completely allows other clinicians to appropriately and successfully implement the procedure.

Fourth, the R&D process deals specifically with clinical experience and allows the investigator to communicate this experience in the final written product. The written description of the model informs the therapist about what types of clients and under what conditions the intervention is most appropriate. In essence, the R&D process can transfer clinical experience with the procedure to the clinician.

A fifth advantage inherent in the methodology is the ability to bridge research and practice. To balance both the demands of research and of consumer needs, the R&D investigator must ask questions and design research in ways that are meaningful to clinicians. If the clinician does not see the value of the research and the results of the study are not easily accessible to the clinician, the investigator has failed in the R&D process.

Finally, this systematic method of developing therapeutic strategy can be used by an investigator in almost any therapy setting. It bridges research and practice by being a clinician-friendly research strategy. R&D is essentially a formalized method of what innovative clinicians are already doing. Consequently, it matches the clinician's way of working and learning from experience.

Disadvantages of the R&D Methodology

Although the R&D process holds promise as a way to systematically develop therapeutic strategies, there are several important limitations that inhibit its use. The most important limitation to the research protocol, and that which stands to inhibit its broader use, is the time commitment involved in developing, refining, and studying therapeutic intervention in this manner. Literally hundreds of hours can be spent in recruiting participants; observing videotapes, transcribing taped data; analyzing, categorizing, and organizing data, observations, and themes; formalizing the model; and designing evaluation studies.

A second limitation to the methodology is that it places a high priority on feedback from research participants through focus groups, questionnaires, and interviews. Participant perceptions of the model and its usefulness become integral in directing the investigators' observations and the development of the clinical model. Although this strategy improves the trustworthiness of a qualitative study (Lincoln & Guba, 1985) and ensures that consumer needs are being met, it is possible that "thank you effects" predominate. Participants may just tell the investigators what they think they want to hear. It may be that the narrative that develops between the investigators and study participants actually creates the model and determines the model's success.

Skills of the Investigator

R&D is a formalized variation of what an innovative clinician would do naturally in developing therapeutic technique. However, because the process is formalized and designed to rigorously meet consumer needs, several skills unique to R&D research should be identified.

First, the investigator should have a working familiarity with both qualitative and quantitative research traditions. Every R&D study designed to develop therapeutic techniques should have a qualitative component and many will have a quantitative component. Qualitative methods will be used primarily to develop the technique, whereas quantitative methods might be most appropriate for evaluation of the effectiveness of the technique. Consequently, the R&D investigator needs to feel comfortable with both qualitative and quantitative methods and value the contribution each can make to the research process. We do not see R&D as either a qualitative or a quantitative methodology but, rather, a framework from which the most appropriate research traditions can be pulled to meet the needs of the consumers.

Second, the R&D investigator needs to possess a great deal of patience with the research process. R&D research can be frustrating for some because it is driven primarily by consumer needs and not by the investigator's own theory. So, investigators may find that their initial ideas about meeting needs will be replaced by consumer-dictated ideas. Also, the researcher must be flexible about the evolution of the research process. R&D research for developing therapeutic technique cannot be planned too far in advance. Rather, decisions about research procedure and analytical steps are made throughout the investigation. This means that the research strategy used in one cycle of research may be very different than the strategy used in another cycle of the same investigation. The researcher needs to be flexible enough with the research design that changes in protocol can be made as need dictates.

SUMMARY

Marriage and family therapy is replete with interventions, yet the development and refinement of techniques have rarely been guided by scientific methods or structured tools. This chapter provides a "how to guide" to the clinician–investigator interested in using R&D strategies to test and improve therapeutic techniques. Family therapy techniques developed by rigorous R&D methods increase credibility, especially as compared to techniques developed by informal methods and sold with evangelical hype.

The R&D strategies presented here are based on an eclectic, mixed methodology that makes use of both quantitative and qualitative research methodologies. Most investigators will not use all the research strategies described in this chapter; rather, investigators are encouraged to select those strategies that will best determine if and how the intervention being studied will meet the identified need.

REFERENCES

Adams, J. L. (1986). *The care and feeding of ideas: A guide to encouraging creativity*. Reading, MA: Addison-Wesley.

Adams, K. A. (1983). Needs sensing: The yeast for R&D organizations. *Educational Evaluation and Policy Analysis, 5*(1), 55–60.

Anderson, C. M. (1986). The all-too-short trip from positive to negative connotation. *Journal of Marital and Family Therapy, 12*, 351–354.

Anderson, G. (1990). *Fundamentals of educational research*. London: Falmer Press.

Anderson, H., & Goolishian, H. A. (1988). Human systems as linguistic systems: Preliminary and evolving ideas about the implications for clinical theory. *Family Process, 27*, 371–393.

Anderson, H., & Goolishian, H. (1992). The client is the expert: A not-knowing approach to therapy. In S. McNamee & K. George (Eds.), *Constructing therapy: Social construction and the therapeutic process*. Newbury Park, CA: Sage.

Bednar, R. L., Burlingame, G. M., & Masters, K. S. (1988). Systems of family treatment: Substance or semantics. *Annual Review of Psychology, 39*, 401–413.

Bischoff, R. J. (1993). *The development of a model of self-consultations*. Unpublished dissertation, Purdue University, West Lafayette, IN.

Bischoff, R. J., & McKeel, A. J. (1993). Collegial consultations. *Journal of Systemic Therapies, 12*(3), 50–60.

Bischoff, R. J., McKeel, A. J., Moon, S. M., & Sprenkle, D. H. (1996). Therapist-conducted consultation: Using clients as consultants to their therapy. *Journal of Marital and Family Therapy, 22*, 335–355.

Borg, W. R. (1987). The educational R&D process: Some insights. *Journal of Experimental Education, 55*, 181–188.

Borg, W. R., & Gall, M. D. (1989). *Educational research: An introduction* (5th ed.). New York: Longman.

Denzin, N. K. (1978). *Sociological methods*. New York: McGraw-Hill.

de Shazer, S. (1994). *Words were originally magic*. New York: Norton.

Glaser, B. G., & Strauss, A. L. (1967). *The discovery of grounded theory: Strategies for qualitative research*. New York: Aldine.

Greenberg, L. S. (1984). Task analysis: The general approach. In L. N. Rice & L. S. Greenberg (Eds.), *Patterns of change: Intensive analysis of psychotherapy process*. New York: Guilford Press.

Greenberg, L. S., & Johnson, S. M. (1988). *Emotionally focused therapy for couples*. New York: Guilford Press.

Heatherington, L., & Friedlander, M. L. (1990). Applying task analysis to structural family therapy. *Journal of Family Psychology, 4*, 36–48.

Hoshmand, L. L. S. T. (1989). Alternate research paradigms: A review and teaching proposal. *The Counseling Psychologist, 17*, 1–80.

Isacksen, S. G., Treffinger, D. J. (1985). *Creative problem solving: The basic course*. Buffalo, NY: Bearly Limited.

Kerlinger, F. N. (1973). *Foundations of behavioral research* (2nd ed.). New York: Holt, Rinehart & Winston.

Lincoln, Y., & Guba, E. (1985). *Naturalistic inquiry*. Beverly Hills, CA: Sage.

Mahrer, A. R. (1988). Discovery-oriented psychotherapy research: Rationale, aims and methods. *American Psychologist, 43*, 694–702.

Morgan, D. L. (1989). *Focus groups as qualitative research*. Newbury Park, CA: Sage.

Rice, L. N., & Greenberg, L. S. (Eds.). (1984). *Patterns of change: Intensive analysis of psychotherapy process*. New York: Guilford Press.

Spanier, G. B. (1976). Measuring dyadic adjustment: New scales for assessing the quality of marriage and similar dyads. *Journal of Marriage and the Family, 38*, 15–28.

Strauss, A. L. (1987). *Qualitative analysis for social scientists*. New York: Cambridge University Press.

Strauss, A., & Corbin, J. (1990). *Basics of qualitative research: Grounded theory procedures and techniques*. Newbury Park, CA: Sage.

von Oech, R. (1983). *A whack on the side of the head: How to unlock your mind for innovation*. New York: Warner.

von Oech, R. (1986). *A kick in the seat of the pants*. New York: Harper & Row.

White, M. (1986). Negative explanation, restraint, and double description: A template for family therapy. *Family Process, 25*, 169–184.

White, M., & Epston, D. (1990). *Narrative means to therapeutic ends*. New York: Norton.

Williams, L. (1991). A blueprint for increasing the relevance of family therapy research. *Journal of Marital and Family Therapy, 17*, 355–362.

Wynne, L. C., McDaniel, S. H., & Weber, T. T. (Eds.). (1986). *Systems consultation: A new perspective for family therapy*. New York: Guilford Press.

Yin, R. K. (1989). *Case study research: Design and methods*. Newbury Park, CA: Sage.

Survey Research

20

Survey Research in Marriage
and Family Therapy

THORANA S. NELSON

BACKGROUND

"Survey," as a verb, means "to examine, inspect or consider carefully" (Guralnik, 1966, p. 749). As a noun, a survey is a "general study: as a *survey* of public opinion" (Guralnik, 1966, p. 749). McGraw and Watson (1976) define *survey research* as "a method of collecting standardized information by interviewing a sample representative of some population" (p. 343). Survey research "studies large and small populations . . . by selecting and studying samples chosen from the population to discover the relative incidence, distribution, and interrelations of sociological and psychological variables" (Kerlinger, 1986, p. 378). Warwick and Lininger (1975) define survey as a "method of collecting information about a human population in which direct contact is made with the units of the study (individuals, organizations, communities, etc.) through such systematic means as questionnaires and interview schedules" (p. 2). Common terms that emerge in definitions of survey research are *sample, information, questionnaire* or *interview schedule,* and, for our purposes, *sociological* and *psychological* variables. The sample is the *who* of the study, the variables are the *what,* and the questionnaire is the *how.* Survey research, then, is a method of collecting data from or about a group of people, asking questions in some fashion about things of interest to the researcher for the purpose of generalizing to a population represented by the group or sample.

Broadly, a sample is a part selected to represent a larger whole (Warwick & Lininger, 1975). The variables are the concepts or information in which the researcher is interested. A questionnaire or interview schedule is a series of questions presented to the sample in person by an interviewer, over the telephone, through a self-administered mailed paper-and-pencil instrument, or in some other way. The data analyses and reports are then used to describe the group or to draw inferences about the variables, their relation to each other, and their relation to the population of interest.

Surveys usually focus on people—facts about them or their opinions, attitudes, motivations, behaviors, and so on—and the relationships between variables under study related to these people. For example, survey research might be used to compare demographic characteristics of a sample of people in a particular location, their access to mental health

447

services, and their perceptions about the efficacy of those services. This information could be used to make recommendations about improving the services for that population or the methods for delivering them. In family therapy research, Wetchler (1989; Wetchler, Piercy, & Sprenkle, 1989) surveyed both supervisors and supervisees about their impressions of their supervision experiences and made some suggestions about marriage–family therapy (MFT) training based on responses to his survey.

For purposes of this chapter, survey research methods do not include those that involve *experiments*—research designed to manipulate participants in some way or to measure changes in people due to interventions, as in therapy *outcome* research. Second, this chapter does not include discussions related to family therapy *process* research—investigations into components of therapy and their effect on participants or on therapy outcome by observing and coding behaviors in therapy. Finally, this chapter does not include discussions of single-case studies, small samples, or observational methods of collecting data. This chapter *does* include discussions of methods related to gathering information from samples of volunteers for the purpose of describing, explaining, and/or exploring particular aspects of the participants' experience, how these data relate to each other and to other data, and how the results of analyses of the data can be used to draw generalizations about larger populations.

The remainder of this chapter describes the history of survey research, various methods related to different stages of conducting survey research, strengths and weaknesses of the method, issues of reliability and validity, researcher skills, and ways that survey research can be used to form bridges between clinicians and researchers. Examples from the Basic Family Therapy Skills (BFTS) project (e.g., Figley & Nelson, 1989) will be used extensively to illustrate various points. Following is a brief description of the BFTS project to provide context for the illustrations. Readers may want to return to the description after reading this chapter and use its information for critiquing the study.

Basic Family Therapy Skills Project

The author and her colleagues (Figley & Nelson, 1989, 1990; Nelson & Figley, 1990; Nelson, Heilbrun, & Figley, 1993) embarked on an ambitious survey of family therapy supervisors and trainers to determine their opinions about the essential skills for beginning family therapists. The study was designed to provide a comprehensive list of skills rather than a consensus report. The study was carried out in several phases. In the first phase, we contacted all American Association for Marriage and Family Therapy (AAMFT) Approved Supervisors and all members of the American Family Therapy Academy (AFTA), describing our purposes and the scope of the study, outlining the criteria for participating (active as a supervisor of beginning family therapists and willing to respond to the questionnaires through several phases), and inviting them to participate in the study. Invitations were personalized by using merge capabilities of a word processor to enhance response rate (Dillman & Frey, 1974). As much as possible, personal touches were used throughout the study.

Questionnaires were sent to those who responded and were eligible (n = 688), asking for demographic information and experience as a family therapist/trainer/educator and soliciting nominations for essential, basic skills for beginning family therapists. Respondents were asked to nominate skills from their theoretical preferences as well as generic basic skills. After the nominations were sorted and consolidated, lists of generic skills were sent to the participants in Phase II. Each questionnaire listed the nominated skills and asked the respondents to rate each in terms of its importance in beginning-level family therapy. Participants were invited to provide comments.

To enhance the response rate of Phase II, the extensive list of items was divided so that each participant received only one-quarter of the nominated items, making the questionnaires more manageable in length for each respondent. Participants were also sent postcards asking them to which of the model-specific questionnaires they wished to respond. Multiple questionnaires of the model-specific items were sent to those requesting them in Phase III of the project. The model-specific questionnaires included the same Likert-type response choices as the generic survey plus several categorical response choices based on feedback from the participants in Phase II. That is, in each phase of the survey, we used information from earlier phases to enhance the quality of the data. In each phase, follow-up postcards were sent to the sample to enhance response rates.

Data from the generic survey were analyzed by computing means and sorting the items accordingly, producing a ranked list. The top 100 items were reported in publication (Figley & Nelson, 1990). Data from the model-specific phase (Phase III) were analyzed by first comparing the responses of those who were self-expressed users of a particular model in their own practices with those who had requested the questionnaire, but who personally used a different model. In no case were the groups judged different (using chi-square tests) in their responses to the items. Items were then ranked by means and standard deviations. Several of the model-specific results have been published (Figley & Nelson, 1990; Nelson & Figley, 1990; Nelson et al., 1993). Other data are currently being analyzed and written up for publication.

A fourth phase of the survey was developed after examining the literature for skills that had not been nominated by our sample. These items were added to the top 200 generic skills and questionnaires were sent to both the original panel and to the editorial advisory board members of important family therapy journals—a different kind of "expert" panel on family therapy skills, perhaps. Data currently are being analyzed and an evaluation instrument is being tested.

History of Survey Research

Surveys have been used for nearly as long as recorded history. Egyptians and Romans used census surveys to gather information about citizenry for purposes of developing tax rates, military conscription, and other administrative needs (Warwick & Lininger, 1975). John Howard, an 18th-century British reformer, surveyed prison conditions in England and their effects on inmates' health. An economist, Frederic LePlay, surveyed income and expenses of households in 19th-century France to aid in social planning. He also checked his information against independent sources: observations and reports of others. In the late 19th century, Charles Book, a statistician, studied poverty in England, asserting that effective change required accurate data on a problem (Warwick & Lininger, 1975).

The 1930s and 1940s saw an alliance between the development of probability sampling techniques from agriculture (developed to estimate crop yields) and controlled interviewing methods (Warwick & Lininger, 1975). Prior to this time, social science considered sampling methods too difficult to gather an accurate picture of a population. Rensis Likert, of the famous Likert (1932) scale used so much in social science research today, pioneered the study of people's attitudes, beliefs, and behaviors. Paul Lazersfeld moved beyond even this sort of descriptive survey to causal explanations and hypothesis testing using survey sampling techniques.

SURVEY RESEARCH IN FAMILY THERAPY

In family therapy research, many surveys have been designed to determine what clinicians think or do. Survey research has been used to ask clinicians about their use of assessment instruments (Boughner, Hayes, Bubenzer, & West, 1994), about how they act when faced with ethical dilemmas (Green & Hansen, 1986, 1989), about their preferred models of therapy (Quinn & Davidson, 1984), and about how they use or view their clinical training (Carter, 1989; Coleman, Myers Avis, & Turin, 1990; Keller, Huber, & Hardy, 1988; Wilson & Stith, 1993). Survey research also has been used to query directors of training programs about their views of accreditation standards (Keller et al., 1988) and admission and program requirements (O'Sullivan & Gilbert, 1989), as well as issues related to ethnicity and gender in their curricula (Coleman et al., 1990; Wilson & Stith, 1993). Students have been surveyed about their ethnic minority status and related experience in training (Wilson & Stith, 1993) and about their experiences as therapists in training (Wetchler, 1989; Wetchler et al., 1989). Supervisors have been asked about their training practices (Lewis & Rohrbaugh, 1989; Nichols, Nichols, & Hardy, 1990), about what they view as essential basic family therapy skills (Figley & Nelson, 1989, 1990; Nelson & Figley, 1990; Nelson et al., 1993), and about the essential elements of MFT and MFT supervision (White & Russell, 1995; in press). Finally, clients have been surveyed as to their opinions about their experiences in therapy, including which components of therapy were most influential for them. Nylund (Nylund & Thomas, 1994) conducted this sort of survey to determine whether or not letters he had written (a narrative approach) had been helpful to his clients and, if so, to what extent. The responses to his survey yielded information not only about his approach for his own enlightenment, but also as a way of informing his clinical practice in the context of managed care and brief therapy.

Delphi models, a particular form of survey research, are often used to query a panel of experts on a topic through several phases of inquiry and feedback—these models are discussed more extensively by Stone Fish and Busby (Chapter 21, this volume). Experts have been surveyed in other ways, however, to obtain their views on a number of topics, including family therapy skills (Figley & Nelson, 1989, 1990; Nelson & Figley, 1990; Nelson et al., 1993) and, interestingly, evaluation of family therapy workshops (Heath, McKenna, & Atkinson, 1988).

On occasion, the general population or a class of clients has been surveyed to determine their experience of a particular issue. Examples include wives' experience of their husbands' posttraumatic stress symptoms or combat stress reactions (Solomon, Ott, & Roach, 1986), couples' experiences of marriage encounter weekends (Doherty, Lester, & Leigh, 1986), and the effects of differing wake–sleep patterns on marital relationships (Larson, Crane, & Smith, 1991). Halik, Rosenthal, and Pattison (1990) measured personal authority (Bray, Williamson, & Malone, 1984) of daughters of Jewish Holocaust survivors or immigrants. These examples of survey research pertain to family therapy by virtue of the constructs measured and are often easily extrapolated into family therapy interventions.

Planning Survey Research

Fowler (1988) suggests a *total design* concept for planning survey research. In this concept, each stage of the project, from determining the goals and purposes of the study through reporting the results, operates recursively with every other stage, each one informing the others until a clear plan emerges. This kind of careful planning helps prevent both sampling error (described below) and nonsampling error, which includes errors related to the questions asked of the participants, their responses, coding and processing the data, analyzing the data, and reporting the results of the study. As much as possible, error should be limited in each area so that the researcher has confidence in the results of the study. The wise investigator puts careful thought into each stage of the project so that error is reduced. Researchers should consult books and articles (e.g., Dillman, 1978; Dillman, Carpenter, Christensen, & Brooks, 1974; Dillman & Frey, 1974; Fink & Kosecoff, 1985; Fowler, 1988; Hackett, 1981; Jolliffe, 1986; Miller, 1986; Warwick & Lininger, 1975; de Vaus, 1986) and statistical consultants and should conduct pilot studies to refine their projects.

Goals and Purposes

The first step in the planning stage is determining the purpose of the project and setting goals. At this time, investigators should think about the later stages of the project: the analyses and report writing. By working back and forth through each stage of the project, the investigator ensures that each stage is strong in the context of the others, limits error as much as possible, and ensures that the project can be appropriately executed.

For example, in the BFTS project, our end goal was a text book for master's-level family therapy students and instructors based on empirically derived basic family therapy skills (Figley & Nelson, 1989). As we thought about this goal, we began to realize that other goals were desirable, including developing instruments that could be used to evaluate family therapy trainees and to determine which aspects of family therapy are predictive of successful therapy outcomes. This new goal required that we rethink the methods of the project, adding procedures that would help develop an instrument.

Research Questions in Survey Investigations

Survey research often is used to determine characteristics or descriptions of samples (and thus of populations). For example, a researcher might want to know the characteristics that are typical of families who enter therapy. Information could be gathered about such variables as age, income, education, ethnicity or race, types of presenting problems, and family structures, and/or about other variables. In addition to demographic descriptions (what the sample looks like), the researcher could gather information related to *who does what, why, how, how well,* and *with what effect.* The researcher could correlate the elicited information with demographic descriptions of the sample.

Research can investigate questions related to behavior, influences on behaviors, attitudes, beliefs, values, and the relationship between beliefs and behaviors. For example, clinicians may believe that they are quite sensitive to and aware of the cultural contexts of their clients. These beliefs can be explored through attitude questionnaires or probing interviews and then correlated with behaviors that have been detected through responses to questions posed after the clinician has read a case study vignette designed to elicit clinical choices and responses. At the same time, clients could be surveyed regarding their experiences in therapy related to contextual issues. All the information could then be analyzed together to provide a picture of how well therapists do what they believe they do. In the BFTS project, we were interested in the kinds of skills supervisors from specific theoretical perspectives thought were most important for beginners. We compared groups on the variable "preferred theoretical perspective" and noted that, for the most part, the groups were similar in the way they rated different skills for particular theories. That is, those who used a particular family therapy theory in their own practices tended to rate the skills in a fashion similar to those supervisors who, personally, preferred other theories. This suggested to us that the skills nominated by our sample were, indeed, derived from theoretical constructs rather than personal practice.

Survey methods use information gathered *directly* from the respondents themselves. However, this information can be compared to other information to answer complex questions. For example, an administrator of a family therapy clinic may want to evaluate the effectiveness and efficiency of therapy performed to enhance an effort to secure a certain kind of therapy contract (e.g., a health maintenance organization panel or a state domestic violence contract). Administrators could survey a sample of the clinic's former clients using a variety of instruments that assess family dynamics (e.g., the Family Assessment Device; Epstein, Baldwin, & Bishop, 1983) and ask questions about the clients' satisfaction with the clinic's services, using their own instrument and/or other questions. Administrators could also ask the therapists about their opinions of the clients' therapy and then compare all the data with clinic records: scores on assessment instruments, number of sessions, presenting problems, economic levels, race/ethnicity, and so on. In the BFTS project, after surveying supervisors regarding their ideas about essential beginning skills, we surveyed the literature, comparing the skills reported there, and generated a new, more comprehensive list of skills.

It is critical for researchers to develop their research questions carefully so that the variables are appropriate and clearly defined and operationalized. A thorough discussion of types of variables and measurements can be found in many standard statistics textbooks. In general, however, investigators must determine the independent and dependent variables and their levels of measurement and whether they want to *describe* a population or *draw inferences* about it, either in terms of how the variables are associated with each other or how groups compare.

The variables of interest and their measurement level (nominal, ordinal, interval, or ratio) determine the way the data will be obtained (forms of questions and collecting strategy) and the analysis strategies. Thus, the research questions must be formulated in the context of other stages of the project. Statistical consultation can be very helpful at this stage to ensure that the form of the data is adequate for the kinds of analyses required to answer the research questions.

Sampling

Although each element of the survey method is critical to the overall design of a good research project, the ability to generalize the results will be only as good as the sampling techniques used (Fowler, 1988). Sampling error is one of the most common and poorly described problems in survey research. *Sampling error* is that error associated with how well or how poorly the sample represents the population of interest. All samples result in some error. That is, no sample is perfectly representative of the population from which it is drawn: by chance, some error will occur. However, sampling error can result from poorly designed sampling strategies or from strategies that are not followed carefully; this is the error that should be avoided.

Sample Size

Although the size of the sample is important, a large sample will not make up for poor selection methods or lack of adherence to the method. Fowler (1988) points out that determining a sample size is a complex process. The aim is to select a quality and quantity of units that will provide sufficient data so that the research questions can be answered with a sufficient level of confidence. Obviously, this is different if the question is, "How much of drug A is required to relieve symptom B without causing side effect C?," than it is if the question is, "What kinds of problems can be addressed using XYZ model of family therapy?" The sample size is also determined by the sampling *method* (smaller size when using simple random methods than when using convenience samples), levels of *variance* in the variables (smaller n for more homogeneous samples), and expected *response rate* (higher n when expected response rate is low) in addition to the level of precision required or power desired.

As the sample size increases, the size of the margin of error increments decrease and power increases. At a certain point, the costs associated with a larger sample size do not justify the slightly higher level of precision and confidence obtained. For a simple random sample with a fairly high expected response rate (60–75%), sample sizes of 150–200 are sufficient for confidence that the sampled mean is, in fact, similar to the population mean, within an acceptable margin of error (Fowler, 1988). (See Kraemer & Thiemann, 1987, for a more detailed discussion of power and sample sizes.)

Representativeness

A critical issue in sampling is representativeness. That is, the sample chosen must represent the population of interest sufficiently that the analyzed data can be generalized to the population. In general, the researcher must be sufficiently confident in the sampling procedures and the results of the study to say that the outcome is probably true for the sampled population. For example, it would not be helpful in an evaluation study to state that clients are generally satisfied with a service if the sampled group did not include those who were least satisfied. In such a case, the researcher must be certain to sample all segments of a population that might give diverse responses to the study's questions.

In family therapy research, we are sometimes less interested in the precision of generalization to larger populations, however, than in feeling rather certain that the information gathered is sufficiently comprehensive that it is useful for informing recommendations or opinions about a topic: Does it represent all or most opinions? In the BFTS project, we were less interested in the precision of the information than in its comprehensiveness and therefore its usefulness to a broader population of family therapy supervisors and their trainees and the field of family therapy in general.

Sampling Techniques

Sampling begins with a decision about the size of the sample desired and the method for selecting the sample. A sampling *frame* is the group or list used for selecting potential respondents. This may be a complete list of the population or some subgroup. Two types of selection may be used: *probability* and *nonprobability* techniques. Probability sampling techniques are less prone to sampling error and thus are more representative of the population of interest. Nonprobability techniques may be used if generalizing to a population is not a critical issue but the information itself is needed and probability techniques are not possible or are too costly. In either case, the limitations of the method must be noted in reports. (See Jolliffe, 1986, for a more thorough discussion of error estimating techniques associated with different kinds of sampling methods; Fowler, 1988, and Warwick & Lininger, 1975 for detailed discussions of sampling methods.)

Probability Sampling. Probability sampling techniques (simple, systematic, stratified, and cluster) yield participants from the population of interest, each of whom has a known chance of being selected for the sample. *Simple random sampling* is considered the best method and the one with the least error (Hackett, 1981; Jolliffe, 1986; Kerlinger, 1986). In this method, a complete list of the targeted population is used and participants are chosen through random selection procedures. This may mean assigning a number to each potential subject and using a computer or table generated list of random numbers to select the sample. Such a method might be useful if one needed a sample of Clinical Members of the AAMFT.

Systematic sampling involves determining the proportion of the population needed in the sample and choosing each nth subject in a list. Instead of using a table of random numbers to determine each member of the sample, the researcher could choose one number from the table and then count out each nth person after that. For example, if there are 5,000 people in the population and 200 are needed for the sample, the researcher would use a table of random numbers to pick a starting point and then select each 25th person.

Stratified sampling involves random selection of participants from essential subgroups of a population (Miller, 1986). This ensures adequate representation from each group for description or comparison. For example, it may be important to describe or compare a population based on race. By chance, too few participants from some racial groups could be chosen using simple random sampling techniques. In this case, a proportionate number (based on known proportions of each group in the population) could be randomly chosen from each group. If the number of cases chosen in this way is too small for some groups, *disproportionate* numbers can be chosen from each group (Miller, 1986). Although the results of the study might not generalize well to the entire population, it is more likely that the data will be comprehensive and representative of the diversity of the population. Congressional district lines are sometimes drawn with this principle in mind: to ensure that certain segments of the population are not excluded by chance or by sheer weight of the rest of the population.

Finally, *cluster* or *multistage* sampling may be used to assist in selecting respondents when the population is very large or there is no available listing of the total population. In this method, participants are selected in stages, beginning by randomly choosing sections of the population and then randomly choosing participants from these sections. For example, if a researcher wanted to survey licensed or certified marriage and family therapists in the United States, obtaining a complete list would be very difficult. However, a researcher could randomly choose several states that certify or license marriage and family therapists and then obtain lists of certified or licensed therapists from those states. Participants would then be selected from those lists.

Nonprobability Sampling. Nonprobability sampling techniques may be used when representativeness of a whole population is not as important as the information itself or when probability sampling is not feasible. Nonprobability sampling significantly increases sampling error and introduces bias into the sample (Miller, 1986). Sometimes, this bias can be accounted for and taken into consideration when reporting the results of the project. At other times, it will compromise the results so badly that they are not useful. This is most obvious when the bias is related to the purpose of the project. For example, a health survey that could not question hospitalized participants could yield extremely skewed and therefore useless data. In any case, the limitations and strengths of the method should be explained in reports so that readers may draw their own conclusions about potential sample bias.

Judgmental, purposive, or *expert* sampling may be appropriate when data from a particular group is required and the researcher uses some rational method for selecting participants. In the BFTS project, we were interested in opinions from those who were most expert at training family therapists. Therefore, we used lists of AAMFT Approved Supervisors and members of AFTA as our expert *panel.* Data from a general list of clinicians would not have been useful because we wanted expert trainers of beginning family therapists. Because we did not have access to a list of *all* supervisors or trainers in family therapy, whether members of organizations or not, ours was not a probability sample and thus contained both known and unknown bias.

Quota sampling involves determining how many people from particular groups or subgroups are needed and then selecting participants nonrandomly until the determined number for each group is reached. Although this method ensures adequate numbers from each group to represent the population, it does not satisfy the criterion that each subject in the population has a known chance of being selected; persons in the smaller groups have a greater chance of being selected than those in the larger groups. However, economy of time and other resources may make this method expeditious, particularly when there are unequal numbers in groups.

A third nonprobability method of selecting participants uses *haphazard* or *convenience* techniques. These methods often entail using participants who are "handy," but the sample will probably not be representative of a population. For example, family therapy researchers may be interested in certain characteristics of couples who enter therapy. It would be very difficult to obtain a list of all couples in therapy, but relatively easy (with permission) to determine the names of couples who are in therapy at the PDQ Clinic. The researchers may draw some tentative conclusions from this sample about couples in therapy, but the sample is actually representative of only the PDQ Clinic at a particular point in time.

Snowball or word-of-mouth samples are also convenience samples (Miller, 1986). In this strategy, participants are solicited who then suggest other potential participants. The danger is that the bias of the sample becomes compounded (students tend to suggest other students, for example). This is a reasonable method, however, when a nonclinical sample is needed that matches a clinical sample in terms of age, education, and economic status. The participants in the clinical sample are likely to suggest people similar to themselves for the matched sample.

All sampling techniques have limitations as well as advantages. It is important for researchers to understand and comment on the limitations of the sampling techniques they use. It is also important to state any deviance from standard techniques. For example, a mail survey may yield an unacceptably low response rate. The researcher may telephone those participants he or she believes will respond with a little encouragement. Although this technique may increase the response rate, it also biases the sample. The trade-off may be worth the bias introduced, but it is important that the researcher include the potential for this bias in the research reports. Suggestions for increasing response rates are included in a later section of this chapter.

Decisions regarding sampling techniques should take into account many factors, including the resources of the researcher as well as the questions being investigated. When precision is required, random sampling techniques that may cost more in terms of time and money are essential. However, when the research is exploratory, the potential population quite large, lists difficult to obtain, the potential biases of a sample well-known, precision or ability to generalize to a population not essential, or the resources of the researcher low, convenience samples may be more appropriate or acceptable. On occasion, a mixed method of sampling will be adequate, with multiple stages and mixes of probability and nonprobability methods. Researchers should be aware, however, that sampling techniques are critical when articles are being judged for publication.

Nonrespondents

It is often as important in survey research to know the biases of the nonrespondent portion of the population as well as the biases of the survey respondents. Because, to some extent, most survey research involves self-selected nonrespondents (those who choose not to respond), the reasons for not responding are often quite important. In the BFTS project, for example, our response rate for Phase IV was lower than in other phases. We surmised that this had as much to do with fatigue from our barrage of questionnaires, waning interest, and competing demands for time as with any other reason. Ideally, we would have found some way to sample nonrespondents to ascertain potential bias. However, this process would have required that these people *respond* to us, something we did not think they were likely to do. Therefore, we examined demographic variables to determine differences between this group of respondents and groups from earlier phases of the project. We noted that the response group in this phase, compared with other phases, contained a higher percentage of supervisors with doctoral degrees, who listed university settings as primary places of employment and "researcher" as a secondary professional identity. We then surmised that these respondents were more likely to participate in the project because the results of our survey might apply to their work or they felt an obligation to help fellow researchers. We also hypothesized that this group included a higher proportion of supervisors working with master's-level graduate students, an ideal situation for our research as we needed those who supervised *beginners* who were working with their first families in therapy and therefore who were in graduate school. If we had been looking for a broader array of items, generalizable to intermediate trainees (i.e., those who were not in graduate school but still under supervision), our results would have been much less useful.

Data-Gathering Techniques

In survey research, the investigator gathers data by asking people questions. Strictly speaking, an *interview* is the format that the investigator uses to ask questions and can be conducted in person, over the telephone, through mailed questionnaires, or in some other way (Jolliffe, 1986). A *questionnaire* is the list of questions or items used in any of the interview methods. Each method has its own advantages and disadvantages.

The format for gathering data should follow from the research questions asked. Researchers also must consider issues related to costs in terms of money, personnel, training time, and so on and choose the best method given the research questions and available resources. Sometimes it is better to reframe a research question so that an appropriate method can be afforded than to choose a design that cannot yield adequate data. For example, the first phase of the BFTS project yielded many hundreds of nominated skill items. Many of these were worded rather vaguely or in ambiguous terms. It might have been better at that point to abandon (or modify) the mailed questionnaire interview format and phone a sample of respondents so that we could ask probing questions. Because ours was an expert panel sample, the data were not confidential and this would have been possible. We might have had fewer respondents (with different limitations) but better data to work with. A colleague (Lee Williams, personal communication, 1991) is fond of reminding us that one can usually have two out of three desirable components: time, money, and quality. That is, one can rarely have a high-quality, inexpensive project that takes a minimal amount of time. One of the three nearly always must be sacrificed and the researcher must find the best balance for the project.

Personal and Telephone Interviews

Personal interviews are the most effective means for gathering in-depth information from people about their opinions, beliefs, or attitudes (Kerlinger, 1986). Skilled and trained interviewers can ask follow-up and probing questions that yield rich data for analysis (Downs, Smeyak, & Martin, 1980; Warwick & Lininger, 1975). Personal interviews also ensure data validity as the interviewer can more easily verify certain kinds of data or give an opinion as to the truthfulness of the subject. Personal interviews are the best means for gathering data that will be analyzed using qualitative methods. Finally, interviewers can keep journals called *field notes* that serve to inform the context of the data and enrich the data source by adding observer data. Personal interviews are also useful when the researcher is generalizing to *theory* rather than to *populations* (Moon, Dillon, & Sprenkle, 1990).

The chief disadvantage of personal interviews for survey research is their cost in terms of time and money relative to the number of participants surveyed. Also, respondents may be less inclined to cooperate with highly personal or embarrassing questions unless the interviewers are well trained and effective at establishing rapport and motivating the respondents. Researchers must be very careful and very clear about the process they use for selecting and training interviewers, for enhancing response rates, and for gathering data.

Telephone interviews offer many of the advantages of personal interviews with different disadvantages. They are more effective when larger numbers of people must be interviewed (Warwick & Lininger, 1975) or when the respondents are known to have a stake in the research and have previously agreed to participate. Participants' responses can be clarified and probed, and costs per interview are lower. They may not be as effective, however, if personal or sensitive questions are asked (Fowler, 1988). A great disadvantage is the increasing tendency of people to refuse to respond. Random digit dialing has the potential for reducing bias in telephone surveys (unlisted numbers can still be dialed), but this practice may have contributed to the increased "bother" factor that leads people to refuse to participate. Response rates may be increased by sending advance letters explaining the purpose and usefulness of the survey or combining phone questions with in-person or mailed questions. In-person interviews may take more time but can be used to "hook" the participants and may be followed by telephone interviews or mailed questionnaires. Participants then are familiar with the interviewer or the project and may be more likely to respond.

The format for the interviews in either in-person or telephone questionnaires can be *structured, semistructured,* or *unstructured.* Structured interviews are those in which the interviewer must follow a set list of questions, using verbatim phrases and clarifying statements which are consistent across all participants. Semistructured interviews ask closed questions which may then be followed by open questions for clarification or depth. They may also ask predetermined open questions, followed by probing or clarifying questions based on the participant's response as well as the interviewer's judgment. This method often provides both quantitative and qualitative data. Unstructured interviews are those informed by the purpose of the study, often using the researcher as the "instrument." Guided by the questions associated with the purpose and theory of the project, the researcher asks probing open questions that may change from respondent to respondent, depending on responses from previous participants (Moon et al., 1990). This kind of interview is not usually done with large samples, however, and the results inform theory rather than describe populations. (See Downs et al., 1980; Tanur, 1992, for excellent texts on interviewing techniques and cognitive aspects of surveys.)

Self-Administered Questionnaires (SAQ)

The most common method of gathering survey data in marriage and family therapy to date is through self-administered, mailed questionnaires (SAQ). Typically, a population is identified, lists of potential participants are gathered and sampled, and questionnaires are mailed to the selected sample. This method has advantages over personal or telephone interviews when the information needed is easily obtained from written, self-administered questionnaires; when the sample is likely to be interested in the subject matter; when larger numbers of respondents are needed than could easily be obtained in personal interviews; and when the researcher wishes to keep the data gathering time to a minimum.

The disadvantages of SAQ formats are not inconsequential. Often, it is difficult or impossible to determine the response bias of the sample. More important, however, is the inability to know the "response set" of the respondents because follow-up or probing questions are uncommon. In the BFTS project, for example, many of the skill items were rather vaguely worded (we used the exact words of the nominated items whenever possible) and so were open to interpretation. We do not know how differently the members of our sample interpreted the items and gave them a Likert score rather than "admit" a lack of familiarity with the item. That is, some respondents may have had a "set" or been predisposed to use the Likert responses. Some may even have had a "set" to answer "very important" more frequently, reducing the variance in their responses.

In addition to deciding how to obtain the information required for the research project, the researcher must also decide how to format the questionnaires. Good SAQs are designed with two issues in mind: (1) motivating respondents to complete the questionnaire and (2) providing reliable, valid data for the research analyses. Questions are typically classified as either closed or open. Closed questions are those that ask for yes–no or fixed-choice responses. Questions about demographic information usually fall into this category, as do checklists, ratings, rankings, or any question that requires simply marking or otherwise indicating a specific response from two or more choices. Closed questions are the easiest to code for analysis and are easily quantifiable. Open questions are those that allow respondents to answer the question in their own words. Although open questions require more from the investigator in terms of coding and analyzing the data, these responses are less restrictive and often contain less researcher bias. For example, the researcher could ask, "What kind of supervision do you prefer: live or case consultation?" The information obtained from this closed question will be very different from that obtained through the open question, "What kind of supervision best facilitates your learning?"

Closed or fixed-choice questions can be followed with probing, open ones. They can also be followed with invitations to add to a list or comment on the question; the researcher can then decide what to do with the data. The researcher needs to think carefully about potential bias in the questions, in their presentation, and in the format allowed for responses. Pretesting or pilot testing is invaluable at this stage. Pretesting also helps determine how long an interview or self-administered questionnaire may take a respondent to complete.

Questions can be asked through the investigator's own, personally developed questionnaire or through one that has been standardized with known utility, validity, and reliability. Most research uses a combination of standardized and self-developed questionnaires. Many standardized instruments have themselves been developed using survey methods.

The researcher must take great care to construct questions that yield usable responses. In the BFTS project, we solicited Likert-type ratings of many different nominated basic skill items. After the first phase, we needed to add several categorical response choices for further phases because our sample told us that they did not understand the meaning of some items and needed, for example, "don't understand this item" as a response choice.

Good questions are short and simple, ask only one question, are unambiguous, are not leading, are positive (do not use "not"), tap knowledge the respondent has (rather than asking for information about something unfamiliar), will be understood similarly across respondents, and are not unnecessarily detailed or objectionable (de Vaus, 1986). In the BFTS project, we did not define *skills* for our sample, resulting in responses that included what some might call *personality characteristics*. This was serendipitous for us, but investigators should be careful to anticipate their respondents and make sure that they will get usable information by not asking ambiguous questions. Pilot testing is invaluable for this purpose. Other factors must be balanced in terms of the time it takes participants to answer the questions, the face validity of the instrument, and the comprehensiveness of the questions.

In addition to thinking about the particular questions asked, the investigator should pay careful attention to the ordering, formatting, and esthetics of the questionnaire. Questions in different forms can be asked in different orders to reduce fatigue or boredom. Mailed or self-administered questionnaires should be easy to read, with sufficient white space so that respondents are not daunted. Type style and size should be plain and clear and instructions placed frequently so that respondents do not need to page back and forth to find response choices. Response rates can be increased by making sure the questionnaires are appropriate for the average reading level of the sample and pleasing to the eye. They also should be free of typographical and spelling errors. These ideas may seem obvious, but more than one poorly proofread questionnaire has been tossed into the round file. Pilot studies can reduce this particular cause of nonresponse. Warwick and Lininger (1975) include an excellent, timeless discussion of the elements associated with a good questionnaire.

Good survey researchers pay a lot of attention to the questions they ask and how they ask them. Spending time on the design of the project at this stage can save a lot of headaches and problems later on. Many researchers have been unable to publish their results because a critical element was overlooked in the planning stage and questions about an important variable were omitted from the questionnaire.

Increasing Response Rates

Methods for carrying out mail survey research and increasing response rates have been suggested by Dillman (1978), Dillman and Frey (1974), and Dillman et al. (1974). When followed, Dillman's methods yield acceptable response rates (60–80%) for generalizing at least some information to the population of interest and for reporting both aggregate and comparative data analyses. In general, the procedure is to send the questionnaire instruments with cover letters and self-addressed stamped envelopes. Reminder and/or thank-you postcards are sent about 10 days later. Ten days after that, the researcher sends a second set of instruments to nonrespondents with a third set mailed after that. Response rates tend to be better in projects in which the sample is likely to be interested in the topic of the research.

Dillman (1978) also suggests using personalized letters, not difficult even with large samples, using merge capabilities of computer word processors. It should be noted that Dillman's beliefs that these methods increase mailed survey response rates are based on his research with the general population, not with such specialized populations as those used in family therapy research. Cover letters should be inviting and simple, rather than technical and complex, friendly but not too familiar, and should clearly express the potential benefits to the respondents and the field.

Data Coding and Storing

After the data are collected, they must be analyzed in some fashion. To do this, they must be transformed into usable data units for either quantitative or qualitative analysis. Many researchers do not put enough thought into this phase early enough in the project and begin coding and entering data into a database without carefully considering how the data will be analyzed. Consultations with data managers or statisticians can be very helpful at this time. Researchers also should think about how they want to handle missing data: drop cases, use means (or some other measure of central tendency), or allow the statistical computer package to use its default mode. Manuals for the statistical computer package that will be used can be consulted for advice, along with a statistician.

Data from survey research are usually converted to numbers of some kind, with each number representing either a category of information (e.g., race) or a numerical value placed on an item by the subject, as with Likert-type ratings. In either case, and however the researcher wishes to code and store data, a code book is essential. This book should list all methods in the study, including research variables, their positions in database records, and the meanings of different values. It is useful to know the details of how the statistical software manages data while setting up the code book and database structures. The data code book also should include a narrative developed over the life of the project, describing decisions, procedures, and so forth. Although this may seem cumbersome and time-consuming, it can be invaluable later on when a manuscript reviewer asks, "What about . . . ?" or when the researcher wants to recall why a particular decision was made.

As with all other research, it is extremely important to "proof" or clean data that have been entered into a database. Each record in the database should be compared to its corresponding raw data and corrected in the master database. Once the master database has been "cleaned," it should be stored in some form that cannot be changed and a written copy kept in a safe place. It also is useful to include descriptions of the data in the database in the form of "comments." Too much data have been scrapped because no one knew the meaning of numbers in a database. This sometimes can be reconstructed from raw data if the data have not been transformed or reorganized in some way (and the raw data is available). However, it is much better to take time to keep careful notes during the project and to explain the data as much as possible in comments in the data base. Current computer database capabilities make this relatively easy.

Data Analysis

Data from survey research are analyzed according to the kinds of research questions asked and the kinds of data gathered. That is, are the research questions asking for *descriptive*, *associative* (correlational or comparative), or *predictive* results? Are the data *qualita-*

tive or *quantitative; nominal, ordinal, interval,* or *ratio?* Other chapters of this book, other texts, and statistical consultants can help determine the best analytical methods for the project. A thorough discussion is beyond the scope of this chapter and the following material is introductory only.

Statistical analyses can be grouped as *univariate, bivariate,* or *multivariate,* depending on the number of variables being considered. Univariate statistics provide descriptions of single variables: frequencies and distributions of values (how did this sample respond in an overall picture), statistics of central tendency (what is the average or most frequent response), and dispersion (how much variability is there in the responses; what is the range) (Miller, 1986). These analyses yield results that describe the sample on the variables of interest, both independent and dependent. Reports usually include descriptions of demographics or independent variables. Analyses of dependent variables usually require adhering to assumptions about *randomly selected samples* and *normal* distributions of responses or scores; therefore, it is important to report sampling methods and descriptive statistics so that readers can judge the appropriateness of the inferential analyses or so they can compare other samples to the one reported.

Bivariate and multivariate analyses are usually considered *inferential* because they infer characteristics or comparisons of random samples rather than directly observe them. Bivariate analyses consider two variables simultaneously. *Cross tabulations* are frequency tables that group nominal variables against each other in distributions. For example, a researcher may want to know how variables are distributed across sex and educational level. Researchers may want to know how variables are associated (correlated or compared) and how strong the association is. This requires analyses such as *correlations, chi-square, t tests,* or *analyses of variance.*

Multivariate analyses involve more than two variables, either independent or dependent, using *canonical correlations, multiple analysis of variance* (MANOVA), and analyses that take into account variables that *covary* in some way (*analysis of covariance,* ANCOVA). Multiple variables can be collapsed into new variables with underlying common dimensions using *factor analyses.* Factor analysis is especially useful in developing new instruments. Respondents can be formed into groups according to shared patterns of responses using *cluster analyses.* Finally, dependent variables can be predicted from multiple independent variables through analyses such as *regression, discriminant function analysis,* and *path analysis.* Path analysis and other structural modeling tools can be used to test hypotheses of how variables should relate according to theoretical principles. The Survey Research Center of the Institute for Social Research at the University of Michigan has published a book that leads the researcher through a decision tree to appropriate statistical tests that can be used for data analyses depending upon levels and number of variables and how the researcher wants these variables treated (Andrews, Klem, Davidson, O'Malley, & Rodgers, 1981). This should not substitute for trained knowledge or statistical consultation, however.

Reporting

A very important and little discussed issue relates to how and where research is reported. Survey research has many uses and can be reported in many legitimate forums including newspapers; refereed journals; and state, regional, national, and international conferences. At least as important as where the research is reported is *how* it is reported. Rsearchers should think carefully about their audience and write toward the needs of that audience. For readers to gain as much as possible from the report, researchers must include clear descriptions of the research questions; the methods used for sampling the population and gathering the data, including methods used to increase response rates; incentives; a description of the sample; interview strategies; descriptions of the questions on the questionnaires; analysis methods; and analysis results. Interview strategies should describe unusual features of a questionnaire format and how interviewers were trained and supervised. Researchers should take particular care in describing the limitations of the research, including sample bias and any information that may be known about those who did not respond to the survey. Conclusions and recommendations should clearly relate to the data, with logical connections that will make sense to the audience. Results and speculations that do not relate clearly to the research questions or data can be confusing and misleading.

DISCUSSION

Strengths and Weaknesses

The greatest strength of survey research lies in its ability to gather large amounts of data from a number of participants in a relatively short amount of time. It is the method of choice when the researcher wants opinions from a number of readily identified people who are willing and able to answer the questions and when they are the *only* ones who can answer the questions (about beliefs, opinion, attitudes, or values, for example) (Miller, 1986). For appropriately conducted, large-sample research, researchers are able to make inferences about a population with reasonable certainty. It certainly is the method of choice when general descriptions about "normal" distributions of variables in a population are required. It is an extremely flexible method, allowing much latitude in the variables studied and the strategies for studying them. Surveys that question clinicians and report the results in forums and formats that are useful to them add to the credibility of the field of family therapy research.

The greatest weakness of survey research is the ease with which each step can be done carelessly, adding considerably to both sampling and nonsampling error and thus producing biased or nonvalid results. Each step assumes certain things and, to the extent that these assumptions are violated, the method will produce results that are not valid. Survey research is not useful when respondents may be unwilling or unable to provide accurate, reliable information. For example, asking families how cohesive they are would probably yield biased data, whereas an indirect method of asking for this information (e.g., FACES; Olson, Portner, & Lavee, 1985) would yield data that have relevance as compared to the researcher's definition (rather than the family's) and as compared to a normative sample.

It is often difficult to replicate survey research, even when each step has been clearly described in the research report. There are many unknown aspects of the process that cannot be replicated or controlled: the response sets, recall ability, or unique reactions of the respondents, for example. In this sense, meta-analytical methods may be more appropriate for discerning "true" distributions of variables.

A final concern about survey research relates to its meaning. Scientific inquiry is usually interested in the statistical significance of research results. In the field of family therapy, we are also interested in the practical or clinical significance of results. This means that analyses may produce results that suggest that two or more groups are, indeed, statistically different, but this difference may not make a practical or clinical difference—may not have meaning to either the researcher or the readers of a report. In discussion sections, this is the "so what" of the research: what difference does this finding make, beyond its veracity, to further research or to clinical practice? For example, two groups may be statistically different in terms of scores on a marital satisfaction questionnaire. This may have been concluded because there was a sample of sufficient size and an instrument with sufficient power to produce a difference at the $p < .01$ level. However, the test could have been so powerful that a difference in means of only 2 points produced these results; that is, the test showed that the probability of finding this result due to chance only is less than 1%. The practical difference of 2 points on the measured scores is something only the researcher can determine.

In-depth conclusions cannot be made from results of this kind of research because its purpose is to provide *aggregate* accounts of groups. Instead of being scrutinized for their meaning, outliers are sometimes discarded as products of error rather than as true data. This means that statistically significant results of data analyses from large numbers of participants may have less meaning for both researchers and clinicians than might trends derived from closer examination of in-depth data from fewer participants.

Survey research is usually carried out from a perspective of attempting to discover some "truth" or fact about a population or sample, without taking into account perspectives that might suggest alternative ways of viewing the problem (is it indeed a problem? for whom?), the constructs behind the questions, and the multiplicity of ways that respondents make meaning out of what is presented to them. That is, survey research may produce accurate numbers about a variable, its distribution in a sample, and its relationship to other variables. What the descriptions and relationships *mean*, however, is a subjective issue of interpretation. Researchers should be careful to distinguish the difference.

Reliability

Research is useful only if the information received is reliable and valid. In survey research, the reliability, or accuracy and dependability, of responses is greatly affected by many factors in the participants' contexts, many of which cannot be controlled by the researcher or are unknown to the researcher. Fortunately, the reliability of averages is greater than the reliability of individual responses (Kerlinger, 1986). That is, although a single subject may respond differently to a questionnaire depending on mood, current issues, or misunderstanding, many participants as a whole are less subject to the same variations. Outliers do not affect results as much. In the BFTS project, we believe that many suggestions for what is a necessary skill for beginning therapists depended upon recent experience of the respondent. That is, if the most recent trainee had exhibited poor skills in moderating intense interactions, the participant was more likely to nominate "ability to control in-room interactions" than if trainees recently had demonstrated good control of interactions. These kinds of responses, if surveyed a second time, might have less likelihood of appearing on a list of nominated items. However, given the *number* of participants responding to the survey (more than 600), the nominated items were likely to reliably reflect opinions of the sample.

Researchers should use statistical tools to determine the reliability of their surveys. A subsample may be asked to respond to the instrument a second time, some weeks after the first administration of the instrument. This method has obvious drawbacks in terms of the bias introduced with such a self-selected sample. Wetchler (1989; Wetchler et al., 1989), however, asked respondents in the first survey if they would be willing to participate in a reliability test–retest study. He then randomly sampled from this list of respondents. Because survey research, by definition, entails the use of self-selected samples in many ways, this method may compound the bias. A second method is to resurvey a randomly selected subsample. Self-selection is a factor in this method also, but less so than in the first. The responses can be compared using agreement correlations, frequently Cohen's *kappa* (Cohen, 1960, 1968). Other statistics (e.g., Cronbach's [1951] *alpha*) may be used with some instruments to determine the consistency of the participants in responding to questions that are part of a composite or global measure.

Reliability can be increased in survey research through several methods, most of them quite reasonable. The easiest method is to make sure that the questions are clear and unambiguous so that the responses are not as likely to change from respondent to respondent depending on their interpretations of what they think is meant or wanted. Reliability also can be increased by having a sufficient number of items for all subscales and by making the length of the survey reasonable so that fatigue does not hinder the participants' ability to be thoughtful rather than careless about responding to the items.

Validity

Data are useful only to the extent that they correspond to the research questions and measure what they are intended to measure. There are basic kinds of validity: criterion, content, and construct. For criterion validity, the data are compared to existing measures of the same concept or phenomenon. This is often difficult in MFT research. For example, attempts to measure Bowen's (1978) concept of differentiation of self are notoriously difficult (Nelson, 1987). For content validity, different aspects of the content of the question are tied to definitions of the concept. For example, in the BFTS project, we asked our respondents to consider *basic* skills for *beginning* family therapists and sampled only those supervisors who had recent experience with beginning trainees, defined as "less than 100 clinical contact hours" rather than the respondent's personal definition of "beginner." Finally, construct validity is established by noting a questionnaire's performance compared to theoretical notions. Less experienced therapists, for example, might have experience with fewer ethical dilemmas than more experienced therapists and therefore list few dilemmas in a survey. This may not mean that they are not aware of ethical issues in family therapy but simply that they are less experienced with them. "In the end," however, "there is no ideal way of determining the validity of a measure" (de Vaus, 1986, p. 49). If there were, direct observations of the phenomena would suffice.

In family therapy survey research, validity is often established through careful examination of the items used in the inquiry. Independent judges, knowledgable in the topic of interest, can make recommendations about how well the items address the researcher's questions. Because most surveys are unique and the questionnaires may not have already established reliability and validity, comparing whatever information is possible can help establish the validity of the data. For example, if the researcher claims that the sample is representative of the population on many demographic variables, evidence of this in terms of known demographic statistics would enhance the researchers' claims to validity. It is essential to pilot test the instruments and instructions and then incorporate feedback into the design of the project.

One difficulty in establishing validity relates to the response set of the participants when they respond to the questionnaire. Not only does mood affect the reliability of the information given, it also can affect the validity, especially when the questions are ambiguous or worded in ways that require a particular response set. For example, asking which items are most important from a list is very different from asking which items are important; the first "set" may assume that *all* items are important to some degree whereas the second suggests that some items are important and others are not. The researcher must be very careful in interpreting data from such questions because claiming that items with low scores are "not important" rather than "less important" may not be a valid conclusion of the study. Again, using opinions from independent judges, with expertise in the subject matter and who might be similar to the surveyed sample, can increase the strength of the data.

Skills

To a great extent, the survey researcher must possess the skills of both the experimental researcher and the case study researcher. As in all research, the project is only as strong as its total design, from formulation of research questions or hypotheses through design of the procedures and sample selection, careful choices or design of instruments, and good knowledge of research analysis and reporting procedures. The survey researcher must also be a skilled consumer of research. That is, in order to obtain good results and report them in a meaningful way, the researcher must be familiar with the field of study, issues of sampling and potential bias, and the meaning of the data in the context from which they are drawn and in which they are reported. It does little good to survey family therapy educators about the strengths and weaknesses of their programs if the researcher is not familiar with the external standards or institutional constraints on programs and recommends sweeping and impossible reforms without this contextual information.

An essential skill for the survey researcher is in consulting with others. Good researchers use experts to help formulate questions for interviews or questionnaires, run pilot tests on knowledgeable participants to refine the questionnaire content and appearance as well as the data-gathering procedures, and consult with statisticians about the design of the study early, before needing help with analyses of data. It is interesting that some of the best reported research was accomplished by doctoral candidates for their dissertations, under the watchful eye of committees. Although students perennially complain about the rigor of research done in this context, the results are often more meaningful and less wasteful of resources. In some ways, editors and reviewers serve a similar function, but at the end rather than at the beginning of the project. Researchers can keep this in mind, however, as they design their studies.

The survey researcher must have patience and an ability to plan with great detail. This same patience can make analyzing the data more fruitful when the researcher is skilled at seeing patterns in data that may not be apparent in the numerical statistics generated from the data. That is, in looking over the questionnaires, or listening to recorded interviews, the researcher may begin to see patterns that suggest further interesting analysis, refinement of the research, or future studies.

Bridging Research and Practice

Survey research is a good way to bridge the gap between researchers and clinicians because it can easily use clinicians and their clients as participants. Other survey research in family therapy has questioned training programs and supervisors; these data are of interest to clinicians because we all have opinions about the strengths and weaknesses of our training and about what should be included in family therapy education. In other ways, survey research responds to questions that clinicians ask: What are people doing, how are they doing it, and what do they think about it? Clinicians should be able to use the results of research to keep themselves current in their practices. Researchers should survey clinicians about what kinds of research they pay attention to, what kinds of research they would like to see conducted, how they would use this research, and how they might be willing to participate.

A most useful way that researchers help bridge the gap between their work and their colleagues' is how they report the results. Publishing articles in refereed professional journals is useful for tenure and promotion but may not be the best way to capture the interest and attention of clinician nonresearchers. Venues such as *The Family Therapy Networker* or conference presentations and workshops may be better suited for this purpose. In these instances, the report language and formatting must be geared toward application, with many examples of clinical usefulness.

FUTURE DIRECTIONS

An interesting phenomenon is just beginning and that entails use of electronic media for conducting survey research. I recently noticed a request for participation in a survey that was posted on an Internet list and I have participated in an electronic Delphi panel for another project. There are numerous specific questions and concerns that come to mind about this practice, but my guess is that the practice will continue and grow. We also have the capability now of sending out questionnaires on computer disks, through modems, or with electronic mail rather than mailed paper-and-pencil instruments. This practice raises interesting questions and challenges as well as advantages that are just beginning to be explored.

The potential for survey research is in its breadth and depth: It can be used to ask many kinds of questions, from many kinds of populations and samples, and reported in a wide variety of ways. Its heuristic value for pointing the field in useful directions is well established because its results often ask more questions than they answer. It is precisely this stance of curiosity and openness that makes survey research in family therapy useful and informative, as researchers and clinicians apply its results to their practices, to their theory, and to further research.

REFERENCES

Andrews, F. M., Klem, L., Davidson, T. N., O'Malley, P. M., & Rodgers, W. L. (1981). *A guide for selecting statistical techniques for analyzing social science data* (2nd ed.). Ann Arbor, MI: Institute for Social Research, University of Michigan.

Boughner, S. R., Hayes, S. F., Bubenzer, D. L., & West, J. D. (1994). Use of standardized assessment instruments by marital and family therapists: A survey. *Journal of Marital and Family Therapy, 20,* 69–75.

Bowen, M. (1978). *Family therapy in clinical practice.* New York: Jason Aronson.

Bray, J. H., Williamson, D. S., & Malone, P. E. (1984). Personal authority in the family system: Development of a questionnaire to measure personal authority in intergenerational processes. *Journal of Marital and Family Therapy, 10,* 167–178.

Carter, R. E. (1989). Residency training and the later use of marital and family therapy in psychiatric practice. *Journal of Marital and Family Therapy, 15,* 411–418.

Cohen, J. A. (1960). A coefficient of agreement for nominal scales. *Educational and Psychological Measurement, 20,* 37–46.

Cohen, J. (1968). Weighted *kappa:* Nominal scale agreement with provision for scaled disagreement or partial credit. *Psychological Bulletin, 70,* 213–220.

Coleman, S. B., Myers Avis, J., & Turin, M. (1990). A study of the role of gender in family therapy training. *Family Process, 29,* 365–374.

Cronbach, L. J. (1951). Coefficient alpha and the internal structure of tests. *Psychiatrika, 16,* 297–334.

de Vaus, D. A. (1986). *Surveys in social research.* Boston: George Allen & Unwin.

Dillman, D. A. (1978). *Mail and telephone surveys: The total design method.* New York: Wiley.

Dillman, D.A., Carpenter, E., Christensen, J., & Brooks, R. (1974). Increasing mail questionnaire response: A four state comparison. *American Sociological Review, 39,* 744–756.

Dillman, D. A., & Frey, J. H. (1974). Contribution of personalization to mail questionnaire response as an element of a previously tested method. *Journal of Applied Psychology, 59,* 297–301.

Doherty, W. J., Lester, M. E., & Leigh, G. (1986). Marriage encounter weekends: Couples who win and couples who lose. *Journal of Marital and Family Therapy, 12,* 49–61.

Downs, C. W., Smeyak, G. P., & Martin, E. (1980). *Professional interviewing.* New York: Harper & Row.

Epstein, N. B., Baldwin, L. M., & Bishop, D. S. (1983). The McMaster Family Assessment Device. *Journal of Marital and Family Therapy, 11,* 171–180.

Figley, C. R., & Nelson, T. S. (1989). Basic family therapy skills, I: Conceptualization and initial findings. *Journal of Marital and Family Therapy, 15,* 349–365.

Figley, C. R., & Nelson, T. S. (1990). Basic family therapy skills, III: Brief and strategic schools of family therapy. *Journal of Family Psychotherapy, 4,* 49–62.

Fink, A., & Kosecoff, J. (1985). *How to conduct surveys: A step-by-step guide.* Newbury Park, CA: Sage.

Fowler, F. J., Jr. (1988). *Survey research methods.* Newbury Park, CA: Sage.

Green, S. L., & Hansen, J. C. (1986). Ethical dilemmas in family therapy. *Journal of Marital and Family Therapy, 12,* 225–230.

Green, S.L., & Hansen, J.C. (1989). Ethical dilemmas faced by family therapists. *Journal of Marital and Family Therapy, 15,* 149–158.

Guralnik, D. B. (Ed.). (1966). *Webster's new world dictionary of the American language.* Nashville, TN: Southwestern.

Hackett, G. (1981). Survey research methods. *Personnel and Guidance Journal, 59,* 599–604.

Halik, V., Rosenthal, D. A., & Pattison, P. E. (1990). Intergenerational effects of the Holocaust: Patterns of engagement in the mother–daughter relationship. *Family Process, 29,* 325–339.

Heath, A. W., McKenna, B. C., & Atkinson, B. J. (1988). Toward the identification of variables for evaluating family therapy workshops. *Journal of Marital and Family Therapy, 14,* 267–276.

Jolliffe, F. R. (1986). *Survey design and analysis.* New York: Halstead Press.

Keller, J. F., Huber, J. R., & Hardy, K. V. (1988). Accreditation: What constitutes appropriate marriage and family therapy education? *Journal of Marital and Family Therapy, 14,* 297–305.

Kerlinger, F. N. (1986). *Foundations of behavioral research.* New York: Holt, Rinehart & Winston.

Kraemer, H. C., & Thiemann, S. (1987). *How many subjects? Statistical power analysis in research.* Newbury Park, CA: Sage.

Larson, J. H., Crane, D. R., & Smith, C. W. (1991). Morning and night couples: The effect of wake and sleep patterns on marital adjustment. *Journal of Marital and Family Therapy, 17,* 53–65.

Lewis, W., & Rohrbaugh, M. (1989). Live supervision by family therapists: A Virginia survey. *Journal of Marital and Family Therapy, 15,* 323–326.

Likert, R. (1932). A technique for measurement of attitudes. *Archives of Psychology, 140,* 52.

McGraw, D. L., & Watson, G. L. (1976). *Political and social inquiry.* New York: Wiley.

Miller, B. C. (1986). *Family research methods.* Newbury Park, CA: Sage.

Moon, S. M., Dillon, D. R., & Sprenkle, D. H. (1990). Family therapy and qualitative research. *Journal of Marital and Family Therapy, 16,* 357–373.

Nelson, T. S. (1987). *Bowen's concept of differentiation of self in clinical and nonclinical couples.* Unpublished doctoral dissertation, University of Iowa.

Nelson, T. S., & Figley, C. R. (1990). Basic family therapy skills, II: Structural family therapy. *Journal of Marital and Family Therapy, 16,* 225–239.

Nelson, T. S., Heilbrun, G., & Figley, C. R. (1993). Basic skills in family therapy, IV: Transgenerational theories of family therapy. *Journal of Marital and Family Therapy, 19,* 253–266.

Nichols, W. C., Nichols, D. P., & Hardy, K. V. (1990). Supervision in family therapy: A decade restudy. *Journal of Marital and Family Therapy, 16,* 275–285.

Nylund, D., & Thomas, J. (1994, November–December). The economics of narrative. *Family Therapy Networker, 18*(6), pp. 38–39.

Olson, D. H., Portner, J., & Lavee, Y. (1985). *FACES III.* St. Paul: University of Minnesota, Family Social Science.

O'Sullivan, M. J., & Gilbert, R. K. (1989). Master's degree programs in marital and family therapy: An evaluation of admission and program requirements. *Journal of Marital and Family Therapy, 15,* 337–347.

Quinn, W. H., & Davidson, B. (1984). Prevalence of family therapy models: A research note. *Journal of Marital and Family Therapy, 10,* 393–398.

Solomon, J., Ott, J., & Roach, A. (1986). A survey of training opportunities for predoctoral psychology interns in marriage and family therapy. *Journal of Marital and Family Therapy, 12,* 269–280.

Tanur, J. M. (Ed.). (1992). *Questions about questions: Inquiries into the cognitive bases of surveys.* New York: Russell Sage Foundation.

Warwick, D. P., & Lininger, C. A. (1975). *The sample survey: Theory and practice.* New York: McGraw-Hill.

Wetchler, J. L. (1989). Supervisors' and supervisees' perceptions of the effectiveness of family therapy supervisor interpersonal skills. *American Journal of Family Therapy, 17,* 244–256.

Wetchler, J. L., Piercy, F. P., & Sprenkle, D. H. (1989). Supervisors' and supervisees' perceptions of the effectiveness of family therapy supervisory techniques. *American Journal of Family Therapy, 17,* 35–47.

White, M. B., & Russell, C. S. (1995). The essential elements of supervisory systems: A modified Delphi study. *Journal of Marital and Family Therapy, 31,* 33–53.

Wilson, L. L., & Stith, S. M. (1993). The voices of African-American MFT students: Suggestions for improving recruitment and retention. *Journal of Marital and Family Therapy, 19,* 17–30.

21

The Delphi Method

LINDA STONE FISH
DEAN M. BUSBY

BACKGROUND

Dear Reader,

We would like to ask your help in a research study of considerable significance for family therapy researchers and clinicians. The present study is designed to compare and contrast the various research methodologies in the field by examining the opinions of prominent family therapists. The completion of the three questionnaires which will make up this study will require a total of no more than one and a half hours of your time. In appreciation of your participation, a complete summary of the findings and a list of the other panelists will be sent to you.

This study will employ the Delphi technique, a widely used method of gathering group consensus from a panel of knowledgeable persons. The Delphi technique assures anonymity of responses, reduces group pressure for conformity, and takes less time for panelists than traditional methods of pooling opinion. As an expert in the field of family therapy, your participation in the present research will be greatly appreciated.

With your help, this research will help clarify various research methodologies and their role in the family therapy field. We look forward to working with you in the weeks to come.

Respectfully,
LINDA STONE FISH, PH.D.   DEAN M. BUSBY, PH.D.

Sound interesting? This is the way Delphi research often begins. Researchers are curious about a particular topic in the field. It may be that they perceive the seeds of an idea germinating in the soil of family therapy (e.g., feminist-informed family therapy in the 1980s) or they perceive discrepancies in ideas that are fueling theory and practice (e.g., how are structural and strategic therapy the same and different). It may be that they have an opinion about a particular topic relevant to the field and want to know how expert colleagues around the country think about the same things (e.g., the strengths and weaknesses of families in the 1990s). Regardless of the idea, the researcher wants to pool experts on the subject. The researcher wants to structure communication about the idea so that consensus can be reached. He or she does not have the financial resources to pay all the experts to meet in one place. The Delphi method provides researchers with a way to gather consensus without face-to-face interaction. They do not want to do traditional surveying because then they just gather everyone's opinions without the benefit of participants receiving feedback from other survey participants. They want more of a dialogue about ideas, and the Delphi method allows this type of dialogue to take place.

Philosophical Assumptions

The Delphi method is based on the philosophical assumption that "n heads are better than one" (Dalkey, 1972). It is a procedure designed to sample a group of knowledgeable persons in order to gain a consensus of opinion on a particular topic. The Delphi method structures the communication of individuals in a way that allows for a group of individuals to deal with complex problems (Linstone & Turoff, 1975).

The Delphi structures the communication by providing a forum in which participants are able to express their opinions anonymously, gather feedback from the group about their views, access other views of the same ideas, and have an opportunity to revise their views. How the researcher designs and implements the Delphi technique is not as important as the philosophical assumption underlying its usage. The Delphi method rests on the idea that it is possible and often quite valuable to reach consensus through a collective human intelligence process (Linstone & Turoff, 1975). The view that truth is relative underlies the attempt to gather myriad opinions on a particular topic. Mitroff and Turoff (1975) explain the underpinnings of the Delphi by utilizing different components of the philosophies of Locke, Leibniz, Kant, Hegel, and Singer. Mitroff and Turoff are quick to suggest, however, that we must be careful not to rigidly define the philosophical assumptions underlying the Delphi. "We certainly no longer seem able to afford the faulty assumption that there is only one philosophical base upon which a technique can rest if it is to be 'scientific.' Indeed if our conception of inquiry is 'fruitful' (notice, not 'true' or 'false' but 'productive') then to be 'scientific' would demand that we study something (model it, collect data on it, argue it, etc.) from as many diverse points of view as possible" (Mitroff & Turoff, 1975, p. 36).

Scheele (1975), another Delphi method specialist, utilizes the ideas of Merleau-Ponty to define the assumptions underlying the philosophical base of the Delphi method. According to Scheele, "the Merleau-Pontyean is concerned with the particular reality created by the 'bracketing' of an event or idea out of the great din of experience, rather than explicating a pragmatic reality that can be used to define possible actions. Truth to the Merleau-Pontyean is agreement that enables action by confirming or altering 'what is normal' or to be expected" (p. 43). The Delphi method attempts to negotiate a reality that can then be useful in moving a particular field forward, planning for the future, or even changing the future by forecasting its events. The philosophical underpinnings of the Delphi, then, are concerned more with the application of useful knowledge than with the attempt to define the truth.

Historical Roots and Development

The Delphi method was named after the Greek town of Delphi. The ancient Greeks believed that Apollo, son of Zeus and god of light, purity, the sun, and prophecy, killed the dragon Python in Delphi. The temple in Delphi then contained the famous oracle, Pythia, whom Apollo chose to speak through to predict the future. She would turn around in a frenzy and utter strange sounds which would then be used for prediction. The Delphi method that is used today, based in a more rational, scientific paradigm, had its first usage in attempting to predict the future.

Although Quade (1967) reports the Delphi method's earliest use in the prediction of horse race outcomes, other leading Delphi specialists argue that the Delphi originated at the Rand Corporation and had its first application in defense and military matters (Dalkey & Helmer, 1963). The first Rand Corporation utilization of the Delphi, "Project Delphi," was an attempt to forecast the probability of a particular event. The Air Force was interested in what U.S. experts believed the Soviet Union thought was the optimal U.S. industrial target and how many A-bombs it would take to reduce the munitions output (Linstone & Turoff, 1975). Had the research team attempted to research this idea utilizing extant research practices, they would have had to use extremely difficult computer programs for the 1950s and would have had to estimate much of the input subjectively. Instead, they decided to gather a consensus of opinion as a means to identify the "truth."

Although defense practices were the first subject for the Delphi technique, it did not receive much publicity until Gordon and Helmer (1964) utilized it to forecast long-range trends in science and technology and their impact on society. This study, coupled with a paper by Helmer and Rescher (1960) entitled "On the epistemology of the inexact sciences," both done through the Rand Corporation, were used as catalysts for many other researchers to utilize the Delphi technique (Linstone & Turoff, 1975). The methodology proliferated in the 1960s and 1970s and continues to find application in fields dealing with other complex problems that face society, such as the environment, health, education, and transportation. The Delphi technique is also commonly used in psychology, sociology, and political science.

The Delphi technique found its way into family therapy through Dr. Sam Cochran of East Texas State University. Cochran utilized his experience as part of the Rand Corporation to bring the Delphi to the psychology department. He became a committee member of Wayne Winkle's family therapy dissertation. Under the advisorship of Dr. Fred Piercy, Winkle used the Delphi to reach a consensus of opinion about a model family therapy curriculum in the late 1970s (Winkle, Piercy, & Hovestadt, 1981). Family therapy researchers have been using the Delphi since the early 1980s, although most of the research utilizing this approach has been archived in dissertation abstracts. While the general field of psychotherapy has seen a number of studies utilizing the approach (e.g., Goplerud, Walfish, & Broskowski, 1985; Kaufman, Holden, & Walker, 1989; Norcross, Alford, & DeMichele, 1992; Thomson, 1990), the family therapy field has only seen a limited number of published articles using this technique.

The Delphi technique has been used in four family therapy research articles since the publication of Winkle's article in 1981. First, Stone Fish and Piercy (1987) used the Delphi to examine the similarities and differences between structural and strategic family therapies. In the second article, Stone Fish (1989) compared the results of the above mentioned Delphi with a Delphi poll conducted by Wheeler (1985) that explored the differences between extant family therapy practices and feminist-informed family therapy. Rago and Childers (1990) used the Delphi to survey family therapists about revisions in family therapy theories that may better accommodate the changing U.S. family. The last article published in the family therapy literature surveyed family therapy experts about the current strengths and weaknesses of family life in the United States (Stone Fish & Osborn, 1992).

METHODOLOGY

Research Questions

As a field undergoing continual transformation and theoretical and practical challenges, family therapy is well positioned to find the Delphi method useful. The family therapy research questions that are best answered by this methodology are those in which the researcher is trying to reach some consensus of opinion about a particular area. An additional use of this method is to develop policy issues for a field or profession regarding a relatively new phenomenon such as AIDS. Often what occurs is that a particular idea or a series of thoughts are germinating in the literature. The Delphi technique is available to help the researcher reach a consensus about particular ideas or predict the future of these ideas in the field.

A good example of the utility of the Delphi occurred in the early 1980s. Structural and strategic family therapies, two of the most popular approaches at the time, lacked both conceptual and practical clarity. There was much confusion in the field about whether to integrate the two approaches. It was often difficult to differentiate them because of overlap in both theory and practice. Clinicians throughout the country were calling themselves structural/strategic family therapists and outcome research combined the two schools into the same category (Stanton, Todd, & Associates, 1982). On the other hand, there were many leading theoreticians in the field (Fraser, 1982; MacKinnon, 1983; deShazer, 1984; Rohrbaugh, 1984) who believed that it would be a grave mistake to integrate the two approaches. A need existed to define both the structural and strategic approaches to family therapy, as well as their similarities and differences.

Although family therapy theorists (e.g., Beavers, 1981; Liddle, 1980; Sprenkle, 1976) were suggesting that the best family therapy practices are linked to some research base, it was proving difficult to research a therapy approach that lacked theoretical clarity. A consensus of opinion from a panel of expert structural and strategic therapists as to the similarities and differences inherent in these two approaches would help clarify the therapies and move the field forward. The Delphi method proved to be an excellent vehicle for researching this dilemma.

Sampling and Selection Procedures

Panel selection is a critical element in the Delphi method. Dalkey (1969) reports that panelists' knowledge of the subject matter at hand is the most significant assurance of a quality outcome using the Delphi method. Therefore, Delphi panelists are chosen for their expertise rather than through a random process. The researcher selects the panelists based on their knowledge of the subject matter of interest. It is also possible to contrast opinions from an expert panel with a panel of non experts.

In the Delphi research comparing structural and strategic therapists, panelists were selected who met three of the following criteria: (1) had published at least two articles or books on structural or strategic family therapy, (2) had at least 5 years of clinical experience in structural or strategic family therapy, (3) had at least five years of experience teaching structural or strategic family therapy, (4) had made at least two national convention presentations on structural or strategic family therapy, and (5) possessed a qualifying degree in a mental health discipline. A list of panelists was generated by perusing family therapy journals and books and selecting authors who wrote about structural and strategic therapies. Those panelists who were asked to participate from this first list were also asked to generate other family therapists who met the criteria listed above. Those generated names were then sent letters asking them to participate. A short demographic questionnaire was sent with the Delphi to confirm the panelists expertise in the subject matter. Of the panelists who were selected for the structural/strategic study, the 32 panelists who agreed to participate and completed the three rounds of the Delphi were quite expert in the field. Twenty-six were educators in the field. The average panelist had more than 8 publications and 10 national presentations.

Data Collection Procedures

Data collection utilizing the Delphi technique is usually a two- or three-part questionnaire. Delphi experts agree "that a point of diminishing returns is reached after a few rounds. Most commonly, three rounds proved sufficient to attain stability in the responses; further rounds tended to show little change and excessive repetition was unacceptable to the participants" (Linstone & Turoff, 1975, p. 229). According to Linstone and Turoff (1975), data collection undergoes four distinct phases. First, the subject is explored by the participants and each panelist gives as much input as she would like about the topic under study. The second phase is characterized by pulling together the individual information and understanding how the group views the subject. The third phase deals with the disagreement encountered by differing views. The final phase occurs after the initial information has been fed back to the individuals for their analysis. How these phases are accomplished is left up to the research team. Most important is the opportunity for panelists to express their opinions about the subject matter and for the research team not to prematurely close off disagreements among members. Usually the team designs a questionnaire that is sent out to a large group of expert panelists. The research team then pools the responses and sends them out again (at least once) to the panelists so that they can reevaluate their answers based on group responses. The research team attempts to reach a consensus of opinion about the initial responses during the last phase of the Delphi.

The Delphi technique, according to Dalkey (1972), has overcome the following drawbacks of the traditional methods of pooling opinion: (1) the influence of dominant individuals, (2) irrelevant and biasing communication, and (3) group pressure for conformity. Anonymity in the Delphi technique reduces the effect of dominant individuals, controlled feedback reduces irrelevant communication, and the use of statistical procedures reduces group pressure for conformity (Dalkey, 1972). It allows greater participation from panel members with economy of time and expense, avoids pressures of face-to-face contacts, and aids the formation of opinion consensus.

The Delphi technique that was employed in the structural/strategic study was a three-part questionnaire designed by the research team (Stone Fish, Piercy, Sprenkle, and Constantine) and sent to each participant. Delphi Questionnaire I (DQI) was an open-ended form with major category headings supplied by the team to stimulate and guide participants' thinking (See Table 21.1). The major headings asked the panelists to associate authors with structural or strategic therapy; identify major theoretical assump-

TABLE 21.1. A Sample Delphi Questionnaire I

Please complete this questionnaire. It is designed to compile a composite profile of structural family therapy. Please answer all the questions, using the reverse side of the paper if necessary. Feel free to make any other major categories or statements you feel would add to an understanding of structural family therapy.

Name: _____

What authors do you associate with structural family therapy?

_____
_____
_____

What are five major theoretical assumptions underlying structural family therapy?

1. _____
2. _____
3. _____
4. _____
5. _____

What are the differences between structural and strategic family therapies?

_____
_____
_____
_____
_____
_____
_____

tions and techniques, how change occurs, and the major goals of therapy; and discuss the differences and similarities inherent in the two approaches.

The completed DQI was returned to the primary researcher, who compiled every panelists' responses, creating Delphi Questionnaire II (DQII) (see Table 21.2). Panelists were then asked to rate the responses listed in DQII on a 7-point scale, indicating their agreement, and return their responses to the researcher. The median and interquartile ranges of the panelists' responses to DQII were computed and sent to the panelists as DQIII (See Table 21.3). In light of this new information, the respondents were asked once again to rate the items on a scale indicating agreement and return them to the primary researcher.

In the structural/strategic study, DQII was sent to panelists with a 7-point scale next to each item. The structural DQII had 213 items and the strategic DQII contained 271 items. Every panelist was asked to rate each item in regard to its importance in defining either strategic or structural family therapy. One indicated complete disagreement with the item being important in defining the different approaches, whereas seven indicated complete agreement (see Table 21.2). The ratings from DQII were analyzed by computing the median, quartiles one and three, and the interquartile range for each item. This statistical information, a new 7-point scale, and each respondents' ratings of DQII items were combined to form DQIII (see Table 21.3).

For the final profile of the strategic and structural questionnaires, medians and interquartile ranges were computed in the fashion of previous Delphi studies in family therapy (e.g., Winkle et al., 1981; Redenour, 1982). A high level of consensus and agreement was set in accordance with Binning, Cochran, and Donatelli (1972) to insure that

TABLE 21.2. A Sample Delphi Questionnaire II

Please circle one number for each item indicating the degree of importance it assumes in the final profiles of structural family therapy.

What authors do you associate with structural family therapy?

Disagree–Agree
1 2 3 4 5 6 7   1. Harry Aponte
1 2 3 4 5 6 7   2. Lynn Hoffman
1 2 3 4 5 6 7   3. Salvador Minuchin
1 2 3 4 5 6 7   4. Ron Liebman
1 2 3 4 5 6 7   5. Braulio Montalvo . . .

What are the major theoretical assumptions underlying structural family therapy?

Disagree–Agree
1 2 3 4 5 6 7   6. Families are hierarchically organized with rules for interacting across and subsystems.
1 2 3 4 5 6 7   7. Family structure is defined by family transactional patterns (rules).
1 2 3 4 5 6 7   8. Family structure determines the effectiveness of family functioning.
1 2 3 4 5 6 7   9. Family members relate to each other in patterned ways that are observable.
1 2 3 4 5 6 7 10. Conflict is not to be avoided but used for change . . .

What are the differences between structural and strategic family therapies?

Disagree–Agree
1 2 3 4 5 6 7 11. The goals and techniques are the same. The degree that each is emphasized is different.
1 2 3 4 5 6 7 12. Strategic therapy focuses more on the presenting problem.
1 2 3 4 5 6 7 13. Strategic therapy focuses more on the rules which maintain the problem.
1 2 3 4 5 6 7 14. The strategic therapist utilizes more direct reliance on paradox.
1 2 3 4 5 6 7 15. Strategic therapists do not use family maps . . .

TABLE 21.3. A Sample Delphi Questionnaire III

Please reconsider your responses to each item on Delphi Questionnaire III in light of the new information presented.

The new information summarizes the responses of all other panelists to each item. The information is reported in terms of the median (MDN) and the interquartile range (IQR). The median is the point below which 50 percent of the responses fell. The interquartile range contains the middle 50 percent of the responses. Its size gives an indication of how widely the responses differed from one another. Your previous answers to each item on Delphi Questionnaire II are given for you to compare. The following is an example.

What authors do you associate with structural family therapy?

Delphi Questionnaire III				Delphi Questionnaire II (Your previous response)
Disagree–Agree	MDN	IQR		Disagree–Agree
1 2 3 4 5 6 7	6.83	0.92	1 2 3 4 5 6 7	1. Harry Aponte
1 2 3 4 5 6 7	3.00	3.50	1 2 3 4 5 6 7	2. Lynn Hoffman

In the example above, the median for Item 1 is 6.83, indicating strong agreement. The interquartile range is .92 which is narrow and indicates a high degree of consensus among panelists. Your response on DQII to item 1 was 7.

The median of Item 2 is 3.00 indicating moderate disagreement. The large interquartile range of 3.50 indicates that there is not strong consensus on this item. Your response on DQII to item 2 was 4.

Please reconsider each item carefully and present new ratings in the scale under Delphi Questionnaire III. Remember to rate each item and to circle only one number for each item.

those items that became part of the final profile were those considered most important by the panelists. Those items that received a median of 6.00 or above and an interquartile range of 1.50 or less were selected as items on the final profile of strategic and structural family therapies (see Table 21.4).

Data Analysis Procedures

Delphi data are analyzed using medians and interquartile ranges. Medians and interquartile ranges are calculated to identify the rates of group agreement and consensus for each item that a panelist makes as a statement. Medians provide information on the central tendency of responses, indicating where most items fall on the disagreement–agreement scale. A median is a measure that divides the distribution into two equal parts if the distribution is a normal bell curve. Another term for the median is the "50th percentile" or the point below which 50% of the cases fall. However, when the distribution of responses is skewed toward the high or low ends of a scale, as it is in many of the questions from a Delphi study where an attempt is made to obtain consensus, the median will often be close to the highest or lowest possible score. An example of a frequency distribution for an item from a Delphi Study is presented in Table 21.5.

The results in Table 21.5 are common for many items obtained in Delphi studies. The median is 6.83, which is almost equal to the highest possible score of 7. This indicates that the distribution is skewed toward the high end of the scale.

The degree to which panelists have reached a consensus of agreement on a particular response is determined by the interquartile range. Interquartile ranges provide information about the variability in the data without being affected by extreme scores. Interquartile ranges are calculated by taking half the difference between the upper quartile, or the point in the distribution below which 75% of the cases lie (the 75th percentile), and the lower quartile, the point below which 25% of the cases lie (the 25th percentile). This type of range statistic provides information about the range of scores that

TABLE 21.4. A Sample of the Final Results of a Delphi Study

Median	Interquartile range	
		Authors associated with structural family therapy
7.00	0.50	Salvador Minuchin
6.96	0.54	H. Charles Fishman
6.87	0.64	Harry Aponte . . .
		Major theoretical assumptions of structural therapy
6.80	0.82	Families are hierarchically organized with rules for interacting across and between subsystems.
6.73	0.85	Insight is not sufficient for change.
6.60	0.90	Normal developmental crises can create problems within a family.
6.67	0.99	Inadequate hierarchy and boundaries maintain symptomatic behavior . . .
		Differences between structural and strategic therapies
6.33	1.17	Different approaches to resistance.
6.30	1.32	Strategic therapists focus more on between session change.
6.07	1.05	The strategic therapist utilizes more direct reliance on paradox . . .

TABLE 21.5. A Sample Frequency Distribution of a Delphi Item

What authors do you associate with structural family therapy?

Disagree–Agree
1 2 3 4 5 6 7   Harry Aponte

Response	Frequency	Cumulated frequency
1	0	0
2	0	0
3	1	1
4	3	4
5	5	9
6	13	22
7	18	40

Mean = 6.1; median (50th percentile) = 6.85; 25th percentile = 6.08; 75th percentile = 7; interquartile range = .92.

lie in the middle 50% of the cases and in doing so provides information about the consensus of response on a particular item.

Table 21.5 contains results that are common for the interquartile range of high consensus items. The upper quartile (75th percentile) is 7 and the lower quartile (25th percentile is 6.08. The interquartile range is calculated by subtracting the upper quartile from the lower quartile (7 – 6.08) which equals .92. This is a small interquartile range indicating high consensus from the panelists.

An attractive aspect of the Delphi method is that most researchers can calculate all of the necessary statistics by hand using simple formulas. The formulas for calculating the 25th, 50th, and 75th percentiles are as follows (Nachmias & Nachmias, 1981):

$$\text{25th percentile} = L_i + \frac{(n/4 - \text{CumF})W_i}{F_i} \text{ or the minimum score}$$

$$\text{50th percentile} = L_i + \frac{(n/2 - \text{CumF})W_i}{F_i}$$

$$\text{75th percentile} = L_i + \frac{(3n/4\ 1\ \text{CumF})W_i}{F_i} \text{ or the maximum score}$$

where L_i is the lower real limit of the interval containing the desired percentile; N is the number of cases; CumF is the accumulated sum of the frequencies of all intervals preceding the interval containing the desired percentile; F_i is the frequency of the interval containing the desired percentile; and W_i is the width of the interval containing the desired percentile.

An example using the data from Table 21.5 follows: To obtain the median the numbers from Table 21.5 can be inserted into the formula for the 50th percentile. It is necessary to know how many people are in the sample; in Table 21.4 there are 40. The researcher then knows that the median will fall in the interval containing the 20th case, in this instance the response choice of 6. The 25th percentile will fall in the interval containing the 10th case, in this instance the response choice of 6. The 75th percentile will fall in the interval containing the 30th case, in this instance the response choice of 7.

$$50\text{th percentile} = 6 + \frac{(40/2 - 9)\,1}{13} = 6 + \frac{20 - 9}{13} = 6.84$$

$$25\text{th percentile} = 6 + \frac{(40/4 - 9)\,1}{13} = 6 + \frac{(10 - 9)}{13} = 6.07$$

$$75\text{th percentile} = 7 + \frac{(3 \cdot 40/4 - 22)\,1}{18} = 7 + \frac{(30 - 22)}{18} = 7.44 \text{ or } 7$$

The 75th percentile cannot be any higher than the maximum score, so although the formula produces a score of 7.44 the answer is 7.

Reporting

Delphi studies, typically reported in the literature as research articles, are commonly published in refereed journals, which publish research articles. A review of the literature about the content of the report is followed by a methodology section, which both describes the Delphi and the particulars of the specific application the Delphi had in the research study. Findings are reported in both narrative form and in tables. Conclusions are usually drawn about the results in a discussion section following the results. The discussion section also includes the idiosyncratic and interesting challenges that occur throughout the research process. For example, in a recent Delphi study, Stone Fish and Osborn (1992) asked family therapists to express their views about family life in the United States. In the discussion section, they report:

> There is a final profile of the U.S. family with which family therapy panelists from diverse backgrounds are able to reach consensus. There were, however, great misgivings by many, when asked to reach a consensus about U.S. family life. Panelists wrote on the edges of their surveys and on additional pieces of paper. The content of these misgivings had to do with the panelists' reluctance to make general statements about all families today when families are so diverse, depending both on the culture they are embedded in and their own shape and size. (p. 414)

DISCUSSION

Strengths and Weaknesses

The Delphi approach is particularly well suited for emerging areas of inquiry and for building consensus among a group of experts. When it is used for these purposes, few weaknesses exist. Still, there are several pitfalls that researchers should be aware of when conducting a Delphi study.

Regression to the Mean

It is common for respondents to change their answers to become more similar to the group mean if too many iterations are conducted. In other words, after three questionnaires are administered the only significant change that occurs in the responses is that they begin to cluster closer to the mean. This problem is most easily avoided by only sending out one questionnaire in which respondents are aware of the group means. This is usually the last questionnaire.

Diversity Is Minimized

In most instances the researchers are searching for consensus from a sample of very diverse people. Because the final items that are selected often are dependent on small inter-quartile ranges, diversity is sacrificed for consensus. It is possible to report the outlying responses or to allow bimodal distributions in which groups of experts split into different camps if the researcher is flexible enough to relax the standard of tight interquartile ranges. A scatterplot is particularly useful for determining if bimodal or other types of unusual distributions exist in the data.

Time Commitment

The respondents, if they take the time to carefully think about their answers, can often expend several hours to complete the questionnaires. Because panels of experts are typically surveyed, and experts are usually very busy people, there is an immediate difficulty in obtaining an adequate sample. However, some people respond to being called an expert and will complete the surveys just to be included in the expert group. In other instances financial incentives might be used or shorter questionnaires can be constructed.

Narrow Perspectives

Experts with time in the field can become more and more specialized. This can produce a perspective that is too narrow to be useful or one that is impossible to mesh with others' views. If the researcher is interested in opinions about issues that are likely to involve complex systems, it is questionable whether the specialized expert is the best person to provide useful opinions.

The "So What" Factor

Finding out that most experts think that families are important has little practical value even though high consensus can be reached. If the questionnaire is not constructed creatively, or if responses are grouped together into categories that are too broad, significance can be sacrificed for consensus. One of the first indicators that the questionnaires are not useful is a low response rate. Additional indicators of poorly constructed questionnaires are small numbers of unique responses on the first questionnaire and uncharacteristically high levels of consensus on the second questionnaire.

Reliability and Validity

Traditional types of reliability and validity are not easily obtained or applicable to the Delphi approach. Because the questionnaires are open ended and general in nature it is probably not useful to conduct typical reliability estimates. The issue of test–retest reliability could be explored by having the same group of experts complete the same questionnaire twice. However, experts are likely to be less tolerant of this repetition than are freshmen students in an introductory psychology class. An estimation of reliability between the first and second questionnaires can be estimated by exploring the consensus rates of the respondents. If a reasonable level of consensus is produced on many items on the second questionnaire, it is likely that the researcher has adequately summarized the meaning behind the responses of the first questionnaire.

The issue of validity is directly related to the selection of the panel of experts. Consensus of opinion is easily obtained with most samples, the important question is whether the experts fit the area of inquiry. If the criteria for selection of the experts is evaluated for content validity by several professionals in the field, this can go a long way toward ensuring some level of validity. Whenever an open-ended approach is used, the researcher takes a bigger risk in the area of validity. Validity asks the question: Am I really measuring what I set out to measure? Because the panel of experts is only given general topics to follow, it is possible that many of the experts may diverge from the topic of interest into their own pet issues. As with qualitative studies, it is possible that the end product will reflect a different topic than the beginning research question. The only solution to wandering is to tightly define the area of interest. This may improve validity but most experts will show a surprising ability to break free from restrictions on their freedom of expression. An example of this was evidenced in Stone Fish and Osborn's (1992) article where the experts simply used the margins and other pieces of paper to freely express their opinions that did not fit into the predefined categories.

Skills

The Delphi method does not demand special statistical skills or clinical expertise. Medians and interquartile ranges can be computed by hand or with a calculator. Some creativity is necessary to capture the interest of the experts and to sell the idea of the research project. One study has demonstrated that the number of words needed to describe a topic area or event is related to amount of information and consensus rates that are obtained (Linstone & Turoff, 1975). This finding suggests that authors need to avoid using too few or too many words when constructing Delphi questionnaires if they hope to elicit accurate responses and build consensus.

Bridging Research and Practice

The characteristics of the Delphi make it particularly well suited for bridging the gap between research and practice. This approach does not demand large samples, statistical expertise, or a great amount of financial resources. As a result, clinicians could use the Delphi method to survey "expert" clients, expert referral sources, or any other group of individuals whose opinions are important. It is especially useful for developing policies about new problems that can crop up in agency work. When offered the choice of completing a few short questionnaires or attending several committee meetings that are likely to produce endless dialogue, most practitioners would elect to complete the questionnaire.

The results from the Delphi questionnaire are presented in the language of the respondents rather than shrouded in excessive theory or statistical jargon. This attribute alone can help bridge the gap between research and practice in that the interest level is usually higher when readers can speak the same language as the authors.

FUTURE DIRECTIONS

As the helping professions continue to struggle with populations that are more diverse and a delivery system that is experiencing dramatic changes, opinions of leaders in the field will be helpful for developing new programs and policies. It is likely that the Delphi approach will become as common in all fields of psychotherapy as it is in education and political science. It is surprising how few studies there are in marriage and family therapy that use this technique. In order for this approach to become more common-place in the field, students must be exposed to it in the early stages of their training. It is a method of inquiry that could easily fit the skills and interests of graduate students who are attempting to complete dissertations and theses.

The Delphi approach would be particularly useful for organizations such as American Association for Marriage and Family Therapy or the National Council on Family Relations, which are trying to meet the needs of a diverse and ever-growing population of professionals. What better way to keep an organization headed in the right direction than to collect opinions from experts in the field on what the future is likely to bring. There are few organizations or agencies that could not benefit from the Oracle of the Delphi.

REFERENCES

Beavers, W. R. (1981). A systems model of family for family therapy. *Journal of Marital and Family Therapy, 7,* 299–307.

Binning, D., Cochran, S., & Donatelli, B. (1972). *Delphi panel to explore post-secondary needs in the State of New Hampshire.* Manchester, NH: Decision Research.

Dalkey, N. (1969). Experimental study of group opinion. *Futures, 1,* 408–426.

Dalkey, N. (1972). *Studies in the quality of life.* Lexington, MA: Lexington Books.

Dalkey, N., & Helmer, O. (1963). An experimental application of the Delphi method to the use of experts. *Management Science, 9,* 458–467.

deShazer, S. (1984). Fit. *Journal of Strategic and Systemic Therapies, 3,* 34–37.

Fraser, J. S. (1982). Structural and strategic family therapy: A basis for marriage or grounds for divorce? *Journal of Marital and Family Therapy, 8,* 13–22.

Goplerud, E. N., Walfish, S., & Broskowski, A. (1985). Weathering the cuts: A Delphi survey on surviving cutbacks in community mental health. *Community Mental Health Journal, 21,* 14–27.

Gordon, J., & Helmer, O. (1964). *Report on a long-range forecasting study.* Santa Monica, CA: The Rand Corporation.

Helmer, O., & Rescher, N. (1960). *On the epistemology of the inexact sciences.* Santa Monica, CA: The Rand Corporation.

Kaufman, K. L., Holden, E. W., & Walker, C. E. (1989). Future directions in pediatric and clinical child psychology. *Professional Psychology Research and Practice, 20,* 148–152.

Liddle, H. A. (1980). On teaching a contextual or systemic therapy: Training content, goals, and methods. *American Journal of Family Therapy, 8,* 58–69.

Linstone, H. A., & Turoff, M. (1975). *The Delphi method: Techniques and applications.* Reading, MA: Addison-Wesley.

MacKinnon, L. (1983). Contrasting strategic and Milan therapies. *Family Process, 22,* 425–437.

Mitroff, I. I., & Turoff, M. (1975). Philosophical and methodological foundations of Delphi. In H. A. Linstone & M. Turoff (Eds.), *The Delphi method: Techniques and Applications* (pp. 17–36). Reading, MA: Addison-Wesley.

Nachmias, D., & Nachmias, C. (1981). *Research methods in the social sciences* (2nd ed.). New York: St. Martin's Press.

Norcross, J. C., Alford, B. A., & DeMichele, J. T. (1992). The future of psychotherapy: Delphi data and concluding observations. *Psychotherapy, 29,* 150–158.

Quade, E. S. (1967). *Cost-effectiveness: Some trends in analysis.* Santa Monica, CA: The Rand Corporation.

Rago, A. M., & Childers, J. H. (1990). Perceived changes in theories of family therapy in response to the changing American family. *TACD Journal, 18,* 23–45.

Redenour, C. (1982). *A Delphi investigation of alternative futures for Texas marriage and family therapists.* Unpublished doctoral dissertation, East Texas State University, Commerce, TX.

Rohrbaugh, M. (1984). The strategic systems therapies: Misgivings about mixing models. *Journal of Strategic and Systemic Therapies, 3*, 28–32.

Scheele, D. S. (1975). Reality construction as a product of Delphi interaction. In H. A. Linstone & M. Turoff (Eds.), *The Delphi method: Techniques and applications* (pp. 37–71). Reading, MA: Addison-Wesley.

Sprenkle, D. H. (1976). The need for integration among theory, research, and practice in the family field. *The Family Coordinator, 25*, 124–127.

Stanton, M. D., Todd, T. C., & Associates (1982). *The family therapy of drug abuse and addiction.* New York: Guilford Press.

Stone Fish, L. (1989). Comparing structural, strategic, and feminist-informed family therapies: Two Delphi studies. *The American Journal of Family Therapy, 17*, 303–314.

Stone Fish, L., & Osborn, J. (1992). Therapists' views of family life: A Delphi study. *Family Relations, 41*, 409–416.

Stone Fish, L., & Piercy, F. P. (1987). The theory and practice of structural and strategic family therapies: A Delphi study. *Journal of Marital and Family Therapy, 13*, 113–125.

Thomson, B. R. (1990). Appropriate and inappropriate uses of humor in psychotherapy as perceived by certified reality therapists: A Delphi study. *Journal of Reality Therapy, 10*, 59–65.

Wheeler, D. (1985). *The theory and practice of feminist-informed family therapy: A Delphi study.* Doctoral dissertation, Purdue University, West Lafayette, IN.

Winkle, W. C., Piercy, F. P., & Hovestadt, A. J. (1981). A curriculum for graduate-level marriage and family therapy education. *Journal of Marital and Family Therapy, 7*, 201–210.

Program Evaluations

22

Program Evaluation Research
APPLICATIONS TO MARITAL
AND FAMILY THERAPY

DOUGLAS LEBER
MICHELLE ST. PETERS
HOWARD J. MARKMAN

BACKGROUND

Since the early 1970s, there has been tremendous growth in the importance and impact of marital and family therapy (Gurman, Kniskern, & Pinsof, 1986) and greater concern with the efficacy of marital and family therapy (Garfield & Bergin, 1986). Outcome research suggests that family therapy holds great promise and may be an effective intervention for families with members displaying a wide variety of disorders (Gurman et al., 1986).

However, little attention has been given to how well marital and family therapy is practiced in the field. Few marital and family therapists engage in any sort of systematic evaluation of the services they offer clients. A recent survey of 598 clinical members of the American Association for Marriage and Family Therapy (AAMFT) who currently practice marital or family therapy revealed that approximately one-third used assessment instruments in their practice (Boughner, Hayes, Bubenza, & West, 1994). Moreover, the instruments reported used most frequently by these AAMFT members, the MMPI-2 and the Myers–Briggs Type Indicator (MBTI), are not sensitive to the kinds of changes likely to result from marital therapy.

In addition, it is a common lament that academic research rarely has an impact upon clinical practice (Liddle, 1991; Olson, 1976; Wynne,1983). Many practitioners are unsatisfied with how academic research has addressed the questions of program effectiveness and treatment outcome. Few are persuaded to follow the lead of researchers, and many do not respect the value of empirical research.

As the system of health care delivery evolves, it is certain that practitioners will be asked to demonstrate that the services they provide are indeed effective for the clients they serve. Perhaps a more important concern is that practitioners have an ethical obligation to offer clients the best services possible, given the present state of knowledge regarding program effectiveness. In our view, program evaluation research offers an ideal set of tools that enables practitioners, administrators, and agencies to document how well services and interventions address the problems they were designed to resolve (Smith, 1990). Although evaluation research is often used to assess large-scale social programs and interventions (Rossi & Freeman, 1993), practitioners and researchers can apply evaluation research methods and techniques to meet the needs of small agencies and practices.

Early in the development of programs and services, evaluation research focuses on how interventions are conceptualized and designed and how they are implemented. In later stages of program development and implementation, evaluation centers on whether programs meet goals and objectives in terms of cost and effectiveness and desired impact upon the target population (Rossi & Freeman, 1993). Evaluation gives early warning of things going wrong and can be an excellent guide for improving programs and practices (Weiss, 1990). For example, carefully monitoring clients' responses to programs may guide "on-line" changes and adaptations of programs to meet the needs of specific target populations. However, systematic evaluation of theoretically guided programs, especially preventive interventions, can do more than test the efficacy of specific programs—it can answer questions about the etiology of disorders, and identify new approaches to familiar issues (Coie et al., 1993).

In this chapter we offer examples of how program evaluation may be used to develop new programs and services, and evaluate existing programs. However, one of the most important reasons for conducting program evaluations is to show what practitioners actually *do*. With this information, researchers gain valuable feedback regarding what is being done (or not done) with their findings, and they may learn how to design studies that provide information that practitioners can use to the benefit of their clients.

Roots and Development of Program Evaluation Research

Evaluation research is a relatively new field and has experienced tremendous growth since the late 1960s. Since the interdisciplinary journal *Evaluation Review* was first published in 1976, about a dozen journals have been established that are primarily concerned with evaluation research (Rossi & Freeman, 1993). Before World War I, large-scale evaluations of education programs (e.g., literacy and occupational training) and public health initiatives (e.g., mortality and morbidity from infectious diseases) were conducted, and during the Great Depression of the 1930s, there was a rapid growth in the number of evaluations of human services and community action programs. Throughout World War II, there was extensive monitoring of the effectiveness of propaganda campaigns and other efforts to improve civilian and soldier morale. After World War II, systematic evaluations were conducted of the impact and implementation of urban development programs and social programs targeting prevention of delinquency; reform of prisons; improvements in public housing; and medical, psychotherapeutic, and psychopharmacological treatments (Rossi & Freeman, 1993).

The 1964 Economic Opportunity Act was a centerpiece of the Johnson Administration's War on Poverty. It created several major projects targeting the needs of poor adults (e.g., unemployment, crime, urban renewal, and mental health care programs) and children (e.g., Head Start) (Valentine & Zigler, 1983; Zigler & Styfco, 1993). Each of these programs included evaluation components. More recently, in the 1980s, the Reagan and Bush administrations intensified efforts to justify the benefits of social programs in relation to their costs. Fiscal accountability and effective management of social programs became high priorities (Rossi & Freeman, 1993).

These trends continue in the current political and social spheres. Choosing which social problems to concentrate on, and assigning priority to which types of interventions, is an extremely important task for administrators and funding agencies. Especially in managed care settings, practitioners and administrators must show that existing programs are effective and efficient in meeting their goals, and researchers must demonstrate the virtues of new or modified programs in order to obtain funding for implementation (Markman, 1992).

METHODOLOGY

Research Questions

Methods of program evaluation research can be applied to address a number of important questions related to marital and family therapy. *Needs assessments* identify populations that are underserved in the community and describe populations being reached by existing programs. This information can be used to document needs for new programs or justify maintaining existing services. *Formative and process studies* describe how services are being delivered by practitioners and agencies, and whether interventions are being delivered in the field as they were intended by the designers. Formative studies tell researchers how their ideas and information are being applied in the field. *Pilot studies* are small-scale investigations designed to examine how new interventions and services are implemented, providing crucial feedback to practitioners about changes that need to be made in order to avoid future problems. *Evaluability assessments* are designed to determine whether existing or proposed programs are capable of being evaluated (e.g., Are there explicit and clearly defined program goals and objectives?) and to guide changes to increase accountability (Wholey, 1977). *Outcome evaluations*, the most popular kind of evaluation study, examine the impacts of interventions on the target population. Practitioners can use outcome evaluations to track what happens for clients over time, to see whether therapeutic objectives are being met on a consistent basis, and to discern which kinds of clients do best with the services offered by practitioners.

Above all, it is important that the evaluation strategy chosen for a particular study accurately reflects the goals and purposes of the evaluation. There is no single "correct" way to conduct an evaluation. However, designing an appropriate evaluation strategy is easier when there are specific program goals and objectives and the objectives of the evaluation are clearly specified.

In this chapter, we offer guidelines illustrated with specific examples of ways to use program evaluation research. Many of the examples are drawn from our experience in evaluating the processes and outcomes of the Prevention and Relationship Enhancement Program (PREP) (Markman, Stanley, & Blumberg, 1993; see Table 22.1).

Some kind of evaluation component should be included in each stage of program design and implementation, and evaluation of existing programs should include collecting data describing program delivery and monitoring how clients participate in the program services.

In the next sections, we briefly describe needs assessment and formative evaluation studies. The remainder of the chapter emphasizes issues involved in planning and conducting outcome evaluations.

Needs Assessment

Needs assessments (also called *feasibility* studies or *front-end* analyses) are conducted to determine whether there is sufficient justification for a proposed program or interven-

TABLE 22.1. The Prevention and Relationship Enhancement Program (PREP)

The Prevention and Relationship Enhancement Program (Markman, Stanley, & Blumberg, 1993) was designed to prevent divorce and the development of marital distress. Dysfunctional interaction patterns precede the development of marital distress (Markman, 1981), and once formed, these patterns are difficult to modify (Raush, Barry, Hertel, & Swain, 1974). By observing how couples interact *prior* to marriage, researchers can predict with a high degree of reliability which couples will subsequently divorce (Gottman, 1994). The quality of couples' communication is one of the best predictors of marital success (Markman et al., 1993), which provides a powerful argument for intervention with premarital or newlywed couples.

In PREP, couples learn communication skills and develop ground rules for handling conflict and promoting intimacy. PREP is typically conducted in six sessions, each lasting about 2½ hours. In a typical session, couples spend some time with other couples listening to lectures presented by the group leader, but most often, couples practice apart from the group, developing skills or discussing various issues with the aid of a consultant.

Longitudinal evaluation of outcomes of PREP has been conducted at the University of Denver since 1980, funded by the National Institute of Mental Health.

tion, outlining the nature and scope of a specific social problem and estimating the size and characteristics of the target population (Royse, 1992). Both primary and secondary sources of data are used in needs assessments. Primary data are gathered directly from the target population or clientele to be served by the proposed program, using results of questionnaires, surveys, or face-to-face interviews.

For example, we are currently conducting a feasibility study for a proposed intervention, based on PREP, designed to prevent postpartum depression. To assess the need for the intervention, we are surveying women who obtain prenatal care at a community medical center. To determine who is at risk for postpartum depression, we ask pregnant women to complete a questionnaire which asks questions about current relationship status, satisfaction with and conflict in their relationships, and current or past episodes of depression. We also ask whether they would be willing to participate in a program to prevent postpartum depression. The goals of this feasibility study are to estimate the size of the population of pregnant females at risk for postpartum depression and to demonstrate that it is possible and workable to recruit subjects from a community medical center.

Sources of secondary data include public documents, records from human service agencies, surveys of experts in a particular program area, and reviews or research in the professional literature. Using these data, researchers learn about the incidence and prevalence of particular social problems as well as the successes and failures of existing programs. However, because secondary data are not gathered directly from the target population to be served, the validity and reliability of secondary data must be carefully examined (Rossi & Freeman, 1993). Also, it is common for different kinds of secondary data to yield a wide range of estimates of the prevalence and incidence of social problems. One way to deal with this problem is to use a variety of sources and then integrate and synthesize information to draw a more precise portrait of the social problem and the target population's needs.

For example, in conducting a needs assessment for the PREP program, we used secondary data to find out the incidence and prevalence of divorce at both the national and local levels using data obtained from the *Current Population Reports* (published by the U.S. Bureau of the Census) and the *Monthly Vital Statistics Report* (published by the National Center for Health Statistics, Centers for Disease Control and Prevention, U.S. Department of Health and Human Services). Converging information about the negative effects of divorce, degree of marital discord, and the extent of depression among married couples was obtained from articles published in professional journals and books on marriage and divorce. In the future we plan to conduct telephone surveys of couples and professionals dealing with families (e.g., clergy, school personnel, social workers, and therapists) regarding perceived needs for divorce prevention programs.

Formative Evaluation

At each stage of program development, formative and process evaluations assess whether interventions are implemented as planned. These studies examine program quality and processes, documenting what services were provided, to whom, when, how often, and in what settings (Royse, 1992). Process studies emphasize how the program is delivered and the ways clients participate in the program, describing how the program functions, often including the perspectives of staff, clients, and community.

Monitoring Program Delivery

A crucial step in the early stages of development of an intervention is monitoring how the program is being implemented in the field. Many programs have failed because the program designers did not carefully track how the programs were being implemented (Rossi & Freeman, 1993).

Pilot studies are extremely useful "pretest" and program development tools. Well-designed pilot studies, conducted with small samples of participants or at a limited number of sites, allow procedures and instruments to be "debugged," and programs can be adjusted to deal with unanticipated problems in delivery.

We are presently engaged in pilot studies of a new intervention for couples at risk for marital aggression. Since 1992, in collaboration with Amy Holtzworth-Munroe at Indiana University and Peter Neidig and Daniel O'Leary of the State University at Stony Brook, we have modified the PREP program to target newlywed or engaged couples who are at risk for domestic violence. The new intervention, PREP/SAVE, is a combination of PREP and the Stop Anger and Violence Escalation (SAVE) workshop (Neidig, 1989a, 1989b). At sites in Denver, Indianapolis, and Stony Brook, pilot studies of the program have been conducted with groups of three or four couples. Initial pilot efforts have focused on refining program content and structure of the PREP/SAVE sessions and monitoring client participation and response to the program sessions and testing procedures. After each program session, participating couples completed brief evaluation forms, which solicited comments regarding highlights and weaknesses of the session. Further comments were obtained from group leaders and staff. Feedback from participants and group leaders led to substantial modifications of the program (e.g., session length was reduced, program materials clarified, redundant sections of lectures were eliminated, and new exercises were developed).

Currently we are planning an extensive evaluation of PREP/SAVE. For this proposed study, we developed a variety of procedures for monitoring program implementation. For example, we constructed adherence checklists for program leaders and staff to complete after each session. These checklists assess key features of program implementation (e.g., keeping to time limits and whether specified content in lectures and exercises was included). We proposed audiotaping program sessions and training coders to check the content of lectures and client participation in the sessions. Also, a checklist describing participants' behavior was developed (e.g., completing assigned homework, session attendance, and response and participation in lectures and exercises).

Monitoring Client Participation

When program participation is voluntary, it may be difficult to attract members of the target population, especially when participants are asked to learn new skills, attend lectures, receive instruction, or otherwise change their habits (Rossi & Freeman, 1993). A key issue for program developers is how to motivate members of the target population to seek out the program and participate in it.

When target clients refuse to participate or do not volunteer for a program, bias due to self-selection may be introduced because the clients who choose to participate may have characteristics (e.g., age, education, and income) that distinguish them from those who participate fully. Also, "drop-out" clients, those who begin a program and fail to complete it, may differ from clients who complete the program.

Bias due to self-selection or dropout may severely threaten the validity of a program's outcome assessment because evaluators may not be able to generalize results obtained from study of the biased sample to the target population as a whole. Another concern is whether the program reaches its intended beneficiaries or serves only a limited subset of the target population.

Keeping records of relevant demographic data on clients served (and if possible those not served) is one way to keep track of potential bias in program impact. What demographic data to collect depends on program goals, interests of funding agencies, and the characteristics of the target population.

For example, useful demographic information may include age, sex, socioeconomic status, ethnicity, religion, geographic location, and residential mobility, as well as problems (e.g., unemployment), difficulties (e.g., lack of access to transportation), and mental and health conditions (e.g., depression, and high blood pressure) (Rossi & Freeman, 1993; Smith, 1990).

Outcome Evaluation

Outcome evaluations focus on the impact(s) of existing or newly developed programs on their target populations, determining how extensive and what kind of changes were introduced in target populations by the programs or interventions. Outcome evaluations are most appropriate in the later stages of program development, when it makes sense to evaluate whether and what kinds of successes or failures a program or intervention has created. "Success" is usually determined by whether stated goals and objectives are met. Researchers also attempt to identify whether the outcomes observed may be due, at least in part, to events or processes *unrelated* to the intervention (Rossi & Freeman, 1993).

Determining the impact of programs requires some type of comparison. This can be done by comparing participants with nonparticipants, or by obtaining measurements of participants before and after interventions are implemented. Without such comparisons, it is difficult to estimate the effects of interventions or to consider other factors that may affect the behavior of clients participating in the programs (Rossi & Freeman, 1993).

In our longitudinal research with the PREP program, we examined three sets of outcome variables: marital satisfaction, relationship problems, and the incidence of marital separation or divorce. Initial studies showed that immediately after intervention, couples that received the PREP intervention showed increased skill in communication and reported greater relationship satisfaction compared to control couples that did not receive the intervention. These gains were maintained at 1- and 3-year follow-ups. At 4- and

5-year follow-ups, the PREP intervention couples, in comparison to control couples, were less likely to divorce and had higher levels of marital satisfaction (Renick, Blumberg, & Markman, 1992).

Many agencies or practices do not have the financial or staff resources to conduct a thorough outcome evaluation, including interviews, questionnaire data, and so forth. Mail or telephone surveys can often be used to gather outcome data with less expense and staff resources. Several excellent texts are available that describe the process of constructing and conducting mail and telephone surveys (e.g., Frey, 1989; Rea & Parker, 1992).

Steps in Program Evaluation Research

Plan the Evaluation

In the following sections we outline steps involved in planning an outcome evaluation. Many of these steps also apply to needs assessments and formative studies.

Two key aspects of planning an evaluation study include identifying (1) the audience(s) for the evaluation findings and (2) goals and objectives. Knowing the audience(s) for evaluation findings is crucial because successful evaluations should be designed to answer a specific set of questions that decisionmakers and "stakeholders" consider relevant (Berk & Rossi, 1990). All people who may be interested in the outcomes of the program evaluation (e.g., participants, program staff, administrators, funding agencies, and community groups) are stakeholders (Pietrzak, Ramler, Renner, Ford, & Gilbert, 1990).

Usually, the questions answered by the evaluation should be closely related to the goals and objectives of the program. Goals are broad statements about the outcomes of a program or intervention, whereas objectives are more specific statements about how program goals are to be achieved (Smith, 1990). If program goals and objectives are not already specified, one of the first steps of the evaluation should be to derive a set of program goals and objectives. Statements of goals and objectives should include detailed descriptions of how they are to be achieved. Having specific, measurable goals and objectives increases the likelihood that the program will be effective and also determines how well its evaluation can be conducted (Rossi & Freeman, 1993).

Goals and objectives for PREP are specified in manuals for leaders and consultants. For example, the primary goal of PREP is to provide an educational experience for couples that will enable them to increase their communication and problem-solving skills, skills which research has shown are associated with effective marital functioning and the prevention of future marital distress (Markman, Stanley, et al., 1993). Examples of major objectives for PREP include (1) developing and guiding practice of constructive communication and conflict resolution skills, (2) clarifying and modifying relationship beliefs and expectations, (3) expanding sexual/sensual knowledge and attitudes, (4) exploring the role of fun and friendship in intimate relationships, and (5) having the couple leave the program with an agreed-on set of ground rules for handling disagreements and conflict (Markman et al., 1993).

Choose Methods of Evaluation

Once a set of evaluation questions has been developed, the evaluator must decide how to answer them. In general, the overriding goal of evaluation research design is to provide a valid and sensitive test of the effectiveness of an intervention or program. However, in designing the study and considering the kinds of data to collect, the evaluator needs to keep in mind which kinds of data the audience(s) for the evaluation findings find persuasive and compelling. For example, practitioners may be interested in gaining a rich description of how the program works, seeking answers to the question, "What's going on here and why?" (Moon, Dillon, & Sprenkle, 1990). For this audience, qualitative data may be most compelling, yielding concrete, meaningful descriptions of program functioning and impact on staff and participants with a persuasiveness that quantitative data often lack (Miles & Huberman, 1994). In contrast, quantitative data may be necessary to persuade such audiences as program administrators and funding agencies, which are often interested in formulating valid and reliable statements regarding program effectiveness. Increasingly, given the diverse audiences for evaluation findings, researchers choose to gather both quantitative and qualitative data, creating a need to link qualitative and quantitative analysis (Miles & Huberman, 1994; Robson, 1993).

In an outcome evaluation, the evaluator wants to be able to detect any important differences or changes that may occur for participants as a result of intervention. This is a question of design sensitivity (Lipsey, 1990). At the same time, the evaluator needs to know whether observed changes are due to influences of the intervention or to forces *other than* the intervention (e.g., random factors or other uncontrolled influences). This is a question of internal validity (Cook & Campbell, 1979), which we discuss in the section on choosing a research design.

Design sensitivity is affected by several factors, including sample size and the size of the effects produced by the intervention (Lipsey, 1990). Sensitivity is also greater when there is less heterogeneity in response to the intervention. That is, if there is wide variation in how individuals respond to the intervention, it will be more difficult to determine the overall effectiveness of the intervention. Sensitivity is also affected by research procedures and measurement. When study participants are treated in identical or substantially similar ways, sensitivity increases. Also, it is important that measurement instrument(s) are sensitive to changes in the outcomes of interest to the evaluation. Finally, when evaluators are able to apply more powerful statistical techniques to the data, differences between groups are more likely to be revealed.

The evaluation research design specifies (1) sampling and selection procedures, (2) research design, and (3) how data will be collected. Sampling and selection procedures include who will be measured and how participants will be selected. The research design specifies how the intervention program will be delivered, timing of measurements, and how participants will be assigned to treatment or comparison groups (e.g., an experimental design might include random assignment of participants to an intervention group or to a no-treatment control group). The data collection strategy specifies when and where measurements will be taken and what instruments will be used for assessment.

A number of texts provide guidelines for planning evaluation studies and selecting appropriate research designs (see, e.g., Fitz-Gibbons & Morris, 1987; Pietrzak et al., 1990). In particular, Kazdin (1992) offers an excellent discussion of research design issues relevant to therapy outcome studies, and Bloom and Fischer (1982) discuss numerous ways to design evaluations of practices and agencies. Miles and Huberman (1994) and Patton (1990) provide guidelines for designs that incorporate qualitative data or combined strategies of quantitative and qualitative data collection. In the following sections we briefly review important issues in the design of evaluation studies.

Choose Sampling and Selection Procedures

How participants are selected for the evaluation will vary depending on the specific goals of the evaluation study and characteristics of the target population. Outcome studies require samples of sufficient size and representativeness in order to maximize generaliz-ability to other settings and times or to the population of clients of an agency or practice.

However, a pilot or formative study may require only a few subjects, enough to examine a specific aspect of the program being tested, and establishing generalizability may be less important than refining procedures and measures.

In general, "representative" samples are drawn from a population of people who share important characteristics in common with the target population (e.g., age, eth-nicity, and household income). In an outcome study, researchers usually want to be able to generalize findings derived from the study to the target population. Generaliza-bility is greater when the characteristics of the target population are well specified and when random sampling is used to select study participants from the target population.

When the target population is well specified, it is easier to see whether the study sample resembles the larger population. Random sampling is the preferred method for selecting participants because it minimizes selection biases. Random sampling methods ensure that each member of the target population has an equal chance (or at least a known likelihood) of participating in the study.

For small programs (25–50 people), it may be possible to recruit everyone as par-ticipants. However, in most cases it is not feasible to include all members of the target population in the evaluation study, and some kind of probability sampling technique (e.g., a random numbers table) should be used to select sample subjects from the target population.

How large a sample should be selected? There are no hard rules for determining the appropriate sample size for an evaluation study. The crucial question is what kinds of data are to be gathered. In general, gathering quantitative information from a larger sample of subjects allows the evaluator to be more confident about generalizing results from obtained to the larger population. However, evaluators must usually contend with practical limits on the number of participants that can be studied. For example, there may be little time available before a decision is needed, or a large evaluation study may not be possible due to limited financial and staff resources.

In treatment effectiveness research, relying on quantitative measures, the average sample size is about 40 per group. However, for qualitative studies, pilot studies, and formative evaluations, useful information may be gathered with much smaller samples.

Evaluators must make decisions regarding how precise the estimates of population characteristics need to be, how large an effect the intervention is expected to produce, what level of confidence in estimates is desired, and how important it is to detect an effect of the intervention, if in fact there is an effect. Limited space does not allow for elaboration here; however, Smith (1990) and Royse (1992) offer "how to" approaches to calculation of sample size for evaluation studies. Cohen (1992) and Kraemer and Thiemann (1987) present clear discussions of the relationship between sample size and statistical power.

Smith (1990) provides a useful illustration of the importance of sample size. He suggests thinking about whether or not it would be misleading to use a percentage figure in reporting findings from the study. For example, if the sample included only five cases, each case represents 20% of the total sample. In this case, it would be misleading (although accurate) to say that 60% of the sample displayed a certain outcome because only three cases would be represented. With small samples, the outcomes of one or two cases can have major effects on estimates of population characteristics. However, if 25 program participants were included in the sample, 60% of the sample represents 15 cases, and the influence of the outcomes of one or two individual cases is less dramatic.

Selecting participants for the evaluation of PREP took into account that the pro-gram was designed as a preventive intervention addressing a major social problem. The target population for PREP includes all couples planning marriage or remarriage. In order to simplify evaluation, recruitment of participants for the longitudinal study was restricted to couples planning marriage for the first time. Other studies were designed to look at the effects of PREP for couples in which one or both partners had been married previously.

Communitywide publicity (advertisements in community and metropolitan newspapers, radio and television announcements, etc.) was used to recruit couples, who were asked to participate in a study of relationship development. Prospective participants were told that participation required completing a minimum of three 2-hour sessions over a period of 8 to 10 weeks, and that they would be paid $25 for participation.

Over the first and second years of the project, a total of 135 couples entered the study. During year 1, 73 couples were recruited, and an additional 62 couples were recruited in year 2.

The selection procedures resulted in a sample drawn from metropolitan Denver that was predominantly middle class and white. The average age of husbands when they entered the study was 24.1 years, and wives' average age was 23.3 years. Sixty-five percent of couples were formally engaged at the time they began the study; 41% were living together; on average, partners had known each other approximately 2.5 years before entering the study (Markman, Duncan, Storaasli, & Howes, 1988).

A number of concerns about the sample used for this evaluation should be raised. First, the sample is not representative of the nationwide population of couples marrying for the first time. This may place some limits on the generalizability of results of this study. Second, because couples were recruited in two cohorts, there is some possibility that couples recruited in different years may differ in important ways. Analyses of demographic and relationship variables did not reveal any important differences (Markman et al., 1988). Even so, it is possible that couples marrying in one year may differ from those marrying in another year because of history effects (important differences in economic climate, natural disasters, events such as the Challenger explosion, invasion of Kuwait, etc.). Third, although a small payment was offered for participation, all couples were volunteers and may differ in important ways from couples that chose not to respond to an advertisement for research participants.

Choose a Research Design

The evaluation research design specifies how participants take part in the study, including how they are assigned to intervention or comparison groups and when measurement will take place.

When deciding what type of design is most appropriate for a study, it is important to consider questions of *internal* and *external* validity. Internal validity refers to whether it is possible to make unambiguous inferences regarding whether differences observed in the study are due to the intervention or due to other causes not related to the intervention. That is, are the "effects" observed due to the intervention or to something else? *External validity* refers to whether findings derived from an evaluation study may be generalized to other populations or settings. The aspect of external validity that is most important for evaluation studies is whether the results of the evaluation are generalizable to the populations or settings that currently receive the intervention or are proposed to receive the intervention in the future. Table 22.2 reviews a number of factors that may threaten the internal or external validity of evaluation studies.

It is not always possible to select a rigorous design that will minimize factors that pose threats to the internal or external validity of an evaluation study. However, it is

TABLE 22.2. Threats to Internal or External Validity

Threats to internal validity

1. *History*. Some external event may have an effect on subjects in the intervention or control group. Limiting the time between measurements will decrease the influence of history.

2. *Maturation*. Changes occurring in the subjects may result from the passage of time and not from effects of the intervention. As time between measurements increases, maturation becomes a more important factor. Maturation is an especially important factor to consider when doing research with children.

3. *Testing*. If the same test is administered a number of times, changes in scores achieved on the test may be due to previous experiences with the test. Subjects may "figure out" the test or become bored or careless in responding to the test.

4. *Instrumentation*. Changes in the measurement instrument, either across subjects or across time, may lead to error in measurement. Care should be taken to ensure that tests are administered in the same way to all subjects (i.e., in the same or similar setting, following the same rules, with the same instructions). When coders are used to score observations, reliability among coders or interviewers should be checked periodically. Coder "drift" across observations may be due to differences in experience, fatigue, or boredom with repetitive tasks.

5. *Differential selection of participants*. If experimental and control groups are not equivalent *prior* to intervention, some differences in outcomes between the groups may be traced to these preexisting differences. Random assignment to groups is the best way to ensure there are no systematic differences between experimental and control groups. Even so, random assignment to groups may still result in experimental and control groups that differ in important ways (i.e., are not equivalent).

6. *Mortality*. When subjects are lost over the course of a study due to refusals, dropouts, or failures to contact, outcomes can be biased. Characteristics of dropouts may be different from characteristics of subjects who stayed in the program.

7. *Statistical regression*. Because measurement instruments are not perfectly reliable, some changes in scores will occur from pretest to posttest due to measurement error alone. Clients who have extreme scores, either high or low, on the first administration of an instrument are likely to have scores that are closer to the mean of all clients' scores on the next administration of the instrument.

Threats to external validity

1. *Population validity*. The extent to which results from a study may be generalized to a larger population of subjects. To increase the likelihood that results from a study may be generalized to the larger target population, researchers should select subjects at random from the target population. Another population effect occurs when the treatment is more effective for some target subjects than it is for other target subjects.

2. *Ecological validity*. The extent to which the outcomes of the study may be generalized to other settings and environmental conditions. Replication of a study in different settings or environmental conditions is the best way to assess the ecological validity of findings. To assist replication, researchers should provide precise descriptions of how the study was conducted and how data were collected and analyzed so that the study may be carried out in another setting by another researcher. In many program evaluations, ecological validity is not a high priority because the evaluation seeks answers to specific questions (e.g., how well is this program functioning in this particular setting, with this population of clients).

3. *Reactive effects of pretesting*. When clients are pretested before receiving an intervention they may become more sensitive to the intervention. Thus, if pretests are not included in the implementation of the program, there may be a threat to external validity of the evaluation (Huck, Cormier, & Bounds, 1974).

most important to control factors that might affect the internal validity of the study because without internal validity, data derived from the study are difficult or impossible to interpret. One reason that random assignment of subjects to experimental and control conditions is desirable is that it is the most straightforward way to maximize internal validity.

Fitz-Gibbons and Morris (1987) suggest that there are three basic choices in how an intervention may be delivered to participants in an evaluation study. The first alternative is to have all participants take part in the intervention. This is a *single-group* design. A second alternative is to randomly assign some participants to an intervention group and the remainder to a no-intervention control group. This is an *experimental* design. The third alternative is to assign participants to an intervention group or to a comparison group by some nonrandom process. This is called a quasi-experimental design.

Experimental designs are the most rigorous designs and provide the best basis for making inferences regarding whether an intervention did or did not have an effect. In an experimental design, subjects are randomly assigned to either an intervention or a control group. Random assignment maximizes the probability that the two groups will be similar in relevant characteristics and that differences in observed outcomes are in fact due to the intervention and do not result from systematic differences between the intervention and control groups.

Quasi-experimental designs also compare two groups of subjects, members of the intervention and the control group, but the difference is that random assignment was not used to assign subjects to groups. Quasi-experimental designs are useful because random assignment of subjects to groups is not always feasible because of practical or ethical concerns (we address the ethics of random assignment in the discussion section). If random assignment is not employed, it is usually best to recruit a control or comparison group of subjects who are similar to the intervention group in terms of such background characteristics as socioeconomic status, ethnicity, income, level of education, occupational status, and so on (Campbell & Stanley, 1963).

Another important concern of research design is *timing of measurements*. Fitz-Gibbons and Morris (1987) outline three choices for when measurement may take place: (1) after the intervention (posttest only), (2) before and after the intervention (pretest and posttest), or (3) time-series measurement, in which participants are measured at several points in time, before and after implementation of the program.

Although the technical procedures for analyzing *time-series designs* are complicated, the ideas underlying these procedures are straightforward. Analysis of time-series designs involves comparing trends or outcomes occurring *before* the intervention was implemented to trends or outcomes observed *after* the intervention has taken place. Time-series designs can be used when there is only an intervention group available, but these designs are strongest when combined with an experimental design, so that, over time, outcomes for an intervention group are compared to those occurring in a control group.

A time-series experimental design was used in the longitudinal evaluation of PREP. Couples were recruited for participation in a study of relationship development and were randomly assigned to the intervention group or to a no-intervention control group after completing the preassessment sessions. This allowed creation of a true control group because the participants had no advance expectation of taking part in an intervention or treatment program. However, it also increased the likelihood that some couples assigned to the intervention condition would decline participation. In fact, a number of couples chose not to participate in the intervention. Thus, subsequent data analyses were conducted on three groups: intervention, control, and "declines."

There have been numerous phases of data collection for evaluating the long-term outcomes of PREP, including preassessment, intervention, postassessment, and follow-up assessments. During preassessment, couples participated in two laboratory sessions in which they were interviewed and completed questionnaires. Couples also engaged in several interaction tasks, which were videotaped and coded (see Markman et al., 1988).

Select Instruments

A crucial part of the design stage of evaluation is selecting instruments that have the potential for determining whether the program has met its goals and objectives. Whatever instruments are selected (semistructured interviews, questionnaires, surveys, observational coding systems, etc.), they need to be able to discriminate "successful" from "unsuccessful" outcomes among program participants. Instruments selected or developed for the evaluation study need to have good psychometric characteristics and also be reliable and valid indicators of what the program is trying to do (Royse, 1992). Reliability generally refers to consistency of measurement (Kazdin, 1992). Validity refers to the degree to which an instrument measures what it was designed or intended to measure. What is validated is not the instrument itself but rather the utility of the instrument (Carmines & Zeller, 1979).

One way to ensure that instruments have good psychometric properties is to use instruments that have already demonstrated reliability and validity. However, in evaluation research it is often necessary to modify existing instruments or design new ones to meet the specific needs of an evaluation study. When instruments are modified or newly constructed, it is important to demonstrate that they display sound psychometric properties.

Two types of validity are especially important for evaluation research: *criterion-related (or predictive) validity* and *content (or "face") validity*. Predictive validity is revealed when scores on an instrument are correlated with a behavior that is external to the measuring instrument. In particular, scores from instruments chosen for the evaluation study should be related to specific behaviors or outcomes related to the objectives and goals of the program. Content validity refers to the extent to which items on an instrument represent a specific domain of content or behavior (Carmines & Zeller, 1979; Cook & Campbell, 1979). Participants, staff, and decision makers may place more confidence in the findings of the evaluation if items on evaluation instruments are clearly program-related behaviors or outcomes.

Reviewing the professional literature will show whether there are some "favorite" or customary instruments and data collection methods used by the field to assess concepts or constructs relevant to the evaluation study. Also, journal articles usually include information on the reliability and validity for the particular instruments used in the study, or they refer to articles and studies from which such information may be gleaned. Table 22.3 lists a number of sourcebooks for marital and family assessment instruments.

However, evaluators often face the prospect of designing new instruments to assess specific aspects of the program. Robson (1993) offers practical guidelines and suggestions for constructing questionnaires, telephone surveys, and semistructured interviews.

When there are clearly defined, specific program objectives, it is easier to develop questionnaires and measures for evaluation. For example, when program objectives outline specific performance goals as outcomes for clients, a *criterion-referenced test* may be developed as an evaluation device. According to Nitko (1984, p. 12), a criterion-referenced test is "deliberately constructed to yield measurements that are directly interpretable in terms of specified performance standards." However, it is important that performance goals refer to a well-defined set of behaviors or tasks. (Berk, 1984, offers guidelines for constructing criterion-referenced tests).

Evaluation instruments may include open-ended items as well as closed questions. Open-ended questions allow respondents much more freedom in responding, which may

TABLE 22.3. Sourcebooks for Marital and Family Assessment Instruments

Corcoran, K., & Fisher, J. (1987). *Measures for clinical practice: A sourcebook.* New York: Free Press.

Filsinger, E. E. (Ed.). (1983). *Marriage and family assessment: A sourcebook for family therapy.* Beverly Hills, CA: Sage.

Fredman, N. H., & Sherman, R. (1987). *Handbook of measurements for marriage and family therapy.* New York: Brunner/Mazel.

Grotevant, H. D., & Carlson, C. I. (1989). *Family assessment: A guide to methods and measures.* New York: Guilford Press.

Jacob, T., & Tennenbaum, D. L. (1988). *Family assessment: Rationale, methods, and future directions.* New York: Plenum Press.

Touliatos, J., Perlmutter, B. F., & Straus, M. A. (Eds.). (1990). *Handbook of family measurement techniques.* Newbury Park, CA: Sage.

yield unexpected and useful information. However, in comparison to closed items, which offer only a limited set of alternative responses, open-ended questions are more difficult to analyze. For this reason, closed questions are generally preferred. However, open-ended questions are extremely useful when the evaluator does not have a good idea of the range of possible responses. Also, qualitative analysis of responses to open questions can yield important insights. Responses to open-ended questionnaires given during pilot studies can be used to develop closed questions for subsequent evaluations. It is often useful to include a mix of instruments that use open-ended and closed questions.

During the formative stages of evaluation, the reliability and validity of new or modified questionnaires should be tested. Also, even with well-established instruments, it is important to assess reliability and validity if they have not been used with the target population of the intervention.

In evaluating the PREP intervention, our predominant mode of analysis is quantitative, although qualitative measures of couples' responses to PREP sessions have been helpful in revising and refining the program. A key outcome variable for PREP is level of marital satisfaction, which we measure quantitatively. Marital satisfaction is assessed by the Marital Adjustment Test (MAT) (Locke & Wallace, 1959). The MAT is a widely used measure of global marital satisfaction because it shows acceptable levels of reliability and sensitivity to the kinds of changes expected from marital therapy (Margolin & Weiss, 1978; O'Leary & Arias, 1983). For example, in one study, test–retest reliability for the MAT was .75 over 3 weeks (Barling & MacEwen, 1986, cited in O'Leary & Arias, 1987). (The MAT is in the public domain and is published in a number of texts, including O'Leary, 1987.)

Currently, we are gathering extensive qualitative data from clergy whom we have trained to deliver PREP. Our goal is to describe how the program is being implemented in their religious organizations. Over the telephone and in group meetings, we interview clergy. These interviews showed us problems they experienced with the format of PREP, helped us identify successful strategies for recruiting couples, and showed us how staff and participants responded to program materials and manuals, as well as other successes and difficulties they experienced in implementing the program.

Within PREP sessions, we also gather feedback from participants, asking what they liked and disliked about particular sessions, what changes they suggest in program format, and what problems they experience in applying the skills learned to their daily lives.

Analyze Data

The purpose of data analysis is to summarize information collected in the study in order to determine whether the goals and objectives of the program or intervention have been achieved. How data are analyzed depends on the types of data collected.

Data analysis is an extensive discipline, and issues involved in data analysis go well beyond the scope of the present chapter. Care should be taken in designing evaluation studies so that data are collected that can be analyzed meaningfully. An excellent basic resource for quantitative data analysis in evaluation research is provided in a text by Fitz-Gibbons and Morris (1987). Miles and Huberman (1994) provide a good overview of qualitative data analysis, including illustrations of diverse methods for handling qualitative data.

Many experienced researchers find it useful to consult experts in data analysis during the design stage of research and evaluation studies to ensure that data are collected in ways that facilitate subsequent data analysis. Moreover, in many cases, it may be a good idea to get expert assistance in conducting the analyses. Most universities and colleges are good sources of consultants for assisting in data analysis.

Analyzing *quantitative* data (e.g., checklists, rating scales, and observation data) usually begins with descriptive analysis. Descriptive statistics allow researchers to reduce the tremendous amount of quantitative information gathered in their studies to a few numbers that summarize outcomes or characteristics observed in the sample, and from these numbers they derive estimates of what outcomes or characteristics may describe the target population as a whole.

Beyond descriptive statistics, the next steps in data analysis are concerned with making inferences about the effects of the intervention or social program. Usually, what evaluation researchers want to know is whether changes observed in intervention groups are due to the intervention and not to other factors, including chance or random influences.

However, researchers usually want to know more than whether it is reasonable to infer that the intervention produced the observed differences between groups—they want to know whether the differences observed represent meaningful or important changes. The question of what represents an important or meaningful change cannot be resolved by inferential statistics. Before the study is conducted, evaluators should develop specific criteria to be applied to assess whether important or meaningful progress toward achieving the objectives of the research program has occurred. Jacobson and Revenstorf (1988) discuss what represents meaningful change in studies of the effectiveness of psychotherapy. Many issues they consider are also relevant for evaluating marital and family intervention programs (see also Jacobson, 1988; Jacobson & Truax, 1991; Kazdin, 1977).

In contrast to quantitative data analysis, there are no generally accepted conventions or procedures for analyzing *qualitative* data (Miles & Huberman, 1994; Robson, 1993). Qualitative data analysis gives individual judgment and interpretive skill a central place: The researcher becomes the primary instrument of measurement (Miles & Huberman, 1994). The task for the researcher is to read through vast amounts of data (e.g., narratives, accounts, responses to open-ended questionnaires, clinical notes, and case studies) with the goal of deriving a "holistic" view of the context under study, explicating "the ways people in particular settings come to understand, account for, take action, and otherwise manage their day-to-day situations" (Miles & Huberman, 1994, p. 7). Qualitative data analysis aims at capturing what actually takes place, incorporating data gathered from people "inside" the program or context and from the researcher's observation of people, activities, and interactions (Patton, 1990).

Qualitative analysis should center on the organizing questions of the evaluation. A key task for the qualitative analyst is making sense of the overwhelming amount of data obtained through qualitative methods. Smith (1990) provides a system for summarizing information generated by qualitative data: (1) read the descriptive data provided by questionnaires or notes, (2) generate as many descriptive categories as possible as defined by the research objectives, (3) refine categories based on the data, (4) examine examples of each category, and (5) report on the major trends by using key quotes and descriptive passages.

To date, quantitative data from the longitudinal evaluation of PREP have been analyzed in a number of different ways to assess the impact of PREP on the major outcome variables of divorce and marital satisfaction. To examine the effects of PREP on instances of divorce or separation, two stages of analysis were required. First, because the sample was composed of couples planning marriage, it was expected that some couples would break up prior to marriage. Categorical analyses were used to compare the rate of premarital breakup for couples in the intervention, control, and decline conditions. Results showed that through the third and fourth follow-up assessments, fewer intervention couples experienced premarital breakup in comparison to control and decline couples (Markman, Renick, Floyd, Stanley, & Clements, 1993).

A second set of categorical analyses excluded couples who broke up before marriage and examined the instances of marital separation or divorce across the intervention, control, and decline groups of couples. Through follow-ups 3 and 4, which took place approximately 4 and 5 years after the intervention, these analyses showed no significant effects on the divorce or separation rates for intervention couples in comparison to control or decline couples (Markman, Renick et al., 1993).

To examine the effects of PREP on relationship functioning, analyses of changes in marital satisfaction and couples' communication were conducted. A series of 3 × 2 (intervention vs. control vs. decline × male vs. female) analyses of covariance (ANCOVA) and analyses of variance (ANOVA) was used to examine differences between groups at follow-up 3 and follow-up 4. ANOVA was used to examine group differences at each follow-up assessment. ANCOVA were used to examine changes in satisfaction or communication from preassessment to follow-up assessment. To look at changes over time, premarital levels of satisfaction or communication were entered as covariates in the analyses, and group differences in the amount of change occurring during this period were examined.

In these analyses it was important to take into account the likelihood of significant correlations between the scores of husbands and wives on measures of satisfaction and communication. To do this, we treated gender as a repeated measure (Kraemer & Jacklin, 1979). This allowed "couple" to be considered the unit of analysis for change or group differences and also examined differences in outcomes for husbands and wives. Results of these analyses are reported in detail elsewhere (e.g., Markman, Renick, et al., 1993; Renick et al., 1992).

Report Results

Reports of evaluation research differ in format, style, and the emphasis placed on specific parts of the evaluation process according to the audience addressed. For example, when results of a program are presented in a professional journal, certain protocols need to be followed, such as that outlined in the fourth edition of the *Publication Manual of the American Psychological Association* (American Psychological Association, 1994). These reports require a complete description of the process of research in order to assist replication of the study. In contrast, reports to decision makers (e.g., institutional or funding agencies) might emphasize information about how the program fits into a larger context (e.g, how the program can be disseminated throughout the community, or how the costs of the program relate to the benefits of those who receive services).

In general, most reports contain similar types of information and should provide a complete and precise description of the program to allow readers to evaluate the strength or soundness of the study. Following is a summary of the information contained in a typical evaluation research report (Rossi & Freeman, 1993; Royse, 1992; Smith, 1990).

The *introduction* includes a thorough description of the problem, including the significance and rationale for study, questions to be explored,, and a description of the program or intervention.

A *literature review* outlines historical and theoretical perspectives on the problem studied, identifying gaps in the literature, and discusses how the study addresses those gaps.

A *methodology* section outlines design and data collection procedures, including descriptions of subjects in the sample, how subjects were selected for participation, instruments used in evaluation, and procedures for collecting and analyzing data.

A report of *findings* presents results observed in the evaluation study and outlines these results using tables or charts accompanied by tests of statistical significance and discussion of practical significance.

In a *discussion section*, a brief summary of the findings is presented, along with explanations of unexpected findings. In this section, how these findings may be applied to practice is considered and any weaknesses or limitations in the evaluation are reviewed.

A *list of references* includes a bibliography of studies cited in the text, along with sources of testing instruments or procedural techniques.

Appendices are attached at the end of the evaluation report and usually include items such as copies of instruments used, instructions given to subjects, cover letters sent to participants, and tables or figures that were too lengthy to place in the results section.

DISCUSSION

Strengths and Weaknesses

There are a number of good reasons for encouraging marital and family practitioners to use program evaluation methods. When programs are designed with evaluation in mind, there is greater attention to specifying the goals and objectives of the program and including measures to assess whether those goals and objectives are being met. Program evaluation research is very useful in program development, but no less useful for documenting the effectiveness of existing programs, keeping track of services provided to the community and to specific target populations. Systematic evaluation of program implementation gives researchers a way to know how practitioners make use of their findings and allows practitioners to give feedback to researchers regarding program design and specific needs in the community.

There are some weaknesses of program evaluation when applied to marital and family therapy programs. At a pragmatic level, conducting a comprehensive evaluation requires a substantial investment of time, money, and staff resources. Unless program evaluation methods are incorporated into the routine of providing services to clients, evaluation may be perceived as an interference rather than a useful activity. An important part of the evaluation is giving feedback to staff and practitioners and addressing questions of interest and importance to them. Staff and practitioners need to be convinced that the information generated by the evaluation will be put to good use and will result in tangible benefits for practice and clients.

Ethical Considerations

Program evaluations almost always pose ethical dilemmas for researchers, especially in evaluation of existing programs. Alkin (1990) argues that evaluation is very much a political act, with numerous opportunities for conflicts of interest. The process of evaluation can also have numerous unintended side effects, some of which may be harmful.

Promises of confidentiality and performance must be kept. Before the evaluation is conducted, it is a good idea to discuss carefully how evaluation findings are to be used and how confidentiality and privacy can best be protected. If limits to confidentiality are anticipated, these should be made clear to all persons involved in the evaluation.

Random Assignment

Some ethical problems arise from the choice of design of the evaluation. In particular, random assignment of participants to treatment conditions or to no-treatment control groups is a source of concern. From a scientific perspective, random assignment is usually much preferable to alternative assignment mechanisms because it is the most efficient way to achieve "equivalent groups" for purposes of statistical comparison. However, random assignment means that "chance" determines group membership and professional judgment plays no role in determining treatment of a particular case. However, Smith (1990) asserts that this often leads to conflict between practitioners and researchers because human service professionals are taught that they should diagnose and determine treatment for particular clients. Also, experimental studies give clients a less powerful role because they do not have any choice regarding which form of treatment they receive (Smith, 1990).

Another ethical problem is created when a true control group is used. A true control group receives no treatment during the study. This puts practitioners and researchers in the position of denying treatment to clients who may in fact benefit from the treatment. One way to deal with this problem is to create a wait-list control group from among clients waiting to enter the program, thus eliminating concerns about withholding treatment. Also, a contrast group may be used instead of a true control group. A contrast group receives a different form of the program than the target, intervention (experimental) group receives. Alternatively, a pre–post design could be used. In this design, all clients receive the program and data analysis focuses on changes over time for all clients (Smith, 1990; Fitz-Gibbons & Morris, 1987).

Misuse of Findings

To prevent misuse of evaluation findings, it is important that the evaluation result in sound, well-documented, and carefully conceptualized information. When writing up findings, evaluators need to keep in mind that they will be obtained and used by people from many areas (Alkin, 1990).

In particular, family researchers and therapists know that national and local media are very interested in stories on couples and families. However, this can be a mixed blessing. We feel that the field of marital and family therapy has an obligation to "give marital and family psychology away," to enhance mental health of our communities and provide the public with a return on tax dollars spent supporting our empirical studies, professional training programs, clinics, and community services.

The media provide some of the most powerful tools we have to inform the public of our findings. A well-done piece outlining major findings that is broadcast on a network news program reaches a far greater number of people than the audience accorded most scientific journal articles or newsletters of professional societies. In our view, when it is appropriate to publish evaluation findings, evaluators should seek dissemination of findings through media articles and stories as well as through professional publications.

However, evaluators and researchers need to be sure that the media receive the most up-to-date, scientifically valid information on issues concerning marital and family psychology. Unfortunately, when findings are made available to the mass media there is a real danger of generating false or misleading impressions or having valid conclusions distorted by being taken out of context. With this in mind, great care needs to be given to what kinds of evaluation information are made available outside the evaluation process itself. In particular, when reports of evaluation studies are written, evaluators should be aware how their words may be understood (or misunderstood) by journalists.

Before beginning an evaluation, it is important for evaluators to consider how they will deal with information that may be revealed regarding the actual conduct of a program. Of course, all participants in the evaluation process should be made aware of limits to confidentiality (if any), and they should be given a clear understanding of how the evaluation findings are intended to be used.

Bridging Research and Practice

Program evaluation research has great potential for providing a bridge between research and practice in the field of marital and family therapy. From the researcher's perspective, evaluation research provides crucial information regarding strengths, limitations, and needs for modification of programs they design. For example, programs developed in university-based contexts are often adapted and modified in response to the pragmatic constraints of practice. In our view, examining how interventions are implemented is central to the process of designing and developing effective interventions.

For practitioners, well-designed program evaluations go beyond identifying "what works" in practice. Evaluations of theoretically derived programs may give practitioners opportunities to communicate directly with researchers and may help shape the agenda of researchers and program developers.

For example, feedback from clergy who have used PREP in their religious organizations brought our attention to examining the best ways to disseminate prevention programs targeting marital distress. In response to this feedback from practitioners, we began a program of research at our laboratory to examine the effectiveness of training clergy to implement PREP. Each stage of research is being developed with active involvement from the major participants, including clergy from a pilot study who provide us ongoing feedback and the advisory board of the Hunt Foundation, which provided funds for the pilot study. One aim of the research program is to identify problems and difficulties in implementing PREP in religious organizations. An additional aim is to observe how PREP is adapted as it is incorporated into the ongoing services of these organizations.

If evaluation studies are to serve as effective bridges between the sometimes divergent communities of research and practice, researchers need to design studies and present findings in ways that are useful for practitioners. We recommend that researchers write materials specifically for dissemination to practitioners. We have found that practitioners appreciate research-based information. For example, along with program descriptions, research related to PREP is summarized in a text that practitioners can use as a couples' workbook (Markman, Stanley, & Blumberg, 1994).

Practitioners and consumers are key stakeholders, and evaluation findings must address their concerns. To ensure that evaluations address questions of practical as well as theoretical concern, input from practitioners and consumers should be solicited in the design stages of program evaluations. We recommend appointing practitioners and consumers to advisory boards to ensure that evaluations yield information relevant to their needs. In addition, we recommend that researchers actively solicit ongoing feedback from practitioners implementing their programs and consumers receiving program services.

FUTURE DIRECTIONS

In the future we expect to see an increased importance and acceptance of evaluation research within the field of marital and family therapy. For example, the demand for ongoing evaluation may increase as a function of greater acceptance and use of marital and family therapy interventions within managed care and employee assistance programs. Managed care programs, in particular, place a great emphasis on accountability and demonstrations of program effectiveness.

We believe that developing skills in program evaluation should become an essential part of the training and practice of service providers. This will aid practitioners in becoming informed consumers of research and allow them to critically evaluate programs developed by researchers. More important, with this foundation, systematic research and evaluation of programs may provide a central means for practitioners and researchers to communicate more effectively with one another.

REFERENCES

Alkin, M. C. (1990). *Debates on evaluation.* Newbury Park, CA: Sage.

American Psychological Association. (1994). *Publication manual of the American Psychological Association* (4th ed.). Washington, DC: Author.

Berk, R. A. (1984). *A guide to criterion-referenced test construction.* Baltimore: Johns Hopkins University Press.

Berk, R. A., & Rossi, P. H. (1990). *Thinking about program evaluation.* Newbury Park, CA: Sage.

Boughner, S. R., Hayes, S. F., Bubenzer, D. L., & West, J. D. (1994). Use of standardized assessment instruments by marital and family therapists: A survey. *Journal of Marital and Family Therapy, 20*(1), 69–75.

Campbell, D. T., & Stanley, J. C. (1963). Experimental and quasi-experimental designs for research and teaching. In N. L. Gage (Ed.), *Handbook of research on teaching* (pp. 171–246). Chicago: Rand McNally.

Carmines, E. G., & Zeller, R. A. (1979). *Reliability and validity assessment.* Beverly Hills, CA: Sage.

Cohen, J. (1992). A power primer. *Psychological Bulletin, 112*(1), 155–159.

Coie, J. C., Watt, N. F., West, S. G., Hawkins, J. D., Asarnow, J. R., Markman, H. J., Ramey, S. L., Shure, M. J., & Long, B. (1993). The science of prevention. *American Psychologist, 48*(10), 1013.

Cook, T., & Campbell, D. T. (1979). *Quasi-experimentation.* Chicago: Rand McNally.

Corcoran, K., & Fisher, J. (1987). *Measures for clinical practice: A sourcebook.* New York: Free Press.

Filsinger, E. E. (Ed.). (1983). *Marriage and family assessment: A sourcebook for family therapy.* Beverly Hills, CA: Sage.

Fitz-Gibbon, C. T., & Morris, L. L. (1987). *How to design a program evaluation.* Newbury Park, CA: Sage.

Fredman, N. H., & Sherman, R. (1987). *Handbook of measurements for marriage and family therapy.* New York: Brunner/Mazel.

Frey, J. H. (1989). *Survey research by telephone.* Beverly Hills, CA: Sage.

Garfield, S. L., & Bergin, A. E. (1986). Introduction and historical overview. In S. L. Garfield & A. E. Bergin (Eds.), *Handbook of psychotherapy and behavior change* (3rd ed., pp. 3–22). New York: Wiley.

Gottman, J. M. (1994). *What predicts divorce?* Hillsdale, NJ: Erlbaum.

Grotevant, H. D., & Carlson, C. I. (1989). *Family assessment: A guide to methods and measures.* New York: Guilford Press.

Gurman, A. S., Kniskern, D. P., & Pinsof, W. M. (1986). Research on the process and outcome of marital and family therapy. In S. L. Garfield & A. E. Bergin (Eds.), *Handbook of psychotherapy and behavior change* (3rd ed., pp. 565–624). New York: Wiley.

Huck, S. W., Cormier, W. H., & Bounds, W. G. (1974). *Reading statistics and research.* New York: Harper & Row.

Jacob, T., & Tennenbaum, D. L. (1988). *Family assessment: Rationale, methods, and future directions.* New York: Plenum Press.

Jacobson, N. S. (Ed.). (1988). Defining clinically significant change [Special issue]. *Behavioral Assessment, 10*(2).

Jacobson, N. S., & Revenstorf, D. (1988). Statistics for assessing the clinical significance of psychotherapy techniques: Issues, problems, and new developments. *Behavioral Assessment, 10,* 133–145.

Jacobson, N. S., & Truax, P. (1991). Clinical significance: A statistical approach to defining meaningful change in psychotherapy research. *Journal of Consulting and Clinical Psychology, 59*(1), 12–19.

Kazdin, A. E. (1977). Assessing the clinical or applied significance of behavior changes through social validation. *Behavior Modification, 1,* 427–452.

Kazdin, A. E. (1992). *Research design in clinical psychology* (2nd ed.). New York: Allyn & Bacon.

Kraemer, H. C., & Jacklin, C. (1979). Statistical analysis of dyadic social behavior. *Psychological Bulletin, 86,* 217–224.

Kraemer, H. C., & Thiemann, S. (1987). *How many subjects?.* Newbury Park, CA: Sage.

Liddle, H. A. (1991). Empirical values and the culture of family therapy. *Journal of Marital and Family Therapy, 17*(4), 327–348.

Lipsey, M. W. (1990). *Design sensitivity: Statistical power for experimental research.* Newbury Park, CA: Sage.

Locke, H. J., & Wallace, K. M. (1959). Short marital adjustment and prediction tests: Their reliability and validity. *Marriage and Family Living, 21,* 251–255.

Margolin, G., & Weiss, R. L. (1978). Comparative evaluation of therapeutic components associated with behavioral marital treatments. *Journal of Consulting and Clinical Psychology, 46,* 1476–1486.

Markman, H. J. (1992). Marital and family psychology: Burning issues. *Journal of Family Psychology, 5*(3), 264–275.

Markman, H. J., Duncan, S. W., Storaasli, R.,& Howes, P. (1988). The prediction and prevention of marital distress: A longitudinal investigation. *Journal of Consulting and Clinical Psychology, 56,* 210–217.

Markman, H. J., Renick, M. J., Floyd, F. J., Stanley, S. M., & Clements, M. (1993). Preventing marital distress through communication and conflict management training: A four and five year follow-up. *Journal of Consulting and Clinical Psychology, 61*(1), 70.

Markman, H. J., Stanley, S. M., & Blumberg, S. (1993). *The Prevention and Relationship Enhancement Program (PREP) leader's manual.* Denver, CO: PREP Educational Products.

Markman, H. J., Stanley, S. M., & Blumberg, S. (1994). *Fighting for your marriage: The PREP approach.* San Francisco: Jossey-Bass.

Miles, M. B., & Huberman, A. M. (1994). *Qualitative data analysis: An expanded sourcebook.* Thousand Oaks, CA: Sage.

Moon, S. M., Dillon, D. R., & Sprenkle, D. H. (1990). Family therapy and qualitative research. *Journal of Marital and Family Therapy, 16*(4), 357.

Nitko, A. J. (1984). Defining "criterion-referenced test." In R. A. Berk (Ed.), *A guide to criterion-referenced test construction* (pp. 8–28). Baltimore: Johns Hopkins University Press.

O'Leary, K. D. (1987) *Assessment of marital discord.* Hillsdale, NJ: Erlbaum.

O'Leary, K. D., & Arias, I. (1983). The influence of marital therapy on sexual satisfaction. *Journal of Sex and Marital Therapy, 9*(3), 171–181.

Olson, D. H. (1976). Bridging research, theory, and application: The triple threat in science. In D. H. Olson (Ed.), *Treating relationships* (pp. 565–579). Lake Mills, IA: Graphics Press.

Patton, M. Q. (1990). *Qualitative evaluation and research methods* (2nd ed.). Newbury Park, CA: Sage.

Pietrzak, J., Ramler, M., Renner, T., Ford, L., & Gilbert, N. (1990). *Practical program evaluation.* Newbury Park, CA: Sage.

Rea, L. M., & Parker, R. L. (1992). *Designing and conducting survey research.* San Francisco: Jossey-Bass.

Renick, M. J., Blumberg, S., & Markman, H. J. (1992). The Prevention and Relationship Enhancement Program (PREP): An empirically-based preventive intervention program for couples. *Family Relations, 41,* 141–147.

Robson, C. (1993). *Real world research: A resource for social scientists and practitioner-researchers.* Oxford, UK: Blackwell.

Rossi, P. H., & Freeman, H. E. (1993). *Evaluation: A systematic approach.* Newbury Park, CA: Sage.

Royse, D. (1992). *Program evaluation: An introduction.* Chicago: Nelson-Hall.

Smith, M. J. (1990). *Program evaluation in the human services.* New York: Springer.

Touliatos, J., Perlmutter, B. F., & Straus, M. A. (Eds.). (1990). *Handbook of family measurement techniques.* Newbury Park, CA: Sage.

Valentine, J., & Zigler, E. F. (1983). Head Start: A case study in the development of social policy for children and families. In E. F. Zigler, S. L. Kagan, & E. Klugman (Eds.), *Children, families, and government: Perspectives on American social policy* (pp. 266–280). New York: Cambridge University Press.

Weiss, C. H. (1990). Evaluation for decisions. In M. C. Alkins (Ed.), *Debates on evaluation* (pp. 171–184), Newbury Park, CA: Sage.

Wholey, J. S. (1977). Evaluability assessment. In L. Rutman (Ed.), *Evaluation research methods: A basic guide* (pp. 39–56). Beverly Hills, CA: Sage.

Wynne, L. C. (1983). Family research and family therapy: A reunion? *Journal of Marital and Family Therapy, 9,* 113–117.

Zigler, E., & Styfco, S. J. (1993). *Using research and theory to justify and inform Head Start expansion* (Social Policy Report Vol. 3). Ann Arbor, MI: Society for Research in Child Development.

Index

507

DATE DUE